"Leave me alone, you disgusting brute, you hollow libertine, you...

"...you...lecherous swine!" Aimee cried, trying to think of the worst comparisons she could.

To her chagrin, he merely laughed at her, intent on pulling away the last shreds of her attire, until she was completely naked underneath him. Still angry, she had no time to feel the embarrassment as his flame-blue eyes swept over her perfect figure.

Without taking his hands from her arms where they were pinned to the bed, Lucian bent his head to capture her lips, effectively silencing her continued angry tirade against him. Hungrily, she matched his kiss. Aimee groaned aloud, wondering how she could have been so angry with him one minute and now be completely at his mercy. Yet, she wasn't at his mercy any more than he was at hers. There was something inside of her crying for release, crying for fulfillment, and she instinctively knew this man— jaded libertine or not—would be the one who could satisfy her...

Books by Theresa Conway

SILVER CLOUDS, GOLDEN DREAMS
A PASSION FOR GLORY

A PASSION FOR GLORY

THERESA CONWAY

JOVE BOOKS, NEW YORK

This Jove book contains the complete
text of the original edition.
It has been completely reset in a typeface
designed for easy reading and was printed
from new film.

A PASSION FOR GLORY

A Jove Book/published by arrangement with
the author

PRINTING HISTORY
Jove trade paperback edition/October 1986
Jove mass market edition/March 1988

ISBN: 0-515-09557-5

Jove Books are published by The Berkley Publishing Group,
200 Madison Avenue, New York, New York 10016.
The name "JOVE" and the "J" logo
are trademarks belonging to Jove Publications, Inc.

PRINTED IN THE UNITED STATES OF AMERICA

10 9 8 7 6 5 4 3 2 1

A PASSION FOR GLORY

With love,
To a dear friend, Diane Henrich
Farewell

A PASSION FOR GLORY

I

- - - - - - - - - - - - -

WINDS
OF
CHANGE

1

Paris simmered from the heat of political events in July, 1789, as its people prepared to tear down a monarchy that had lasted over a thousand years and replace it with the revolutionary idea of a republic. Louis XVI, awkward, timid, and weak in implementing good ideas, but pressured by his Queen, who could not conceive of the rabble daring to overthrow their masters, made one mistake after another; he attempted to retain both his throne and his dignity, while continuing to placate his spoiled and lovely wife by placing the woefully inadequate treasury at her disposal.

The citizens of Paris were aching for a fight, panicking at the thought of what another poor harvest might do to the price of bread, desperate to save themselves from becoming the faceless crowd that Louis and Marie Antoinette would not choose to see or hear from their lofty position in the fairy-tale palace of Versailles. Theirs was a great blaze of discontent that grew ever hotter in the streets and alleyways of Paris that summer of 1789 —a blaze that required only the presence of strong and centralized leaders to turn it into a conflagration.

But in the rural town of Orléans, some seventy miles from the hotbed of Paris, the heat of mid-summer settled with drowsy heaviness on the thick, verdant squares of green that dotted the gentle hills and patchwork-quilted meadows. Even the flies seemed to have lost their energy and gathered lazily about the remains of lunch spilling from a wicker basket while the energetic young diners, oblivious to the humid heat, played children's games among old trees in the park that had always been their playground.

Set a short distance from the park, topping a gentle knoll, the Castle du Beautreillis stood, a shadowy reminder of the grand castle it had once been nearly four hundred years before. It had housed generations of the de Chartres family, each seeing a subtle wearing away of the once formidable walls until now it stood as a sad monument to the past. But to Aimee de Chartres, the youngest of that present generation, the castle was still magical, its

turrets and towers, its secret corners all known to her and all part
of the make-believe she conjured up to hide its crumbling façade.
In one turret, she could pretend to be a princess, waiting for some
handsome knight to rescue her from a witch's spell; in one other
she might be the wife of a nobleman awaiting her husband's
return from war. Although her bedroom could be frigid in winter
and hot as an oven in summer due to the eroding chinks between
the blocks of granite, she could still believe it was the most
sumptuous room in the world, its faded tapestries works of art
hung for her inspection.

Just now, though, she was not in her bedroom, but playing
among the trees with her older brothers, ignoring the heat of the
day beneath the light weight of a discarded shirt from one of
them. Despite being the only girl and the youngest of six children, it was easy to see that she was every bit as carefree and
adventurous as they as she scrambled about on the branches of
the ancient oaks, dangling bare feet in the air and laughingly
pushing back skeins of shining gold hair that fell forward to cover
the peach of her cheeks.

Suddenly, she dropped from the tree in which she was hiding,
tiring of the game, and seated herself ceremoniously on the old
stump of an oak. "I am the Queen!" she proclaimed importantly,
tapping the youngest of her brothers, eleven-year-old Giles, on
the   shoulder   with   an   improvised   scepter   made   from
the broken branch of a young sapling. The statement was at distinct odds with the picture she presented in her boy's breeches,
castoffs from her brothers, and the too large shirt that enveloped
the still immature, ten-year-old body.

The comical effect was not lost on her eldest brother, sixteen-
year-old Etienne. "Where are your palace robes, my Queen?" he
asked, managing to hide an endearing grin behind his hand.

Aimee pushed back the heavy gold of her hair, the look in her
eyes distinctly condescending. "You dare to speak so to the
Queen of France, knave! My palace robes are of the finest silk
and satin, brought from lands far away—"

"—at great expense to the poor taxpayers of France, no
doubt!" interrupted fifteen-year-old Vachel, who was disgruntled
at this turn in the game he'd been enjoying.

His words had the effect of ruining the play as all of the young
players' faces took on an anxious look. Even Aimee knew of the
burden of taxes and the dread that accompanied the arrival of the
"sub-intendant," the man responsible for collecting the taxes for
the state. Henri Cavat, a man whom her father referred to as "that

groveling bourgeois," made his rounds like clockwork, expecting her father to pay the property tax, the personal tax, the tax on his income, and the poll tax from what meager funds he received as stipends from the government for his service in the King's army and from the once bountiful largesse that had passed down through his noble rank. Once, Aimee knew, her family had been one of the richest in France and one of the highest in rank—but that had been long ago. And though she could still trace her lineage back to King Henry II, the de Chartres du Beautreillis were no longer received at Court and had retired to the clichéd existence of country nobility.

"Why must you bring up taxes?" she implored her brother, setting aside the broken branch and climbing down from the tree stump. "Father talks of little else."

"We cannot escape them," Etienne said and sighed, "although God knows where the money goes."

"It goes to buy the Queen four pairs of shoes a week and diamonds the size of a pigeon's eggs!" piped in thirteen-year-old Charles, who, with his twin, Denis, was sitting idly a few feet away watching the fascinating antics of an ant colony.

"Where did you hear that?" Aimee demanded.

"From Margot," Charles replied with complete confidence.

"She's only an old nurse!" Aimee returned in disgust. "What does she know of such things? Why, even Father admits that the government must have money to run the country and—"

"But what does it do for *us?*" Vachel wanted to know, gaining interest in the subject. "Five miles away the du Poirons live in a magnificent marble château that is well kept and manned by many servants. Yet, their blood is not as pure as ours, nor can their father boast of doing anything but lazing at Versailles with the King and Court!"

"That is because du Poiron fawns over the king and pays pretty compliments to the fair Marie Antoinette," Etienne answered heatedly. "I have heard she is so vain and silly that any man who gives her attention is rewarded with some favor. She dispenses *our* money, paid in taxes, to fools like that, when we sit down to a meal of bread and soup every day!"

"It is better than what Jean eats," Denis put in matter-of-factly, referring to the son of one of the peasants on the estate. He patted his stomach and looked longingly at the remaining crumbs surrounding the wicker basket.

"Pah! He is a peasant and used to getting what he can!" Etienne put in with a narrowminded gruffness that displayed a common attitude toward the lower class that was shared by that Court nobility he professed to despise.

"Oh, dear, I can see the play is ruined." Aimee sighed and walked to the wicker basket to fold the cloth over it. "Etienne, you get such a light in your eyes when you speak of taxes and nobility and the peasants," she continued with a look of reproach in her own green eyes.

"It's just talk," Vachel said soothingly, sorry now that he had brought up the whole thing.

"Yes, just talk!" Etienne echoed back fiercely, as the six children gathered their things and walked to the castle. "Just like the talk of those pompous idiots who have met in the States-General. What do they hope to accomplish with so much infighting among them? Why, every day our father receives dispatches from Paris indicating the frustration among the people from the lack of results of that assembly!"

Although only Etienne and Vachel were old enough to really understand the complicated machinery of the States-General, that body of some twelve hundred that the King had called to Paris in order to straighten out the woeful finances of the government, all the children understood that the meeting was of historical import, for their father had told them that such an assembly had not met in more than one hundred seventy-five years. Always the King had ruled by Divine Right and his own conscience, but now King Louis XVI found his treasury all but empty and there was no one willing to loan money to the government anymore.

Aimee recalled her father's excitement at this turn of events, for he foresaw it as the best of beginnings to equalize the tax laws that barely touched the court nobility and laid the heaviest burdens on those least able to pay them. When the people of France were asked to draw up a formal statement of their grievances and the reforms they favored, the majority had demanded tax reform wherein all would be taxed according to their ability to pay. There had also been demands for confining the government by establishing a constitution that would guarantee individual liberty and the right to think, speak, and write without fear of retribution from the King in the form of the dreaded *"lettre de cachet,"* which threw many innocent men into prison without hope of appeal.

"God, how I wish I could go to Paris and witness the events happening there!" Etienne spoke with youthful zeal. "Instead, I am confined to this crumbling estate where nothing moves, nothing happens!" The fierce look on his face frightened his sister.

"Etienne, you must promise not to leave!" she implored, truly fearful that her headstrong brother would leave and journey to Paris. She had heard much about that city of intrigue and cruelty from her nurse, Margot, an Englishwoman who had come to live in Paris when her former mistress had married a Frenchman. For twenty years, Margot said, she had endured the wickedness and debauchery of a city mad with lust and the yearning for power. She would shudder and pat the shoulder of her youngest charge, expressing her hope that Aimee would never have to suffer the same fate.

Etienne stared at the forlorn face of his sister and struggled to push his frustration aside. With a forced smile, he ruffled the golden strands of her hair and heaved a sigh. "Little sister, I promise I won't leave now," he said seriously, "but there will come a time when I must go."

"As must I," Vachel added valiantly, not to be outdone by the gravity of his brother's words.

"Then I will go, too," Aimee decided with a firm toss of her head. "Heaven knows you will need someone to cook and care for you both!"

Both boys laughed while making some good-natured but somewhat disparaging remarks about the quality of their sister's cooking. Aimee, quite ignobly, stuck out her tongue, then ran as swiftly as a startled doe when Etienne sought to grab her arm in order to administer chastisement.

"Such behavior hardly becomes you should you desire to catch a decent husband one day!" Etienne shouted after her with a grin.

Aimee turned about and faced him, hands on hips, her green eyes dancing with amusement. "Then I shall not marry," she retorted. "At least not until I am too old to have fun any longer—perhaps not until I am twenty-two or so!"

"It shall certainly be before then!" Vachel returned laughingly. "For when all of us boys are married, you will have no one to amuse yourself with and shall be forced to marry for a playmate!"

"Ha! None would have you!" Aimee taunted in sisterly spite. "I shall have no worry on that score!"

Her bright eyes watched the secret look of smugness that passed between her two oldest brothers and she felt, for a moment, shut out of their private worlds. The feeling passed through her like a tug of cold wind and she sought to release herself from it—from the realization that very soon there would come changes in the warm orderliness of her family.

"There's Father!" Giles shouted suddenly, running from the

others as he spied the patriarch of the de Chartres clan standing near the door of the kitchen, watching his wife inside baking fresh-smelling bread.

Philippe de Chartres, still handsome at forty-five, still as erect as he had been as a young soldier in the Army of France, cuddled his son unashamedly and held out his arms for his only daughter, who launched herself at him with unabashed affection.

After a moment, he released them both and mopped at his brow with a well-worn handkerchief. "Such exuberance in youth," he muttered with a shake of his head, "even in the face of this steady heat. You nearly wear me out with your energy, my dears." He fixed his gaze on the oval face of his daughter. "And you, my chick, must get inside and help your mother. The heat in the kitchen is unbearable this time of day, but she insists on doing the baking herself—as though the village girls don't know how to bake bread!"

"Certainly they know how to bake bread," replied Madame de Chartres, a tall, handsome woman in her mid-forties, as she stuck her head out of the half door, "but I will not have them flitting about with their skirts up in the air seeking to turn *your* head, dear husband, while we pay them hard-to-come-by money for kitchen duties!"

Philippe de Chartres harrumphed at this backhanded compliment, but seemed pleased at this measure of his wife's possessiveness, patting her shoulder with the comfortable touch of one who had known and loved the same woman for more than twenty years.

Anne de Chartres smiled at him as she bade her daughter to hurry inside to help her. Aimee sighed, knowing she was being delegated to kitchen duty when she longed to accompany her father and brothers to the sitting room, listening to exciting talk of Paris and the growing anger of the people of that city. Still, without too much balking, she tied the ends of an apron around her waist, glad that at least her mother hadn't commented on her unsuitable attire, a subject Anne de Chartres had long since given up on when she realized she could not control her headstrong daughter's choice of wardrobe, nor could she really argue with the sense of wearing boys' clothing, which was in more abundance in their household than girls'.

Aimee toiled for several hours over the baking, working up a fine sweat as she kneaded the doughy mass, shaping it into perfect, round loaves for baking in the oven. When at last she was finished and had helped her mother clean up the kitchen, she heard the sound of a hard-ridden horse's hooves on the cobblestones within the courtyard of the castle and ran to the hall to intercept her brothers on their way to see the messenger.

The courier, a young man who stopped frequently at their house with news on his way to spreading it in other parts of the town, had already alighted from his steed and was shaking the dust from his shirtsleeves.

"The people of Paris," he announced, "have stormed the Bastille!"

"The Bastille!" Philippe de Chartres repeated with a look of horror on his face at the mention of the old fortress on the eastern edge of Paris that had been turned into one of the most infamous prisons of the city. "But how—why—?" He sought blindly for his wife's hands, knowing somehow that this news meant the beginning of some monstrous chain of events that would affect them all. "Have they all gone mad?" he wondered aloud.

"Yes, the whole populace is mad—drunk with power!" young Conan asserted. "Necker was dismissed by the King four days ago," he went on, speaking of the man who had been assigned to head the assembly of the historic meeting of the States-General. "The King, fearing the power that the Third Estate was gaining over the nobility and clergy, tried to suppress the Assembly and ordered soldiers to patrol in Versailles and Paris . . . most of them foreign mercenaries. The people of Paris would not tolerate the foreigners patrolling their streets and stormed the Bastille yesterday, giving protection to the Assembly and saving the day!"

"I cannot believe such madness," Philippe de Chartres responded, shaking his head in confusion. "The Bastille—"

"Were many hurt?" Aimee interrupted, forgetting her manners in her excitement.

Conan looked at her with clear contempt. "What can a few lives matter when their deaths are offered up to the cause of revolution!" he asked her. "It is being talked of as a triumph of liberty and shall even be declared a national holiday! Everywhere in the streets of Paris the new flag is being flown—the tricolor of red, white, and blue—to replace the white and gold Bourbon flag!"

"So," Philippe said softly, "it has finally happened."

"The revolution, Father?" Etienne asked softly, although excitement was so plain on his face. "And Paris the center of it all—only a day's ride from here."

The meaning of his words sunk through Philippe's brain. "Are there—have there been repercussions among the rural people?" he asked Conan.

"Paris is calling for all who adhere to her ideals to follow her example and overthrow the symbols of intolerance and inequality," he responded, looking around the crumbling courtyard. "But you should have no worries, my good baron, since no one could call this crumbling shell a symbol of anything but the ravages of time!"

Etienne jumped at the young man, seeking to throttle him as his hands closed about his throat. "You'll not be so chipper, de Landry, after you've felt my thumbs in your flesh!" he vowed. It took his father and all of his younger brothers to pull him off the other young man.

Aimee watched anxiously as her beloved brother was wrestled to the ground, huffing and panting, while the courier loosened his collar and took deep breaths into his lungs. She didn't understand why the young man was so smug—he was little better than a peasant, from simple country stock, who had gone to Paris when they could no longer eke out a living on the land. Her father had paid him to bring news to them from Paris on his way to the town of Orléans, where his father's family still lived. He was like a bloated pigeon, she thought, fat on the knowledge he gleaned from others in the city of Paris, full of importance as he bestowed his news with as much greed as a miser might bestow gold on a starving populace.

"I shall not be stopping here again, de Chartres," Conan was saying, still a little breathless as he eyed Etienne with a wary eye. "I can see that your son has little regard for the ideals of the revolution. Like our beautiful Queen, he is daring but lacking in wisdom and judgment." With a nod to the elder de Chartres, the messenger mounted his horse and cantered out of the courtyard into the soft grass of the park that would lead him toward the town of Orléans.

Pushing himself away from his father's hands, Etienne eyed his siblings in disgust. "You would all just stand there and let him speak of our home as though it were nothing better than some trash heap, fit only for vermin!" He gazed at his father reproachfully. "You should have let me squeeze his throat a bit longer, Father, and I would have stilled his insolent peasant's tongue!"

"And have you behave no better than that rabble in Paris?" Philippe responded quietly, his face still reflecting his shock at the news of bloodshed.

Etienne opened his mouth to respond, then stopped at his mother's gentle hand on his shoulder.

"I am frightened," Anne said quietly in a voice filled with a mother's dread. "Does this mean civil war?"

Philippe shrugged, then put his arms about his wife and held her close, his children watching them with a mixture of excitement and uneasiness as each tried to struggle with the meaning of this turn of events.

"I don't know what it means," he said finally, honestly. "I believe this may be the true beginnings of a revolution—and an end to our safe and protected world, my dears. I feel anger at the thought that we, who have so much at stake, can only stand and wait to see what those hotheads in Paris shall concoct. We must not act hastily or irrationally, but must wait to hear more news of what is happening in Paris and Versailles."

"Cannot we go to Paris, Father?" Etienne asked hopefully, his young masculine body tense as a bowstring.

Philippe gazed at his eldest and shook his head. "What good would it do?" he wondered aloud. "We must trust to the conscience of the Assembly and hope that the people of Paris follow their laws."

Aimee watched as her brother turned away in disappointment, and she ached for him, knowing how much he craved the excitement, the drama, that was unfolding in Paris. For herself, she had no wish to go to that wicked city, no wish ever to step inside its gates if its populace was as bloodthirsty as their actions indicated. Perhaps her father was right—perhaps there was some madness abroad that had struck the citizens of that city.

At first the madness that affected Paris was confined to the city itself in the midst of changes that were, on the whole, made in the spirit of liberty and equality that had caused the fall of the Bastille. Quite spontaneously, Paris gave itself a new form of municipal government, superseding the old royal form. A new military force was organized that called itself the National Guard. Even the King himself bowed to the will of the Parisians and came to the city to ratify all the changes.

In the countryside, things did not go so smoothly as radicals urged the peasants to make war against their mostly absent masters. Rabble-rousers with burning eyes, spouting the equality theories of Rousseau, pushed the peasants into acts of violence. Many châteaux were burned out of vengeance, the owners safely

ensconced in their apartments in Versailles, while the farmers of
their estates destroyed the records of feudal dues owed by each of
them. Without these written records, no taxes could be collected
and the peasant rejoiced that these chains, at least, had been
severed.

In early August, the Assembly drew up a report on what was
happening throughout the country: the burning of châteaux, the
assaulting of unpopular tax collectors, even the hanging of some
unscrupulous businessmen. Lawlessness seemed triumphant, and
in Orléans the people were not unaffected.

Peasants had marched on all the châteaux, burning that of the
du Poirons to the ground after first sacking the place and taking
anything of value. Two old and trusted servants had been hanged
unceremoniously from a nearby tree. Anxiously, Philippe de
Chartres had waited for the inevitable, standing tall and proud in
the ancient arch of his castle as some twenty peasants gathered in
front of him, brandishing pitchforks and smoking torches, shouting obscenities and cursing his family.

The largest of them, and the self-appointed leader, finally
strode forward. Aimee, peeking out from one of the small, square
windows in her bedroom, where she had been banished, recognized him as Faron, the miller, a man whom her father had frequently accused of cheating the peasants who brought him their
wheat to grind.

"So, de Chartres, you expected us, no doubt, after hearing the
fate of the Château du Poiron?" Faron challenged.

"Yes," Philippe answered simply, never wavering from his
stance.

"And you know what we want, then?"

"The accounts of the feudal dues," Philippe returned and gestured to a large container at his side. "Here they are—and you
may take them and do what you will with them. I no longer have
any use for them."

For a moment, the miller seemed stunned by this easy victory. "You—you give them to us? You know we will destroy
them!"

"Better to destroy them than to hurt one hair of any member of
my family, Faron," Philippe said quietly. "At any rate, haven't
you heard the news from Paris? It seems the nobility of the Second Estate have all had flashes of generosity since they moved
that all feudal dues be swept away. A veritable frenzy of generosity has gripped the Assembly since all the bishops have renounced the privileges of their order, the parish priests have

renounced their usual fees, and even the judges have discarded their distinctions."

Gesturing once more to the container beside him, Philippe shouted, "Here, take them! I am telling all of you that your work is finished—the Assembly has done it for you. All feudal dues are dead, tithes abandoned, even the guilds have been swept away. Justice is free and distinctions of class have been abolished. You—all of you—know I am not a wealthy man. I have no appointments at Versailles; my children run as yours do in bare feet. Jean, Pierre, all of you I have known for many years and we have worked together to keep food in the mouths of our families. I have no quarrel with any of you!"

Those farmers he had named dropped their weapons in slow shame, realizing they truly had no grievance against this man, whose only difference from them was his old and aristocratic name. But they knew that that name had done no more for him than it had for them.

"De Chartres is right!" one of the mob shouted. "We have no quarrel with him! I say we take the accounts and burn them and go home!"

The men were tired of the ceaseless pillage they had caused. They had had enough—and certainly the Castle du Beautreillis was no satisfactory target for pent-up wrath. With a snort of disgust, Faron signaled for two of the men to hoist the container with the accounts in it and spill its contents to the ground, where he torched the hated papers himself.

Aimee watched from her window as the men turned around and began to march home, leaving her to breathe a huge sigh of relief. She had been positive her father was going to be hurt, and to have the incident end with no bloodshed, no physical activity of any kind, was almost too much to be believed.

Aimee's eyes shone with tears as she gazed at her beloved father—a Daniel facing the lions—and her heart felt as though it would burst with the pride of her love for him. He seemed, at that moment, invincible, and all her child's fears were laid to rest as she realized that as long as he lived, she would always be safe.

2

The next months went by quickly as rapid changes in Paris affected everyone in France. The citizens of that city had become angry again when they realized that all the good resolutions made by the Assembly would take time to be implemented into laws that worked. Two separate parties now appeared in the Assembly: those who upheld the accomplishments of the revolution so far, and those who wished to undo what had been done and recover their losses. Many courtiers had begun leaving France and emigrating to other parts of Europe to escape retaliation by maddened anarchists, some of whom were shouting for the downfall of the nobility, and even of the King himself. Louis XVI did nothing to restore the people's confidence in himself as he listened to the damaging advice of his unsympathetic wife and his ambitious cousin, the Duke of Orléans. The people began to suspect the King's true motives, and coupled with that suspicion was a growing fear of famine as the price of bread continued to climb and desperate mothers marched to Versailles to demand a reduction in bread prices. The outcome of this action was that the King and his family were forced to leave the comparative protection of Versailles and return to Paris to live in the Tuileries. The Assembly was quickly made to follow, and so both King and Assembly were now virtual prisoners, under the supervision of the people of Paris.

Philippe de Chartres shook his head at this turn of events as he and his family sat down to an austere meal of barley soup and bread one evening. "Paris is now our King," he said worriedly, showing the countryman's innate distrust of the city. "And, I fear, she shall rule with no more mercy than poor Louis before her."

"Philippe, you talk as though the King were no more," Anne chided him, though she was plagued by her own doubts as well. "Surely the people continue to listen to him, even to the point of making no new laws without his acceptance of them."

"His hand is forced," Philippe returned pointedly.

"But what of the Declaration of the Rights of Man!" Etienne spoke up excitedly. "Surely that is something good, Father, that

14

has come from the joining of the King and the Assembly. Without pressure from the latter, Louis would never have thought of signing such a document. With its assertions that men are free and equal, that we all have a right to free speech and free assembly—"

"It is only a declaration of rights, my son, not a guarantee of them," Philippe commented thoughtfully.

"So, the fighting is not finished?" Aimee asked between mouthfuls of bread.

Her father looked at her and smiled sadly. "No, my dearest, I do not think so. It is true that King Louis has finally accepted a constitution drawn up by the Assembly, but I cannot imagine his heart is in it. He will look for the chance to degrade it, for its acceptance takes away that power he thought to be divinely his, as it had been that of his father and grandfather and all of the Bourbons before him. According to this new constitution, the King will be a limited ruler with legislative power given over to a single assembly of elected members from the districts. So, the government has been decentralized, but there is still the pressing problem of bankruptcy. No government can survive without funds." His eyes gazed around the table. "Even a bad government can maintain itself if it has prestige, age, and wealth to support it. But not even a good government can maintain itself, despite its age and prestige, if it does not have money."

"But, then, where will it get the money?" Vachel demanded, leaning over his bowl attentively.

Philippe's smile was ironic. "From taxes, my boy. And so, you see, there is its downfall, for the peasants will not pay taxes without a fight, after they thought themselves released from doing so."

"Must we also pay taxes again, Father?" Aimee wondered with a sigh, trying not to think of the fate of the tax collector, Henri Cavat, who had been trussed up to a tree without much ado and left to kick his life out in slow agony.

"It cannot be otherwise," Philippe replied. "From the messages we receive from Paris and those infrequent letters from my dear sister, your Aunt Hortense, the city is chronically in a state of intense excitement; food is constantly going up in price, bread is scarce, business is bad, and unemployment has increased. The bubble will burst soon."

"Hortense—do you think she will be all right?" Anne asked anxiously, watching the lines of worry deepen in her husband's face.

"I have written her, pleading with her to come here and stay with us until the madness leaves the city." Philippe sighed. "But she has always been stubborn and has so far refused to come."

Aimee thought of her Aunt Hortense, a skinny, nervous sort of woman who had never married and seemed in a constant state of motion. She hadn't seen her for at least two years—and couldn't imagine her becoming a part of their family. Still, if it would mean lessening the concern on her father's face, she would welcome her, however grudgingly, into their home.

"I could go to Paris and bring her back with me," Philippe was saying, his words breaking into Aimee's reverie. She looked fearfully at her father, trying not to think of him walking into that mad, fiery pit that was Paris.

"No!" Anne's answer was echoed in Aimee's head. "No, Philippe, you cannot go there now." She clutched her husband's arm as though to physically restrain him.

"I could accompany you, Father!" Etienne burst in excitedly, unaware of his mother's distress, but only seeing the glorious adventure in it. "How I should like to go!"

"But if you go, then so must I!" Vachel reminded him quickly.

"Pah! You cannot even handle a sword with any competence," Etienne cut in spitefully. "You would be no use to anyone, but would only be one more to protect on the road against brigands."

"I could defend myself!" Vachel returned hotly, standing up from the table.

Etienne followed suit and the two of them would have come to blows had it not been for their father's interference. In a stern voice, he banished both of them from the room, stating in no uncertain terms that both were as yet too immature for him even to think of allowing them to venture far from the castle. Wrathfully, both young men stomped away—Vachel upstairs to his room, and Etienne to the courtyard outside.

"They both should have been in the army," Philippe said to his wife as he reseated himself. "There is true spirit there, but they lack the self-discipline of hard training. If I had had the money to buy them posts—"

"Hush, my dear," Anne said softly. "Things will turn out for the best. I only pray that neither of them will ever see a battlefield!" she ended, with a fierceness that surprised her husband.

Aimee was troubled by the conversation of her parents and she laid her soup spoon aside, concerned also about her older brothers' behavior. Glancing at Charles and Denis, who were both greedily slurping their soup, she felt somehow comforted in the very commonness of their needs and desires. A warm fire, a full stomach, the presence of those they loved: Why were those not enough for Etienne? Next to her, Giles was nodding over his bowl. After carefully pushing it out of the way and cushioning his head on a piece of cloth, Aimee slipped away from the table and made her way to the courtyard to check on Etienne.

The late spring evening was chill and Aimee shivered, wishing she'd thought to bring a shawl with her. Hesitantly, she searched the interior of the courtyard, her eyes adjusting quickly to the glow of moonlight. Just outside the archway that led into the park beyond, she spied the silhouette of her brother, leaning negligently against the cold stone, kicking at the ground in impetuous irritation.

"Etienne?"

He started and turned, perceiving her light-colored dress in the moonlight. "Aimee, what are you doing out here? Have you followed me at Father's request?" he wondered sarcastically, crossing his arms as though to contain the emotions inside him.

"No. I was worried about you."

"You waste your worry, then," he returned flippantly. "After all, I am not allowed to do anything but rot in this old castle while all around me things are going on that I cannot do anything about! Ah, if only Father would let me go to Paris, little sister!"

"Would you truly be happy then, Etienne?" she questioned, moving closer to his tall figure for warmth.

He blinked in the moonlight, then put his arm about her shoulders and hugged her tightly. "Yes, I think so," he replied. "I cannot abide this country existence," he continued. "There is no adventure, no excitement to it!"

Aimee thought of the peasant uprisings, the burnings and the murders, and shivered. To her way of thinking, that was excitement enough. What was it her brother was truly seeking—a release for his restless nature? She asked him as much.

Etienne laughed. "You have certainly put the point on it, little one. Yes, I admit to having a wanderlust that can never be assuaged here on this little estate. I must see adventure—yes, even danger—to make life seem worthwhile! We hear the news from Paris and I yearn to go there and see for myself everything that is happening, while Father is content to sit here and wait—wait for *what*, I ask! For the revolution to go on around him? For battles to be fought and wars won and men killed and women taken? And all the while, he sits behind these decaying granite blocks and thinks to be spared the horrifying glory of it all!"

"But what glory is there in battles and wars, in murder and rape?" Aimee demanded, shrugging off the arm around her shoulders. "You talk like a child, Etienne. You speak of dying men as though they were toy soldiers to be picked up after some staged battle; you talk of war as though it were something to be begun or ended on your own whim! I have heard Father talking to others of war and I cannot see anything glorious in it! It is blood and dying and suffering and tears—I hate it!" And she whirled around, eluding his outstretched hand, running back into the safety of those granite walls that she was sure would stand until the end of time.

The remainder of that year of 1790 saw a rapid collage of events that seemed barely to touch those living outside Paris. Because of the pressing problem of the empty treasury, the Assembly decided to confiscate and sell properties of the Church, which had always been exempt from taxes. The common people cheered this development while not understanding the sheer logistics of such an enormous feat. It would take a long time to sell all these lands and to get the money for them. Meanwhile, the government issued new paper money, called "assignats," which was issued against church property as security. The owner of these assignats could not demand gold for them, and the danger was that more paper money would be issued than the value of the property behind them, which would cause the depreciation of the paper—something no one cared to think about when the assignats were first issued to the value of one hundred francs in coin. But by 1791, the paper money had already dropped to only eighty-two francs in coin.

Also, with the confiscation of the Church's land came the abolition of monasteries and convents, and by November 1790, the National Assembly passed a law requiring all former clerics to take an oath concerning the Civil Constitution of the Clergy or forfeit their positions, which meant that the priests and bishops must choose between allegiance to the Church or the State. This created a schism between the oath-takers, many of whom were the highest-ranking members of the Church in France who had long been used to nonsecular ways at Court, anyway, and the non-oath-takers, many of whom were parish priests, devoted to their old religion and the strict observance of its rules as handed down by the Pope in Rome.

Added to the confusion of the religious question was the decision by the Assembly that all titles and coats of arms were to be abolished. Nobles were instructed to use only their family names, and even Louis XVI was to be known as Citizen Capet.

The year 1791 saw many problems that caused internal disorder. Among them were the high cost of living, the non-oath-taking clergy, the peasant uprisings, and the rise of certain "clubs" in the cities whose struggle for power in the government threatened to tear it apart. One of the most notorious of these clubs was the Jacobins, who were represented in Paris by Robespierre, Danton, and Marat.

Philippe de Chartres, reading of these men from a new journal, the *Moniteur,* which had been sent to him from his sister, Hortense, in Paris, was amazed at the bloodthirsty ideals that seemed to be equated with them. He worried more and more about his sister, whose adamant refusal to leave her beloved city he could not understand. Thousands of royalists had already fled from France rather than risk their gold or their lives to the ravening wolves of the revolution, which seemed to be gaining in momentum. Philippe wondered where it would take them—and when it would end.

All hope of a quick and reasonable resolution ended when he learned of the royal family's ignominious flight from Paris and their capture at Varennes on the night of June 20, 1791. The King and Queen were arrested and conducted back to Paris amid outrages and insults, and the people's fear, fed by the radical Jacobins, that the King would betray them. They were now made to realize that the King was dispensable, that the government could continue to work without him.

"I fear for King Louis and his Queen," Philippe said one day in the autumn of 1791. Two long years had passed since the original States-General had met by order of the King, and now that body of men had declared its work completed and had given power over to the new Legislative Assembly, whose first session was held in October. "According to all the reports and journals, the people are beginning to distrust the monarch more and more, especially when he uses his power to veto the decrees of the Assembly."

"Then why does he veto them?" Giles asked earnestly, interested in spite of the fact that he was nursing a terrible head cold. Aimee watched sympathetically as he blew his nose and wiped at the moisture in his eyes.

"Because he feels he must listen to his own conscience," Philippe answered.

"He listens to the Queen's conscience," Vachel broke in. At

seventeen, he was nearly as headstrong and outspoken as his eighteen-year-old brother, Etienne. "There's talk that many of the emigrés who have fled from France have been smuggling in secret notes to the King filled with ideas of counter-revolution! They have threatened to return to full power by using our enemies, the British and the Austrians, against us!"

Philippe chuckled and shook his head. "Another firebrand in the family! Vachel, do you never think that some of those emigrés you speak of so sourly are probably distant cousins of yours! Have I truly brought my family up as that of a solid bourgeois?"

"No, Father!" Aimee spoke up with spirit. "Etienne and Vachel are always speaking down about the King and Queen, but I feel sorry for them!"

"Pah! Sorry for them! You're a sentimental goose, little sister," Vachel retorted in disgust. "Look at how they tried to escape to Austria just a few months ago to betray government secrets to the enemy! And do you think they suffer for it? No! They are once more cozily ensconced in the Tuileries with plenty to eat and with servants at their beck and call!"

"Vachel, perhaps you are being too harsh," Philippe advised his son. "Both you and Etienne seem to blame the monarchy for the state of our own finances. It is true we are not wealthy, but you are still an aristocrat, my son."

Vachel simmered for a moment, then left the room, apparently to find his older brother, who was conspicuously absent from the family gathering. Aimee watched him go, knowing he would make his way into town, where he would eventually find Etienne drinking with a handful of other young men who expressed their ideas in heated debates while they gulped down quantities of wine and spirits.

Denis and Charles excused themselves from the room and went about whatever activities interested them. The twins had always been quiet, docile boys who, even now, at fifteen, seemed worlds apart from their two older brothers.

After Giles had gone with his mother to the kitchen in order to take some herbal remedy for his cold, Aimee sat alone with her father, watching the waning day outside through the mullioned panes of the windows until only the fire in the grate shed any light into the room. She sat by her father's knees on a small stool, her bright hair catching the light from the flames as it rested on the arm of his wing chair. Absently, Philippe touched the fine, silken gold, a gentle smile touching his lips.

"So," he commented after a moment, "I have at least one child who remembers she is an aristocrat by birth."

"I shall never forget that, Father," Aimee returned, lifting her head to scan her father's face. She could see the deep lines of worry etched into his forehead and cheeks, the whitening of the hair on his brow and temples. She knew how concerned he was over his sister in Paris and wished there was something she could do to alleviate his worries. Silly woman—why did she insist on remaining in a city that was on the verge of some great explosion? The political upheaval was increasing, as was the danger to those of aristocratic blood. She was foolish for not fleeing to the provinces while she still could.

"Have you heard more from Aunt Hortense?" she wondered aloud.

Philippe shook his head. "Nothing in the last week. I hope she received my last note, begging her to reconsider her decision to stay in Paris. With all the turmoil in the city, though, it would easily be possible for the mails to be tied up. I am hoping to receive something from her soon."

"And if not?"

"Then I may journey to Paris myself to persuade her to come with me."

Aimee's face paled at the thought. "Father, you mustn't go!" She turned toward him, her face registering appeal.

Philippe laughed and took her face between his hands, shaking it slightly and rubbing his thumbs against the softness of her flesh. "What's this?" he wondered. "My little aristocrat in whose veins courses the blood of noble knights and brave warriors is afraid? That cannot be, my daughter, for now is not the time to surrender to fear. Fear makes the evil stronger. We all need courage to do the tasks set aside for us. If it is God's will that I go to Paris to rescue my sister, then I will certainly go."

"It is not God's will, but that silly old woman's!" Aimee returned heatedly. "If she insists on remaining in that place after all your pleadings, then let her stay!"

With a sigh of resignation, Philippe brushed back an errant strand of silk from his daughter's brow. "Let us not talk of your aunt now, my dear, for I would not have us both arguing as your brothers do. I am worried for their sake, too."

"Father, they would jump at the chance to go to Paris," Aimee put in grumpily. "Let them both go and fetch Aunt Hortense back with them!"

He laughed as though vastly pleased at the idea. "Your

brothers think themselves grown men already, talking of fighting and revolution with a zest that only points out their immaturity. Protected behind these granite walls all of their lives, sheltered from the dire aspects of poverty and crime that run rampant in cities like Paris, they believe that their youth and passion are indestructible. How little they really know! How quickly their fine ideals would be crushed beneath the abject misery and the heartless cruelty of the city! And yet, I know that I can no longer protect them as I would like. Paris stretches out her fingers to the provinces even now. . ."

Aimee nodded. "In the tavern I know Etienne and Vachel both get their fill of talk of Paris and the revolution."

Philippe nodded thoughtfully. "So much of the new Legislative Assembly is composed of inexperienced men who are suspicious of the King. Certain political clubs have loomed up threateningly as possible rivals of that Assembly. A power struggle goes on in the city and both sides seek recruits from the country."

"I have heard Etienne talk of the Jacobins, Father."

"Yes, as have I, little one. It is a club that has been growing steadily since the beginning of all this change, and which has grown more radical as the revolution progresses. There have been smaller clubs of theirs established throughout the country. I fear Etienne may become one of their recruits."

"But he is of the nobility!" Aimee said quickly. "They would not allow him to be one of them!"

"But he has never known the privileges of true nobility," Philippe explained. "I think your brother suffers from the misconception that because of our lack of finances and social position, the Court nobility owes him something. He thinks—"

"Yes, Father, what do I think?"

Philippe and Aimee looked up, startled at the appearance of Etienne in the doorway. He stood tall and handsome, golden-haired and muscular as he gazed down at the pair of them. Aimee stood up, noting the slight unsteadiness in his gait as he entered the room to sit in a chair close to the fire. He ran one hand through his hair, and she could see the flush of drink on his cheeks.

"You are home earlier than usual," Philippe observed dryly.

"Am I?" Etienne returned carelessly. "I had thought you would be pleased, then."

"I am," Philippe agreed. He was silent, knowing that his son would speak when he wanted to.

"Jacobins were in Orléans recruiting today," Etienne finally went on, leaning his head back wearily in the chair. "It seems they are rapidly extending their influence all over France, Father. Robespierre, their leader, seems to be the man of the hour."

"I have heard him labeled a radical democrat, but a monarchist still," Philippe observed.

Etienne shrugged. "They tell me he is a strong leader, an inspiring man who believes in the right of equality and justice for every man. I have no idea if this is truth or lies. He is strongly against the other powerful club in Paris, the Cordelier Club, which has Danton as its leader. He's a ruthless lawyer, I've heard, a man whose chief influence is with the working class of Paris—the stuff of which mobs are made . . ."

"Both clubs are trying to impose their will on the Assembly," Philippe stated. Then, after a long breath, he added, "What have you decided, my son?"

Etienne stared at his father. "I have decided nothing," he replied softly. "Nothing, except that I distrust both sides of this affair and, before making a decision, I will wait and see what comes about in the next few months."

Philippe got up from his seat and went to embrace his son heartily. "Perhaps," he said with a light laugh, "there is still hope for you, my son."

Aimee's young heart swelled with relief as father and son embraced. The family was whole again, united in spirit against the unknown. They had survived the first raw shock of the revolution—and it would remain to be seen how they would fare against the devastating aftershocks.

3

"France has declared war on Austria!"

Vachel's excited cry echoed through the long main hall of the Castle du Beautreillis, where Aimee was seated in front of an embroidery frame, painstakingly attempting to finish the fine, delicate stitches in the pattern her mother had given her. She had just turned thirteen that month of April and, although she still preferred to don her brothers' castoff clothing and ride one of the stable mares or climb high up into the branches of an oak to look down on the world below, Anne de Chartres had decided that her daughter must begin to learn some of the more womanly arts that would be expected of her. She was, Anne declared, growing into a young lady in spite of herself, and that meant conducting herself with more decorum.

At first, Aimee had fought against the physical changes in her body that separated her more and more from her brothers. The budding breasts, the mysterious flow that afflicted her once every month—these things made her different from her brothers, and it made them act differently toward her. She wished she could have remained a child forever, never changing, continuing through life as always, joining in her brothers' activities without hesitation. But her brothers, too, were growing up and, despite all of Aimee's fervent prayers, nothing could change the steady clock of time—so that finally, much to her parents' relief, she accepted her young womanhood. She might still, at times, seem ungracious about it, but she was trying her best to please the expectations of both her father and mother. Hence, the hours spent at the embroidery frame, though she disliked having to sit still when she would much rather be out riding with the twins or swimming with Giles.

Now, as she heard Vachel's passionate declaration, she completely gave up on the embroidery and jumped up from her seat, her green eyes brilliant in her excitement. "Father's not here. He's gone into town with Etienne. Oh, Vachel, has war really been declared! Do we even have an army big enough to make war?"

24

"Of course, we have an army—the Army of France, you dolt!" Vachel replied impatiently, clearly disappointed that he could not share his momentous information with anyone other than his little sister. "But where is everyone else?"

"Mother is weeding the kitchen garden with one of the village girls. The twins are out riding and—"

"Never mind!" Vachel interrupted with exasperation. "Father and Etienne are probably at the Café Foy. I'll go there myself, although I'm sure the news must have reached them by now. It was only by luck that I happened to intercept the messenger on his way to Orléans from Paris."

"Wait for me!" Aimee implored, racing after him, lifting her long skirts to give her more freedom of movement, wishing she'd put on a pair of breeches instead. "I want to go, too!"

"Don't be ridiculous! You don't go into a tavern, Aimee!" Vachel called back, running headlong into the stable in order to grab his horse before the servants unsaddled it. "You wait here until we get back!"

"No, I'll not wait!" Aimee replied angrily, but she realized her brother was not listening to her. Stamping her foot, she continued after him, certain that this time she would not be excluded from all the excitement. It was bad enough that she'd been sitting at that embroidery frame for hours this morning; she was not about to go back to it now.

As she entered the stable, Vachel dashed past her on one of the horses, throwing her a lopsided grin, fully expecting her to have a tantrum, but in the end to stay at the castle as any young lady should. But Aimee had other ideas, ordering another mare saddled hastily while she slipped on a muddy pair of her brother's riding boots, having no time to go back inside to get her own. Once the horse was saddled, Aimee scrambled onto it, heading it toward the road that led to Orléans. Determinedly, she raced over the neatly maintained road, past the newly planted fields, oblivious to the occasional farmer or peasant wife who gazed at her in surprise and annoyance as her unbound hair streamed in a bright cascade behind her and her skirts rode high on her finely shaped legs.

It took her only a short time to gain the town and she slowed her mount to a more sedate walk, remembering to pull down her petticoats as she went through the streets, scanning the signs on the edifices, searching for the one proclaiming the Café Foy, the most popular of the gathering places, which had taken its name from the famous café in Paris. Finally, she saw the picture of a hearth outlined in red against a bright blue background with white lettering, obviously recently repainted in the tricolors of liberty. She called a small boy to watch her horse, noting the red-white-and-blue cockade he'd sewn to his shirt.

The excitement she'd sensed upon entering the town seemed intensified a thousandfold as she walked through the door of the café into a smoky, warm common room filled all around with men who all seemed to be speaking, shouting, or whispering at the same time. Trying to make herself as unnoticeable as possible, she circled the perimeter of the room, searching for the faces of her father and brothers. In some surprise, she noted the tricolor cockade displayed everywhere in the room, especially on the shirts and hats of the men present. Some had even adopted a small, red cap as a symbol of liberty, while many were wearing the long trousers of the *sans-culottes*, who were all the rage in Paris.

As Aimee trod cautiously about the room, it was inevitable that a brown and gnarled hand would shoot out to capture her about her waist and pull her toward a dingy shirtfront that showed the remains of the wearer's last meal as well as a few fresh splashes of beer. With a squeak, Aimee was thumped onto a well-padded lap while a warm, moist breath heavily laden with onions and beer ruffled the hair at the back of her neck.

"A bit young for your trade, aren't you, girl?" a gruff voice questioned in her ear. "Ordinarily, all this talk of war would mean slim pickings for your kind today, but damned if I'm not feeling randy just looking at your sweet flesh!"

"I'm looking for my father!" Aimee explained, turning her head to stare into the surprised eyes of Faron, the miller.

"Holy Christ! What are *you* doing here, wench? Don't you know, women—at least your kind—aren't allowed in here?" His surprise did not prevent him from continuing to hold tightly to her waist, and his small eyes kept on devouring the peachlike skin of her cheeks.

"My father is here, with my two oldest brothers," Aimee said, seeking a way out of his firm hold.

"He is, is he? Well, I've not seen him, girl. Of course, I can't say I'd imagine him here, among all these true patriots of France —him with his 'noble blood' and all. I'm surprised he's not turned tail and run with the rest of those damned emigrés, most of them going over to Austria, inciting them to war!"

"My father is as loyal to France as you are, Monsieur Faron!"

Aimee interjected heatedly, forgetting her precarious position on this huge man's lap.

"That's *Citizen* Faron, my girl, don't be forgetting," he replied, winking slyly. "Why, to hear that from you, a body might think you haven't been listening to the laws the Assembly's been passing. No one has the right to be called 'Monsieur'—not even your noble father!"

"And least of all *you!*" Aimee spat, becoming angrier by the minute. She hated this beefy man pawing at her waist, breathing his obnoxious smell into her face. He was odious! If she could only turn herself around, she'd get free and kick him in the shin for his trouble!

But the miller seemed ill-inclined to let her go as he took one hand from her waist and stroked her bright hair thoughtfully. His small, mean eyes took in the budding young womanhood and, despite his knowing the danger he might be provoking, he couldn't resist keeping her there, almost as much for her own beauty as for the fact that he was finding an outlet for his resentment and envy of her father.

"Let me go!" Aimee said tightly, her revulsion preventing any fear from showing. "If you do not want my father and brothers to carve you up into small pieces among them, Citizen Faron, you had best release me now!"

"Ha! Those young popinjays! Why, I could crush both their skulls with my own two hands!" He laughed, amused by her anger. "As for the noble Philippe de Chartres, let him come! I would like to see what the man is truly made of—I doubt that much else but scented water flows through his veins!"

"Release my daughter immediately!"

Aimee turned around to see her father, his face bloodless with rage, staring down at Faron, his dark blue eyes terrible to behold as they took in the man's hand at her waist and on her hair. For the first time in her life, Aimee felt shame color her cheeks as her father looked at her. Despite everything happening without her provocation, she could not but feel she had failed her father in some intrinsic way. Behind Philippe stood her two brothers, equally as angry as he, and Aimee found she could not meet their eyes. It was almost as though she were made to stand naked in front of them, her womanhood revealed. She hung her head in pain, letting the curtain of her hair shield her face from them.

"I told you to release my daughter!" Philippe repeated, and Aimee could not know the terrible pain in his own heart at that moment.

"Why, of course, Citizen de Chartres," Faron replied with a toothy smile, standing up so that Aimee slid unceremoniously to the pine floor of the café.

Acutely embarrassed, Aimee picked herself up, aware of dozens of pairs of eyes on her, wondering if the entire assemblage were staring at her. With a lump in her throat as big as a pigeon's egg, she moved toward her father, hardly able to bear the terrible fury in his eyes, even though it was not directed at her.

"Vachel, take your sister outside," Philippe said quietly. "Citizen Faron and I have something to discuss."

"Father—" Aimee stopped at the look Philippe gave her.

"Aimee, go with your brother."

Aimee hesitated, all her instincts pleading with her to run from the room, but pride rescued her from ignominious flight and, holding her back straight, her head high, she walked from the room, Vachel's hand on her arm.

Outside, she would have liked to collapse against her brother, but his words stopped her. "What a stupid thing to do!" he uttered harshly. "You haven't an ounce of sense in you to come riding into town and swishing into the Café Foy as brazen as some city whore! Men like Faron are always in cafés waiting for women. I *told* you to stay at home and wait, didn't I?"

Tears stung Aimee's eyes at the fury of his attack. No words of defense could come to her lips and she stood dumbly, trying not to let the tears overflow onto her cheeks. Angrily, Vachel retrieved her horse from the boy, giving him a coin for his trouble, then cupped his hands to help Aimee mount the mare.

Suddenly, the noise of fighting—the cracking of chairs, the shouts of men, the roars of angry voices—could be heard coming from inside the Café Foy. Without thinking, Vachel drew his sword and rushed back inside the building, leaving Aimee to her own devices.

Terrified, Aimee could hear the splintering sound of crashing glass and the ring of cold, hard steel clanging inside the café. Her heart pounding, she stood next to her horse, wondering what she should do. Every fiber of her being wanted to reenter the building and make sure her father and brothers were all right, but good sense held her back, as she realized she would only be something else for them to worry about. And yet, she couldn't ride back to the castle now—no, she must wait and make sure they were all right. All of this was her fault! If only she hadn't been determined to follow Vachel!

It seemed that everyone had joined into the fray inside and that the very walls of the place were going to collapse. In the street, curious townspeople gathered, wondering what the commotion was about.

"Have they caught a royalist spy?" someone wondered aloud.

"It must be an Austrian spy!" a woman shouted. "He'll try to kill us all in our sleep!" She wailed frantically and clutched her children to her skirts before hurrying away.

Several men of the town were trying to shoulder their way inside the café to bring some order, and Aimee watched, her heart in her throat, hoping her family was all right. Finally, the fracas seemed to be dying down and several of those involved lurched outside the door, spitting teeth, nursing cuts and bruises, and trying to stand upright on shaky legs. With a glad cry, Aimee saw her father, supported by both her brothers, exit onto the street, and she ran to help them, forgetting the earlier shame she had felt.

Her father, too, seemed to have forgotten his earlier ferocity, for he smiled at his daughter almost merrily, although immediately his hand went to his cheek and he spat out a loosened tooth. Aimee tried not to cry as a trickle of blood inched from his mouth and she scanned his face frantically for signs of wounds.

"Just a few bruises, my dear," Philippe said, noting her anxious look.

"The fat Faron cannot boast the same," Etienne assured her with a grin that also showed a missing tooth on the side. "I think," he said to Vachel, "you broke his arm, little brother! Did you see the way his hand dropped as though it had just caught a cannonball!" Etienne laughed, then stopped as a pain smote him.

Sporting a cut over one eye and a nasty-looking bruise high on his cheek, Vachel grinned back, looking especially proud to have proved himself in front of his older brother. He put one arm around Aimee's shoulder to support himself as he favored one leg. "Damn! I think someone must have scraped me a good one on my shinbone," he commented, limping noticeably by the time they got to their horses.

By the time all four returned to the castle, twilight was settling in and Anne de Chartres was gazing anxiously out the door of the courtyard. Upon seeing the state of the three males in the group, she drew in a deep breath and hurried to help them dismount. She gave Aimee an anxious look, but seeing nothing wrong with her outwardly, she bawled out orders to the gaping servant girls to get fresh cloths and water and her special liniment from the medicine cabinet.

"What have you been up to?" Anne finally asked as the three men were seated in the kitchen and treated to warmed mugs of ale while the women tended to their wounds. Giles and the twins had arrived and were watching with a mixture of excitement and worry as their father and brothers groaned painfully throughout the ordeal.

"That disgusting miller Faron overstepped himself today," Etienne explained heatedly, wincing as Aimee bandaged his ribs where several purple bruises showed.

"He's been spoiling for a fight with Father ever since he was bested that night he came for the feudal tax accounts," Vachel supplied, trying to remain manfully still while a kitchen girl doctored his eye.

"Mother, it was my fault!" Aimee interjected, moist-eyed. "If it hadn't been for me following Vachel into town—"

"Aimee, it was bound to happen!" Philippe interrupted her quickly. "You were only the catalyst, my dear, for something that's been brewing for some time now. Faron has always hated me because I don't allow him to charge my tenants exorbitant prices for grinding their wheat. His ideals are totally alien to me, as mine are to him. It was inevitable that we would clash some-day— especially with the heightened emotions caused by the revolution. He's an ardent sympathizer of the Jacobins."

"Is he a dangerous man, Philippe?" Anne asked anxiously, then quieted at a stern look from her husband.

"He is no more dangerous than we allow him to be," he answered.

"He's a stupid oaf!" Etienne cut in. Then he boasted, "I should have liked to use my sword on that fat stomach of his, but Father—"

"He had no sword of his own, Etienne," Philippe reprimanded him.

"But if the situation had been reversed, do you think he would have hesitated to use *his* sword?" Etienne demanded.

Philippe was silent and Aimee bit her lip, knowing what the answer would be. It might be true that Faron did not have intelligence on his side, but he did have a nasty cunning, and she wondered if he would take retribution for this drubbing the de Chartres family had given him. The thought was sure to have occurred to her father, she knew, as evidenced by his next words of caution.

"I would rather the twins not go riding too far without one of their older brothers with them for a while," he said. "Aimee, I would have you stay close to the castle, and you, too, Giles, until the results of today's work have become a distant memory. The townspeople will talk about it for some time, but I have an idea that with everything that is happening in Paris and around the country, they will soon have other topics to discuss."

"The war!" Etienne responded, as though just remembering.

"France is welcoming this opportunity to spread her revolutionary ideas beyond French borders," Philippe said wearily. "She urges this war on her young men only because the Jacobins want it to prove that the King is secretly a traitor to France, that he is in intimate relations with her enemies. It will be disastrous for the poor, young inexperienced men who will go into battle with absolutely no idea of how to fight or take orders."

"Etienne and I will serve brilliantly, Father," Vachel assured him.

"You will not go—not yet, my son," Philippe returned implacably. "I shall not have you butchered on the battlefield because of incapable officers or poor weapons."

Vachel would have argued, but he covered his impatience as well as he was able, helped, no doubt, by his wounds, which made him want to do nothing else but sleep. After he and Etienne had gone upstairs to their rooms with the rest of the children, Anne and Philippe remained awake, talking quietly in the sitting room. Aimee, unable to sleep and restless, returned downstairs several hours later only to find them still talking.

"Aimee, haven't you slept, my dear?" her mother asked, going to put her arms around her daughter.

"It's hard tonight," Aimee said simply. "I can't help thinking of that horrible Faron."

"He is not worth your troubled thoughts, daughter," Philippe said comfortingly.

"And yet—the way he spoke to me—held me—"

Philippe whitened at the remembrance. "Indeed, my dear, you are no longer a child in the eyes of many. To your mother and me, you are still our littlest, our baby, but to men like Faron—" He stopped and his mouth tightened in anger.

"You are growing up," Anne said with a small sigh. "And no matter how your father and I think of it, in times like these when the world seems turned upside down, it is hard for girls to grow to womanhood. We have talked about it, Aimee, and we think it would be best for you to go to the Convent of Saint-Vincent in Orléans for a time."

"No!" Aimee nearly shouted, upset at the idea of being separated from her family.

"Yes, my dearest, I'm afraid you will go," Philippe said with a gentle sternness. "I . . . I cannot risk anything happening again like what happened today. You will be safe within the walls of the convent, for even though all Church lands have been confiscated, the good sisters are still allowed to do their work there—at least for the time being."

"But why are you doing this to me?" Aimee wondered. "Is it because of my own foolishness in going into the café?"

"It is for your own good," Philippe emphasized stubbornly, not likely to be swayed by guilty confessions. "That is my word on it, daughter."

4

—◦—◦—◦—

The glorious war to spread the revolution began disastrously when, instead of easily conquering Belgium, which belonged to Francis II of Austria, the French suffered severe losses. One of the reasons was what Philippe had feared: the resignation or emigration of all the nobility in the army who made up nearly all of the officers. Another suspected reason was treason by the King and Queen, who, it was whispered, must have informed the Austrians of the French campaign plans. When Louis boldly vetoed two important decrees by the Assembly, ordering all non-oath-taking priests to penal colonies and providing for an army of twenty thousand men for the protection of Paris, the storm broke. Several thousand working men, wearing the liberty cockades and carrying standards with the Declaration of the Rights of Man written on them, went to the hall of the Assembly and marched through it, shouting that the will of twenty-five million people could not be balked by the will of one man. Further inspired by the Jacobins to force the King to sign the two decrees, the crowd went to the Tuileries, forced open the gates, and penetrated to the King's apartments. Louis stood before them in the recess of a window, protected by some deputies for three hours while the crowd shouted to him to sign the decrees. Louis gave no promises but donned a red hat and drank a glass of wine with them. There was no violence, but the King had received a bitter humiliation that only hardened his resolve to work against the revolutionary ideals.

"I must go to Paris and bring my sister home with me," Philippe said solemnly after reading the news in a Parisian journal. "This insanity is becoming much worse and she will certainly be threatened, even imprisoned, if she doesn't leave her hotel in the city."

Aimee's heart froze at the dreaded words. She was still at home, her departure for the convent having been delayed because of an investigation into the workings of the institution by the city council. Now, to hear her beloved father talk of actually going to that place of evil! Why didn't that stupid woman listen to the

33

voice of reason and journey out of Paris herself? Things were only worsening as Prussia had joined Austria in the war against France and had issued a manifesto to restore Louis XVI to the throne, threatening to destroy all of Paris if this were not done, causing the people to become incensed with patriotic anger. All aristocrats were being looked upon with suspicion and hatred, commoners pointing the finger of guilt at them, accusing them of being spies against the revolution.

"When will you leave?" Anne asked with resignation, knowing she could do nothing to dissuade her husband from going.

He took her hand and smiled with love. "Within the week, my dearest. I should like to go as soon as possible—so that I may return that much more quickly."

"Will you . . . take Etienne and Vachel with you?"

Philippe leaned back in his chair and rubbed his eyes. "I do not want to risk their young lives—"

"But they will want to go," Anne pointed out, although it broke her heart to remind him. "And you cannot go alone, Philippe."

He sighed and nodded. "Then I shall take one of them with me, as well as two of the menservants. I shall leave four here with you and one of our older sons for protection." He rubbed his temples. "It shall be Etienne who comes with me—and Vachel who remains here."

Aimee felt a tight constriction in her chest as she imagined her oldest brother entering the gates of hell itself. And yet, it was what he had always wanted, always dreamed about. His joy would know no bounds. And poor Vachel, his loss would be bitter as he was forced to remain behind with the women and children. Nothing his father might say in regard to protecting his mother and siblings would erase the blow to his manhood, Aimee was sure.

Three days later, they were ready to leave, packed and mounted, each man well armed against highwaymen along the road. Aimee and her mother were hard put to hold back the tears as they bade good-bye to their loved ones. Vachel manfully hid his hurt, although his eyes were moist as he bade his brother farewell. Aimee hugged her father close, wishing for an instant that she might go with him, even though she was truly frightened of the city. It was hard to take her arms away from him, and when he gently set her aside the tears burst forth in torrents and she hurried from the courtyard, running upstairs to her room.

Wretchedly, she gazed out her window, watching her father

and brother as they started on the road to Paris. Behind her, she could hear her old nurse, Margot, creeping about the room, trying not to disturb her.

"What are you about, old woman!" she finally cried out in her fear and anger.

"Nothing, child, just straightening your bedclothes," the woman replied, taking no offense at what she knew to be a case of strained nerves.

Aimee was silent a moment, facing the window again. "They're going to Paris, Margot," she said finally.

"Yes, lamb, a wicked, wicked place, I know."

"More wicked now than when you lived there," Aimee said, turning around to face the old woman curiously.

"Yes," Margot agreed quietly. "Much worse than before, I'm afraid, little one. When I came to Paris, she was still happy and gay; she still had a king to rule her and a queen whom everyone adored. The crimes were many, 'tis true, but the worst of those were lechery and greed. Now the city is no longer gay, its people are mad with fear, and the thirst for vengeance rules everyone."

"And that is where my father is going," Aimee said with a clutch of fear. "I pray God go with him."

Two weeks later, Aimee was alerted to the main hall by a cry from her mother. Running from the kitchen, she hoped against all hope that it was her father and brother returned from Paris with her Aunt Hortense unharmed. Entering the hall to see Etienne sinking exhaustedly into a chair, her hopes plummeted and her legs seemed to go numb as she walked with difficulty the rest of the way. Her brother's face was worn and haggard, his clothing dirty and obviously unchanged for some time. Seated beside him, Anne de Chartres was pouring a glass of wine, offering it to his lips and waiting for him to speak.

Vachel, Denis, Charles, and Giles came in, halted, too, by the sight of their brother in his state of exhaustion. Quietly, they sat around him, waiting to hear what he had to say, all hoping the same thing, but fearful that Etienne's words would soon crush those hopes.

"Father—is—in—prison," Etienne gasped finally, taking deep breaths after swallowing the wine in one gulp.

There—it was said. Their fears were realized, but at least, Aimee prayed, he was not dead.

Anne's face seemed carved from stone as she gazed at her eldest son, a thousand questions on her lips, but able to ask none of them, not wanting to know the answers. Finally, she asked, "You have returned alone?"

Etienne nodded. "The menservants deserted us as soon as Father was taken away to prison—they are probably new recruits for the Army of France," he ended ironically. He seemed unable or unwilling to say more, and Anne poured him more wine, which he drank as quickly as the first glass. Everyone waited with strained quiet to hear more.

Finally, Etienne continued. "The second day after we arrived in Paris, while we were trying to find out the whereabouts of our aunt, another insurrection occurred. At nine o'clock in the morning, a large crowd attacked the Tuileries. By ten, the royal family left the palace and sought safety in the hall of the Assembly. They remained there for thirty hours while outside a furious combat raged between the Swiss Guard at the Tuileries and the mob. No quarter was given, Mother," he said, his eyes sickened by the remembrance. "I heard later that five thousand were killed that day, twelve hundred in the first two hours! Meanwhile, the Assembly continued to debate—it was madness, madness unlike anything I've ever experienced. They voted to depose the King and call for a National Convention to draw up a new constitution.

"Father and I managed to avoid the outbreaks of fighting. The next day, there was still some battle continuing in the streets, but we were able to find out Aunt Hortense's whereabouts, and the reason she had not been able to leave Paris. She had been placed under arrest, incarcerated in an old convent with several hundred other aristocratic women. There were channels, the intendant informed us, that we must go through in order to secure her release. We went through them and Father had to appear in front of the Jacobins at their Revolutionary Commune of Paris, which seems to be the true ruler of Paris and all of France now. Father presented his case and they agreed to release Aunt Hortense to his custody."

Etienne's eyes closed and his head dropped forward. "We took Aunt Hortense to her hotel, which had been boarded up after her arrest. Father made plans to leave as early as possible the following day, but—before we could go, *they* came for him. I don't know what happened, Mother, I honestly don't. Everything seemed to be going smoothly and then someone decided that Father should be arrested, that he was an aristocrat, a probable spy against the government of France! Could anything be more ridiculous? Father didn't resist them—he was sure that he would be released immediately. The next day, we were informed that he

was to remain in prison for an 'undisclosed' amount of time—
that could mean forever!"

"And so you came back," Anne said woodenly. "Thank God
for that, at least."

"But what about Aunt Hortense? Why didn't you bring her
back with you?" Aimee questioned, trying to think of anything
but her father stuck in some dark prison.

"The old crone wouldn't come!" Etienne huffed in a spurt of
anger. "She claimed her imprisonment had weakened her so that
she couldn't possibly make the journey! I told her she could rot in
that damned hotel of hers and I left at night, hoping I wouldn't be
detained at the gates. The guards there were suspicious at first,
asked me if I knew the words to their patriotic song, 'La Marseil-
laise.' I made a break for it and managed to escape them, but lost
my horse. I've been walking for five days!"

There was a strained hush in the room for several minutes as
each one of them digested the horrifying news. Anne was the first
to recover as she looked at her son with a mother's love and
sympathy. "I am so glad you are home with us again!"

Etienne's pain was evident as he returned her look. "I'm
sorry, Mother! I could do nothing to save Father . . . there was
nothing—"

"It's all right." She soothed him. "Better to have you here and
alive than imprisoned with him, without our knowing anything."

"But, Mother, I'm afraid for him," Etienne whispered, struggling against tears. "Paris is worse than anything you can imagine. People being arrested and dragged off to prison—sometimes
ten and twenty at a time! The Paris Commune talked of making
France a democracy, and yet, still, they seek out revenge against
anyone of noble blood. It's like some gigantic lunatic asylum!
They have even arrested the King and Queen and imprisoned
them in the Temple."

"What should we do, Mother?" Vachel asked, fear edging his
voice. "We cannot leave Father in prison, at the whim of such
monsters!"

Anne looked at her family, then stared most fiercely at her two
eldest. "You will *not* go to Paris," she directed in a hard voice. "I
will not lose anyone else I love to this madness. Your father is
capable of taking care of himself. He will surely find some way
to convince this . . . this Commune of Paris that he is guilty of
nothing! It would only cause him more pain to find that anyone
else he loves has been imprisoned. And you two"—she nodded
to Etienne and Vachel—"you have a responsibility to me and to

your sister and brothers. You cannot leave us unprotected. You must stay here—all of us must remain here and wait and hope . . . and pray."

When both older boys would have protested, Anne's eyes stopped them. "Your father would not wish you to endanger yourselves on his behalf now," she said matter-of-factly. "He can concentrate better on freeing himself, knowing that we are all safe here."

"Will our father come home—soon?" Giles wanted to know, and Denis and Charles echoed the question anxiously.

"I don't know," Anne answered honestly. "That is why we must all send our prayers to God for his swift release from prison."

"The waiting is hard for me," Vachel said softly.

"It is hard for all of us," Anne returned.

The next few weeks seemed to go at a snail's pace as everyone awaited word from Paris. A note, a line or two, anything would have been welcome—but nothing came, and so, finally, Anne concluded that, as a prisoner, Philippe would not be allowed to write to his family. Even though she had expected as much, the blow was still a hard one to withstand as she tried to think of the days going by without hearing anything. Not even a letter from Hortense was forthcoming, and Aimee was hard put to hide her bitterness, thinking of the sacrifice her father had made for such an undeserving human being.

Her acceptance into the convent was further delayed, mainly because no one talked of it, and Aimee was content to remain at home. She would certainly want to be there when her father returned, as she was sure he would one day.

The news from Paris, however, was not good. Freedom of the press was suppressed, and so there were no journals coming from the city. People in the provinces had to rely on infrequent messengers on their way to other points in the country. The de Chartres family did learn, however, from one of these infrequent couriers that, as Etienne had suspected, the Revolutionary Commune, or City Council of Paris, was the real ruler, and not the Legislative Assembly—at least until the meeting of the National Convention. News of the war was not good either as a feeling of panic began to spread throughout France as the Prussians and Austrians besieged Verdun, which was the last fortress on the road to Paris. A frenzy gripped the capital as hundreds of persons were thrown into prison in a continual stream—all being suspected accomplices to the invaders.

The Commune tried to raise and forward troops to Verdun, but some members began to stir up more unrest and unease by saying that before the troops were sent to the front, the traitors within the city should be put out of the way. The common working men of Paris began to fear leaving the city, wondering if while they were at the front, the prisoners might escape and murder their wives and children. Marat, one of the most bloodthirsty advocates of the revolution, echoed and reinforced their fears until, finally, the result was the infamous September massacres.

With huge eyes and cold hearts, frozen by fear, the family heard the terrible news of the massacres—cold-blooded murders of priests who would not take the new civil oath, and of many people suspected or accused of being aristocrats. The butchery was systematically done by men hired and paid by certain members of the Commune, and the Legislative Assembly was too terrified to stop the bloody carnage. Nearly twelve hundred persons were "executed," and Aimee and her family had no idea whether her father was among the victims.

"This is too much!" Anne sobbed, having been crying for two days after hearing the news. "How can men continue to murder and maim for no good cause? Why does God not strike down these evil men?"

"There is no God in Paris," Etienne mumbled, unable to comfort his mother in his own pain.

"But surely this cold-blooded massacre will discredit the cause of the revolution!" Vachel said heatedly. "Surely people will begin to see its insanity!"

Two weeks after the massacres ended, the Prussians were miraculously stopped at Valmy, thus relieving the tension in Paris and allowing the prisoners who had not already been killed to breathe easier. Five days later, Anne received a hastily scrawled note from her husband.

The note, written on a torn and dirty piece of linen, said only that he was as well as could be expected and was hopeful of being released shortly. The words cheered Anne considerably and she begged the messenger to stay and sup with them, even though she feared the fare they could offer was poor indeed. The traveler, Citizen Pélagie, accepted with gusto, assuring Anne that anything she could offer would be better than what he'd been used to, despite his having heard that the harvest for this year of 1792 had been an excellent one.

"You wouldn't know it in the city," he said, slurping his soup down energetically and attacking ravenously the plain bread and preserves. "Everything is so damned expensive, although certain parties seem to be well supplied with whatever they desire," he added, winking conspiratorially at her.

"And what of those in prison?" Anne asked quickly, hungry for news.

"I myself was a prisoner in Saint-Lazare in the Faubourg Saint-Martin when I was first arrested," he began, tamping a fresh pipe and filling the hall with the tobacco's aromatic odor as he settled back in his chair. "Prisoners there could bring their own beds; some even brought complete sets of furniture! Even though two or three persons were generally in a room together, the rooms were quite large and airy, not what you'd expect of a prison. Of course, most have been converted from former convents because the capacity of the old prisons has long been filled. Ah, madame, it was as though you were not even in a prison; there were no bars on the windows, no bolted doors. Everyone occupied his time by playing ball games or with music or painting or sketching. I'm telling you, I was sorry to leave that place after my first hearing with the Assembly."

"Were you transferred to the same prison, then, as my husband?" Anne asked.

He nodded. "Les Ecossais du Luxembourg—not as pleasant as Saint-Lazare, mind you, but not altogether unpleasant for a prison. Many of the prisoners are allowed to play chess and whist at least once a week, and everyone gets regular exercise outside in the courtyard. It's lacking in some comforts, but the communal life of the prisoners gives one a curious sense of freedom."

"How were you able to escape?" Aimee wondered impatiently.

Citizen Pélagie laughed amiably. "I did not escape, my dear. I proved to the Commune that I was not a true aristocrat, but only a wealthy bourgeois from Lyons, having got mistakenly caught up in the furor of the capital."

"Is it true that you are not an aristocrat?" Aimee continued.

The man blanched and glanced around, as though seeking someone in hiding. He laughed again, but nervously this time. "Of course it is true, my girl; I have already proven it to be so!"

"Were you there during the September massacres?" Vachel asked.

The man nodded, his face drawn at the remembrance. "Yes. I could look out my window and see six large carts rolling down that I took to be cattle trucks. But then I realized my mistake as they got closer and I could see they were full of men and women who'd just been slaughtered and whose legs and arms and heads dangled on either side of the carts. My God, I'd never seen such gore, even on a hunt. With trickles of fresh blood falling and staining the road—it was the most gruesome sight I've ever seen. If I live to be a hundred, I hope I never see its like again." He shook his head and puffed for a moment on his pipe.

"But let's not talk of such events," he said hurriedly. He looked at the young, eager faces around him and pointed to the boys with a little wink. "Ah, you would make fine new recruits for our National Guard. They need strong young men like yourselves to fight those cursed Austrians and Prussians. Resplendent they are in their fine royal blue coats with white linings and scarlet facings and gleaming yellow epaulets on their shoulders. They'd turn a pretty girl's head with no trouble," he added, extending his wink to Aimee's flushed face.

"They do sound splendid!" Vachel said enthusiastically. "Are they still needing volunteers?"

"Yes, they need many more to swell the ranks for war, boy. Most of the volunteers come from the bourgeois—lawyers, merchants, artisans, and men of independent means—like yourself."

"What has happened to the nobility?" Anne asked, deliberately changing the subject. "I mean those not imprisoned."

"It's impossible for all the nobility to be put in prison," Citizen Pélagie agreed. "Many have renounced their coats of arms and either obtain false papers or simply stay away from the authorities. Some have become wig makers, dancing teachers, café waiters, and doormen. It amuses the bourgeois to have their former masters as their servants now. Before I left Paris, I saw the former Comte de Vieuville shining shoes at the corner of the Place d'Erlanger. The Marquis de Montbazet is a lamplighter and the Chevalier d'Anselme an actor. Even the Comtesse de Virieu, whom I knew personally, though only slightly, was darning stockings on the pavement outside the Palais Royal! I tell you, the world is topsy-turvy these days when the rabble sits in the Tuileries and the nobility are out in the street!" He shook his head again.

"You are most fortunate, then, Citizen Pélagie, in having been able to return to your home in Lyons," Anne put in warmly. "I hope my own husband will prove to be as fortunate as quickly as possible."

"I heartily hope so, madame," Citizen Pélagie returned. "And now, I must be on my way since I have far to go and I would like to put as much distance between myself and Paris before I sleep tonight—ah, if you catch my meaning, madame."

Anne nodded. "Although you are welcome to stay the night here—"

"Ah, thank you, but no," he replied, already rising to retrieve his coat. "This place, I'm afraid, is still much too close to Paris for my own peace of mind." He bowed over her hand, saluted the youngsters, and then was gone.

After he left, everyone sat soberly for a while until Anne retrieved the precious piece of linen and clasped it to her breast, bursting into sudden tears. Immediately, the others gathered around her, trying to offer comfort and to receive it as best they could. Just knowing their father was still alive was almost a miracle.

"We must keep on praying," Anne said through her tears. "Look how Citizen Pélagie was able to obtain his freedom. If he can do it, so can your father."

"But aren't *we* aristocrats, Mother?" Denis asked in confusion. "How can we claim to be bourgeois? I mean, the records would state clearly that our blood has come down from Henry the Second."

"You forget, son, that all Church lands have been confiscated by the State and all documents destroyed. Country nobility like us are in very little danger so long as we stay where we are and do not draw attention to ourselves. The Court aristocrats, however, were known to many in Paris, and so they are much easier targets for their wrath."

"The du Poirons?" Charles wondered suddenly, remembering the once beautiful château that was now only charred ruins.

"We must pray for them also," Anne said promptly. "I do not know their fate, my dear ones, but let us hope they are safe, too."

After that, news was even harder to come by. What news there was was mostly of the state of the war, which seemed to go back and forth with little victory for either side. The National Convention held its first meeting and voted to abolish royalty immediately, thus provoking a frenzied quarrel between the Jacobins and their enemies, the Girondists, as to who would have supreme power over the Convention.

The de Chartres family continued to hope for more letters from Philippe, but none was forthcoming and their hopes began to slide when they heard the astounding news that the King had actually, finally, been arrested for treason. A secret iron box had been found in the possession of the King that contained treasonous papers. The Jacobins, who held no mercy toward the King, demanded he be executed as any traitor would be, but the Convention finally agreed that he should be allowed a trial, which would begin in December.

King Louis XVI, Citizen Capet, did receive a trial that lasted over a month, but the verdict would have been the same had it lasted over a year—Louis Capet was found guilty on January 15, 1793, and on the morning of January 21, he was guillotined in the square fronting the Tuileries. The people of Paris cheered and proclaimed a victory for France, while many others outside Paris were numbed with shock at what had happened. More importantly, after the King's execution, England, Russia, Spain, Holland, Germany, and Italy all sided with Austria and Prussia in the war against France.

The National Convention voted three hundred thousand troops immediately for the war effort. They also created a Committee of General Security, a Committee of Public Safety, and a Revolutionary Tribunal to try those accused by these two committees. Meanwhile, the Girondists and Jacobins were still struggling for power and civil wars were breaking out in the provinces against the power of the Commune of Paris. Hastily, the Convention drew up the Constitution of 1793, but then just as hastily suspended it because they said a strong, central government was needed to wage war against the invaders. Therefore, they created a provisional government that would inaugurate the Reign of Terror.

5

Aimee de Chartres stood halfheartedly on the narrow stoop before the old iron door of the Convent of Saint-Vincent in Orléans, waving good-bye to her brother Etienne as he started back to the Castle du Beautreillis. Resignedly, she picked up the small trunk she had brought with a few dresses in it (the good sisters would never have allowed her to wear boys' clothing) and picked up the large brass knocker, which reverberated against the old door with a deep, hard thud. Shortly, a tall, large-boned nun, dressed in severe black, accentuated only by a pristinely white collar at her throat, opened the door, obviously expecting her. With a wave of one plump hand, she ushered the young woman inside to a wide, arched hallway with cold, stone flagging that echoed the click of Aimee's heels.

"You are Citizeness de Chartres?" the nun asked pleasantly.

"Yes." Aimee glanced at her surroundings with an uninterested eye, noting the shadowy alcoves in the wall where tallow candles stood, glowing softly in front of statues of saints and other holy icons.

"I am Sister Marie-Marguerite, my child, and you are welcome here," the nun said formally. "Follow me, my dear, and I will present you to our Mother Abbess." She led Aimee down the wide entrance hall until they passed into a small chapel where several nuns were at vespers, the sound of chiming bells overhead scattering a half dozen birds into the rafters. "We have heard your dear father was only recently a victim of the guillotine," Sister Marie-Marguerite whispered sympathetically. "We have been offering prayers for the repose of his soul."

The words sent an arrow of pain through Aimee's chest and she choked back tears at the unexpected reminder of her father's death. She had not wanted to think of it now; she had willed her mind to become numb so as not to feel the pain anymore. It had seemed forever that she had cried when the news came to them that Citizen Philippe de Chartres, having been found guilty of treason against the State, had been sent to the guillotine on the morning of May 2, 1793. His body had been buried in a communal pit in the outskirts of Paris, so even the comfort of seeing her father decently buried was denied her. She had tried to obtain some measure of comfort from her family, but their pain had been too great to offer her consolation.

Sister Marie-Marguerite, a kind woman, saw the tears in her young charge's eyes and patted her shoulder consolingly. "It is hard, my dear, but remember that he has gone from this world of terror and uncertainty to a far better place where there is no more pain and no more worry. His soul rests with God, and that should be some comfort to you in your pain."

Aimee shook her head stiffly. "It is little comfort to me, Sister, when I no longer have my father here with me. They named him a traitor, yet he loved France with all his heart! The charge of treason was ridiculous!"

The nun sighed. "Do you think they did not know that, my dear? It is so with anyone suspected of being part of the nobility. Even though they are innocent of any wrongdoing, the people of Paris continue to demand blood and retribution. The Committee of Public Safety, which *is* the voice of government now, seeks to secure its own precarious position by giving the people what they want. I have heard it said that a man is informed at ten in the morning that he is to appear before the Revolutionary Tribunal for trial at eleven. The tribunal sentences him to death by two in the afternoon, and at four o'clock he is executed in the square amid the cheers of the deathmongers. Such a travesty of justice!"

"And yet, you can still believe there is a God!" Aimee wondered, her green eyes hard as emeralds as she studied the nun's face more closely, noting the youth still reflected in the warm, blue eyes and nearly translucent skin.

"Yes, I still believe in God," Sister Marie-Marguerite returned, leading Aimee down a narrow corridor off which were several doors leading into different wings of the convent. "It is not God who commits these injustices against us, but men, who, in their free will, choose the work of the devil!"

"Then it must be the devil who rules in Paris—who rules all of France!" Aimee exclaimed bitterly.

"He lays claim to the weak, the ignorant," Sister Marie-Marguerite answered calmly. "That is why you are *here*, my child, to grow strong and intelligent, so that you will never turn to Satan despite the evil that men may do to you."

She turned down another hallway and opened a door that led into a spacious room, furnished austerely with the rudiments of comfort, the focus of which was a large bowed window, looking out onto the town of Orléans, in front of which was placed an impressively large desk. Seated behind the desk, looking equally as impressive, was a middle-aged nun, tall and regal, with sharp, piercing blue eyes that seemed to penetrate through Aimee's skull. Aimee sank automatically into a curtsy, amazed at the imposing stature of the woman before her who must be the Mother Abbess. Keeping her head down, she heard the scrape of the chair on the wooden flooring and the deliberate footsteps of the nun as she came around the desk to stand in front of her. Two cool, fine-boned fingers lifted her chin so that she could look into the dark, intelligent eyes of the older woman.

"Welcome, Aimee de Chartres," the Mother Abbess said in a husky, almost melodious voice that seemed at odds with her physical presence. "You have been sent by your family to be instructed in the ways of God and to learn the finer points of young womanhood, is that not so?"

Aimee nodded, feeling her rapid heartbeat returning to normal as the abbess gestured to her to resume standing. The woman gazed at her thoughtfully so that Aimee wondered if she were examining her very soul. Finally, she nodded to herself and returned to her seat behind the desk. "Come closer, my child, over here by the window. I should like to see you in a better light."

Aimee obeyed dutifully, wondering if the reason for the elderly nun's hard stare was simply poor eyesight. But she realized that was not the case when those striking, dark blue eyes continued to assess her silently, missing nothing. The warm, spring light from the large window seemed to bathe Aimee in a shimmering warmth as she stood, close by the desk, turning her attention to the wonderful view the window afforded her of the town of Orléans, spread out in picturesque fashion in front of her. Situated on the top of a small rise, the convent had the advantage of a wide kaleidoscopic view of the town and surrounding countryside. Straining to see her own home, only a few miles distant, Aimee thought she could just make out a gray turret rising above the castle, and her heart leaped with joy, eased somewhat by that familiar gray stone with which she had grown up. Once having made that discovery, she let her eyes fall to the town in front of her, a city that stood straddling the banks of the Loire, to the south of which she could see the small Saint-Marceau quarter, where the loveliest roses in France were sold.

The main part of the city, which rose on the north bank of the Loire, was the oldest section, surrounded by wide boulevards and picturesque quays along the river. Close by, she could make out the towers of the Gothic-styled Sainte-Croix cathedral, which had been largely destroyed by the Protestant uprising more than two hundred years before, but had been faithfully rebuilt over the last two centuries, and was nearly the same size as the famous Notre Dame of Paris. She remembered her mother telling her tales of the famous siege of Orléans and how the young Jeanne d'Arc had brought troops from Charles VII and provisions for the combatants inside the walls to save the day against the English. Orléans was a city full of the history of France, a history of bloodshed and defeat and of miracles and victory. Hard to believe that less than a hundred miles away, the city of Paris rose up, dirty and evil, a miasma of blood and hatred.

Watching the young girl from her vantage point, the Mother Abbess could see the change of emotions flickering across her face, deepening the color in her cheeks and changing the shade of her green eyes. She was, the mother noted, a tall girl with excellent bearing and an impressive tilt to her somewhat pointed chin, which made the nun wonder if she might prove intractable. She had suffered a terrible loss at the death of her father—sometimes young women in her situation turned toward God for comfort; other times they turned away from Him with a vengeance. This, the nun decided, would be her task in the coming months, then —to make certain that Aimee de Chartres turned to God and good works and spurned the temptations of Satan that might await her.

And so, the walls of the good convent closed in protectively around Aimee—a protectiveness that was nearly stifling for the young woman who was so used to open spaces. Her companions, she soon found, did not appeal to her very much, for they were mostly from the bourgeois families in the city of Orléans. These young women despised the young aristocrat in their midst, reminding her that she was no longer any different from the rest of them and that, in fact, she was worse off since her father had been branded a traitor, and heaven knew the whole family was as poor as church mice.

As the days turned into weeks, Aimee found herself submerged, in spite of herself, into the life of the convent, a stricter life than what she'd had before, but with a certain comforting sameness to it that sheltered her from the horrors of the revolution. For now that the Committee of Public Safety, with Robespierre at its helm, had taken over the government of France, the people in the provinces lived in fear of its long arm reaching out to overpower them. Robespierre believed in using fear to create loyalty, and commissioned committees of surveillance throughout the country to find spies in every city, town, and hamlet. Arrests of suspected persons were made en masse, and judgment and execution were summarily rendered. There were more guillotines erected in two of the public squares in Paris, and each day saw executions of priests who would not take the civil oath, emigrés who had tried to sneak back into France to secure their possessions, and losing generals who had been warned that they must lead their armies to victory or they would lose their heads.

In Paris, fear and panic were widespread. With the precarious food situation and the depreciation of assignats, there were bread riots and angry mobs demanding food for their families. Death was decreed for all food monopolists and profiteers; and all foreigners who had come to France after the fall of the Bastille were ordered arrested. The terror was spreading, building slowly, fed by news of the army's defeats and the certainty of the people that England had spies everywhere, plotting the downfall of France.

The contrast between the world of the convent and the world outside was like night and day. All the young charges, under the strict tutelage of the nuns, learned theology and logic. They studied Latin out of heavy, dull tomes whose pages were yellowed and cracked, and geography and history from maps and journals that presented everything in the dullest of terms. Attention was paid to keeping tallies of household accounts in neat and precise columns and to the art of letter writing, which was considered a must for genteel young ladies. Next in importance was the attendance to the humblest of chores in case reverses in one's fortunes came unforeseen. Aimee took to these with more grace than many of her companions, they having come from wealthy merchant families for the most part and being unused to housekeeping. They would tease Aimee, remarking slyly on how well she looked as she scrubbed the floor or worked in the kitchens. But, in the end, it was not Aimee whose back ached and whose knees were bruised. Her healthy body did not mind in the least the work that she had been used to for most of her life.

Lastly, the charges were taught to dance and how to curtsy properly, how to play the harpsichord, how to converse intelligently, and even how to handle a fan. Very little outside news was allowed to trickle down to the students from the Mother Abbess. If she was concerned with the general lawlessness and brutality of the people outside the convent, she said nothing to the young women entrusted to her care. She could not conceive of anyone daring to touch the sanctity of her religious order, nor could she comprehend the bestiality of peasants gone mad with hunger and fear.

But as the months went by and things worsened and the harvest of 1793 was even more meager than anticipated, the peasants began to grow more and more desperate. There were shortages of sugar and bread, and travel became nearly impossible; at each village, one had to stop, show one's passport, reply to interrogations, and, at the least suspicion, appear before an examining committee, then cool one's heels in a detention house while things were cleared up. Frustrations were building and it was only a matter of time before they would blow up completely.

In mid-October, news came that the Mother Abbess felt compelled to share with her charges. On October 16, Marie Antoinette was sent to the guillotine after being found guilty of treason to her country. Many of the girls wept in mingled shock and disbelief, but just as many turned hard faces to the Mother Abbess and whispered among themselves that that was exactly what the "royal whore" deserved, sentiments expressed by their fathers throughout the city of Orléans.

In early November, Aimee, who had been grumbling at the slowness of mail service in bringing letters from her family, was surprised and delighted by an unexpected visit from her brothers Etienne and Giles. Vachel had been left at home to protect their mother and the rest of the family. At first, Aimee was so pleased to see them that she hardly noticed the look of strain on their faces, but once they were seated in a small room for privacy, she detected their anxiety and demanded anxiously to know what it was all about.

"We've been burglarized three times in the last month," Etienne said gloomily, although his eyes darkened with anger. "Peasants have been sneaking in at night, stealing chickens and pigs; even one of our horses is missing. Mother was nearly scared out of her wits one night when she caught a poacher inside the kitchen. He was brandishing a knife at the kitchen wenches, who were too frightened to yell for help. Luckily, no one was hurt, but we lost one of the girls when she refused to come back to work, and two of the stablehands have run off to join the army."

"The peasants know we've very little protection," Giles grumbled. "And we never know when they're going to hit us, although there seems to be a system to their robbery. Almost as if there are some brains behind the whole business."

"You suspect someone?" Aimee asked quickly.

"Faron. Who else?" Etienne responded. "Even after Father's

death, he has continued to hold a grudge against our family, and he leads the others around like stupid cattle. He fills their heads with lies, telling them that the aristocrats are only waiting for the right time to put someone else on the throne and then their children will be killed, their wives raped, and their homes burned. Better to hurt them first, he says, and then proceeds to do so! We're not the only ones who've been harmed. Several of the other châteaux, those still standing, have been robbed, too!"

"And you cannot appeal to anyone?" Aimee asked, her dark blonde brows knitting in consternation.

Etienne snorted in amusement. "To whom would we appeal? Paris is mad with the terror, and Robespierre is the only law there, and he has no love for the 'former nobility.'"

"We must end this thing with Faron ourselves," Giles spoke up stoutly.

Etienne agreed and Aimee saw the hard glint of malice in his blue eyes that frightened her. "He cannot continue to rob us blind without paying for it!"

"But you must be careful, my brothers," Aimee pleaded. "And you must never leave our mother alone, especially at night. Etienne, I know that you and Vachel enjoy coming into Orléans for your...entertainment, but you cannot continue with that until this thing is solved."

"Of course," Etienne agreed, shrugging away her flushed cheeks. He deliberately changed the subject. "But you, my sister, how are you doing here? It seems you do not get much news inside this ancient edifice."

Aimee shook her head. "The Mother Abbess has strict rules about that. She does not want panic to spread among the girls, nor does she feel gossip should interrupt our studies."

"Gossip! She's as strict as a Jesuit!" Etienne laughed, then quieted at his sister's look of disapproval.

"What news of the war is there?" she asked, eager to know more before they had to leave.

"In August, we lost the port of Toulon to the English, which set off intense emotion in Paris and the rest of the country. There's hope now, though, that we may be able to reclaim it and drive the British ships from the harbor. After the fall of Toulon, Paris issued orders for conscription of all young men to fight in the armies. Buildings, horses, and all available arms have been requisitioned by the government. Just last month the Committee of General Security was reorganized and is now responsible for internal policing and preservation of order, second only to the Committee of Public Safety."

"And last month that same committee decreed the Law of Suspects," Giles put in with sarcasm. "It orders the arrests of so-called 'suspect persons.' They have even issued pamphlets explaining to the populace exactly what a suspect is!"

"And what *is* a suspect?" Aimee demanded, trying not to let her fear for her family show in her eyes. Protected and safe behind the high stone walls of the convent, she had no idea that all these rules had been instigated.

"Bah!" Etienne interjected quickly. "Anyone who shows himself to be an enemy of liberty or who cannot justify their means of existence is a suspect. All emigrés and husbands, wives, fathers, mothers, sons, and daughters of former nobles who have not constantly manifested their attachment to the revolution."

"But, then, *you* are in danger—we, all of us, are in danger!" Aimee cried, jumping from her seat to stare in horror at her brothers.

Etienne shook his head and searched in his pocket to produce a small piece of folded paper. "This protects us," he assured her. "It is our certificate of civism, our passport through the country. We had to obtain them from the local committee here in Orléans, and we must carry them on our person at all times. Lucky for us that Father had more than a few friends here, enabling us to get them. If it had been up to Faron, we would have been thrown into the deepest dungeon!" He dug once more in his pocket and produced an identical square of paper that he presented to his sister. "Here is your passport, Aimee, which you mustn't lose." There was a constrained look about his eyes as he leaned forward and said earnestly, "You must be very careful, my sister. News has come that Paris is becoming even harsher toward Roman Catholics. The Paris Commune is controlled by the most violent party of the revolution. Hébert and Chaumette are its leaders, and they know how to use the rabble for their own purposes. They have de-Christianized the calendar and set up a new religion of their own—the religion of Reason, they call it. Heaven and hell have been abolished, and without the hope or fear of eternal reward or punishment, the rabble will do as they like. One hope is that Hébert and Robespierre are at each other's throats in their quest for power and perhaps they will be unable to act as violently as they might like. Still, Hébert was able, just three days ago, to have the great Cathedral of Notre Dame converted into a 'Temple of Reason,' where Reason is supposedly enthroned, but the scandal is that orgies take place there every night. Within a month, he vows that all the churches will be converted into these temples."

"We worry for you, Aimee," Giles said seriously, taking his sister's hands in his. "We know there seems to be protection behind these old and hallowed walls, but with the changes that Paris is bringing about, we cannot be sure of anything anymore, only that everyone must be careful."

"You must have your passport on your person at all times," Etienne said sternly. "Giles or Vachel or I—one of us—will try to visit you each month to bring you news since your Mother Abbess deems it unacceptable for your ears. She is a foolish woman to hide the events of Paris from you, for that is the only way to stay one step ahead of those who would see us imprisoned."

Aimee nodded in agreement. "And you, too, must be careful. If Faron is as bent toward vengeance as it sounds, he will stop at nothing to discredit our family and harm our persons. I fear more for you than for myself, dear brothers!"

"We can take care of ourselves!" Giles returned stoutly.

The three siblings stood up and embraced, a little awkwardly as teen-agers would do, but there was love and warmth in their hearts as they separated in the great hall of the convent. Aimee was forbidden to go to the door with them, but Sister Marie-Marguerite accompanied them to the stoop while Aimee called out words of care.

After they had gone, Aimee went to her room, a small cell, austerely appointed, its one great fixture being a large wooden crucifix overlaid in gold leaf and studded with small rubies where the wounds of Jesus were shown. She knelt before it now, her heart troubled and her mind filled with images of what her brothers had related to her. But the praying was hard this night and for a long time she could only stare dumbly at the cross, unable to reach out to a God that seemed to have deserted the people of France.

The winter of 1793–94 seemed to drag by on leaden feet while Aimee continued her studies at the Convent of Saint-Vincent. By the first of the year, true to its promise, the Paris Commune had proclaimed as the official religion of the country the Worship of Reason, and within a month nearly three thousand churches were converted to temples, assigned to lead their congregations in that worship. The Mother Abbess told her charges of the ridiculous decree and smiled grimly at the notion that any of her students would purport to worship such silliness. The little bourgeois girls looked at one another and thought of the notes they'd received from their fathers—saying that under no circumstances were they to assemble for vespers, nor were they allowed to have crosses or statues in their rooms. Fear had descended on the upright citizens of Orléans. Many, in fact, began taking their daughters out of the convent, not wanting to be thought of as participating in keeping the old religion alive. There was even talk of closing down the convent, forcing the nuns out, and making them take the civil oath, but such talk died down in March when the shocking news came from Paris that Hébert and his followers in the Paris Commune had been arrested and executed.

Danton, who had heretofore been allied with Robespierre and the Committee of Public Safety, was now sick at heart of the bloodshed and recommended that the terror be eased. Now that Hébert was out of the way, Robespierre found he had another mortal enemy who must be taken care of, and so, in early April, Danton was committed to the guillotine, leaving Robespierre, "the Incorruptible," as the most popular and powerful man in France. Little did the people realize that they had given Robespierre almost limitless power over them and that this small, provincial lawyer would become practically a dictator in the next four months. With his ascendancy came the "Great Terror" and new dictates were made law. Now, Robespierre decreed, the accused would no longer be automatically given the right of counsel, nor did witnesses have to be heard for the defense. Any opposition to the government was punishable by death. A swell of panic and anger gripped the populace, not only in Paris, but all over the country as a frenzied fear made men go temporarily mad, murdering their brothers, accusing their own fathers of treason, imprisoning their wives for some imagined words against the government. The world had, indeed, found itself in the clutches of the devil.

6

Aimee lay in her bed, staring up at the whitewashed ceiling of her room, unable to return to sleep after being awakened by something she could not quite identify. Everything seemed normal. She glanced out the small window and could see that dawn had nearly arrived as the sky was growing pink with the promise of a crisp, April day. She had celebrated her fifteenth birthday the night before, receiving unexpected gifts from her family, which had cheered her considerably. Noiselessly, she rose from the bed, dressed in the white cotton gown that each student was issued upon entering the convent, and went to the window, her nose suddenly picking up the smell of smoke not too far distant.

Her eyes sharpened as she looked out the window and saw gray smoke darkening the dawning sky in the direction of the kitchen buildings. Had the cook left the fire too hot? Perhaps some errant coals had fallen away from the banked fires and ignited some piece of furniture. Curious now, but not afraid yet, Aimee turned to put on a dressing robe when suddenly a loud clanging sound broke the early dawn, followed by a frantic ringing of the big bell in the chapel tower.

At first, Aimee was so startled she could only stand frozen in her room, but then the acrid smell of smoke, followed by the crackling sound of a fire, seemed to permeate her room and she dragged on her dressing robe, not even troubling to pin up the long tail of her braid or to find her slippers. Quickly, she opened her door onto the hallway that was filling up quickly with smoke.

Coughing, Aimee could hear other students, awakened either by the fire or by the chapel bell, sputtering and shuffling in their rooms, trying to orient themselves to the reality of what was happening. A chill spread throughout Aimee's body as she passed down the hall and into another passageway that was thick with smoke, at the end of which long tongues of orange flame were already greedily consuming anything combustible. A sudden explosion wracked the building as something ignited close by and Aimee was thrown to the floor. Before she could get back to her feet, she was nearly trampled by several panic-stricken girls, fleeing their rooms, unable to figure out which way to go.

Gaining her feet again, Aimee ran in the opposite direction from where she sensed the explosion had come from, following a bevy of white-nightgowned girls who were seeking fresh air. Another passageway was already bright with flames and real panic ensued as girls started screaming in terror, tears streaming from blackened faces.

"This way! This way!" It was one of the nuns, waving frantically, calling the girls toward her. Her concern was so great for her charges that she didn't even notice the bright flame tearing greedily at the hem of her robes. In the space of a minute, the woman was a mass of flames, her screams of pain and horror throwing the girls who had been running toward her into a frenzy of fear.

"We'll all be killed!"

"We must get out before the flames reach us!"

Frantically, falling back like the crest of a wave, the girls retreated from the hungry flames, running into one another, knocking some down as they tried to get away. Aimee was jostled and spun about as she tried to figure out which way to run. Already her lungs were burning, her eyes smarting from the smoke. It was hard to breathe and she knew she must find fresh air soon or she would not get out of this inferno alive.

Gasping, she found herself back in her own room again. With frantic eyes she searched for something to break the paned glass in her room and focused on the glittering cross at the head of her bed. Determinedly, she wrenched it from the wall and smashed it against the glass, drawing in huge lungfuls of blessed air, coughing out the smoke that had threatened to choke her. As she looked from the window, she saw peasants, men from the city and surrounding countryside, gathering around the convent, jumping down from its walls. At first, she thought they had come to rescue her and she waved frantically, but suddenly she saw the hated face of Faron, the miller, leading a group of peasants toward the chapel. One of the nuns ran to him, beseeching him to help in the rescue efforts of the students. With a vicious swipe of his knife, he sent the woman into the dirt, a gaping wound in her breast.

Faron! Could he have led a group of men to the convent deliberately to set it on fire? Could he have done such a thing, harming the lives of innocents—for what? And then she knew. She stared at the gold-leafed cross in her hand, its rubies winking like drops of blood at her. It was for the gold, the ornaments of the chapel, that they had come—money to exchange for bread for their starving families. Their hunger had finally broken their reason. Hell had been abolished by the government and religious buildings were fair game for their hatred. Aimee nearly sank to her knees at the horror if it.

But the immediacy of her situation came back to her and she scrambled to her feet, still clutching the crucifix. Behind its face there was a small compartment with a hinged door to carry a rosary, a jar of holy water. Aimee opened it and took her passport from the pocket of her convent uniform to stuff it in the opening. After securing the compartment, she tied the crucifix around her waist with a sash and threw a gown over her nightdress. She would need shoes to save her bare feet from being burned and she quickly donned them, knowing the smoke was getting thicker and she would have to leave the room, despite her need for the fresh air from the open window. The cross felt heavy at her waist as she crouched low and ran out into the hallway once more. Stumbling almost blindly through the passageway, she tried two doors, only to find the fire had already reached those areas. Finally, the third door she tried yielded an escape way and she followed it to the end, where it opened onto the great hall with its flagstone flooring.

Other girls shivered in nightgowns, their faces black with smoke, their eyes huge with fright, looking for guidance out of this nightmare. Aimee called to them, urging them to follow her out of the hall and outside to fresh air. A short distance away, she could hear the bellowing voices of the peasants as they ransacked the chapel and knew it would not take them long to come here to the hall.

"We must get out of here!" she told the others.

"My sister is not here!" someone shouted in panic. "She must still be in one of the passageways! I must go after her!"

"No! You must come with me! There are men here, men who started this fire!" Aimee shouted. "If you don't flee now, they will find you!"

"They would not harm *me!*" someone returned, coughing violently. "My father is the most respected draper in the city—they will not harm me!"

Aimee wanted to shake her. "These men don't care who your father is, you little fool! If they did, do you think they would have set the place on fire! Now come with me, or you will be killed—or worse!"

"No, *you* go—you *aristocrat!*" someone shouted. "You are

the one putting all of us in danger! If it had not been for your being here, they would never have dared this!"

With a look of disgust, Aimee turned from the others and hurried to the great door that led to the outside, but before she could take more than a few steps toward it, it burst open on its hinges, allowing eight or ten dirty, wild-eyed men into the hall. Shrieks of alarm issued from the girls behind her as Aimee side-stepped to one of the alcoves. These were not just unhappy farmers, she realized, but desperate men, some perhaps even criminals, that Faron and his followers must have gathered together to perpetrate this terrible deed. Sharp knives gleamed at their belts and they all wore the long, striped trousers of the *sans-culottes*, their dirty feet bare on the stone flagging.

"Pretty pickings for the likes of us!" one of the men crowed greedily, eyeing the screeching girls in the nightgowns. "Much more *appreciative* of a man, I'll warrant, than those whores on the quay!"

Aimee shrank back into the stone of the alcove, her heart hammering against her breast in fear. There was no way through the door, past those men who had spread out into the hall now and were advancing with grinning, evil faces toward the group of students whose continued screams seemed to echo and bounce off the high, arched walls of the great hall. Frightened out of her wits, she pressed her back to the cold stone at the side of the alcove, praying desperately that she would be given a chance to make her escape before they discovered her hiding place.

Unable to stand there and witness the savagery of rape, Aimee swallowed a demented cry and ran from her hiding place, her eyes focused on the doorway, where she knew freedom awaited her on the other side of the road. Once beyond the stoop, she could make her way down the small hill to the city below. One man tried to stop her, his hand brushing her sleeve, but she wrenched her arm from his grasp and went on, the elusive doorway coming ever closer.

But, just as she reached the archway, with the dawning sun hitting her full in the face, the huge figure of Faron, the miller, seemed to fill the doorway, blocking out the sun—and hope.

"Why, what do we have here?" he hissed, scanning her face in instant recognition. "A little aristocrat, I'll be bound!"

Aimee stopped dead in her tracks, her eyes opening wide at the sight of the man. She took only a moment to calm the wild beating of her heart before she drew herself up to her full height, throwing back her head to gaze up at him defiantly. "You here,

Faron? I am not surprised, for you always seemed to be heading the rabble! Get out of my way!"

"You are so brave, my little aristocrat," he chortled, moving closer to catch her arm in a grip that hurt.

Her anger against this man swelled inside of her as she reached inside the bodice of her dress and pulled out the crucifix, bringing it up so rapidly that Faron had no time to react to her movement. With the steady quickness of a snake, Aimee brought the crucifix toward his face, jabbing it with as much strength as she could muster.

With a howl of pain and rage, Faron released her and grabbed at his face, his fingers seeking to squelch the blood that flowed from one eye. His screams of pain continued to echo in the hall, and for an instant Aimee was galvanized where she stood, but as a torrent of crude oaths issued from his mouth, she took to her heels, running out into the open air, intent on reaching the comparative safety of the city until she could make her way back to the Castle du Beautreillis in order to warn her family of Faron's intentions.

"Ho! Stop! Wait!"

Aimee heard the cries and continued to run blindly, jabbing at the air with the crucifix, determined not to be caught again, for she knew Faron would probably kill her. But suddenly several pairs of arms were holding her while anxious men's faces looked into hers, demanding to know where their daughters were. Looking up, Aimee realized that these men were from the city, the fathers of the students at the convent who had been alerted by the clanging bell. Breathlessly, she told them of Faron's treachery and of the criminals he had added to his followers. Aghast, the men hurried up the hill, looking somehow incongruous in their flapping coats and polished shoes—these few were going to fight against the maddened mob in the convent, Aimee thought in surprise.

Wearily, she sat down on the ground, feeling her whole body tremble with reaction, beginning to feel the effects of the horror she had witnessed. The sounds of fighting swirled around her as she leaned her head forward over her knees, still clutching the crucifix in one hand. Almost automatically, she stuffed it back inside her bodice, remembering, even in her shock, the importance of the square of paper inside it. Perhaps using that paper somehow, she could convince the police in Orléans to provide her family with some protection against Faron and his men.

With renewed determination, she lifted herself up, rubbing her arm where Faron had twisted it, and made her way into the city, stepping carefully through the streets, some cobbled, some not, providing risky footing at best when coupled with the mud and refuse.

A rough hand caught her arm, spinning her around to face a shabbily uniformed man with the tricolor cockade sticking out from his hat. Behind him, two more similarly dressed men stood at attention with their swords at their sides.

"She's the one!" the first man said swiftly. "An aristocrat, Citizen de Landry told us. She must be partly responsible for the sacking of the convent. That mob wouldn't have dared so much without her kind giving them the reason for it! Come along with me, girl, if you know what's good for you! My captain will want to question you about the fire."

"Don't be stupid!" Aimee said angrily, squirming along in his grasp. "I had nothing to do with what happened!"

"You had everything to do with it—you are an *aristocrat!*" the man spat. He pulled her inside the building, into the ante-chamber, where a harried-looking official sat behind a desk, going over papers.

"I found this one walking the street, Captain," the man said, practically hurling Aimee toward the desk. "She's from the convent where twelve of our men were sent to restore order some minutes ago." He leaned toward the captain meaningfully. "She's an aristocrat, sir, one of the family of de Chartres."

The captain looked up, rubbing his eyes behind the spectacles on the bridge of his nose. With a sigh he took them off and shoved the paperwork aside. "So, citizeness, can you explain what you were doing in the street?"

Aimee looked at him incredulously. "Is it a crime to walk the streets now?" she wondered in dismay.

The captain cleared his throat and fixed her with an irritated look. "If you are an aristocrat, citizeness, it may well be a crime," he assured her. "Your father was guillotined as an enemy of France; therefore, you are under suspicion. How is it that you were allowed to attend the Convent of Saint-Vincent?"

Aimee shrugged. "My father had set aside money for the good sisters to take me in as their student. My brother took me there after my father was . . . murdered," she ended, tossing the word at him with defiance.

"Your father was a traitor to his country," the captain returned, standing up behind his desk and walking around to place himself before her. "You are a suspect, citizeness, not only because of your relationship to an enemy of France, but because of your attitude. All of you aristocrats seem to think we should still be bowing and scraping to you, but times have changed, citizeness, and there will be no more of that!"

"If you know anything of the de Chartres family, you would know that we have never expected that of anyone!" Aimee answered, straining for calm. "We have always lived in peace with our neighbors and our tenants. My father welcomed the beginning of the revolution because he saw it as a way to ease injustice and to destroy the old feudal laws that were keeping France from becoming the great country she should have been! Please, Captain, you must at least go to my family's home and see to their safety. I fear this Faron, who was truly the ringleader of the acts of violence on the convent, will stop at nothing to hurt them. He said as much to me in the convent. You must, at least, send someone to warn my family of the danger they are in."

"I will think on your words, citizeness," the captain said ambiguously. "Meanwhile, you will be obliged to stay the night in one of our rooms while we go through legal channels to see what we are to do with you."

"I have a passport!" Aimee said suddenly, remembering the precious paper inside the crucifix. "Surely that will clear me."

The captain seemed nonplussed at this unexpected turn of events. But recovering, he said only, "You may keep it on your person, but have it ready should anyone require you to verify it, citizeness."

"But, you cannot hold me if I—"

"Silence! You try my patience, wench! Take her into one of the cells!" he ordered his subordinate.

Aimee was unceremoniously thrown into one of the "rooms" used for detaining suspects found within the city walls. In the cramped, square room there were both men and women, some of whom she knew slightly as former servants and bailiffs of neighboring châteaux, others whom she did not recognize.

Miserable, thinking of her family, she tried to settle down as comfortably as she could, stealthily checking the compartment inside the crucifix to make sure that her passport was safe. Lying drowsily on a splintery bench without benefit of blanket or pillow, Aimee dozed fitfully throughout the day, waking up when it was time to eat, using as little as possible the slop bucket that was situated behind a wooden screen, in some deference to privacy. She found the food adequate: hard, crusty bread and soup that was more water than broth, but at least it was something to ease the hunger pangs of her stomach, and she wolfed it down unashamedly.

The night dragged by slowly and she woke up several times not knowing for a moment where she was. All around her people talked or moaned in their sleep. As dawn proceeded to lighten the sky outside the one narrow window, Aimee arose and stretched heavily, feeling the tight knots in her back and shoulders and rubbing the sleep from eyes that she knew were puffy from strain. She felt as though she had hardly slept, and to think of having to face the captain again made her sigh with frustration. So she kept her own counsel, walking impatiently in her cell, waiting to be released while the day died away and another night took its place.

By the time the next morning dawned, Aimee was nearly beside herself with anger. It wasn't until ten o'clock that she was released and allowed to leave with the sharp admonition from the captain that, should he see her in his offices again, she would not be so lucky the next time.

Despite her lack of sleep the previous two nights, Aimee hurried as fast as she was able through the streets of Orléans, keeping her eyes open for patrolling militia, remembering the captain's threat. Dodging into an alley, she watched silently as two uniformed officers passed by her hiding place, then scurried away as a suspicious washerwoman shrieked at her to be gone. She continued to watch behind her until she passed out of the city gates and was in the openness of the countryside.

Now her heart lifted as she recognized the greening meadows, the newly sprouted leaves on the trees and bushes along the roadside. The road wound between copses of oaks and birch and she could see the sparkle of the Loire just beyond a wooded grove of orange trees where songbirds lifted their musical voices to the sky. She was almost skipping as she came through the wooded area beyond which was the park that belonged to Castle du Beautreillis.

But her breath caught in her throat as she was confronted by the terrible spectacle before her eyes. The stable was still smoldering from a fire, as were several other outbuildings that surrounded the main castle. The castle itself was charred and blackened on two of its towers, its once solid wooden gates hanging limply on their broken hinges. With her heart beating in her throat, Aimee entered the courtyard, aware only of the stench of blood and smoke. No living thing moved as she made her way inside the great hall.

She found Giles first, lying in a pool of blood, face down beside the tall clock in the hall where he must have been running to hide. With tears in her eyes, she gently turned him on his back, brushing back the sandy-colored hair, avoiding the gaping wound in his throat. With a numb coldness, she moved through her home, noting the brazen destruction of anything that could not be removed by force. Everything of value had been taken.

In the kitchen, sprawled in front of the huge pantry where death had caught them, lay the twins, Denis and Charles, their identical faces showing nothing of the terror that must have besieged them before they were so brutally murdered. Aimee stood for a moment, taking deep breaths and stepping outside into the calm April day. She saw her mother lying in the warm, rich earth of the garden that she had tended with such loving care. Beside her, his bloodied sword still in his outstretched hand, lay Vachel, his face pale in death and his blond hair red with the wound that had crushed his skull.

Falling to her knees, Aimee vomited what little she had in her stomach, then thrust her face into her hands. Her sobs were heart-wrenching, sobs of pain and fear mixed with cold anger.

A heavy footstep behind her made her whirl around, scrambling to her feet, her hand on the crucifix to use as a weapon. Etienne's blue eyes stared back at her bleakly, his face a mask of emotions, of which hatred was the most intense.

"Faron," he said grimly.

Aimee ran to him, needing his strength in this hour, but found him strangely reluctant to offer comfort, as though he could not bear to listen to her sorrow. "Etienne, how is it that you were not hurt?"

"I was not here," he answered slowly.

She looked at him in disbelief.

"We had heard about the firing of the convent and the rabble that Faron had picked up in order to further his own greedy plans," he said. "Mother was nearly torn in two by her fear for you and she sent me the next day to find out what news I could and to locate your whereabouts."

"I was detained in the prison," Aimee said wearily. "They would not release me because I was a former aristocrat! Instead, I was forced to stay there two nights while they took their own time about letting me go! I begged them to send a warning here so that you might all be put on your guard!"

"No warning came," Etienne said. Suddenly he put his face in his hands, a shameful sorrow in his voice mingling with the sobs

at escaped him. "When I found that you had not been hurt but
ere detained in prison, I went to the Café Foy. I wound up
unk and . . . with a woman who took me to her room, where I
ayed the night. I should have come back here to help Vachel
fend our mother, but instead I was with some whore, my head
uffed with drink! Oh, God, it should be me lying there dead!"
gasped, berating himself with self-loathing.

"You could not know!" Aimee said quickly, seeking to com-
rt him somehow.

He shook his head in disgust. "I should have come back to
otect Mother and the rest of them. I have failed our father and
r name, Aimee! Because of me—"

"Hush! It was not because of you, Etienne!" she admonished
rcely, seeking to drive some sense back into his head. "What
ood would you have done here? There were too many of them
and they were not the peasants and farmers you might have
ought! No—I saw them in the convent! They were criminals,
ienne, thieves and murderers, desperate men who wanted any-
ng that Faron could promise them! You would have been
atchered with the rest of our family—and I couldn't have borne
at! I couldn't have gone on alone, Etienne!"

"I am unworthy to be your brother. I am unworthy to be
ve!" Etienne insisted. "I would be better off dead than with this
rden of guilt upon me!"

"No! Listen to me, Etienne! We will not let Faron and his
llowers do this to us! We will rebuild Castle du Beautreillis,
en grander than it was before. We will—"

"With what?" Etienne asked incredulously, looking at his sis-
r as though she'd lost her mind. "There is nothing left! I have
ready been upstairs, and they have taken everything, even
other's clothing . . . the portrait frames in the sitting room! How
n we rebuild anything without money!"

Aimee was at a loss. She looked around as though expecting
find something of value on the ground. Beside her, she heard
r brother's sobs lessening and looked up hopefully. What she
w chilled her to the bone, for Etienne's face had hardened with
purpose, a purpose that gleamed out hatefully from his blue
es, that made his jaw rigid with its intensity.

"No, Aimee," he said in a voice deceptively soft. "We will not
ay here while the murderer of our family goes free. We will
llow him to Paris, to the very gates of hell, dear sister! We will
t rest until he has been made to suffer as we have suffered."

"But there is danger in Paris, Etienne," Aimee warned him.

He looked at her and scoffed, his eyes losing none of th
purpose. "There is danger here, Aimee. Look at the poor bod
of our mother and brother and tell me that Paris could be a
worse!"

"But—"

"I am going to Paris," he stated deliberately. "If you do
want to come with me, you will have to make some arrangeme
here, my sister. I will stay only long enough to see our fam
decently buried; then I will go."

"But where will you stay, what will you do, how will y
live?" Aimee asked practically, feeling helpless before the ha
implacability in her brother.

"We do have an aunt who lives in Paris," he returned. "S
should be able to provide a roof over our heads and food for c
mouths. I do not expect any more of her."

"And how will you find Faron, Etienne? Paris is much bigg
than Orléans, and I've heard tales that anyone who wants to c
get lost inside of it!"

"So shall we, then, my sister, get lost inside of it!" Etien
returned briskly. "And I will find Faron—even though it m
take me the rest of my life, I will find him!"

Aimee bit her lip, running a hand through her hair, surpris
to realize it was still in the same braid she'd left it in three mo
ings before. "All right, Etienne, I will go to Paris with you," s
said finally, softly.

7

In answer to their repeated knocking, the door finally opened a crack, emitting a pale light from a tallow candle, held in a nervous hand, as it sought to shed light into the darkness of the street outside. Aimee tried to discern the figure behind the outstretched arm, but was prevented by the position of the door from seeing into the hallway of the house. Behind her, she could feel Etienne's impatience at being kept in the street so long. They were both very tired from the three-day journey from Orléans to Paris on foot. They had been lucky enough to sleep undisturbed one night, but had had to keep guard the second night because of the uncommon number of travelers on the roads. Then there had been the repeated stops once they got closer to Paris because of the many road outposts where armed militia demanded to check their passports and question them as to their reasons for being on the roads. It had been all Etienne could do to keep his temper as the same questions were repeated over and over again, to which they always replied the same answers. Finally, they had reached the gates of Paris and Aimee had walked through them with foreboding, wondering if she would ever be able to leave through them again.

Since they had entered the city just before evening, they had been one of the last groups of travelers to be allowed in. The National Guardsmen were especially sharp with their questions, for even stricter laws had been imposed since Robespierre had come to be practically the dictator of Paris now that his enemies had been sent to the guillotine. Aimee and Etienne had been forced to stand patiently while their passports were checked and they were interrogated as to their reasons for entering Paris. Finally, satisfied, the officer of the watch warned them that they'd best have somewhere to go, for there was a strict curfew being enforced, and should they be found roaming the streets of Paris after ten o'clock at night, they would be thrown into prison.

So they had made their way through twisting alleys and darkened streets lit only by the lights coming from establishments where the sounds of drink and hilarity mingled with women's laughter and high-pitched shrills. Twice they had gotten lost among the alleyways and yards of Paris where only those born to the city could find their way without too much trouble. Luckily, Etienne was able to recall street markers and certain establishments from his journey with his father nearly two years before. Finally, they had found themselves in the Faubourg Saint-Denis, dismayed at the state of disrepair of the Hôtel de Chartres, whose exterior was lighted somewhat by the glow of an oil lamp on the street in front of it.

"Who is it?" a quavering voice asked.

"Aunt Hortense, it's Aimee and Etienne de Chartres," Aimee answered urgently. "Please open the door so that we may come in before the night patrol finds us standing out here in the street!"

"De Chartres, you say?" The voice came again, seeming disembodied in the warm night air. "My name is not de Chartres," she continued, becoming almost shrill. "It is Descartes. You must have the wrong number. Now go away!"

Before the door could be slammed in their faces, Etienne put out his arm and caught the edge of it, pushing with all his might so that, at last, the woman behind the door fell back and Aimee and Etienne both tumbled in, finding themselves face to face with a withered, skinny middle-aged woman who looked at them as though they might be sent from hell.

"How dare you break into my house, you young rogues!" Hortense de Chartres shrieked at them. "Get out of here before I call the watch!"

"You foolish old woman!" Etienne shouted back, losing all patience. "Do you think I do not know you? You are the one my father lost his life in trying to save! Yes, your brother was guillotined as an aristocrat by this stinking government of Paris—and he would never have come here if your stupidity and stubbornness hadn't forced him to it!"

The woman clutched at her throat above the severely cut dark cloth of her gown and her eyes bulged beneath the nightcap that hid strands of gray hair that might once have been blond. Aimee felt pity for her, despite her role in the death of her father. It was evident that the woman was wildly fearful.

"Let me help you up, Aunt," she said softly, bending down to aid the woman to her feet. "Please do not turn us away now. It's true that the night watch is patrolling already and my brother and I have no one else to turn to."

"Why have you come?" Hortense asked a little breathlessly. *"Why* have you descended on me now, when everyone had ceased to remember me, when I can come and go as I please without fear of someone spying on me? Oh, yes, I went through trying times for nearly two years after I was released from prison. After my brother was executed, it worsened. Always a policeman at my heels, waiting for me to do something that could be construed as treason toward the government. But I was much more clever than they thought, and I did absolutely nothing to arouse their suspicions!" Her eyes narrowed as she studied the faces of her two uninvited guests. "And now *you* come here! You—the offspring of a convicted traitor to France! What shall they think if they try to follow me again, eh? What shall they think if they find me harboring two suspects from the law?"

"No one needs to know of our existence," Etienne said quickly, turning to bolt the door closed once again and retrieve the precariously situated candle. He held it high to reveal the penury of the hallway, its once gloriously bright carpets faded and smudged, the deep, shining panels gone dull from lack of buffing. "We only require lodging and food. Our business does not involve you!"

"Food! Food is scarce, my boy, especially here, from where almost everyone has fled in the last two years! Go to the bourgeois districts in the Faubourg Saint-Germain and the arsenal districts! Do not expect me to feed two more mouths when I can barely keep myself from starving!"

"Listen to me, foolish woman!" Etienne said heatedly, taking a deep breath to keep himself from throttling the old crone. "You *owe* us lodging and food! If it hadn't been for our father getting you released from prison, you would probably be dead by now! You're an ungrateful, wretched woman whose heart must be as shriveled as your skin!"

"Etienne! There is no need to badger her!" Aimee reproached him. She turned to the woman beseechingly. "Please, Aunt Hortense, do not send us away. We have no one but you left to turn to. Our mother and brothers were murdered in Orléans by a group of criminals led by one of our father's tenant farmers! He has come here to Paris and we—"

"Do not tell me of your plans!" Hortense yelled, covering her ears with her bony hands. "Enough of bloodshed and murder and revenge! I am sick of it!"

Etienne snorted in disgust. "You must have something to eat here! We are starving. We've been on the road to Paris for three days and haven't eaten anything but a bit of cheese and some bread."

Hortense's shoulders seemed to sag suddenly and she looked at them bleakly. "All right, all right. I will give you something to eat, but then you will have to go. I cannot risk having you here in my house!"

"You have nothing to fear, Aunt Hortense," Aimee reassured her. "We have our passports in order and had no trouble getting through the gates of Paris. There is nothing for you to worry about."

"Ah, child, you do not understand," the woman returned with a sigh. "Once they have singled you out, once you have been imprisoned or suspected of treason, life can never be so carefree for you. Always, there are secret police checking up on you, making sure that nothing changes in your life. Justice is dead in Paris these days. Anyone can point the finger at you and say you are a spy for the enemy, and if you happen to be an aristocrat or even a bourgeois who has become too rich or too powerful, it is off to prison with you. And the prisons are no longer the comfortable places they were before. I know of a woman who was only just released after a stay of six months at L'Abbaye, and her health had deteriorated shockingly because of the damp and chill of the cell she'd been thrown into. They say sickness and disease run rampant in the prisons, and if the guillotine does not get you, the disease will! I have no desire to be thrown into a place like that, child!"

"Nonsense! You won't be put into prison for extending a welcome to your niece and nephew in from the country," Etienne remarked reasonably as they entered the kitchen and stirred the fire in the grate to bring it to life.

Hortense shook her head. "I cannot allow you to stay more than one night," she said firmly, though her voice shook a little in her fear.

Etienne glared at her as he asked where the food was kept. Resignedly, Hortense took the key from her waist and opened the lock on the pantry, revealing a veritable hoard of food stored inside. Eagerly, Etienne reached inside for a joint of mutton, while Hortense cried out in distress that she could live off that joint for a month!

"Start the water to boiling, Aimee, and we'll feast tonight!" Etienne cried merrily, ignoring his sputtering aunt. He searched through the pantry for more, hauling out sugar and flour and vegetables and salt that Aimee could make into a soup. Little screeches of outrage issued from Hortense as she saw her hard-won storehouse of food being squandered in one night. Angrily, she denounced the two of them, claiming they would soon have her starving in the streets if they did not leave anything for her.

"And wine, Aunt—do you not have anything to drink?" Etienne asked, his blue eyes bright from the fire and the promise of a masterful dinner.

"Bah! Wine is twelve hundred fifty livres a half bottle, young pup! You'll drink water or cider that I've stored in the cellar and be glad to have it!"

"All right, then, cider it is!" Etienne cried.

While he went to search out the cellar, Aimee continued busily to cut up vegetables and thicken the soup with flour, turning the mutton on a spit until its juices were dripping appetizingly into the fiery coals. Hortense watched in misery, although her own salivary glands were beginning to work at the prospect of such a fine feast—one she'd denied herself in her fear of not having enough to eat.

"Is food truly as scarce as all that?" Aimee wondered aloud.

"Once that pantry is bare, I'll be lucky to get a few crusts of bread and a glass of beer for my dinner," Hortense grumbled testily.

"And yet, there must be food somewhere that you can buy," Aimee said wonderingly, stirring the soup again as she heard Etienne's footsteps coming up from the cellar.

"Who has money to buy it?" Hortense asked wearily. "The paper assignats that were issued seem to be dropping in value daily. Milk and cream are twenty sous now, and even cheese has gone up to twelve sous. A fat pullet is nearly ten livres. No one but the wealthy bourgeois have that kind of money—they and the mighty in government. 'Tis said that Robespierre feasts every night on whole chickens and sides of beef that he washes down with the best of wines. And everything is 'donated' to him with no expectation of payment—except perhaps for a few favors that he might deign to grant them!"

"How can Robespierre stay in power?" Aimee asked.

"Because the people fear him," Hortense returned. "Ever since Danton was executed, Robespierre has tightened his grip on the government reins. Executions are a daily occurrence, and the people have gotten so used to them that the crowds in the public squares are practically nil. A man, jealous of his wife, can point the finger at her, denounce her publicly, and have her guillotined as a traitor!"

"But that is madness!"

"Yes, madness, my child, but there is nothing to be done about it!"

"Come, come, don't talk about such gloomy things when we have a feast nearly ready before us!" Etienne said, plunking down a jar of cider that was cool and sweating from the cellar. "I forbid talk of this damnable insanity while we fill our bellies. No one can think on an empty stomach!"

Despite Hortense's grumblings, she joined in as heartily as her guests when the feast was set down on the kitchen table. Sitting back later, replete, she even deigned to smile, announcing that she might be starving tomorrow but that she would remember this meal for some time to come.

"See, Aunt, how in one night we have managed to brighten your existence?" Etienne asked. "You cannot turn us away now."

Hortense straightened. "Of course I will turn you away. Have you not been listening to anything I have been saying! You *cannot* stay with me! I will not be put into such jeopardy!"

Etienne leaned closer to her; gone now was the smile that had lightened his face briefly. "Perhaps we should throw *you* out into the street for the patrol to haul off to prison," he suggested threateningly. "My sister and I easily outnumber you, dear aunt!"

Hortense paled and looked, for a moment, as though she might bring up the excellent repast she'd just enjoyed. Aimee, distressed at her brother's menacing attitude, stood up and went to put a hand on her aunt's shoulders. "Etienne, you are being heartless—"

"And she is not?" he questioned.

"Enough!" Hortense stood up, her thin, sallow face still weak, but with a touch more determination than previously. "I will consent to allow your sister to remain with me in this house," she said finally. "You are right, Etienne, and it is the least that I can do in memory of your father. But I beseech you to see reason and realize you cannot stay here! You, a young man—what is it?—twenty-one years now! What would it look like to people across the street and next door who have never seen anyone besides myself and perhaps an occasional servant here?" She begged Etienne with her eyes. "If you truly wish to protect your sister, you will go."

"No, Etienne!" Aimee realized the woman's tactic and ran to her brother. "If you go, then I will go!"

"You are better off with me, here," Hortense went on swiftly. "Outside the streets of Paris are death to a young girl like yourself. Men wait in alleys to knock you out and sell you to the highest bidder at the houses of the whores in the rue Saint-Honoré and the rue de Beaujolais. They would turn you into a courtesan, a woman who belongs to no one man, and yet to any one who will pay for your services."

"But what of my brother? How can he survive in the streets of Paris?"

For once, Hortense's face took on a crafty look. "Oh, there are ways for young men to survive. He could enlist in the National Guard, or join the army. He could join one of the cutthroat gangs in Paris. You said you were looking for someone who had wronged you—well, there you have it! These gangs roam the streets at night looking for something to do. Join them and you can find that someone much easier than you might alone."

Etienne's eyes darkened and he smiled wickedly. "Why, my dear aunt, it seems you are more than you seem. Where did you learn such deep, dark secrets?"

She smiled thinly. "Everyone knows of the street gangs. They do not bother to keep themselves a secret. Neither do the whores in the rue Saint-Honoré. Your sister is young and fresh—she would not last one night in the streets with you."

Etienne stared at his aunt for a moment. Then his eyes moved to his sister, whose green eyes pleaded with him to stay with her. With a sudden decision, Etienne straightened himself and bowed over his aunt's hand. "Ah, Aunt Hortense, I know that I can count on you to ensure my sister's safety while I go to do that which I am compelled to do—find my family's murderer and administer justice to him!"

"She may stay here as long as she likes," Hortense promised, a sigh of relief issuing from her. "But you—" And she raised her brows worriedly once more.

"I shall trouble you for one night's lodging only," he assured her with a half smile. "I think it is well I do not venture out tonight, for I know nothing of the city and could easily find myself with my throat cut. Better to start the search tomorrow—which will find me outside your door before dawn, I can assure you."

"Well, then, now you are talking sense," Hortense returned with an injured air. "Your sister and I will fare much better that way."

"But how will I know where you are, and if you are all right?" Aimee asked anxiously, her green eyes dark with apprehension.

"I will find ways to get messages to you," Etienne returned comfortingly.

"You promise, Etienne?" she whispered, her eyes not quite believing him.

He smiled jauntily. "I promise, little sister."

Aimee settled in with her aunt as comfortably as was possible in the next few weeks. Hortense de Chartres was truly a nervous and timid woman when it came to dealing with the realities of the revolution, but of one thing she was certain—without food they might as well offer themselves up to the guillotine, and so she was extremely frugal about what might be taken from the pantry. At fifteen, Aimee had still kept a bit of baby fat on her body that slowly began to dissolve because of the low rations of food on which her aunt kept them both. In the space of a few weeks, her breasts became more defined, her waist whittled down, and her arms and legs lost their adolescent plumpness and became more sinewy. She kept active around the house, dusting and grooming the rooms under her aunt's orders, putting up jars of preserves made from the fruit of a tree that Hortense had somehow cajoled to grow in the back of the house. Despite her initial reluctance to have a companion, Hortense was surprised at how much she came to rely on her niece in the following days. Now there was someone to talk to, to order about as she had been used to in the days of the old regime—when one could not afford servants, one simply had to make do with family, Hortense told herself with satisfaction.

Aimee was not unhappy. She missed her brother terribly and wished for more frequent news of him. True to his word, he made sure to smuggle a note to her at least once every two or three weeks, but Aimee longed for a visit from him, to be able to see for herself how he fared in this evil city. For her own part, Aimee did not venture from the Hôtel de Chartres. Hortense was very strict in keeping the girl close to home, terrified of what might happen should the patrol get wind of her new houseguest. Despite all Aimee's assurances, Hortense would not be mollified, and it got to the point where the old woman would complain when Aimee stepped to the back of the house to gather fruit from the apple tree outside.

It was on one of these occasions, when Aimee had stepped outside on a mild day in early June while her aunt was upstairs in bed sipping the tea Aimee had brewed for her, that Aimee made the acquaintance of one of her neighbors. At first she was not aware of anyone watching her as she expertly climbed the apple tree to shake down some of the higher fruits, but after a few minutes with her dress hiked up around her hips and her petticoat showing to anyone who cared to look, she began to feel uncomfortable, as though a pair of eyes was on her. Glancing about suspiciously, she spied a boy lounging on top of the low wall that ran the perimeter of her aunt's backyard.

"What are you doing there?" she asked sharply, pulling her skirt down from her waistband. It was an old skirt she'd altered from her aunt's wardrobe. She flushed suddenly, unexplainably, as the boy continued to stare at her.

"I said—"

"I heard what you said," the boy answered breezily, dropping down from his perch and landing lightly on the balls of his feet just a few yards from where Aimee stood watching him.

"Then why didn't you answer me?" she questioned him tightly, thinking how merry his brown eyes seemed in a face tanned by the sun and framed by an unruly mop of chestnut curls.

He shrugged. "I was watching you, citizeness."

Aimee flushed at his boldness and turned away to gather the apples that had fallen to the ground into a large wooden basket. In a moment, the boy had swooped down next to her and was tossing apples into the basket with a disdainful air.

"Careful, you will bruise them!" Aimee cried, unable to think of anything else to say.

"Don't be silly, they are already bruised from their fall from the branches," the boy replied practically. "If you didn't want them bruised, I could have climbed the tree for you and you could have caught the apples I threw down."

"I don't need your help," Aimee replied primly, gathering the remaining apples with more care and placing them with the others. "I don't even know who you are."

"Jean-Baptiste Aubray, citizeness," he told her with a little bow and a devilish grin. "My uncle lives a few doors down the street and I am staying with him for a while—and you?"

Aimee hesitated, all of Hortense's warning clanging in her head. But what had she to fear from a boy who looked hardly older than herself and was barely an inch or two taller? "Aimee de Chartres. My aunt lives here," she supplied with a sudden shyness that felt alien to her.

"So you are not from Paris?" he wondered aloud, picking up one of the apples and shining it on a rather threadbare sleeve before sinking his teeth into it.

She shook her head. "I am only visiting."

"I have lived here all of my sixteen years," he informed her, continuing to enjoy the apple as he leaned against the tree and watched her. "I have seen the beginnings of the revolution and the rise of Hébert and Danton and Marat. I saw Charlotte Corday on trial for the murder of Marat and watched her guillotined in the Champ de Mars. I saw the King and Queen guillotined— what a fine day that was! Of course, it was cold when Louis was executed, but none felt it as they watched the downfall of a tyrant!"

"No more a tyrant than this Robespierre, who drowns the streets of Paris in the blood of innocents!" Aimee replied, throwing caution to the winds as her anger was provoked.

The boy smiled lazily and finished the apple, throwing it negligently into the basket with the others. "You talk like an aristocrat, citizeness," he said.

Aimee stepped back in horror, feeling a sudden, dreadful fear wash over her. What had she done? She had talked freely to a stranger who might be a spy for the government. Who was his uncle? Did he really live here? She knew none of these things for certain . . . Oh, her aunt had been right to keep her confined to the house, for she had made such a mess of things!

Jean-Baptiste smiled again. "You seem to have difficulty keeping your feelings hidden, citizeness," he told her with amusement. "Could it be you have betrayed your true feelings to me?"

"Get out of here!" Aimee said angrily, picking up the basket and striding toward the house. "I did not invite you here—and my feelings are none of your business!"

With masculine authority, he pulled the basket from her hands, shouldered it, and took it to the back door of the house, his eyes peering inside the window glass to see what was inside. "Anything else to eat?" he wondered hopefully.

"Not for you! I think you have already proven yourself rude enough, startling me as you did and eating one of my apples—"

"One of *your* apples?" he asked, his chestnut brows rising inquiringly over the twinkling brown eyes. "But, citizeness, according to the Worship of Reason, these apples are the fruit of the earth, and thus are fair game for anyone. If I wished, I could take the whole basket, for I am sure my need is much greater than yours."

Aimee studied him, noting the general shabbiness of his clothing, the streaks of dirt on his forearms, and the hollowed cheekbones beneath his eyes. As she stared, he smiled again and drew closer to her so that she stepped back warily, her cheeks once more flooding with color.

"Ah, that is much better," he said happily. "You are so much more delightful when you are shy and unsure of yourself than when you are spouting sentiment for the aristocrats or telling me what an unworthy scoundrel I am! I assure you, Jean-Baptiste Aubray is every bit of a scoundrel! If I were not, I should not be alive now, I can tell you! One has to live by his wits in the streets of Paris, my dear, or one does not live at all!"

"The streets of Paris? But you said that you lived with your uncle—"

He cleared his throat, but hardly looked nonplussed. "If I would have told you I lived in the streets, would you have talked to me?" he queried.

"My brother lives in the same streets," Aimee said, her voice taking on a hard edge of concern. Then her green eyes brightened hopefully. "Perhaps you know him? Etienne de Chartres—he looks very much like me, except his eyes are blue."

"Hmm, and yours are as green as the sea, aren't they?" Jean-Baptiste clarified somewhat bemusedly. "No, citizeness, I'm afraid I have not heard that name, although many people do not use their real names in the streets. Your brother is new to Paris, too?"

Aimee nodded. "We came here—to look for someone," she ended lamely, not willing to trust this boy with any more information.

"And as soon as you find him, you will leave Paris?" he asked. After Aimee nodded, he continued. "Then I shall hope that it takes a long time, Citizeness de Chartres, for I have already determined to visit you again very soon."

"Oh, no!" Aimee cried in horror. "You cannot come here again. My aunt . . . is . . . unused to strangers and she would not think well of me should I bring one to her home. You mustn't come again, Citizen Aubray, I beg you!"

"Call me Jean-Baptiste, and I shall think on your request," he said merrily. "And, of course, you will do me the honor of telling me your first name—"

"Aimee."

He laughed. "It sounds positively *aristocratic*," he said, leaning closer to her once more. "Now, tell me, Aimee, you really don't want me never to visit you again, do you? I should think a young girl like yourself would look forward to having me around for company if all you have inside is some maiden aunt who is afraid of strangers." His brown eyes seemed to be coming closer to her, and Aimee looked away, as though afraid of becoming mesmerized by them.

"I suppose you shall do as you like," she said quickly, "no matter what my feelings are in the matter."

He laughed again, delighting at her indirect compliance. "I shall come again, then," he said quickly, stealing another apple from the basket before bowing and hurrying over to the wall, which he climbed with speedy agility before looking back at her and blowing a kiss.

Aimee's cheeks warmed again, but she felt a strange tingling within herself and a kind of disappointment, perhaps, that he was already gone.

8

In the days that followed, the Great Terror was instigated by Robespierre, whose bloodlust seemed to know no bounds. Either drunk with his absolute power or perhaps seeing imagined enemies on all sides, he ordered the arrests and executions of almost fourteen hundred people in the months of June and July. In two days during July alone, one hundred fifty people were sent to the guillotine. Day after day the butchery went on, until the people of Paris finally sickened of it and, on July 27, 1794 the National Convention voted for Robespierre's arrest. Later he was executed with twenty of his most ardent followers amid the loud cheers of the populace. In the two days following the execution, eighty-three more met the blade of the guillotine until the Convention was convinced that all of Robespierre's followers had been weeded out of the government.

The people of Paris turned their thoughts toward the war again as the French Army took the offensive, capturing Brussels and Antwerp. With the army winning decisive victories, the people began to protest the continuation of the terror, but the new leaders still wished it to remain so long as there were plots afoot by foreign agents to effect a royalist restoration and to assassinate the remaining leaders of the revolution.

Aimee had grown used to her somewhat lonely existence with her aunt, with only infrequent notes from her brother that said very little, but she began to chafe at her enforced inactivity and longed for the wide-open fields and meadows of the Castle du Beautreillis once the hated Robespierre was deposed and she felt as though her aunt might leave the hotel once in a while. But Hortense de Chartres remained adamant in her refusal to leave her home, afraid that it would be locked up should she try to gain entrance again. That, or her carefully hoarded food might be eaten up by scavengers.

Aimee continued to grow more and more restless, and it was in this mood that she saw Jean-Baptiste Aubray again as she sat sulking underneath the shade of the apple tree one day in September. His whistle alerted her at once and she scrambled to her feet, her heart beating faster in spite of herself as those merry brown eyes seemed to assess her appearance from head to toe.

"Hello, Aimee!" he called, jumping down lightly from the wall. "Have you missed me, little aristocrat?"

"Yes," Aimee replied without artifice. "I've been lonesome here with my aunt—and, worse, I feel pent up so that I can barely breathe. The summer has already gone and I've spent all of it indoors in that musty old hotel, surviving on as little food as she thinks we can survive on!" She stamped her foot petulantly. "I cannot go on like this, yet she refuses to leave the hotel!"

"Ha! I don't blame you for sulking, my beauty," Jean-Baptiste said with a sad shake of his head. "I would have come back to see you sooner had I but known how desperate you were for company. Listen to me! Why don't you come with me today on my sojourns through Paris and have a little fun, eh? Marat's body is to be transferred today to the Pantheon, which has become the revolutionary hall of fame. In exchange, Mirabeau's body is to be removed in disgrace."

The names meant little to Aimee, but her eyes brightened considerably at the prospect of seeing the city, of leaving the confines of the hotel. But common sense held her back as she realized that she knew very little about this boy. Her aunt's warnings continued to haunt her and she agonized between wanting to be free, if only for a little while, and her distrust of the companion who offered that freedom to her.

Jean-Baptiste, sensing her hesitation, came closer and caught her hand, despite her attempt to pull it from his grasp. "Aimee, I swear no harm will come to you," he told her seriously. "I will bring you back here whenever you wish. You could not be safer if you were with your own brother."

"My brother," she echoed dismally, aching for the sight of her handsome sibling. "It seems Paris has swallowed him up, for I haven't heard from him for a long time."

"Come with me and I promise you I will find your brother and bring you word of him," Jean-Baptiste swore, squeezing the hand he held, feeling the blood coursing swiftly through the veins in her wrist.

"Why would you do this for me?" she wondered softly, daring to bring her eyes up to meet his.

"Because you are too lovely to pine away in this musty old place," he replied promptly. "And also because I am a vain scoundrel who fancies all the girls falling head over heels for me," he continued with a faint trace of mockery, "and I would eel enormously disappointed if I could not count your heart as mine as well."

Aimee laughed and removed her hand from his. "I should be most afraid of entrusting my heart to you, Jean-Baptiste, for I do not think you treat young girls' hearts well."

He joined in her laughter, glad to see she had some wit about her. "Then you'll come with me today?"

She glanced at the tall hotel, at its sightless walls that seemed to smother her, knowing her aunt lay abed this morning, as she did every morning, expecting her to be about her duties, which never varied from day to day. She looked back at Jean-Baptiste, his smile as warm as the September day, his eyes twinkling with the prospect of a day of fun. It was not a hard decision for a fifteen-year-old to make.

"Yes, I'll come!" she said swiftly with a little trill of laughter. "But hurry, let's go before my aunt calls for me."

"Or before you lose your nerve!" Jean-Baptiste laughed, taking her hand and pulling her over to the wall, where he gave her a leg-up with his cupped hands, exclaiming as he did, "Whew! You're as light as a feather, my girl. Your aunt must be starving you, indeed! Ah, we'll feast today, though—you'll see!"

He lifted himself up with his usual sprightly agility and landed on the balls of his feet on the other side. "Come on," he urged, "this house is empty. We can go through here to get to the street." So saying, he took her hand once more and pulled her through the hotel, giving her no time to catch her breath until they stood out in the street, where there was a medium amount of activity going on.

"The milliners and the haberdashers live just down the street," Jean-Baptiste said. "Would you like to see the shops of some of the most fashionable seamstresses in Paris?" He smiled at her self-conscious blush as she realized the outdated fashion of her own plain clothing. "Come along, then, it will do your female heart good to see what wonders the fashionable are wearing these days!" He took her hand again, keeping to an energetic walk as they traversed the rue Saint-Denis, heading for the long rows of shops that were closer in to the heart of the city.

As they got closer to the Seine, the crowds on the streets seemed to increase until it was necessary for Aimee to clasp Jean-Baptiste's hand tightly so that she would not become separated from him and get lost. He squeezed her hand for courage and brought her to the most fashionable shops of Paris, pointing

out the items in the windows while Aimee's eyes grew round
with excitement.

She had never seen such fashions before and felt even dowdier
in her clothing as she took in the gowns of fine cloth with their
double collars and satin jackets and the lesser width of the skirts
which required fewer petticoats. The hats made her catch her
breath in sheer feminine delight at the sight of the tulle and satin
creations, the straw hats with their satin rosettes, the bonnets of
ribbons with elegant, dyed ostrich plumes.

"Oh, look how the hair is done!" she cried, pointing to a
woman who was just leaving the shop, her hair in loose curls
done in a rather unsophisticated style that was in great contrast to
the high, towering wigs of the era of Marie Antoinette. Aimee
touched her own bright wavy lengths, realizing how unaristo-
cratic she must look with the simple hairstyle she had affected
from childhood.

Another woman exited a shop, looking coyly fresh in a striped
cotton gown with a matching short jacket, decorated with a
bowknot at the bodice that helped to fasten a gauze fichu around
her throat. She wore her unpowdered hair in loose rolls at the
sides and wavy in the back, while perched atop her head was a
small straw hat that decorated with long ribbons. Aimee clasped her
hands together and allowed herself a small sigh of envy.

"I must look positively provincial," she said aloud to herself.

"You look like the rest of the working class of Paris," Jean-
Baptiste told her, laughing at the frown with which she favored
him. "That lady is one of the rich bourgeois. Her husband is
probably a banker or a lawyer and they are the ones who have
money to buy fripperies like that. Hard to believe that only a few
streets away, people barely have enough money to buy bread."
He shrugged philosophically. "And yet, Paris decrees that fashion
must go on, despite famine and war and revolution."

"Let's do go on," Aimee said quickly. "I could stand and gaze
at these people all day, but I want to see as much as I can before I
have to return to the hotel."

"I am at your command, my lady," Jean-Baptiste returned,
heading her away from the fashionable congestion.

They took several turns through alleyways that seemed a maze
of twisting, turning tunnels to Aimee as she watched with huge
eyes as they passed yards filled with rotting debris and trash and
dirty back stairs where wild-haired children played games and
stared back at her curiously. Sometimes another boy about Jean-
Baptiste's age would make a sign to him and Jean-Baptiste would

nod or return the sign with crossed fingers. Aimee wondered what this meant and determined that she would ask him about it when they returned to the hotel.

"The Palais Royal!" Jean-Baptiste pointed out as they closed upon a magnificent structure of stone and marble that had once belonged to the Duc d'Orléans. "Here is the forum of the revolution," he told Aimee. "The center of café life is here with restaurants and bookshops, even a circus! There are all kinds of entertainment, but you must tread carefully, for it is also the stomping ground of agitators and scandalmongers who stand on their soapboxes and deliver oratory for unceasing hours on end. Would you like to walk through?"

Aimee shook her head hesitantly. The cafés looked inviting, but there were literally hordes of people coming in and out, men escorting women, groups of men and even one or two women alone, venturing into the establishments that featured good food and wine, but, more importantly, stimulating conversation. She felt out of place among the fashionable men and women, the firebrands of the revolution and the officials of government. Here, too, there were quite a few militiamen, some assigned to the protection of Paris, others home on leave from the front, and the sight of their red-white-and-blue uniforms caused a feeling of unease in Aimee as she recalled her uncomfortable stay in the jail in Orléans.

They passed through the crowds on their way to the Tuileries, which Aimee gazed at in awe. Adjacent to the Tuileries was the Jardin des Tuileries, a fashionable parade ground where one could hear the latest news. Here, Jean-Baptiste insisted on escorting her through the park with its flowering hedges and neatly trimmed shrubbery. All around her, Aimee was aware of fashionable young dandies who seemed oddly out of place beside those idealists who still wore the *sans-culottes* uniforms of the beginning of the revolution. On the arms of the dandies were young ladies dressed in elegant gowns with moleskin patches cut into intricate designs on their cheeks.

"How does the revolution tolerate them?" Aimee asked Jean-Baptiste in a low whisper as they walked along the promenade.

The boy shrugged. "They're called Muscadins, many of whom are moderates and former royalists. They attend the meetings of the Convention and try to shout down the Jacobins, who are on the decline anyway. Fréron is their leader, and despite their foppish looks they delight in joining in street brawls with the *sans-*

culottes, who despise them. I have heard they are advocating clemency to the remaining prisoners still being held from the terror."

"For that, I applaud them," Aimee said sincerely, although she still could not look at the mincing dandies without wondering how in the world they could bring themselves to fisticuffs with the street brawlers of the city.

She was so intent on watching these fashionable apparitions that she did not watch where she was going and ran headlong into a National Guardsman whose hands immediately came out to steady her, lingering overlong on her shoulders. Aimee looked up in surprise, noting the ready smile on the soldier's face. Confused at such a reaction, she ducked her head shyly, searching for her companion, relieved to see Jean-Baptiste on hand to spirit her away.

"He liked you," Jean-Baptiste whispered conspiratorially.

"Don't be silly. He was simply being rude!" Aimee replied quickly, keeping her eyes in front of her now.

"Aimee de Chartres, you are the oddest young lady I've ever been with. Don't you know you are most charming and really quite lovely?" Jean-Baptiste continued. "Did no one in your province ever try to steal a kiss from you?"

Aimee shook her head. "No, because I had five brothers who would have sent anyone sprawling who dared!"

Jean-Baptiste laughed and drew her closer to him suddenly, placing one hand on the small of her back so that she could not wriggle free. "You are lovely, Aimee, with your green eyes like the sea and those peachlike cheeks of yours. A young man begins to wonder if the rest of your skin could possibly look the same. And your hair—the brightest gold gleaming in the sunshine. Ah, if I were an unscrupulous man, I'd draw you behind one of these bushes and seduce you!"

"One doesn't seduce girls in a public garden!" Aimee reproached him, looking into his warm brown eyes and wondering what it might feel like to be seduced by him.

"Perhaps not in Orléans, but certainly in Paris," Jean-Baptiste returned, bringing his mouth closer to hers so that they were almost touching. "One kiss, little aristocrat, and I shall be your slave forever!"

Aimee wanted to laugh and wondered if he was teasing her. But the look in his eyes was suddenly serious, and in the next moment she felt his warm mouth on hers, tasting her lips with a tenuous movement that would have deepened had she not pushed him away.

"I'm sorry," she said, immediately contrite at his flabbergasted air. "I haven't gotten used to Parisian traditions. I'm afraid you shall have to be patient with me, Jean-Baptiste."

The smile returned to his lips. "If there is hope, I shall be as patient as Job," he responded, taking her hand once more.

As they walked, it was impossible to avoid bumping into ladies and their gentlemen, and Aimee begged her own escort to take her out of the garden. Jean-Baptiste complied immediately and Aimee wondered for a moment at his ready compliance. She saw a self-satisfied look on his face as they passed out of the garden and walked past the Tuileries again toward the Louvre, heading in the direction of the river. Finally, she asked him the reason for it.

"I've seen a good day's work this day," he told her with a wink.

"What do you mean?"

He patted the pocket of his vest. "A pocket watch, a couple of snuffboxes, and one or two handkerchiefs, plus a lady's silver comb."

"You're a thief!"

Jean-Baptiste grinned. "Yes, petty larceny, my pet. That's what keeps food in my mouth and clothes on my back. How do you think I'm supposed to live?"

"I thought . . . well, I didn't really . . ."

"Everyone's got a right to live, don't they? And these few trinkets won't be missed, I'm telling you." He leaned toward her and touched a rough finger to her nose. "You've been a boon to business, Aimee. Those stodgy old gentlemen are so busy looking at *you* that they don't notice me with my fingers inside their coat pockets. We've made a rather good team today."

Aimee gazed at him sourly. "Well, don't expect me to accompany you on your thieving expeditions all the time!" she huffed in righteous fury. "In Orléans, pickpockets got their hands cut off!"

"In Paris, you can get your head cut off!" Jean-Baptiste told her with a light air about him. "And yet, what's the difference if you're starving to death!"

"You're not starving!"

"No, because I'm industrious," he went on, unperturbed. "My friends and I do pretty well at it, I'm telling you. I've never been caught yet—and I don't intend to be. It's been close sometimes, but with you next to me, it's a snap. Maybe you'll come out with me again and I'll show you a few of the tricks of the trade!"

"I should think not!" Aimee returned, aghast at the idea.

"Douse the pretty airs," Jean-Baptiste told her seriously.
"What will you do when you and your aunt run out of food,
wench? Are you going to go into the streets and beg? I doubt it.
What are the other alternatives?" He eyed her deliberately.
"You're certainly pretty enough to sell yourself to a man, but I
don't think you could do that either." He noted her fiery cheeks at
the notion. "Of course, there are places that'll do the selling for
you. Madame Dupéron at the Palais Royal will set you up and
you can make twenty-five livres a night if you like, if you're
lucky. If you're not, you could end up further down the scale at
only six livres."

"I don't want to hear—"

"Don't be a goose! You live in Paris now, not the provinces!
Life isn't kind to people like you, Aimee, who aren't industrious.
You and your aunt have too much pride to do anything but rot in
that old hotel. Do you think someone will rescue you? It's everyone for himself in the city. Why do you think former aristocrats
have turned to other professions—dance teachers, music performers, even petty thievery? They've got to live!"

"But why does life have to be so hard? I thought the grand
revolution was supposed to change all that! I thought those precious ideals that everyone was spouting when the King was guillotined meant that everyone would have an equal chance at life
no matter what their station!"

Jean-Baptiste clapped. "Bravo! Little aristocrat, you are turning into a firebrand," he said with a sarcastic twist to his mouth.
"But to answer your question, my dear, those wonderful ideals of
Diderot and Rousseau and Danton sound wonderful when one is
shouting from a balcony overlooking the square, but in substance
they mean very little. No one can make a peasant equal to a
nobleman, just as one does not cast pearls before swine. It is
enough for the people to hear such democratic ideals. No one
really expects them to be carried out. That is why the working
class and the poor of Paris have learned to be more clever at
making a living. Look at me! If I did not rob the wealthy bourgeois, I would not be alive today."

They had come to the edge of the Seine and Aimee would
have liked to say something in return, but the heavy crowds from
the Pont Neuf were a jostling, vivacious bunch that allowed only
limited conversation. With a pout, she wondered if Jean-Baptiste
had steered her deliberately this way so as to avoid having to

argue further with her. At any rate, she was soon swept into all the noise and activity all around her and decided to shelve her arguments for a more opportune time. With renewed delight, she listened to the cries of the hawkers, their flattery and ballyhoo, as they assailed her ears with the worth of their goods. Everything from books to flowers and all kinds of food could be gotten for the price of a few sous. There were also rope dancers, jugglers, and sleight-of-hand artists who were the delight of the children. There was activity everywhere along with a veritable rainstorm of pamphlets, most of them having to do with those same revolutionary ideals that Aimee and Jean-Baptiste had discussed earlier.

Across the Seine, connected by the Pont Neuf, was the Ile de la Cité, where the tall Gothic towers of the Cathedral of Notre Dame stood imposingly. Aimee stared breathlessly at the old stone, then begged her companion to take her there. He shook his head implacably.

"Nothing there to tempt you, Aimee. You'd be disappointed with how it looks now that they've outlawed all religion except for the Worship of Reason. The scandal sheets cry out against the nightly orgies conducted there by government officials."

"Such things should be outlawed!" Aimee cried in disgust.

"No doubt they will be now that Robespierre is dead and more conservative elements are beginning to take over. But come along, we can see all that another time. Aren't you hungry?"

Aimee nodded, realizing it was long past the noon hour and she hadn't eaten anything since early that morning.

"Let's see now, what would tempt your palate?" Jean-Baptiste wondered. "We can go back along the rue Saint-Honoré and go into one of those cafés close by the Palais Royal."

Despite her earlier reluctance, Aimee nodded enthusiastically. "Yes, that would be wonderful—but with what shall we pay for our lunch?"

"Come along, we'll make a little detour along the way. I know someone who will give us ready cash for these little trinkets I picked up today."

So saying, Jean-Baptiste led her along the street, then down a sidestreet and through a back alley, twisting and turning until they came to a small shop, its disheveled exterior belying the neat shelves of goods it displayed inside. A gnarled old man with a gray beard and beetling brows gazed out over the rim of his spectacles, smiling almost grimly as he recognized Jean-Baptiste.

"Aha! You've brought me something," he said. "And what is

it this time? A pair of silver candlesticks? An ornamented rosary, perhaps? Or some lady's trinkets?" He waved his hand behind him at the rows of goods on the shelves. "Those are the most popular, my lad."

Jean-Baptiste emptied his pockets, displaying his day's catch with an air of pride. He picked up one of the snuffboxes, displaying the artistically carved sides and the fluted top, which was pure silver. "Look at these, gray beard! I've done well today, thanks to the help of my companion here."

The old man gazed at Aimee with compressed lips. "Eh, what did she do?"

"Provided diversion so that I might get on with my nimble fingers," Jean-Baptiste said and laughed. "But hurry along, old man, for she's hungry and so am I. We need money to buy a meal or two."

"Ah, you spend it as soon as I give it to you!" the man said, shaking his head at what he considered a lack of wisdom in the boy. "But you're right, these are nice pieces here, and the silver comb. The handkerchiefs are worth a few sous at most, but come, I can be generous to one of my favorite suppliers." And he pressed a handful of coins into Jean-Baptiste's palm. "I am giving you good prices here."

"Better than old Flaubert a few streets over," Jean-Baptiste assured him. "I'll make sure my friends come by."

Once outside, Aimee had a thousand questions on her lips, but Jean-Baptiste brushed them aside, telling her that one could not talk on an empty stomach. Dismissing the subject, he brought her to one of the smaller cafés near the Palais Royal that was, nevertheless, still quite crowded.

"The police don't frequent here as a rule," Jean-Baptiste whispered to her. "Always have to keep my eyes open in my business, you understand. Once the law gets your number, they're like bulldogs, hovering about your heels, waiting for you to make one wrong move. Then it's into the Conciergerie with you, and it's up to their pleasure whether you get out again."

They seated themselves at a small round table, bearing traces of the previous patron's lunch. Jean-Baptiste ordered herb soup, potatoes, and cheese along with two glasses of beer—a typical working-class lunch, he said to Aimee with a smile.

Aimee found the food quite good, the beer a little sour, but palatable. When they had finished their repast, she leaned back in her chair, feeling a little tired from the day's adventure, but hardly looking forward to the dismal hotel with Aunt Hortense. She said as much to her companion.

"Stay with me, then," he advised with a wicked air.

"But where is that?"

"Anywhere I can find shelter. A deserted hotel, the steps of a cathedral, a statue in the Place de Grève."

"I don't think I should like that very much," Aimee returned honestly. "Don't you ever worry about what might happen? And what of the night patrol? If they catch you—"

"But they don't catch me," Jean-Baptiste interrupted cockily. "Think of all the spies and murderers and profiteers in the city of Paris. Why should the police bother too much about a petty thief?"

Aimee admitted that his reasoning seemed sound, but there was always the chance that his luck would run out.

He shrugged, then leaned across the table to take her hands in his. "But what do you say to my proposal, Aimee? Would you like to spend the night with me? I know of an empty house in the Faubourg Saint-Germain that still has a bed in it. We could stay there."

"My aunt would be worried to death," Aimee put in quickly. "I couldn't leave her alone after all she has done for me. If she hadn't taken me in, I would have been destitute in the city."

"And yet, just a moment ago you said you weren't looking forward to going back there," he reminded her with irony.

She reddened a little, but stood her ground. "I have to go back."

For a moment, he looked as though he might like to continue the argument, then sighed and gave up. "All right, then, I suppose we should be getting back. It's late afternoon already and you'll not want to be out after twilight."

Aimee nodded and they exited the café, making their way through the colorful crowds once again, passing mountebanks, with their puppet shows, and vendors of licorice water who hawked their merchandise in strident voices. With his last sou, Jean-Baptiste bought Aimee a nosegay from one of the little flower sellers, presenting it to her with a sweep of his arm as he bowed from the waist. Aimee protested his spending his last coin for her, but he insisted and she took the nosegay with a smile, breathing in its fragrance, which couldn't quite dispel the other smells of the city—those of the soap factories and ironworks and the pervasive, noxious odor of garbage that ran all along little channels cut into the streets. The air smelled foul and seemed suddenly oppressively hot. Jean-Baptiste noticed the girl's sudden quiet and asked her what was the matter.

"I was thinking how stifling the city seemed," Aimee answered him thoughtfully. "I suddenly found myself longing for Orléans and the Loire, for long vistas of green hills and fields, not this cold stone and gray buildings that close in all around me."

"I cannot imagine anything else," Jean-Baptiste said quietly, glancing around him with a familiar air of confidence.

"I worry about my brother, Etienne," Aimee went on as though she had not heard him. "I think of him in these dark streets, running through alleys, living from hand to mouth." She shivered unconsciously. "I only pray he is all right."

Privately, Jean-Baptiste doubted it. How could a young provincial from the country hope to learn the ways of the streets of Paris in a few weeks? Still, he didn't want to deaden his companion's hope. "I'll be on the lookout for him," he promised, "although I don't think he would be using his own name. Most people in the streets use tags, nicknames, like Honest Jean, Pretty Boy, the Gypsy. It's easier and keeps the law off their necks."

"Do what you can?" Aimee asked hopefully. They had come to her street, and it was time to part. She held out her hand and felt Jean-Baptiste's answering squeeze. "I'll look for you again —soon." She smiled.

"What about your aunt?"

"Oh, I shall simply have to explain something to her," Aimee replied airily, although she was secretly dreading having to face her aunt, who, by this time, was probably nearly apoplectic with anger and worry over her niece's disappearance.

Jean-Baptiste laughed, seeing through her subterfuge. "I'll try to come back around next week—and hopefully have news of your brother." He released her hand and started off down the street with a jaunty air, leaving Aimee to stand watching him rather forlornly.

9

·—●—●—●·

In the weeks that followed, Jean-Baptiste came often to the rue Saint-Denis, finally becoming bold enough to knock on the back door of the kitchen so he would not have to wait in order to catch Aimee outside. The weather was turning chilly and Aimee was not out in the apple tree as often as before. Aunt Hortense nearly had a seizure when Aimee informed her about her companion. In no uncertain terms, she expressly forbade Aimee to see the young scamp again, but Aimee ignored her, feeling the time with Jean-Baptiste, away from the gloomy hotel, was too precious to give up. After a time, Hortense stopped grumbling, merely warning her niece that should she find herself in trouble, she would not be there to pick up the pieces.

In spite of her earlier high-minded ideals, she had lapsed quite easily into the routine of petty thievery with her companion. She met several of the gang with which Jean-Baptiste ran, and was amazed at how young some of them were, only nine and ten. But all of them had one thing in common—they were all orphans, children of the Paris streets. Their ability to find their way through the city continually amazed Aimee, and their knowledge of police whereabouts and the changes in the patrols were invaluable in their occupation. Soon, she was able to take things to old Graybeard by herself, feeling immensely pleased at the coins she'd secured—money to pay for food that she and her aunt needed to live. A stolen Chinese fan, carelessly dropped from a lady's hand, was the price of a new pair of shoes, needed for the coming winter. A man's pair of gold-rimmed spectacles or a lady's jewel-encrusted mirror would supply her aunt and her with warm clothing and food in the coming months.

By the time the new year rolled around, Aimee had become quite an accomplished little thief and, despite the January cold, it seemed Jean-Baptiste was not about to stop doing what he did best. The harvest of the year before had been severely damaged by storms, and the people of Paris were hungry again because of a bread shortage. It took more money to buy a loaf of bread or a bag of vegetables, and Aimee's pilfering increased so that she was out more often with Jean-Baptiste than she was at home. Some evenings she arrived at the hotel totally exhausted, her feet numb with cold, her fingers reddened and cracking from the dry north wind.

The terror that had been instigated by Robespierre was beginning to die as the Revolutionary Tribunal was reorganized. Large numbers of prisoners were released and freedom of worship was again permitted. The committees of Public Safety and General Security were revised and brought under the National Convention's control.

In January, a mob of Muscadins burned Marat in effigy in the garden of the Jacobin Club; the incident provoked street fights all over Paris between the two groups. These brawls resulted in the closing of the Jacobin Club by a decree of the convention and many people cheered at the news, tired of that group of men holding sway over the city. Aimee was obliged to remain at the hotel during this time, for Jean-Baptiste insisted things were too dangerous with the increased patrols all around the city.

Aimee chafed at the enforced inactivity and at her aunt's harangues on the immorality of her behavior. By the time it was safe again, in Jean-Baptiste's opinion, to resume her thievery, Aimee was nearly speechless with excitement. The only sad note to her successes was the fact that she had still not heard from Etienne, despite all Jean-Baptiste's efforts to find him, and the attempts of his friends. Either Etienne was in prison, had fled Paris, or was dead. Aimee refused even to think of the last condition and told herself that her brother was probably somewhere in hiding within the city, still hoping to find the fat Faron and administer justice.

On a cold, blustery day in late February, she waited impatiently at the hotel for Jean-Baptiste, realizing it was well past the appointed time of his visit. She paced around the kitchen while her aunt lectured her on her growing attachment to the vagabond boy who would probably break her heart one day. Aimee scoffed at her aunt's words, assuring her that Jean-Baptiste was at all times a gentleman with her, although privately she admitted to herself that, as they had grown closer through the last months, he had become more and more attached to her, loath to leave her at the hotel and find a bed somewhere for himself alone. His kisses were more frequent, his hands seeking to explore the growing curves that he perceived even through the warm layers of her clothing.

At last, over three hours late, Jean-Baptiste's familiar knock sounded at the door. Aimee uttered a cry of alarm when she opened the door to see him stagger into the kitchen, his hair matted with blood from a long gash over his forehead. Quickly, despite her aunt's screeching, she drew up a chair for him and set out a bowl of soup to cool. Then, despite her own queasiness, she attended to the wound while he told her what had happened.

It seemed the patrols were becoming more vigilant, he explained. He and some of his fellows were at old Graybeard's when, suddenly, a pack of policemen came storming in with their swords and clubs, placing them all under arrest. Well, he told her, they weren't about to be carted off like sheep and there was a nasty brawl. Graybeard was dead, as were two of Jean-Baptiste's gang. But twice as many policemen had been dispatched, he boasted, then winced as Aimee applied a compress to his wound.

"How did you get away?" she inquired as he began eating the soup with a ravenous appetite.

He waited until he'd taken several spoonfuls in rapid succession. "Old Graybeard was dying and I had fallen next to him. They must have thought I was dead, too, for they took those still standing and hustled them into the cart outside. That was my chance to slip around behind the counter and out the back door. It was a good thing, too, since they searched the place before barring it shut. All the goods have been sequestered, more's the pity."

"And your companions?"

"In the Conciergerie," Jean-Baptiste replied glumly. "And not likely to get out very soon either. Not everyone was there, so we've still enough to band together again, but it won't be the same." He shook his head. "And on top of everything else, this damned weather has been so cold you could freeze your ears off!"

"Better than starving to death!" Aimee put in.

"I don't mind telling you I'll be glad to see spring again!" Jean-Baptiste said fervently, finishing the last of the soup in his bowl and looking for more. "Then we shall have much better pickings, since everyone will not be so bundled up. I'll tell you, Aimee, I could almost think of laying off until the end of March, except that I'd have nothing to eat."

"You could get a regular job," Aimee told him, pursing her lips.

"You mean *gainful* employment!" Jean-Baptiste cried, rolling his eyes in comic horror. "But, my dear, children of the streets don't do such things. No, they graduate from petty thievery to grand larceny, and then—who knows? Some become quite able with a knife and pistol; others become the chieftains of beggar bands."

"And others find their necks stretched over *la guillotine!*" Aimee snorted.

"That is true, my dear. But *I* do not plan to be one of them!"

After this incident, Jean-Baptiste was more careful, and, indeed, as he'd said, the pickings were slim. Food was terribly scarce and Aimee finally had to part with the gold-leafed crucifix with its ruby wounds in order to purchase food for herself and her aunt, as well as for Jean-Baptiste, who had taken to staying at the hotel, for the protection of the ladies, he assured an indignant Hortense, although Aimee knew it was really because he had nowhere else to go and it was too cold to sleep outdoors.

The spring finally made a late appearance in mid-April and Aimee gloried in the feel of the sun on her face as she sat in the yard with Jean-Baptiste, inspecting the apple tree for winter damage.

"I think," she said with a decided air, "that I shall plant a vegetable garden here. Jean-Baptiste, you can get some of your friends to help turn the soil and ready it for planting."

"And where will you get the seeds?"

"I shall buy them."

"Ah, that will be a steep purchase, citizeness. It looks like we shall have our work cut out for us, eh?" He winked at her and, with a natural motion, brought his arm around to enclose her shoulders and draw her nearer to him. "Your cheek is as firm as an apple," he declared, rubbing it with an index finger. "I should love to bite into it!" And so saying, he brought his mouth down and nipped at her skin, then nuzzled her neck and turned her around to fit her against the length of him.

Aimee, not unused to his rough caresses, was not in the mood for them this morning and pushed him back in irritation. To her surprise, instead of releasing her as usual, he continued to hold her while his mouth explored the top of her bodice.

"Enough!" she cried, struggling to be set free.

Then he released her, an angry look to his brown eyes and a frustrated set to his shoulders. "Damn it, Aimee! Why will you not let me make us both happy? Believe me, I would be proud to initiate you into the arts of love, my dear. Come, let me teach you." He would have drawn her to him again, but she shook her head and stepped away from arm's reach. He frowned. "You are a prude, as bad as that spinster aunt of yours! Look at her, Aimee, old before her time, withered and dry as a sheaf of wheat. You are only sixteen, but it will not take long once you let your heart dry up inside of you!"

"My heart is not dried up, Jean-Baptiste!" she answered fiercely. "But if I gave it to you, you would cut it up into little pieces. I would begin to sigh for you, to grow eager at your coming and fearful when you left. You would no longer be free, and neither would I. But it would be you who would leave in the end! You would grow tired of me and find your fun elsewhere after a time! No!" She held up her hand when he would have interrupted. "I have seen how you treat other girls. You become hard and mean to them when you've used them up. I will not have it, Jean-Baptiste! If you cannot be content to be my friend, then we should part now!" Her eyes were a blazing green with her convictions, and Jean-Baptiste choked back his anger with difficulty, telling himself there would be another opportunity.

"All right, then," he said, the edge of frustration still sharp in his voice. "But then you will excuse me if I seek my physical pleasures elsewhere!" And with a flourish, he leaped over the wall and was gone, leaving Aimee feeling proud of her victory— and yet, somehow empty, as her healthy young body yearned for something she could not name.

Thereafter, Jean-Baptiste was reckless in his forages through the city. With Aimee at his side, he had the temerity to steal the watch seals from a uniformed official. While Aimee asked him for directions, Jean-Baptiste sneaked up behind him and took the watch and chain, crowing about it to the rest of the gang later. They all marveled at his pluck and Jean-Baptiste became determined to be even more daring, so that Aimee finally pleaded with him not to be so foolish. He consented for a little while, although she suspected him of continuing his daring escapades when she wasn't around.

One sunny day in May, they were strolling close by the headquarters of the Convention, enjoying both the weather and the great number of bourgeois who were taking their constitutionals, their striped vests bulging with heavy purses of which Jean-Baptiste was only too happy to relieve them. The crowd, though, was unnaturally cluttered with working class that day and the pickings from them were not worth the risk, Jean-Baptiste said with a yawn. He could feel the weight of the coins inside his coat and thought of the cozy little body of Marie, who would be waiting for him at Madame Dupéron's that night.

Somewhere among the crowd, a brawl began. Aimee could hear someone bawling for help and could see a deputy of the Convention being set upon by some of those men of the working class. In a sudden frenzy, several more men joined in the fray and it looked as though an insurrection was beginning to mount in short order. Shouting that they had Fréron, the leader of the Muscadins, the working-class men cried out their hatred for him, accusing him of being a royalist and wanting to see a king over them again.

The poor deputy told them they were mistaken, but they would not believe him, and, to Aimee's horror, the unlucky man was decapitated before the Convention steps. Feeling utterly sick, she turned her head into Jean-Baptiste's arm as some of the mob put his head on a pike and took it inside to parade around the Convention's meeting room. In spite of her horror, the bustling, surging crowd was pushing her into the Convention hall, and to her despair she lost hold of Jean-Baptiste in the mob and was forced to go along with the surge or be ground underfoot.

She looked away from the grisly sight on the pike of the leader of the mob, but then her eyes fastened on the face of that leader and a low gasp escaped her as she recognized the beefy visage of Faron, the miller from Orléans, the man who was responsible for her family's death! Hatred bubbled up within her as she stared at the man, noting that he had become even more gross since she had last seen him a year before. He wore the dress of the sans-culottes, the striped trousers of which strained to stay buttoned around the bulging belly. His chest and arms were massive, looking ridiculous confined to the short jacket. But her eyes were drawn back to his face, where a black patch covered one eye decorated with a cockade of the colors of liberty. So she felt satisfaction knowing that she had at least blinded that eye with her attack. If only she knew Etienne's whereabouts! Here was the man he had sworn to slay!

Watching attentively now, she heard the chairman of the Convention refusing to let the meeting continue as long as armed men remained in the house. The crowd booed stridently and seemed to be gaining in strength, menacing the remainder of the members of the Convention with drawn knives and pikes.

"We want to voice our grievances!" Faron was shouting.

Some of his followers overturned a table and, after sticking the pike into one of its legs, Faron stepped across it and began haranguing the members with his ideas of what was needed to make Paris happy again. As he was about to sum up his clumsy speech, the doors of the chambers burst open with the timely arrival of armed Muscadins who effectively prevented more serious trouble.

Seeing their enemies, the crowd of working-class men shifted uneasily, then made a break for the doors, streaming out of the room, leaving the pike with its gruesome reminder for all to see. Struggling through the room, Aimee kept her eyes fixed on Faron, an easy target as he was at least a head taller than most of the others.

Once outside, she felt someone grabbing her arm and turned to see Jean-Baptiste. "Come on, Aimee, let's get out of here while we've the chance! I don't like all these uniforms surrounding me!"

"No!" Aimee broke away from him, locating Faron once more in the crowd. "That man, the one with the patch over one eye—he's the one my brother and I were seeking in Paris! He is the one who set the torch to my home and killed my family! I must follow him!"

"But he's with a mean crowd, Aimee. You can't risk it!" Jean-Baptiste said soberly, running behind her as she hurried to keep up with Faron.

"It doesn't matter—I must see where he's going! Perhaps I can find out where he lives!"

"And then what?" Jean-Baptiste asked her, catching her arm once more and spinning her around. She struggled away from him, turning her head to keep her eyes glued to Faron. "Let me go! If you are afraid, then go on!"

"Don't be a fool, Aimee! The Convention will order the arrests of all of those Jacobins. The one with the eye patch will be arrested, too, and put into prison with the others. What can you do? Follow him to the cell! Do not be so stupid!"

"Then I will kill him before he can be arrested!" she shouted into his face, her green eyes huge and dark, her face white with strain. And without further ado, she wrenched her arm from his grasp and continued following Faron and his men down the street, keeping to the cover of the porches of buildings. Behind her, she heard footsteps and knew that Jean-Baptiste was doggedly staying on her trail and blessed him for it. God knew what would happen once Faron got to his destination, but of one thing she was sure—she was not going to lose him again! She would find out all she could so she might make sure he paid for what he had done to her family.

The crowd continued to march on with shouts and oaths punctuating their footsteps as they passed windows where women called out to them and joined in their singing. Aimee thought they would march forever, and then, finally, little pieces of the group started to break away, going to their own homes, leaving only Faron and about a half dozen men who eventually made their way to the Faubourg Saint-Antoine, a part of town with which Aimee was not familiar. Here were the furniture workshops, the dyeworks, tanneries, breweries, and tapestry works, all emitting a most unpleasant stench into the air.

Finally, Aimee saw Faron stop and enter a large, dingy building where the noise and lights inside told her there was drinking, and there were women for sale. Behind her, Jean-Baptiste had stayed close and now he caught her hand in his. "That is the Café Caveau," he whispered. "It is not a place for us to be found, now that evening is getting on. Come on, Aimee, you know where he can be located now. Some of the boys and I will investigate this more thoroughly another time!"

"But what if he goes elsewhere?" Aimee wondered, feeling exhausted, but not willing to lose this small thread.

"He won't. If he's leading those men there, this would be the best place for them, for it caters to their kind. A few inquiries can be made." He patted the pocket of his coat meaningfully. "But, come along, before we become the victims in this sad place." He pulled her along behind him, even though Aimee craned her neck backward to make certain Faron did not leave the establishment. Her heart raced at the thought that very soon vengeance would be hers.

But vengeance had to wait, for the next morning the Convention ordered the arrests of the Jacobins who had been involved in the insurrection. The Faubourg Saint-Antoine was put under martial law and, inside of two days, more than ten thousand arrests were made. Pacing the kitchen of the hotel, Aimee waited impatiently for news from Jean-Baptiste, telling herself that she would put herself in jail if it meant finding Faron and administering justice to him. She truly had no idea how she was going to kill him, only that he must be killed and that he must know who was responsible for exacting the revenge.

Jean-Baptiste finally appeared on the doorstep breathless from his activities and Aimee ushered him inside. "What did you find out?" she demanded.

"He was not arrested with the others," was the welcome news. "He must have some hiding place that is not known to the officials, for everyone was searching for the big man with the eye patch—after all, he did stand out in the crowd! Obviously, his friends are loyal, for the police got no information from the Café Caveau, nor from any of those arrested. It seems he is part of a fine network of informants, for he has been one step ahead of the police for the past two days."

"Good," Aimee said with satisfaction. "We will give him another few days to become careless once more."

"And then?" Jean-Baptiste asked. His brows drew downward as he looked at the change in the young girl. There was a fiery purpose about her, a strained look about the eyes that paled them to the lightest green imaginable. She seemed as tense and taut as a bow-string. "Are you going to kill him yourself?"

She brought her eyes back to him, seeming disconcerted at the idea at first. But then her expression hardened and she nodded. Jean-Baptiste whistled sharply and shook his head.

"You are crazy, Aimee! You cannot just go up to the man and kill him! He is, for one thing, much larger and stronger than you. He could overpower you instantly, and then what would you do? Do not think he would be kind, my dear, for men like him are desperate and inclined to shrug off additional crimes they might commit. He has already killed your family and the deputy in the square. God knows there are probably quite a few more on the list we don't know about. Killing you would be child's play for him!"

"Words, words, I am sick of them, Jean-Baptiste!" Aimee cried, bringing her hands to her ears.

"Because they are the truth!" he replied quickly. "Aimee, you must listen to reason. You cannot possibly kill this Faron! I doubt if one *man* could even do it!"

"Then what is the alternative?" she demanded. "I have sworn to see justice done to the murderer of my family! I cannot let him slip through my fingers this time!"

"Let the militia do the work for you! If we can locate his hiding place and give the alarm, they will take him off to prison and summarily execute him."

For a moment, Aimee hesitated, unwilling to allow the killing of Faron to be left to others. But then sanity prevailed and she realized that it was truly the only way to make sure Faron's life was ended. "But how can we lead the militia to him?" she answered Jean-Baptiste, who grinned in relief that she had accepted his plan.

"My boys and I can locate his hiding place. We've been making discreet inquiries at the Café Caveau, with the explanation that we're interested in joining Faron's group. The keeper of the café is a very suspicious soul, especially where the welfare of his best patron is concerned. He doesn't reveal much, but if we continue to show our good faith and frequent the place often enough, we're bound to run into Faron himself. Then we can plead our cause to him. Since he's lost a lot of his followers in the arrests, I think he'll be more than pleased to gain new ones. We must convince him of our dedication to his Jacobin ideals. Once inside his gang, we should be able to find out where Faron hides out. Then you will have to lead the police there." Jean-Baptiste smiled disarmingly. "I wouldn't want to have too close a dealing with the police myself, you understand. One brush with the law is enough. Too many and they remember your face too well!"

"But will they listen to me?"

"If you tell them you know the whereabouts of Faron, the murderer of the Convention's deputy, they will come with you," Jean-Baptiste assured her.

"And how long will this take?" Aimee wondered.

"Give it at least a month," Jean-Baptiste answered, raising his hand to silence her protests. "If we try to hurry too much, we'll botch the job and Faron will smell a rat. Leave the timing to me—I'll contact you when you're needed."

"But what shall I do in the meantime?"

He smiled again. "Do as you have been doing. Keep your hand in the work, and you and your aunt won't starve. Who knows—you may even find your brother one of these days. And then you will be able to tell him that your mission has been carried out."

"I know he would wish to be there to see Faron's fat face when he realizes he has been deceived," Aimee said with a cold smile. Then she looked hard at Jean-Baptiste. "Do you truly think it will work? Do you promise me that Faron will be in prison, awaiting his execution in the next month?"

Jean-Baptiste crossed his fingers and spat, the pledge of loyalty in the underworld of Paris. "I promise I will do everything I can to help you put him there, Aimee," he answered seriously. "And now," he continued with a mischievous grin, "fix me something to eat, wench, for I'm starving. If I am to do your dirty work for you, I expect you to cater to me, at least a little bit!"

Aimee laughed at his good-natured teasing, her mind at ease about the fate of Faron.

True to his word, Jean-Baptiste gathered a half dozen of his friends and proceeded to the Café Caveau every day, hoping to see Faron show his face there. It was disappointing when, after a week, nothing had happened. But in the next week, the tavern keeper admitted that he expected Faron sometime later in the week and that the boys could talk to him then. Eventually, Jean-Baptiste made contact with the former miller, now turned revolutionist, and after a thorough check into his background, Faron accepted him and his companions into his group.

Aimee's excitement grew by leaps and bounds as Jean-Baptiste reported his progress to her every night. Unfortunately, once he was allowed into the group his outside activities were curtailed, as Faron did not want his people far from him, lest he grow suspicious of their motives. So, Jean-Baptiste told her he would probably not see her for a while, and as Aimee clung to him, he grinned and kissed her gently, telling her not to worry and that everything would be done according to their plan. He would make sure to smuggle a message out to her so that she might bring the militia at the proper time.

Weeks went by and things were changing once more in the government. In June, the official use of the word *revolutionary* was suppressed and the Revolutionary Tribunal passed into limbo by official decree. In July, the Dauphin died in the temple, easing the minds of many who would not tolerate a return to a monarchy. The Convention was now controlled by moderates who were republicans and saw to it that a milder regime was begun. With Prussia, Holland, and Spain suing for peace in the summer of 1795, the task of the Convention was made easier, and work was begun on a new constitution, the third one in France in six years. It only remained for them to weed out the last of the Jacobins, the insurrectionists who still threatened to overturn the government at the least provocation.

As the Convention sought to solve its problems, Aimee anxiously awaited news from Jean-Baptiste. With the summer, her trade had grown easier and, by now, she had become so expert at pickpocketing that it hardly seemed a challenge. She could usually count on a man to be watching her face so closely that she needn't worry about him watching her hands. With her increased income, she could afford to begin making more extravagant purchases as well, and, much to her aunt's consternation, she began to frequent the dress shops, oohing over the delicate cotton and lawns that had replaced silk and satin in dressmaking as the dresses became less shaped and simply fell from a sash below the breasts. With a natural generosity, Aimee bought gowns for her aunt, who was scandalized at the sheerness of the materials and refused to wear them. Aimee laughed at her dismay and assured her that that was all to be had at the dressmakers' shops and that she could wear a cashmere shawl or embroidered cape over them if she chose and still look fashionable. Aunt Hortense warned her that such fashion would lead to pneumonia if she wasn't careful, but Aimee shrugged aside her words, delighting in the freedom the gowns lent her. It also was not bad for business, for the gowns that were draped snugly around her healthy, young body kept a man's eyes from roving anywhere else, and Aimee was amazed at the ease with which she relieved them of their treasures.

One day in August, as she was walking in the gardens of the Tuileries, drinking in the lovely scents that emanated from the rosebushes and the orange trees in their tubs, she saw a young man, perhaps ten years older than she, strolling through the park, dressed conservatively in a dark green cloth coat, beige trousers, and knee-length leather boots. His light silk waistcoat and short walking stick gave him an air of fashionable dash that appealed to Aimee as she continued to eye him through her lashes, following him at a discreet distance. He seemed to be alone and, by the look of him, probably had quite a bit of money on his person. With a carefree recklessness, Aimee decided to find out.

Walking a little faster, she had nearly overtaken him, when he turned around suddenly eyeing her from dark blue eyes that seemed to freeze her to the spot. Unaccustomed to wariness on the part of men, she smiled tentatively, hoping to see the full-lipped mouth in the clean-shaven face smile back. Instead, his dark brows drew downward as he assessed her from head to toe.

"Good morning, citizen," she managed to squeak, finding outrage building inside her at his rudeness.

"Go about your business!" he said suddenly in a deep voice that startled her. "I'm not in the mood for your favors, citizeness."

"My—" Aimee's own blond brows drew down now and she drew herself up to her full height, which was still not quite up to his chin. "I think you are mistaken," she said icily. "I was merely being pleasant on such a beautiful morning as this. Forgive me if I have annoyed you!"

The dark blue eyes showed a shred of doubt and his mouth softened considerably as he bowed suddenly, taking off the light-weight beaver hat to show thick, sable hair that curled disarmingly at his collar. "Forgive me, then, citizeness. I apologize most sincerely for my rudeness. Would you care to walk with me for a while?"

Aimee, disconcerted by his about-face, eyed him warily now, not sure at all that she wanted to accept his offer. There was something about him that warned her off. Certainly he *seemed* like a respectable citizen taking a stroll in the park, but his attitude was too wary, his eyes too piercing to make her feel comfortable. She started to back away, a slight smile on her lips. "No, thank you, citizen. I must be going—"

His cane came out and hooked expertly about her wrist, pulling her toward him. "But I insist! I should feel quite guilty about my treatment of you if you do not reconsider!" He smiled now, quite charmingly. "I had thought you to be one of those stupid little *merveilleuses* who plague strollers in the park, but I do apologize for the thought, citizeness."

Aimee felt miffed at having been mistaken for one of those women of low morals who wore Grecian tunics of great transparency and paraded about the public squares on the arms of their dandies, those men who had affected the wearing of large golden hoop earrings and spent their time gambling and chasing prostitutes. How could this overbearing man have mistaken her for someone of that caliber? Self-consciously, she straightened her bodice, knowing that despite the softness of the white cotton, the neckline was high enough to discourage anyone from staring at her breasts. She hugged the lightweight shawl closer about her and fixed him with a cool stare from her sparkling green eyes.

"If you will detach your walking stick from my arm, citizen, I shall stroll for a short distance with you," she decided, realizing that unless she took his offer he would probably not release her. Certainly, she had become quite wary of trying to cut the purse of this man.

"Good. Then I shall replace my stick with my arm," he said, proffering his bent elbow to her. They walked for a short way, conversing mundanely about the weather after first exchanging names. Aimee found that he was one Lucian Napier, but when she asked him his occupation, he seemed disinclined to enlighten her and, instead, adroitly steered the conversation to another topic. She found, too, that when he inquired into her past, she avoided talking about it, causing him to lift his eyebrows in curiosity.

Aimee realized with a kind of surprise that she was well aware of the masculine figure next to her, not only because of the ripple of muscles that glided beneath her fingers, but because of the welcoming smiles he continued to receive from female passersby, some painted women of the streets, but others ladies of quality who were obviously attracted by his handsome maleness. Aimee had never thought about men in regard to their attraction to her sex. She had always been surrounded by the protective shield of her father and brothers so that no boys ever ventured too close. Even in Paris, she had managed to avoid the cruder aspects of the exchanges between men and women. She had sometimes heard some of the boys in the gang crowing about Marie or Justine or Giselle at the Palais Royal, but the gist of the conversations had only come to her in the vaguest of terms. Despite an occasional kiss or embrace from Jean-Baptiste, Aimee was still an innocent.

"So you live in Paris, citizeness?" Lucian Napier asked suddenly.

Aimee nodded. "Yes. And you?"

His affirmative nod was typical of his whole range of conversation when it came to personal questions, and Aimee began to feel even more uncomfortable with him. She stopped and leaned over to lace her shoe, giving herself time to think of a way to be rid of him. When she straightened, she smiled and stretched out her hand to say good-bye. "You must forgive me, Citizen Napier, but it is time for me to be off. I have several errands to run—"

"Excellent. I have a carriage just around the corner that I feel obliged to put at your disposal, Citizeness de Chartres. If you will allow me?" And he took her hand again, leading her past a line of shrubbery to the street where a carriage was, indeed, awaiting him.

"I am surprised to see you have a carriage," Aimee said lightly, though her green eyes were beginning to darken with anger. "I had thought most diligences were requisitioned by the government to help in the war effort."

"That is true, but I have been able to procure the use of one," he told her.

Aimee balked at his unsatisfactory explanation. She did not want to get into the carriage with him, for she had no idea what he had in mind once they were inside. Was he a government agent, perhaps? Jean Baptiste had taught her to be very careful of strangers. Perhaps he was some terrible man like the Marquis de Sade, who it was said liked to lure unsuspecting young women into his coach and then spirit them away to his castle. She stared at Citizen Napier beneath lowered eyelashes, wondering just what he was up to. And, then again, perhaps he was up to nothing and was just being helpful.

As she stood in front of the carriage door, trying to make up her mind, Lucian Napier made it up for her as he took her arm and guided her through the door so she found herself, in short order, sitting on a leather seat opposite the man who was beginning to prove quite intriguing.

"Do you usually offer complete strangers the use of your carriage?" she inquired.

He smiled. "Not unless they are lovely young women like yourself, citizeness." He leaned toward her and his smile deepened. "Do you know that you have a most unusual color of eyes, citizeness?"

Her cheeks colored slightly.

"A most unusual color," he continued, "and one is not likely to forget them once having seen them." He leaned back again and continued to regard her through half-closed eyes. "Have you always lived in Paris?" he wondered a moment later.

Aimee stiffened at the question. "No," she answered slowly. "I have come to Paris only recently."

"Then you must be staying with friends?"

She shook her head. "I live with my aunt. My parents are both dead," she continued. She glanced out the window of the carriage, trying to find some familiar street marker that might tell her where they were. When she spied a dressmaker's shop that she knew, she pointed it out and insisted that he stop the carriage, as she had to visit the shop.

He did her bidding, asking the driver to bring the vehicle to a stop. "Shall I wait for you?" he wondered, helping her down from the carriage.

Aimee shook her head quickly. "No, thank you. I have rather a long list of things to purchase and I would not like to put you out," she answered quickly. With a friendly smile, she took her leave of him, glancing back once to see him watching her with an enigmatic expression. Once inside the establishment, she peered out the window curtains, waiting for him to move on before leaving the shop.

As she walked on the street, making for home, she had the

oddest sense of being watched, and several times she turned around, expecting to see Lucian Napier striding behind her. For some reason, she could not shake the feeling of discomfort she was experiencing in regard to that man. What was it about him? His blue eyes had been disturbing the way they'd stared at her, as though trying to discover all her secrets. She felt relieved she'd disengaged herself from his company, yet the unease remained, as though there had been some purpose to everything that had happened this morning.

When she found herself in the rue Saint-Denis, the feeling of being watched grew stronger, and now she turned her head several times, hoping to catch whoever it was lurking behind her. But always, there was no one conspicuously following her, although it was difficult to tell for sure as the crowds thickened. In a hurry now to reach the hotel and safety, Aimee quickened her steps, nearly breaking into a run as the hotel came into sight. Hurrying up the front steps, she paused a moment to catch her breath, glancing back one more time, thus catching a glimpse of someone furtively ducking behind the corner of a building. Could it be the generous Lucian Napier, or was it one of Faron's men? But that was ridiculous; there would be no reason for Faron to have her followed. He had no idea of her existence here in Paris.

Thinking of Faron depressed her as she recalled that Jean-Baptiste had not come with information in a long time. She hoped he would do so soon. More than anything else, she suddenly wished to return to Beautreillis, to try somehow to rebuild it. But she could not leave Paris until she was sure Faron was dead and her brother alive. With such thoughts on her mind, she did not see the stealthy man a few buildings away, taking note of the number over the door behind which she disappeared.

10

·-■-■-■-·

Aimee soon dismissed the intriguing Lucian Napier from her mind, for the next evening she received an unexpected visit from Jean-Baptiste. He was dressed poorly in the ragged outfit of the *sans-culottes*, but he told her excitedly that he had now, he felt, gained Faron's complete trust. Since Faron was a wanted man with the police, he had to entrust certain members of his gang to do his errands for him within the city walls. Jean-Baptiste was enthralled by the size of Faron's network, which included former Jacobins, revolutionists, and insurrectionists, many of whom were wanted by the law for everything from inciting riots to murder.

"The man is very dangerous," Jean-Baptiste said quickly. "Not only because of his own lack of principles, but because he leads so many who are of the same temperament. I think, Aimee," he said honestly, "it will be hard to flush him out in order for the police to take him."

"Do you think he suspects anything?"

"No. The boys and I have been very careful. That is why I haven't been able to see you in all these weeks. I do know that Faron is planning something big as soon as the Convention gets ready to dissolve itself after finishing the new constitution. Faron has talked about gaining the reins of power, of becoming another Robespierre!"

Aimee shivered at the mention of the name that conjured up memories of the Reign of Terror. And she knew that Faron would be doubly worse. At least Robespierre had had a good law background behind him, but Faron had only his experience as a miller. What kind of government could he back? It was true that he had probably gained experience as the leader of his band of cutthroats, but he would be lost in the sea of government policies that awaited him. Would he simply sweep them all away and proclaim himself dictator? Somehow, Aimee knew this would appeal to him. She shivered at the thought that, with government in Paris so fragile, it would not be hard for someone as determined as Faron to get his foot in the door. It remained, then, for her to see that he did not get even that far.

She questioned Jean-Baptiste about what it was that Faron was planning, but he had no details to give her. "As soon as I know, I will find some way of getting a message to you," he promised. "It will be difficult as the time comes nearer, for Faron is a man who gets very nervous before the culmination of any plan and he sees traitors everywhere among his followers. I may not be able to get away."

"You must try to get a message to me, Jean-Baptiste," Aimee said urgently. "This may be something too good to pass up. If he is planning any kind of mob activity, it will be child's play to inform the police ahead of time and have him arrested on the spot." Her eyes glowed. "And then I will step forward and look into his face and tell him exactly how he was caught."

Jean-Baptiste looked at her and his brown eyes were warm and concerned. "And then, once you have your revenge, what will you do?"

Aimee looked at him blankly for a moment. "Why, then I suppose I shall go home." Home, she thought—but home to what? There was no longer a Castle du Beautreillis. Orléans had never been her home, and she was already under suspicion by the law there. Without her brother, Etienne, could she face the endless days and nights, trying somehow to rebuild her family's castle. She recalled the graves that she and Etienne had dug into the soft earth in the park. Tears came to her eyes and she covered them with her hands, sobbing softly for a moment. "I don't know what I shall do, truly," she told Jean-Baptiste, who reached out to comfort her.

"You can always stay here in Paris," he told her. "You know how much we all would miss you, Aimee." He put her at arm's length and looked steadily into her eyes. "Besides, you must continue the search for your brother. You will find him one day, I am sure of it."

She nodded, wiping at her eyes with a square of linen she had pickpocketed the day before. Looking at it, she began to laugh, wondering at the depths to which she had been driven. Who would have guessed that Aimee de Chartres, the daughter of Baron de Chartres and in whose blood ran a long line of noblemen, knights, and courtiers, would ever have become a common cutpurse? She laughed wildly at the notion, burying her face into

Jean-Baptiste's vest, sighing when he pushed her away gently, telling her he had to get back to Faron or risk being missed too long.

With a lingering kiss, he took his leave of her and Aimee waved to him from the doorway, admonishing him once more to be careful and to get word to her as soon as he was able to find out anything more about Faron's plans.

It was not until mid-September that Aimee heard from Jean-Baptiste again. She had taken to staying at the hotel with her aunt, reading from the surprisingly well-stocked library, which featured heavy tomes of philosophical bent as well as some of the racier novels of the day. In surprise, Aimee read through *La Religieuse* by Diderot, *Nouvelle Héloise* by Rousseau, and *Justine* by the Marquis de Sade, all of which featured the torture, whether physical or mental, of innocent young girls. It was an education all in itself when Aimee became engrossed in the adventures of de Sade's heroine, who seemed to get into one sexual depravity after another, from being tied down for bloodhounds to savage to falling into the clutches of a saber-happy mass murderer who tried to vivisect her.

Hortense, catching her reading some of the more questionable material one afternoon, snatched the book from her, her face crimsoning in embarrassment. "You will not be reading such filth, niece!" she thundered, her skinny body shaking with outrage.

"But what is it doing in your library, Aunt?" Aimee inquired with suave innocence.

"Humph! That is hardly your business, Aimee! But as you will undoubtedly continue to wonder, I will tell you that all of these types of books were gifts from a suitor in my earlier days. To tell you the truth, I had forgotten their existence, else I would have thrown them out!"

Hortense grabbed up all the offending material, marching with it outside the room, presumably to see it burned in the kitchen fire. Aimee sighed, wondering about those earlier days of her aunt when she was, perhaps, pretty and sought after. Aimee herself had never had a beau, nor had she ever seriously considered marriage. Things had happened too swiftly in her young life and there had never been time to speak with her parents of the future in such terms. And, even if life had not taken such a drastic downturn for her, there would not have been too many young men knocking on her door asking for her hand in marriage. The de Chartres family, for all their ancient bloodlines, were poor when measured by the standards of wealth and position. The best Aimee could have expected was for some comfortable bourgeois in Orléans, a lawyer, perhaps, to ask for her hand. Doubtless, he would have had to be more interested in obtaining an old and valued name rather than the pitiful dowry that Philippe de Chartres would have been able to provide for his only daughter.

Her thoughts were interrupted by the return of her aunt, whose tight-lipped countenance revealed the state of her feelings. Sourly, she informed her niece there was a vagabond at the door who had some sort of message for her. Aimee hurried to the foyer of the house, welcoming in little Bernard, one of Jean-Baptiste's cohorts.

"I am to give you a message from Jean-Baptiste," Bernard said swiftly, his tattered exterior belied by the warm smile he bestowed on Aimee. "He says to tell you that something is being planned for October. He doesn't know all the details yet, but he will try to give you enough time when the moment arrives."

"That is all? Nothing more?" Aimee asked hopefully. And when the boy shook his head, she sighed. "All right, then, Bernard. Come in and have some soup or a bite of lunch." She took the boy to the kitchen despite her aunt's protestations.

The last days of September went by slowly for Aimee, although Paris was once more simmering at the Convention's decisions about the new government. The deputies had decided that to make the government republican, they would require a legislative body of two separate parts: one part to be called the Council of Five Hundred, which would consist of men who were at least thirty years old and had lived at least ten years in France, to be elected by the people and which would originate all legislation; the second part to be called the Council of Ancients, which would consist of two hundred fifty men, forty years of age or older and having lived in France at least fifteen years and who would have the power to veto the resolutions of the Council of Five Hundred. An administrative body would have to be named, and would consist of an Executive Directory of five members who would be chosen from former ministers or deputies. What put Paris up in arms was the high-handed tactics of the Convention deputies who decided that in order to have a smooth change-over from Convention to Directory, they would retain control of the new government, by decreeing that two-thirds of the legislative body must come from existing members of the Convention.

Paris roared its outrage at the news and there was a general stirring among the people that hadn't been seen for some time. Everyone held his breath waiting to see what would happen next.

Aimee, though, grew tired of waiting, and in early October she and a few others of Jean-Baptiste's gang went for a stroll near the Palais Royal to see what pickings they could find. Winter was not too far away and they must get what they could before people began bundling up again. Once more, the harvest had been disastrous and Paris was girding itself for a long winter.

As Aimee moved among the crowds, she could sense tension all around her, as though the populace was waiting for something. She glanced around, carefully picking her way among the dandies and their ladies, speculating about a fat-paunched old gentleman who might or might not have ready cash on his person. So concerned was she with her occupation that at first she did not see Jean-Baptiste running toward her, hatless and out of breath, his eyes bright with expectation. Tugging at her sleeve, he brought her to a private part of the garden.

"Aimee, today is the day!" he said in an urgent whisper. "It's been rumored that the bourgeois and some of the wealthier people in Paris have organized an insurrection against the Convention. The National Guard has pledged to join them so there will be thousands in front of the Louvre. In all the hubbub, it will be easy for Faron to make his move. He will bring his working class into the crowd and begin his coup d'etat of the government. His grand ideas even include having himself as head of the new system he would see set up!"

"But he is only a miller!" Aimee protested.

"That may be, but in all these months he has planned this very carefully, and he has many intelligent men on his side. Men with intelligence, but no power, who itch to see themselves in government. Most of them hate the Convention and will not mind the spilling of blood as a means to their ends!" He looked around quickly. "I must go back now. Faron is readying his men and expects me to be there with them. You must get word to the authorities somehow, Aimee. Do your best to alert the Paris police!" And then he was gone, hurrying through the crowd while Aimee watched him with a sudden lump in her throat.

So, it had finally come! The culmination of her revenge—yet, she felt suddenly afraid. How could she, a nobody in Paris, hope to persuade the police of what was to happen? She noticed the crowd beginning to tighten up, more and more men coming together while an angry buzzing began to swell in the crisp October air. Merchants, lawyers, bankers, respected middle-class citizens who were getting tired of the way the government was being run. Something was about to happen, and Aimee realized she must hurry in order to escape being drawn along with the crowd. Quickly, she pushed her way through the crowd, bumping into a red-faced merchant who nearly knocked her down. Without thinking, by habit, her deft hand reached into his pocket and relieved him of his purse, dropping it smoothly into the pocket of her apron. The merchant, though, was not as oblivious as he looked and immediately tried to grab hold of the girl, claiming loudly, "I've been robbed! Help me! Police! I've been robbed!"

Police, who were already mingling with the crowd, closed in around the blond-haired girl. The merchant, still shrieking, was stirring up the crowd and it was difficult for the police to catch her. Frantically, Aimee ducked beneath the outstretched arms of one man and dodged another. She could see the entrance to the Palais Royal grounds just ahead. With one more effort, she could make it and be able to get lost among the crowds outside.

But, suddenly, a hand on her shoulder spun her around and her wrists were caught in a punishing grip that brought tears to her eyes. Looking up, her mouth fell open in shock at seeing the man called Lucian Napier, his blue eyes like frozen chips of ice, gazing at her with a stern satisfaction on his face.

"So, citizeness, it seems you have been caught red-handed!" He signaled to one of the policemen. "I think the Conciergerie will be most happy to take you in for the winter, little thief." He released one of her wrists, but kept a firm hold on the other one as his hand dove into her apron pocket, pulling out the evidence. "Officer, here is one of the Aubray gang you have been trying to round up."

Aimee stared up at him. "But—you knew—you knew before—?"

He nodded. "You happened to steal a valued pocketwatch from a very good friend of mine—who happens to be a deputy in the Convention. He happened to remember those green eyes of yours, which I admit are hard for any man to forget, citizeness."

"So, you are nothing more than a policeman!" Aimee said, curling her lip in sneering disappointment.

Lucian Napier smiled in grim amusement. "Are you so disappointed, wench? I suppose you thought it was your beauty that induced me to offer you a ride in my carriage that day?"

"I should have known better," Aimee retorted sarcastically, "for, from the first, I did not think you were a gentleman!"

He laughed outright this time, then sobered as the policemen came up to take the girl away. Aimee saw them, too, and anxiously, recalling her mission, she looked back to Lucian Napier. "Please help me!" she cried hastily. "I have important work to do! There is to be an insurrection today!"

"What trickery is this? I'm afraid your petty lies will not keep you out of prison, little thief!" Lucian returned, unperturbed.

"But you must listen to me! There is a man called Faron who killed one of the deputies of the Convention. He is going to bring his followers to the insurrection and use it as a shield in order to try to take over the government! Please, you must believe me! I have to talk to someone in authority! If you are truly a member of the police—"

"Alas, I am not!" Lucian returned quickly, seeing the evident disappointment on her face. "Ah, first I disappoint you because you think I am a policeman, and now I disappoint you again." He looked about him and noted the tension in the crowd, the gathering numbers, and his brows drew downward thoughtfully. "But I think, perhaps, you should be questioned further on your accusations, citizeness."

"There is no time for questioning!" Aimee shouted at him. She appealed to the police officers. "Are you idiots that you cannot see what is happening all around you? Listen! Look, even now the crowd is growing and soon they will begin to move to the Tuileries and the Convention meeting rooms." She looked back at Lucian. "You stand here lecturing me when very soon a man who is a murderer will be coming from the Faubourg Saint-Antoine to put all the deputies in great danger!"

Calmly, Lucian surveyed the crowd, seeing the beginnings of a mob. His blue eyes looked back to Aimee. "It's true that we have been searching for the man called Faron, who is wanted for the murder of Deputy Féraud last May. But what connection do you have with this man?"

"He is the murderer of my mother and brothers!" Aimee returned, her green eyes pleading with him to believe her. "I came to Paris to see justice done to him."

Lucian studied her a long moment, then signaled to the police. "Come, then, let us go and see what can be done. You men stay here and control the crowd as much as possible. I will try to have reinforcements sent shortly." He began pulling Aimee behind him, making his way between the tightening lines of the crowd, pushing people aside with an ease that amazed Aimee. "We must persuade the army to offer protection to the Convention!" he threw back at her as he quickened his pace once they were out of the main part of the crowd.

As they ran through the streets of Paris, hordes of National Guardsmen were beginning to join the crowd, which was beginning to grow angry and march toward the Tuileries. The Guardsmen's tricolored uniforms and deep-throated cries mingled with the voices of the stolid merchants and lawyers, causing a wall of noise as they came forward. By the time the crowd had reached the Tuileries, its number had multiplied to several thousand, one of whom must be Faron, Aimee was sure.

"There!" She thought she caught a glimpse of a tall, beefy man with a black eye patch, but in a moment he was swallowed up by the crowd and she searched frantically before Lucian pulled her away, sensing the urgent need to get help for the Convention before anything else. Aimee cried out in anger, unwilling to see her prize snatched away from her. But her companion was deaf to her cries and quickly shoved her through a doorway that led to a long corridor, down which he ran until he came to an anteroom where a captain looked up sharply.

"I must see Barras immediately," Lucian said. Leaving Aimee under the watchful eye of one of the guards, he disappeared through a doorway, leaving her to cool her heels in frustration.

Meanwhile, outside the crowd had grown into an angry mob. They were losing patience with the men who were trying to keep them from their goal. The timid bourgeois had not counted on the highly charged emotions of the National Guard, nor on the added agitation caused by Faron and his men. The Paris troops were called out to protect the Convention and fighting began in the streets. Aimee tapped her foot in frustration, staring at the door, willing Lucian to appear. She longed to know the fate of Faron, and of Jean-Baptiste, who had risked so much for her. She fumed at the whim of destiny that had placed her in the hands of Lucian Napier, while her whole reason for coming to Paris was outside, as free as he pleased.

Finally, while the uproar was at its height and windows were being smashed everywhere, Lucian Napier reappeared, accompanied by a middle-aged gentleman whom Aimee recognized as Paul Barras, Commander of the Army of the Interior, a position for which he was woefully lacking in experience, being more a politician than a soldier. Next to him was a slight man with a rather pointed face whom Aimee thought might be Joseph Fouché, the head of the secret police. Her eyebrows shot up and she wondered at the company kept by the man called Lucian

Napier. But she had no time to think about just who her captor really was; he came up to her immediately and asked her to relate her story about Faron's activities to the two powerful men in front of her.

"And this Faron is the man we've been seeking for months now!" Fouché reiterated, stroking his chin. "You are sure he is the one, citizeness?"

"Yes, yes!" Aimee cried, her agitation getting the best of her. "Why are you standing here when your government is about to come down around your ears? You must act quickly if you do not wish anarchy on your hands!"

"I have no head for military maneuvers," Barras said rather apologetically to the other two men. "But I know of a Corsican officer who seems to be rather brilliant in that area." He called to one of the guards to fetch Brigadier General Napoleon Bonaparte. "I will put him in charge of our defense," Barras continued. "He is ambitious and will do well when he realizes how it will shine on his military record." He looked at the lovely young Aimee, who was trembling with anger and anxiety, then winked slyly at Lucian. "I wouldn't be so hasty to put this little pullet behind bars, my friend, for she looks a tasty morsel." He smiled and bowed to Aimee, hurrying down the corridor after Fouché, apparently to see the defense coordinated for the Convention.

Quickly, cannon were placed about the Tuileries through the efforts of Bonaparte, Joachim Murat, and several cavalrymen who were under Bonaparte's command. It was now nearly four-thirty in the afternoon, and the fighting was out of control. Standing at a second-story window, seeing the seething, swirling mob below, Aimee wondered where Jean-Baptiste was and if Fouché had been able to find Faron among all that human flesh. And then, just as it seemed the mob would gain entrance to the Tuileries, the cannon roared and grapeshot scattered throughout the crowd, causing cries of pain and agony as those closest seemed to fall like wooden dolls. Aimee watched in amazement as more grapeshot was poured into the mob until they began to retreat and finally to flee.

"It seems this Bonaparte is a genius in military matters," Lucian observed dryly, his eyes noting the dead and dying scattered about the street. There were at least four hundred casualties, but at least the mob had been turned back and dispersed. There would be arrests made, inquiries into the reason for the insurrection, legal procedures that would attempt to make sure such a thing did not happen again. But for now, Lucian realized he must deal with this lovely little criminal. He turned his attention back to her. "Come along."

Aimee stared up at him in surprise, forgetting him standing there so quietly when such violence had been enacted below. "I must see about my friends," she said firmly.

"And your enemies?" he queried. "Do not worry about this man Faron. Fouché is quite thorough, and he undoubtedly already has him in custody. He will most likely be executed for his crimes within the month."

"But I must see for myself!" she cried.

Lucian shook his head. "I'm afraid that you have a rendezvous with the Conciergerie, my dear. Your escapades are known too well to the police and—"

"I don't care! You would take away the culmination of my revenge!" she accused angrily. "You are more cruel than I thought, Citizen Napier! Can't you understand the reason for one's revenge! Can't you understand that to take away that revenge is to destroy me, to take away my reason for being here!"

The man's lips whitened for a moment. "Yes," he said quietly, "I can understand, citizeness, despite whatever you may think of me." He opened the door for her, letting his guard slip for just a moment.

But it was all the time that Aimee needed as she spied a large vase on a pedestal near the door. Without time for thought, she picked it up as he turned to the doorway and brought it smashing down on the back of his head. She watched him fall to the floor, a trickle of red issuing from beneath his hair onto the collar of his shirt. She looked at what she had done with a touch of horror, but told herself it had been necessary. She didn't trust this man, who seemed to run with some of the most powerful men in the city. She had never trusted the mighty, for hadn't it been exactly those men who had killed her beloved father?

Quickly, she escaped the scene, fleeing downstairs and out into the street, where patrols were already beginning to load the dead onto carts and take the wounded to hospitals. Frantically, Aimee passed through the melee, searching for the face of Jean-Baptiste, gasping with relief when she didn't see him among those already in the death carts. She moved away from the main part of the street, wondering if Lucian Napier had regained consciousness and was, even now, ordering someone to pursue her.

She hurried down the street, hoping to find Jean-Baptiste somewhere along the way, disappointed when she did not. After an hour of searching for him in the streets, she went home, wondering what had become of him. At the doorway to the hotel she met her aunt, staring at her with pale cheeks and nearly speechless.

"Aimee!" Her aunt motioned her to hurry. "Aimee, your friend—he has come here! Hurry, for I think that he is dying!"

Aimee felt the blood drain from her own cheeks as she hurried inside to find Jean-Baptiste on a divan, the warm brown eyes filled now with excruciating pain as he clutched his stomach. Horrified, Aimee could see blood seeping from between his fingers and she hurried to kneel next to him.

"Aunt Hortense, hurry and fetch a physician!" she ordered.

"No!" Jean-Baptiste said with a short gasp. "It is too late for a physician, my dear." He coughed and the pain in his eyes increased. "Ah! This damned grapeshot has made a mess of my insides," he said and sighed, as Aimee searched for a handkerchief or a piece of cloth to cover his wound, but the blood was coming too fast now and the linen was soaked in a moment.

"Oh, Jean-Baptiste, what happened?" Aimee asked softly, brushing at the chestnut hair that had fallen over his forehead.

"Got in the way of a piece of cannon," he answered, trying to smile. "I . . . I came here, hoping to see you again before—" He swallowed and was silent a moment before continuing. "Faron— I think he got away," he continued slowly. "He was to my left, on the opposite side of the cannon. There were all of his companions surrounding him, and when the grapeshot went off I saw him begin to run down the street with the others!"

"It doesn't matter, Jean-Baptiste," Aimee said gently, though her heart ached to think of poor Jean-Baptiste lying here dying, while the monstrous Faron roamed free somewhere in the city. So her revenge was not complete—Faron had escaped and Fouché would not find him. Aimee felt a grinding disappointment that threatened to overwhelm her.

"I am sorry, Aimee," Jean-Baptiste said softly, and Aimee gently cradled his head with one hand as she leaned close to him, her eyes wet with tears.

"You were my only friend here in Paris," she told him, trying not to give way to the sobs that choked her throat. "What shall I do without you, my friend?"

"Tears—for me?" he wondered, his breath coming with more difficulty. "I would wish you not to waste them, for I . . . might begin to think . . . that you held some feeling toward me."

Aimee smiled through her tears, but her heart contracted as

she saw his eyes close, then open once more with an effort. "I am sorry, Aimee . . . sorry to be . . . leaving . . . you . . ." He breathed softly and was gone.

Aimee gave full vent to her grief. Poor Jean-Baptiste, poor child of the streets of Paris, homeless and unwanted. The streets had given him life; the streets had taken it away. She wept over his poor, broken body, wondering at the injustice of life that would take Jean-Baptiste and leave Faron still alive.

"Aimee? It is terrible," Aunt Hortense said, realizing that the boy was dead. "But you cannot . . . You must have the death cart take him to the Place de Grève," she said.

"I will not give him up to a nameless grave!" Aimee said fiercely.

"But, Aimee, you have no money—" Hortense was interrupted by a firm knocking on the door. In a moment, it was pushed in and several armed police entered the foyer. Directing them was a young lieutenant whose eyes scanned the scene with some surprise.

"We are here for one Aimee de Chartres," he said formally, taking in the appearance of the disheveled girl. "You are under arrest, citizeness, for the crime of thievery and for assaulting one Citizen Napier, who is, at this moment, recuperating from the blow you dealt him."

Aimee was incensed by the officer's unfeeling obligation to his duty. "Can you not see that someone has died—wounded by grapeshot flung at the crowd?" she demanded. "Do you expect to have me come with you and leave my aunt to take care of the burial of my friend?"

"I have my orders," the lieutenant reminded her crisply. "Come along."

"No!" Aimee stood up and stepped back, shaking in reaction to the events of the day, coupled with the shock of the death of her friend. "Are these orders from Citizen Napier?"

"No, they are from my captain, citizeness. You are to be taken to the Conciergerie this moment. If you do not come along quietly, I will have to take you by force." He signaled to his men.

"Aimee, good heavens, go with them!" Hortense shrieked shrilly, thrown into a fit at this unexpected turn of events and worried for her own skin. "What have I told you all these months? Yes, and it has finally happened! Now you have ruined me! Go with them!"

"Aunt Hortense, you must promise to see to the burial of my friend. You know where I have hidden money. You must promise

—swear an oath to God that you will do it for me!" Her eyes narrowed at her aunt's reluctance. "You will swear or I will implicate you in my arrest!"

Horrified, Hortense agreed readily to do as Aimee wished. Then, after planting a kiss on Jean-Baptiste's brow, Aimee took her leave of her aunt with no emotion. The latter did not even embrace her niece as she was taken away by the police, but closed the door quickly as though to keep her from ever coming back.

11

Aimee's stay at the Conciergerie was a brief one. The captain of the guard consigned her to one of the low jails of the Châtelet. Aimee was thrown into a dark, foul-smelling cell with several other young women, all complaining of their fate and cursing God for landing them in this place. Although it was still only early October, the interior of the jail was icy and damp, and Aimee huddled in some straw that had been scattered around the floor, trying to keep warm without a shawl or outer covering of any kind. Some of the women were dressed in the costume of the truly poor: the coarse, woollen cloth sewn into shapeless garments that covered them from breasts to ankles, tattered in many places; some were not even able to afford stockings.

Although Aimee did have stockings, her feet were cold from the lightweight flat-heeled slippers she had purchased just a few weeks before—fashionable but highly impractical for a stay in the jails of the Châtelet. Moreover, she was dressed in a cotton gown whose scooped neck left her collarbone bare and made her shiver for lack of a shawl or fichu to drape around it. She must have lost her scarf during the ride from the rue Saint-Denis to the Conciergerie. Meanwhile, she realized she would be obliged to sleep in this place as well as she could and determinedly leaned against one of the icy stone walls, trying to warm the spot with her body.

In the morning, she was roused by the clanking sound of metal keys in locks and the high-pitched squealing sound of the doors swinging open. A constable of the watch shined the light of his lantern into the gaping, dark hole of the cell and informed all therein to show themselves, as they were to be brought to trial today. Tiredly, the women got to their feet and filed out of the cell into the dimly lit corridor, where four or five soldiers waited to escort them to the judge's chambers.

Aimee stumbled along behind the rest of them, still sleepy from the night, rubbing her eyes and shaking her head, trying to draw her wits about her. She still felt cold and rubbed her arms nervously, trying to keep the sluggish blood flowing. The soldiers escorted them through endless corridors until they came to a large hall covered in cloth of red, white, and blue, with standards bearing the same colors draped around a semicircular platform where there stood a kind of pulpit. Behind the pulpit sat a small, roundshouldered man in a black robe with a small white neckband and a long white wig. Another, holding a bundle of papers dangling with official-looking seals, stood beside him, talking quietly as he pointed out certain things about the prisoners, outlined in the documents. Aimee and the others were pushed forward to the foot of the platform, where each was obliged to call out her name and former residence for the court clerk.

It did not take long for sentence to be passed. Because of the high numbers of prisoners stemming from the outbreak in front of the Convention, these women must be dealt with quickly. They were sentenced to a whipping in the courtyard of the Châtelet, their hair was to be shorn to serve notice to the public that they had been prisoners inside the Châtelet, and all pickpockets were consigned to the workhouse in the factory district until such time as they could find suitable lodgings, either through the aid of relatives or employment by an upstanding citizen. Aimee smiled grimly to herself, imagining her Aunt Hortense coming to her rescue. She may as well get used to the idea of the workhouse, for she had the idea that her aunt would count herself lucky to be rid of her. Aimee shook her head, remembering the wealth of food and new clothing her thievery had enabled her aunt to have. What would happen to her now that her only means of buying bread had been taken away from her? She almost laughed, trying to imagine her aunt learning the ways of the cutpurse from one of Jean-Baptiste's companions. Well, she was no longer her concern—as long as she saw to Jean-Baptiste's burial, Aimee could call it even with her aunt.

She felt a soft jab in her back and realized that she was supposed to follow the others out of the hall in order to receive punishment. First, the dozen or so women were taken into a domed enclosure whose old stone walls looked as though they had been standing for centuries. This room seemed almost colder than the jail cell, and Aimee shivered as a soldier came up to her and ordered her to turn and face the wall. She felt his hand on her neck, pulling at her long golden hair—the hair her father had used to love to stroke so often when she sat at his knee. And then, with rough scissors, the soldier hacked away at it until all the gleaming gold lay at her feet and nothing was left but a bare nape. Aimee tried not to let the tears overflow, but she hung her head in shame as the soldier turned her around to face front once more, stuffing the long, shimmering cascade of hair into a cloth bag, perhaps to be sold at one of the wigmakers' shops in the rue Saint-Honoré. With a trembling hand, Aimee felt the bareness on her neck.

"Don't worry about it, my dear, it'll grow back," one woman said sympathetically to her. "Anyway, don't you know the style is short now. I've seen many a merchant's wife prancing about with her hair hanging in her eyes in front and nothing in back. Besides, they could have shaved the whole head—and then you would have looked a fright, let me tell you!"

Aimee nodded, trying to draw comfort from the woman's words. She and the others were pushed outside into the October air, grateful for the sun on their shoulders. But in the next moment, Aimee knew even a deeper shame as the guards on duty ordered the women to strip to the waist. Those who hesitated were "helped" along by the soldiers, brusque, rough men who had no time for the niceties of etiquette. Before one could strip away her bodice, Aimee unbuttoned it with nerveless fingers, hanging her head so that her flaming cheeks were not readily apparent. Quickly, she turned so that her back was presented for the soldier's ready hand.

Suddenly, she felt the sting of the lash on her exposed back and winced, trying not to cry out. All around her, other women were feeling the same, while half of the women waited on the other side for their turn with dull eyes and slack expressions. Aimee kept her head down, feeling the sun on the nape of her neck, closing her eyes and straining against the touch of the cold leather on her skin. A dozen lashes and it was over. Aimee quickly pushed her arms back into the sleeves of her dress, buttoning up and trying to ignore the smarting of her wounds at the touch of the cotton.

"You have blood on your back," one of the women observed dryly. "Wouldn't you rather wait for it to dry before you ruin the back of your dress?"

Aimee shook her head. She was then led, with the others, beyond the walled yard and back into a cart, watched over by three soldiers. The cart rolled along quite a distance to the Hôpital de la Roquette, which served the poor and where they got off the cart and filed into position in front of the administrator, who assigned half of the women to work in the hospital and the other half to work in the workhouse a few blocks away. Aimee was lucky enough to be sent to the workhouse—lucky because she would not be exposed to the plethora of contagious diseases that the others would encounter in the hospital. Smallpox and tuberculosis were virulent among the hospital wards, and many of those who were consigned to the hospital broke out in protest before soldiers took them away.

Aimee was made to walk the few blocks to the workhouse, a large, low building of stone where she would work at a spinning loom sixteen hours a day and take care of her duties in her own sleeping ward, which many times would include cooking for herself and seventeen other young women who shared the ward, turning the mattresses, and washing the bedclothes or scrubbing floors and walls. She would get approximately six hours of sleep at night, perhaps less if she was not able to finish her quota of cloth in the time allotted. With a shiver, she entered the building, hearing the heavy, iron gates clang shut at her back. Bleakly, she gazed at the dark windows of the workhouse and tried to imagine her life behind them. How would she ever escape this prison? Some said one could work here until the life drained out of them, others barely lasted a year, unable to keep up with the demands of the superintendent as well as the foul air, the constant sitting at the loom, which constrained the muscles, the lack of good food. Aimee straightened her back, still smarting from the lashing she'd received, and walked into the archway, determined that she would not give in to these obstacles. There was much she still had to do. Faron, she reminded herself, was still free. Her brother was somewhere in Paris, still alive, she hoped. Perhaps he would come back for her one day at her aunt's hotel and then he would come for her here and take her away from all this misery. Then, too, she held a grudge against the blue-eyed Lucian Napier, who had engineered the arrest. Though his had not been the order that had sent her to this place of misery, she could not help but lay some blame on him. With a smile and narrowed eyes, she hoped that she had laid him out good and that he would not be recovering from the bump on his head for quite a long time.

II

WINDS
OF
FORTUNE

12

·—■—·—■—·

Aimee de Chartres, seventeen now and in the full flush of young womanhood, sat quietly with the confessor priest of the workhouse, Father Vincent, an aged man with a kind face who had been nearly killed when the terror had tried to guillotine every priest who would not take the Oath of Civility. But now that religious freedom was once more tolerated by the new Directory, he had been returned to his calling and served to help those unfortunates of the workhouses and factories in the district. Since the year before, in 1795, when the Convention had dissolved itself, there had been fewer and fewer restrictions enforced on the populace. A general amnesty had been declared for all except deported priests and emigrés. The death penalty would be abolished as soon as general peace was made with the enemies of France and the name of the Place de la Révolution, where the guillotine had stood, had been changed to the Place de la Concorde. People breathed easier, and there rose up among the wealthier bourgeois a new kind of "aristocracy," which began to gather for huge celebrations, keep mistresses, and hold sway in the salons of Paris.

The Directory had been chosen, and Paul Barras became its leader. They were assigned to the Luxembourg Palace as their official residence, which was separate from the Council of Ancients, which met in the Tuileries, and there was the Council of Five Hundred, which met at the Manège. In March of 1796, Bonaparte, who had behaved so masterfully in pushing back the mob the previous October, was named general-in-chief of the Army of Italy and triumphantly entered Milan, taking over most of Italy. Things seemed to be going peacefully and Paris had settled down in the past six months since Aimee had come to the workhouse.

She gazed with a soft smile at the priest sitting next to her, having made her confession and received absolution, a ceremony frequently executed among those poor young women of the workhouse, although what sins they could possibly have time to commit, the priest didn't know. They were unceasingly busy, with very little time left over to do anything but sleep.

125

"I think I have found a sponsor for you, my child," Father Vincent said to the young woman at his side. He moved to study the high-boned cheeks, pale after the winter and her enforced duties inside the building. His attention turned to the gleaming brightness of gold that had grown to the top of her shoulders and hung in soft waves, framing the face and its emerald-green eyes, which shined clearly now, not full of the depressing listlessness of many of the others who had been here longer.

"A sponsor, Father?" Aimee inquired, thinking she should really be getting back to her work, but willing to sit in the April sunshine a moment longer before the superintendent accused her of lolling too long outside.

The priest nodded. "Monsieur de Brueys, a wealthy shop-keeper in the Faubourg Saint-Germain. He and his family are in need of a serving maid—"

"A servant?" Aimee's brows drew downward. "That is impossible, Father. I could never work for a bourgeois as a servant!"

"And why not?" he wondered. "You have been to the Châtelet. Is that not true? You have been a thief, a pickpocket, and have worked for six months in the workhouse along with various other young women from the poorest sections in Paris. I think the sin of pride sits ill on your young shoulders, my daughter!"

Aimee stood up, wringing her hands together nervously. "It is difficult to keep one's pride while emptying the slops of others, scrubbing windows and floors until your hands are cracked and bleeding, Father, but I have managed to salvage some of it. My father would turn over in his grave if he knew I had consented to servitude for a bourgeois!"

"He would be sadder still to see you spend the rest of your life in this workhouse, Aimee de Chartres!" the priest replied sternly. "Have you not learned anything here, my child? Have you not learned that life is more precious than any stupid human pride— that you must be true to yourself, be honest and moral above all, in order to be happy? Would it suit that noble spirit of yours better to be committed to the humdrum existence of this work-house when you could be living comfortably with a decent family who, out of the charity of the hearts, accepts you under their roof?"

Aimee looked away from the good priest, feeling foolish and ungrateful. He was right, of course. Many of the others inside would kill for the position being offered her. She met the priest's eyes and nodded. "I will think on it, Father Vincent."

"Remember, too, that you cannot seek out your brother inside these walls, my daughter. This would be an opportunity for you to find out his whereabouts," he said suavely, knowing of her wish to be reunited with her brother. Aimee had not told him about Faron, nor about Lucian Napier. She would be chided sternly by him concerning the wickedness of vengeance, she knew. He had, he'd told her, already forgiven those who had chased and tormented him throughout France in the years before.

"Move your pins, wench!"

Aimee looked toward the thin, sallow face of her superintendent, and then turned toward the priest. "When is this de Brueys to come by, Father?" she asked quickly.

The priest smiled. "He is away on business in the south of France, my child, but he will be back by the first of May. Shall I tell him you are interested in his offer?"

Aimee hesitated, stared back at the cold stone walls of the workhouse and the sallow face of the man who called her inside, then turned back and nodded to the priest. "Yes, I am interested." She started to move away, then stopped and came back to hug the surprised priest. "And, thank you, Father Vincent!"

It was on an overcast Tuesday morning that Aimee beheld her future employer for the first time as she waited in the workhouse vestibule, the only room that was decently furnished, with its thin carpet covering the nicked and scarred wooden flooring and several old, but comfortable chairs placed before a tapestry worked with the colors of the revolution. Monsieur de Brueys seemed a rather pompous man, nearly as round as he was tall, implying that his table had not suffered much during the Reign of Terror. He was fairly jovial, having the looks for that temperament, with his balding pate fringed with graying hair, a round, rather florid visage from which looked out two round blue eyes, and square hands with blunt fingers that he rested on his ample thighs, which seemed to be straining the material of his breeches. His blue eyes were now resting on Aimee de Chartres and his rather thin-lipped smile broadened his face even further as he seemed to make up his mind quickly.

"Yes, Monsieur Gesvres," he was saying to the superintendent, who watched the proceedings with his usual sour visage, "I really do think this young lady will make a fine serving maid for our house. She certainly seems strong and quite healthy, rather intelligent—"

"She was a baron's daughter before the revolution," the superintendent put in flatly, as though to warn him that the girl might, in fact, have too much intelligence and a great deal more spirit than a mere serving wench should possess.

"And her reason for being sent here?" Monsieur de Brueys wanted to know.

"Thievery."

"Hmm." Monsieur de Brueys rubbed his round chin and eyed the girl more speculatively. "Has her behavior been other than reasonable while she was here?"

"No, she has been a model of good behavior," Gesvres admitted almost spitefully.

"Ah, then it is settled. Father Vincent has recommended her very highly to me. Where are the documents that need to be signed?" He stood up from the chair and went after the superintendent, into the latter's office to take care of the necessary legal elements wherein he was actually taking responsibility for the care and behavior of the young woman.

Aimee sat alone in the vestibule, her hands holding the coarse stuff of her workhouse uniform for want of nothing else to grasp. She had no belongings, only the dress she was wearing, the cloddish shoes that were required on the frigid floors of the workhouse, and the dress she had arrived in nearly seven long months before, which had been donated to the charity hospital for the poor. She felt curiously afraid, feeling as though she needed the support of belongings to make her feel a whole person. She tried to remember Father Vincent's kind words, reminding her that she must always be obedient to God, kind and obedient to her new employers, and, above all, true to her own self. Someday, he assured her, Etienne would be found. She held on to that thought, repeating it over and over in her mind until Jacques de Brueys returned from the superintendent's office.

With a kindly smile, he nodded to her to follow him outside to his coach, a rather modest outfit for which he apologized before he realized he was not talking to the daughter of a baron any longer, but to his servant. "The larger coach was requisitioned by the government for the war," he explained bluntly, getting in first and signaling to Aimee that she should sit up top with the driver.

Aimee climbed up nimbly enough with the help of the driver, who introduced himself as Pierre after gazing with appreciation over the slender-waisted figure who seated herself almost daintily next to him.

The drive was not long, but Aimee found herself breathing in the smells and sights of the city of Paris with renewed enjoyment. How could she ever have thought the air was foul-smelling, the sounds overwhelming—in comparison to the smells and sounds of the workhouse, this was like paradise! She found herself smiling, her eyes avidly touching on the smooth-flowing Seine, the crowded Pont Neuf, and the other bridges that crossed the river. All around there were people doing their marketing, taking children to tutors or dance masters; all seemed bustle and congestion under the overcast gray sky. They passed a poorer section of Paris, a place of wretched existence, illness, deprivations, where the women looked at the coach with dark-ringed eyes as they held their babies on their hips and begged for bread or coin. Aimee closed her eyes, unwilling to let this crushing existence dampen her enthusiasm for the city, but she could not help wondering how the revolution had changed *their* lives. It had, in fact, done nothing for the truly poor who made their pitiful wages from such occupations as wafer vendor, pastry cook, laundress, and fishwife. There had been many of these in the workhouse, pleased to be in a place that at least always had a warm fire in the grate and something on the table for dinner. Some of the girls had told Aimee about the public houses where they had gone on Sundays to meet a lackey or a sergeant of the guards where drunkenness played with obscenity. Some of them would even sink to whoring to gain enough money to enable them to buy food for their families. Pitiful figures dressed in faded finery to parade up and down the rue Maubíe or the rue Pierre-au-lard. Aimee thought of the young women she had known in the workhouse and was glad for them in a way, because at least they no longer had to sell their bodies for a crust of bread or a bowl of soup.

She was curious to see this new home that was to be hers, trying to imagine what the house of a respectable and wealthy bourgeois might look like. She recalled the hollow emptiness of her aunt's hotel, the many rooms with dust-laden furniture that no longer saw any guests. She was anxious to see who lived at the house of Monsieur de Brueys. Did he have children? What was his wife like? Shortly she would find out, she realized, as the coach stopped before a several-storied house of wood and brick in the rue de Varennes, not far from the Fair of Saint-Germain and the nearby college.

Aimee stepped down from the coach, her eyes taking in the well-tended rosebushes on either side of the front door, and the square of grass that separated the building from the main part of the street. Surely, the merchant must be prosperous, for the house looked as though it had only recently received a new coat of paint. Tentatively, she stepped toward the front door, when she felt Monsieur de Brueys's hand on her arm.

"Ahem! I'm afraid we don't allow our employees to use the front entrance," he explained to her with an almost apologetic air. "There is a back entrance around the walk there. You will see the stables in back and the small yard. The door leads into the cellar, and from there through the pantry into the kitchen." He motioned her to walk around while he advanced to the oak-paneled door in front.

Aimee did as she was told. Certainly, it didn't make any difference to her through which door she entered. And the cellar was probably cooler in these warm months anyway. Curiously, she went around the side of the house and followed the steps the merchant had described until she found herself in a multiwindowed kitchen managed by a rotund cook whose doughy face looked out beneath a pristinely white bonnet.

"You must be the new girl," the cook said with a dignified air. "You'll sit yourself down and have a bite of something to eat before you're to meet the mistress." And at Aimee's hesitation, the cook snapped, "Sit down, I said! Monsieur de Brueys will have nothing more to do with you. It's his wife who makes the rest of the decisions, believe me." The cook padded over to the fireplace to slap the careless girl who had let the soup boil over in the kettle. The girl cried, raised a hand to her cheek, then began to stir the pot, still sniffing a little. Satisfied, the cook poured out a portion of soup for her new charge and set it down on a rough, wooden table that had not a splinter left, it had been scoured so often.

"Now, then," the cook began familiarly, setting her own bulk on a nearby chair after glancing at the lazy kitchen girl once more, "you'll tell me your name, dear."

"Aimee de Chartres," she replied, spooning the delicious soup into her mouth with ever increasing strokes of her hand. It was surely the best soup she'd ever had, she thought, and told the cook so.

The cook laughed. "I'm not surprised you'd think so, having been fed dishwater over at the workhouse for so long."

"You know about me?" Aimee wondered, surprised.

"Monsieur de Brueys informed me a few days ago that we would be getting a new upstairs serving maid. Do you know what your duties will be?"

"No. I've . . . never been a . . . serving maid before," Aimee replied tensely, finding the soup suddenly sticking in her throat.

"From what I've been told, you'd never been a pickpocket

before either, but you seemed to learn with remarkable ease, eh?"
The cook laughed, tapping Aimee's arm and then leaning back in
her own chair. "A serving maid's job is easier than being a thief,
my girl, believe me! For one thing, you do your work indoors—
no more freezing to death in the middle of winter trying to make
ends meet. You've got a bed of your own and enough food to
keep you healthy, plus you get fifteen livres a month wages, and
no worry about your pimp trying to steal them away from you!"
She smiled, showing rows of gleaming white teeth that looked
almost feral.

"I didn't have a pimp!" Aimee returned, turning red at the sly
look the kitchen girl gave her. "I didn't do *that* sort of work. I
lived with my aunt and had no need of anyone to take care of
me."

"Well, maybe if you'd had someone you wouldn't have ended
up in the workhouse, now, eh?" the cook went on, unperturbed.
"Rosine, stir that soup and quit gawking, or you'll receive the
back of my hand again!" she threatened, turning her attention
back to her kitchen help.

She turned back to Aimee. "Rosine, there, could have had the
post you've been given, but she's too lazy, more's the pity.
You're not lazy, are you, girl?"

Aimee shook her head. "Not likely," she assured her. "I
worked even when I lived with my family near Orléans. We
weren't rich," she added in a small voice.

"Well, let's not get to talking of the past," the cook advised
her. "My name is Lila and you'll be taking your orders from me,
or from Madame de Brueys. Besides Rosine, who helps out in
the kitchen, there's Jacinth, the scullery maid, Pierre, the coach-
man, and the two stableboys, Bernard and Nicholas. Madame de
Brueys is very strict about any of the house girls mingling with
the men in the stables." She eyed Rosine as though directing the
warning at her. "We've already lost one girl because she found
herself pregnant by the likes of Pierre. She was kicked out right
away, believe me!"

"Who are the members in the family?" Aimee inquired, and
received a severe look from the cook.

"You'll not be talking about them, girl. I'll inform you about
your duties and you shall meet the rest of the family when you're
presented to Madame de Brueys. Now, then, as the upstairs serving maid you'll see that madame's dresses are laid out before her
evening social activities. Although she has her own maid to help
her dress, Marisa has little clothes sense, and madame doesn't

like to be bothered with making the choices herself. Since you've a good background, I'm sure you'll have no trouble there. Also, you'll see the beds made and the rooms straightened every morning. You'll scrub the floors and beat the rugs once a week and wash the curtains once a month. The walls should be done every other month and the silverware and crystal must be polished before any entertaining. Madame de Brueys enjoys entertaining friends, let me tell you!" The cook thought a moment. "Of course, you'll be expected to conduct yourself with the utmost deportment. You'll answer the front door to guests and see that the fires are lighted in the morning. Bernard or Nicholas can bring in the wood from outside for you.

"You'll share a room with Rosine. You'll have your own bed and blankets, a new suit of clothes, and four clean aprons." She stopped as a bell rang on the wall. "Ah, that's madame now. She'll be wanting to talk to you before you move in permanently. Monsieur de Brueys can be turned by a pretty head, especially when there's nothing underneath." Once more she gave a meaningful look at Rosine.

Aimee stood up, automatically brushing at the front of her dress and pushing her hair back where it had escaped from its coiffure. Thus readied, she followed Lila upstairs to the third floor, where Madame de Brueys received her in her dressing room.

Aimee looked around in amazement at the snow-white walls of the room, painted along the ceiling with fat, rosy-cheeked cherubs blowing trumpets and holding out hand mirrors to an invisible mistress. In the center of the room, and its crowning glory, was a mirrored dressing table, swathed in white muslin like an infant's cradle, decked with lace and littered with trinkets, philters, cosmetics and creams, rouges, and perfumes. Madame de Brueys sat before the mirror, while her maid, Marisa, combed out her hair in preparation for the day's coiffure. Regarding her new servant from the mirror, Madame de Brueys's dark eyebrows went up speculatively.

"So, you are Aimee de Chartres." Her dark eyes seemed to miss nothing of the girl's appearance. "My husband did not tell me how lovely you are."

Aimee did not know if she was required to answer, but as the lady did not say anything else, she hastened to put in, "I am very grateful that your husband decided to employ me, madame. I—"

"Do be quiet!" Madame de Brueys interrupted with pursed lips. "You must learn, Aimee, that you never speak to your employers unless you are first given permission or asked a direct question. I'm afraid you are not in the position you may have been used to in Orléans."

Aimee was surprised at the woman's intolerance, but kept her silence, wondering privately at the extreme differences in Monsieur de Brueys and his wife. This woman seemed extremely straitlaced and stiff-backed, not one to laugh very much and certainly one who expected only the best behavior from those in her employ. She turned around in her seat and looked directly at her new employee.

"You seem ill at ease, Aimee. Are you having second thoughts about your new position?"

"No, madame."

The woman seemed very pleased at Aimee's short answer. "Good. Then I expect you to begin work immediately. My daughter, Lavinia, should be coming down directly. She is under the care of her governess, of course, Mademoiselle Nina, who sees to all her needs. You, however, are in charge of keeping her room neat and taking her breakfast to her if she desires it. My son, Henri . . ."—she stopped and her eyes flew upward to meet the innocent green gaze of the other girl—". . . uh, my son can take care of his own room. He has his personal valet for that, and so there is no need for you to make contact with him. Do you understand me, Aimee?"

"Yes, madame."

"Good." She seemed pleased once more, although her severe mouth barely smiled. "Now, before you leave here, you may choose something for me to wear—something befitting an afternoon's walk in the gardens of the Tuileries. I do think blue is my best color, but see what you think." She dismissed her to her closet with the sweep of her hand.

Aimee, unsure what was expected of her, walked to an adjoining door that opened blessedly into a huge, narrow room that was lined with walls upon walls of clothing, some rather outdated from a few years before and other items quite fashionable. Aimee began to wonder just how rich this shopkeeper was. Surely he must have an immense fortune in order to outfit his wife in such a manner. But Aimee had the sudden intuition that Monsieur de Brueys enjoyed dressing his wife thus, for she seemed younger than he and was certainly darkly pretty, if she ever deigned to smile. Aimee wondered what her entertainments were like.

After choosing Madame de Brueys's strolling outfit and running up to the fifth-floor attic, where the room she would share with Rosine was located, in order to fetch an apron and a white bonnet that would conceal all but the front part of her hair, Aimee quickly returned to the floor below, which housed the bedrooms of Lavinia and her brother, Henri, plus three other guest bedrooms. These she tidied up quickly, having learned to work with great efficiency in the workhouse. She stayed away from Henri's room, which she remembered she was not to enter. The directive seemed odd, but Aimee dismissed it from her mind, deeming it unworthy to be bothered with.

As the weeks went by, she learned a great deal about the family, much of it from the talkative Rosine, whose favorite pastime was to sit up and talk at night when Aimee wanted nothing more than to catch a few extra hours' sleep before the following day's drudgery began. Although Rosine was kept busy under Lila's watchful eye, she still found times to catnap in the cellar or nod off when she was supposed to be stirring the broth for the evening's meal.

"And Monsieur Henri—ah, that one is very handsome," Rosine would say, sighing a little as she looked out the small attic window. "He is attending the university now, but will be home at the end of the month. His mother is very jealous of him and guards him very well when he is home. She does not want his head turned by little chits who fancy themselves the perfect wife for him."

"But doesn't she want him to be married?"

Rosine shrugged. "I suppose, but it must be to the perfect young lady—meaning the one who can bring a lot of wealth and prestige into the marriage. Our mistress has big plans for her children, believe me. She was born in Passy, the daughter of a well-to-do butcher. I suppose she feels she must rid herself of the stench of butchered meat, and so she puts on airs and pretends to everyone that she was really the daughter of a poor country nobleman who was forced to do hard labor in desperate times. She is some twenty years younger then her husband, who was married once before to a former marquise who left him for another man. Oh, my dear, it is all quite unbelievable, let me tell you!"

"Good heavens, Rosine, I'm not all that interested in the background of my employers. Just as long as they pay me my wages and give me a decent bed and board until I can save up enough to leave them and search for my brother, Etienne."

"Oh, but you can't leave them just like that!" Rosine explained quickly. "Monsieur de Brueys signed a document that he would have custody of you. Legally, it's almost like you are his ward—and there's no way out of it, unless he throws you out!"

Aimee hadn't realized this and her heart sank with the knowledge. If she tried to run away, she could be caught and turned over to the workhouse again, or, worse yet, sent back to the Châtelet. She chewed her lip thoughtfully. Perhaps in time, she could buy her freedom from the de Brueys family, or persuade Monsieur de Brueys to allow her to leave to find her brother. She thought about the hard, dark eyes of Madame de Brueys and her heart lurched, knowing very well that the cold woman would never let her leave so easily.

She tried not to think of her dilemma in the following days of her servitude. The war outside France seemed to be going splendidly, and the exploits of "The Little Corporal," as his men called Napoleon Bonaparte, was on everyone's lips in Paris. This made the men of the Directory feel a bit shaky in their positions and they were careful to keep Bonaparte out of the capital. He was given just enough time to marry the lovely but adulterous Josephine de Beauharnais before the Directory requested him to direct the first Italian campaign. Bonaparte went, as any good military man would—for he was certainly clever enough to realize that the more army campaigns he was able to turn into victories, the better for his own future.

Monsieur de Brueys seemed to think a lot of the man, as Aimee heard him exclaim over dinner many times to visiting guests. She loved to stand just out of range of anyone's sight and listen to the conversation that flowed around the usually boisterous dinner. She realized that the de Brueys family was quite affluent, certainly better off than she and her family had ever been. They had a music room on the second floor with a beautiful pianoforte that had cost, she remembered Monsieur de Brueys boasting, more than one hundred fifty livres. He owned an estate in Auteuil with vineyards from which he received quite a good income, and which was run by a trusted bailee who had been with him for several years. He did have a coach and was able to make a few excursions around Saint-Prix and in the forest of Montmorency with his wife and daughter.

Lavinia, Aimee soon learned, was a rather spoiled child of twelve with terrible manners and rotting teeth because of all the sweets her father allowed her. Her day ran like clockwork, thanks to her mother's strict discipline, and Aimee knew at all times of the day where the girl would be. She would usually eat a rather spartan breakfast very early in the morning, then would practice at the pianoforte. Then, with her governess carrying the bouillon and bread soup in a tin container, she would go to her drawing class. She would be home promptly at three o'clock for a rest and then would have more pianoforte practice until the tallow candles were lit. She would read to Mademoiselle Nina from Ovid or Horace until dinner, then afterward would read for her own entertainment. It seemed a rather regimented life for a young woman, Aimee thought, remembering her days of carefree adventure with her five brothers.

Lavinia did not seem to mind in the least. She was only glad, she told Aimee, that she was not obliged to attend one of those horrid convents where everything was too, too routine. Aimee had to laugh at such a comment, considering the kind of life Lavinia had. She seldom saw her mother, for Madame de Brueys did not get out of bed until nearly eleven in the morning. Then it would take almost two hours for the unfortunate Marisa to dress her properly. And finally Madame de Brueys would pay her daily round of social calls that were interrupted by shopping and the odd visit to the theater. Once, Aimee had heard her say that she had seen a very interesting tragedy at the Théâtre de la République; it was called *Nero and Epictetus,* and it had nearly made her weep. Anything that could make the madame weep was, in Aimee's opinion, quite miraculous!

But she and Rosine had their entertainments, too. Although Aimee did not wish to spend too much of her earnings on frivolous things, she did go to a lecture given by one Dominique-Joseph Garat at the Lycée entitled "The Ancient History of the Peoples of the Orient." It had been fascinating and had left her thirsting for more. Rosine preferred lighter entertainment and dragged Aimee off to the theater to see *Michel Cervantès* one evening, and they had both come away laughing.

Aimee could not truly complain about her life with the de Brueys family, for she was treated well, had plenty to eat, and slept soundly every night after a hard day's work. And yet, she hungered for something . . . Rosine would give her a sly look and confirm for the hundredth time that she was seventeen and should expect to feel certain "needs." When Aimee questioned her further, she would giggle, roll her eyes, and shake her head, assuring her that she would find out soon enough what it all meant. Rosine herself had a steady lad, an apprentice at the goldsmith's shop who was quite handsome and would certainly be rich enough some day to afford a wife and children.

Aimee would laugh away the idea of a beau. She assured Rosine that she did not need any of those kinds of entanglements now. She had goals to achieve, work to do; a boy would only complicate matters.

She had told Rosine this same thing only the night before the day that Henri de Brueys was to return home from the university. All day, Madame de Brueys had been giving orders to everyone in the house, including her husband and daughter. Lila had outdone herself making a feast fit for a wedding: pie, pâté, baked cod and potatoes, salads, apples, cheeses, gingerbread, coffee, and brandy. Aimee's mouth watered at the sight of all that food heaped upon the long sideboard in the dining room. Guests had been invited and most had arrived early, before the young man himself had arrived.

Aimee stood in the wide foyer of the house, smoothing her crisp, white apron for at least the tenth time, stealing a moment to glance into the hall mirror to see that no hair was out of place beneath the snowy cap. When the brass knocker sounded for perhaps the twentieth time that evening, she straightened her back and went to open it.

Her green eyes beheld a young man with curly dark hair and laughing eyes staring back at her in friendly fashion. His thin-lipped mouth, so like his father's, smiled with an easy charm as he made his way inside, aware of the effect of his charm on the young girl before him. He was barely an inch taller than Aimee herself, but proportioned so well she thought him much taller. She realized, after a moment, that she was staring at him in a completely unservantlike way and quickly looked down to the carpeted floor.

"You're new, aren't you?" the young man asked politely before setting his hat and gloves into the crook of her arm. "I would certainly have remembered such a delightful little maid before I left for the university!"

"Yes, monsieur," Aimee returned, feeling strangely tongue-tied as this handsome young man continued to spend time with her when all the guests eagerly awaited him inside. How different from the attitude of his mother, she thought, with pleasure sparking her breast.

He reached under her chin familiarly and she felt his fingers touch the smooth skin there in a half caress. She might have been angered if anyone else had presumed so much, but this young man seemed so easy, so friendly, she could hardly take offense at it and smiled up at him, meeting his dark eyes almost curiously. They stared back at her a long moment, seeing the lovely features of a young girl, almost a woman, who was unaware of the sweet blush on her curved cheeks or the decided sparkle in those unusual green eyes. Henri de Brueys found himself aroused at the sight of the young maid and immediately told himself he must make better acquaintance of her in the near future.

"Henri! I thought I heard the door!" Madame de Brueys hurried out of the salon, her dark eyes brightening at the sight of her son. "Whatever are you doing out here, my dear? Come in, come in and see everyone! We have all been waiting!" She planted a motherly kiss, full of pride, on his cheek, then took his arm to persuade him into the crowded room beyond.

Aimee watched the pair leave, wondering at the change in the woman she had always deemed rather hard and cold. Here, though, was her reason for living, obviously, for mother love was stamped on every feature of her face, lighting it up and making it appear quite agreeable. She was still thinking on this when Henri appeared once more from around the corner, making Aimee start almost guiltily at being found daydreaming.

"I almost forgot, I've left my bags outside with the cab. Would you have them brought in?" he asked, taking out ten livres and putting them into her hand. "Oh—er—I've forgotten to ask your name," he ended rather apologetically.

"Aimee de Chartres," Aimee replied a little breathlessly.

"Aimee? How unusual—as different as those lovely green eyes of yours," he said with a smile before leaving her standing alone once more in the foyer.

Rousing herself, Aimee took the money to the driver outside and told him where to take the bags. He gave her back one of the livres, explaining the cab fare was only nine livres from the university to the Faubourg Saint-Germain. Aimee stared for a moment at the money in her hand as though wondering what to do with it. The driver winked at her.

"Sweeting, don't say anything about it—I'll never tell. It'll be a little extra you've probably earned anyway, eh?" He winked again and drove his vehicle away.

Later that evening, after the guests had all gone and everyone had retired, Aimee lay in bed, thinking of that single livre. It would be quite easy to pocket it for herself, as the driver had suggested, but somehow she couldn't do it. Doubtless, Rosine told her archly, she was merely looking for an excuse to talk to young Henri again. Aimee threw her a scowl and turned her back on her. But *was* she doing exactly that? she wondered. Had her head been turned so completely by the bourgeois son? Admittedly, Henri was a charming young man, but being a student at the university, he had had plenty of chances to cultivate that charm, she was certain, for it was well known what rogues the student lads were among the taverns and cafés of Paris.

Aimee reflected, for an odd moment, on the lack of young men in her life. She could recall, as a child, hearing her brothers talking about their exploits among some of the tavern girls in Orléans and remembered, more recently, Jean-Baptiste's kisses. But she had certainly not felt toward Jean-Baptiste as she seemed to feel toward Henri. There was a feeling of anticipation, of suppressed excitement at the thought of seeing him again. Rosine would call it "puppy love" or infatuation, and Aimee wondered if that weren't so. Certainly, she had never had a beau, a young man to bring her flowers and read poetry to her, to take her hand when they walked or escort her to the Palais Royal for a Sunday stroll. Would Henri be like that?

Aimee shook herself almost angrily. Silly thoughts, really. She kept forgetting she was no longer Aimee de Chartres, the daughter of a baron of France, but that she was simply a servant, under the employ of Monsieur de Brueys and his wife. Her beaux should rightly come from the working class—for that was what she was now, she realized with a start. She had become grouped in with that wide, seething mass in Paris who worked hard for their bread, who hated the aristocrats, who had, for all intents and purposes, started the grand revolution! She shivered at the thought, trying to imagine herself one of *them*. Had she truly lost her identity? It made her sad to think so. She thought of her father, of her mother—what would they think if they could see her fallen upon such straits? Surely, they would be happier to see her alive and healthy, rather than walking the streets of Paris, bearer of a once proud name, but reduced to begging for her bread. She comforted herself with the thought, recalling what Father Vincent had once told her—that from such experiences, a finer human being was made. From her experiences at the convent, to her sojourn in Paris, to her employment as a servant in the de Brueys household—all had combined to shape and mold the personality that was hers alone. What, she wondered, would have happened if the revolution had never come? Would she now, at seventeen, be married to some bourgeois attorney from Orléans? Would she still be running freely about the estate of du Beautreillis, like a young hoyden, uncaring as to what others thought of her adventurous spirit?

And yet, that spirit was still very much alive within the maid, Aimee de Chartres, she reassured herself. It only required a reawakening. And that time would come, she thought, when she could leave this place and find Etienne. Together they would build their ancestral castle into what it had once been—even finer than she had ever known it. And, with that rather comforting thought, she finally fell asleep.

13

- - -

"Do hurry, Aimee, or we will be late!" Rosine urged her friend as she glanced once more into the fragment of mirror over the washstand in their room.

Aimee tied up the last of her dress laces, wishing she had something grander than the same old dress she always wore on their entertainment outings. Still, the dark green broadcloth did deepen the color of her eyes attractively and made her hair seem even brighter in the summer sun. It was her best outfit and, with the little straw hat she had bought for herself from one of the hawkers on the Pont Neuf, it suited her very well. She patted her hair, which Rosine had fixed into the latest style, drawing it up in a soft coil in back and leaving the front in rather a disarray around her face, then took a few folded assignats to put in her pocket and announced she was ready.

"Good!" Rosine squeaked happily. "I have heard so much about this new comedy! The title is *Honorine, or the Woman Difficult to Deal With*. Can you imagine how delightful it must be with such a title!" She laughed and tossed her head brazenly. "Afterward, we shall stroll along the rue Saint-Honoré and roll our eyes at all the young gallants. Perhaps, if we've enough money, we could stop for an ice at one of the smarter cafés?"

"Or perhaps we could persuade some of the gallants to buy us one!" Aimee laughed, feeling in a gay mood today. It was Sunday and her workload had been very light. Lila had grudgingly allowed both girls a short holiday since there was really nothing for them to do that couldn't wait. Lavinia was with her governess, Monsieur and Madame de Brueys had gone for a drive in the country, and Henri was with friends. All was relatively quiet and Lila hadn't the heart to keep the young things home any more than they had to be. With a motherly cluck, she watched them go out the back door, warning them to be home before dark—for her worst fear was that they might be accosted by some of the hoodlums who made it a practice to rob young women without escorts. Their kind seemed to be sprinkled throughout Paris in the summer months, and Lila gave them one last warning as she watched them go.

"Poor Lila, we should have asked her to come with us!" Aimee said, waving a friendly hand back at the cook.

"Pooh! She would have spoiled our fun!" Rosine said, ignoring her. "Why, what young gallant would pay any attention to us with such a tight-lipped guardian hovering nearby?"

"Rosine, you have no heart!" Aimee accused her, but laughed at her friend, realizing suddenly that Rosine was the first real female friend she had ever had.

"Ah, God, sometimes I wish I didn't!" Rosine complained with a shake of her head. "There's times I'd like to think I didn't really love my little apprentice, but then I think of those gentle brown eyes of his and my heart turns inside out!"

"So now you are planning to turn the head of another gentleman in the rue Saint-Honoré?" Aimee inquired guilelessly.

Rosine shrugged. "He's turned the heads of a few little laundresses, plus a flower seller he swore he was going to marry someday—of course, that was before *I* came along!" She laughed, linking her arm in Aimee's and pulling her along.

By the time they reached the theater, it was already crowded with patrons, and the mid-June sun promised them an uncomfortable wait for the performance. Aimee and Rosine looked around appreciatively at the bevy of ladies, all dressed rather daringly in the fashion of the period. Many wore the new *sans chemise* look, which consisted of a thin, see-through muslin dress in white— with nothing underneath! The most daring among them had sponged the dress material to make it even more see-through. It would have been a terrible scandal in any other time, but now immoral conduct seemed to suit the mood of Paris. Because it was a generation who lived in war, whose young men, alive today, might be dead tomorrow, whose money was always worth less today than yesterday as the assignats continued to plunge downward, there seemed no reason not to live as one pleased. Ladies of the highest rank conducted their affairs freely and openly, and even the new bride of the young Bonaparte had not denied herself lovers while her husband was away on his army campaign.

Aimee had ceased to be shocked at the immorality around her, although she did not necessarily agree with what many people did; the many months spent in Paris had begun to take their toll on her innocence. She had not yet become jaded, as opposed to many who did after they had been in the capital for a length of time. She was still squeamish at the sight of an occasional execution, still grew flushed upon seeing through a café window a half-naked woman sitting on the knees of a student, and refused to accompany Rosine to the Hôtel Richelieu, where profiteers and speculators made free with pretty street girls. But, yes, she did enjoy some of the bawdy comedies that Rosine suggested and laughed at some of the tasteless jokes that were printed in pamphlets about the wives of the generals.

She had learned, more than anything else, how to survive in all the madness that was Paris during the post-revolutionary period. If she did not laugh, she would eventually go mad. And besides, who was there to care if she sat at home in her attic bedroom doing nothing but praying during her free time? She was her own mistress now, and at the age of seventeen there was too much life and vivacity inside of her to live the life of a pious nun. Yes, she breathed in the sights and smells of the city and reveled in the celebration of life that went on all around her.

"Here are the tickets!" Rosine said, proffering Aimee hers. "Whew! The assignats have dropped even lower since the last time we were here—it cost nearly double for these!"

They walked inside the theater, finding seats in the floor section of the building where all the working-class people were relegated. Aimee sat on an orange crate, feeling warm beneath her dress, glancing over at a young lady just above her in one of the reserved boxes whose attire consisted of one of those white muslin sheaths, her only decoration the red ribbon about her throat that aped, in dreadful fashion, those who had been guillotined. Casually, her eyes moved among the boxes, picking out ladies and gentlemen of quality, wondering if they were former aristocrats who had, somehow, managed to keep their fortunes hidden during the torment of the Reign of Terror.

As her eye roved over the boxes, she stiffened suddenly and stared for a moment at one particular box where a man sat, legs crossed indolently at the knee, one arm casually surrounding the shoulders of a young lady in white muslin. Could it be—could it be? Quickly, she turned around, trying to shield her face with the brim of her hat. Good Lord! Surely she was mistaken, but if she wasn't, pray God he hadn't seen her!

"What is it?" Rosine asked curiously, seeing her friend grow pale. "You look as though you've seen a ghost."

"Something like that," Aimee murmured. "There is a man in one of the boxes up there. The last time I saw him, we parted under rather strained conditions."

"Yes?" Rosine asked eagerly.

"I had just cracked him over the head with a vase!" Aimee said quickly. "I really don't think he would be pleased to see me again. If he thinks of me at all, he would imagine me hard at work in the workhouse, not here in the theater!"

"Oh, my dear, which one is he?" Rosine asked quickly, her eyes eagerly searching the boxes. "Certainly not that distinguished-looking man with the silvered temples? Or that charming young man with the shaggy haircut and the golden loops in his ears? Oh, but it must be *that* one—for he is looking straight at your head, my dear! The one with the dark hair and—oh!—such piercing blue eyes that I feel quite breathless! Hmm! I should feel flattered to have him look at *me* that way! Aimee, do turn around and wave to him, for I'm bound he's not going to let up until you do!"

"Rosine, for heaven's sake!" Aimee pleaded helplessly. "If you value your life, you will please stop waving and smiling at him!"

Rosine made a pout, her dark lashes covering her brown eyes for a moment, before she patted her dark brown hair and reseated herself correctly, facing the stage. "Pooh! He didn't look so terrible! In fact, I should think having his attentions might be quite pleasant. You can be such a fool about men, Aimee!"

"That one is just one I don't care to have any communication with," Aimee returned lightly. Then: "Do look again and tell me if he is still watching me, Rosine."

Rosine risked a quick, upward glance and shook her head. "No, he's talking to the young lady beside him, smiling at her. Ah, it seems he's no longer interested in you!" she said with a faintly malicious air.

"Good! Perhaps he didn't recognize me!" Aimee felt relieved. She certainly did not want to come face to face with the man who had so ignominiously arrested her in the gardens that day so long ago. It had been he who had started her present position in life, although, to be fair, she could not lay the blame totally on him. It was true, he had collared her for pickpocketing, but she could never be sure if it had been his order that had sent her to the Châtelet. She preferred not to know; that part of her life was over. Jean-Baptiste was dead, Faron still lived somewhere in Paris, but she could not think of that now.

Still, as the curtain went up and the play began, she found she could not concentrate on the actors no matter how she tried. Those freezing blue eyes kept coming to mind, and his lips form-

ing words: "I'm afraid you have a rendezvous with the Conciergerie, my dear." Oh, she tried to shake away the thoughts. He
was a witness to her shame and she wanted no part of him.
Stubbornly, she turned her attention back to the stage and tried
once more to follow the plot of the comedy.

All around her there was laughter and she smiled rather
vaguely, wondering what on earth they found so funny when all
she could think of was being exposed by the man in the box
above her. She glanced at Rosine. She knew that Aimee had been
in the workhouse because of the charge of pickpocketing, but she
was her friend, she could trust her. That man above her—she
could not trust him! Hadn't he told her that Faron would be arrested and executed? And yet, Faron still lived as far as she
knew. Her heart felt like lead as everything came back to her; she
did not want to think of this now. It seemed so incongruous as all
around her giggles mixed with belly laughs and chortles of mirth.
Why did she feel so miserable suddenly?

"Rosine, I . . . I think I shall have to excuse myself for a moment," Aimee told her companion several minutes into the play.
"I just need a little fresh air. The people pressing in—and this
heat! I'll be back shortly."

Rosine gave her a curious look, then shrugged and turned her
attention back to the play. Aimee made her way out cautiously,
careful not to tread on anyone's toes, trying not to block the view,
not wanting any attention drawn to her leaving. Once she was out
of the main part of the theater, she walked quickly to the edge of
the lobby, looking outside, between the colonnaded veranda and
the square of green lawn. She put her hand to her forehead, trying
to push aside thoughts of Lucian Napier and her past. A sudden
longing came over her to see her brother, Etienne, and she wondered, for the first time seriously, if he were dead.

"Mademoiselle, are you ill?"

Aimee turned to see a stagehand looking at her anxiously, his
plain, good face showing his concern. She shook her head with a
tentative smile. "No, no, thank you." She watched him walk
away, grateful for this small show of human kindness. Suddenly,
the close, sweaty rabble inside no longer appealed to her. She
didn't want to return to the floor of the theater, rubbing elbows
with strangers, inhaling cheap perfume and the smoke of pipes
and cigars. It was pleasant out here, where a soft breeze vied with
the warmth of the June sun to create a small idyll for a weary
soul.

Unfortunately, her solitude was brusquely interrupted as she heard booted footsteps coming her way on the floorboards of the wide porch. She trembled instinctively and wondered why he would have followed her out here.

"Good afternoon, mademoiselle." The deep voice saluted her, forcing her to turn her head and encounter the deep blue eyes that silently assessed her from head to toe. She remembered the look from many months before and smiled a little.

"Hello, again, Monsieur Napier—although before, when we met, it was *Citizen* Napier, wasn't it?" She was surprised at the calm beating of her heart.

He seemed, for a moment, taken aback by her placid composure. "So it was. But much has changed since I saw you last, mademoiselle."

She nodded. "The government seems to be more lenient. Tell me, monsieur, do you still hold friends in high places?" she wondered, tilting her head a little and surveying him from beneath her lashes.

He smiled, the firm lips parting to show even, white teeth that presented themselves well against the darkish tan of his skin. She didn't recall this fact from before, nor the way his sinewy-muscled thighs strained against the fabric of his breeches. With his Hessian boots and wide-shouldered stance, he looked quite well, Aimee thought, not surprised that Rosine had been so excited about him. Of course, she reminded herself, looks were certainly not everything, and there was much more to this man than what he looked like, as she well knew.

"I have many friends—and many enemies," he said slowly, realizing she was studying him with a look that was somehow provocative without her trying to be so. Somehow, he hadn't remembered her being quite this attractive, with her tall, slender body and bright, sparkling green eyes that gazed steadily at him without artifice. "At our last meeting—"

She colored quickly and her eyes broke away from his gaze. "Oh, yes, about that bump I must have given you—" She cleared her throat and continued: "I am sorry, Monsieur Napier, but you must understand I did the only thing I could in order to find out for myself what had happened to Jean-Baptiste—and to Faron."

"I shall certainly never trust myself to turn my back on you again, mademoiselle," he said ruefully, unconsciously rubbing the spot at the back of his head in remembrance. "You're stronger than you look!" He came closer and waved to a chair, several of which were scattered about the long porch. When she had seated herself, he pulled one close to her and asked, "Did you find your friend, and Faron?"

Aimee shook her head. "Faron had escaped arrest, and Jean-Baptiste . . . he died from grapeshot wounds," she ended with sadness in her voice. "He had gone to the house of my aunt in search of me, and when I found him he was already half dead. He told me Faron had escaped and—afterward—the police came to arrest me." She looked up at him. "Did you send them?"

He shook his head. "How could I? I was still out cold from that nice bump on the head you'd given me. To tell you the truth, I didn't know what had happened to you." He leaned closer. "What *did* happen?"

She hesitated, wondering at his reason for wanting to know. Was it just a guilty conscience? Still, there was no harm in telling him, for she was doing nothing wrong. "I was taken to the Châtelet," she told him, shivering at the memory. Unconsciously, her hand touched her hair, remembering how they had cut it all off. He noticed the gesture and felt somehow touched by it. "Afterward, I was sentenced to the workhouse in the factory district. The life was not bad, but very regimented. I missed having my freedom. Then one of the priests who came to say mass for all the young women there told me of a wealthy bourgeois family that needed a serving girl. It was a chance to escape the drudgery of the workhouse—and I took it!"

"And so, here you are, a respectable working girl, having her Sunday off and attending a new play at the theater," he mused. "Somehow, I had not thought that would be what would become of you, mademoiselle."

"And what is wrong with that?" she wondered, anger tinging her voice. "What did you expect would happen to me? Were you perhaps thinking that I might remain forever in the Châtelet, or that I might find a man to take care of me, or perhaps I might take to walking the streets in front of the Palais Royal?" She stood up, irritated, without knowing the precise reason for her irritation. "I can assure you, Monsieur Napier, I can do whatever must be done to survive. Until I am certain of my brother's whereabouts, I will continue working at the home of Monsieur de Brueys!"

"The shopkeeper de Brueys?" he asked, ignoring the rest, much to her further irritation. "I know of him." He was silent for a while, watching the angry color fade from her cheeks.

"Well . . . is that all you have to say?" she demanded.

He shrugged. "What would you like me to say?"

She reared back, as though stunned. "What would I *like*, Monsieur Napier, is for you to leave me alone. I do not require your company. Indeed, I would do better without it!" Even as the words tumbled out, she was not sure of her reason for saying them. Why was she so angry with him?

He stood up also and bowed. "As you wish, mademoiselle."

Aimee watched him walk away, feeling a raging mixture of emotions inside herself. Why had she sent him away so meanly? He had, after all, behaved very well toward her. Perhaps he truly had a guilty conscience and only wanted to know what had happened to her. And instead of feeling pleased by his interest, she had insulted him and made herself out to look like some strident harpy! And she was not really like that!

By the time Rosine came out in search of her, she had worked herself into a rare lather. "Come on, Rosine, weren't we going to ogle the gallants and find something daring to do tonight?" she asked her, her cheeks highly colored, her green eyes sparkling with a reckless gleam.

Rosine studied her for a moment. "What has happened?" She looked around. "Did that man you were so worried about come out here after you?"

"Him? Heavens, I wasn't worried about *him,* Rosine. He's . . . nothing to me. Someone from my past, nothing to fear—actually, for all his handsome exterior, he's quite mundane inside. A preening peacock, interested only in himself and his conquests! Let's forget about him and go on!"

"Aimee, you are funny today," Rosine remarked as they walked away from the theater. "First you act as though you are frightened to death, and the next moment you're like a wild woman! Don't forget, we must get home before dark or we'll have Lila so worried—"

"Oh, Rosine!" Aimee interrupted airily. "Don't start lecturing me. Can't we have one night of fun!" She twirled around and laughed at her friend. "Now, you're always accusing me of being straitlaced and a prude! Look, tonight I am not going to be a prude. We'll go to one of those fashionable dance halls and dance until the wee hours. I have a passion for dancing." She sighed, aping Lavinia, who spent hours a week with her dancing master. Mimicking the dance master, she said in a nasal voice, "In step . . . steady . . . turn now . . . head high, mademoiselle . . . turn, I say, *turn,* Mademoiselle Lavinia!"

Rosine broke into laughter at Aimee's excellent impersonation. "Ah, you have him down perfectly!" she cried gleefully, wiping the tears of mirth from her eyes. "But first, before we go dancing, we must have something to eat. I'm famished!"

"As you wish," Aimee agreed, although food was the last thing she wanted.

She allowed Rosine to lead her to one of the lesser cafés where the prices would not be quite so outrageous. Once seated, feeling very daring, they watched the crowd surrounding them, which consisted mostly of the working class, some soldiers, and a few of the less well-off bourgeois. There were enough women in the place so that they felt quite comfortable as they ordered from the barrelchested man who claimed his was the best wine in Paris. Rosine and Aimee exchanged looks, then shrugged and ordered a bottle.

The wine went down Aimee's throat like a fiery stream, making tears come to her eyes before she swallowed it. She looked over at Rosine, whose face was a mirror of her own, and they both burst into laughter.

"Good heavens, we mustn't get drunk before we can go dancing!" Aimee exclaimed. A soldier came over to their table expectantly and she favored him with a look of annoyance. "Go away, clodhopper! Can't you see we are decent women?" At his look of surprise, she burst into more laughter, noting that the bottle was nearly gone.

It seemed forever before their food was served, a tasty soup and hard, crusty bread that Aimee felt ill-inclined to eat. The wine had filled up her stomach so that she had very little room for anything else, and, shortly, she pushed away her bowl, barely touched. Rosine, on the other hand, had nearly drained her soup, obviously being a bit more used to spirits. She favored Aimee with a studied look. Glancing at the clock on the wall, she turned back to her companion.

"It's nearly eight o'clock, Aimee, and nearly pitch-dark outside. We'd best forget the dancing tonight and get home."

Aimee shook her head. "No, Rosine. Who knows when we'll have another evening like this! We'll have a grand time tonight, and tomorrow you'll go back to being just a kitchen girl and I'll be a mere upstairs maid." She sighed. "Come along, don't desert me!"

"What if we lose our positions?" Rosine asked practically.

Aimee shrugged. "Then we shall get new ones!"

Rosine would have protested, but Aimee was dragging her along at a faster pace now. Rosine had no doubts that her companion was in her cups, but allowed herself to be pulled along, not wholly against having a little fun. They were soon in front of Lucquet's, a fashionable dancing establishment that catered mostly to bourgeois families.

"Not here!" Rosine whispered quickly when the doorman asked for the six livres it would take to admit them. "Too rich for our blood," she said to him, leading Aimee to another establishment, a little farther down the street, called The Paphos, which counted more working class among its clientele and whose entrance fee was a mere two livres, which included the price of a litre of wine to go to the musicians.

Aimee felt strangely excited, keyed up, as she entered the large hall, with its arched ceilings and low sideboards running the length of the hall on either side where people sat talking and laughing. Everything here was gay and charming, she decided. No dour looks, no moralizing—just fun and entertainment, that's what she wanted! There was a dizzying array of dancers, most of the women dressed in their sheer gowns, dancing the quadrille and the polka with their partners, rough men for the most part up from the docks or the factories to have a little fun on a Sunday night.

Aimee and Rosine seated themselves close to the musicians. "The music is lovely," Aimee drawled, leaning toward her friend and nearly dropping her chin into her lap. Rosine looked closely at her, seeing the glassy look about the eyes and the flushed cheeks that was a result of the cheap wine.

"Ho! You know you shouldn't drink, Aimee," she advised with a whistle. "You look as though you're about to fall down, let alone do any dancing!"

Aimee laughed away her concern. "I can dance as well as anyone! Don't forget what the dance master says: 'A flowing pace . . . more assurance in the expression . . . that's all it takes!' You see, Rosine, anyone can do it!"

She turned her attention to the bearded man whose girth was nearly three times her own. He was a lighter from the barges of the Seine and his clothes still bore the foul smell of the river, but Aimee smiled with dazzling charm as he asked to dance with her, pushing Rosine's arm aside. The barge man took her out onto the polished wooden floor and Aimee felt as light as air as he twirled her about until she was breathless. His grip on her waist was tight and she realized how he must hold the hooks onto the barges to unload the crates and boxes. After a while of this, she began to feel a little nauseous and begged him to take her back to her seat. Rosine was not there and the lighter moved away to find someone else as Aimee insisted she must sit down for a while or pass out. She leaned against the wall behind her, willing her head to stop spinning. Ugh! If this was the result of cheap wine, she vowed never to have any again! When she felt sufficiently rested, she leaned forward once more and, almost immediately, several young men were next to her, begging for the next dance.

And so it went, on into the night until Aimee thought her feet would fall off. Most of the young men were surprisingly courteous, their rough manners hiding rather shy beings who were awed by the beauty of this golden flower among them. Her hair was like a banner waved in the breeze, for by now she had lost her hat and was dancing without it, the careful coiffure in a tangle down her back. Her eyes were shining, her lips red and full, her cheeks flushed becomingly. What man could see her and not want her? At least, so thought Lucian Napier as he studied her from his vantage point in a darkened corner of the room.

He had followed her on impulse when he perceived her and her friend going in the direction of the cafés. He'd watched them eat and drink, not unused to this sort of activity, having been given many spy missions in his service in government. He thought of his poor companion at the theater—doubtless, she had been absolutely miffed at his quick leavetaking, but he was sure she had probably found another partner by now. He was more concerned about Mademoiselle de Chartres, who was very drunk, he surmised, and quite liable to find herself in a lot of trouble if she didn't stop batting her eyelashes at every man who asked her to dance. Her friend seemed a more practical sort, but he wasn't sure that she would be able to extricate them from any trouble in which they might find themselves. These men could be rough, if they chose, and two young women, unarmed, would not prove very difficult to overpower.

He continued to watch Aimee as she was whirled about the floor, wondering at the strong stomach she had that enabled her to keep the wine down. He was certain that she would find herself retching it all up before the night was over, but she continued to amaze him with her stamina. He glanced at the tall clock in another corner of the room, noting it was already after ten. Surely, if she was in the employ of the de Brueys family, she should be getting home; otherwise, she would most likely lose her position. It was not often that Lucian Napier cared what became of a girl who got drunk and put herself in the position that Aimee was putting herself in, but there was *something* about this girl, he admitted. It was not the mere fact that she really was

quite lovely, but he felt almost an obligation to see her safely
home, especially after upsetting her at the theater. He didn't like
to think that her irrational behavior was a direct result of their
meeting, but he wasn't at all positive that it wasn't!

Aimee, unaware of those dark blue eyes watching her across
the room, was beginning to feel both tired and sick. Her excitement was wearing thin and all she wanted to do was go home to
her attic room with Rosine and tumble into bed. It was definitely
time to go, she thought, but her partner had other ideas as he
continued to hold her for the next dance.

"I'm afraid, no more," Aimee explained, trying to smile, but
nearly too tired for that.

Her partner, a tall, wiry man whose garlic-flavored breath was
making her feel faint, shook his head. "No, no, one more dance!"
He laughed.

Aimee tried to push him away weakly. "No, I . . . I am going
to be sick!" she explained nervously, turning her head away from
him.

His eyes gleamed. "Let me take you outside," he suggested,
already planning a quick tussle on the grounds, hardly unheard of
in these times. "You need a little air, that's all. I'll help you."

Aimee leaned against him, swallowing hard and willing her
stomach to stop tumbling inside out. "No! I have to go. Where is
my friend?" She looked around and saw Rosine laughing into the
face of a tall, blond giant. Trying to signal her, she felt her arm
grasped and turned to confront her partner once more.

"I will take care of you," he said again, beginning to pull her
to the doorway. "Lean on me, my beauty, and we'll soon be
outside."

Aimee could hardly do anything else, although her tired mind
began to realize that she was putting herself into some kind of
danger. Growing a trifle panicky, she watched the blur of faces
dancing by her as the man led her out of the dance hall. She
closed her eyes only a moment to try to regain her balance and
felt the cooler air outside close in around her. Her partner's hands
were already on her shoulders, pushing her back against the wall
of the building while his lips sought hers in the dark.

Suddenly angry at his fumbling, Aimee pushed him away, but
he came right back, growing angry himself. "You'll not tease me
inside, then refuse me out here!" he told her venomously. He
pinched her arm until it bled. "I'll not be satisfied with a few
paltry dances, sister. Now, be nice to me and I'll be nice to you!"

"Why, you oaf! How dare you speak to me so familiarly!"

Aimee cried, beginning to recover a little in the night air. "Let me go or I'll call the watch!"

He laughed nastily. "Do you think they'll come flying at a scream from some skirt? Not likely, wench. Now, stop threatening me, or I might not be so gentle with you."

Aimee shrank back against the wall, trying to think of something through the fog that still surrounded her brain. She could scream, but what if he was right and it only increased his anger? Desperately, she flattened herself against the stone behind her, wishing she could melt into it. He was so close that she could barely breathe, and his face seemed to be swimming before her eyes.

"Let go of that young woman!"

Aimee's eyes flew open at the sound of Lucian Napier's voice. She searched for him in the darkness, so relieved she thought she would faint. Where had he come from? How had he found her? She started toward his voice, but felt an arm across her chest, holding her where she was.

"I said, let her go!" Lucian repeated quietly, but with a deadly earnestness in his voice.

"Now, now, who's to tell me what to do?" the man asked, trying to make out the figure of his opponent. "You the girl's father?" he wondered.

"No, I'm afraid the lady is my wife," Lucian drawled without hesitation. "We had a bit of an argument earlier this evening and it's taken me all this time to find the little hoyden. Now, if you'll excuse us?"

"Not so fast, not so fast," the other man said, obviously disappointed that his prey was to be snatched from him so easily. "How do I know she's your wife?"

"You can ask her, if you want," Lucian replied lazily. "Of course, she may deny it if she's still angry with me. On the other hand, perhaps I ought to let you have her—the minx gave me such a bad case of the pox last month that I'm only now able to move about." He heard Aimee's outraged gasp as well as the man's indrawn breath of alarm.

"Well, now, maybe you're right," he said, backing away from Aimee and wiping his mouth with the back of his hand. "If you say she's your wife, then I don't see as how you'd be lying to me!" And he quickly retreated, leaving Lucian to face an enraged Aimee.

"How dare you say such a thing!" she hissed, completely

mortified. "First you lie about my being your wife, and then . . . and then . . ."

"I just saved you from being raped, my dear. Or would you rather I call back the man and tell him there's been a mistake, that you're not my wife, and he's welcome to a quick tumble out here under the moon! Of course, you don't know, but maybe *he* has the pox and would have given it to you as a parting gift!"

"Oh, you!" She flew toward him, her fingers outstretched as though to claw out his eyes, but he caught her easily enough against him, subduing her with ridiculous ease. "Ooh!" He felt her forehead pressing into his chest and heard her hiccough. Only just in time, he pushed her over the side of the porch and heard her retching into the bushes below.

"That will teach you to drink cheap wine," he murmured as she continued to empty her stomach. He led her from the porch to a small fountain in the yard below.

Gratefully, Aimee plunged her face into the cool water, cupping her hands to drink and wash out her mouth. God, she felt much better, although there was a light film of perspiration on her neck and arms. Wearily, she straightened herself, feeling suddenly very tired.

"Would you like me to take you home?" Lucian wondered with an underlying sarcasm that Aimee barely noticed in her condition.

She nodded. "I . . . I'm sorry to have seemed so . . . ungrateful," she stammered.

He smiled in the darkness and gave her his handkerchief to wipe her face. "Let me hail a cab and I'll place you in it. Then I'll get your friend and take you both home."

She nodded again, feeling as though a heavy weight had been lifted from where it had been pressing down on her head all evening. Now she actually felt quite light and, standing there, she wavered back and forth as though she were a young sapling being buffeted by a strong breeze. Lucian couldn't hide his amusement as he put one arm about her shoulders to help steady her, then walked with her to the street, where he was able to find a cab to take them home. After seeing Aimee safely inside, he went back into the dance hall to find a relieved Rosine looking frantically for her companion. Explaining the situation concisely, he persuaded the girl to accompany him to the waiting carriage, where Aimee was already half asleep on one of the seats. After giving the address to the driver, he pushed himself next to Aimee, allowing Rosine, who still seemed a bit unsure of him, to have the other seat to herself.

"It seems this was not the best of ideas," he commented as Rosine watched him with big, dark eyes. "It's much too late for two such innocents to be about." He smiled to himself as Rosine bridled a bit.

"Why, I can assure you *I* knew what I was about!" she said in self-defense. She looked at Aimee with her head quite comfortably ensconced in the lap of the man she had been so worried about in the theater that afternoon. "It's she who can't handle the wine, monsieur! And she was the one who insisted on going to the dance hall," she added as Lucian's brow arched upward in mock disbelief.

"I see," he said softly, "and you are, then, a woman of the world, mademoiselle?"

Rosine smiled, showing the dimple in her cheek. She wondered if she should risk flirting with this stranger, then thought better of it. Perhaps Aimee was frightened of him for good reason. There did seem a secretive air about him, as though he wasn't the type who'd appreciate too many questions. She lowered her lashes primly and responded, "Not exactly a woman of the world, monsieur, but I do know how to hold my liquor."

Lucian would have laughed at that, but was afraid he might hurt the girl's feelings. She seemed a good enough girl, a trifle more experienced than Aimee, but that meant nothing in this day and age. Everyone was experienced except for young provincials who didn't know what they were getting into when they came to Paris, he thought, looking down at the sleeping girl in his lap. Amazingly, although with many women he would have found himself becoming aroused at such a position, he didn't feel that way now. Perhaps if she didn't seem so *vulnerable*. Then he laughed to himself, remembering the way she had clobbered him with the vase at the Tuileries.

"We're there," he said as the carriage came to a halt.

Rosine hopped out of the carriage, showing very few ill effects from the night's events, but Aimee was dead to the world. Swiftly, Lucian picked her up in his arms and carried her around to the back of the house, where a shocked Lila met them in the kitchen.

"Don't worry, Lila. This is an old friend of Aimee's," Rosine supplied glibly. "I'm afraid she's had a little too much wine, and this man kindly gave us a ride home." She realized she didn't even know the man's name.

"Lucian Napier," he supplied, bowing to the still surprised and somewhat suspicious Lila. "Would you like me to take her up to her room?"

"Heavens, no!" Lila exploded, trying not to imagine what Madame de Brueys would think if she saw this tall, dark-haired stranger taking one of her servants upstairs. "I mean, thank you for your trouble, monsieur," she amended as gracefully as she could, "but I'm afraid our mistress will be quite distraught if she finds out about all this. If you don't mind, I'll pour a little coffee down her throat—enough to get her upstairs to her room on her own two feet."

Lucian nodded, bowed once more, then took himself out of the house, leaving an astonished Lila to gaze uncomprehendingly at Rosine.

"What happened? If you two got yourselves into some trouble, you'll find yourselves out in the street should madame hear about it!" she threatened, setting the pot to boil. She glanced over at Aimee and shook her head. "Who would have thought it of her?" she wondered.

Nearly an hour later, a still groggy Aimee was "escorted" to her room with the help of Rosine and Lila, whose puffing and panting up the stairs threatened to rouse the entire de Brueys household. As Aimee sank to her bed, she heard Lila muttering to herself that if anything like this should happen again, she'd wash her hands of both of them. Contentedly, she snuggled down into her bedclothes, so tired she didn't even want to take off her dress—but something was jiggling at her, nagging at the back of her mind.

She sat up, the fog having cleared somewhat from her mind. "Lucian Napier!" she exclaimed, remembering. "Did he bring us home?"

Rosine nodded as she dressed herself for bed. "He certainly did—and was quite the gentleman about it." She looked at her friend closely. "I don't quite see what you were so worried about, Aimee. He certainly saved our skins, you know."

Aimee sighed. "Yes, I know. I probably didn't even thank him." She gazed at Rosine, trying to sound casual as she began to undress. "Er . . . what exactly did I do?"

Rosine laughed tiredly. "You fell asleep in the carriage with your head in his lap!"

Aimee colored with humiliation. First she'd retched up the wine in front of him. Then she had fallen asleep in his lap! What he must think of her! She certainly hoped she never saw him again! "Thank goodness that's all over," she said aloud, stepping into her nightgown. She looked once more at Rosine across the room. "Is that all?" she wondered, trying to hide her flaming cheeks as Rosine went to blow out the candle.

Rosine nodded and blew out the candle. Then across the darkness, her voice floated: "Yes, that's all—except that . . . well, when you had your head in his lap . . ."

"Yes?" Aimee asked in a strained voice.

"You were snoring terribly!" Rosine laughed and heard the groan of disgust that issued from the other side of the room.

14

Days later, Aimee had still not stopped thinking about her complete humiliation of that night. She had awakened the next morning with a dreadful headache and a complete disinclination to begin her usual duties around the house. It had even occurred to her to plead sickness in order to stay in bed, but obviously she could not fool Lila, who would probably have insisted she get up in order to teach her a lesson. Every sound, every clang of the kitchen pots, every step of someone on the stairs seemed to reverberate through her head and she had spent a miserable day, nearly mad with relief when it was over.

Now that part of it was behind her, but she still fumed about her foolishness of that night until Rosine grew tired of listening to her and told her not to think about it any longer. Aimee sighed and shook her head as she dusted the dressing table of Madame de Brueys. The lady of the house was still abed, snoring gently in her adjoining bedroom, and Aimee tried to make as little noise as possible. She was being so quiet that it startled her when she heard a step in the room.

"Good morning!" Henri de Brueys said, obviously in a cheerful mood.

Aimee brought a finger to her lips. "Your mother's still abed," she explained, moving out of the dressing room and closing the door behind her. Henri had followed her and was standing next to her in the hallway. His nearness caused a strange constriction in her breathing and Aimee cleared her throat quickly, ostensibly to move on to another part of the house.

"No, don't run away from me!" Henri laughed, catching her elbow so that she could not escape. "Every time I run into you, you act like a frightened doe. Are you afraid of me, Aimee?"

She turned to regard him, her heart leaping at the charm in his face. Mentally, she compared him to Lucian Napier, finding fault with the latter immediately. Henri's face was so much more open, so boyish and honest—nothing like Lucian's secretive look— and those piercing blue eyes watched everything she did. "No, monsieur, of course I am not afraid of you," she said softly. "But you are the son of my employer and I have no right to be standing here talking with you when I have other duties to perform."

He seemed disappointed. "Oh! I had thought we might talk a little while," he said, surprising her. "My father has very little time for me, and Lavinia is such a spoiled little thing, she can't really communicate with me. All of my fellow students have their own homes in the country where they spend the summer."

"Your mother—"

He looked at her with a resigned air. "My mother loves me—too much," he told her. "Her favorite topic is the wonderful marriage she wants to arrange for me as soon as I am ready to leave the university and enter into Father's business."

Aimee flushed at his divulging of private conversation. He noted it and his own cheeks reddened a little. "I'm sorry, I suppose I shouldn't have told you that, should I?"

"Your mother wouldn't appreciate it, I'm sure," Aimee put in, "but I don't mind your telling me," she added hastily, wanting to reassure him.

He smiled again. "You really are quite lovely," he told her. "Lovelier than any of the girls who hang around the university. Wherever did my father find you?"

Aimee didn't want to tell him that she had been found in the workhouse, put there because she'd been arrested after committing a crime. She wondered if he would be appalled at such an idea. "It doesn't really matter," she said lightly. "But you must excuse me, monsieur, for I do have work to attend to."

He caught her arm once more. "I will excuse you, Aimee, only if you promise to meet me somewhere this afternoon."

She was taken aback by his request. "This afternoon? But I can't possibly leave the house. Your mother—"

"Then when?" he pleaded almost fervently. "When do you go out? Surely you have some time off. Come, meet me sometime and we can talk all we want," he said quickly. "It would mean so much to me, Aimee."

She was at a loss. Was he so lonesome here in his own home, then? She knew that it was true his father paid little attention to him. His mother doted on him so much that there was little time left for his father anyway. Perhaps he held that against his son. And Lavinia was in her own separate world, far removed from both her father and her mother. Her world revolved around drawing lessons and geography lessons and dancing lessons. Certainly, Henri was right in thinking her an unsatisfactory conversation partner. She suddenly felt sorry for the young man

—so bright and charming, she imagined he was quite a wonderful student. To come from the university into this home, where his mother smothered him with her attentions and his father barely knew he was alive—how sad it seemed! She knew he was about her own age, perhaps a year or two older. It seemed easily explained why he would turn to her in desperation for someone to talk to.

Making up her mind, she nodded to him. "I will be off again on Sunday afternoon," she replied. "Rosine and I usually go out together, but I'll tell her that I have other plans. We could meet somewhere." She was still conscious of the need to keep such a meeting secret. She was sure that if his mother ever found out about it she would be livid, and Aimee would be without a position—or perhaps, worse yet, back in the workhouse.

Henri seemed ridiculously pleased at her agreement. They arranged a place to meet, a public place where it would be difficult to find them—the Fair of Saint-Germain; it was close by and they could go from there to a quiet café to talk.

The days seemed to drag after that until Sunday. Aimee went through her work, judiciously avoiding Henri whenever his mother was about, unwilling to allow her any suspicion. She found herself anticipating their outing with a kind of eagerness that she could not quite understand. Surely she couldn't be falling in love with a young man she barely knew? And yet, her heart was light, her head filled with ideas for conversation with him. How wonderful it would be to find herself on his arm, strolling through the Fair of Saint-Germain, entering one of the cafés with him! She hummed while she worked and even Rosine told her she was so sickeningly cheerful she was getting on her nerves.

When Sunday finally arrived, Aimee dressed with care in the same green outfit she had worn to the theater on that fateful day when she had met Lucian Napier again. She looked at her sparkling eyes in the mirror and blew a kiss to her reflection, confounding Rosine, who was already upset that their outing had been canceled by Aimee's "other plans." Cheerfully, Aimee set off for the prescribed meeting place, seemingly floating along the street with anticipation.

At the fairgrounds, she noted the two large wooden market halls that housed nearly four hundred bays between them where vendors displayed and sold various merchandise. There were traders from as far away as Amiens, Rouen, and Marseille. The Portuguese set up shop there, now that the war had lightened up somewhat. Their stalls were filled with delicate porcelain that Aimee looked at with awe. There were lemons and oranges, rugs and cheeses; almost anything one wished to buy could be found at the fair. Besides the traders, there were magic acts and freak shows, animal exhibitions, cock fights, and gambling tables set up. Aimee passed through all of the noise and crowds, wondering suddenly if she would be able to find Henri in all of this.

She looked with sudden panic for the sight of his dark-haired form, wondering if he was, perhaps, already here and looking for her in a different part of the fair. She hurried among the stalls, her eyes moving among the crowd until she spotted the picturesque fountain in the center of the square. She remembered Henri had suggested that as a meeting place and settled down by it with relief. It was still early; he would probably not come for a few more minutes.

Aimee sat at the fountain for a long time, watching the crowds, the people passing to and fro, wishing she had Rosine with her to help to pass the time. An hour crawled by and Aimee looked around in concern, wondering what could be keeping Henri. Hadn't he said four o'clock? Now it was nearly five, and still he had not made his appearance. By six o'clock, Aimee's concern had given way to a steady anger as she realized he might not show up at all. She recalled how he had pleaded with her for this meeting and how she had finally agreed. She could not equate the charming, boyish face with this rudeness of missing an appointment.

Finally, as twilight settled in and many of the people started to head for their homes, Aimee realized that he was not coming. Weariness and outrage warred within her, each vying for supremacy. By the time she arrived back at the de Brueys home, she felt totally dejected. Rosine had not returned yet from her outing. Only Lila was there to offer comfort.

Setting down a plate of food in front of her, Lila patted Aimee's shoulder with a motherly air and asked, "Did he stand you up, then?"

Aimee looked up in surprise. "How did you know—"

"Ah, I'm not that surprised, you know. When he brought you home that night, I told myself he must care for you quite a bit—"

"Who are you talking about?" Aimee inquired, at a loss.

"Why, Monsieur Napier, of course. Wasn't he the one you were so eager to meet earlier today?" Now it was Lila's turn to look confused.

Aimee flushed, wishing she could lie to the cook, but she

knew her eyes would betray her. "No, it wasn't him," she said quickly. "It was someone else."

"Oh." Lila was silent for a time. Then, shaking her head, she said softly, "I was sure it'd be him. What a charmer he looked, and so gentle with you—"

"Let's not talk about it," Aimee interrupted, hardly aware of what she was eating or what Lila was saying. All she knew was that Henri de Brueys had not shown up at their meeting place— and she wanted to know why. She glanced over at the cook, trying her utmost to sound casual. "What did the de Brueyses do today?"

"Aimee, you know I don't snoop as to the whereabouts of our employers. And I've told you before, I don't like talking about them!" She gave her a severe look. Then, relenting a little, she informed her, "I do know that they spent some time—the whole family did—at the home of the Linots."

Aimee did not recognize the name, but seized on the niche she had made in Lila's usually impenetrable wall. "The Linots—who are they?" she wondered idly.

"Monsieur Linot works for the government, my dear. They are quite an up-and-coming family, as madame likes to say. I believe he is an attorney and works directly under Monsieur Barras. Doesn't that sound exciting!" At Aimee's shrug, she went on commandingly: "What's more important is that he has been favored by the Directory, which bodes quite well for the marriage of his *three* daughters!"

"Three?" Aimee repeated, suddenly realizing exactly what the cook was getting at. "You mean a marriage to one of them for Monsieur Henri?" Her heart sank at the cook's satisfied nod. "But what about the year he has left at the university. Surely his father would not wish him to curtail his education—"

"It appears to me," Lila interrupted coolly, "that you're entirely too concerned about Monsieur Henri and what his father wishes for him. Naturally, theirs can be a long engagement. The documents can be signed before Monsieur Henri returns to school, and a sweet little wife will be awaiting him when he gets out and comes home to join in his father's business."

"I . . . see," Aimee said, feeling as though she had swallowed a wad of stockings. "Well, I am sure his mother must be thrilled with such a match," she added with a sarcasm that sat ill on her lips.

"You'll hold your tongue on that," Lila warned her. "Madame

de Brueys doesn't request the opinions of her servants in such matters."

"Of course not," Aimee returned automatically, then left the table.

The next day, as Aimee was taking down the curtains to wash them, she heard Henri's voice behind her. "Here, Aimee, let me help you with those heavy things," he said practically, as though nothing was amiss between them. "They are much too cumbersome for you to handle alone."

"Rosine will help me as soon as she is through in the kitchen!" Aimee retorted, still put out by his rudeness of the day before.

She heard him sigh. "I'm sorry about yesterday," he got out. "I had every intention of meeting you as we had planned, but there were . . . other plans made by my parents."

"Yes, I know!" Aimee snapped, unable to help her shrewishness. "You were taken over to the Linots to be shown and stared at like some prized stud at market! I can imagine the three daughters of Monsieur Linot were quite agreeably admiring!" She climbed down from the stool she had been standing on, shaking out the curtains before folding them neatly.

"How did you know?" he wondered.

She looked at him, unable to help the lurching of her heart at the sweet-sad look on his face. "Oh, Henri, does that matter? I was hurt because you did not even bother to send me a note, to let me know that you were not coming. I sat for over two hours at the fair waiting for you yesterday!"

"Ah, sweeting, my name sounds like music on those sweet lips of yours," he said, ignoring her words. "You cannot imagine how bovine those daughters of Monsieur Linot looked when I compared them to you. Dearest Aimee, I simply must have you all to myself one day!" he said, coming toward her to take one of her hands. "Would you consent to meet me next Sunday at the same place?"

Aimee gazed at him, unbelieving. How could he have the gall to ask her that? And yet, he seemed so sincere, so sweet, she thought, feeling her anger slowly evaporating. After all, was it his fault that his mother was so determined to make a match for him? No! She smiled, astonished all over again at the charm in his answering smile. She felt a strong urge to hold him close against her and somehow protect him from a mother who really didn't understand him.

"All right, I will meet you next Sunday." She sighed, hoping she was not making another stupid mistake. She wanted to tell him that if he didn't make the appointed time next Sunday, he would not have another chance, but he looked so pleased that she truly wondered if she would not forgive him all over again.

Thereafter, they met every Sunday in the same place. Aimee found herself completely content to remain in his company for as long as possible, listening to the words that fell from his lips like gemstones, every one of them filled with a fascinating intelligence, she thought. He held her hand while they sat across from each other in the café, eating and drinking nothing half the time as they drank in each other's words. Aimee found herself anticipating Sundays, feeling disappointed when he told her he could not make it because of some commitment. She began to feel horribly jealous of his visits to the home of the three Linot daughters, wondering what they looked like, which one of them he liked the best. She could barely sleep on Saturday nights, so anxious was she for the next day to bode well for their meeting.

Rosine, unable not to notice the change in her friend, tried talking to her about it, surprised when Aimee refused to divulge who it was she met every Sunday. Curiously, Rosine asked if it was Lucian Napier, and Aimee, looking away from her and biting her lip, nodded her head, deducing that it was much easier to let Rosine think it was Lucian Napier, rather than have her find out it was Henri de Brueys.

The summer months passed too quickly for Aimee as she became more and more caught up in the magical web of first love. She looked forward to each little word, however casual, that Henri would say to her in the house, each little touch that he could get away with: a hand on her arm, a passing touch when he handed her a plate or a piece of fabric. Breathlessly, she would feel her skin tingle where their flesh touched and wondered if Henri felt it, too.

Finally, there came the day that Henri kissed her, a sweet, gentle kiss that made her heartbeat speed up and caused conflicting emotions inside her—one part of her truly happy with that kiss, and another part of her wanting more than just that. It frightened her to think how much she loved him. She asked him ten times a day if he loved her, too, and he would always answer yes. Then why, she would demand, must he continue his visits to the Linot home? He would sigh and look away from her, touching her arm and telling her how much he wished his father and mother did not demand them from him. But demand them they did, and he had little choice but to obey, since he depended on his father for his income. The admission surprised Aimee, for she never thought of money in terms of how important it might become to their intensifying relationship. However, she told herself, she was lucky to have Henri thinking of it, a trait he must have inherited from his father's practical bourgeois nature.

She told Henri of her background, hesitantly at first, but as he insisted on hearing it, she related her early years at Castle du Beautreillis, her freedom with her brothers, and the unusual way she'd been brought up for an aristocrat. She had not liked to use the word around Henri, but he liked to hear her say it, he told her, holding her close and kissing her soundly. Bit by bit, she related the rest of her story, her father's death, her journey to Paris with her brother, and the embarrassing part of her life when she had stooped to thievery to put bread into her mouth. Henri had been gentle with her, wiping the tears from her cheeks and telling her he understood, that he didn't mind in the least and could certainly understand why she had done what she had.

Aimee basked in his adoration. Her cheeks seemed rosier, her eyes more sparkling, her laugh huskier as each day she fell more and more under his spell. She even allowed herself to think that one day they would marry. The idea, once implanted in her mind, would not leave her and she would agonize about it at night, knowing the obstacles were nearly insurmountable, beginning with his mother's sure objections and ending with the fact that neither of them had much money of their own.

Suddenly, it was the end of August and Aimee realized that, very soon, Henri would have to leave Paris to go back to the university in Toulon. Her heart ached at the thought of the long separation, for he would not come home, except for Christmas. She wondered how she could bear to be away from him for such a long time, without his kisses and embraces that made life seem so much more bearable.

Henri, too, expressed his need for her. They were sitting at their favorite café one afternoon, looking into each other's eyes almost fearfully as they realized he would be leaving in less than a week. Aimee was hard put not to give vent to the tears that were threatening to spill down her cheeks. Tenderly, Henri reached over to wipe her eyes with his handkerchief, causing the floodgates to burst as Aimee sobbed uncontrollably.

When she had recovered a little, he urged her to drink a little wine to steady her nerves. "My poor Aimee," he said. "You have come to mean so much to me. I do love you, you know. I only wish that I were done with my education and that I wasn't obliged to be leaving you, my dearest."

She nodded. "I wish I could come with you, Henri," she said, knowing it was impossible. "You know you shall carry my heart with you while you're gone."

"And you, mine."

They sat silently until Aimee saw the shadows beginning to lengthen outside. "We must get back," she said gently. "I'll go along and you come later."

"Not yet," he begged. "Can't we be together a little longer?" He looked about the room, noting the wooden staircase running to the second floor, where rooms could be rented. "Come upstairs with me, my heart," he whispered to her, holding her hands tightly. "You know how much I want you, my dearest!"

Aimee shrank back a little at what he was asking of her. God, she loved him so much, but this! She felt herself trembling at the idea of going to bed with him. She knew, instinctively, that he would be gentle with her, that he would be patient and caring and loving. But still her heart trembled and fear seized her at the notion. And yet, she stared at his beloved face and saw the pleading in those dark eyes. Could she refuse him if she loved him?

"Oh, Henri, I do love you, you know that!" she told him passionately. "But—"

"You will not let me have all of you?" he finished, unable to hide his disappointment. His mouth turned down and he disengaged his hands from hers. "I suppose I cannot blame you. What have I to offer you? An unsure future, at best. I cannot even promise to marry you, my love, for we both know all the obstacles that stand in our way." He bent his head and she thought she heard him weeping.

"Dearest Henri, you are the gentlest soul I have ever known," she said softly, reaching out to touch his dark curls. "But don't rush me in this. We still have time—and then, perhaps, I will be able to grant you what you request of me." She thrilled at the passionate look he gave her, her dark eyes eagerly passing over her form, as though anticipating the delights he would find in her.

"My dear, I shall hardly know what to do until next Sunday!" he replied, taking her hands once more and squeezing them.

All that week, Aimee hardly knew what to do. She wavered continuously between giving herself to him and holding back that last precious gift. So caught up was she in her dilemma that she finally asked Rosine for advice, not knowing who else to turn to. The other girl looked at her curiously. "You mean," she asked her slyly, "you've not given up your maidenhead yet? With all the sighs and cowlike looks you've been giving everyone, I would have thought for sure you were head over heels in love with the man!"

"I am, I am!" Aimee sighed. "But he's left the choice to me and—"

"Left the choice to you?" Rosine finished curiously. "Why, that's something I never would have figured from a man like Lucian Napier. You'll pardon me for saying, my dear, but he seems the type of man who takes what he wants—with or without your permission." She smiled smugly. "Personally, I like that way much better; you don't have to fret so about making the right choice when it's taken away from you like that."

Aimee nodded, wishing she could confide in Rosine, but still finding she could not quite trust anyone else with the truth of her love. She had no doubt that the other girl was right insofar as Lucian Napier was concerned. Most likely, he carried little regard for the feelings of his paramours. If they didn't do his bidding, out they'd go! She smiled thinking of her gentle, sensitive Henri. How different he was from that swaggering rogue whose eyes raked over a woman as though disrobing her in broad daylight! Her Henri was much too caring and loving to do such a thing. Her heart turned over, remembering the look on his face when she had told him she would give him her answer this Sunday— tomorrow!

Later that day, she listened for Henri returning home with his father. They had gone down to the latter's business offices and then had stopped at the Linots' for a few glasses of wine. Aimee burned at the thought of the Linot females making over *her* Henri! But, of course, he had told her often enough how unlovely they were. When she heard him and his father returning, she hurried to the door to open it.

To her surprise, they had another man and a young girl with them. Aimee stared for a moment at the group, before their curious gazes made her remember what she was about. Hesitantly, she widened the door, staring frankly at the pretty face of the girl, whose blue eyes stared back at her as though wondering if she was demented.

"Aimee, you are feeling all right?" Monsieur de Brueys questioned politely. "Please tell cook we'll have two more for supper tonight—Monsieur Linot and his daughter Clarisse."

Aimee's eyes skidded back and forth between the girl and Henri's flushed face.

"Henri?" Clarisse questioned uncertainly, holding her hand out for Henri to take in order to escort her in.

For the space of a heartbeat, Henri hesitated. Then, without a word, he gave her his arm and brought her into the house, leaving Aimee standing at the door, watching them, a stricken expression on her face. Gathering her wits about her, she closed the door mechanically and went to tell Lila of the additional guests for dinner. All that evening she worked like an automaton, although she burned to speak alone with Henri.

On the other hand, the guests were quite gay. Monsieur and Madame de Brueys were in hearty moods while Clarisse gazed at Henri with undisguised admiration. Aimee watched her spitefully, noting the limpid gaze she bestowed on *her* love, and wished a thunderbolt might strike her at any moment. She could not believe Henri's treachery, did not wish to think that he had only been toying with her heart. Certainly he was not capable of such betrayal! She warmed herself with memories of their meetings, of sharing dinners together at the café, of looking into each other's eyes and realizing how much they cared for each other. And yet, as time wore on, she could see Henri responding to the look in Clarisse's eyes.

After dinner, both fathers retired to Monsieur de Brueys's study, while Madame de Brueys tactfully allowed the couple a few moments together. Clearing the dishes from the table, Aimee shot Henri a bitter look, which he intercepted. His cheeks grew ruddy and he looked, for a moment, quite miserable, appealing to her with his dark eyes. Aimee turned away from him, no longer able to bear the sight of him with Clarisse Linot.

Finally, the evening wore to a close and Monsieur Linot and his daughter said their good-byes. Aimee watched them leave and closed her eyes as she leaned against the door. She opened them, hearing Henri's step close by. Their eyes met and she saw misery in his as well as a certain acceptance that nearly broke her heart. Hesitantly, she started to walk to him, not knowing what to say. But whatever she might have said was broken up by the appearance of his mother. For a breathless second, Madame de Brueys studied the pair, her cheeks slowly reddening and her brows coming down over her eyes. There was no doubt that she could guess there was something between her son and this servant wench. Nevertheless, Aimee was surprised when she said nothing.

"Good night, Henri," she said lightly, giving him a motherly kiss. "I hope you realize what this marriage means for your future," she added, giving Aimee a vicious look. Then, as she climbed the stairs, she called out, "You are coming up, aren't you, Henri?"

Aimee watched dully as he dutifully followed his mother up the stairs, wishing he had more backbone when it came to resisting his mother's commands. Close on his heels, Monsieur de Brueys came out into the foyer, wishing Aimee a pleasant goodnight in his usual absentminded way. Aimee watched them for a moment before turning away.

The next morning, she was up at her usual early time, although her heart was not in her work. She recalled that today was Sunday—she was to have given Henri his answer today. She laughed mirthlessly to herself, thinking how very lucky she was to have seen the machinations of his parents last night insofar as his marriage was concerned. She would certainly have given herself to Henri this afternoon, given herself to him freely and lovingly. She shuddered now at the thought, hating herself for being so foolish.

"Aimee, wait!"

Aimee hurried away, not wanting to hear any more lies from the lips of her beloved. The pain in her heart was already too great to bear any more hurt. But Henri seemed determined to speak with her and caught up with her, holding her arm to detain her.

"Aimee, please, let me explain," he pleaded.

"You don't have to explain!" she said, turning around to tear into him. "I remember what you told me—that you couldn't promise me marriage, but somehow I didn't think that you meant for me to be your mistress! How could you, Henri? Leading me on, making me think you were going to find a way for us to be together!"

He shook his head. "Please, Aimee, I do love you! I would give anything if it were possible for me to marry you—but it isn't! My parents and Monsieur Linot have already made the arrangements for me to marry Clarisse as soon as this last term is out."

"But you knew all along that the arrangements were being made!" Aimee accused him bitterly. "You cannot expect me to believe that they were kept secret from you!"

His silence was damning and Aimee felt bile rising in her throat, the bitter taste of betrayal. "Leave me alone," she said listlessly. "I don't want to talk with you now."

He squeezed her hand. "My dearest, my heart will always be

yours. When I return from the university, perhaps things will have changed. Perhaps Clarisse will receive a better offer from someone else. She's a pretty enough girl, and I'm sure she would have no trouble finding someone to marry her."

This last admission was like an arrow piercing Aimee's heart; it hurt worse than anything else. Taking her hand from Henri's, she spun around on her heel and stalked away, wishing the floor would swallow her up. She was not to get far, though, before Marisa, Madame de Brueys's lady's maid, caught up with her and requested for her to come to Madame de Brueys's dressing room.

Once arrived there, Marisa took her leave, shutting the door, leaving Aimee to face Madame de Brueys alone. If there had been any doubt that she knew about the relationship between her son and Aimee, it was dispelled quickly as the woman came directly to the point.

"You and my son," she said, gazing into the mirror, her eyes on Aimee's reflection, "have behaved . . . indiscreetly, Aimee."

Aimee stood silently, so much in pain she didn't have the heart to defend herself. What was there to defend? It was the truth.

Madame de Brueys turned around and her eyes were dark and bitter, showing no pity as she gazed at the slender, lovely girl before her. "It does not matter to me whether my son led you on, or if you enticed him. The fact is that I cannot have this sort of thing in my household. I believe I warned you about staying away from Henri." Her eyes flicked over the girl's face. "I know you are quite, quite lovely, Aimee, and I feared that Henri might be taken with you, but I suppose I thought your background would save you from such behavior as you have displayed." She stood up, fingering one of the boxes on her table. "Of course, you realize that I must dismiss you from this position."

Aimee swallowed, trying not to think of the workhouse.

"Have you . . . you are not . . . pregnant, are you?" Madame de Brueys asked with difficulty, avoiding the girl's eyes.

"No!" The word came out in a rush as Aimee crimsoned at the idea.

"Good!" Madame de Brueys lifted her eyes to Aimee's. "I do not think it is necessary to inform any of the staff about this, nor do I intend to tell my husband. You will pack whatever clothing you have upstairs—and you will leave, telling no one! Do you understand me?"

Aimee looked at the woman curiously. "You are not sending me back to the workhouse, madame?"

"I should like to very much," Madame de Brueys ground out bitterly, "but because of the delicacy of the marriage contract we are negotiating with Monsieur Linot, I cannot afford to make public my reasons for letting you go. The workhouse would demand an investigation, facts would be discovered, my son humiliated—and the marriage would be off."

"What if I refuse to leave?" Aimee asked, watching the woman go livid.

"You *must* leave!" she cried. "Do you think I want to risk a continuation of this affair? Eventually, you *would* get pregnant! And do you think," she asked cunningly, "that my son would ever marry you? Of course not! Henri may be stupid in his personal affairs, but he does have a good head for business. He knows where his future lies. He would set you up as his mistress if you begged him for that, but he would never marry you. Surely, a young woman of your aristocratic background would never settle for such an offer?" she asked, appealing to Aimee's pride with a spider's wiliness.

Aimee realized that she would not. "I believed that I loved your son, madame," she said with quiet dignity. "I believed that he returned that love—and for many weeks now we have been happy together. But you are right, I do not want to come second in his heart."

Madame de Brueys winced at the words, then straightened as she realized the girl was accepting her terms—to leave without a word, to disappear into the streets of Paris, to allow her son his richer destiny with Clarisse Linot. She did not dwell on the fact that she was actually turning the girl out with no employment, no references, and very little money. She only wanted to be rid of her—and if the girl did not ask for anything, she would not offer it.

"I will go upstairs and pack my things," Aimee said, going to the door to open it. "And you needn't worry, madame, I will never trouble you again!"

Madame de Brueys sniffed disdainfully as Aimee exited.

Aimee hurried upstairs, packed her things in a small cloth case, then hurried back downstairs. She wanted to avoid any questions from Lila and Rosine, so she took the front way out, recalling with some irony how Monsieur de Brueys had first told her that no servants could use the front door. Well, she was no longer a servant of the de Brueys household. Madame de Brueys would tear up the legal documents binding her to the family, therefore giving up any responsibility for her. It was enough, Aimee thought.

As she plunged into the sunny street in front of the house, she heard her name being called and turned automatically, her heart constricting when she saw Henri running up to her, out of breath, his face flushed.

"Aimee, did you think I would let you leave without saying good-bye?" he wondered, looking truly heartbroken.

Aimee marveled at his powers of deception. "Good-bye, then, Henri," she said swiftly, turning away from him purposefully.

"Dearest, is that all?" he asked her, catching up once more and looking at her hopefully. "You can say good-bye like that and leave me alone?"

"You have left me alone," she said resolutely. "Because of your fickle attentions I have lost my employment and must now live as well as I can. I do not pity you, Henri, nor do I despise you. I just want you to leave me alone." Her heart felt as though it were cracking into little pieces. A harsh ending to a young girl's first passion.

"But, Aimee, please—"

"Good-bye, Henri!"

Aimee turned away and hurried off, but not before he caught her once more. "Here—at least let me give you this," he told her, placing a bag of coins in her hand. "There are fifty livres in there. It was the best I could do, and I knew my mother would not give you anything. With what you have saved I should think it will keep you up until you can find some other employment. Believe me, Aimee, I wish things could have been otherwise." He looked at her solemnly, his dark eyes so sincere that she almost believed him. "I will always remember you, my darling," he said almost reverently, and quickly, before she could protest, he bent and kissed her lingeringly.

Tearing herself away from him, turning swiftly so he could not see the tears in her eyes, she headed down the street, never turning back. She would not allow herself to think of him now; she would need all her strength and all her wits about her, she thought, as she plunged back into the city of Paris.

15

•—•—•—•—•

"Hola, wench! Look here and come buy a dainty for those lovely lips of yours!" a hawker shouted.

Another smiled widely. "A pair of stockings, girl, for only one hundred livres!"

"No, buy here, wench! Genuine Marseilles soap. Only forty livres!"

Aimee walked along the Pont Neuf, immune to the cries of the vendors, her thoughts far away as she braced herself against a chill wind. Winter had come early to Paris, and although it was only October, it felt more like December, as she tugged her woollen shawl tighter about her shoulders and bent her head forward, trying not to think of the fact that her shoes had holes in them and her feet were nearly freezing in the rain puddles along the bridge.

Ever since that day almost two months before when she had left the employ of the de Brueys family, she had been unable to find permanent work. She had no references to offer suspicious ladies who needed chambermaids. She didn't know how to sew cloth for the seamstress who needed an extra apprentice to help her. Occasionally, she would put in a few hours' work for the flower sellers, bundling up bunches of flowers into little nosegays to sell to the passing populace. But now that the cold had arrived, the flower sellers had packed up, some heading south and others retiring for the winter into the snug, little houses off the rue Saint-Marcel.

Aimee tried not to think of where she was going to live once the last of her money was spent. That was why she didn't buy herself new shoes; she must hoard every last livre for a roof over her head and a fire to warm her at night. She had thought of going back to her aunt, but dismissed the idea almost immediately. Aunt Hortense wanted nothing to do with her. She would not allow her in her house again after what had happened the last time. Besides, it was too much for Aimee to have to swallow her pride and go to beg Aunt Hortense for shelter. She would exist as well as she could, hoping that the next day would bring a chance at employment.

Wearily, she realized the sun was going down and she would have to return to the miserable boardinghouse where her rooms were currently located. The house was in a section of Paris called the Montmartre, where many of the poorer middle class lived. For the most part, the women who stayed in her boardinghouse were good people, many of them fallen on hard times like Aimee. Some were even former aristocrats whose husbands had been sent to the guillotine during the height of the revolutionary fervor. Now that some aristocrats were once again coming into favor, many of them were returning to their homes that had been sealed off by the government, but for these husbandless women, there was no chance at hope, for it was as though they no longer existed. The government did not wish to hear their tale of woe, nor did they want to become responsible for them. They needed no more "charity cases" and refused to see them.

Aimee thought of their desperate circumstances, realizing they were actually worse off than she, for they had absolutely no skills to gain employment. Some halfheartedly mended shirts and stockings for a living; others hired themselves out as music teachers, voice teachers, or governesses. So lost in her thoughts was she that Aimee didn't see the tall figure step out in front of her as she rounded a corner until she'd bumped into him. As two strong hands came out to steady her, Aimee felt a fleeting hope that it might be Henri, having come after her to rescue her after all. But she cruelly crushed the hope, realizing that Henri was back at Toulon, learning how to be a businessman while his father signed the legal documents that would cement the marriage between him and Clarisse when he returned to Paris.

She shook away the proffered hands and murmured an apology before going on, not even bothering to look up to see the identity of the man. Still, somewhere in her subconscious she became aware of the steady rhythm of footsteps matching hers exactly. Someone was following her! Careful not to look around, she hurried her steps, checking the sign marker to make sure she was not too far from her boardinghouse. The steps behind her increased as hers did, and by the time she arrived at the building she was nearly breathless, the sharp wind stabbing at her lungs as she took in deep breaths to steady her.

"Aimee, why do you insist on running away from me?" came the deeply amused voice behind her, which she recognized instantly.

Whirling around, she saw the familiar blue eyes and sable-dark hair of Lucian Napier, a smile creasing his lips as he returned her stare. "Why! Why, how dare you scare me as you did!" she accused him, anger bubbling up her throat. "Why are you following me?"

"I wanted to talk to you," he answered calmly, noting the green eyes hardening into twin emeralds. "Don't be upset. I have good news for you—"

"I'm surprised to see you," Aimee cut in huffily. "Although, truly, the way you step in and out of my life, I suppose I shouldn't be. At any rate, I don't want you to feel responsible for me!"

He laughed. "I don't feel responsible for you, my dear, but I must admit to a certain concern for you that enables me to keep up on your whereabouts." He looked about him, then noted how she was hugging her arms and stamping her feet to keep warm. "But can't we go inside now? It's too cold to continue our conversation out here. I won't have you freezing into a statue on me!"

"Inside!" Aimee exclaimed with horror. "Monsieur, you don't understand. This is not my home, but a boardinghouse where I rent a room for my own use. I cannot simply bring you into the parlor and offer you tea!"

His eyes showed his amusement. "Of course, I know it's a boardinghouse. But don't young women like yourself have gentlemen up to their rooms all the time? What could be so unusual about my coming in with you?"

Aimee stiffened, her already red-with-cold cheeks crimsoning. "Perhaps not unusual for the kind of company *you* keep, monsieur!" she replied scathingly. "But, certainly, I am not used to having gentlemen up to my room!"

He smiled disarmingly. "Forgive me, Aimee. I only meant that no one would question the fact that I accompany you to your room. I'm sure many of them have had gentlemen callers in, whether brothers or friends or . . . anything else," he ended with a sardonic look that enraged her.

"Will you just say what you have to say and get along?" she asked him bitingly. "I can assure you, I never expected to see you again, and, now that you're here, I would appreciate your going right back out of my life!"

"Impossible!" he returned amiably, leaning against the wall as though he had all day, and, indeed, Aimee thought with fury, he was probably better insulated against the cold than she with his top boots and the great heavy coat he was wearing. Meanwhile, she would probably catch pneumonia, the scourge of the poor in winter.

Clenching her teeth, she glared at him, as icy as the north wind, then nodded. "All right, you may come in for a time, monsieur. But I would hope you manage to make your visit as brief as possible! You can relay your news to me—and go!"

He bowed, holding the door open as she went inside. Aimee felt embarrassed as she looked at the dirty hallway, the litter on the stairs. Why was it that he always saw her at her worst? she wondered, recalling the last time she had seen him, at the dance hall. Her cheeks colored at the memory. They walked up six flights of stairs, up to the top floor, where the brisk wind could be heard quite clearly howling under the eaves. Unlocking the door to her room, Aimee searched it quickly, relieved that she had remembered to straighten it up before her departure earlier that morning. Behind her, she heard him walk in and close the door.

She took off her wrap, unconsciously straightening her coiffure, wondering how woefully windblown it had become while she was outside. She wished she had a mirror to see how she looked, but shrugged suddenly, realizing it didn't matter how she looked for Lucian Napier. She hoped he would stay for only a very brief time.

Lucian Napier surveyed the little room casually. He noted the shabbiness of the two chairs pulled up to a small wooden table near the window, and the narrow bed brought as close to the fireplace as possible. Except for a few odds and ends, there was nothing else, not even a rug for the floor, which he suspected would be freezing in winter. Carefully, knowing her pride, he took off his coat and draped it over the end of the bed, setting his hat beside it.

"Can I light the fire for you?" he asked, seeing there were logs in the fireplace, probably in preparation for this evening.

It was on the tip of Aimee's tongue to tell him no, for those logs were all she could use for the rest of the night. She had to stick to a quota or she would be out before she knew it. But her pride refused to allow her to be humbled in front of him, and she nodded airily.

"Pity you don't have coffee," he murmured, seeing no sign of kitchen utensils about the room. Her money must be going fast, he thought, if she had to eat out every day. For boiled beef and broth, it would cost at least seven hundred francs in assignats a week. He wondered how close she was to being penniless.

Aimee watched him straighten up after he'd gotten the fire going, trying to imagine Henri standing there instead. Was this how it would have been had they run off and gotten married, despite his parents' protests? She had to admit the idea held no appeal for her. Having been away from him for two months, she had had to face the fact that Henri was a weak man, and she could never have been happy with him.

Wordlessly, she watched as he brought over the two chairs next to the table so that the two of them could sit by the fire. With a sigh, she sank into one of the chairs. Despite Lucian's presence she was determined to make good use of the fire. After removing her shoes, she stretched her naked feet out toward the flames, wriggling her toes in appreciation.

Lucian watched her and felt a stirring of emotion deep inside himself. Was it the sight of those poor, naked feet? he wondered. Or something else? At any rate, he realized he must tell her the news he had, or she would soon turn once again into the suspicious, emerald-eyed hoyden he had met below. He gazed at the smooth white column of her throat for a moment before beginning.

"I have been trying to find you for over a month. It seems you don't like to stay in one place too long. Of course, I knew that you were the serving maid for the de Brueys household, and one day I came to call on you and was informed by the girl I seem to recall was your companion at the dance hall that you had disappeared."

"Disappeared?"

"That was her word," he returned casually. "She told me that you had simply up and left one day without telling anyone—even your best friend. She seemed quite put out by that and told me in no uncertain terms that you were among the most ungrateful women who ever walked the face of the earth."

Aimee bit her lip. Of course, she wouldn't have expected Madame de Brueys or her son to tell the truth about her departure. But then she shrugged. Perhaps it was better this way. It seemed as each chapter of her life ended, she would turn the page and everyone in the last chapter would be gone—except one, she realized, gazing over at Lucian Napier, whose dark blue eyes seemed lit by the flames from the fire. How funny that this man should linger from her past! She felt herself caught in his blue-fire gaze as though she were helpless to look away. Then, recovering, she turned her eyes away from his, wondering at the strange feeling that had come over her.

"At any rate, I could get nothing out of her as far as your present whereabouts was concerned, so I left," he went on, unaware of a sudden, unforeseen notion that he wanted to kiss her. The thought surprised him utterly, for he had never really thought of this young woman in those terms before. Of course, it could be partially a feeling of pity, he told himself, for certainly she looked a little of the termagant with her wind-tousled hair and the tired shadows under her eyes.

"How did you find me?" she asked, leaning back in her chair and closing her eyes, letting the warmth of the fire make her drowsy. Somehow, she was not alarmed at finding herself alone with Lucian Napier. She felt comfortable with him, as though she had known him for a long time. Growing more and more relaxed, she was pleasantly drifting through space, listening to the sound of his voice.

Lucian watched the long lashes closing over the magnificent emerald of her eyes, saw the cheeks flushed with heat, and realized she was about to fall asleep. Her breathing grew more regular and he watched the rise and fall of her breasts beneath the dark green broadcloth of her gown. The dress, he decided, would not be much help against the real cold of winter, for it was too lightweight to keep her really warm. He remembered seeing her in the same dress at the theater when he had gotten reacquainted with her.

Contentedly, he leaned back in his own chair, his mind not on the young woman beside him, but on the work that lay ahead of him. Employed by the French government, it was Lucian Napier's job to keep a finger in every branch of it. As a master spy himself, he must watch closely the activities of other known spies, especially those of the enemies of France. His work took him to other parts of the country, but most of it was confined to Paris, where the most secret activity transpired. He had always worked for the military, ever since he could remember being a young man in his middle teens, listening to his father telling about his exploits as a soldier of France. His mother had been an American, and he had traveled to that new country just after their own Revolutionary War, marveling at the industry of the people and the splendor of their land. He sighed unintentionally, recalling his meeting with General George Washington, who had been elected President of the new United States of America.

Then he shook his head. Now was not the time to think about that part of his life. He was involved in keeping a close watch on the immigration of the former emigrés back to France from England and Austria. They were seeping in gradually through the borders, taking care not to draw attention to themselves. Still the government feared them, feared that they might still try to instigate a royalist insurrection, putting the former King's nephew on the throne now that the Dauphin had died.

One of the wiliest of those emigrés had only just returned from exile in England in September. Charles Maurice de Talleyrand-Périgord, an aristocrat by birth, but a revolutionist at heart, or so he liked to proclaim, was back in Paris and Lucian was trying to find out what his motives were. He knew almost all there was to know about the man, who, at forty-two, was fourteen years older than he and probably much more cunning. Lucian knew that he had been raised in the country surrounding Paris, for his family, though aristocratic, was poor. He had acquired his deformed right foot when he was a baby and a wet nurse had not been watchful, allowing him to fall off a table. The man still walked with a slight limp and made good use of walking canes, although that had never seemed to stop the ladies from clustering around him. Even when he had been ordained Bishop of Autun, before the revolution, he had had several mistresses and many bastard offspring. Once the revolution had come, he had been created a "constitutional" bishop under the new Civil Constitution of the Clergy. When things began to get a bit hot for him in Paris, he arranged to have himself sent on a diplomatic mission to London, later becoming an emigré when it was time to return to Paris. And now he had returned, four years later, and Barras was proposing that he be appointed Minister of Foreign Relations.

Lucian shook his head. The wily Talleyrand was maneuvering for just such a position ever since his return to Paris, and Lucian didn't quite trust his reasons. He knew for a fact that Talleyrand liked the English—but just how much he liked them, he wasn't sure. Did he like them well enough to sell French secrets to them? Lucian shrugged. With Fouché's network of spies, he would find out soon enough.

He sighed ruefully, glancing over at the sleeping girl beside him. With all this on his mind, he surprised himself by keeping tabs on her. There was really nothing special about her. She, like Talleyrand, was born a poor aristocrat, had come to Paris on a mission of vengeance after her family had all been killed, had become a pickpocket to earn a living, and was now barely making ends meet after being thrown out of the de Brueys household. Still, why did he feel somehow responsible for her? Was it really responsibility that drove him to find her—or something else?

He looked at her objectively. Surely he had had women more beautiful than she, certainly richer, and most certainly more experienced. He was a man who had spurned the entanglements of marriage, mainly because of the dangers prevalent in his work. Having a wife and children would not have suited his life-style. He had undressed a countess while searching beneath her bed for documents that would have put her husband in prison for treason; he'd caressed the wife of a wealthy bourgeois while trying to find out what time an insurrection was being planned the following day. He wasn't necessarily proud of his duplicity, but he found that many times women were the best informers, whether because of jealousy or passion or bitterness toward their husbands or families.

This girl beside him would never understand his work, or his reasons for doing it. He felt sure she would have been outraged to think that anyone could have sex without feeling love first. He smiled at her naïveté, but felt oddly touched by it, as though it were a cool draft of water among all the hot, clinging, passionate women who had surrounded him throughout the years. Perhaps it was for this reason that he had kept up with her, had investigated all he could about her. So rare to find an innocent like her in Paris these days, he thought grimly, wondering with a certain cynicism how long it would take her to become one of those women who dispensed her favors with false smiles and coy promises. Would she sink that low? She had to eat, she had to survive! What else, in the end, waited for her, unless—

She stirred in the chair, bringing his attention back to her face. The classic profile arched toward him, the full lips parting softly with her breath. He spared a brief glance toward the bed, then caught himself. No, he wouldn't destroy her dreams, he thought resolutely. He had come to help her and then he would go. She would have to make her own life, for he could not always be there to help her.

Gently, he touched her cheek, grazing its curve with one finger. "Aimee?" He shook her softly, watching as she opened her eyes.

Aimee gazed for a long moment at the man who bent over her. She had been dreaming that she was back at Castle du Beautreillis, that her brothers and she were playing a game. She was the Queen of France and they were her subjects. The sun had been warm on her legs, she had felt freer than she had for a very long time—and happier. She felt a man's soft touch against her cheek and heard her name spoken. Was it her father's voice? Or Etienne's? Perhaps it was Henri's. She'd opened her eyes and in the firelight could see only the shadow of a face bending down to hers. Automatically, she smiled up at it, her eyes still dreamy with sleep.

Lucian caught his breath at that look. Almost kittenish, totally feminine, she drew him irresistibly forward, his hands cupping her face until his mouth could capture hers. Gently, his lips felt the texture of her mouth, molding it to his own, shaping and remolding it in an ever-increasing rhythm. He felt the response deep within himself as his body quickened at the nearness of an arresting young woman. His hands slipped from her jawline to the slim column of her throat, then down to her shoulders, where the rough cloth felt like an insult to the smooth skin beneath.

But already Aimee was reorienting herself, beginning to draw away from him. For a moment longer he held her, then released her, opening his eyes to see her own staring back at him, confusion mixed with distress in their depths. Then as he watched her, she purposely pushed all the other emotions aside and her eyes hardened into the emeralds he had seen before.

"Why did you do that?" she asked him flatly.

He looked at her trembling mouth. "Because I wanted to," he replied simply.

She drew back sharply, as though he had slapped her. "Oh, and I suppose you always take what you want, don't you, Monsieur Napier?" she asked him cuttingly. "I should have known better than to trust you in my room. You really are not the sort of gentleman on whom a lady can count."

He laughed then, breaking the tension. "But I am precisely that sort of gentleman, Aimee. I will prove it to you, in a moment."

She snorted her disbelief, then leaned down to put her shoes back on. They were still damp and she grimaced for a moment, noting at the same time that the fire needed to be stoked. She got up from the chair and poked at it a moment, glancing around to see him watching her thoughtfully.

"Well, I am waiting for proof," she reminded him, irritated that he simply sat there while she did the work.

"All right, then. Forget the kiss, Aimee—let us just say it came out of habit. Whenever I see a pair of beautiful lips such as you were presenting to me, I just naturally want to kiss them. I don't think there's a man in all of Paris who could say different."

He smiled as she was about to offer some scathing retort. "What I have to tell you will erase all your irritation about that kiss, let me assure you."

"Unless you have found a way to make money appear out of thin air, I'm not interested," Aimee said coldly, still upset and troubled that he had taken advantage of her.

"Listen to me, vixen. I have found your brother for you."

Aimee's eyes grew huge at the news. "What?" she asked, coming closer to him, knowing she would kill him if he was lying to her.

"I must admit I have taken an inordinate interest in you. At any rate, I undertook, through various connections, to find your missing brother—Etienne, I believe his name is."

"That's right," Aimee said, hope shining in her eyes now.

"It seems he has been ensconced in the Châtelet for nearly a year for attempted robbery. It seems such crimes run in your family," he said with a sardonic grin that she chose to ignore. "He was released about the time we had our first meeting in the Tuileries gardens. I suppose he went into hiding for a time, for there was no information on him after that. Now, though, he runs with a gang of former aristocrats like himself. He has been mixed up with a few break-ins on the left bank, but nothing concrete so that he could be put back into prison." He leaned closer to her. "Your brother has been walking a very thin line, my dear. You must warn him, when you see him, to be very careful."

"But when will I see him?" Aimee wondered.

"I can take you there tonight. He frequents the Brazen Bull with his fellows. He'll probably be there this evening, and you can see him then."

"But . . . why . . . why did he never get in touch with me?" Aimee wondered.

Lucian looked at her expression, knowing that doubt was warring with anger in her mind. "I don't know, my dear. Perhaps he thought you safe with your aunt; perhaps he went there to find you and your aunt told him you'd been taken away by soldiers. It would be hard for him to trace your whereabouts after your arrest. That's ground he would most likely not wish to tread on, since it would bring him too close to the authorities."

"Yes, of course, that must be it," Aimee told herself, clinging to this straw of hope, refusing to believe that her brother had simply forgotten about her. She gazed at Lucian gratefully. "Forgive me—for berating you earlier," she said haltingly. "You must understand that I—"

"I understand," he said quickly, feeling uncomfortable with her apology.

"So you will take me to the Brazen Bull tonight?" she asked him, excitement in her voice.

"If you wish."

"Yes, yes!" She stood up, her mind full of what she would say to her brother. Etienne—she would see him again at last! Together, they could make plans for the future—hadn't they both had enough of Paris? "Monsieur Napier, you have made me so happy that I can no longer begrudge you that kiss! In fact, I could kiss you again!" she chirped happily.

Lucian held up his hand as though to fend her off. "I am content with the one kiss," he assured her, his eyes crinkling with laughter. "But I beg you to call me Lucian—it sounds much more agreeable."

Aimee nodded, her eyes still sparkling. She could barely wait to see her brother, and when Lucian suggested that she should get something to eat first, she shook her head, not wanting to waste a minute before she was with Etienne.

Despite the chilly night, Aimee barely felt the cold as they hailed a carriage to take them to the Brazen Bull, a tavern located close to the Seine, a place where lighter men and dockworkers frequently went to have a quick meal and a drink before returning to their families.

By the time Lucian and Aimee arrived, it was nearly full to bursting with rowdies and giggling strumpets, not at all the kind of place Aimee would feel comfortable in if it weren't for the protection of Lucian Napier. She stared at the colorful crowd, wondering where in this mass of humanity her brother was.

"Perhaps he won't come tonight," she said to Lucian, obliged to put her lips next to his ear to make herself heard.

"No, my sources say he usually always comes here," Lucian replied, trying to see through the haze of smoke. The place was crowded and it was difficult to discern features among the blur of faces. "Does he look just like you?" he wondered, leaning down toward his companion.

Aimee nodded. "He has blond hair like mine and fair coloring, except his eyes are blue. He's very handsome," she added proudly, unable to prevent herself from saying so.

Lucian smiled to himself and continued to peruse the room. He realized, though, that standing in the center of the floor, they were making something of a spectacle of themselves, and many of the males in the room were casting suspicious glances at them.

"I think we had better find ourselves someplace to sit," he suggested to Aimee, guiding her through a maze of arms and legs to a chair. He sat down and dragged her onto his lap. At her look of amazement, he smiled wryly. "We'd best look like the rest of the customers or they might become suspicious and think we're looking for someone."

"But that's exactly what we are doing!" Aimee protested, feeling his hard thighs beneath her bottom with a sense of unease.

"Of course, but it doesn't pay to let them know. Most of them are probably wanted by the police for something. If they thought we were police, they'd be more than likely to slit our throats!" Lucian warned her. He gazed warily at the group of people surrounding the table opposite them. Thugs and cutthroats, most of them, he thought, noting the various weapons stuck in their belts and bulging out the sides of their jackets. He hugged Aimee tighter until she squealed in protest, pushing against his chest to put more distance between them. Her green eyes began to flash a warning, when suddenly they softened and her mouth formed an "oh!" of surprise.

"Etienne!" Her voice was lost in the crowd, but Lucian followed the direction of her eyes and saw a young man with untidy blond hair and a three-day growth of beard on his cheeks, sitting in a chair with a half-naked prostitute on his knees. He was drinking with about four other men, taking sips from his glass and alternately fondling the breasts of the woman on his lap.

"That's him! That's my brother!" Aimee cried, her eyes drinking in the sight of him, barely noticing the woman. "I can't believe it!" she exclaimed, tears flowing down her cheeks.

"Come along, don't make too much of a commotion," Lucian warned her, standing up as casually as he could and throwing an arm about her shoulders. "You're sure that's him?"

"Yes, yes, I would know my own brother!"

He hoped she did because this was a rough crowd and he was feeling pretty uncomfortable at some of the glances they were receiving. Slowly, they inched their way to the wooden booth where Etienne was sitting.

"Etienne!" Aimee shouted, unable to contain herself.

The young blond man turned at the sound of his name and his face registered a blank for a moment before his mouth turned upward in a smile and he stood up, carelessly dropping the whore to the floor of the tavern.

"Aimee!" He hurried toward her, enveloping her in a tight embrace.

For her part, Aimee was speechless with joy and could only cling to her brother, feeling as though a long journey was finally over. They continued to embrace until Etienne finally disengaged himself and pulled her over to the booth, where his companions were watching the scene in surprise.

"Fellows, this is my baby sister!" he announced.

For a moment, they all looked stunned. Then loud guffaws greeted his words. "Baby sister!" echoed one before breaking out into a fit of laughter.

"Sure she is," joked another.

Etienne smiled good-naturedly at their ribbing, but shook his head in all seriousness. "No, she really *is* my sister," he said. "I've not seen her since we arrived in Paris two years ago." He turned to Aimee, taking her hand. "But where have you been, Aimee?" he wondered. "What are you doing here? I thought you safe with Aunt Hortense."

"You don't know what happened?" she asked, realizing that he had not gone to Hortense's to inquire after her. Her hopes fell at his thoughtlessness. "I was arrested for pickpocketing," she told him.

Her words brought more laughter from the table. "Why, she's Etienne's sister, all right!" one of the men swore. "Already seen the inside of the jails, and only here two years!"

"Quiet!" Etienne ordered gruffly. "Tell me everything," he demanded, indicating his vacated seat in the booth.

Gingerly, Aimee stepped over the woman who was still half reclining on the floor in a drunken stupor. She eyed the man next to whom she sat with some anxiety, for, despite his apparent youth, he had a wicked look about him that boded ill for anyone who crossed his path. In fact, she realized, all of these men had that look — a look of desperation, of devil-may-care that would see them alive and spending their spoils one day, dead the next. She looked up at her brother and saw the same look on his face — and her heart despaired.

"I fell in with a boy and his gang," she explained slowly, keeping her eyes on the table. "After I was arrested for pickpocketing, I was sent to the Châtelet to be sentenced. They sent me to the workhouse, where I stayed for seven months until a merchant sponsored me. In other words, he hired me away from the workhouse, taking legal responsibility for me. I was there for the summer and then . . . I lost my position and was forced out into the streets."

Etienne looked concerned, but his first question surprised her.

"So, you're no better than I, eh? I mean, you've no money either?"

She shook her head. "I'm living in a boardinghouse in the Montmartre, but I'll soon have to vacate that, for I've very little money left."

"How did you find me?" he wondered.

"Through Lucian Napier—"

"Who?"

"Lucian Napier, the man standing—" Aimee turned to look for Lucian, but found him gone. She searched the room with her eyes, but could see no sign of him. Somehow she felt horribly desolate at finding herself in this place without him. She had been wrong to think her brother would protect her, that they could find a new future together away from Paris. From the look of him, he was in worse shape than she was, and had every intention of continuing this squalid life as long as he could. She glanced briefly at his choice of companions.

"It doesn't matter how I found you, Etienne," she said, trying to make her voice light. "Now at last we are together again."

He looked distinctly uncomfortable. "I'm glad to see you again, my sister, but surely you realize you can't stay with me." He indicated the foul-smelling room and the half-naked whore with a nod of his head. "I'd have no place to put you, Aimee, for I've really no place to call my own. I live hand to mouth, stealing what I can get, unloading barges if the pickings get too lean. I sleep in the alleys of Paris or on the bench of a tavern or in the arms of one of the whores along the river. You can't lead that kind of life."

"And you can?" she challenged him.

He shrugged and looked away from her. "I have managed these last two years."

"Rubbish!" she said angrily. "You've spent more than half that time in the Châtelet!"

He jerked his head up to stare at her, his blue eyes suspicious. "And how would you know that?" he snapped.

"I heard it," she said vaguely, not wishing to implicate Lucian, who obviously had thought better of sticking around. She wondered at his desertion of her, feeling a little sorry for herself, but angry with her brother for his totally unacceptable way of life.

"Etienne, what has happened to you, my brother?" she asked him softly. "Where is the young man I knew when we first came to Paris? What of your quest for vengeance? Do you know that I nearly had Faron in my grasp? Yes, I did! But he eluded capture and is still at large for all I know."

"Faron no longer concerns me," Etienne mumbled into his beer glass. "Vengeance is a luxury reserved for those who have the money to pay the right people to do their dirty work for them. All I'm concerned with is staying alive."

"Oh, Etienne, why can't we leave this ugly place and—"

"And do what?" he interrupted almost viciously. "Where would we go, Aimee? Back to Orléans, back to a castle that's a shambles, back to milking cows and gathering chickens' eggs?" He shook his head fiercely. "Don't be stupid, little sister. There'll be no more of that for me."

"So what will you do? Continue with this life until you're dead of the drink or the pox or a policeman's sword in your back?" Aimee pleaded, unaware of the tears on her cheeks. "Etienne, I know you are good and kind and brave and strong. You can't go on living like this—unless your heart is truly dead!"

"Then it *is* dead!" Etienne threw at her, draining the last of his beer and bellowing for another. He looked at her stricken face and relented a little. "I'm sorry, chick, but what else is there? I have no money, and no means of making any more than I need to survive. What hope is there for us?"

"There must be something you could do—something that would keep you out of places like this," she said, her eyes intense.

He sighed and his blue eyes looked weary. "Aimee, I don't know. I just don't know. I love you, you know that, but I don't know what I can do to help you now. My friends and I, we get on by the skin of our teeth. We can't afford a female slowing us up, making us vulnerable. You do understand, don't you?"

She shook her head. "No! Etienne, you were never this stupid before! What has happened? Have you dowsed your brain in so much liquor you can no longer think?" She stared at him hard, wiping the tears from her cheeks, "Surely you can think of something!"

One of his companions hiccoughed and leaned forward. "Yes, little pullet, we've got lots of ideas," he said sarcastically. "We've thought of inciting a riot and putting your brother up as the new King. We've thought of selling secrets to England and lining our pockets with gold. We've even thought of selling our souls to the devil—but he wouldn't have them on a platter!" He laughed drunkenly.

"He already has them, you fool!" Aimee retorted, not ready to back down even when he fixed her with a glaring stare.

"Hey! What about our idea of working out in the country?" one of the others asked, winking broadly at Etienne. "You know, our little scheme to get rich quick?"

Etienne laughed. "Hey! That's just the thing, Pierre." He seemed to mull over the idea for a moment. "I like it more and more. Pierre's right," he told the others, "it's time to get off our lazy backsides and do some work to earn some money!"

Aimee felt excited at this positive transformation and eagerly asked her brother what it was he had in mind. Etienne gave her a comical look, tilting his head and pursing his lips as though imparting a secret.

"Why, we've hatched a scheme to become highwaymen, little sister!" he whispered into her face. "Ha! We'll rob the rich and give to the poor—our poor! There's many who can waylay a weary traveler on the road from Orléans to Paris and come away with riches! These fat, pompous merchants who travel on business with large sums of money on their persons are ridiculously easy to rob!"

Aimee's eyes widened at her brother's suggestion. "But, Etienne, highwaymen, when they are caught, are always hanged!" She paled at the thought of her brother swinging from a gibbet.

"No, no! We've been thinking on this for some time, little sister. It just took a timely appearance from you to set the wheels in motion. By God, we'll do it!" he cried, raising his glass for a toast with those around the table. He looked down at his sister, seeing her white face, her rather woebegone look—and his brotherly heart was touched.

"Don't worry, my dearest," he begged her. "Come, I'll take you back to your rooms. If you've a fire and enough space, perhaps you could put me up for the night. I'll be happy to sleep on the floor. Then we can talk in the morning."

Aimee nodded, realizing how very tired she suddenly felt. So much had happened since this afternoon, she truly felt overwhelmed by it all. She tried to keep telling herself that everything would be all right, that somehow she and her brother would get through this trying period and come out on top—but doubt lingered in her mind and her heart was heavy as she felt her brother's arm on her shoulders. Gone was her playmate of childhood; in his place was a man, old before his time, laughing in the teeth of disaster, snubbing his nose at the devil. She shuddered to think that the demon was only biding his time before he gathered in the chips.

16

•—■—•—■—•

Aimee blew on her fingers to keep them warm beneath the woollen mitts, then leaned over to quiet her horse as it pranced nervously in the road, its ears pricked forward and its nostrils blowing. She looked up to search the stretch of road ahead, watching for a coach or a group of travelers on their way to Paris on the road from Orléans. She touched the scarf wound around the lower half of her face and pulled the brim of her untidy hat down lower over her eyes so that her visage was almost totally hidden from view. It was not because of the chill March wind that she was grateful for the covering, but because in the last months of serving as lookout for her brother's gang of highwaymen, she had learned that disguise was vital to the operation.

Once put on the course of an idea, Etienne never gave up on it until it had reached fruition. He and his four companions, all former aristocrats with chips on their shoulders, decided that highway robbery would be nothing more than child's play. After surviving for two years in Paris, Etienne felt he was ready for any challenge, and this sort of adventure was exactly the kind of thing that appealed to him. They had made their plans in the small room that Aimee rented in Montmartre, throwing out some ideas, revising others. Aimee realized that this was something they had obviously already discussed and, though she hated the idea of lawlessness attached to it, she felt duty-bound to lend a voice of reason to the proceedings.

She pressured her brother on the trustworthiness of his four comrades, wondering aloud at how they would react in a pinch. Would they turn tail and run, or would they fight along-side their captain? Etienne assured her that all four of them were gentlemen and that they all could be trusted. Every one of them hated the government in power—and that hatred spread to the bourgeoisie who had seen their fathers and mothers sent to the guillotine. It was time to be repaid for the miseries they had endured.

Aimee knew very little else about the other four men; only

their first names were known to her and she wished it that way. If she should ever be captured, she would not, under any means of interrogation, reveal their identities. And so, Pierre, Joseph, Paul, and Jean became her little family.

At first she had refused to be a party to the actual robberies, content to wait for the gang at a small cottage they had found to be abandoned and used as their hideout. She spent her time cooking their meals, washing their laundry—being indispensable, as she laughingly pointed out.

But as the small band graduated from attacking lone travelers and groups of fewer than three or four, to robbing coaches and mail vehicles, they had needed extra help in their mission. Reluctantly, Aimee had found herself drawn into the actual robberies, acting as lookout to see what coaches were coming while the others stayed low behind trees and undergrowth. Many times, too, she kept her position while the robbery was being committed, signaling with loud whistles should she see anyone else on the road. Twice already she had saved the day by these tactics, for being involved with the fleecing of the passengers, the gang would have been ill-prepared for a contingent of soldiers coming through. After both these incidents, Aimee had begged her brother to stop this adventure, telling him the risks were becoming too great, but Etienne had laughed and shaken his head, chucking her beneath the chin and comforting her with the thought that they would stop "someday," after they'd gathered enough money to live comfortably.

Aimee thought many times that that day had come, for after five months of highway robbery there was quite a stash set aside for each man, as well as a substantial amount for Aimee. She received as much as each man, even though she did not risk physical harm as they did. Her greatest contribution was in knowing the right contacts in Paris where they could exchange their items for money—not the paper assignats that had finally been repudiated by the government, but golden louis d'or and livres whose worth would never be devalued.

There had been a few weeks in February when they had had to curtail their activities because of extra soldiers escorting travelers on the roads to Paris in order to stamp out the highwaymen's means of securing revenue. But the soldiers had had to be taken off that duty since Bonaparte had renewed his offensive against Austria and every available soldier had to report to the front.

Once again, the highwaymen had had their pick of prosperous merchants, trembling, old bankers whose clawing hands had to be forced open to relieve them of their money, and wealthy bourgeois whose paunches indicated the easy life they enjoyed. Etienne liked to think he had every right to relieve these "new rich" of their treasures, for hadn't they done the same to the old aristocracy? It was only justice, he told his sister. Many of the men they robbed had grown fat from the sale of aristocrats' lands and possessions—it was only right that they take that money back.

Aimee now waited in the chill March afternoon, narrowing her eyes to enable her to see as far down the road as possible. There was nothing today, she thought, feeling irritated at having to wait in the road all this time for nothing. But then, suddenly, she saw a speck coming forward on the narrow ribbon of road leading from Orléans. As it came nearer, she recognized a coach with but one driver and waved her arm behind her as a signal to the men waiting. Then, slowly, she moved her horse behind the shelter of the woods, waiting until the coach passed. Once it did, she would turn her horse around and go in the opposite direction so that she might see the road from Paris, where it was more likely soldiers or police would be dispatched. There was always an element of risk involved between the time the coach passed her and the time she could get far enough ahead on the road to see, but it was the only way to work the operation, Etienne had informed her.

After the coach had passed, she raced the horse around through the woods, hearing the shouts of her comrades attacking, the slowing down of the horses, a few warning shots fired over the head of the driver to make him believe they meant business. She glanced over her shoulder and saw the coach halted, the driver out of his seat lying prone on the ground, with one of the men holding a pistol over him, while the other four took care of removing the valuables from the passengers, who were made to stand in single file outside the coach. Aimee could see only two passengers; both looked like students, with reed-thin bodies and bookish expressions and she knew Etienne would be frustrated by such poor pickings. A lot of trouble for very little, he would say. But it was getting late and there would probably not be any more coaches before dark. Etienne refused to work after nightfall for fear someone might escape in the dark, or that it would be easier for one of the passengers, who could possibly be armed, to get to his pistols.

She turned her head forward again, knowing that Paris lay no more than twenty miles northeast of this spot. After the gang retired to their cottage to sort the day's booty, she would return to Paris in the morning to fence the goods they'd collected this week. She made only one trip to the city each week for this purpose, for it was too far to do it every night. And Etienne feared for her safety when she was carrying so much on her person. He and the others would escort her through the gates of Paris, then loiter at some river tavern while she made her rounds. She took care to dress so poorly, with the goods hidden in special pockets sewn into the lining of her petticoat, that no one would think to try to rob her.

It took no more than twenty minutes for the men to do their work, and then, hearing their whistle of forewarning, Aimee would disappear once more into the trees while the coach sped by to cover the last miles to Paris. She waited a few more minutes, then went in search of her companions, whose irritation was written plainly on their faces.

"Barely a sou between the both of them!" Jean said disgustedly, showing a pitiable purse.

"Students on their way to the Sorbonne," Paul got out, spitting on the ground to show his distaste. "God, the pickings have been slim this week, fellows. There'll not be much for our Aimee to take to the fences."

"There's enough." Etienne shrugged. "Come along and we'll divide the money at the cottage before turning over the jewelry and such to Aimee." He led the way back to the crossroads beyond which was a small, overgrown path large enough for their horses to trod that led them to the small woodcutter's cottage they used as their base.

Inside, they sat at the table and divided their spoils, which they hid beneath the floorboards. Aimee was given all the jewelry and trinkets, unless someone wanted to keep for himself a special piece, which was deducted from his portion.

"Ah, this is a sparkler!" Joseph exclaimed, holding up a winking, blood-red brooch that seemed to catch fire from the flames in the grate. "I'd like to give this to the girl I'm seeing— she'd probably by my slave for life!" He laughed.

Etienne looked at him good-naturedly. "She might ask questions you couldn't answer, Joseph," he warned.

Joseph shrugged and tossed the brooch back into the pile.

"Jesus, I can remember my mother wearing things like this," Pierre said wryly, holding up a pair of pearl earrings that dangled between his fingers. "Beautiful, aren't they?" he asked Aimee, swinging them before her eyes.

She nodded. "Whoever they were intended for must be tearing herself to pieces about losing them."

"Probably some bourgeois cow," Jean put in with a frown, grabbing the earrings and throwing them into the pile.

When they were finished, the things were put into a bag for Aimee to place inside her petticoat the next morning. Wearily, she got out cooking utensils and prepared dinner, noting the men all seemed in solemn moods this night.

"Soon, winter will be over," Paul said, picking at the table with the tip of his knife. "Spring will bring back the Fair of SaintGermain, the traveling gypsies, and all the whores along the Seine." He looked at his fellows. "I wouldn't mind being back there rather than coughing up summer dust and sweating behind the disguises we're forced to wear."

"I'd rather have the money," Pierre insisted. "You can't have the whores for free, you know. There'll be time to enjoy them— higher-class women, too—when you've made your stake!"

"I've had enough of this life!" Jean grumbled in frustration. "A little here, a little there, and each time we risk our lives—for what!"

"You can leave whenever you like," Etienne put in somberly. "I've no hold on you, and if you can't stomach the work, we don't want you in." He eyed the other young man with a shrug. "I can't promise you there's not a gibbet waiting for you down the line, but we'll enjoy what we can now. If you have regrets, you can have what's yours and go, Jean."

Jean looked uncomfortably around at the others. "Well, I only meant that it's a shame we're not hauling in more."

"Once the warmer weather arrives, we should get more people out for drives," Joseph suggested meaningfully. "You know how those bourgeois women love to dress for their silly picnics and social gatherings. And more people will be coming to Paris from the provinces. Things should pick up considerably."

"Well said." Etienne laughed, slapping Joseph on the back. "Winter's not easy on travelers—"

"Or highwaymen," Aimee put in beneath her breath. She set their supper out in bowls and sat down beside her brother to eat.

The next morning, they all set out for Paris at a brisk pace, Aimee dressed once more in a conservative peasant skirt and loose-fitting blouse with a warm shawl, looking appropriately tattered, instead of wearing the man's breeches and coat she normally donned during operations. Seeing the gates of Paris ahead of her, she thought back to that time more than two years ago when she had first seen them. How forbidding they seemed now, she thought disconsolately. They seemed to swallow people up whole so that they lost their identities inside and were never heard from again. Had that happened to her? Was she no longer Aimee de Chartres, the daughter of Philippe de Chartres, a baron of France? Who was this ragged, pale-faced young woman of nearly eighteen who rode toward those gates now? Was this what she truly wanted for the rest of her life? Was this what her father would have wanted—would have expected? She knew the answer to that was a resounding no. Yet, what else was there? She had asked herself the same question too many times. Always she came up with the same answer—there was nothing else for her now. She was tied by blood to her brother; otherwise she had no one. She could not survive alone in the city, nor could she survive anywhere else by herself. A young woman alone, who had no protector, was soon eaten up, tossed out, and left broken and sad, like those dark-ringed prostitutes in front of the Palais Royal. Aimee had seen them, staring out from their windows at the dandies who paraded below them. Their one sad hope was that one of those men would take them away from the life they led, take care of them and be true to them. Alas, most of their hopes were soon forgotten in the struggle for survival when some horrid disease attacked them, took away what beauty they had once had, and left them with nothing more to offer. Cold and lifeless, they would later be dredged up from the Seine, taking the only way out of their miserable existence they could.

Aimee shivered and drew her shawl closer about her shoulders. She vowed that she would never end up like one of those lost, sad souls. Once more, from hidden reserves inbred in her family since centuries before, Aimee drew on her strength to stiffen her back and clench her jaw. She would survive this—she would! And with the money she earned she would go back to the country and live a quiet, peaceful life without the foul stench of Paris forever in her nostrils. The thought comforted her and she parted from her comrades at the gates after making arrangements to meet them in a special place the next day.

She stabled her horse and went on foot to the men who would examine the treasures she brought them and give her, more or less, a fair value for them. It took her most of the day to take care of this business, for each man would take only a few things: some interested only in fine, old pieces of jewelry that could be sold without alteration; others interested in the jewels themselves, which could be put into new mountings and sold for ten times more than what they gave Aimee. Some preferred not to deal in jewelry at all and wanted soft goods, clothing, handkerchiefs, scarves, and the like.

By the end of the day Aimee was feeling very tired, and she saw her boardinghouse rise up in front of her with a feeling of relief. But her eyes narrowed as she perceived a tall figure leaning against the wall—obviously waiting for someone. Cautiously, she advanced, fairly certain she knew the identity of the man even before she caught a blue flash from beneath his hat and heard the deep voice salute her.

"Hello, Aimee."

"Lucian, how nice to see you again," Aimee said, forcing her voice to sound light, heavily aware of the coins in the pocket of her petticoat. She hoped he wasn't going to stay, but her hope soon died when he followed her inside the building up to her room.

Casually, he glanced about the room, noting the addition of a new coverlet for the bed, a cloth to put over the table, and a small stove to heat up drinks to ward off the chill outside. Also, there was a huge stack of firewood beneath the window, plus a bucket of coal near the fireplace. Obligingly, he started a fire for her, while offering slight comments on the weather, the war, and the state of Paris in general. He noted that her responses were mostly mechanical and there was a distinct air of weariness about her coupled with an anxiety at his presence.

"I haven't seen you for some time," he explained finally, settling himself in a chair as she heated water for tea. "I remember how happy you were to see your brother again." He looked around. "And yet, I don't see any sign of his presence here. Have you lost him again already?"

"No, but he doesn't stay here with me," Aimee said, keeping her voice calm. "He has his own rooms."

"I see," he commented, taking the cup of tea and sipping at it thoughtfully. He watched her sit down, removing the shawl from her shoulders as the heat of the fire permeated the room. Casually, his eyes moved over the high, impudent breasts that rose and fell with increasing rapidity as he watched them. He could see telltale color rising in her throat and noticed her

hands were not still in her lap as the fingers laced and unlaced
nervously.

"What brings you here?" she finally asked bluntly. "I had
thought, after you took me to Etienne, that I would not be seeing
you again."

He smiled. "Oh, I always have time for you, Aimee. I can go
months without seeing you, and then, suddenly, I'll think about
you and wonder how you are doing. There's something about
you—I suppose I should just admit that I couldn't bear the
thought of never seeing you again."

Aimee bit her lip, barely registering his words. She only
wished he would say what he had to say and go—for as sure as
the sun rose in the east every morning, she knew Lucian Napier
had come here for a purpose. All this blather about wanting to see
her to make sure she was doing all right was probably just a ruse
to keep her guessing. She hated these games he played with her,
but knew she could only sit and wait, simmering while he took
his own sweet time getting to the point.

"You seem to have stumbled on to some money," he commented, indicating the accouterments added to the room. He
waited for her explanation, inspecting her over the rim of his cup.

"Yes," she said finally, brightly, "I prevailed upon my aunt
to loan me a sum of money—"

"Your aunt no longer lives in Paris," Lucian said, still amia-
ble, though his blue eyes had darkened at her blatant lie.

Aimee whitened.

"As a known former aristocrat, your aunt is kept under routine surveillance by some of Fouché's men. Some three months
ago, she closed up her town house and retired to one of her
estates in Amiens," Lucian continued, keeping a close eye on
the range of expressions that flitted across Aimee's face. He
put down his tea cup and leaned forward. "Try again, my
dear."

As always, when backed into a corner, Aimee relied on
anger to bolster her confidence. "I don't *have* to tell you anything, Lucian!" she got out, standing up to pace angrily in
front of him. "What am I supposed to do—report to you when
I decide to make a purchase, or change my life-style? Believe
me, your interest in me is not something I cherish!"

He leaned back in his chair, regarding her with a mocking
gleam in his eyes. "I don't think you understand, Aimee, that I
am simply trying to help you. You're still a babe in arms when it
comes to street sense. When I last saw you, you were down on

your luck, afraid of burning an extra log in the fireplace. Now, suddenly, you have several added amenities. Now, in my experience, reversals like that are usually due to something illegal or immoral—which is it, Aimee?"

She stubbornly compressed her lips, then turned to flop unceremoniously into a chair. The clanking sound of coins seemed overloud in the room and Aimee's face paled as she realized she'd forgotten about the coins in her petticoats. At her abrupt movements, they had clashed together. She looked over to Lucian, her heart sinking at the look he gave her.

"It sounds like quite a few coins," he said softly, standing up to come closer. "Aimee, you're not back to pickpocketing again, are you?"

She shook her head. "No!"

"Ah, well, that is a relief, yet, why are you carrying so much coin around on your person, I wonder?" He seemed to ponder for a moment. Then his blue eyes brightened. "I know of several ladies who like to wear a special petticoat under their dresses. When they get paid by a gentleman for their services, they slip the money in there so they won't get robbed." He eyed her with amusement. "Don't tell me you've prostituted yourself, my dear?"

Aimee's face tightened as though he'd just delivered a blow to her stomach. Then she stood up, stiffening her spine and looking at him through green eyes as hard and bright as emeralds. "Yes, Lucian, I'm afraid you've discovered my secret," she lied. "Now you can see why I'm able to afford the additions to my residence."

"I see," he murmured, coming closer. "And from the sounds of it, you must be quite good at your work." He was so close that she felt the need to step back, but was prevented from doing so by the chair behind her. "Hmm. Yes, I can see where you'd make quite a lot of coin in a single night, Aimee. You are very beautiful, you know, and quite desirable—in a lower-class sort of way."

Riled, she stood up to him. "You—you peasant!" she cried. "How dare you say such a thing! Why, my blood holds generations of noblemen, bishops—"

"Hush! I don't want to know about your blood, my dear," he continued in that soft voice. "Just name your price and I will pay it."

"Oh!" Without thinking, she slapped his face, feeling the sting of his skin meeting her palm. She stared at the livid mark on his cheek, then looked into the blue eyes that were hard and unyielding. Without a word, he caught her by the shoulders, pushing her backward, causing her to stumble over the chair and land in a heap close to the fireplace. The pocket inside her petticoat was ripped and coins rolled out onto the floor.

"A very good night's work," Lucian said calmly, watching her on the floor while he unbuttoned his coat. Slowly, he untied his cravat, pulling the tail of his shirt from his breeches and slipping it over his head so that he stood before her half naked, his broad, dark chest catching the gleam of the fire as it played across the lean, sinewy muscles. "Well?" he asked coolly.

Gathering her senses, Aimee glared up at him. "You had better leave, Lucian Napier," she warned him.

He laughed, throwing back his head, exposing the strong muscles of his neck and throat. "I don't want to leave, Aimee—I want *you!*"

"You can't have me!" she cried, fear edging her voice. "I'm . . . I'm . . . not . . ."

"A selective whore," he mused, kneeling beside her, making her cringe as he leaned down to untie the lacings of her blouse. The garment slipped from her shoulders with ridiculous ease, revealing the slender arms, the willowy waist, and the soft, white slopes of her breasts. His eyes wandered to the dusty-pink nipples, and Aimee thought she would die of shame.

"Lucian, please," she whispered as he came down to hold her head, lacing his fingers through her hair and bringing her lips up to meet his.

She was caught in a sudden maelstrom of male passion as he moved one hand from behind her head to her back in order to press her body against his. The points of her breasts, hardened already from the cool air, stabbed at his chest while his lips shaped and molded her mouth, moving them with utter confidence as he began to ignite a passion inside her, a new, primitive feeling she had never had before. His lips were alternately demanding and gentle, insinuating their magic to hers, nipping and pulling at the flesh of her mouth so that she opened her lips of her own volition, allowing his tongue an entrance. The touch of it against her own made her start at such an invasion of privacy and she tried to push him away, but he would not have it. His hands pressed her body closer to his while his tongue continued to play havoc with the interior of her mouth, tasting the sweetness, running along the edge of her teeth, dancing with a fencer's skill.

Aimee felt as though she could not breathe, that she could not fill her lungs with enough air in order to keep from fainting. Like a wounded bird, she stirred against him, arching her back and throwing back her head so that he was bound to release her. She gasped for breath, but he did not wait before moving down from her lips to her throat, imprinting hot, slow kisses down her neck before licking one ivory shoulder. He dragged his tongue from her shoulder to one firm slope of her breast, circling the nipple until it was turgid with desire. Gently, he circled inward, until he could capture the hot little point with his teeth. Aimee groaned at the exquisite sensation he was provoking, having never felt anything else like it.

His hands were not idle, for he had set her head back down on the floor and was caressing one firm breast while his mouth toyed with the other. His fingers brushed the sensitive peaks while his lips planted kisses on them, then gently nuzzled and pulled until Aimee thought they would burst with sensation. She couldn't help the sigh that escaped her and Lucian smiled, knowing he had caused it with his arousal techniques.

"You are fashioned for love, my little beauty," he murmured, licking the underside of one breast, while his fingers continued to brush the nipple of the other.

Aimee was not listening to him, so lost was she in her own bodily sensations. Never had she felt such exquisite tinglings inside, emanating from her breasts to her thighs and centering in that private part of herself that no one else had ever seen. She closed her eyes tightly and brought her arms up to clasp around her seducer's head, bringing him back up to her lips, which now matched him kiss for kiss. Her tongue fenced shyly with his own, causing the sensations to intensify, especially as he continued to caress her breasts, teasing the sensitive peaks once more into dusty-rose points of desire.

His hands moved slowly from her breasts to the flat of her stomach, the thumbs hooking into the waistband of her skirt. Aimee felt the touch of his hands on her belly with a sudden shock. Her eyes flew open and she gazed into his face with genuine alarm. His blue eyes looked back at her, the look intense, filled with such desire that she felt it almost physically. And yet, every signal inside her was begging her to stop him. She could not allow him the ultimate seduction. He was, she realized, treating her like a prostitute—because he thought she was one. She was, as yet, too inexperienced to realize how very gently he was actually treating her, especially in the face of his own raging desire.

Warily, they stared at each other, realizing already that the tenuous bond of friendship was changed forever. Even if she denied him this last act that would complete her seduction, she would never be able to look into his eyes and forget that he had touched her breasts, had kissed them and kissed her lips as no mere friend ever would. She wanted to weep with the frustration of it—the change in emotions as she looked into the handsome face of the man who was waiting for some signal from her to continue. She was at a loss, and could only find herself wishing that this had never happened.

"Lucian?" she asked tentatively, her green eyes wide and pleading.

Lucian, caught between the tide of his own raging desire and the realization that he would carry an unwilling victim with him should he continue, ground his teeth in suppressed fury. Softly, so as not to alarm her, he placed his head on her bosom and closed his eyes, breathing deeply so as to regain his composure. He hadn't meant to go so far with her—but God knew once he'd started and seen that sweet, ripe flesh, his emotions had swept him away from reason. She was lovelier than anything he had ever seen—and he found he wanted her more than any other woman with whom he'd ever been. But the dawning shame in her eyes, the unshed tears that she was rigidly trying to hold back, the certainty that she was most definitely not a whore, but probably still an unbreached virgin made him fight to regain control—although it was costing him dearly. He felt the sheen of perspiration on his forehead and licked his suddenly dry lips, willing the painful erection between his legs to go away before he had to stand up before her.

"Lucian?" Once again her voice came uncertainly, almost painfully.

He raised his head and managed a rugged smile, sliding off of her and getting to his feet, reaching for his shirt. The sight of her half-naked form, lying so unconsciously provocative at his feet, made him bite back a groan and, with more gruffness than he intended, he threw her blouse over her and told her to get up.

Clutching the material to her breasts, Aimee scrambled to her feet, her eyes huge with the need to understand. "I—why did you—"

"Don't worry about it!" he snapped at her, buttoning his shirt and tucking it into his breeches, sincerely relieved he had not removed them before. "Nothing happened. Nothing is changed," he said, realizing that he was lying—that much had changed between them.

"Lucian, you're angry with me—and I don't understand why," she said, donning her blouse awkwardly, her cheeks suffused with color as she retied the lacings.

"I'm sorry, Aimee. I'm not angry with you—I'm angry with myself for allowing this to happen. I—lost my head."

"Because you thought I was—"

"No!" he shouted. He wanted to say simply that he wanted her not because he had thought her a whore, but because she was so lovely and vulnerable and achingly innocent, but instead he merely shook his head and retrieved his coat.

Aimee watched him, feeling worse every moment that ticked by. She wondered what would have happened had he not stopped when he did. The thought made color flow into her face once more and she turned away from him, busying herself with picking up the coins that had fallen from her petticoat.

Lucian noticed her movements and frowned, realizing the question of the money had not been satisfactorily answered. He suspected, of course, that she had gotten it through some illegal means, but suddenly he didn't want to know how. He told himself he would not see her again—that her life would be her own now. What mistakes she made, she would answer for. He could not continue directing her life, taking time out from his own work to help her. He told himself these things even while he knew he would have to see her again, someday.

Aimee was aware of his quiet, and she turned around, letting the coins fall from her hands onto the bed. "This money—" she began, not quite sure how she would relate the extent of her activities to this man who was so involved in government.

"Is yours," he finished quickly, buttoning the last button of his coat and tilting the tall hat on his head. "I've no right to ask you where you got it, Aimee."

She swallowed, visibly relieved at the reprieve he'd given her. "Thank you, Lucian."

They stood there awkwardly, each deep in thought, both sad at the loss of innocence that had accompanied this day. Finally, Lucian roused himself.

"Well, I suppose I should be off, Aimee. I'm sure you probably have better things to do than entertain me for the rest of the day. Possibly you have an assignation with your brother later on this evening?"

She shook her head.

"No? Well, perhaps—" He stopped. It was on the tip of his tongue to invite her to dine with him, but he realized it would only prolong the awkwardness. Instead, he bowed abruptly. "Good night, Aimee," he said, turning on his heel to go.

"Good night," she whispered, watching him as he strode out the door, slamming it behind him.

17

•-•=•-•=•-•

The days passed quickly, a cycle constantly repeated throughout the spring and summer of 1797 as Aimee and her brother continued their life of crime. To Etienne, it was not really crime, but a wonderful adventure that was justified because they were robbing those bourgeois who had backed the revolution that had robbed them of their birthright. More than once, he had remarked to his sister how exhilarating the element of danger was, how exciting to think that he courted disaster nearly every day—and somehow returned again to thumb his nose at it. Aimee couldn't understand this need for danger and adventure. She grew weary of the constant necessity for vigilance, of the visits to the men who fenced their goods. She told her brother more than once that they had amassed, by now, a good-sized nest egg with which they could begin to rebuild Castle du Beautreillis. He would laugh and kiss her cheek, telling her there wasn't nearly enough.

Aimee would grow angry, suspecting the reason for this was that Etienne spent much of the money he earned at the whorehouses along the river, or gambling at the Palais Royal. Her heart ached to think how foolish he was with his money, but there was nothing she could do to stop him. There was always more to replenish what he spent, he assured her. Every day more and more wealthy victims would pass along the road to Paris—and promptly be relieved of their goods.

But as the summer came to an end and fall began, Aimee remembered the cold winter nights of the year before and began to dread the passing days. Then, too, the watch had been plumped up for a time, making it dangerous to stop coaches. Jean had been wounded by a passenger's bullet and was not mending as he should, causing him all manner of problems riding his horse and holding a pistol. Aimee told him he should see a physician and not rely on the questionable skills of the young prostitute he was seeing in the rue Saint-Antoine, but Jean refused. By September, when a royalist upsurge in Paris threatened to unseat the Directory, Jean's wound had putrefied and he was unable to accompany them on their robbery missions. In a few days the insurrection was squelched through a purging of those who were royalists—and Jean was dead.

This chilled some of Etienne's gaiety for a time, and he suspended any more "jobs," causing hope to stir in Aimee's breast that perhaps her brother had finally seen the light of reason. But, unfortunately, this state of things lasted only a few weeks, and Etienne found himself low on money from his constant spending. It was back to the cottage and the road to Paris.

Fearfully, Aimee continued on as lookout, but her need to quit this dangerous adventure became more urgent within her as she saw her brother taking foolish risks by intimidating the passengers, bragging about the power he held over the road to Paris. Inevitably, it would bring the police down about their ears, she was sure.

Their luck worsened when, in October, Austria sued for peace and the Treaty of Campo Formio was signed, wherein Austria gave up her possessions in Belgium and the left bank of the Rhine to France. With only England as the enemy, there were not so many soldiers needed at the front, and many of the coaches began bearing military escorts on command from the Directory since too many passengers were complaining of the crime-ridden roads. The wealthy bourgeoisie were voicing its complaints to a government that was already shaky at best with young General Bonaparte scoring brilliant military victories. Quickly, the Directory appointed Bonaparte Commander of the Army of England. And while he went away to plan the conquest of Egypt, the Directory breathed a collective sigh of relief and went about the business of keeping their people happy. One of the ways of doing this was to clamp down hard on the crime that was running rampant on all the roads that led to Paris.

It was a particularly cold day in January of 1798 that Aimee sat on her horse, rubbing her arms to try to keep warm, thinking longingly of the warm fire that would await her at her little room in the Montmartre. Oddly, this day her mind had gone back to that evening the previous March when she had last seen Lucian Napier. Had it really been nine months? It was hard to believe; she had almost become used to his popping up at odd moments of her life. Once, she had thought she recognized him in front of the Tuileries, but he had passed so quickly from her view that she couldn't be sure. The events of that night had blurred a little in her mind—whether by choice or the inevitable passage of time, she wasn't sure. Oddly, she found herself missing him, wondering what he had been up to in all this time. Did he still carry out some shadowy dictates of the government? Was he working for Fouché? Or did he carry some post within the Directory itself? Perhaps she could have endeavored to find out, but something held her back. Maybe it was the wish that she remain forever out of his life now that their relationship had changed. Precisely what that relationship had truly been, she wasn't sure. How oddly lives were entwined, she thought dreamily. If things hadn't happened as they had, if her father hadn't died, if Faron had not taken out his revenge on her family—if, if, if! Aimee shook her head. There was no good in wondering about other possibilities. What had happened had happened—and there was no changing it. Now, she had to worry about keeping her brother and herself alive within the ever tightening net of military and police who were threatening to capture all highwaymen in the vicinity and throw them into the Châtelet for summary sentencing to the gallows.

Aimee's eyes sharpened as she saw a speck on the horizon that promised to turn into a coach on its way to Paris. She waited until she was sure no military escort was with it and, when satisfied that there was no one besides the driver, she gave the signal to her brother and the other three waiting several yards away, before turning her horse into the woods and speeding around to the other side. She could hear the rumbling coach behind her, suddenly stopped, the shouts of her brother and Paul and Joseph and Pierre calling a halt. In the crisp, cold air, every sound seemed to come back at her clearly, and so, when she heard her brother cry in a loud, strident voice, "Faron!," she caught her breath and felt her heart begin a rapid tattoo before wheeling her horse about abruptly, back to the scene of the robbery.

Never before had she been this close and she watched for a moment in fascination. Etienne and Paul were on one side of the coach, Joseph and Pierre on the other, pistols raised, masks covering their faces. Three men stood next to the coach. One was the driver, another was a mere passenger—but the third man, huge and red-faced, a grotesque caricature of the Faron she remembered grown hugely fat and even more oily looking than she recalled, was the one to whom her attention was riveted.

"Stand carefully!" Etienne was warning, his blue eyes above

the mask, slits of hatred and revulsion as they centered on Faron. Here stood the murderer of his mother and brothers, the man whose hatred had caused the collapse of his home, and, indirectly, perhaps, had caused Etienne de Chartres to embark upon a life of crime. "You!" He pointed to the driver. "Empty your pockets—slowly!"

The driver complied, throwing out small articles onto the ground.

"Bah! The pickings are lean at best!" Paul snickered, unaware of the tension in his captain.

"Now you!" Etienne pointed to the other passenger, who also was obliged to empty his pockets. "Aha! Don't forget the diamond I see nestled so snugly in your cravat, my friend!" He laughed, jabbing his pistol in the air in the direction of the same diamond. Quickly, the man complied, although he scowled up at Etienne as though trying to see through the mask that covered most of his face.

Etienne turned his attention to the last one. "And now, you, fat man!" he jeered, his voice razor-sharp. "You seem the plumpest of the lot—and probably the most prosperous, eh? What wonders have you got to show us?"

"I'll show you the end of my pistol!" Faron ground out, his face sweating.

Etienne laughed. "You will, will you? I don't think so, fat one. I want to see that pistol—and everything else in your pockets—thrown to the ground!" He lowered his own weapon, aiming at the huge stomach. "And do be careful you don't make me nervous—so nervous that I fire this pistol!"

"You cursed dog!" Faron muttered, emptying the pockets of his coat, his face growing redder every second. "How dare you rob decent citizens within the very limits of the capital! You'll be sorry for this, I swear!"

"*Decent citizens!*" Etienne whistled. "Now, that is something, I think. How can I be sure that you are more decent— more deserving—than I, my fat friend? Surely we all carry secrets in our past, don't we? Who's to say that you were not, at one time in your life, even lower than I? Who's to say that you didn't stoop to all manner of crimes in days long past? Perhaps robbery, perhaps arson, perhaps murder—perhaps all three and more?"

"No need for conversation, Captain," Joseph called from the other side of the coach. "We've got the goods. Pick 'em up,

Paul, and we'll leave these gentlemen to get on with their travels."

"Not quite yet," Etienne returned, confounding his fellows. "For I do think I recognize this fat pumpkin of a man in front of me. Yes, indeed, I believe he is Faron, a revolutionary of Paris, a criminal insurgent who has escaped justice."

"What? What are you talking about?" the fat man puffed, casting sidelong glances at his companions. "My name is not Faron."

"Hmm. I couldn't possibly be mistaken," Etienne continued, toying with him. "No one could be as fat as you, nor as adept at lying, I'm sure. You must have done quite a bit of lying, in fact, to have turned yourself from Faron, the former miller of Orléans, into a respectable bourgeois of Paris."

The man's face was turning purple with rage. "I told you—I am *not* this Faron you speak of!" he shouted, moisture glistening in every fold of his face.

There was silence for a moment and Aimee thought her nerves would snap. She herself was sweating, waiting to see how much longer her brother would toy with this dangerous man. Faron was much too slick, too cunning for Etienne to take a false step, and Aimee watched the scene sharply, keeping her eyes on every movement of Faron, every flicker of his eyelids. She wanted desperately to call to her brother to quit this dangerous game and get on with his revenge. For revenge was what they must have!

She had never completely forgotten about Faron and his part in her past. She would never forget the feel of the crucifix in her hand, nor his howl of pain as she plunged it into his eye. Now, she saw that he wore no eye patch, but allowed the hollow socket with its disfigured lid to remain visible. Perhaps the eye patch would have given away the man who had been known in Paris as Faron. With the additional weight, the absence of an eye patch, and the respectable clothing of a prosperous merchant, he thought he could pull off the disguise, for whatever reason he had effected it. No wonder the police had never captured him! He had been living in Paris all this time, right under their noses! A bittersweet memory of Jean-Baptiste jabbed at her skull and she glared at this man who had caused so much pain to others.

"You *are* Faron!" Etienne finally said in a deeply deliberate voice. "And for your many crimes, you will now pay!"

Faron's purple face whitened suddenly, as though all color had been drained from it. "You must be mad, young fool! I don't know who you are, or why you are having these delusions, but I tell you, I am not the man you speak of! My name is Thierry and I am quite a respectable merchant, as you say, returning to Paris from business in Poitiers!"

"It is *you* who is the fool, Faron!" Etienne shouted, his anger rising at the man's refusal to admit who he was. "For your crimes—for the murders of my brothers and my mother—you will now receive justice!"

At these words, Faron's one good eye narrowed in cunning. He knew now who it was he was facing. Aimee could almost see his thoughts revolving inside his brain, wondering how this one had escaped him. He was putting everything together—the bandit's knowledge of his past, his memories of the family of de Chartres. But, quickly, the cunning was masked, for he was not ready yet to admit to anything that would make his fate irrevocable.

"If I am," he said in a slower voice, "who you say I am, how is it that I would be here, like this? Surely, common sense would tell you that the police would have caught up with me long ago. Fouché's secret police are trained well. I could not have escaped him." As he talked, Faron's gaze was moving between Etienne's face and his pistol on the ground. "Listen to reason. You have my valuables—let me go now in peace! I am not the man you think I am! I have a wife and two children at home awaiting me! Have mercy on me, I beg you, for their sakes!" He fell to his knees in dramatic fashion, lowering his head and clasping his hands together in supplication.

Etienne watched him unmoved. Beside him, he sensed Paul's confusion. The man who knelt so pitifully on the ground must die, Etienne told himself firmly, but not before he was made to suffer the same emotional torment he must have inflicted on his family.

Aimee, from her position, watched the actions of Faron, the former miller, the former revolutionary, the former criminal, and felt hatred within her breast. The man was a quivering mountain of fat, fearful for his miserable life! What did she care about his family? Had he cared about hers? She glanced up at her brother, wishing she could speak, but knowing how important it was not to betray her identity. The scene seemed frozen in time, with no one moving, no sound coming.

And then, in the near distance and closing in fast, came the unexpected, startling sound of another coach on the road to

Paris! Aimee spun around, her eyes widening as she realized that by deserting her post she had left them all exposed to very real danger. She looked along the road and saw an armed mail coach speeding toward them—but, more importantly, three soldiers were riding even faster in their direction, having observed what was happening. A scream of alarm issued from her throat.

Suddenly, as though her scream had catapulted him into action, Faron hoisted himself to his feet, bringing his pistol up with him! With an evil glee, he laughed into the face of Etienne de Chartres and fired the pistol. Etienne moved quickly to avoid the bullet, but his scream of pain told Aimee that it had found its mark somewhere on his body. With a cry of pure hatred, Aimee ran her horse toward the unsuspecting man who stood gleefully malicious as he watched Etienne fall from his horse. The driver and the other passenger, seeing that help was on its way, cowered beneath the coach while Pierre and Joseph went to attack the three soldiers in order to give their captain time to recover, if possible. Paul, who seemed in a daze at seeing his chief fall from his horse, sat in confusion, unable to move.

"Go back and help the others with the soldiers!" Aimee snapped at him, uncaring now as to whether Faron recognized her voice.

She watched Paul hurry to do as he was told while she wheeled her horse up, its hooves pawing at the air in front of Faron, causing him to cower backward beneath the flailing hooves. Despite her knowledge that she was safer on her mount, Aimee realized she must get to her brother's pistol, which had fallen to the ground when he had been wounded.

With a slithering speed, she clambered down from her horse to the spot where her brother lay bleeding. Behind her, she could hear Faron recovering himself, his hot, heavy breath filling her ears, blocking out all other noise. Her fingers closed around the pistol and she whirled just in time to feel the flat of Faron's huge hand strike her across the face. The action unsettled her mask and made her reel backward, nearly losing her footing.

Shaking her head, willing herself to remain upright, Aimee pushed the pistol out in front of her in a reflex action. For an instant in time, she looked into the one eye of Faron and saw the knowledge written there. She saw the hatred, the rapacious glee as he realized she was only a girl and how easily he could subdue her. She saw the recognition and all it meant to him—

the loss of his eye, her refusal to submit to his rape at the convent.

Then, closing her eyes as he advanced nearly on top of her, she fired her brother's pistol at point-blank range. In a moment, she felt the enormous weight of Faron fall heavily into her, knocking her to the ground. Opening her eyes, she looked into the eye of Faron, rapidly clouding over with death. For another second she saw the look of hopeless rage in that eye, before it was extinguished forever.

With difficulty, she dragged her body out from beneath him, feeling as though every bone in her rib cage had been bruised from the force of his weight toppling onto her. Blood was spattered on her clothing, her face, and automatically she picked up the disguising scarf and wrapped it around her mouth and nose once more. She heard her brother close by, groaning softly now. Fearfully, she crawled to him, unaware of the noise of battle ensuing between the highwaymen and the military escort a few yards away.

The twilight was thickening and it was becoming more and more difficult to see. Aimee went to her brother and turned him over as gently as she could, gasping at the blood that was seeping from the wound in his side.

"Etienne," she sobbed, hardly able to bear the thought that she might lose her brother, and by the very same hand that had killed her other brothers and her mother.

"Aimee, get out of here!" Etienne ground out painfully. "For God's sake, go! They have me, but I couldn't bear the thought of you ending up at the gibbet because of that murderous bastard!" His blue eyes pleaded with her through the growing darkness. "Please!"

With a half sob, Aimee turned and saw that the fight was nearly over. One of their comrades, she couldn't tell who, was lying wounded, possibly dead, on the ground. The other two were surrendering their weapons. With a surge of strength, Aimee leaned over to kiss her brother's face.

"Etienne?" she whispered.

"Go!" he pleaded once more.

Quickly now, without hesitation, Aimee obeyed. Despite her own aching body and sore heart, she got to her feet and ran for the cover of the underbrush at the side of the road. Hopefully, no one of the military escort would have seen her and she would be able to get away under cover of darkness. Softly, trying not to make any sound, she moved among the bushes and tangled weeds, but her heart leaped as she heard one of the men calling to say that a highwayman had escaped into the woods. Next, she heard the sound of a galloping horse, closing in on her position.

Terrified, memories of the Châtelet flitting through her brain along with half-forgotten visions of the workhouse and then the hangman's noose in the square, Aimee threw caution to the wind. She had to escape! Wildly, she ran through the underbrush, hoping against hope that it would serve to slow down the progress of the horse. The thick, naked branches barred her own path as she pushed at them with her hands and face, receiving scratches and welts even through the protection of her gloves and scarf. Her lungs felt the cold, January air like knife points as she ran faster through the icy darkness.

Faster she ran, half stumbling over exposed tree roots, but still hearing the persistent sound of the horse's hooves behind her. Her legs were weakening, her lungs were bursting, she could hardly see in the dark—but still she ran on. She could no longer hear the horse behind her, but now the sound of running, booted feet had taken their place. Horror skidded up her backbone as she stepped into a rabbit hole and twisted her ankle. But, ignoring the pain, she continued, knowing that the slight hesitation had caused her pursuer to gain on her.

"Ah! Got you!"

A hand grabbed her by the edge of her coat, nearly pulling her feet from the ground as she flew forward on her hands, rolling in a somersault on the frozen earth. Dazed, she lay for only a moment, trying to clear her head, when a pair of hands pulled her up roughly to her feet.

With her ankle smarting painfully and her ribs hurting even more, Aimee stood there, heaving to catch her breath, while the man who held her labored to do the same. Then he pushed her two hands behind her and secured them with a length of something—his belt, perhaps; she was too much in pain to wonder. It felt as though he were trying to pull her arms from their sockets and she let out an involuntary cry against the pain.

"What's the matter? You've got the stomach for murder, but not for your own pain?" her captor snarled.

Nevertheless, Aimee stiffened, for she knew that voice, despite not having heard it for so very long. Dear God! It couldn't be! But she knew it was. Fate had ordained that her captor be Lucian Napier. Despite her pain, she could only hope that he would not recognize her in the dark. She felt his hands at her waist, pulling aside her coat in order to search for weapons. She gasped at his hands brushed over her shirt, touching her breast. He stopped his search abruptly with a low whistle. Then, hesitantly, he slipped between the buttons of her shirt and felt the warm, living flesh of her breast, brushing the nipple with his palm.

"A woman, by God!" he muttered in some disbelief. His hand lingered for a moment, warming itself next to her flesh. Then abruptly he withdrew it, not bothering to rebutton her shirt or her coat. "A little cold air might do you some good," he murmured to himself.

Walking around behind her, he pushed her forward, uncaring if she stumbled on her inflamed ankle, ignoring her moans of protest when he drove her through a group of naked trees, the rough bark of which scraped her skin.

"You'll not talk, eh?" he snapped, and Aimee could hear the curiosity in his voice. By the time they'd reached the road again, she was half fainting from the pain in her ankle and the cold that was biting at her breast. "Hey! You, there! Lieutenant, bring that torch this way—I want to have a look at this bird!"

Aimee cringed away from the light, knowing the pain she felt now was nothing compared to the shame she would feel when Lucian recognized her.

"No, you don't, you'll not escape us!" Lucian said fiercely, bringing her back toward the torch, catching her jaw cruelly in one hand and forcing her face forward. Aimee closed her eyes, hoping that the blood and dirt on her face would prevent her from being recognized. She felt the heat of the torch on her upturned face, felt the scarf dragged from her mouth as she was inspected by Lucian and the lieutenant. Her hat was pulled summarily from her head so that her long hair tumbled out, catching the shimmering light from the torch. She heard the gasp that escaped from the soldier.

"Hair that color will fetch a pretty price from the wigmakers when they shave it off!" He whistled as though expecting to pocket the money himself.

"Hmm." Lucian seemed too quiet and Aimee held her breath. "Open your eyes, wench!" he commanded suddenly, and Aimee wished she could die right there. "You heard me!"

Obediently, dully, Aimee opened her eyes, meeting the harsh glare of the torch. She shivered, knowing those sharp blue points of flame that were *his* eyes were probing her face, tracking down the opened front of her clothing.

The lieutenant shook his head. "Green eyes—an unlucky color, sir!"

"Unlucky for her," Lucian offered grimly. "All right, take the torch and see to the two men on the ground. One of them is dead, but the other I'm not sure about."

"Yes, sir!" The lieutenant walked off with the torch, leaving Aimee and Lucian in the shadows.

Aimee heard his breath coming slowly, deeply, as though trying to absorb everything. She barely breathed herself, wishing somehow that she could make herself invisible. She closed her eyes again and lowered her head, unable to look at him, unable to see the damning evidence in his eyes.

"So, this was how you earned your money?" he questioned slowly. Then, after a deep breath: "You would have done better to prostitute yourself, my dear."

She did not answer him. What was there to say? It was true. She was a member of a gang of highwaymen and now a murderer. And yet, she knew she would not have changed that last for anything!

He stood in front of her and she felt his hands on her naked skin, refastening her shirt and the coat. "I'm sorry—about that," he murmured awkwardly. "If I had known who you were—"

Aimee wished he would leave her alone. Why didn't he just take her to the coach to await the others? Why must he submit her to this humiliating ordeal?

"Dammit! Say something!" he finally burst out angrily. "What are you going to do—go to your death in proud silence? Dammit! That's exactly what you will do, too, isn't it? This isn't the same as picking the pockets of dandies in the gardens of the Tuileries, Aimee!"

She looked at him, her own anger flaring at his harsh words. "I'm cold!" she pronounced, her back stiffening despite the pain.

He laughed grimly. "Yes, you'll be even colder a month from now, when they dump your body into a criminal's grave! Is that what it's to be, Aimee! For God's sake, tell me why! Was this your brother's way of protecting the little sister who had come to him for help? Jesus Christ!" His fury was directed more at Etienne than her. How could he have done this to her?

"The fat one is dead," the lieutenant informed them unnecessarily. "The other highwayman has a wound in his side, but he's alive. Of the three who attacked us, one is dead, the other wounded, and the third with only minor scratches."

"Thank you," Lucian said in clipped tones. He turned back to Aimee. "Since fate has decreed that I be riding as escort to important documents in that mail coach, I suppose you should be glad since I could very easily make you walk all the way back to Paris!"

"My brother—" Aimee began, hoping that Lucian would allow him to ride in one of the coaches.

"Which one is he?"

"The one with the wound in his side."

"He can ride inside," Lucian said, guessing her plea, "but what difference does it really make, my dear, when in a fortnight he'll be swinging from a gibbet in the executioner's square!" His words were harsh, grinding, as he fought back the anger at this girl. When she refused to be baited into responding, he snorted in disgust and called to one of the other men to watch her while he spoke to the driver and remaining passenger of the first coach, explaining the need for sequestering their vehicle. He told them both to sit on top while they loaded the bodies of the dead and wounded into the coach.

Aimee waited patiently, feeling a curious sense of numbness. What did it matter what they did to her? she thought with a strange feeling of carelessness. Yes, Lucian was right. She would be tried and sentenced to hang for her crimes. But she would not change anything if it meant that Faron would not now be dead! The price of his life, she was willing to pay, and gladly!

When Lucian returned, she expected to be taken to the same coach where her brother had been carried, but Lucian instead swept her up onto his horse to sit in front of him. He had taken the belt from around her hands and she steadied herself with the aid of the pommel, feeling his arms go around her waist to catch the reins of his horse. She shivered; she told herself it was from the cold, as his arms necessarily pressed against her, bringing her back against him.

They set off at a slow pace, partly because of the wounded and partly because of the treachery of the icy road now that darkness had descended fully and only the low glimmer of the coach lights lit their way. Lucian allowed the coaches to go ahead of him. Aimee felt his warm breath close to her ear. She wished they'd given her back her hat.

They rode in silence for some time until Lucian finally sighed aloud. "Tell me, Aimee . . ."

Aimee closed her eyes for a moment and leaned against him,

welcoming the warmth against her back and neck. "It was Faron," she stated simply.

"Faron?" Lucian seemed to be thinking. "Not the man you said had killed your family? The reason for your coming to Paris?"

"Yes. He was the fat man who was dead. When we were robbing the coach, Etienne recognized him. I was supposed to be watching the road, but when I heard Etienne's cry, I had to come back and see for myself."

"But his papers claimed he was a Monsieur Thierry, a merchant residing in the Faubourg Saint-Germain."

"Lies!" Aimee snapped with loathing. "Your Fouché is obviously not as thorough as you led me to believe! It was Faron! I don't know how he managed it, but he changed his name and his identity! The butcher who killed my family somehow became a respectable merchant in these last years. Etienne was going to kill him, but when you happened upon us so unexpectedly, he looked away, giving that wily pig the time to pick up his own weapon and shoot my brother!" The hatred was fierce in Aimee's voice. "I was not going to let him get away from me again!" she went on. "So I killed him!"

Lucian seemed to be thinking for a moment. "That does alter some of the events. Perhaps a judge might be able to dismiss murder charges when he realizes the reasons for what you did."

"But the other," Aimee put in dully.

"The highway robbery," Lucian muttered, still thinking.

"I have no defense against it."

"Are you so set, then, on dying, Aimee?" Lucian wondered, irritated at her dismal outlook. "God, I should have seduced you nine months ago and made you my mistress! At least that would have kept you out of this trouble!"

"What makes you think I would have consented to become your mistress?" she asked angrily, disliking the way he felt he had to take charge of her life.

"You would have had very little choice in the matter," he told her with a certain smugness in his voice that further irritated her.

"Why, you conceited, pig-headed, *policeman!*" she lashed out. "I wouldn't have been your mistress if you had tied me down and locked me in a room! I wouldn't—"

"And yet," he interrupted, his lips at her ear now, "it seemed to me that you were very close to surrendering that time before. I don't think," he continued, his breath tickling her ear lobe, "that you would have made too much of a protest."

She shivered again—and this time she knew it was *not* from the cold. Still, unwilling to fall under his spell, she stiffened her spine. "Well, it's rather senseless to talk of such things when that is all in the past—and the future seems pretty bleak! I'm afraid, Monsieur Napier, you will have to find some other biddable young woman to do the honors of being your paramour!"

"We'll see," he said enigmatically, and hastened his horse to a trot.

18

Aimee waited in the antechamber with trepidation, remembering only too well the icy-cold dampness of the prison called the Châtelet. She was alone, except for two soldiers who sat talking around a desk that was piled with papers. She had been waiting here ever since Lucian deposited her on the bench after they had been brought in. She had no idea where her brother was, though Lucian had promised to try to get him some medical attention. She felt bone-weary suddenly as she reflected on the sequence of the night's events. One thought shined above everything else— Faron was dead! It didn't matter what happened to her now, for she had accomplished her revenge. If she died on the gibbet for murder, so be it!

It seemed hours had gone by and her head was slowly tipping forward, falling to her chest, when she heard the sound of Lucian's voice in the hallway. Immediately, she sprang to attention, wondering what news he had for her.

Upon seeing the grim expression on his face, her heart sank. "Etienne has died," she said dully.

"No," Lucian returned soberly, "but that event will be arranged for later next month. I'm afraid there's very little I can do for your brother, Aimee. As the leader of a band of cutthroats—"

"Cutthroats!" Aimee interrupted with a sad laugh. "Why, they never harmed any of those they robbed. Lucian, my brother wasn't capable of cold-blooded murder—he hesitated even at killing Faron, who truly deserved to die! Surely you can convince the magistrate of that!"

"My dear, I'm afraid I am not a magician. The laws were not made to be broken for friends and loved ones. Your brother will die next month on the gallows, as will his accomplices . . ."

Aimee whitened at the inference.

"All except one," Lucian continued, his blue eyes on her face with an intent seriousness.

"So, you *are* a magician," Aimee murmured, unable to believe that Lucian had gotten her off so easily.

"I managed to convince the provost that you were only a dupe in the plan, an innocent who had been conned into acting as the lookout while your brother and his comrades did the actual robbing. Because of your previous arrest record, though, he is unwilling to let you roam Paris at will. You will be put under the close watch of a guardian."

Aimee's cheeks flamed. "And, I presume that *you* are that guardian?" she queried, unsure whether she felt relief or anger at this maneuver.

To her complete surprise, he shook his head. "Not I, my dear. I could not claim responsibility for you because of . . . certain circumstances. But you will become the ward of a very high personage, someone whose elevation in the government will keep you beyond any reproach."

"And may I ask who this statesman is?" she asked curiously.

"Not at this time," he said flatly, indicating the two guards who were listening to the conversation with indifferent interest. "I'm afraid for the time being you will be escorted to the prison of Saint-Lazare, to remain there until further instructions are issued."

Bewildered at this unexpected turn of events, Aimee stared at him openmouthed. "I don't understand. This seems a strange way to treat a prisoner of no account," she said. "You can save me, yet you cannot save my brother?"

"It is not possible," Lucian said flatly.

Aimee stiffened, then held her head up high, her green eyes clashing with his blue ones. "Then take me to the jails below, monsieur, for I cannot remain alive and well while my brother languishes in prison and ends up on the gallows. *I* was the one who committed murder—and I deserve to hang for it. The laws are inflexible, as you told me. I cannot avoid my deserved fate!"

Lucian laughed suddenly, the sound almost jarring in the high-ceilinged room. "Ah, what a vexing young wench you are, Aimee de Chartres." He laughed, his blue eyes creased with humor. "Here I offer you freedom of a sort, a chance at life—and you refuse it! And why? For a brother who obviously did not have your best interests at heart when he allowed you to accompany him on his dangerous missions. You would die with him, would you?" He came closer and grasped her by the shoulders. "I am tempted to let them throw you into the prison and be done with you, my dear! For I have the distinct notion that I shall rue the day I did not!"

"Could it be you are afraid of me?" Aimee asked with unintentional coquetry, letting her eyes slide up beneath her lashes.

He laughed again, but not so heartily. "If I am afraid of you, wench, it's only because I have the feeling you shall be my cross to bear in life. Because of you, I have already risked much in seeing that you are kept out of the Châtelet. I have promised everything to people who will always be greedy for more—and yet I am not even sure I can keep those promises. And now, with your proud little head held high, you tell me that I can keep all of my good intentions, thank you, and you would just as soon accompany your beloved brother to the gallows!" He sighed deeply. "You make me feel very foolish, little one. And there are very few women who can boast of that."

"I am not boasting of anything," Aimee said firmly. "I only wish for my brother to receive a reprieve. I—"

"You ask for a reprieve as though asking for another slice of bread," Lucian put in roughly. "The Directory is not in the mood for reprieves, my dear."

For a long moment, they stood facing each other, his hands on her shoulders, staring into each other's eyes. Suddenly, he grinned most charmingly, as though having made up his mind to do something. Aimee watched him, hardly daring to hope that he would somehow be able to grant her request. His next words shocked her.

"Let this one cool her heels in one of your detention rooms," he told the officers who awaited his orders. "She needs to learn a little lesson in humility, I think."

Aimee's face whitened, then flamed with anger. "What are you doing?" she demanded. "You—you—told me—you—"

"Now, now, don't tell me that you are the one who is afraid now, Aimee," he said softly. "Do you think, perhaps, that I will desert you, my dear?" He shook his head. "You will just have to trust me." Bowing slightly, he walked quickly out of the room with the air of one who has better things to do than indulge a prisoner of the Châtelet.

Aimee stared after him in disbelief. Was he going to make good his threat to allow her to go to the gallows with Etienne? She could not believe he would allow it; yet, here she was being taken to a small, damp room off the main corridor. Had she overplayed her hand? Had she pressed him too much? Obviously, she deduced that Lucian Napier did not enjoy being made to look foolish; yet, his idea of punishment did not appeal to her in the least.

As the hours rolled slowly by, Aimee paced her cell, building up her anger at Lucian for his perfidy. How dare he play these kinds of games with her? If he was going to have her released, then why force her to spend time in this room? If he was going to see her hanged, then why wasn't she below in the jails with the rest of the condemned? She shook her head, realizing she did not understand the man. And so long as she couldn't understand him, she was not about to place all of her trust in him.

While Aimee paced her cell at the Châtelet, Lucian paced the antechamber in front of Monsieur Charles Maurice de Talleyrand-Périgord's offices in the Tuileries. He tried to think of the most logical way of tackling the problem before him, but a lovely little face with provocative green eyes kept getting in his way. He chuckled to himself, trying to imagine how on earth he allowed himself to get so involved with the little chit. It seemed she truly was destined to be his cross to bear, for once she had immersed herself into his life, there was no way for him to rid himself of her.

The interesting thing about it was that it wasn't only the physical pleasure he could imagine enjoying in her arms or the pride he would feel at showing her off to society as his mistress—but he genuinely liked the little vixen. He was interested in her—he found her stimulating, interesting, and wholly entertaining. He liked being around her; she added spice to his life, a spice of which he fully intended to have more helpings.

But how to get around this sticky problem of her brother. As he had told Aimee, he had already promised much to the wily Talleyrand. He had practically signed over his services for the rest of his life to the minister of foreign relations, and now he had to promise something more. He tried to think about everything he had heard about the cunning Talleyrand.

Lucian knew that upon Talleyrand's graduation from the Collège d'Harcourt, he had been sent to the famous seminary of Saint-Sulpice in Paris, much against his wishes. He had not wished the life of a priest, but it had been forced on him, partly because of the injury to the right foot that caused the limp that had kept him out of military service, and partly because he loved women, wine, and the good life too much to make a very good cleric. But, after being ordained a priest at

Reims and becoming Monsieur l'Abbé, he had found that all manner of things were opened to him, including the salons, the government cabinets, and the ladies' boudoirs. Even after he became Bishop of Autun, he continued with his mistresses and his gambling. When he was elected to the first States-General in 1789, it was Talleyrand who had proposed selling the assets of the Church in order to refill the coffers of government. He was created a "constitutional" bishop under the Civil Constitution and was summarily excommunicated by the Pope, an action about which he could not have cared less.

In 1792, his name had been put on a list of traitors to be arrested and sent to the guillotine, but he had escaped to England. After being exiled from that country, he had gone to America for two years only to return from exile in triumph. Upon arriving back at Paris, he had been pressed into service by the Directory and given the title of Foreign Minister. Unfortunately, before having served in that office for a full year, he had already made a serious blunder, one that he was eager to cover up in order to regain his position of trust with the government. The blunder had been rather serious and could easily succeed in discrediting Talleyrand altogether, which would please his enemies only too well. It had come about because of the French search and seizure of American ships in open waters. There had been a large measure of good feeling on the part of the new republic of America for the French, but that good feeling was being eroded quickly because of the unlawful seizing of American ships, goods, and seamen.

President John Adams had asked his Cabinet what to do and had been advised to send a mission to Paris to try to negotiate with the Directory, which had refused to accept an American ambassador. Nevertheless, three Americans came to Paris, knowing that the Directory would refuse to see them. When their fears turned out to be correct, the three had not known what to do, and Talleyrand, seeing a chance to fool the gullible Americans and make something for himself, had sent a messenger telling them that he wished to see them.

At an appointed time, the three Americans met three Frenchmen, who would identify themselves only as Messieurs X, Y, and Z, but they were apparently there on direct orders from Talleyrand. These three, Messieurs X, Y, and Z, suggested to the three Americans that the United States, in order to gain access to the Directory, must pay 32,000 florins for some worthless Dutch bonds and, in addition, present a gift of

$250,000 to Monsieur Talleyrand. Only then could negotiations begin. The Americans had been deeply shocked at his bald-faced order for a bribe, and had returned home in haste. Now, reports were being received that American ships were destroying or capturing French warships—this at a time when the French Navy could not afford any losses as Bonaparte planned the conquest of Egypt.

Talleyrand was, indeed, in serious trouble, and Lucian hoped that he might be able to offer him some kind of life raft—in exchange for two insignificant lives.

When, finally, he was admitted into Talleyrand's office, Lucian saw immediately that the Foreign Minister did look a bit harried. Of medium height and well proportioned, the man was very dashing in his dark clothing, which accentuated his light features. Not classically handsome, he nevertheless was appealing, with a retroussé nose, sardonic mouth, and a superior, aloof air that seemed to entice many women to try their seductive wiles on him. He accepted most with little resistance and was known as a great womanizer despite his deformed right foot and his forty-four years.

"Yes?" Talleyrand looked up, his bushy, light brows drawing together at the sight of his visitor. "Well, Monsieur Napier, hadn't you only left me earlier this morning? I see you are back already. What is it this time?"

Lucian got to the point immediately. "As you know, Monsieur Talleyrand, you have already granted my request of a reprieve for a young woman who was involved with her brother in a high-waymen's gang outside Paris. I have come back because this stiff-necked wench will not accept my help unless I also retrieve her brother from the gallows."

Talleyrand stared at him with sharp blue eyes. "This woman means so much to you, my friend?"

Lucian allowed himself a smile. "We earlier discussed her worth, monsieur. Under your influence and protection, she can be taught the things she will need to know in order to undertake the bold mission you brought forth earlier. I know how very much you wish to extend the borders of France—even beyond the Atlantic to the Americas themselves."

Talleyrand stood up, walking thoughtfully over to the window, his hand clasping the ever-present walking stick that relieved him of most of his limp. "Yes, indeed, my friend, I hold high hopes that one day France will extend her domination over entire countries. That is why, as you are aware, we have been negotiating a secret treaty with Spain, trying to get them to sign over that piece of North America that is theirs. In the last century, Spain has lost much of her power and her glory. I believe it would be well for France to get the Louisiana Territory back from a jittery Spain in order to put direct French military pressure on United States policy. We cannot have this new republic back-sliding into the hands of the British!" He turned to Lucian and his eyes were fierce. "For the glory of France!" he added with a flourish.

"I know that you have high hopes of succeeding with a treaty," Lucian responded. "But, as yet, there has been little success, with Spain proving more than obstinate. Meanwhile, America grows angrier at our warships' searching her naval vessels on the ocean, and now she is beginning to turn from us. We have received varied reports of the Americans enlarging their army and building a navy in order to prepare for eventual war."

"I fear that as they strengthen themselves, they will have the ability to take the port of New Orleans and the Louisiana Territory away from Spain before France is able to get them back. And now"—his cheeks reddened a bit at the admission—"I have bungled badly in this X, Y, Z affair. I have put distrust in the heart of even our staunchest ally in America, Thomas Jefferson. As Vice President under Adams, he could have helped us a great deal, but now—" He held out his hands and shook his head.

"Let me propose a solution to the problem," Lucian said, gaining the other man's attention effectively. "You know of my considerable skills as statesman and spy, which I have used for a good many years in the service of France."

Talleyrand nodded. "And let us not forget your military background," he added with a wink.

"I propose that you send me to America as a personal emissary directly from you, acting for the government of France, to Jefferson. Let me talk to him. As you know, my mother is an American, and Jefferson and I have met already on several occasions on his visits to Paris before the revolution. I believe he holds me in as much esteem as I hold him. If I tell him that you will be able to persuade the Directory to end this undeclared war between us, it would certainly be a coup for you, monsieur!"

"I see what you're getting at, Napier. Reopening diplomatic channels between our two countries would lessen the pressure on the Directory. They've got all they can handle from England—not to mention the glory that Bonaparte is amassing as he continues with his military victories. Believe me, Napier, Barras has mentioned more than once how nice it would be to hear a report that young Bonaparte has met with an untimely cannonball to the head!" He laughed sardonically. "I have an idea, though, that that is most unlikely to happen. In fact, were I Barras I might begin to worry about my own head!"

He met Lucian's frank gaze and smiled. "And so, I suppose for this service you are doing the French government—and me, personally—you expect not only the life of this young lady, who you assure me will make a loyal and useful spy for France, but also the life of her brother."

"Exactly." It was Lucian's turn to smile.

"You are aware, are you not, how tenuous is the life of a spy, my friend?" Talleyrand spoke warningly in a deceptively soft voice. "I could denounce you as a traitor at any time and your old friend Fouché would probably delight in seeing your head fall under the blade."

"The thought *has* occurred to me," Lucian admitted, although he continued to smile.

The two men stared at each other a moment longer. Talleyrand leaned on his cane, trying to gauge the trustworthiness of the young man who stood before him. Finally, he nodded.

"I haven't very much choice, really," he admitted with a sigh. "This affair has left me rather an outcast with the Directory, and I must put credibility back into my position; otherwise, I am lost." He went back to his desk and sat down, scribbling quickly on a document. "Here is the arrest order for one Etienne de Chartres," he said, holding it out to Lucian. "I have written the order for his reprieve, as well as the information that he shall be allowed his full freedom, including the right to leave Paris, should he so desire. There will be put at your disposal, my friend, the usual sums of money for your mission." He cocked his head and gazed at the younger man. "I must confess an interest in this young lady for whom you have asked so much—and promised so much. When is she . . . ah . . . to be delivered to me?"

Lucian smiled, knowing the proud Aimee de Chartres would have her dainty hands quite filled while he was away, trying to keep away the advances of the amorous Talleyrand. Somehow, though, he was sure she was equal to the task. "I have arranged for her to be put in the Châtelet detention room overnight. From there, she shall be taken to the prison of Saint-Lazare, where her brother will also be sent. She will insist on remaining with him until his wound mends, after which time I hope to persuade him to return to his estate near Orléans, along with a tidy sum to begin rebuilding. I should say that Aimee de Chartres shall be presenting herself at your house in the rue du Bac sometime in April." He bowed and hurried out of the office, his mind already planning the details of his departure.

19

Aimee de Chartres settled herself uncertainly in the proffered seat to which a pretty, young maid had led her inside a splendidly appointed salon room. She was dressed in clothing suitable for a countess, she thought rather dazedly, looking down at the rich silk of the gown that had arrived at the prison of Saint-Lazare for her this morning. After many weeks of becoming accustomed to the plain prison garb, the soft richness of the high-waisted gown felt like some obscene luxury. Even her hair had been styled for this occasion by a fussy young man who had wanted to hack away at her splendid golden curls in order to reduce them into the short hairstyle that represented a Grecian statue and which, he assured her, was so much in vogue now. At her piteous plea, he had consented to leaving the back long, swirling the thick golden mass into a tight coiffure at the back of her head, but insisting on cutting the front and sides into the wispy tendrils so in style and designed, he told her, to frame the face most effectively.

Having just turned nineteen, Aimee had responded enthusiastically to the fuss made over her appearance. She had been in awe of the number of jars and tiny pots the hairdresser had pulled from a cloth bag. A touch of red to her lips, a pink stain on her cheeks, a fine line of kohl to the top of her eyelids—the little magician seemed to be preparing her for employment in a bordello, she thought humorously, but held her tongue lest she offend him. She remembered Lucian Napier's telling her that she was to meet a very influential personage once her brother had recovered and they were both released.

The thought of Lucian made her suddenly wish desperately that he were here with her now. She was very nervous in this strange salon, in a strange and splendid house, meeting an unknown man. She looked down at her finery, reflecting that she had never been dressed thus, nor would she have been even if she had become the wife of Henri de Brueys. *Lucian, where are you now?* she wondered. She recalled the last time she had seen him nearly two months before.

He had arrived in the detention room, freshly shaved and appearing to have received an excellent night's sleep. She, on the other hand, felt tired and haggard, having slept not at all on the hard mattress that had been rolled out at nightfall for her. She had gazed at him with emerald eyes, trying to hold down her fury, but unequal to the task in the face of his optimistic heartiness.

"Well?" she blurted out, crossing her arms over her breasts and tapping her foot impatiently. "How can you stand there, grinning at me so charmingly, when I long to scratch your eyes out for making me wait all night in this room! If you want to see me hanged, then do it now, for I cannot stand another night in this place!"

"But, my dear, you wound me to the heart." He had merely laughed, sidestepping her neatly when she launched herself at him, fingers outstretched like claws. "Listen to me, vixen!" he added, catching hold of her arms and pinning them firmly at her sides. "You will not have to spend another night in this place, I promise you. I have done all that you requested, my lady."

As his last words sank in beyond the anger, Aimee raised surprised eyes to his. "You mean—"

"You and your brother will not be called upon to stretch your necks on the gallows," he told her, smiling at the look of joy that transfixed her face.

Without artifice, Aimee flung herself at him, wrapping her arms around his neck and pressing her face into his shoulder. She was crying and her whole body shook against his as Lucian's arms came up to hold her protectively.

"Oh, Lucian, I am so sorry! Can you ever forgive me for doubting you?" she asked him, turning her face up, the tears wetting her cheeks and the material of his shirtfront at the same time.

He kissed her lightly, unable to resist it, tasting the saltiness of her lips. "I forgive you," he assured her, "but I'm afraid you cannot be set free immediately. You and your brother will be transferred to the prison of Saint-Lazare. It is much more comfortable than this, and you will be able to tend to your brother's wounds. When he is able to get around on his own, he is to be sent back to your home in Orléans with enough money to start rebuilding your ancestral castle. I'm sure a man of his spirit will find a suitable young wife without a problem. By this time next year, he should be a happily married man starting a family and reclaiming his birthright."

"Oh, it does sound too good to be true!" Aimee sighed, imagining her brother with a pipe between his teeth and a pretty, young wife at his side within the Castle du Beautreillis. She looked up at Lucian with a question in her eyes. "And what about me, Lucian? Have you decided my fate also?" The question was put to him without sarcasm.

"You will be taken to the home of a very wealthy man in government."

"For what purpose?" she asked, aware of a grain of suspicion in her breast.

He avoided her eyes, deeming the time not right to explain the dubious joys of being a spy for one's government. "You will be safe there," he hedged. "Your duties will be few—and things will be explained to you in slow stages."

Aimee's golden brows drew down in consternation. "You are not . . . selling me . . . to some lecherous lord as his mistress, are you, Lucian?" she wondered aloud, and this time the sarcasm stained her words.

He laughed and kissed her again, but she pulled herself from his arms and gazed at him determinedly. "Do not try to get around me," she warned him, tilting her head to one side. "I want to know what is to become of me."

"You will be safe," he said again, thinking how delicious she looked with her hair tousled and her green eyes seeming sleep-deprived. The thought of being away from her for several months caused a strange pang in the region of his heart.

"Safe from whom?" she asked. "You, Lucian?"

He shook his head. "No need to worry about me, my dear, for I shan't be troubling you for some months. I have business of my own to attend to that requires extensive travel."

The anger left her eyes at this bit of unexpected news. "You . . . are leaving me?"

Her innocent words caused a stab of desire in Lucian, but he was careful to mask it. "I shall return, sweetheart. You've no need to worry on that score. But, while I am gone, you must do your best to listen to the advice you will be receiving from a certain gentleman."

"But, I don't understand—"

He stopped her questions with a finger to her lips. "You will understand soon enough, Aimee."

And she hadn't seen him after that, she thought, wondering what business it was that had taken him away from Paris. He had told her she would understand soon enough, but here she was in this grand house without one shred of knowledge as to her reason for being there. She comforted herself with the knowledge that

Etienne had indeed gone back to Castle du Beautreillis with the intention of rebuilding the castle, all thoughts of wild adventure having fled from his system. He had had enough of that in Paris and was ready, at twenty-five, to settle down. The idea made Aimee wonder again about Lucian Napier; he was nearly thirty, yet he had not settled down, nor did he seem to have any intentions of doing so.

Her thoughts were interrupted by the slight noise of a walking stick on the polished oak floor of the hallway outside the salon. The sound riveted her eyes to the doorway, in which a slender figure appeared, dressed in black to contrast strongly with his fair features, leaning slightly on the curved head of an ebony cane. There was a superior air about the man, as though, she thought, he had descended from royalty and was only biding time until the madness of the revolution had passed and he could take his rightful place among the true nobility. His light blue eyes passed quickly over her entire person as she sat in the chair, watching him with some trepidation.

"You are Mademoiselle de Chartres?" he questioned finally, making his way into the room without difficulty. Indeed, the limp was barely noticeable and Aimee was so riveted by his eyes that she would not have noticed anyway. At her nod, he smiled suddenly. "You seem fearful, my dear. Please do not be, for I have no intention of hurting you."

Aimee swallowed and nodded once more. "Who are you?" she managed to squeak.

"Ah, you do not know me, then." He bowed grandly. "I am Talleyrand, the Foreign Minister of the Directory." As enlightenment showed in her eyes, he seemed pleased. "What have you heard of me?"

"Only that you are as cunning as a fox," she said carelessly. It was true, she did recognize the name and knew him to be one of the wiliest men in France. It had been whispered about at one time that he had sold his government's secrets to England, then had done the same to the Americans. He had nearly been sent to the guillotine, but had escaped the Reign of Terror by the skin of his teeth. After living in exile for some years, he had returned to Paris to acclamation and the offer of a government job that held high prestige and monetary gain.

"Cunning as a fox," Talleyrand repeated, taking a seat close beside her. "I suppose I do like the sound of that, my dear, especially from your lovely lips. One has to be cunning in order to survive the madness of this world, don't you agree?"

Aimee wasn't sure what to say. "I'm not very cunning," she said.

"And yet, you are a survivor," he pointed out. "Why is that?"

"I suppose it is because I was lucky enough to have made a friend like Lucian Napier—"

"Who has enough cunning for both of you," Talley rand murmured to himself. Then, louder, he said to her, "Luck is almost as important as cunning sometimes, my dear. And beauty"—he leaned closer to her, his eyes running appreciatively over the pale slopes of her bosom, revealed by the low cut of the gown— "can be even more important—when it is used properly."

Aimee leaned away from him, her eyes revealing her confusion. "I . . . I don't know what you mean, monsieur."

He smiled again. "Lucian has sent me an innocent," he said, rubbing his chin with his index finger. "Ah, well, I have always loved a challenge."

"Lucian did not inform me as to what my exact reason is for being here," Aimee said carefully. "He told me that everything would be revealed in time."

"And so it shall be," Talleyrand assured her. "But for now, you are simply my ward. There is a room in this house that will be yours. You will have your own servant to see to all of your needs. I require only that you tell me when you are going out and where you are going, for the present. As to your duties"—he lifted his eyebrows speculatively—"we shall see about them after you have settled in."

Aimee was not sure she liked the sound of that. She had heard about the famous Talleyrand's womanizing. His amorous exploits had been bandied about in public on the Pont Neuf, in the scandal sheets, and at the Fair of Saint-Germain. He enjoyed women a great deal and his reputation was such to prove that they enjoyed him also. Aimee did not trust him at all, especially when he looked at her with that speculative glance, as though assessing her reactions to various proposals he might make. What had Lucian promised him? she wondered. She tried to keep her trust in her friend, but found it hard in the face of these new complications.

After chatting amiably about unimportant matters and household details, Talleyrand had a servant lead her upstairs to her rooms: a suite of three rooms that comprised a bedchamber, a closet for her wardrobe, and a dressing room, all of which were appointed beautifully. In awe, Aimee let her fingers run over the softness of the counterpane, the richness of the draperies at the windows, the carved furniture pieces that were more splendid than anything she had ever seen. The closet was empty, awaiting gowns that she herself would choose the next day when she saw the dressmaker. Her head felt totally muddled as her young maid, named Yvonne, directed her attention to the sumptuous dressing table and the delicately molded silver bathing tub. Yvonne handed Aimee a list, written in Talleyrand's own hand, of the various people with whom she would be acquainting herself: the dance master, the drawing instructor, the tutor who would freshen up her knowledge of math and writing, and the young lady who would instruct her in the social graces, something in which she had definitely been lacking during her escapades in the streets of Paris, Aimee thought with a half smile.

"But why is Monsieur Talleyrand doing all of this for me?" she wondered aloud. "He doesn't even know me."

Yvonne seemed at a loss. "I don't know, mademoiselle, but I suppose it is not unusual for a great lord to do as he pleases, no matter how strange it seems."

Aimee had to agree, but still she wondered. She recalled that Lucian had told her he had promised much in order to gain her release from prison and the gallows: Had he promised to deliver a new mistress to the Foreign Minister?

As the days of spring rolled into summer, Aimee delighted in the life she led as the protected ward of the Foreign Minister of France. If some highborn ladies snickered behind their hands and wondered openly at the relationship between the forty-four-year-old libertine and the young and beautiful woman whose background was something of a mystery, Aimee chose not to see it. While it was true that Talleyrand sometimes allowed his eyes to rove over her form on the rare occasions he had supper with her, she contented herself with the knowledge that he had never done anything else to deserve reproach. In fact, much of the time he seemed barely interested in her, his mind full of details of government or the juggling act he must do between two of his mistresses, both of whom were married ladies. One of his lovers, Madame Grand, Catherine Worlée, was even friendly to Aimee, taking her with her on shopping sprees and allowing her to accompany her on walks through the Tuileries gardens on those days when Talleyrand was engaged elsewhere. Rather birdlike and silly, Catherine seemed not to have a mean bone in her body, and Aimee accepted her friendship happily, for she longed for someone with whom she could really talk. She was too much in awe of Talleyrand, her brother was full of his own concerns in Orléans, and Lucian had still not returned. She thought of Rosine sometimes and wondered what she would say should Aimee make an appearance at the home of the de Brueys, but, most likely, Madame de Brueys had poisoned her against Aimee and Aimee wasn't sure she could face the cold unfriendliness of the girl who had once been her only close companion. Besides, she had no wish to see Henri de Brueys again, or hear of his splendid marriage.

Fortunately, she was too busy to be depressed. Besides Catherine's excursions, she had her dancing and drawing classes and her lessons in deportment. Talleyrand had allowed her the use of his library, and she also wandered the huge gardens at the back of the house, gathering blooms for the vases inside the house. Talleyrand, on those occasions when he was home in the evenings, even consented to teaching her the game of whist, which he enjoyed greatly and claimed that Catherine was too stupid to learn.

It was on one such evening, while Aimee looked over her cards and thought of appropriate strategy, that Talleyrand informed her he had received news from Lucian. His eagle eyes noted the glow in her green orbs as she asked him for more information.

"He should be ready to return from his trip shortly," he told her, deliberately being nonspecific. "I expect him back toward the end of summer."

"That seems a long time away." Aimee sighed, practicing her newly acquired pout on her companion.

Talleyrand chuckled as she batted her eyelashes at him in perfect imitation of the young lady who had been teaching her social graces. "Not so long, my dear. In fact, it seems too soon, for I've an idea that when Lucian returns I will not have so many free evenings for whist—and your delightful company."

"Why should Lucian's return keep us from enjoying our game?" Aimee queried, remembering to tilt her head provocatively as Madame de Vois had suggested.

"Because with his return, your real education will begin," Talleyrand returned enigmatically.

This effectively stopped any more flirtatious measures from Aimee as she leaned forward earnestly, all artifice dropped. "And what exactly is this real education?" she asked. "For a long time, Monsieur Talleyrand, I have been wondering about the reasons for my welcome in your home. You are not a married man, and although you care little for your own reputation, I am still young enough to worry about mine," she added with refreshing candor.

"Your reputation is hardly the issue," Talleyrand said dryly. "People will think what they like. It would make little difference if I was married—or even if you were! Vicious minds pounce on any shred of gossip that will enliven their stupid, mundane lives." His blue eyes looked at her with a touch of calculation. "You, my dear, would not wish to grow up and become one of those stupid, mundane women I speak of, would you?"

"I don't think so," Aimee said cautiously. She was not quite sure what Talleyrand was getting at.

"Good. For you, life should be a continual adventure, an exciting game—much more exciting than this quiet game of whist." He stood up suddenly, throwing his cards down on the table. With his cane, he walked around to Aimee's side of the table, putting his free hand on her shoulder where the material of her dress stopped to reveal the tender flesh along her collarbone. "You are much too lovely and too intelligent to become one of those women whose lives revolve around whom her next lover is going to be, or which dress she will choose to wear to the next ball. Life is too short for such paltry titillation." As he talked, his hand unconsciously slid back and forth across her shoulder, raising goose bumps on Aimee's exposed flesh.

"But what else is there?" She sighed, fighting the urge to lean her head back in an attitude of surrender. How potent were his caresses!

"There is real life, my dear—there is travel and the gathering of knowledge and the meeting of exciting people! Your Lucian is one who thrives on such lively arts, and you would do well to emulate him!"

"But how could I propose to do that?" Aimee asked, aware that Talleyrand's hand had slipped lower and was brushing against the upper slope of her breast.

"Through the real education I was speaking of, my dear," Talleyrand continued, his voice growing husky with desire. "If you prove yourself an apt pupil, you will go far, of that I'm sure. You have the tools and the inquisitiveness—now you must learn to sharpen your skills."

His words meant little to Aimee as she became aware of nothing but the increased rapidity of her heartbeat while Talleyrand's hand slipped inside the bodice of her gown and expertly fondled her breast. There was a tightening inside of her, a tingling sensation that seemed to emanate from her breast to that secret place between her thighs.

Glancing down at the heightened color in the young woman's cheeks, and noticing the increased rate of breathing, Talleyrand smiled to himself. Certainly she was proving an apt pupil in the game of love, he thought wyrly. Would she apply herself as well to the more serious game of spying for her country? Her beauty could prove deadly in such a game, for what man would not be moved by it? Certainly Talleyrand, quite jaded after a life of debauchery, felt an old spark kindling deep within himself at the idea of making love to her. He wondered, curiously, if Lucian had already tasted this one—and the thought of Lucian brought him back to reality and the real reason for his guardianship of the girl. Regretfully, he removed his hand, sliding it up her throat and awarding a final caress to her cheek.

A sigh escaped Aimee as she half turned to regain the feeling that had been extinguished with Talleyrand's removal of his hand from her body. But he was already moving toward the sideboard, intent on pouring himself something to drink.

"You almost make me forget how much trouble I am already in with women." Talleyrand sighed with a half smile.

Aimee colored, realizing how she had just displayed a perplexing wantonness that dismayed her. Talleyrand would think her a fool, she thought dismally, risking a peep at him from between her eyelashes. To her relief, he did not look at her as though he thought her foolish.

"I think I shall have to visit Catherine tonight," Talleyrand said ruefully after finishing his drink. "You are quite enough to ignite a man's blood, my dear."

At her silence, he went on. "You should feel flattered, not ashamed, Aimee. Most beautiful women use their bodies blatantly to get what they want from a man, while you, by withholding your favors, may have found the means to bring them to their knees. It is quite a remarkable trait, quite devastating."

Aimee was not sure whether to thank him for the compliment.

"At any rate, my dear, Lucian will be returning from his mission shortly and you will find out from him all you need to know about why you are here. He is more experienced in these matters —and certainly as experienced as I with women, despite his comparative youth!" He laughed cynically. He came back to the table and reseated himself. "You miss him?"

"Yes," Aimee responded automatically.

Talleyrand frowned. "Ah, you would do well not to put so much of your heart into it, little one. Despite the fact that I find your honesty refreshing, it can sometimes do you more harm than good. I have learned to keep my true feelings hidden in most cases; it is the best way I know to protect one's inner self."

"But, then, you are deceiving only yourself," Aimee murmured candidly.

Talleyrand blinked at her perception, then laughed aloud. "Aha! Perhaps Lucian was right—you may be the perfect one for our little mission, my dear." He leaned closer. "Of course, it may do you well to learn a little deception yourself!"

It was Aimee's turn to get to her feet and pace along the edge of the carpet. "I do not care for dishonesty, monsieur," she said.

The man's blue eyes narrowed. "Strange words from a former pickpocket and highwayman," he suggested smoothly, seeing the blush on her cheeks at his words. "No, do not try to persuade me of your innocence," he went on, holding up his hand. "It matters not at all to me." He watched her for a few minutes as though to gauge her reaction to his next question. "Do you love your country, Aimee?"

She stopped her pacing to stare at him. "Of course! I love France as much as my father loved her—despite the fact that he was tried for treason. It was a false charge, Monsieur, I can tell you! He loved his country more than many of those rabble-rousers who cheered his death!"

"I did not ask you to expound on your father's patriotism, my dear," Talleyrand said calmly. "I only asked for your views. Would you, for instance, do something *dishonest* if it was for the good of your country?"

Aimee hesitated. "That would depend," she hedged.

Talleyrand smiled. "You give the answer of a born statesman," he said, applauding her. "No, I will not press you further for now." He stood up and bowed to her. "I think it is time for me to bid you good-night, my dear. I've enjoyed our little chat, believe me—and I look forward to more of the same at a later date. If you will excuse me?"

Aimee nodded, bidding him good-night, watching as he made his way out of the room, presumably to spend the rest of the night at one of his long list of lovers' residences. She thought about what he had said concerning Lucian, recalling his inference that the younger man was every bit the connoisseur of women that he was. Aimee dropped into a chair, staring out the window at the summer darkness, thinking about the man of whom she knew so little, yet to whom she felt a special attachment. Memories of her near seduction by Lucian at the boardinghouse in the Montmartre came back to her, and the thought occurred to her that perhaps she should have not been so eager to stop his advances. The idea made her cheeks burn and she stood up, suddenly angry with herself for thinking such a thing.

"I owe him a great deal for saving my life and the life of Etienne," she said aloud, addressing the silent stacks of books around her. "But he cannot *buy* my embraces! We shall see about this 'education' Talleyrand keeps hinting at!"

20

While Aimee awaited Lucian's return to Paris, Bonaparte continued his military campaign against the English, sailing from Toulon and landing with the French fleet in Egypt on July 1, 1798. Three weeks later, the Battle of the Pyramids was fought, and the French won a decisive victory, but news reached Paris in August that the English admiral, Nelson, had practically annihilated the French fleet, leaving the army cut off in Egypt. Meanwhile, more bad news came to the attention of the people. All of Bonaparte's conquests in Italy and Germany had been freed and a combined English-Russian force had landed in Holland. The people were grumbling against the government, and in the elections of that year, the Jacobins were voted into office. The Directory had the election results annulled, unwilling to lose its power to the political party that had spawned the terrorist governments of the early revolutionary years.

Aimee, living in the same house as the French Foreign Minister, could not help but be aware of the tension in the government. Talleyrand was taciturn and unwilling to spend any evenings playing with his ward. Everyone in the house was obliged to walk around on tiptoes so as not to disturb their master while he deliberated behind closed doors in his library. Catherine Worlée was very often red-eyed from crying when she visited Aimee, complaining that her dear Charles no longer was as attentive to her as before.

Toward the end of August, Talleyrand surprised Aimee by requesting her help in planning a soirée.

"I will provide the list of invited guests," he told her briskly. "They will include anyone who has the slightest hold on the power in government." He eyed his ward warningly. "You must learn, my dear, never to settle too comfortably into any position, because there is always someone who would like to see you pushed out of it. But if you know your enemies, they can never surprise you."

"So you will be inviting your enemies to a party?" Aimee queried with raised eyebrows.

He smiled. "Exactly. Who knows who will be in power tomorrow? One can't be too careful—one must cultivate friendships on both sides in this war!"

Aimee settled in to the task he had given her, asking, and receiving, the help of Catherine Worlée, who tittered excitedly at being able to give aid to the ward of the man she most wanted to marry in the world. Aimee was grateful for all of her suggestions, for the diplomatic refinements of negotiating such a gathering were still beyond her reach, having had no experience in such matters.

On the appointed day, the house was a beehive of activity as extra help, hired especially for the occasion, made sure that the salon floors were waxed to a shiny gloss, that all the silver was polished and the china was gleaming. The orchestra that Catherine had suggested for the evening had just arrived when Aimee, feeling a bit frazzled, dashed into her dressing room, calling for Yvonne to ready her gown for the evening. Although she barely had a moment to spare, she nevertheless had to take the time to bathe, for she'd been in the wine cellar, the pantry, and the garden all day, picking the flowers that would adorn the large tables and making choices for the food and drink that would be served to the guests.

After a scant fifteen minutes in the warmed, perfumed water, Aimee toweled herself dry and swiftly rolled up the clocked silk stockings in a flesh-tone shade that were all the rage in Paris that summer. Yvonne handed her a single silken petticoat that fit closely to her hips and waist and then pulled the white muslin gown over her head, tying the wide green sash that spanned the area beneath her breasts, which were pushed up enticingly by the low-cut scoop of the bodice.

Aimee sat before the mirror of her dressing table, watching her reflection impatiently as Yvonne collected the thick, gleaming mass of golden curls onto the back of her head, securing them with dozens of tiny pins, each pasted with a brilliant so that her hair seemed to sparkle like the stars. The front was combed forward into calculatedly disheveled locks "à la Titus," which framed her face and set off the green jewels of her eyes. Talleyrand had suggested a single length of green silk around her neck to match the sash of the dress, making her attire quite simple, but completely charming. Aimee reflected on how some ladies would sponge the entire length of the chemise gown in order to make the material cling indecently to their bodies, but she declined the idea, knowing instinctively that was not the image she, nor Talleyrand, wanted her to display this evening.

After donning a pair of white, elbow-length gloves, Aimee twirled around for Yvonne's smiling inspection, then hurried out of her room to meet Talleyrand downstairs before the guests began to arrive. She found him inspecting the several different kinds of hors d'oeuvres that were packed in ice before being set out when the guests arrived.

His fingers grasping a piece of boned, truffled quail, Talleyrand laughed at her automatic look of reprimand, then popped the hors d'oeuvre into his mouth. "Mmm. Quite delicious, my dear," he pronounced. His eyes traveled the length of her figure. "As are you in that ravishing ensemble. You will certainly set the ladies to buzzing about our 'relationship' tonight, and the men to hoping to unseat me in your affections."

"That would be impossible." She smiled, flashing him a flirtatious look from sparkling green eyes.

He answered the look and took her arm to lead her into the wide foyer of the house, whose Corinthian façade was brightly lit with lanterns on this warm summer night. They checked with the cook as to the time when supper would be served, then instructed the orchestra on what time to begin playing the dance music. Aimee anxiously rechecked the menu, noting the pork-and-cabbage soup would be the first course and admonishing the cook to keep it hot. Afterward, there would come a real pumpkin, hollowed out, used to hold pumpkin soup, then large crayfish shells used to conceal squabs in ragout, one of Talleyrand's favorite dishes. Stuffed turkey with raspberries was the main course, with green-bean salad and chicken-and-pork pies. Iced cheese and sugar and honey wafers with marzipan tarts would make for a sumptuous dessert spread. Satisfied, Aimee left the kitchen to greet Catherine, who had come early to help with any last-minute details.

"I think your young pupil has done everything to perfection," Talleyrand told the older woman. "This night shall be a great success for her."

"Oh no!" Aimee protested quickly. "I shall certainly remain in the background, monsieur. With all these politicians and their wives, it will be dangerous ground for me to tread. I shall be content to watch you shine among them!"

Talleyrand nodded in acknowledgment of her gallantry. He gave his arm to Catherine, who took it with a giggle, then led her to the arched doorway in the foyer, through which all the guests would arrive.

Aimee stood nervously beside Catherine, trying not to stare as the guests started arriving, each woman seemingly more audacious with her dress and her jewelry than the next, as though there were some competition to see who could outshine the other. The men were more soberly attired, but even they were quite in fashion with their short, shaggy haircuts and the diamonds and sapphires they wore at their wrists and shirtfronts.

Before the last guest had gone through the short receiving line, Aimee thought her hand would remain limp for the rest of the night, so many times had it been grasped and held and kissed and squeezed. Many of the men had allowed their eyes to delve curiously into the décolletage of her gown, while the women— some of them—had looked daggers at the fresh appeal of her outfit. By the time dinner was announced, Aimee felt as though she had been put up at auction for all to inspect.

At the interlude between eating and dancing, she realized she was expected to keep the ladies entertained in one large salon, while the men talked in another. This proved less difficult than she feared, for the women naturally began talking animatedly as soon as the door closed on the males. Aimee tried to make herself quite indistinguishable from the woodwork, listening almost idly as the mistress of Paul Barras exchanged barbs with one of his former mistresses, now married to the young General Bonaparte, Josephine.

"Your husband has embarrassed himself quite thoroughly during this affair in Egypt," the current mistress said acidly. "He has lost nearly the entire fleet of French naval ships to Lord Nelson and has no way to return to France."

"Napoleon will find a way," Josephine spoke up quickly. "He will not stay away from Paris any longer than necessary. And when he does return, my dear, you had better take care of yourself as well as your paramour, for my husband intends to have a much greater say in the government!"

"Listen to you, warning me!" the other woman returned nastily. "You had better watch out for yourself. You seem to forget, dear Josephine, that you are a married woman! Taking one lover after another is not the best way to soothe that little hot head of a husband of yours!"

"I can handle my husband, Elizabeth," Josephine responded with a sneer.

"No doubt. But you will have to be careful, for the scandal is that he has had relations with a dozen Egyptian women during this campaign, and God knows what sort of disease he may bring back to you, my dear!"

Aimee moved carefully out of earshot, not wishing to hear any more of such a conversation. She wound her way gracefully around the room, trying not to hear the comments whispered about her as she passed. Most had to do with whether she was Talleyrand's mistress or his long-lost daughter, whom he refused to recognize. Most decided she was definitely his mistress and that she would surely be the one who would finally get the libertine to settle down and marry.

With relief, Aimee heard the knock sound on the door to announce that the men were finished talking and wished the ladies to rejoin them. While the orchestra tuned up, Aimee took the opportunity to talk with Talleyrand, who was anxious to know how she had fared.

Aimee related the guesses as to her identity and her reason for being in Talleyrand's household, to which Talleyrand laughed so loudly that several people stared. Aimee urged him to be quiet, pointing out that her reputation was nearly beyond repair as it was.

"Don't worry about your reputation, my dear," Talleyrand informed her. "It matters very little in the scheme of things. What else did the ladies discuss?"

"General Bonaparte's wife and Barras's current mistress nearly came to blows," she reported with a shrug. "Josephine saved face over the Egyptian bungling by saying that her husband expected to return to Paris shortly—and when he did, he would be having a much greater say in the government."

Talleyrand nodded thoughtfully. "So, our little Corsican aspires to higher things," he murmured to himself. He glanced at the girl with a smile. "My dear, you have done well for me. I shall, sooner or later, turn you into quite an efficient little spy, but it seems you already have a natural talent for it!" So saying, he bowed and left her to claim the first dance with Josephine Bonaparte.

Aimee thought for a moment on his words; the use of *spy* tasted rather sour on her tongue. Spies were cold, calculating people who cared only for the money they were paid and had absolutely no qualms about exposing the secrets of any person or government whose enemies could pay him the highest price. She would abhor such a person, she was certain, and should Talleyrand expect her to continue to come to him with such tales, she would most certainly have to set him straight on that account.

It was several hours later, when most of the wine had been drunk and several of the orchestra members had fallen asleep, that Aimee stifled a yawn and turned to the doorway to see Lucian Napier watching her with those flaming blue eyes she remembered so well. A smile of joyful welcome shaped her lips as she disengaged herself from the drunken dancing partner who was stepping all over her satin slippers and hurried to greet him.

"Lucian, how wonderful to have you back at last!" she cried honestly, wishing she could throw her arms around him, but remembering decorum at the last minute and restraining herself. Instead, she offered her hand, but her eyes danced at the comical look he gave her, as though to mimic the assembled guests who were in varying stages of drunkenness and fatigue. "They should be leaving soon," she added beneath the noise of the orchestra.

"Good. I should like to have you all to myself," he told her, resisting the urge to gather her in his arms and kiss that exquisite mouth of hers. His eyes took in the simplicity of her ensemble and, despite his own tiredness, his heart quickened and he felt desire shoot through him. "You look very beautiful tonight, my dear."

Aimee gazed back at him, aware of the dashing figure he displayed in the dark blue, double-breasted coat with the white waistcoat and a pair of buff-colored nankeen breeches. He did not look, she thought, as though he had only just arrived in town, and she said as much to him.

"I have to admit, I suppose, that I arrived earlier this morning, but before you harangue me because I did not call upon you immediately, let me tell you that I have been engaged in important meetings since ten o'clock. I got away only two hours ago, which gave me time to bathe and shave and change my attire. Then I came here immediately, hoping the party would be over and I would have some time alone with you."

"Oh, I wish it *were* over!" Aimee gave forth a heartfelt sigh. "These people are so—so—"

"Unreal?" Lucian supplied knowingly. "So artificial? Yes, I would dare to agree with you on that, Aimee, since the simple fact is that most of them *aren't* real—they don't have souls, you see."

"Souls?" Aimee smiled, wondering if he was making fun of her.

"Yes, you know that essence we are supposed to be born with that makes us different from the animals. These people, I'm afraid, are no different—except for you, of course. Your soul shines through those green eyes of yours every time you speak. God, it is refreshing!"

"Lucian, you are teasing me," she accused him.

"All right, if that is what you think, there'll be no more talk of souls. Just come and dance with me, sweetheart, since that is the only way I can feel my arms around you."

But before Lucian could do more than lead her out onto the dance floor, Talleyrand had spotted him and was making his way through the crowd to collar him. Reluctantly, Lucian blew Aimee a kiss and followed the older man to where a circle of government officials was conversing. Aimee watched him go with a sense of loss and the distinct feeling she would not get that dance —at least not this night. Halfheartedly, she accepted the proposal of another young man, whose energy knew no bounds and nearly wore her out before the dance was over.

After that, the endless succession of partners seemed to blur together as the evening wore on. Aimee found herself feeling shamelessly light-headed as another glass of champagne was pressed into her hands by a fervent young man who asked her to walk outside with him in the gardens. Aimee laughed and shook her head, gulping the cool drink as the warm breeze blew in from the opened windows and fanned her hot cheeks. She looked for Lucian, but he had disappeared into Talleyrand's library several minutes before. Disappointed, she accepted another young man's proposal to dance.

It was well past midnight, into the wee hours before dawn, before the last remaining guests made their way outside to their waiting vehicle. Aimee leaned against the doorframe, feeling her eyes drooping heavily as the clock sounded four o'clock in the morning. She felt so tired she would have gladly fallen asleep in the hallway, but realized it would never do for the servants to find her curled up on the rug. With a yawn, she made her way upstairs, wondering how people ever built up the stamina to stay awake all night at such social functions. She had noticed Talleyrand, still smiling and paying compliments to the end, and had been amazed at how well he had stood the test of the evening. For herself, she could hardly wait to sink beneath the covers in her own bed.

But no sooner had she dismissed Yvonne and slipped a clean, white nightgown over her head, she heard a discreet tapping at her door. Grumbling, and wondering what on earth Talleyrand might want to discuss now, Aimee opened the door a crack to reveal Lucian Napier waiting for her to let him in.

"Lucian? My goodness, I'd forgotten you were here," she whispered, aware of the darkness in the house and of the fact that she had only a single candle lit in her room to see what she was doing.

He smiled. "You cut me to the quick, my dear. How soon you forget those who admire you! But I suppose with all the probable swains you picked up at the gathering tonight, you don't need me to pay you pretty compliments anymore." He shouldered his way lightly into the room and closed the door behind him.

"Well, you can hardly expect for me to have you on my mind, when the moment you arrived, you were swept away by Talleyrand. I daresay you didn't spare a thought for *me* all night!" she accused him, watching as he blew out the candle she held and strode over to the long windows to open them to the waning moon's light.

The half light filled the room, a single moonbeam lighting Lucian's tall form as he walked back toward her. "You're wrong," he declared with a light laugh. "I did spare more than a few thoughts for you, my dear, which is why I wanted to stop by your rooms before you fell asleep."

"It's too late," she grumbled, sitting on the bed and rolling back the coverlet. "I've already fallen asleep, I'm afraid."

He laughed and sat down beside her, sweeping her into his arms, feeling the softness of her body beneath the nightgown. "You don't look asleep," he accused her, bending his head to plant little kisses all around her face.

"I would have been had you not stopped by," she protested, trying to shove him away.

He only held her that much tighter. "Then wake up, Aimee," he urged her softly. His lips found her soft, pliant mouth and he kissed her soundly, forcing her head back as she clung to him with both hands to keep herself from falling backward. "Now, do you believe I was thinking of you?" he wondered aloud, staring down into the lovely face and seeing her eyes closed, her lips parted.

Aimee opened her eyes. "Yes," she whispered.

"Good. And did you miss me all these months that I have been gone?" he prodded, still holding her with one arm while his free hand stroked her neck and throat.

She nodded. "You know very well I did, Lucian," she said sleepily. It was so pleasant here in his arms, she felt a tired wave wash over her as she leaned back against his arm and closed her eyes once more.

Lucian looked down at the young woman, so vulnerable and yet so trusting, and felt desire rage through himself. The sight of her throat disappearing into the lace at the top of her nightgown made him want to plant his mouth there and suck the life from the pulsating vein he saw. Swiftly, he bent his head and planted warm kisses on her throat, stopping at the lace only long enough to undo the fastenings of the bodice before delving farther down until his lips were caressing the softness of her upper breasts. Beneath his lips, Aimee stirred at the sensations he was evoking, feeling the points of her breasts stand turgid and hard in expectation of having his lips encircle them. A long sigh escaped her, after which she felt Lucian's mouth climbing back up to meet hers.

His kiss was hard, becoming more demanding, and Aimee tried to push away a little, her mood wishing for the soft, gentle feelings he had inspired before. "No," she protested sleepily. "No more, Lucian, please," she added when he took no heed of her protestations.

Lucian, despite his own weariness, felt his loins tightening, his manhood stiffening with his desire, but the object of his affections was so obviously uninterested in such things at this moment that he felt guilty insisting. With regret, he lay her back among the pillows, noting the sweet curve of her mouth as she smiled up at him, bleary-eyed. It was certainly not the easiest thing he had ever done—to stand up and tuck in bed such a ravishing little beauty, when all he wanted to do was sink down beside her and make love to her.

As he straightened, he saw her looking up at him, the smile still curving her lips. "I'm so glad you're back, Lucian," she whispered. "Good night." And she turned on her stomach, burying her face into the pillows and bending one knee so that her bewitchingly rounded bottom stood up enticingly beneath the cover.

Lucian groaned and set his teeth with his frustration, unable to resist one last caress on the curve of that bottom before standing up and walking softly out of the bedchamber, closing the door behind him.

Once out in the hallway, he shook his head and returned to the bedroom that Talleyrand had offered him, trying not to think of that tantalizing little vixen only a few feet across the hall, sleeping an innocent dreaming sleep, while he was doomed to toss and turn in bed for nearly an hour before finding his rest.

21

The next morning, Aimee opened her eyes to strong sunlight streaming through the opened windows into her bedroom. She was not at all surprised to find that she had slept past the noon hour and sat up to stretch hugely, satisfied at the cracking noises that came from her spine. The sun, combined with the heavy moisture in the air, made her feel sticky and hot beneath the coverlet, and she threw it aside to step out onto her bare feet, stretching once more before ringing the bellpull for Yvonne.

"Has Monsieur Talleyrand already left for the day?" Aimee inquired absently as she splashed cool water on her face to wake herself up.

"Yes, mademoiselle. He and Monsieur Napier left for the Tuileries earlier this morning." Yvonne pulled the nightgown from her mistress and settled a fresh slip and gown over her head. "The dancing master has already called twice, and your drawing teacher sent a message, wondering if you would be at class today."

"Goodness, I suppose I shall have to cancel all but Madame de Vois today," Aimee said. "I should like to take the air before it begins to cloud over and rain."

"But, mademoiselle, it is so hot!" Yvonne protested primly.

Aimee shrugged. "I won't melt," she said to her maid with a smile. "Besides, I must visit Madame Worlée in order to thank her properly for all her help during the party last night. It was a success, don't you think, Yvonne?"

The maid nodded vigorously. "Oh, yes, mademoiselle! I heard so many guests commenting on the food and the wine and the music—and on you, too, mademoiselle!" she added, her plump cheeks pinkening a little.

Aimee decided not to ask the exact nature of those comments. Heaven knew what sort of rumors were being bandied about and it would only frustrate or hurt her to know them all. She recalled the cattiness of Josephine Bonaparte and her rival last night and realized how cutting the remarks might be by two such "sophisticated" women of the city.

When she was dressed and had received her deportment tutor, Madame de Vois, for an hour, she sent a message to the other instructors, declining their services for the day, and selected a charming yellow umbrella to act as a sunshade for her walk out of doors. Yvonne would accompany her to the home of Catherine Worlée. Then Aimee wished to persuade Catherine to take a few turns about the Palais Royal or the Tuileries gardens, hoping to catch sight of Lucian. She recalled with a cloudy vagueness the events of the night before, when Lucian had kissed her goodnight. There was a distinct sense that something had been left unfinished, and the feeling persisted even now.

By the time she reached the house of Catherine Worlée, the sun had all but disappeared behind thickening gray clouds that promised rain later that evening. The air was heavy with moisture and Aimee felt tiny dots of perspiration on her forehead and beneath her arms, obliging her to stay and converse quietly in Catherine's salon instead of pursuing the walk she had planned.

Catherine was immensely pleased to see the younger woman, repeating over and over how beautiful she had looked at the party and how well she had behaved. "Why, I overheard dozens of young men expressing their amorous feelings toward you!" she tittered, fanning herself with a nervous gesture. "I'm sure Charles was not immune either, my dear." She cast her a sidelong look. "Of course, you have no interest of *that* sort in the Foreign Minister, do you, Aimee?"

Aimee shook her head. "No, Catherine, and neither does he in me. There is no need for you to feel jealous at all! Why, Talleyrand thinks of me as a—a daughter!" she proclaimed, trying not to think of the caresses he had bestowed on her during their games of whist.

Catherine sighed heavily. "Ah, I am so pleased to hear that, my dear. Of course, with the dashing Lucian Napier hovering about, I'm sure you would have no time for my dear Charles. What a scamp that young man is!" Catherine leaned forward suddenly, as though imparting a huge secret. "But you must be careful around him, my dear, for he really has no heart, I've heard. Several of my friends have been wooed by him; he takes what he wants from them and then discards them like a pair of old shoes. Such a man is completely dangerous and not to be trusted!"

"Catherine, you are really too silly!" Aimee put in, flabbergasted at her friend's accusations. "Why, Lucian is nothing but a gentleman to me! It's true he is quite handsome, but certainly that is no reason to claim he breaks women's hearts without a care in the world. I do think you are mixing him up with someone else!"

Catherine studied her friend for a moment, then shrugged. "Possibly, possibly, my dear, but please do be careful around him. He is—what? —at least thirty and not married yet. That must mean *something*, don't you think?"

"Talleyrand is over forty and not married yet," Aimee pointed out in exasperation.

"Yes, but that is only because he was a member of the clergy for so many years. Somehow, I do not think that is the case with Monsieur Napier!"

"Catherine, I simply will not listen to you!" Aimee put in. "You are acting as though Lucian is some ogre I should avoid at all costs. He has already done so much for me—and has asked nothing in return!" Her thoughts turned back to her brother, living a contented life now in Orléans.

"Men always ask for *something*," Catherine put in rather slyly. "You should know, my dear, that it may not come for a long time after the favor, but the time will come when Lucian will demand something for all of his help!"

"Well, then"—Aimee laughed suddenly—"I will simply have to refuse his demands, won't I? Now, Catherine, let us talk of something else, for this conversation is really beginning to become most irritating for me. Tell me about the latest fashions—I had wanted to go shopping with you today, but since it looks like rain, we shall have to postpone such delights."

Thereafter followed a deliciously feminine discussion of the latest in hats and fripperies, gowns and shoes, during which time Aimee sent Yvonne back to Talleyrand's home to fetch the carriage. The clouds had thickened and the sun was completely hidden and Aimee feared the rain would start before she had time to return home on foot.

By the time the carriage returned for her, Aimee heard the pitter-patter of raindrops splashing against the windows and was glad she had thought to send Yvonne back earlier. She took her good-bye of Catherine, promising to lunch with her the following week and spend some time shopping for new clothing for the fall. Holding her sunshade over her head for some protection, Aimee ran from the front door to the carriage, jumping in the open door quickly.

"Good afternoon!"

Aimee was surprised to see Lucian Napier seated in the carriage, smiling invitingly at her as she shook out her umbrella and waited for the footman to close the door. "Lucian, however did you get here?" she asked. "How did you know I was visiting with Catherine?"

"I had just arrived back at Talleyrand's when your maid returned," he explained, taking her umbrella and laying it on the floor beside him. "I offered to come with the carriage. Are you pleased to see me?"

Aimee nodded, but her thoughts returned insidiously to the conversation with Catherine. She studied Lucian thoughtfully, noting the devilish blue eyes that certainly seemed capable of masking the truth. His mouth was strong, but not too full, designating no sign of weakness, and the strong square of his jaw only emphasized that impression. Aimee noticed the impeccable clothing, the thick, wavy hair of softest sable, and decided that Catherine might easily have been correct in assuming this man could break women's hearts.

Lucian could not help but notice the slow stare he was receiving from his companion. "Don't tell me I've sprouted horns." He grinned, leaning forward to take her hand in his two big warm ones.

Aimee colored and shook her head. "Forgive me for staring, Lucian. I was just thinking of something Catherine was telling me."

"About me?"

She nodded truthfully. "She said you were a dangerous man."

He frowned. "Dangerous? In what way, I wonder?"

"Dangerous to women," Aimee explained, trying not to feel too foolish.

He laughed, causing her blush to deepen. "Catherine is a rather silly woman, Aimee. I wouldn't put too much faith in what she says."

Aimee bridled at this slight to her friend. "Well, is it true, though?" she questioned stiffly. "Certainly, you are handsome and unmarried. She said you enjoyed wooing women and then casting them aside when you . . . when you finished with them. If that is true, certainly I am putting myself in some danger by being with you so much."

"Do *you* think I'm dangerous, Aimee?" he asked, pressing her hand softly.

She studied him, feeling the blue eyes delve deeply into hers, as though trying to read her thoughts. "I'm not sure," she pronounced. "I do wonder why you troubled yourself with me and my problems. Surely there are other things that would command your attention—yet, you helped my brother escape the gallows, even arranged for him to get the money he needed to start to rebuild our family castle. And here I am, living with one of the most powerful men in Paris—and having no idea why I am there."

Lucian released her hand and leaned back in his seat, continuing to study her through half-closed eyes. "I'm not sure you will like it when I tell you why you are with Talleyrand, Aimee."

Aimee felt her heartbeat grow faster as she waited to hear what Lucian would tell her. "Tell me, Lucian. You promised you would tell me when you returned from your journey."

"That is true." He nodded, stroking his chin thoughtfully. Before he could continue, though, the carriage was already arriving back at Talleyrand's mansion. Aimee quickly hid her irritation at the interruption and waited patiently as the footman opened the door and Lucian handed her her umbrella. Together, they raced into the house, dripping small puddles onto the waxed floor as they stood in the foyer.

"You'd best go upstairs and change," Lucian instructed her.

"But I want to hear from you why I am here!" Aimee insisted, stamping her foot decidedly.

"I promise I will reveal everything to you, Aimee, if you will go upstairs and change before you catch cold. There's no reason for you to stand there shivering and wet!"

"What if Talleyrand returns before I am changed?" Aimee wanted to know. "That will give you another convenient excuse to put off telling me what I want to know."

"I left Talleyrand an hour ago. He will be in several long meetings with the members of the Directory for the rest of the evening. He is trying to convince them of a proposal he has had in mind for several months now."

Aimee looked at him distrustfully. "You promise not to disappear by the time I return?" she asked him.

He laughed and gave her a little push toward the stairs. "I promise! I'm going up, too. You don't think I relish having this wet coat on, do you?" He accompanied her upstairs, depositing her at her bedchamber door before going on to his own.

Aimee entered her rooms to find Yvonne already laying out fresh, dry clothing for her to wear when dinner was served. "Yvonne?" Aimee asked thoughtfully. "Is Monsieur Napier a frequent guest in this house?"

"Yes, mademoiselle. He stays quite often."

"Do you know where Monsieur Napier's house is in Paris?"

"No, mademoiselle. I would venture to say he has no permanent address," Yvonne responded carelessly, helping her mistress out of her wet clothing.

"You mean he doesn't live in Paris?"

"I don't know," the maid answered with a shrug. "But he seems always to be coming and going. I'd say there was no point in him having his own home, he'd be there so little."

"I see." Aimee thought about the idea as Yvonne slipped a fresh white gown over her, tied with a wide pink sash, then brushed out her damp hair before pinning it up in back in loose curls, secured with a narrow fillet around her forehead.

When she was dressed, Aimee hurried to Lucian's room, not wanting to wait until they were both downstairs. She knocked quickly, then entered before waiting to hear Lucian's voice bidding her to do so. To her surprise, he seemed to have disappeared. Frowning, she searched out his rooms, but found no trace of him except for the discarded wet coat he had been wearing.

Feeling the frustration building inside of her, Aimee hurried downstairs to question the servants to see if any of them knew the whereabouts of Lucian Napier. The majordomo, a dignified middle-aged man who never seemed as if he approved of anything, looked down his nose at her and told her that he had received a message for Monsieur Napier and had taken it up to his room himself, whereupon Monsieur Napier, after perusing the message, had hurried to change his coat and then had gone back out in the carriage, without telling him what time to expect him back.

"Do you have the message?" Aimee asked curiously, receiving a scathing look of shock from the majordomo.

"Of course not, mademoiselle. I do not take it upon myself to read other people's messages, nor do I keep such messages for later perusal."

"I'm sorry, François, but I must know where Monsieur Napier went," Aimee said firmly.

"I believe the footman who delivered the message said he was from . . . uh . . . Madame Bonaparte," François returned distastefully.

"Josephine Bonaparte, the wife of the general?" Aimee asked in surprise.

The servant shrugged. "I wouldn't know, mademoiselle. Is there anything else?"

"Yes, please tell cook not to serve dinner in the dining room this evening. I don't expect Monsieur Talleyrand or Monsieur Napier to be home, and I myself would prefer a tray sent to my room." And she turned on her heel, tramping back upstairs angrily, frustrated beyond belief that Lucian had once again managed to elude her questions. And why, she wondered, would Josephine Bonaparte want to see him? Did they know each other well?

In spite of herself, Aimee couldn't help remembering Catherine's admonitions about Lucian's interest in other women. Aimee shook her head angrily. Certainly, it wasn't any of her affair if he wanted to entertain Josephine or any of the other beautiful women in Paris, yet her teeth were set on edge at the thought of Lucian's leaving her alone in order to spend time with any of them. For what reason would Josephine wish to see Lucian? The only one that came readily to mind made Aimee angrier than ever—although why she felt angry she wasn't completely sure. Yes, she admitted to liking Lucian a great deal. He had helped her through quite a lot and she had come to feel almost protected by his mere presence. He asked so little of her in return, she realized, thrusting away the memory of his near seduction of her in the little room in the Montmartre. Even then, she conceded, he had stopped when she had asked him.

Oh, it was maddening to feel this way! Why should she care where he was or with whom he was! Perhaps Catherine had been telling the truth! Perhaps he was simply a libertine, like his mentor, Talleyrand. It would not be so hard to believe. Lucian was handsome, charming, and quite at ease with women; it would be ridiculous to assume they could remain immune to him. Even she herself had fallen under his spell, she realized morosely. Well, no more of that! As soon as he returned, she would demand to know why she was here and what it was he wanted from her. If he could not answer her questions to her satisfaction, she would tell him quite simply she was leaving. She would return to Orléans and live with her brother! With that thought in mind, she told Yvonne she would wait for Lucian in his room, so that he would not be able to escape her questions.

After eating her dinner, Aimee went to Lucian's room and settled herself in one of the wide, comfortable chairs, turning it around so that she had a good view of the door through which he would enter. With grim determination, she watched the door, listening to the rain outside beating furiously against the windowpane.

The room was completely dark except for the occasional flashes of lightning outside the windows. Aimee changed positions in the chair, trying to get more comfortable, realizing she had dozed off for nearly an hour before something had awakened her. Staring through the darkness, she saw the door from the hallway opening, revealing a tall, lean figure outlined by the candlelight in the hall.

"Lucian?" she whispered.

"Yes. Is that you, Aimee? Where are you?" he asked, coming in and closing the door softly behind him.

She waited until he had lit a wall sconce inside the room, throwing it into an eerie half light. "I've been waiting in this chair several hours," she said rather primly. "I think you must have forgotten that conversation you promised me."

He chuckled. "No, I didn't forget it, my sweet, but I was called away unavoidably. I'm sorry."

"Oh?" Aimee asked, pretending ignorance. "What was it—a message from Talleyrand?"

"No," he answered, surprising her with his truthfulness, but he didn't elaborate on who had sent the message.

"Was it business?" she pressed, wanting to catch him in the lie so that she could turn her righteous fury on him.

"Yes," he said slowly, removing his coat and seating himself on the edge of his bed in front of her in order to take off his boots, which were dripping onto the rug.

"Business!" Aimee stood up, pacing around him, watching him as he laid his boots aside and stood up in his stockinged feet. "Business—with a woman?"

"Aimee?" He laughed suddenly at the look on her face. "Why all these questions? Are you angry because I was called away? I assure you I could do nothing else but go. It was most important."

"Most important," she mocked with a sneer. "Well, I suppose it was! As I recall, Josephine Bonaparte is quite a beauty. Of course, I have heard it said that she takes many, many lovers while her husband is away on his military campaigns. I suppose you couldn't help but add yourself to the list!"

He reached out to catch her arm, but she sidestepped him, her eyes flashing green sparks in the dim light. "Don't lie to me, Lucian! I know that the message came from her! How dare you make me think it was business!"

"Sweetheart, it *was* business," he assured her, still chuckling. He hesitated. "Believe me, please. It has to do with her husband and the government of France and Talleyrand—"

"Rubbish!" she threw at him angrily. "You are exactly what

Catherine said you were!" she went on. "A man not to be trusted, a liar, and a . . . a libertine!"

He laughed outright at that. "Is that all?" he wanted to know when he could speak. "I assure you, my dear, you haven't told me anything I don't already know—although I must admit I have tried to be as truthful with you as I possibly could be." He moved toward her, but once again she eluded him, intent on nurturing her own anger.

"Laugh about it!" she cried. "I don't care what you think, Lucian Napier! If I am so funny to you, then why do you keep me here? Well, it won't be for any longer, I assure you, for I'm leaving to return to Orléans tomorrow!"

"You can't leave, Aimee," he said quietly, the laughter leaving his face.

"Yes, I can! And you won't stop me!"

"I *will* stop you!" he corrected her. "I'm afraid there was a price for saving you and your brother from the gallows, my dear."

So! Just as Catherine had suggested, now came the price he wanted her to pay for his favors, Aimee thought in growing rage. Catherine had been right about him all along! She watched him warily, aware of the strength, the quickness that emanated from his tall, lithe body. But she was not afraid of him—she was far too angry to be afraid.

"I owe you nothing!" she flung at him proudly.

"Listen to me, little fool!" he said angrily, losing patience with her. "I told you I had to promise much in order to save your ungrateful little neck. *You* were part of the bargain!"

"What do you mean?" she cried. "I'll not stoop to becoming Talleyrand's mistress, I can assure you of that, so if that's—"

"That's not it!" he interrupted.

She caught her breath and glared at him. "And I won't be *your* mistress either!" she proclaimed with a toss of her head.

"Dammit! I wouldn't have you as my mistress if you offered yourself to me!" he threw back at her, seeing her wince at the humiliating remark.

"Of course, I'm forgetting about all the women you've known," she said, her heart stinging from his barbs. "Certainly, you must have quite a few to turn to for that kind of comfort. I'm sure their experience and jaded appetites could tempt you more than my clumsy naïveté!"

"You are absolutely correct, my dear," he returned, attempting to gain control over his emotions. "Your stupid childishness could hardly compare to their passionate spirit, I'm afraid."

Stung, Aimee continued to glare at him, wishing she could tear his eyes out with her nails. Warily, she walked around him, keeping well out of arm's reach. "I'm glad you feel that way, for it would make me physically ill to think that I would be forced to succumb to your lecherous advances!" she threw at him, enjoying the anger she could see in his blue eyes. "I should hate to think of having my first experience in such matters tarnished by your own jaded spirit!"

"First experience?" he queried through clenched teeth. "Now who is lying, my dear! You cannot expect me to believe that through all those months in Jean-Baptiste Aubray's gang, you were 'unsullied' by him and his companions! Nor the months you spent with your brother's gang. I'm sure they all found your female attributes quite handy and more than willing on those days when there was nothing else to do!"

"How dare you!" she squeaked, throwing caution to the winds and leaping at him in order to scratch his eyes out. With an angry cry, she felt her nails meet the flesh of his cheek and was satisfied to see the long furrow she left in his skin. But before she could do more, he had caught both her hands in his and was twisting them behind her back. Struggling furiously, she tried to bite him, kick him, do anything to hurt him as he had hurt her. But to her further humiliation, he made it seem ridiculously easy to subdue her by grasping her around the waist and throwing her uncere-moniously onto the bed.

"Well, well, now!" He laughed, holding her down as he climbed over her. "What do we have here! An angry, spitting little kitten—well, we'll soon tame her, by God!" And with an easy efficiency, he reached down and ripped the front of her gown, tearing the fragile muslin from neckline to skirt.

"Leave me alone, you disgusting brute, you hollow libertine, you . . . you . . . lecherous swine!" she cried, trying to think of the worst comparisons she could.

To her chagrin, he merely laughed at her, intent on pulling away the last shreds of her attire, until she was completely naked underneath him, even to the point where her shoes had been thrown over the edge of the bed. Still angry, she had no time to feel the embarrassment as his flame-blue eyes swept over her perfect figure, taking in the high, rounded breasts, the slender waist, and the firm-fleshed thighs between which grew bright, golden curls that matched those on her head.

Without taking his hands from her arms where they were

pinned to the bed, Lucian bent his head to capture her lips, effectively silencing her continued angry tirade against him. Aimee felt his mouth on hers, rough, demanding—and the reaction inside of her shook her to the marrow. Hungrily, she matched his kiss, moving her lips provocatively beneath his, fencing her tongue with his when he opened his mouth. She felt his tongue travel along her teeth and test the soft inner sides of her mouth and her heart began to beat faster as a burning-sweet feeling seemed to envelop her from breast to hips.

A soft sigh escaped her when he finally took his mouth away and moved downward to find her breasts. Expertly, he circled the nipples with his tongue, laving the undersides and sucking gently at the firm, full flesh that offered itself to him. Tentatively, he took his hands from her arms and was rewarded by the soft twining of them around his neck, pressing his face closer to her breast. With nimble fingers he caressed the flesh offered to him while his mouth continued to work its magic until the points of her breasts stood turgid and full.

Aimee groaned aloud, wondering how she could have been so angry with him one minute, and now be completely at his mercy. Yet, she wasn't at his mercy any more than he was at hers. There was something inside of her crying for release, crying for fulfillment, and she instinctively knew that this man—jaded libertine or not—would be the one who could satisfy her.

He pulled away from her a moment, leaving her feeling bereft in the semidarkness, but when he returned to her, she felt his naked legs against hers and the shock of it made her tremble. Naked, they moved together on the bed, kissing until Aimee gasped for breath, throwing her head back and arching her back against him so that the points of her breasts stabbed against his chest. His hands worked their way down her body, following the curve of her waist and the small, flat cushion of her belly. At the juncture of her thighs, they hesitated before pulling her legs apart and raiding the soft moistness there.

Aimee cried out at the entry of his fingers in her most private place, but the fever inside her seemed to be rekindled when he softly rubbed the moist flesh with gentle caresses that seemed to be making her increasingly breathless. With little cries of wonder and surprise, she took in the sensations he was making her feel as he continued to work some kind of magic. Breathless one moment and panting hard the next, Aimee moved her head from side to side, arching her back and pushing his face back to her breasts. Passionately, he obliged her, suckling the sweet morsels so temptingly pushed at him while he relentlessly continued the sweet torture between her thighs. Aimee could feel the tension inside of her building gradually, the tingling spreading outward from the junction of her thighs until, with a gasp, she felt a curious kind of release that made her tighten her muscles reflexively before releasing them and collapsing with a moan on the bed.

Lucian withdrew his hand and gently caressed her quivering thighs. He reared up a little so that he could see her beautiful face before he looked downward and pushed her thighs open so that he might fit himself between. Settling down lightly on top of her, he positioned his aching member into that moistness he had precipitated just a moment before. With gentle strokes, he strove to breach the opening while his mouth caressed hers with soft murmurings. His hands toyed gently with her breasts and he felt the rapid beat of her heart beneath his fingers.

Aroused once more, Aimee began to move beneath him with instinctive stirrings that tried to match his own movements. As passion built within, Lucian groaned aloud and pushed deeply, feeling the tiny barrier give way beneath his onslaught and her warm flesh welcoming him. He had the fleeting notion that she had not been lying—that she had been a virgin still—before all thought left him and he could concentrate only on the fulfillment of pleasure.

With smooth, steady strokes he brought her back, taking away the momentary pain and replacing it with the delicious tingling that made her tremble and shiver beneath him. Her movements drove him mad and the stroking grew deeper and faster so that Aimee brought her knees up to hug around his sides, clasping him around the neck as she sought his mouth once more. Hungrily, they kissed, and at the same time his movements grew so furious that Aimee felt nearly buffeted by them. Inside her, a tiny ripple grew fiercely, sending quiverings all through her body as she felt him release a wet warmth within her. She shivered and felt his answering shiver before he kissed her once again and settled heavily on top of her.

When Aimee drifted back to reality once more, she became aware of the rain still beating against the window, the distant crackling of thunder, and the weight of her lover pressing her into the mattress. A strange feeling enveloped her: a sense of loss for her girlhood, mixed with a trembling fear that her relationship with this man had changed forever. She felt him lift his head from her shoulder and turned her face away, wanting to avoid this direct contact with him.

"Aimee? Are you all right?" Lucian asked, a tender note of concern in his voice.

She nodded.

He waited for her to speak, and when she did not, he continued. "Sweetheart, don't be ashamed with me. You have a beautiful body and I'm very happy to have been the first to awaken you to that fact."

Aimee was not quite sure how to cope with this different sort of tenderness from this man, this sense of intimacy that made her feel her life must be forever intertwined with his now. She was aware of his concern, and it only made her more uncomfortable so that all she wanted was to get away from him.

"You're too heavy," she said softly, needing distance between them. His moist hard flesh on hers seemed an affront somehow now that the act was over.

He obliged her by shifting his weight to the side, leaving her free so that cool air washed over her body. She shivered a little, but pressed away from him when he would have pulled her back into his arms.

"I should be getting back to my rooms," she said, clearing her throat and sitting up gingerly.

"Aimee? What's wrong?" Lucian asked sensibly. He, too, sat up and took her hand in his, trying to see through the curtain of her hair.

"My dress," she said, seeing the garment lying on the floor in a white pool, "you've ruined it!" Somehow she felt close to tears and she wanted more than anything else to get away from this man who aroused this curious and scary feeling in her.

"Aimee, forget the damned dress!" he returned. "Look at me! What's wrong?"

She looked at him, seeing the blue eyes resting with sincere concern on her face. Suddenly, she started crying, sobbing heavily, putting her face in her hands as though her heart were broken. Lucian, startled at such a reaction, drew her into his arms and rocked her back and forth tenderly, knowing the storm must drain itself dry before she would be able to talk sensibly.

With a last sob, Aimee pulled herself away and looked at him. "Lucian, you . . . you took advantage of me," she accused in a low voice. "You made love to me . . . without really loving me! You've used me as you use other women, for your own enjoyment, and I'm afraid I'm . . . too new at this to be able to handle that!"

"Aimee, I care for you a great deal!" he assured her, trying to catch her in his arms again, but she pushed him away.

"No, please don't, Lucian! I hate dishonesty—and I wouldn't want to hate *you!* I suppose we could simply say that this was bound to happen between us, wasn't it? I mean, there is something between us after all the time we've known each other. I just don't want our friendship to be gone!"

"Aimee, we can still be friends. Sweetheart, who told you that lovers weren't meant to be friends?"

"But I don't love you, Lucian!" she proclaimed honestly, knowing that she felt *something* for this man, but not quite sure what it was.

He seemed taken aback. In his experience, after the passion had been assuaged, women always needed to be told they were loved, and they needed to tell him that he was loved. It was a polite little game that was played between casual lovers—seeing to the niceties so that no one's feelings were hurt. But here was this little chit, telling him that there was no need to speak of love! He gazed at her with raised eyebrows, wondering where she had learned so much.

"I must get back to my rooms," she was saying rather absently, searching around the bed for something to put on.

He stood up and padded around to pick up her dress. In the half light, Aimee could see the magnificent physique that couldn't fail to impress her, even in her distraught state of mind. Quickly, she took the garment he held out, wrapping it haphazardly around her as best she could.

"You could stay here," he coaxed, suddenly wanting to feel her soft body next to him again. "You could sleep with me tonight, Aimee."

Her cheeks grew warm at the invitation, but she shook her head firmly. "No. I . . . I don't want anyone to know of this, Lucian, *please!*"

"Aimee, I just can't forget it happened—and neither can you," he told her reasonably. "Is it so terrible to have others know we are lovers?"

"We are *not* lovers!" she said firmly. "This must not happen again, Lucian."

He laughed lightly. "Darling, you cannot convince me of that. I'm sure you can talk to yourself until you're blue in the face, but

at night, when you start to think of me—of what I can give
you—"

"Stop it!"

He sobered at the ragged edge of anger in her voice. "All
right, my dear, it shall be our secret," he promised, tilting his
head sideways to study her. He watched as she walked to the
door, opened it, and checked the hallway before making her departure. "Good night, Aimee!" he called, seeing her turn back to
hold a finger to her lips. "And tomorrow, I promise we shall have
that conversation we seemed to have forgotten about tonight!"

Aimee stiffened, recalling the reason for her vigil in his room
—the vigil that had gotten her into this mess to begin with. And
here, she still didn't know what it was that he and Talleyrand
expected of her. The thought rankled for a moment—that she
should have kept her mind to her business instead of losing her
head to anger and making herself vulnerable to Lucian the way
she did. Well, she promised herself, tomorrow she would find out
what this was all about!

22

.-.-.-.

Aimee sat at the dining table, hardly tasting the breakfast that was set before her, waiting anxiously for Lucian to make an appearance. She hadn't slept at all the rest of the night and felt slightly groggy still, as though a vise had settled down over her forehead. She had tried not to think of what had happened between her and Lucian, but he had been right—she was unable to put it out of her mind. There was an insidious urge to go back to his room, to snuggle in his bed with his strong arms around her, shivering at the thought that sometime later he would once more become the demanding lover and she would meet him urgently, gloriously, enjoying his caresses with every fiber of her being. The thought came to her that he had probably gone directly to sleep, able to find dreams easily while she tossed and turned in her own bed.

As Lucian finally made his morning appearance, though, his face seemed to belie her ideas, for he, too, looked as though he had spent a sleepless night. Upon seeing her, his blue eyes flamed brightly, reflecting the memory of last night so that her cheeks crimsoned and she dropped her eyes to her plate.

"Good morning, Aimee," he said with a charming grin, passing by her seat in order to bestow a rather chaste kiss on her cheek.

"Good morning," she returned, aware of the serving maid at the sideboard.

"Did you sleep well, my dear?" he inquired, his eyes touching on the violet bruises beneath her eyes.

She glared at him without answering. After being served breakfast, Lucian dismissed the servant with a wave of his hand and dug into his food, obviously eating with much gusto. Aimee watched him in disgust, knowing the evidence of her own poor appetite would probably cause some wry comment from him sooner or later.

"Well?" she asked finally, when he seemed content to continue eating, ignoring her presence.

He looked up and smiled. "Yes, my dear? Forgive me for

proving to be a terrible table companion this morning, but I really am famished. A good hop in bed with a beautiful young woman always causes that in me!"

Aimee flushed and longed to slap his face as she glanced around quickly to see if anyone was about. "Will you be quiet about that!" she said angrily.

His blue eyes mocked her. "No one is eavesdropping, Aimee. There's no need for you to have that guilty look on your face."

"I just would rather not discuss that this morning, if you don't mind."

"All right," he conceded. "I suppose you would just as soon pretend it didn't happen, but for the life of me, I can't understand why. It was an immensely enjoyable experience for me—and for you, too, I think! Are you afraid that you'll become more vulnerable, less independent?"

"Please, don't go on!" she hissed, shoving aside her plate. "I suppose you won't be satisfied until I go on about what a *glorious* night it was, what a wonderful lover you were, and how I'm weak in the knees at the mere sight of you this morning!"

He grinned. "Hmm. It does sound rather pleasant hearing such words of praise from you, my dear."

"Well, enjoy them while you may, for you'll not be hearing them again, I can tell you!"

He gave her an intense and enigmatic look from his blue eyes. "That remains to be seen."

She flushed, but went on determinedly. "At any rate, we have other things to discuss. For instance, what is my *real* purpose in being installed in this house, as the ward of Monsieur Talleyrand? Where were you all these months since you saved Etienne and myself from the gallows? And just what kind of business did you really have with Madame Bonaparte last night?"

"Jealousy becomes you, sweetheart," he returned laconically. "It makes those eyes of yours sparkle like emeralds."

"You are procrastinating!" she accused.

"Indeed, I am." He sighed, wiping his mouth with a napkin and throwing it on the table before standing up and pacing around to her side with his hands clasped behind his back. "Actually, Aimee, I suppose I do owe you a full explanation. After all, your cooperation is going to be needed in the months ahead, and I realize that without total honesty between us, neither is going to be able to trust the other."

"Exactly," Aimee agreed.

He took a chair next to hers and leaned forward, his eyes

taking on a serious look. "I have told you that I work for the government of France. The exact nature of the work I have left purposely vague. I believe you thought I was connected with the police of Paris at one time, and then perhaps you thought I worked for Joseph Fouché, the Minister of Police, who also happens to operate a large network of secret police."

"Who *do* you work for?" Aimee prompted.

"Essentially, I work for myself," he told her. "I am . . . uh . . . an intelligence gatherer of sorts, you might call it. If the Directory, or Talleyrand, or Fouché needs information that I am able to get for any of them, I'm paid to supply it."

"A spy!" Aimee said, her eyes widening.

He smiled. "Yes, exactly right, my dear. I am a spy, right now commissioned by our dear Talleyrand to gather information about America's intentions to go to war with France over our impressment of seamen and capture of their vessels. That is where I have been these past months—in America talking with Vice-President Thomas Jefferson, who carries a great deal of sympathy for our country. Alas, his superior, President John Adams, does not carry as much sympathy, but still lacks the arrogance to proclaim an outright war with us. Eventually, peace will have to be made. Talleyrand's plan was to send me in a diplomatic posture to ask Jefferson, in private, if there was something we could do about averting war. Jefferson has persuaded Adams to send an envoy—a man called Victor Du Pont, whose family is French. Du Pont will act as a private emissary to Talleyrand to discuss mutual ways to warm up the public relations between France and the United States."

Aimee could only nod, her mind trying to reject the image of spy she held—the heartless, cold-blooded man who would sell his country's secrets for the price of a good meal. "So, that is where you have been," she said softly, trying to digest everything. "But that does not explain why you had to visit Madame Bonaparte. Certainly you cannot expect me to believe that she holds some key to our relationship with America."

He laughed. "No. But Josephine is married to a young man whose ambitions are very high. Napoleon Bonaparte has proven himself courageous, intelligent, and a born leader. All these qualities combine to make him a very dangerous man in the eyes of the Directory. In essence, they fear him. They know that he is the kind of leader who can rouse the populace in his favor—who could topple the Directory from their positions very easily."

"But what of this Egyptian campaign?" Aimee wondered.

"Surely he has made a terrible mistake in allowing the English to destroy our navy."

"He is wily enough to turn that mistake to his advantage. Josephine gets occasional letters from him. Their content is quite remarkable, I can assure you. Our Corsican general definitely plans to rule France one day—and he believes the hour is close at hand. As does Talleyrand."

"Another revolution?"

Lucian shook his head. "Nothing so dramatic. More of a quiet takeover, I should think, though anything is possible with military hotheads in the thick of things."

"So you went to Josephine at her request, because she had received more information from her husband?" Aimee guessed. And at his confirming nod, she added, "But why should she give you that information, Lucian? Why should she trust such potentially dangerous information to a man who could very easily sell it to the Directory, who could set a trap for Bonaparte, or even try to kill him before he can return to France?"

"I gave her my word that I would not let the Directory know of it," he said casually.

Aimee sat back in her chair, regarding him with gleaming eyes. "And besides, everyone knows how immoral is our dear Josephine. What better lover to have than a spy for France, one who already knows her secrets and can be trusted to keep his mouth shut?"

Lucian's smile was mocking. "I admit that I was not immune to Josephine's considerable charms, but after the first passionate flush, I'm afraid it sank into nothing so much as mundane business between us," he assured her, noting the heightened color in her cheeks.

Aimee stood up, pacing nervously for a moment. "So, you are a spy, Lucian. Now I know the truth—but what has that to do with me? It still doesn't explain why I am here."

"I told you before that I was forced to promise Talleyrand quite a lot in order to save your neck and that of your brother. Firstly, I promised him my services on an exclusive basis for an undisclosed amount of time—I assume until there is some change in the government, either with Bonaparte as part of it or not. Secondly"—and his blue eyes burned as they watched her face—"I promised him *your* services, my dear."

She stood stock-still, digesting his words, her eyes wide and her mouth forming an "oh!" of surprise. "What do you mean?" she whispered.

"I mean that you will be a spy for France, just as I am, my dear."

"You—you promised that—without my knowledge!" she cried, her anger building. "You told Talleyrand I would become like *you*—a person who schemes and sneaks and makes love to other people all for the sake of finding out their secrets!"

"Wait!" He stood up, too, and caught her hands, though she tried to pull them from his grasp. "Is that what you think of me, Aimee? I can assure you, I have my own code of ethics, just as you do! Was it those ethics that forced you to steal for a living when you came to Paris, to kill Faron, to act as lookout for a gang of thieves—"

"Enough! I did those things because I had to!" she cried, finally wresting her hands from his. "Not because I was *paid* to do them!"

"What difference?" he asked her. "We all do what we have to do, Aimee, to survive! I have a talent for what I do. Sometimes it is risky, dangerous, but I do it because I *have* to, just as you did those things you did!"

"But I don't have to be a spy!" Aimee argued.

"I'm afraid you do," he returned tightly.

"That's ridiculous! I know nothing of spying. I wouldn't know the first thing about what to do!"

"There you are wrong. Talleyrand has already informed me how you listened in on the conversation between Josephine and Barras's mistress at his soirée."

"That! But that was eavesdropping, nothing else!"

He shrugged. "Even so, it was a way of gathering information. You see, Aimee, how simple it really is. You don't have to kill people when you're a spy, you don't have to hurt anyone, or even make love to someone you don't want to—"

"It doesn't matter!" she interrupted firmly. "I can't do as you ask, Lucian! I can't!"

"Aimee, you must! Would you rather your brother be arrested and taken back to prison? Would you rather risk his life—and yours?"

She looked at him narrowly. "That's impossible!" she scoffed. "How could they arrest Etienne when he has done nothing wrong?"

"It would be a simple thing for the Directory to send out an order for his arrest. Talleyrand could initiate it himself."

"You are lying to me—I won't believe it! Talleyrand has

shown me nothing but kindness since I've lived here. He wouldn't do such a thing!" Aimee protested.

"Ah, my dear, how little you know of the great ones." Lucian sighed pityingly. "If you do not serve their purpose, they crush you like an ant! I'm afraid there is no way out of this predicament but to submit to a will greater than your own. Take heart, you will be with me, and I will protect you always."

"I do not wish your protection!" she cried. "It was you who got me into all of this!"

He started to remind her that it was necessary in order to save her life, but sighed and shrugged his shoulders. She was in no mood to listen to him now, he knew. He had been stupid to let his emotions override his intelligence last night; he should never have made love to her. It had changed their relationship too much, made her untrusting of him. And yet, he had to admit to himself that he could not take back last night if he wanted to— and he definitely did not want to!

"Why don't you speak to Talleyrand this evening," he suggested finally.

Aimee nodded vigorously. "Yes, that is exactly what I will do! And you will see, Lucian Napier, that I will not become your accomplice in any of your sordid affairs!"

"Monsieur Talleyrand, I must speak with you!" Aimee's voice held a quality of urgency in it that piqued the Foreign Minister's curiosity, and, despite his throbbing headache, acquired from all-day meetings at the Council of Five Hundred, he nodded his head and indicated that she follow him into his library.

Once seated, he behind his desk and she in front of him in a straight-backed chair she had moved forward, he asked her politely, "What can I do for you, my dear? You sound as though whatever it is must require my immediate attention."

"Yes, monsieur. I do hate to bother you at this hour upon your return from business, but I must discuss something of great importance to me. I . . . I have spoken to Lucian Napier this morning—about my reasons for being under your guardianship."

"And he told you?"

"Yes."

"So?" Talleyrand cocked an eyebrow, feeling the headache tighten irritatingly around his head. "Any questions you have should be brought up with Lucian, Aimee. He knows far more about this business than I. Trust him, my dear."

Aimee stood up, the interview hardly going as she had

planned. "But I'm afraid, monsieur, that I . . . I cannot accept such . . . such a task from you. You ask me to become a spy for France, yet I know nothing of such work! You must believe me when I say my heart would not be in it!"

Talleyrand also stood up, clasping his cane, for his foot ached him especially tonight after the torrential rains they'd been receiving. "My dear mademoiselle, many things we are called upon to do—and our hearts are not in it. Do you think my heart is in my work when it requires me to sit for long hours at a time trying to talk sense into complete idiots! I sit there and speak of the importance of France's strategic positions in the New World, and those morons in the Directory look at me like I'm speaking of the moon! They cannot understand how America could possibly have any importance to us—why, they say, it is an ocean away! And the fools will not keep their independence long. But it is Barras and the rest of them who are the fools—they cannot see beyond their own borders! Only with someone with vision, someone like General Bonaparte—" He stopped suddenly, afraid he had revealed too much.

"Monsieur, your plans mean very little to me," Aimee reassured him hastily, noting the suspicious glance with which he favored her. "In fact, that is exactly my point. I don't care what happens in government, nor do I care about any secrets you may have, or General Bonaparte, or anyone! All I care about is my brother, that he be happy!"

"And yourself, Aimee?"

"Etienne would welcome me back at Castle du Beautreillis," she said staunchly.

"Can you be so sure of that, my dear?" the statesmen asked craftily. "He wants to take a wife and start a family; that requires money. He wishes to rebuild his ancestral castle; that, too, requires money. With all his capital outlay, do you think he would welcome another mouth to feed? A sister whose dowry must be paid in order to marry her off to some respectable bourgeois?"

"But, Etienne would not think of it that way," Aimee protested.

"My dear young woman, people begin to think differently as they grow older and find they've acquired more responsibilities. Besides, if you truly care so much about your brother, wouldn't you want to keep him from having to worry about your welfare?"

"Of course, monsieur, but—"

"Listen to me, Aimee de Chartres. Your interests, and those of your brother, are best served by your cooperation in this venture.

There are plans afoot that will add to the glory of France—a glory in which you can participate!"

"I do not care for the glory of France!" Aimee put in sulkily.

Talleyrand laughed. "Ah, but you must! The glory of your country is everything, my dear. It is what makes men fight wars and go into battle with trumpets sounding and banners flying. It can make beautiful women cry and men fight duels—all for the honor and the glory of their country. You must put yourself beyond the pettiness of spying, my dear, and realize that you are only a small part of a whole—a whole that is working for France, for her glory and that of her people!"

"Very patriotic, Talleyrand, but I don't think the young lady is swallowing any of it!" Lucian Napier injected sarcastically, clapping his hands as he entered the library.

Talleyrand bristled a moment, then smiled tiredly. "Ah, I mustn't forget how very good a spy you are, Lucian. Have you been practicing your skills at the keyhole, my friend?"

Lucian shrugged. "I wanted to see if your eloquent tongue could sway our stubborn guest."

Before Aimee could reply, Talleyrand said smoothly, "She will come around, my friend, for there is nothing else for her to do. You have chosen her for the job yourself, and I put my complete trust in you." Talleyrand directed himself to Aimee, who was standing quietly enough, though her bosom was rising and falling doubly fast. "Lucian's taste has been unerring in the past, my dear. And I believe he is right about you. There is a great potential in you—a young woman of the old aristocracy with all the manners and graces inbred through generations, but with a delightful mix of cunning and intelligence learned from the 'tragic' events in your life of the recent past. You have obtained a sense of the Parisian streets, of how to survive. That is most important for anyone, but triply so for a spy who must live by his wits at all times. You are the perfect choice, my dear, for if my plans go well, you and Lucian will be working together closely for a while, and my instincts tell me that would be most agreeable for the two of you!" He laughed rather lewdly.

"Well, your instincts are wrong about that!" Aimee snapped angrily, looking to Lucian as though accusing him of revealing to Talleyrand what had transpired between them the night before.

Lucian gave her an innocent look, then smiled roguishly. "Anyone would be looking forward to . . . uh . . . working closely with Mademoiselle de Chartres," he said with a little bow.

"Precisely," Talleyrand said. "Now, mademoiselle, I really do not feel the need to continue this discussion any longer. Any more questions, you may direct them to Lucian. Good night, my dear." He bowed, nodded to Lucian, and retired, leaving Aimee to face her companion alone.

"How could you have done this to me!" she accused spitefully. "Now what a tangle it all is! I can hardly say no, else Talleyrand will have poor Etienne thrown back into prison!"

"I'm sorry for that, Aimee, but there was no other way out of it. Now, if you will just calm your ruffled feathers and sit down with me, I'll tell you what it is you will be required to do."

"How do you know you can trust me?" she grumbled, sitting down next to him in the proffered chair. "What if I turn on you and your plan goes awry?"

"Then I shall be forced to punish you most severely," he returned, his blue eyes gleaming with mocking malice. "I can't say the idea doesn't appeal to me, Aimee, so do be careful."

She longed to stick her tongue out at him in a childish display of anger, but held on to her temper with difficulty. "All right, then, tell me what it is you wish me to do."

"I want you to marry me," he answered her seriously.

"What!" Her green eyes widened. "What—did you—say?"

"I want you to be my wife, Aimee de Chartres," he repeated. "Is the idea so hard for you to grasp?"

"Marriage! But you . . . you made no mention of it last night when you—" She blushed, then started over. "Do you really want me to marry you, Lucian? Why?"

"My dear Aimee, I wish I could say, in all honesty, it was because I loved you, but I'm afraid my reasons are less glorious than that. You see, it is all part of a plan of Talleyrand's for France to obtain a piece of the Americas. He knows that a French position on the Mississippi River in North America would put an end to American dreams of expanding the length of the continent. It would give France a base of operations with which to threaten Canada and support the French islands in the Caribbean. Right now, Spain holds the lease on that land, called the Louisiana Territory, but I believe France has been negotiating for the rights to that land for the past three years. Spain has so far refused to give it up and there have been numerous breaks in the discussions, making it very frustrating for Talleyrand's high ambitions."

"But if the Directory does not concur with his ambitions—"

"Exactly, my dear. Those men are too frightened for their own positions to worry about trying to expand French borders. But the people are sick of this chaos and ready to be ruled by one man. Talleyrand thinks highly of Napoleon Bonaparte's chances to be that man. He already has the popular support of the citizens of Paris and much of the rest of France. How can one not love a military hero?" he asked sardonically.

"And I suppose you have confirmed Bonaparte's ambitions through his wife's letters?"

"Yes."

"But, why should that prompt you to propose marriage to me?" she asked, somewhat bewildered. "I would think there is very little else to do but wait until Bonaparte makes some move, or the Directory is persuaded to do something about Spain's reluctance to sell the land."

"Ah, but one cannot predict for sure that Bonaparte will gain the upper hand—and even if he does, Talleyrand cannot be sure that he will be any more easily persuaded of the wisdom of his plan than the Directory was. So Talleyrand must send someone to the Louisiana Territory to send back firsthand reports on the advisability of purchasing the territory. Such reports will make their way to the proper people and help in their persuasion, you see. It is also a good way of keeping an eye on the Spanish government in New Orleans who may or may not wish to release the land even if their mother government in Spain commands them to. All in all, a very sticky situation."

"And I suppose *you* are the person Talleyrand will be sending on this 'fact-finding' mission?" Aimee queried.

"Precisely. And to add immeasurably to my cover as a roving French diplomat will be you, posing as my wife, a delicate, high-born young lady whose social graces can be counted on to get us invited to all the right parties and gatherings of the political contingent. Now do you understand?"

Aimee nodded, feeling a sudden sadness. Now, why was that? she wondered. Certainly, she couldn't have hoped that Lucian's proposal had anything to do with love—she must have realized it would be all part of his "business." She sighed and closed her eyes for a moment, wondering how foolish she would be to accept what he was offering her.

"Do we really have to get married?" she asked in a low voice. "I mean, we could pretend to be married, couldn't we?"

Lucian shrugged. "In my business, you must lend as much authenticity to the part as possible. Besides, my dear, you shouldn't worry about being attached to me for life. You know how easily civil divorce is obtained these days. It is only a matter of standing up before the judge and signing a paper." One dark brow was raised quizzically. "Or is the idea of being my wife so abhorrent to you, even if it is, as Talleyrand would say, for the glory of France?"

"Lucian, I cannot in all truth say I like the idea," Aimee said honestly, bringing a glimmer of respect to his eyes, "but I suppose I have little choice in the matter." She glanced at him from beneath her lashes. "But this marriage will be in name only."

He smiled mockingly. "As you wish. But, do remember, it was *your* wish that it be so—and not mine."

23

The brief civil ceremony was over and Aimee walked quietly beside her husband into the October air, feeling his arm beneath her hand, tensing a little as she stumbled over the last step. Tenderly, he inquired if she was all right—exactly as he would if he was her real husband, she thought with a note of despair. Then she realized that he *was* her real husband, and that they were now bound together by law. Unable to stop the flow of her thoughts, Aimee recalled her mother telling her about her own memories of her wedding to her father. How grand it had sounded, Aimee thought with a sigh: the traditional white wedding gown with its yards-long train and veil, the numerous attendants, and the elaborate wedding feast afterward. Today, there were no attendants; not even Talleyrand had been able to come. There would be no wedding feast, for Lucian would be leaving her shortly for meetings at the Tuileries. A sob was caught in Aimee's throat, but she was determined that her husband would not be aware of it. Dully, she glanced down at the golden band that encircled her finger, feeling it like a brand on her flesh. She felt a sudden urge to tear it off and throw it to the ground, to run away from all it represented, but she stifled the urge with an effort.

"Darling, I must be leaving you now," Lucian was saying, and Aimee hated him for his mock-tenderness. "Shall I call you a cab, or would you like to take the air for a while?"

"I prefer to walk, thank you," Aimee replied stiffly. She was not afraid to be on the streets of Paris alone during the day. After so many years in the city, she had become nearly as familiar with them as the native citizens. It would be nice, she thought, to walk along the Pont Neuf and buy a waffle from one of the vendors, or perhaps a bouquet of posies from one of the flower sellers.

"Why, look, I do believe that is Josephine Bonaparte's carriage," Lucian intervened, nodded discreetly to a vehicle parked across the street. "Let me take you over and introduce you, Aimee. You never know what you might find out about the good general."

"I don't want to meet Madame Bonaparte," Aimee said rebelliously. "Will I have to put up with her simpering over you while I stand there feeling foolish?"

"I told you, Aimee, that those days are over. Josephine and I are nothing but friends now. Besides, if you are so jealous of my seeing her, why don't you cultivate a friendship with her and then it can be up to you to hear about her husband's correspondence!"

"I could not care less!"

Lucian stopped walking and turned her around sharply to face him. A barely contained anger emanated from him. "Listen to me, Aimee! I know you don't give a damn about Bonaparte or his wife, but you had better follow my advice, or you may find yourself in hot water rather quickly. It pays to keep your eyes open as well as your ears in the position you find yourself now. You can help me immensely if you'll only forget your childish ways and start acting like a woman—my wife!"

"Your wife!" she sneered, hating him at that moment. "Do you think I am overjoyed at the idea? Yes, yes, I know I agreed to this farce, but now I find myself regretting it more and more!"

"That is your misfortune, my dear, for I shall endeavor to keep you around a little while longer until your usefulness has worn itself out. Then I will gladly agree to a divorce—and you will be free to do whatever you wish!" His contemptuous smile matched her curled lip and she felt the greatest urge to wipe it from his mouth, but she controlled her anger, reminding herself that now was not the time to confront her new husband.

"Now, if you will allow me to escort you, we will walk over to that shop where Josephine is browsing and I will introduce you. I'm sure you will find her quite lively and entertaining, my dear. Much better than returning home to an empty house, awaiting my arrival this evening with bated breath!"

"Ha!" Aimee cried. "I'll be in bed asleep by the time you return home!"

His smile was positively licentious. "Good. That is exactly where I want you, my good little wife. It certainly saves time and the husband's pride to find his dutiful wife awaiting him in the conjugal bower!"

"You conceited boor!" Aimee spat. "I just hope—"

"Lucian!" A woman's soft voice interrupted before Aimee could give full vent to her anger. Both she and Lucian turned abruptly to see the small, well-endowed figure of Josephine Bonaparte stepping toward them from the shop where she had been making her purchases.

"Josephine, how nice to see you," Lucian said gallantly, bowing to her in his most courtly fashion.

Josephine smiled, the smile transforming her ordinary pertness into something quite lovely so that even Aimee was caught for the moment by her charm. "It is always nice to see you, Lucian," she was saying. Then, turning to Aimee, she said, "But what have we here, another companion to steal your heart away from me?" she teased.

Lucian returned her smile. "Josephine, I believe you have already met this charming young lady at the home of our Foreign Minister, Talleyrand, on the occasion of his party last August."

Josephine wrinkled her brow, trying to remember, then brightened. "Oh, yes. Monsieur Talleyrand's ward, I believe?"

"And now my wife," Lucian put in smoothly, seeing the raised brow this announcement caused. "Allow me to present Aimee Napier, the former Aimee de Chartres of Orléans."

"Charmed," Josephine said, clasping the younger woman's hand in her own. "You must feel quite lucky to have landed such a charming rogue as this," she added. "I must say, if my dear Napoleon hadn't already ensnared my heart, I would have been hard put to stay away from this one."

Aimee smiled, despite her irritation at the woman's flirtatious deceit. "Thank you, madame, but perhaps you may have him yet—when I have grown tired of him," she added impertinently, causing Josephine to look at her in surprise.

"Hmm," Madame Bonaparte said thoughtfully, "I think you and I will get along quite well, my dear. Can I take you somewhere in my carriage?"

"That would be nice, Josephine," Lucian answered before Aimee could say no. "I was just telling my wife it would be good for her to cultivate friendships like yours. She really has not had much of a chance to make many friends during her stay in Paris, and I think she feels the loss deeply. I should like you both to enjoy each other's company while I'm at business. Do you mind?" he inquired politely, his blue eyes jumping from one female to the other.

"Not at all. Come along, Aimee, and we shall have a good time while our husbands are toiling at their respective jobs, eh?" Josephine laughed, taking Aimee's hand. She winked at Lucian. "My friend, you have a spirited one here. I trust you treat her as she deserves."

"Have no fear, madame," Lucian returned. "I will treat her

exactly as she deserves." And so saying, he bowed once more and retreated from the two ladies.

Aimee watched him go, unable to believe that he was actually her husband. She turned back to Josephine with a sigh. "Madame, I do thank you for your proposal, but I should like to be alone right now and—"

"Nonsense! A new bride must not be left alone!" Josephine intervened quickly. "Come along, my dear, and we shall make a little tour of Paris. We can eat at one of the best cafés, drink wine with some cavaliers, and walk in the gardens. Your husband has his mind on his business. Shame on him! But as long as he chooses to ignore you, so you should teach him a lesson!"

"Madame—"

"And do call me Josephine, my dear. I may be older than you, but madame is simply much too formal, don't you think, between friends!"

Aimee acquiesced as gracefully as she could and found herself pulled into Josephine's carriage and treated to a whirlwind tour of the city. They stopped at various shops so that Josephine could make several purchases, raving about this dressmaker or that milliner. She talked nonstop about her husband's courage and military prowess so that Aimee was obliged to smile and nod and agree with practically everything she said. They lunched in the Café Royal Purple and watched the whores plying their wares on the street outside. Josephine seemed to enjoy this immensely, although Aimee couldn't help but feel sorry for the poor creatures. More shopping followed, and then came several hours at a smoky café filled with all manner of citizens where Josephine urged Aimee to share a bottle of wine with her.

"I do love an afternoon's activities shared with a friend," Josephine was saying brightly, having already finished off her third glass of wine. "I do think we can be friends, don't you, Aimee?" She closed her eyes for a moment, then opened them and smiled sadly. "I get lonely often without my husband. He is gone so much," she related. "Italy, Austria, Egypt—I hardly remember I am married half the time. I suppose one cannot blame me too much for taking lovers. Napoleon has his affairs when he is away from me, I know."

"Madame—Josephine, I hardly think you should discuss such intimate details with one you hardly know," Aimee protested, feeling distinctly uncomfortable at such talk.

"Why not? Everyone in Paris knows I take lovers," Josephine said rather pathetically. "Men are charming to me and I cannot help but respond to their charm. I suppose that is why Napoleon fell in love with me, you see. He was so small and shy—so terribly young—when I first met him. And now he has grown stronger, wiser, more sure of himself. Very soon, he will realize his greatest ambition—and I am afraid, Aimee, afraid that he will cast me away from him!"

"Josephine, don't talk nonsense," Aimee said softly, feeling suddenly touched by the woman's situation. "You are so lovely, and when your husband is away so much that will only make him miss you the more."

"Ah, if only it were so!" Josephine sighed. But then she brightened. "You and Lucian—ah, now, there you are, such a lovely couple," she said. "He is so handsome and romantic, and you so young and beautiful. I must admit it was a shock to hear he had married—not a few young ladies will find their hearts broken at the news, my dear. But at least this will quell all those nasty rumors of your relationship with the decadent Talleyrand!"

Aimee flushed. "I don't understand why such rumors must be circulated, Josephine, when the relationship was completely innocent."

"Oh, my dear, I can assure you that I did not believe the rumors for one moment!" Josephine hastened to tell her. "Still, there are those who enjoy throwing mud at one's reputation, probably because they are overly zealous of their own! At any rate, such people hardly matter in the scheme of life, do they, my dear? Life is really much too short to let such people ruin it for you."

Aimee nodded in agreement. She was about to make another comment on the subject, when she heard her name called from somewhere in the room. Turning curiously, she was startled to see the boyish face and curly hair of Henri de Brueys as he smiled widely at her. Without a word, he rushed to her table and seated himself beside her, taking her hand in a gesture that sat ill with Aimee, and she snatched it away, wondering what on earth induced him to be so forward.

"Aimee, how fortunate I am that my friends decided to stop here on their way home from their employment!" he cried gladly, totally ignoring Josephine, who was watching the proceedings with interest. "How are you, my dear?"

"I am well, Henri," Aimee returned stiffly. A host of memories flooded through her for a moment as she recalled the "puppy love" she had felt for this young man at one time. She had entertained hopes of marrying him, she remembered, but the idea seemed ludicrous now as she compared him mentally to Lucian Napier. He seemed so young, so unsophisticated—a bourgeois, she told herself with a mental sneer.

"Ah, my dear, how many times I have wondered what ever became of you when you left me," Henri went on passionately.

"But you did not bother to find out?" Aimee accused him softly.

He had the grace to redden at her words. "No, you are right. I—"

"It's all right, Henri," Aimee interrupted. "I have landed on my feet, as you can see, so now you may set your heart at rest as to my fortunes."

"But, are you truly all right, my dear? I . . . I am in a position now where I can offer you help. We could—come to some agreement—"

"Agreement?" Aimee questioned, feeling a slow anger beginning to boil within her. "What sort of agreement, Henri? I would become your mistress and you would help me financially, is that it?" She pulled away from him, disgusted at the truth in his eyes. "I have no need of your money."

"I'm sorry, Aimee. The idea was not worthy of you, I know. But seeing you again—and you've grown so much more beautiful—I lost my head! My God, when I think that without my mother's intervention you would have been mine!"

"I thank God for your mother's intervention," Aimee said bitingly, "for it prevented me from making a stupid mistake, Henri. I was prepared to give myself to you—and now I realize you would have used me until you grew tired of me. I would have been your castoff affair, and you would have felt very little remorse."

"No, Aimee! How could you think I could be so crude to you? I cared for you a great deal, my dear."

"So much that you married Clarisse, with her big dowry?"

He looked down at the table, then back at her again. "I admit to being a weak man, my dearest. Yes, I married Clarisse, and I am now partner with my father in his business."

"It is what your mother wanted," Aimee replied without bitterness. "I am glad for you."

"But the marriage . . . is not what I had expected," Henri admitted. He tried to take her hand again. "I—we could have been so happy together," he ended wistfully.

"No, Henri. We would have been miserable. You would have

grown to hate me because I would have brought nothing to a marriage between us."

"But—but you said that you loved me!" Henri accused her incredulously.

She shrugged with unintentional cruelty. "I was still a child then, Henri. You were the first young man who was kind and interested in me. I thank you for that, but I feel nothing else for you."

For a moment he looked crestfallen, then seemed to notice Josephine's presence across the table. "Gracious lady, I am sorry to cause you embarrassment, but surely there must be some way you can help me convince Aimee that she should listen to my plea. I would promise to give her anything she wanted. I have the means to do so, I can assure you."

Josephine, who had been listening avidly, tittered at his request. "Oh, my poor young man, she is in no position to say yes when she herself is married!"

Henri turned to Aimee in shock. "You are married?"

She nodded. "Yes, Henri. So you see, this must be good-bye between us." Aimee looked at the young man, wondering what in the world she had ever seen in him. He had not changed at all since she had left him so long ago. Whereas, she felt as though she had aged considerably. He had the gall to propose she become his mistress. What would he say, she wondered, should she inform him that she was the ward of the Foreign Minister of France? She sighed, telling herself there was no reason for her to gloat over her good fortune. She only wished he would go away and leave her alone. All his attention was becoming embarrassing.

"Aimee, my dearest, I hardly know what to say," he chirped, still finding it difficult to believe she was married.

"There is no need for you to say anything, Henri," Aimee replied coolly. "Good-bye, and I do wish you every happiness in your marriage, as I know you wish me in mine."

Dispirited, Henri stood up, his face alternating between sadness and bitterness. Aimee watched him walk back to his companions, who immediately barraged him with questions, all of which he refused to answer. After downing a glass of brandy with a quick flick of his wrist, he left the place, much to Aimee's relief. She glanced over at Josephine and found the latter gazing at her with new interest and some speculation in her eyes.

"So, your past is no more immaculate than your new husband's," Josephine said thoughtfully.

"Don't be silly," Aimee rebuked her. "Henri meant very little to me—even then. He was the first young man to show a serious interest in me, and I clung to that. I met him during a very difficult time in my life. He married another and that was that. Please don't make anything else out of it, I beg you!"

Josephine's lids came down to hood her eyes as she shook her head with a smile. "Why, of course not, my dear. Really, there is no sense in being ashamed of a young man's passion toward you—just the thing, really, to put Lucian in his place, I think."

If Aimee had any doubts that Josephine would spread the gossip about her meeting with Henri de Brueys, they were confirmed quickly. A few afternoons later, she was reading quietly in the garden, enjoying the still-warm days of autumn, when her husband strode up to her, his face a tight mask of irritation that warned her he was displeased with something. Since she had barely seen him since the day they were married, she couldn't conceive of anything she had done wrong, but he quickly enlightened her.

"I hear you ran into an old paramour while you were in the company of Josephine Bonaparte," he began, holding on to his anger, though keeping a tight rein on it.

Aimee looked up from her book, wondering what on earth he was talking about when she remembered the meeting with Henri at the café. She sighed. "I asked Josephine to say nothing about it, Lucian, but I suppose she can't be trusted."

"I don't give a damn about her trust, it's you I'm wondering about," he stated succinctly.

She looked at him in bewilderment. "What do you mean?" she asked. "If you say she told you of that incident, you must realize how very little it meant to me."

"Josephine led me to believe that this young scamp proposed for you to become his mistress!"

Aimee blushed. "Yes, but—"

"And why would he think you would agree to such a thing?"

Aimee couldn't make sense of this attack on her. "I have no idea, Lucian, but I can assure you I set him straight immediately. He was Henri de Brueys, the son of—"

"I know who he is, my dear," Lucian interrupted.

"Well, then, you know as much about him as I do," Aimee responded quickly. "I admit to a friendship with him when I was in the employ of his father, but I can assure you it was no more than that. When he was engaged to be married to his present wife, his mother threw me out of the house. I never saw Henri again until a few days ago. I've never even thought about him," Aimee added, realizing with some surprise that it was true, she had dismissed him from her mind quite easily.

Lucian felt the tightness leaving his chest. He hated to admit to jealousy, but he was very much afraid he had been feeling exactly that. It was stupid—and dangerous—of him to feel that way when he knew that when he and Aimee began their "work" in America, it might be necessary for each of them to forget their marriage vows. Besides, the marriage was a farce—they both knew that, he reminded himself. She would be only too happy to obtain a divorce once her obligation was repaid in full. Still, the thought of a former lover offering to set her up as his mistress had galled him considerably. He was a proud man, and he wouldn't have another man dallying with his wife while he could help it!

He glanced in a rather shamefaced manner at the young woman, who was studying him with concern, anxious to make things right with him. He felt a tugging at his heart, a sudden desire to take her in his arms and make passionate love to her. He had to admit that one taste of her was hardly enough; he wanted more. Controlling himself with an effort, he said hastily, "I'm sorry, Aimee. I suppose I jumped to the wrong conclusion, but Josephine is extremely good at presenting only one side of the case. I thought of how blatant she is with her lovers, and wondered if, perhaps, you'd been taking lessons from her!"

Ruffled, Aimee stood up. "That shows how little you know me, Lucian!" she responded. "Actually, I'm surprised at you. I would think a spy of your caliber would be able to sift truth from lies. Perhaps you are not as good at your work as you've tried to make me believe," she challenged him.

He grinned. "Perhaps I'm not," he conceded.

Aimee smiled then, too, glad that a truce had been called. She would thank Henri de Brueys for that, if nothing else. She still wasn't completely sure why her husband would be so angry about the whole episode. Certainly he wasn't jealous, when she was positive he could have any woman he wished—and probably had made full use of several while her marriage bed remained empty of him. She recalled uneasily how he had reminded her that *she* had been the one who had demanded this marriage be one in name only. If it had been up to him, she knew he would have taken full advantage of the situation to visit her every night. The thought made her flush, but the idea was not as unpleasant as she had once thought.

Lucian watched the play of emotions on his wife's lovely face and wondered what she was thinking about. He knew it was not Henri de Brueys. Was she thinking of himself? he wondered. The idea warmed him and he drew closer to her in order to take her in his arms. The garden was fairly secluded; Talleyrand was not at home. What better spot to make love to a beautiful woman than among the last blooms of the season?

Aimee's green eyes darkened as he stepped toward her and put his arms around her waist to draw her close to him. Involuntarily, she twined her arms around his neck, tilting her head back to receive his kiss. Lucian smiled at the picture of surrender she made and bent his head to touch her lips, softly at first, then with growing passion as he clasped her closer. For a long moment, they stood holding each other, kissing, feeling the texture of their lips, the taste of their tongues.

Then, with a groan, Lucian pulled her down to the sun-warmed grass. Aimee felt as though there were no resistance in her. Supinely, she lay beneath him, still kissing, their legs tangled together, her arms holding him fast. She opened her eyes and looked at his face, passionate, the desire obvious in every line of his mouth, even in the curve of his jaw. God, how beautiful he seemed to her! How much she wanted to be his! She did not try to question this perverse wish inside her, did not remember how much she had sworn that never again would he have her at his mercy like this. None of that mattered! She was a young woman, a healthy animal with a husband who could satisfy completely her budding desires. There was no reason to keep denying them, she told herself. She would not become like poor Josephine, taking one lover after another to satisfy the hole in her heart that only her husband could truly fill.

With a sigh, she surrendered to her husband's ardent demands, turning in his arms, feeling his hands unfasten the bodice of her dress. Soon her breasts would be freed and he would caress them and kiss them, driving her mad with desire. The thought made her shiver deliciously and she closed her eyes, feeling the sun on her face.

A sudden clearing of someone's throat made Aimee jump, her hands going reflexively to her bosom to cover it from a stranger's gaze. Above her, Lucian started and his eyes flew open to reveal a fierce irritation in their depths.

"Do forgive me, Lucian," came Talleyrand's amused voice,

making Aimee's cheeks flush with her embarrassment. "I'm sorry to . . . intrude on your little interlude here in my garden, but I have important news for you, my friend."

Refastening Aimee's bodice, Lucian stood up and helped his wife to her feet, sparing a glaring look at Talleyrand, who continued to stand quietly, content to smile at their embarrassment.

"Your timing is atrocious," Lucian said angrily, feeling the frustration between his loins.

"Ah, I have been accused of that before," Talleyrand returned. "Still, I must give you this news immediately. I have finally convinced the Directory that there is some merit in my plan for North America. They agree to the advisability of dispatching someone to send back reports to us as to the general state of the Louisiana Territory and the Spanish government there." Talleyrand smiled hugely and slapped Lucian soundly on the back. "They have appropriated funds for our venture, my friend!"

"How will the Americans interpret our friendly overtures to the Spanish government there?" Lucian asked. To Aimee's chagrin, he seemed to have forgotten her for the moment.

"Not well, I'm afraid. We shall have to keep this as quiet as possible. You will have to travel to Brest and commission a ship that will take you to the port of New Orleans. I have tried once more to suggest, delicately, to the Directory that they put an end to the sea war with the United States, but they have so far refused to allow the order. They claim our naval seizures have been quite lucrative. The fools don't realize that our relations with America are rapidly deteriorating!"

"I am surprised you were able to get their consent to this scheme of yours," Lucian remarked, casually taking Aimee's hand as they returned to the house.

At his touch, Aimee felt her heart beat rapidly and wished she could make it slow down. She felt, with disturbing intensity, the warmth of his fingers on her arm and wondered what Lucian might think of her change in attitude if he knew. Maybe he wouldn't care, she thought sadly. With his reputation as quite a lover among the ladies, perhaps the addition of another conquest would have little effect on him. Her feet seemed to move slower and slower as they entered the house. She knew what Talleyrand's words had meant for her; she would be leaving Paris, leaving France very soon, journeying to an unknown land with only Lucian as her companion, a man whom she hardly really knew. She felt a sudden sense of panic now that the moment had finally arrived. Did she really understand what she was doing?

Did she really want to be bound to Lucian Napier and sail with him for a place she had barely heard of? She shivered.

"Aimee?" There was a tender note in Lucian's voice, but Aimee was too distraught to hear it.

She looked up at him blindly. "If I am to be leaving France, I should like to go home to visit my brother for a short time," she said quickly, afraid that he would refuse her.

Talleyrand's brows drew downward. "Damn, but it is inconvenient," he told her initially. But upon seeing the drowning look in those wide, green eyes, he relented. "All right, you can leave as soon as you wish—but the visit will have to be brief!"

Aimee nodded. "I would like to leave tonight—this afternoon!" she concluded urgently, missing the hurt expression on Lucian's face. But he quickly covered it so that by the time she did look at him, he was once more the smooth, unruffled man in control whom she knew.

"All right," he said curtly. "If you must go for one last look at your old home, you may as well go today. That will leave me time to make the necessary arrangements without the . . . distraction of your delightful presence." He smiled sardonically.

Aimee fought back the unexplained tears. "Thank you. I will pack a few things to take with me, and then, if I can prevail upon you to supply a vehicle and driver?"

It was on the tip of Lucian's tongue to volunteer his own services in that capacity, but he bit back the words. Obviously, she was having a change of heart from the warm sweetness he had sensed in the garden. Stiffly, he nodded. "I'll arrange it," he promised her.

Talleyrand looked at the pair of them and wondered if he had truly made a mistake in interrupting the sweet interlude in which they had been enmeshed before. Surely, he thought, they hadn't fallen in love with each other! He sighed. He learned long ago that love was a luxury he couldn't afford—and neither could either of them. They must have all their wits about them in entering into this mission of theirs. He wanted them to do their work well in order to persuade the Directory, or whoever else was in power, that his plan was feasible and for the good of France. He had always been able to rely on Lucian before. Now he wondered as he watched the look in the young man's eyes as he gazed at the departing form of his wife as she hurried upstairs to pack.

III

WINDS
OF
DESTINY

24

The fresh sea breeze blew briskly over the deck of the *Hélène* as Aimee stood at the railing, gazing toward the horizon, where the sun was just setting. They had been six weeks at sea already and she was heartily sick of this ocean voyage. She thought longingly of home, of the shores of France and of her brother, who had bid her a tearful farewell when she had had to leave the Castle du Beautreillis. She remembered her visit fondly, recalling how well her brother had looked, completely recovered as he was from his wounds. She had met his wife, a plump little bourgeois who looked at Etienne with continuous adoration. With her dowry and the pension he received from the government, Etienne had begun the restoration of the castle, a long and arduous process that would take several years to complete. Still, he and his wife lived cozily enough in a few rooms off the great hall, and he had been bursting with pride to inform her that he was to be a father by spring. Aimee had felt his happiness within her, even as she also felt a sense of loss that she would not be able to share in the happy event.

She had been able to parry successfully Etienne's questions about her own surprise marriage. He had wondered why she had consented to marry a virtual stranger and Aimee had hedged the issue, telling him just enough to satisfy his curiosity, while not revealing much at all. She didn't tell him it had been through Lucian's efforts that he had been released from prison and saved from the gallows. She knew it would only give rise to further questions. She simply told him she was happy in her marriage and that, when she returned from her journey to America, she would bring her husband out to meet him.

Etienne had wondered at the nature of her trip to America, but Aimee had only said it had to do with her husband's work. He seemed satisfied with that answer, although Aimee could not be sure. At the last, when she had been obliged to leave, he had hugged her close and tilted her chin up to look into her green eyes.

"Aimee, I know you're hiding something from me, little sister," he said gently. "And I know it isn't any of my business—I have very little right to interrogate you on your reasons for doing what you have to do after all you have managed to accomplish for me. Still, I want you to remember that I love you and that you will always have a place here if you should find you need it."

So much for Talleyrand's theory that her brother would not be pleased to have her as a permanent member of his household, Aimee thought with some satisfaction. She had hugged her brother close and promised she would write as often as she could. It had been harder than she'd realized to leave the home she had known for so long, the castle where all her dreams had been expressed when she was a little girl and where there were so many memories. She had visited the graves of her family and prayed, hoping her mother could somehow guide her in the months ahead.

Now, as she looked out over the calm ocean, Aimee wondered at what those months would bring. Ever since she had arrived back in Paris there had been a strain between Lucian and herself, a kind of visible constraint that kept them from talking to each other on any deep level. She was at a loss to know its cause, and even more at a loss to understand what to do about it. Lucian seemed completely wrapped up in his work, taking time only to brief her about certain necessary things. They did not even share a cabin; Lucian explained he believed she would be more comfortable with her own room. The physical separation only enforced the emotional one and Aimee felt miserable, coming to believe she had made a grave mistake in ever accepting this assignment. She began to feel that Lucian had his doubts, too, for he looked at her sometimes with an odd gaze in his blue eyes that confused her.

"What are you daydreaming about?"

Aimee turned around, smiling automatically as Lucian came up from belowdecks. "I was just watching the sun go down," she explained.

"Haven't seen any ships on the horizon, have you?" he asked, leaning against the railing and watching her with a half smile. "We wouldn't want to come face to face with a British man-o'-war, or an American sloop determined to retaliate for our impressment of their seamen!"

"I haven't seen anything," Aimee said flatly. "Nothing but water everywhere! I'm so tired of this voyage, Lucian."

He nodded in agreement. "I am, too. Normally, I enjoy the ocean, but this voyage is different."

His words hung in the air for a moment and Aimee wondered if it was because of her that he was not finding this trip enjoyable. "How much longer until we reach New Orleans?" she queried.

"Less than two weeks, I should imagine. Let's hope for continuing good weather. How are you feeling about what we're going to be doing?" he asked her with a sensitivity that amazed her. But then Lucian Napier had never fit the usual pattern of most men.

She shrugged her shoulders. "Somewhat ambivalent. Sometimes I feel that it is very important and my small contribution may make France the greatest country in the world. Other times, I wonder how my insignificant addition to the scheme of things can really matter. I mean, what is it we are really trying to do, Lucian? Will Talleyrand be able to persuade the government of France to get back this territory they gave to the Spanish? And what is so crucial about it? It seems too far away from France to make any difference."

Lucian looked out over the ocean for a moment, thinking of what he would say to her and how he would make her understand what it was they were trying to do. "First of all, despite the ocean miles, the continent of North America could prove very important to France one day. The United States is a growing republic, still young, I agree, but stretching its muscle, learning to use force to get what it wants. They have already begun to build up their navy, and they certainly have the heart and will to make good on their threat to harass French and British ships. The only thing that holds them back now is that we have a friend in Thomas Jefferson, the Vice President of the United States. He feels it is quite unthinkable for two republics like America and France to go to war against each other—and wait for Britain to divide the remains. And yet, he hasn't much influence, or at least not enough to persuade others in high office to follow his ideas of friendship toward France."

"But what does all this have to do with the Louisiana Territory?"

"Very simply, America does not want France to take back the territory from Spain. A decadent Spanish government, without the power or the inclination to defend its large territory in North America, provides very little threat to the United States. On the other hand, a strong French government which, with Talleyrand's backing, pushes for the defense of such a territory could be a very big thorn in the Americans' side. Unfortunately, the Americans do not realize that should Spain and Britain become strong allies, the Spanish could look to the English for help in defending their territory. This could be extremely dangerous since the British already control Canada."

"You sound as though you are overly concerned about the American interests in all of this," Aimee commented.

Lucian smiled smoothly. "Only insofar as they coincide with French interests, my dear. Unfortunately, many Americans look with suspicion on the motives of the French ever since that stupid Edmond Genet made a bungle of things when he came to America as our ambassador five years ago."

"What happened?"

"He was sent as the not-so-secret agent of world revolution. His specific instructions were to pry Canada away from British influence, and Louisiana and Florida away from the Spaniards. The French intentions were to attack Spanish New Orleans and Mexico and initiate them into the republican form of government. Genet learned of Jefferson's French leanings and courted him outrageously. He learned that Jefferson was a Republican, which meant he was a friend of France and universal humanity, so to speak, and also a representative of the southern American interests, most of whom are planters."

"But that all sounds good for France," Aimee interjected.

"But there is another side to the coin. The government in the United States is made up in a two-party system. One side is the Republicans, and the other side is the Federalists, who are pro-British and antirevolutionary, representing the northern commercial interests of the United States."

"Heavens, it seems so confusing," Aimee put in quickly. "Cannot the north and the south of the United States agree on their ideals?"

"It is no different from France in that respect," Lucian replied, smiling at the interest in her eyes. "When do the northern provinces ever agree with the southern areas? The people of Normandy will always distrust those of the Languedoc, just as most of the country provinces look with suspicion on the citizens of Paris."

"That's true," Aimee agreed. "Even a revolution could not bring all the provinces together."

"Exactly. So it is in the United States—and it was this division that Genet counted on when he tried to get Jefferson to back his ideas and present them to his government. Unfortunately, both north and south agreed that they did not wish to go to war with the British again for the sake of French interests. Genet badly jeopardized the French position in America and caused Jefferson, our greatest friend, to resign in some disgrace.

"The French ambassadors who succeeded Genet have been under orders to try to prevent the United States from coming to any agreement with Spain with respect to the navigation of the Mississippi River—the river that empties into the Gulf of Mexico at the port of New Orleans. It is the longest river in America so far as we know, and now you can see the importance of New Orleans and the surrounding Louisiana Territory."

"So Talleyrand believes that if we can persuade Spain to sell us New Orleans and the rest of the territory, the French will have a strong foothold in America," Aimee deduced.

"And greater leverage as to American policies regarding England, France's eternal enemy," Lucian added. "To that end, the Directory dispatched a secret agent, a General Collot, to navigate the Ohio and Mississippi Rivers in order to map out their features with a view to future military operations. I have his reports with me, advising France to seize certain portions of the American western territories adjacent to these rivers in order to safeguard French possession of the Mississippi River valley. Accordingly, French agents like ourselves have been sent to the Louisiana Territory, only their missions have been to go among the Indians to urge them to take to the warpath against the American settlers."

"It seems . . . so cold-blooded," Aimee commented, not sure she liked the sound of what her own countrymen were doing.

"It is," Lucian agreed. "But the Americans are apprised of the situation, which only makes them more hostile to France."

"But what of Spain? I would think she would be very nervous about her possessions in America, what with both France and England looking at them covetously, not to mention the Americans."

"She is indeed nervous," Lucian confirmed. "In fact, her whole policy is limited by her fears. She simply negotiates with everyone and hopes for the best."

"It all sounds muddled to me," Aimee said, shaking her head in confusion. "I know that Talleyrand has France's best interests at heart, yet I abhor the idea that we must go around so sneakily, trying to subvert Indians to kill American settlers."

Lucian regarded her with an enigmatic expression. "It's the nature of countries to be distrustful of one another," he finally said quietly. "That is why there is the need for agents—spies. Spain has them, as do the British, as do the Americans."

"Do you know who they all are?" Aimee wondered.

For a moment, Lucian seemed taken aback at the question, but he smiled, recovering his previous control. "I know *some* of them," he told her, but would say nothing more, even as she probed for answers. Finally, he laughed and took her hand in his. "I didn't realize what an inquisitive mind my wife has."

Aimee looked into his flame-blue eyes and felt her cheeks grow warm at his use of the term *wife*. She had nearly forgotten they were actually married, they had been so distant to each other. Lucian was gazing back at her with a sober look in his blue eyes, a questioning look that disturbed her. Feeling suddenly uncomfortable, she looked away from him.

"What's the matter, Aimee?" he asked her directly.

"I don't know," she answered him softly. "I feel . . . somehow inadequate for this task you expect of me. Sometimes . . . sometimes I think how much happier I would have been had I married and settled somewhere in one of the provincial towns, living the life I had before I came to Paris."

"You regret coming to Paris?" he asked.

Some magnetic quality seemed to draw her eyes back to his. "No," she replied in a low voice. "I would never have met you," she added.

For a moment he looked somewhat astonished at her admission. Then a pleased smile settled over his features. "You give me heart, my dear. Perhaps we will make an advantageous pairing in this venture. I certainly hadn't hoped for such cooperation from you when I first proposed it."

Aimee frowned at his words. What was he spouting? She had admitted to him she would have felt empty without having met him, admitted he meant something to her—and here he was going on about how advantageous that feeling was in their work together! What about their marriage together! She wanted to tell him of her feelings, but caution warned her to wait and see how he acted toward her. She had already admitted much, and he had not admitted anything as far as his feelings toward her were concerned.

"Yes, I'm sure we shall make wonderful agents for France!" she returned with sarcasm. "And that *is* what is important to you, isn't it, Lucian?"

He blinked at the hidden fires in her voice. "Of course it's important, my dear. In this work, one must be sure of one's partner. Without trust there is no advantage to it."

"I agree completely," she returned bitingly.

He watched her, trying to read the reason behind her words. She was angry with him, but he wasn't certain as to the reason. She had already told him she wanted this to be a marriage in name only. Her cooperation was guaranteed because of the leverage he had held over her brother's fate. But was she hinting now at something more? He couldn't be sure, and in his business he had grown used to exercising caution. He could not just jump in and make a clean breast of it with her; that went against all of his instincts. No, he would wait and try to pick up signals from her, figure out what it was she wanted. The thought came to him that perhaps she was piqued because he hadn't been paying much attention to her during the voyage. His masculine ego liked that idea and he smiled to himself, thinking there was little reason to continue to forgo his own pleasure with her if she was willing to cooperate.

"Aimee, are you angry with me because we haven't been enjoying our . . . rights . . . as husband and wife?" he asked, watching her green eyes sparkling in the last rays of the setting sun.

Aimee felt incensed at his words. His rights! Whatever did he mean? She didn't want to hear about his *rights;* she wanted to hear about caring and a measure of feeling for her that had nothing to do with his rights!

"Why, no!" she answered brightly, fighting down the urge to ball her hand into a fist and do what damage she could to that smiling, handsome face. "Heavens, Lucian, I'm sure I will have more than enough of that sort of thing once we begin our work. I mean, I'm sure you will expect me to obtain information from certain men in whatever way I can—isn't that right? Certainly, even should it require methods of . . . uh . . . seduction?" She lifted her eyes innocently to his, quite pleased at the angry surprise she saw there.

"Madame, I brought you on this mission as a partner, to aid me in my work—not as a whore! I'll thank you to remember that."

She pouted and wrinkled her nose. "But really, Lucian, we must be completely honest with each other. Our marriage means nothing to either of us. After all, it is simply a cover so that you can more easily do what is required of you. I am merely here as an ornament. You shouldn't be bothered too much by the methods I use to obtain useful information."

"Aimee, I'm warning you—you go too far with this jest!" he growled, feeling a sudden urge to grab her by the shoulders and shake her. Abruptly, he turned on his heel, leaving her by the railing, wondering if she had gone too far.

Dinner was a rather stilted affair that evening. Aimee contributed very little to the conversation, which was mostly carried by the captain and his first mate. Lucian, too, was on the morose side, drinking more than he usually did and leaving most of his food untouched on his plate. Aimee excused herself early, intending to go to bed and fall asleep. But her mind would not allow her to rest and she tossed and turned fitfully for a while, kept awake by guilty feelings about how terribly she had acted toward Lucian and the loud laughter coming from the captain's cabin, where the men were still conversing and enjoying their wine.

She had just begun to drift off when she heard her door open and then close swiftly. She sat up in her bunk, hugging the bedcovers to her breast while she strove to make out the figure of the man in the darkness. He seemed to be swaying a little, whether from the motion of the ship in the water or the simple fact that he was drunk, she wasn't sure.

"Lucian?" she whispered. "Is that you?"

"Yes, madame. It is your husband," he said, the words slurring a little.

"You're drunk!" she accused, a note of disgust in her voice.

"Drunk?" he repeated, lurching toward the bunk. He came up short, barking his shin against the wood, which caused him to curse loudly at the pain.

"Lucian, get out of here and go back to your own room!" she hissed, feeling uncomfortable at seeing this side of him.

"You are my wife," he pointed out, leaning over to feel for the bedcovers.

Aimee jumped when his hands made contact with her. "Lucian, you are in no condition to do anything but go to sleep," she assured him, moving farther over in the bunk in order to move out of his reach.

Lucian's hands followed her, smoothing the covers over her body, feeling the lumps and contours, before lurching forward once more and landing on the bed beside her. Aimee cringed, smelling the liquor on his breath and cursing the captain for allowing him to become inebriated.

"Get out of here!" she ordered him again. "You're intoxicated!"

He laughed. "Ah, yes, intoxicated by your beauty, my lovely,

lovely wife," he replied, then hiccoughed. "You see, I could stay away no longer—and now, here I am, ready to let you play the whore with me. Better with me, my dear, than with a stranger, for I, at least, will stick by you in the morning." He leaned closer, conversing as though he were sincerely trying to convince her of his good intentions. "You cannot play at being a whore without first practicing, my dear wife. And look—I have volunteered for the part. Whore with me all you wish!"

"Lucian, you must get out of here! You know very well I have no intention of—of doing what I said I would earlier. I was just angry with you—you know that!"

"And I am angry with you," he returned, waggling a finger in her face. "You talk of being a whore with others and won't even deign to allow me my husbandly rights. That seems quite . . . unfair to me, my dear." He moved forward clumsily to bury his face in her shoulder.

Aimee shrugged him off and he flopped to the edge of the bunk, nearly cracking his head. She felt his hand on her arm, allowing him to pull himself back up.

"You are a most cruel wife," he muttered. "I should have bargained with some other poor waif who would have been more than glad to do whatever I wanted."

"Oh! I suppose you thought I would grovel at your feet for the chance to be at your side on this mission for France!" she snorted. "Well, you may have held most of the cards, Lucian, but—"

"You are holding the trump!" He laughed jokingly. "Yes, you are, Aimee!" He caught her around the waist and thrust her forward against his chest, burying his face in her hair. "I should never have allowed you to get under my skin like this," he murmured into her hair. "I want you, Aimee!"

The words caused a momentary thrill to run up Aimee's backbone, but she struggled to get out of his hold, detesting his drunkenness, not sure she could believe anything he was saying in his present state.

"Are you sure, Lucian?" she asked. "Changing our relationship might muddy the waters too much for you. After all, you've got your mission to think about, don't you? Talleyrand would be disappointed in you if he thought you allowed romance to get in the way of your work."

"I'm bound to disappoint the old bastard anyway." Lucian sighed, trying to grab hold of her again. He stopped abruptly, as though catching himself before saying too much. Then he smiled again. "Don't worry about Talleyrand, Aimee. He can get his own whores. I want *you!*"

The inference, drunk or not, stung Aimee out of any romantic feelings she might be experiencing. Firmly, she pushed him away. "Well, that's to be expected since I am the only woman on board this ship," she pointed out matter-of-factly. "Since I also happen to be your wife—at least in name—I'm not at all surprised to see you here. But I'm afraid you're bound to be disappointed, Lucian, for I really don't want *you!*" So saying, she pushed him once again, causing him to fall out of the bunk and land with a heavy thud on the floor planking.

"Oh!" Suddenly terrified that she had mortally wounded him, she leaned over the side of the bunk, afraid to hear that he had stopped breathing. But suddenly, a loud snore greeted her, accompanied by a whoosh of liquor-laden breath that nearly nauseated her. He'd fallen asleep! Gritting her teeth, Aimee thought about calling the captain to haul him off to his own bunk, but wasn't sure she wanted him to see her embarrassment in this little episode. Instead, she decided to let him lie where he was. It would certainly serve him right when he awoke with a sore back and a stiff neck—on top of a throbbing head—in the morning! Oddly enough, she found his resonant snores quite soothing all of a sudden, and, settling down as comfortably as she could in the bunk, she was soon fast asleep.

"What in the hell!"

Aimee came awake to the sound of her husband's curses as he awoke to find himself lying flat out on the floor. She smiled to herself, then leaned over the bunk to meet his cloudy blue eyes gazing up at her questioningly.

"You came in last night very drunk," she informed him, trying not to laugh at the bemused look on his face. "I'm afraid you were in no condition to be coaxed back to your own room, so I simply let you sleep there on the floor."

"Damn! You could have let me have half the bunk!" he snapped, wincing and bringing a hand to his throbbing temple. "My back feels as though it's been cut in two from this hard planking! Couldn't you show me a little pity?" he rebuked her, rising unsteadily to his feet, keeping one hand on his head while the other rubbed at the small of his back.

"None, I'm afraid," she returned tartly, then suppressed a giggle at the glaring look with which he favored her. "I couldn't help it if you insisted on presenting yourself to me in the condition you were in. You are much too heavy for me to have attempted to lift you into the bunk when you fell out of it." She gave him an innocent look of reproach from beneath the veil of her lashes. "Really, I hardly see how you can blame me."

He eyed her interrogatively. "Damn! I wish I could remember what happened, but as it is, I suppose I shall have to take your word for it."

"What are partners for, if you can't trust them?" she reminded him gently.

His glare deepened. "I think, little wife, we will have to discuss this at length—after I've recovered a little better from the night."

"Of course," she demurred, acting the perfect wife. "Is there anything I can do for you, darling?"

He winced again. "Not at present," he answered through gritted teeth. Then turning, he made his way out of her cabin quite gingerly, leaving Aimee to roll on her bunk with laughter.

25

Fifteen days later, the ship was in sight of the vast delta that comprised the mouth of the Mississippi River. Bobbing gently on the sparkling waters of the Gulf of Mexico, the ship slid softly through the blue-green waters while the captain made his calculations on how best to navigate the great river. Aimee stood at the railing once more with Lucian close beside her, her eyes avidly drinking in the sight of the unfamiliar terrain. The great mud plain that had been built up through centuries of the river-deposited silt was encrusted with twisted, petrified pieces of trees that extended out into the Gulf waters. The river coursed through these impediments in five separate branches, which the captain referred to as "passes." He had already told his two passengers that they would not attempt to reach New Orleans by any of these five passes since all were much more difficult than another route that had been used for several years. They would sail along the coast a few more miles and then cross Lake Pontchartrain and Bayou St. John, which would lead them into the Mississippi River directly up from the levee of the city.

"How much farther is New Orleans?" Aimee asked, directing her question to Lucian, who was gazing out at the swamps and bayous that seemed to be everywhere along the coast here.

"About a hundred miles from the mouth of the river," he told her absently. "I have heard that it is located within a great bend of the river and that the land is only ten feet above sea level, causing frequent flooding in the rainy season. Why Bienville chose that place for the location of a great city is beyond my comprehension, but I suppose the location on the river more than makes up for any other inconveniences."

"Other inconveniences?" Aimee inquired curiously.

He nodded. "Mosquitoes, fever, hurricanes." He glanced down at her and smiled. "*Minor* inconveniences to those of us who have already lived through the French revolution, right, my dear?"

Aimee smiled and returned his nod. "I suppose so, but I

must admit I am quite anxious to see this city we are going to."

"It will take a few more days before we arrive," Lucian replied. "I suppose we could use the time, though, in order to go over our assignment once more." His blue eyes looked at her testily. "You can't back out on me at this late date, you know."

She laughed. "I promise I will support you, Lucian. I feel in these last few days that we have . . . uh . . . grown closer. Don't you agree?"

He rubbed the back of his head gingerly, as though recalling the night he had spent on the floor of her cabin. Since then, there had been an easing of the tension between them, although he had been somewhat chagrined to realize that she had no intention of inviting him into her bunk. Aimee had been firm in her resolve that this "bargain" between them would not be one of Lucian merely using her to assuage his bodily needs while she could only expect to be "dumped" when the assignment was over and he looked for fresh new adventures to explore. No, he would have to earn her trust first, she told herself. She was not stupid enough to try to tell herself that she was not attracted to Lucian. On the contrary, she knew it would be quite easy to fall completely under his spell and let him do whatever he wished with her. But she was determined not to be an easy conquest for him.

As she looked up into his suntanned face, which had browned considerably from the exposure to the sun during their voyage, she realized how remarkably handsome he was and shuddered to think of all the women who would be more than willing to throw themselves at his feet. He was intelligent, too, and quite sophisticated, which only made him all the more devastating. She sighed to herself, wondering if she would be able to keep her promise to herself and hold him at arm's length. It would be most difficult once they were thrown together closely during their work for France.

"You're staring at me," he accused her with a half smile, raising one dark eyebrow in mock consternation. "Are you wishing you were back in France, contentedly raising chickens on your brother's estate?"

She laughed gaily and tossed her head back. "Not at all, Lucian! I was just thinking how hard it might prove to be to keep my mind on my work with you around," she teased provocatively.

He seemed surprised at her candor. "Aimee, I must say you are not like any other woman I have ever known. You constantly surprise me with your forthrightness. Can it possibly be that you and I will work well together?"

"I believe we will," she answered matter-of-factly. "In fact, I think you should count yourself quite lucky, Lucian Napier, that you chose me for this mission of yours!"

He shook his head and grinned at her. "If your intelligence matches your wit, my dear, I shall certainly have no regrets. I just hope that the first time I ask you to do something that might go against your . . . er . . . principles, you don't turn around and slap my face."

"That depends," she demurred, making a comical face. "For now, I can honestly say I am looking forward to finding out exactly how a spy earns his money." She eyed him directly. "Speaking of which, just how much am I to earn for this dangerous work I will perform for France?"

He seemed taken aback by her directness for a moment, then recovered and let out a sharp whistle. "You are the only woman I've ever worked with who has worried about the pay," he informed her with a sardonic smile. "I suppose most of the women were content with my . . . uh . . . services."

"Shame on you, Lucian!" she reproached him, waving her index finger in front of his face. "That sounds very much like you prostituted yourself—and you can be sure I would never do that for France, or you!"

He was silent, gazing with a degree of awe at this little vixen, who seemed to be able to one-up him all the time. How he would like to have another chance in her bed! he thought longingly. The episode in his room at Talleyrand's when he'd taken her virginity had been nothing compared to what he would teach her in the future. She was really much too unique a young woman to be taken lightly, he decided. Gently, he reached out to brush an errant strand of golden hair away from her face, letting his thumb slide along her cheek and feeling the softness of her skin. She had acquired a fine, beige tint to her skin from the sun after first burning red and then peeling.

Aimee felt his hand against her face, and felt her heart begin to thud at the sensuous gesture. With a nervous little laugh, she jerked her face away and eyed him with some defiance, seeing the knowing look in his blue eyes.

To change the subject, she asked him, "Shouldn't you be telling me more about what it is we are to do once we arrive in New Orleans? I should like to be kept apprised of your plans, if you don't mind, rather than have you simply spring them on me."

"Of course. Accompany me down to my cabin and we can talk in private," he told her, looking for an excuse to get her alone.

Aimee sensed this, but realized it would be easier to talk in his cabin than out here on deck while the sailors were maneuvering the sails and the captain was barking out orders. She nodded shortly and followed him belowdecks, entering his cabin rather hesitantly, not having set foot inside it before today. It was much the same as hers, except that in the center, nailed to the floor, was a square table with maps and papers strewn about, on top of which was some official-looking correspondence signed with Talleyrand's name.

Lucian picked up the paper and held it out for her perusal. "These are our directives," he explained. "We are, first of all, to estimate the mood of the city that serves as capital for the entire Louisiana Territory. Secondly, we are to ascertain how well the people would cooperate with a French government set up to replace the current Spanish one. We are to send back reports to Talleyrand so he can persuade the Directory to beef up the negotiations with Spain in order to buy back the territory. We can also feel out the mood of the Americans, since they are so anxious to add the territory to their United States."

"Are there many Americans living in New Orleans?"

"Quite a few since the last governor of the district lifted most of the restrictions on their commerce. The reports have indicated that there are many American shopkeepers in the city and also quite a few soldiers in the army who, after taking an oath of allegiance to Spain, are allowed to carry arms and have the task of patrolling the city at night after curfew. Of course, many more Americans come in and out of the city on a seasonal basis. These are the ones who seem to be making the most trouble. They're mostly rivermen from the newly organized states of Kentucky and Tennessee who float their goods down on enormous flatboats, trade with the city people, and then go back upriver. It's a thriving commerce, especially since the Spanish have granted them the freedom to navigate the river and consider New Orleans a free port."

"What kind of trouble do they bring?"

He shrugged. "Rivermen caught on the river for several weeks tend to go a little wild once they reach port. I'm sure you can imagine the damage they can do once they've had a little too much to drink. Many of the Creoles of the city detest these Americans and would rather they not float down from their homes, but the Spanish government has long realized the advantage to stimulating the commerce of the city brought about by these floating merchantmen."

"So the Americans are very much a force in all these negotiations," Aimee observed astutely.

Lucian nodded thoughtfully. "They are an industrious, courageous people."

She glanced up at him perceptively. "You sound as though you admire them, Lucian."

He smiled. "I do. I'm one of them."

At her startled look, he explained, "My mother is an American from Virginia. She married my father in France. It was quite a whirlwind romance, I believe, since she was on holiday, touring Europe with her parents and two sisters."

"So she never returned to Virginia?"

"Oh, yes. In fact, I've been there several times myself over the years. After her father died, he left her one-third of the family's large tobacco plantation. We would visit from time to time. I remember my two aunts and my grandmother making quite a fuss over me, as I was the only grandchild. Neither of my aunts ever married and both died fairly young."

"So you are the sole heir to the tobacco plantation?" Aimee asked, feeling complete shock at this side of Lucian she hadn't suspected.

He nodded, looking a bit uncomfortable, but Aimee pursued the topic. "Then why do you continue spying for Talleyrand?" she wondered. "Why don't you retire to your plantation in America, instead of living this dangerous life? Is it because you love France too much?"

He turned away from her probing questions, walking quietly to the sideboard in order to pour himself something from a glass decanter. "I have a competent staff that runs the house and grounds in Virginia," he finally said with a sigh. "An overseer whom I trust completely runs the tobacco fields. I . . . try to visit the plantation as much as possible. In fact, I stopped by there when I went to see Jefferson on my mission for Talleyrand."

"But don't you find something of a conflict of interest?" Aimee asked.

He shrugged. "That is my concern, Aimee," he said evasively.

"But what about your parents?"

"My father died for the glory of France in one of the interminable wars of Louis the Fifteenth. My mother . . . is still alive. She and my grandmother live on my plantation."

Aimee sat down abruptly in a chair, overwhelmed by all these sudden and unexpected revelations about her husband. "Why—why didn't you tell me all of this before?" she inquired helplessly.

"Because I didn't think it was important," he returned, an edginess to his voice. "After all, you must admit our marriage was rather hasty and designed to put a seal of truth on our future adventure together in New Orleans. I didn't think there was any point in telling you of your in-laws, since it didn't seem likely that you would ever meet them."

Aimee stiffened at the implication. "Of course, I understand. And I quite agree. This marriage is one of 'convenience' in every sense of the word, and there is absolutely no reason for you to share your background with me."

He turned to face her, his blue eyes gently mocking her. "I distinctly recall that is exactly what you wished. If I have hurt your feelings in some way, I apologize. I only wish the subject hadn't come out now. I don't want it to complicate your feelings toward me in any way."

"You needn't worry about that," she said airily. "My feelings toward you, Lucian, are most *uncomplicated*," she assured him.

He gazed at her for a moment, then smiled with a shrug. "If that is the case, then you needn't worry yourself about anything but doing what we have to do in order to get those reports back to Talleyrand." He sat down and reached for several papers strewn about the table. "Our contact in New Orleans—the people we will be staying with—is a French Creole couple, Dominic St. Cyr and his wife, Violette. I have met Dominic in Philadelphia and I can vouch for his charm and intelligence. You will be delighted with him, my dear."

"You have never met his wife?"

He shook his head. "No, they have been married for less than a year, but from all accounts rendered by Dominic when she was still his fiancée, she is quite beautiful and the sweetest of women." He cocked an eyebrow at his own wife. "Perhaps you could learn something from her during our stay," he suggested.

Aimee reared back in her chair. "I didn't come on this

voyage to learn etiquette from some pioneer woman!" she said derisively.

Lucian laughed. "New Orleans isn't a backwoods area anymore, Aimee. In fact, it holds quite a bit of charm and a suggestion of old France. You will see when you arrive."

"How will this St. Cyr couple help us?" Aimee wanted to know, dismissing the thought that she could ever love any place this far from her native land.

"Dominic has quite a few contacts among the Spanish officials of the city. His influence will get us into the social functions where you will keep your ears open for any information the wives might let slip, and I will ingratiate myself to the gentlemen. We are distant cousins of the St. Cyrs, in case I forgot to inform you."

"Very distant," Aimee returned with a little laugh. She perused the large map of the port of New Orleans as well as the huge territory that bulged upward into the center of the continent of North America. "If this map is accurate, this land is immense," she concluded. "Why, in heaven's name, did France ever sell it to Spain?"

"Louis the Fifteenth of France was not the wisest of kings, as you may or may not know," Lucian said. "Because of his defeat at the hands of the English during the Seven Years' War in Europe, the French lost whatever hold they had on the great area of India. They also lost Canada to the English, and Louis, considering the Louisiana Territory nothing more than an unprofitable financial burden, gave it to his cousin, Charles the Third of Spain. A stupid blunder, for France lost any foothold at all in the New World. Talleyrand wishes to right that blunder by winning the Louisiana Territory back for France."

"What do the people of the territory want?" Aimee asked curiously.

"That is what we have come to find out," he replied smoothly.

Several days later, Aimee saw her first glimpse of the city of New Orleans, symbolically important to her, since it reminded her of her old home in France. But—oh! Certainly the Orléans in France was a hundred times better than this sprawling town of mud and trees and swamp that had the temerity to call itself the "new Orléans"! The ship anchored in the great river just up from the levee, where Aimee could see several people on the wharf beginning to go about their day's work. The docks did seem to do a bustling business, she noticed, from all the activity of dark-skinned men in straw hats and colorful bandannas who unloaded long, heavy flatboats of boxes and crates. Blacks squatted along the edge of the docks with baskets of yellow oranges, hawking their wares in loud voices that sang out in a certain cadence, accompanied by the strident notes of the banana sellers and other vendors selling cooled ginger beer to the dock workers. She grudgingly admitted that it might remind her a very little bit of the activity on the Pont Neuf, although the crowds were not nearly as numerous in this city.

There were several warehouses along the wharffront where goods were stored, and beyond those she could see buildings in the town proper. A two-story edifice with stuccoed brick walls and a flat roof with flat tiles caught her attention because at its pediment above the central entrance there was emblazoned the royal arms of Spain. She surmised that this, then, must be some sort of government building. Close beside it rose the walls of what was obviously a church, with two hexagonal towers capped with bell-shaped structures and a flat roof enclosed by a balustrade.

Close to the river, she could see from her vantage point one of the twin forts that protected New Orleans from enemy attack. It was pentagon-shaped with a brick-faced parapet and armed with twelve- and eighteen pound cannon, the noses of which stuck out through holes in the wall with a menacing air. Between the two forts a large battery had been installed, and beyond it was a parapet of earth surmounted with a palisade, and around that was a moat.

"It looks like they are ready for any attack," Lucian commented, coming up behind Aimee. "Certainly it couldn't be said that they would give up easily in a fight."

"That depends on what mettle the citizens are made of," Aimee proposed stoutly. "What good are fortifications without the people behind them to make them work?"

"A very intelligent observation, my good little wife," Lucian returned with a smile, leaning over to plant a casual kiss on one smooth cheek.

Aimee felt his lips on her skin and experienced a pleasurable shiver along her spine. She had, only a few minutes before, been looking forward to disembarking with quite a bit of trepidation, but now, with Lucian at her side, she somehow didn't feel so anxious anymore. In fact, with his blue eyes scanning down the length of her, she was glad that she had chosen her gown with care that morning. It was of lightweight cotton; even though the

month was February, it was like springtime here. Short-sleeved
and high-waisted, it dropped gracefully in white folds from the
wide, velvet sash beneath her breasts. A high-crowned hat made
of the same material as the sash set off the green of her eyes and
was festooned with artificial flowers in varying shades of purple.
A cashmere shawl was draped artfully over her shoulders, and to
complete the sense of high fashion she had chosen a pair of Grecian sandals.

"You will impress the provincials most assuredly," Lucian
commented with a note of pride in his voice.

"Thank you, my husband," Aimee returned with a coquettish air, so that Lucian was hard-pressed not to sweep her into
his arms and plant a salacious kiss on that pert and lovely
mouth.

As it was, he took her hand firmly in his and led her to the
gangplank, where he helped her ashore. Once on a nonmoving
surface, Aimee felt as though she were still rolling on water. She
made a comical face at her husband, seeing the same look in his
eyes.

"I suppose we've got to lose our sea legs," she commented
with a shaky laugh.

She was about to comment to Lucian on the activity along the
wharf when a black-haired young man of medium height, who
looked to be about Lucian's age, came up to grasp Lucian's hand,
a beaming smile revealing white teeth that contrasted sharply to
his dark-tanned face. He was dressed impeccably in tan trousers
and pearl-gray waistcoat with a dark brown coat and snowy-white
cravat. A tall-crowned hat sat well on his head, and high polished
boots encased his muscular legs.

"Lucian! Violette and I had begun to think you weren't coming!" the man cried, pumping the other man's hand vigorously.
"Good God, man, it's good to see you! Have you come to see
what our fair city is all about?"

"It is a very fair city," Lucian responded diplomatically.
"Dominic, it's good to see you, too! And please let me introduce
my wife to you—Aimee, this is Dominic St. Cyr, our host for
our time in New Orleans."

Dominic turned to Lucian's wife with a courtly bow, his
dark, snapping eyes registering his complete approval. With a
white smile, he took her hand and planted a very moist kiss on
the back of it so that Aimee couldn't help the blush that rose in
her cheeks.

"Madame, it is New Orleans' pleasure that you have arrived to add even more beauty to her boulevards. Our men will fight among themselves to be your escort." He turned back to Lucian. "You know my weakness for blondes, my friend—it is most dangerous of you to have married one."

"Violette would not like the sounds of that," Lucian teased him.

The other man sighed. "It's true, she is very jealous—and very beautiful in her own right. Wait until you meet her, my friend. Come along. My carriage is waiting. Do you have your luggage yet?"

"It is just now being unloaded," Lucian informed him. He turned to Aimee, who was still watching this dynamic young Creole with some fascination. "Sweetheart, why don't you rest on that crate there while Dominic and I see to the luggage." She nodded and sat down, glad of the wide brim of her hat, which shaded her eyes from the glare of the sun off the water.

When the luggage had been loaded and the passengers installed in the carriage, Dominic gave the order to move and the driver obligingly whipped the horses onto the road that led through the Vieux Carré. Aimee sat back in one of the luxurious seats of fine leather, rethinking her idea on the provincialness of New Orleans. Certainly from the fashionably dressed Dominic St. Cyr, to the well-maintained red-brick homes they were now passing, it seemed to have transplanted a bit of old France to this place in a wild, new world. She leaned forward eagerly, gazing out the window and throwing question after question to a smiling Dominic, who answered as best he could.

She learned that the building showing the Spanish royal arms was indeed the government building of the city, called the Cabildo, where the administrative offices of the governor were located, as well as the rooms where the legislative assembly met. It looked out onto the military square, the Place d'Armes, where several Spanish soldiers could be seen doing their drills. The church, Dominic informed her, was called the Saint Louis Cathedral, so named after Louisiana had been made a diocese.

"Only four years ago, the Vieux Carré was ravaged by a great fire," Dominic told her conversationally. "Six years before that was the first great fire. Much of what you see here was razed, but the spirit of our people is indomitable, and out of the ashes of those two great fires arose the graceful architecture you see now."

Aimee drank in the colorful pictures of the streets of New Orleans, forgetting her earlier summary dismissal of it. Indeed, most of the buildings were built in the Spanish style, with every building either of red brick or white stucco with colorful green- or red-tiled roofs. Dominic informed her that the stucco was obtained by burning the plentiful clam shells that the black slaves gathered up from the beach, and the bricks were made from the sandy clay found along the banks of the Mississippi.

"You see, we provide for ourselves," he said with pride in his voice. "We are very proud of our city, madame. Every house, whether cottage or mansion, has its bricked or flagged courtyard —a patio, as the Spanish call it. Many of them have a fountain in the center, providing cool relief during the hot, moist days of summer. They recall nothing so much as a tropical garden paradise—you will grow to love it, I can assure you."

"What are those planks and boards that run between the street and the houses?" Aimee queried.

"They are called a banquette—a sidewalk—for our citizens to keep the mud from splashing on their clothing. We are quite civilized and nearly as vain as the citizens of Paris, I've been told," he added with a charming smile so that Aimee found it impossible to take affront.

"Actually, you are far ahead of Paris," she returned with an answering smile. "We walked in filth and mud in the spring and summer and were usually up to our ankles in wet and snow in the cold months."

"Ah, we have our sewage problems, too," Dominic acknowledged with a shake of his head. "We are trying to do something about it, since the mosquitoes seem to breed in those places in the summer months, carrying all manner of suffering to us. Many of the citizens are building summer homes on the outskirts of the city, some turning them into large plantations for the crops of sugarcane and rice and indigo."

"I had heard you were having trouble with some insect eating all the indigo crop," Lucian remarked with interest. "But didn't some planter discover a way to press the sugarcane so it wouldn't turn to liquid on the export ships?"

Dominic nodded vigorously. "Yes, Etienne Boré brought up some experienced sugar makers from Cuba and successfully exported nearly twelve thousand dollars' worth of superior sugar only four years ago," he explained. "Many of the planters are tilling their fields for the cane now, and most of the indigo has been dumped. The insect was hardier than the crop, I'm afraid."

"And what of you, Dominic?" Lucian wondered. "Are you

going to become a respectable planter like the rest of them?"

"Alas, no!" Dominic responded. "At least not yet, my friend. Violette insists on remaining in the city year round, and since she is still a new bride, I must indulge her, you see. I would like to get into some land speculation at a later time, though. We have westerners from the American states coming in by the boatload, all wanting their own plot of ground to start their farms. Many of them failed, but there are some who are really adding to the economy. I'm not sure what the Spanish think of the Americans' industry, but I suppose anything that brings added commerce to the city pleases Brigadier General Manuel Gayoso de Lemos."

"General Gayoso?" Lucian repeated. "But I thought Baron de Carondelet was the governor of the province."

"Your reports are outdated, my friend. Carondelet, bless him, has been gone for the last eighteen months. Gayoso took his place, but he falls far short of our expectations. He is a rather mean-minded military man who seeks only profit. You will meet him at a government function next week. The Spanish officers' wives are hosting a fête and, of course, our honored guests from France must come." He winked at his friend conspiratorially.

Lucian raised an eyebrow warningly, nodding toward Aimee, who was still looking out the window. Dominic cast him a questioning look, but remained silent until the carriage reached his town house by way of Dauphine Street, turning west onto Toulouse Street and presenting them in front of a three-story house built flush with the banquette. The carriage passed through the porte cochere, or carriageway, a high, broad passageway that led toward the back of the house.

"It's lovely," Aimee said with awe in her voice, as Dominic helped her out of the carriage into the courtyard from whence a curved, white staircase rose to a second-floor porch that housed the living quarters. Tubs of green plants and bright-foliaged flowers brightened the gray flagstones and, indeed, the aforementioned fountain splashed fitfully in the center of it all. Looking up, Aimee could see the wide porch that ran the perimeter of the interior of the house so that every room had its own doorway leading out to it. The windows were wide and arched, and set in these arches were beautiful fan-shaped transoms.

Standing in front of one of these was a petite, shiny-black-haired young woman who looked no more than seventeen. Her wealth of hair was plaited and coiled and looked too heavy for the delicate, pale oval of her face with its round, black eyes that were just now observing her guests with marked shyness. Smiling hesitantly, she walked down the staircase, looking every inch a duchess, Aimee thought, with her regal carriage and proud bearing.

"Violette! Our guests have arrived, my love. Lucian, Aimee, may I present my wife, Violette," Dominic said proudly, hurrying to his young wife's side and taking her hand protectively. It was easy to see the love shining from his dark eyes, and Aimee felt almost embarrassed to be a witness to it.

"I am so glad to welcome you both to our home," Violette said in curiously accented French.

"My wife's mother was an American," Dominic explained, noting the dubious look on Aimee's face. "There are several languages spoken in the city, my friends, including French, Spanish, and English, plus the numerous dialects of the African and West Indian slaves who are transported here for labor on the plantations."

"My Spanish is rather rusty," Aimee said with a laugh, easing the slight tension in the air. "But my English is passingly good since my old nurse was from England."

"How wonderful!" Violette said, clapping her hands in delight. "I have so few friends who speak my mother's tongue," she went on in English. She smiled at Aimee, her eyes touching on the fashionable outfit she wore. "Come, let me show you upstairs to your room," she continued. "You must rest after your long voyage and then we will talk again at supper."

Aimee and Lucian followed their hosts up the stairs to the wide porch. They passed several doors before Violette opened one that showed them a wide, high-ceilinged room with massive oaken furniture in the traditional Spanish style. Delighted, Aimee hurried inside, watching as one of the servants deposited their luggage in the middle of the room.

"This is charming!" she pronounced, and Violette smiled widely, her whole face becoming animated.

"I am so glad you like it, Aimee. I have been hoping to please you."

"Thank you, Violette, you are more than kind," Aimee said, going over to kiss the young woman on impulse. Violette laughed and the two women knew they were going to be good friends.

The two husbands seemed to let out a collective sigh of relief before the St. Cyrs took their leave. Aimee faced her husband with a slight frown on her face. "But, where is *your* room?" she asked quickly.

"This is my room," he replied quietly, gazing at her with mocking blue eyes. "Certainly, you don't expect me to announce the true state of our marriage to our hosts, do you?"

"But, you can't sleep here—"

"Quite the contrary, my dear. I am sure it will suit me wonderfully." His eyes stared into her green ones with a challenging look. "Are you afraid you will not be able to keep your promises of chastity, my good wife?" he mocked her gently.

Blushing furiously, Aimee stamped her foot and turned on her heel.

26

·—·—·—·

At supper that evening, Aimee sat next to her husband, very much aware of the handsome picture he presented in his dark blue coat and champagne-colored waistcoat. His sable-dark hair shone under the lamps in the dining room, and the white cuffs of his shirt only emphasized the dark strength of his hands. She shivered at the memories of those hands touching her and wondered if she would ever be able to get through this masquerade without losing her heart to the rogue.

Sitting next to her, Lucian also had his thoughts focused on his spouse. He could appreciate the loveliness of her fair features, especially when presented against the strong contrast of the darkly beautiful Violette St. Cyr. Aimee's burnished tresses, artfully arranged by one of the servants into a fashionably curly chignon, seemed the perfect setting for her lightly tanned skin and the incredible green jewels that were her eyes. His hand lightly grazed hers as he reached for his fork and he was gratified at the pink stain on her cheeks. A thoughtful smile shaped his sensual mouth as he looked forward to the evening in their bedroom.

"It is easy to see that you two are very much in love, as are my wife and I," Dominic stated smilingly.

Both Lucian and Aimee started at the pronouncement and looked at each other guiltily, as though each had discovered some secret. Aimee lowered her eyes and concentrated on the food on her plate. She knew that Violette had gone to great lengths to prepare the exotic Creole dishes, but, unfortunately, she could taste nothing. Her thoughts were all on Lucian. They had reached the end of their sea voyage; now was the peaceful interim before they began the first of their findings for France. Knowing Lucian, he would deem this a perfect chance to try to woo her, she was sure. And did she really want to fight him? she wondered uneasily. After all, legally they were husband and wife; she would not be compromising her virtue by giving in to his masculine lust. That last word, formed in her own mind, made her blush, and she pushed the food around on her plate even more nervously, hoping against hope that Lucian was not a good mind reader.

Lucian's interest in his wife's reactions was momentarily diverted by the table conversation as Dominic filled him in on the administrative atmosphere of New Orleans.

"I must be generous to the Spaniards," Dominic was saying seriously. "They have provided good government for our city in these past decades, but the hearts of most of the citizens are still with France, and we would certainly welcome any attempt by that country to regain control of our territory."

"Are there many rumors to that effect floating about?" Lucian wondered.

Dominic shrugged. "There are always rumors, but Gayoso tries to squelch them, determined to rule militarily, which means rather iron-handed. Still, even he cannot turn us against the Spaniards, who really have been, on the whole, rather benevolent governors. When the news came that the revolution had gripped France and caused her King to be beheaded, there was a moment of silence throughout the city. And that, even with the Spanish influence, so you know how much we think of our true homeland, my friend."

"Certainly, then, there would be no resistance to a French takeover?" Lucian asked smoothly.

"I don't think so. Perhaps from the American sector, for they are determined to add us to the United States." Dominic laughed. "It would be a curious marriage, my friend."

Lucian shrugged. "And yet, it could have its advantages," he pointed out.

"True," Dominic agreed. "It is one thing to feel a love for one's homeland, and quite another to feel a political closeness to a country an ocean away. The United States is only just up the Mississippi River, and we thrive on the commerce they bring on their flatboats. The French ignored us even when we were under their rule, and the Spaniards are not much better. Of course, we have little to trade with their islands in the Caribbean. America has a lot more to offer in the respect of trade and economy."

The two men eyed each other carefully. "And you are a true patriot of your city, aren't you?" Lucian asked.

Dominic nodded vigorously. "I want what is best for her," he admitted. "I have seen her grow out of two devastating fires. I have seen the diversification of products and people. I know she would prove a valuable port for anyone with interests in the New World. Do you truly think the Directory has such an interest?" he wondered, more to the point.

Lucian shook his head. "Those men have little interest in anything but themselves," he conceded.

"What of the American President, Adams?" Dominic wondered. "Our newspaper, *Le Moniteur de la Louisiane,* has published several editorials on the worthiness and unworthiness of that man—it is hard to know what to believe."

"I rather like his Vice-President, Jefferson," Lucian returned honestly. "Of course, it helps that he is a fellow Virginian, like my mother—"

"And you?" Dominic questioned rather cunningly.

"I am only part American," Lucian reminded him, refusing to be baited.

Fortunately, the servants arrived to clear the table at that time and Violette announced that they would withdraw to the salon to listen to her young cousin play the pianoforte for them.

"Do you sing?" she asked Aimee politely as they entered the blue-and-gold-decorated salon that sported a beautiful white marble fireplace at one end and two long, French-paned windows that opened out onto the patio at the other.

"I'm afraid not," Aimee responded with a merry laugh. "My brother, Etienne, used to accuse me of screeching when I was a child, when I was sure I was the most clear-throated soprano."

"Your brother lives in Paris?"

"No. He lives in our ancestral home just outside Orléans."

"Ah, what a favorable omen! You have come from old Orléans to New Orleans," Violette observed with a smile.

Aimee smiled back at her while fervently hoping that it was meant to be a favorable sign. She seated herself in a straight-backed chair of blue brocade, settling her watered-silk skirts around her, aware of her husband seated directly behind her so that his eyes rested annoyingly on the bare surface of skin exposed by her upswept hairdo. She could feel those flame-bright eyes on the nape of her neck, causing a tiny shiver to run through her and the points of her breasts to harden unexpectedly.

Her attention, fortunately, was diverted by the arrival of a young girl of twelve or thirteen who looked something like her cousin. After introductions were made, the girl sat down at the highly polished pianoforte and began to play some beautiful Bach pieces that made Aimee close her eyes and think of Paris and the days of the Court. Although she had never seen the Court of Marie Antoinette and Louis XVI, she had heard much about it from their neighbors, who were received at Versailles, and the tinkling notes of the pianoforte seemed to bring back those memories rather unexpectedly.

Halfway through the program, Lucian leaned forward, his breath warm on her neck, and asked, "Are you enjoying yourself, my dear?"

Aimee nodded, opening her eyes and becoming, once more, aware of him behind her. The rest of the program was lost to her, as she could concentrate only on Lucian's gaze at her back and the knowledge that he probably was not listening to the concert either.

When it was over, everyone clapped politely and the young girl retired to her room, where her parents would pick her up in the morning. Violette took Aimee by the arm in sisterly fashion and guided her out the long windows to the patio beyond, the men following at a leisurely pace.

Outside, the splashing fountain and the cadence of the crickets seemed the perfect sounds to go with the star-spangled night sky and the slight breeze that caused a slight swishing sound in the palmettos and ferns that grew inside the courtyard. Aimee sat next to Violette on a small stone bench and felt utterly at peace.

"It is beautiful here," she murmured in appreciation to her hostess.

"Yes," Violette agreed. "I am so happy to have the opportunity to live in this house. When Dominic asked me to be his wife, I thought I would faint from the joy of it." She looked over at her guest. "But I suppose you know the feeling."

Aimee started, feeling somehow guilty that she did not know the feeling. She could recall very little of Lucian's proposal of marriage, other than the fact that it had been the expedient thing for him to do under the circumstances; he had needed a wife for his mission of intrigue, and, she supposed, having already taken her virginity, he had thought her perfect for the role. And yet, perhaps she was judging him too harshly, she told herself.

Surreptitiously, she glanced over to where he stood, smoking a cigar with Dominic. His tall silhouette, highlighted by the lanterns hung around the patio, caused a familiar thrill in the region of her heart and she wondered what lay behind those mocking blue eyes that could sometimes be so wonderfully sensitive and understanding. He had told her once that he cared for her—of course, that had been in the aftermath of his seduction of her. Had he really meant it? She wondered. Sometimes, she argued, he could be so hateful, so boorish toward her that she wanted to strike him, but other times he could be so tender and so attentive that she found herself actually enjoying his presence.

She shook her head at the jumble of emotions, telling herself it was due to her inexperience in matters of the heart. After all, what did she have upon which to base her judgments? There had been the friendship of Jean-Baptiste, the innocent affair with Henri de Brueys—she spared a drop of sympathy for the young man who had not seemed at all happy when she last saw him in Paris—but that was all. On the other hand, she was quite sure that Lucian was vastly experienced with women. Was that good or bad? Had he been able to learn more from his experience than she had learned from her relative inexperience? Or did men ever learn anything from their amorous adventures?

Finding herself in something of a quandary, she decided to postpone the argument for now. It was really too beautiful an evening, and she truly wanted to learn more about her host and hostess. She turned back to Violette, who had been watching her husband with a look of adoration.

"Tell me about your life in New Orleans," she said simply.

Violette seemed pleased at her interest. "My family has been here a very long time," she responded eagerly. "My father's family dates back to some of the first Colonials who came here with Bienville when he formally founded the city. My mother's family had relatives here, too, but her grandfather left New Orleans for the wilderness of what is now the state of Kentucky, upriver from our city. He had several adventures with the Indians, my mother has told me, and then moved east to Pennsylvania, where he was involved in the French and Indian Wars. My mother can remember him leaving her and the rest of the family to go off to war at periodic intervals. I suppose he was a soldier of fortune at heart. Anyway, she was born in the United States, making her an American, but she and her mother returned to New Orleans after my grandfather was killed in an Indian skirmish. My grandmother was a most elegant widow and the people of the city came to respect her. My mother grew up quite protected and, although the family didn't have much money, many of the most eligible bachelors in New Orleans courted her. My father, though, was much more dashing than any of them, she told me, and her heart could not resist him."

"So they were married and lived happily ever after," Aimee said with a sigh.

Violette laughed at her romanticism. "Yes, that is true, Aimee. And they are still living happily. They have only recently moved out of the Vieux Carré into the outskirts of the city. Their plantation home was finished only last year; it is quite beautiful. You will have a chance to see it in the very near future, for my father's birthday is in April and we always have a birthday party for him—all my relatives and Dominic's will be there. It is quite a festive occasion really!"

"My birthday is in April," Aimee realized with a laugh. "Goodness, I'll be twenty!"

"Then we shall include your birthday in the celebration," Violette promised good-naturedly. "My father will be honored."

Aimee thanked her rather shyly. "I know I will be happy during my stay here," she added.

"I am glad. It will be nice to have a friend to go shopping with. We have several fine stores on Saint Peter and Saint Ann streets, as well as the French market on the lower side of the Place d'Armes. For a long time, the market vendors—Indians, Negroes, trappers, and hunters—would display their wares in the open air, but the city has had a shed built, which is only to be the first of many such structures. It is quite a bustling place, Aimee, and I think it might remind you of the activity of your Parisian streets."

"Only if they have pickpockets and juggling acts lining the streets!" Aimee laughed jokingly and Violette joined in her laughter.

"What has tickled you both?" Dominic asked, walking over to where they sat with Lucian behind him.

"Aimee has quite a good sense of humor," Violette related.

"Good, we Creoles have sometimes been blamed for having too little," Dominic said. "In fact, I'm afraid we've something of a reputation for hotheadedness, Aimee."

"It's true," Violette concurred. "So many duels have been fought over alleged violations of honor that it no longer causes alarm when we hear of another. The authorities look the other way—it hardly matters to them if the Creoles kill each other off," she added with a touch of bitterness.

Dominic put his hand on her shoulder. "Perhaps we need more immigrants like our guests here to add humor to our flashes of temper," he suggested with a smile.

Violette nodded.

"Aimee, I do think we'd do well to retire," Lucian spoke suddenly, causing Aimee to stare at him in the star-filled night.

"Already?" she asked tentatively.

"Certainly, you must be tired," Dominic agreed. "I have been a thoughtless host in keeping you up so late. In the morning, you and Violette will make a few social calls, do some shopping, while Lucian and I talk business."

Aimee sighed, defeated. "All right, I suppose I am feeling a bit sleepy," she admitted. She stood up and felt Lucian glide beside her to take her hand and put it in the crook of his arm. "Good night, Violette, good night, Dominic," she said softly.

After bidding their own good-nights and walking them up the graceful outside staircase, the St. Cyrs parted for their own bedroom, leaving Aimee and Lucian standing outside their room. Lucian pulled her inside gently, closing the door but leaving the windows open slightly to allow the gentle breeze to keep the room cool. He watched as Aimee started to ring the bell that would bring a servant to help her undress.

"I can do that," he said deliberately.

"But—"

"Let me," he continued softly.

Reluctantly, Aimee pulled away from the bell rope, watching as Lucian came toward her, walking lightly on the balls of his feet, having already removed his boots. She presented her back to him and felt his nimble fingers on the fastenings of her gown, opening the back and displaying her skin above the fragile lace of the chemise beneath it. She closed her eyes, feeling his lips moving against her exposed back, imprinting tiny kisses on her spine and shoulder blades. With gentle movements, he pushed the gown from her shoulders so that it fell in a shimmering puddle around her feet. Next, he pushed down the straps of her chemise, kissing her shoulders and the backs of her upper arms, pulling the straps down to her wrists and exposing her breasts.

Frantically, Aimee pulled them back up and turned around to face him, her green eyes wide, the pupils dilated. "Lucian, I'm not sure—"

"Don't fret," he advised her softly, pulling her forward to melt against his chest. His lips bore down on the top of her head as he kissed her hair and bent sideways to nibble at her ears.

Shivers began to run riot through Aimee's body as she closed her eyes and let the sensation of feeling shoot through her. His breath was warm, his lips soft, his teeth gentle as they nipped at her earlobes and moved to the side of her neck, where the vein pulsed wildly beneath his mouth. Gently, he nipped it and then moved lower to the hollow of her throat. Aimee arched her neck, bending her head backward, this time making no resistance as he pulled the chemise straps down and over her wrists, taking the garment with them.

She was naked except for her stockings and garters and the Grecian sandals. Slowly, Lucian knelt in front of her and leaned down to remove the sandals. His hands caressed her stockinged legs, removing the garters and rolling the silk down very sensuously so that goose bumps pricked Aimee's skin from thigh to ankle.

She stood trembling as he continued to kneel in front of her, his hands sliding back up her calves, up to her knees and the backs of her thighs. Gently, he pushed her forward from the thighs so that his face came in contact with the juncture of her legs. For a moment, Aimee was at a loss as to what he was doing until the warm, soft moistness of his tongue flicked out to touch the burnished curls between her legs. His hands moved around from the back of her thighs to the front, curving around the firm flesh so that his thumbs could part the swollen lips of her femininity, allowing his tongue better entrance.

With a cry of shock, Aimee stepped backward, moving away from him. He looked up at her and saw the anxiety on her face and shook his head. "Aimee, let me love you tonight," he said pleadingly. "I promise I won't hurt you."

"Lucian, I—I don't know—"

"Hush," he whispered, drawing her back soothingly toward him. His hands regained their position on her legs and once more she felt his mouth move upward from her knees to her inner thigh and higher. But this time she seemed powerless to stop him as his head pressed forward and the heat of his tongue seemed to transfer itself to that very core of her womanliness.

Throwing her head back in sudden abandon, Aimee pressed her pelvis forward, opening herself to her husband's knowing mouth and tongue, shivering so that she was sure she would collapse at any moment. Waves of pleasure seemed to radiate from that spot where his face was pressed until she became aware of a curious kind of building, an ascending pleasure that seemed to build and build until she uttered a soft cry and would have fallen if he hadn't clasped her firmly about her buttocks, continuing to torture her exquisitely even as she was in the throes of the climactic moment.

Finally, he released her and she sank against him, allowing him to pull her down so that she was kneeling in front of him. His mouth reached for hers and she opened her lips automatically, seeking the tingling sensation from the delicate fencing of their tongues. His hands were on her back. Then they moved around to clasp her breasts, caressing them gently at first, then more urgently, pulling softly on the nipples and rolling them between thumb and forefinger as they rose into tiny, hard points.

Very gently, he lowered her to the ground, allowing her to unfold her legs so that she was lying prone on the softness of the Turkish carpet, her body pressed lightly against warm flesh—his flesh. She hadn't even realized when he'd finished undressing himself, she thought with some surprise. His body was hard, unyielding, with the carpet pressed against her back. For a moment, she lay barely breathing, her eyes closed.

Lips, warm and seeking, pressed against her temple, then moved slowly down her face. His arm at her waist kept her pressed against him while he leisurely explored her face and neck with his mouth. Suddenly, it slid upward from her neck, fastening upon her lips again, shaping them, molding them so exquisitely that they parted without her conscious volition. The kiss seemed to last forever and Aimee felt as though she couldn't endure the breathless, incredible moment while he seemed to suck the very life from her.

Lucian's hand moved lazily to graze her breast, drifting over the upper swell of her bosom and brushing the tender spot beneath her arm and to the side of her rib cage. Fingers traced the outline of her breast from her side to the stiffened nipple.

Aimee gasped as that desire began to rage through her body, making her move her hips restlessly against her husband's. With a half smile, Lucian kissed her closed eyes, then moved down to the breasts, teasing and sucking gently so that Aimee was obliged to bring her hands up to press into the softness of his hair, pressing his face into her flesh, arching her back to meet his mouth. Her fingertips brushed the sensitive nape of his neck where the hair curled slightly, then brushed along the sides of his face, stretching along his jawline.

"Lucian," she whispered, opening her eyes to the darkness of the room, lit only by the starlight from outside the windows.

He needed no urging, concentrating his attention on her breasts, sensing her extraordinary sensitivity to his teeth as they pulled at the nipples and then bit gently at the flesh surrounding them. Aimee couldn't help the movement of her hips once again, looking down at the dark head on her breast and wondering when he would end this exquisite torture.

With a muffled laugh, Lucian swept his hands down her sides and brushed the springy curls between her thighs before opening the damp entrance to his knowing fingers. A small sigh escaped Aimee as she felt his fingers within her, busily working their own special magic as she tossed her head from side to side.

Lucian sensing how finely tuned her body was, how taut she was drawn, pulled his own body upward, bringing his hands to hold her shoulders and his mouth to capture hers as he poised himself above her parted thighs, prolonging the joy for both of them for one sublime moment, before thrusting deep and true, taking her breath away. Aimee pressed her hands to her husband's neck, clasping him close as she felt the sure, deep strokes inside of her, causing such a sensation of feeling in her lower body that she cried out with the wonder of it.

Lucian heard her cry of ecstasy and matched it with his own as he thrust once more and spilled his liquid warmth inside of her, feeling the pleasurable reverberations and thrusting gently still, meaning to give her as much pleasure as he had gotten himself. Slowly, their breathing returned to normal and Aimee felt his lips on hers again, kissing her deeply even as he remained within her.

Softly, Aimee let her hands roam over his well-muscled back, feeling the cords bunch under the touch of her fingers. She roamed lower to the taut buttocks and then back to his neck to press his mouth to hers. She opened her eyes and met his blue ones, cloudy with pleasure attained. He smiled at her and she smiled back, feeling unreasonably happy at that moment.

"I think we should forget about keeping this a marriage in name only," he joked.

Aimee sighed and nodded. "How could we fail to wind up in each other's arms with two such lovebirds as hosts?" she queried with a comical lifting of the corners of her mouth.

"Everything was against us," he agreed humorously. "The perfect night, the soft breeze, the romantic noises outside. I'm afraid there was simply no defense against it, my lovely wife."

"I agree," she answered, kissing him on the tip of his chin.

"And now," he began, moving a little, as though testing the waters, "what would you think, my dear, if I proposed another go? Would it shock your sensibilities too much?"

Aimee was glad of the darkness that covered her flushed cheeks. "I'm afraid nothing you do would shock them," she admitted, remembering her earlier initiation when he had knelt in front of her.

"Hmm—that gives me hope," he remarked, beginning to move more rhythmically as he watched her eyes widen and the pupils dilate with lazy desire. He brought his mouth down to cover hers, delighted at the heartfelt response he received—so much so that he redoubled his efforts, determined to give her even more pleasure the second time than the first.

27

The next morning, Aimee awoke in the wide bed, forgetting for a brief moment where she was when she realized she was no longer in the narrow bunk on board the *Hélène*. So much had changed since then, she thought, glancing with a new tenderness at her husband, who was still asleep beside her. Last night had been so very wonderful that she looked upon this morning with a bit of trepidation, as though wondering how they could improve on the oneness they had shared the night before. Her cheeks grew rosy as she thought of the sensual orgy of bliss they had enjoyed— never before had she thought that married life could be so satisfying. As she felt Lucian stirring lazily beside her, she felt a hurried panic, as though wanting to pretend to be asleep again before he could awaken and find her watching him.

It was already too late anyway, for those blue eyes were gazing up into her face, crinkling into a lazy smile as he stretched his arms out over his head. "Good morning, Aimee," he bade her pleasantly, his eyes beginning to dance with mischief as they roamed over her naked shoulders and touched on the sheet she was holding to her bosom with one hand.

"Good morning," she said with a little shyness.

He waited for her to continue speaking, and when she did not, his smile widened and his eyes moved suggestively down the rest of the covered form. "Did you sleep well last night?"

He was rewarded by a deepening blush on her face.

Finally, when she was silent too long, he pulled her close to him with his arms and kissed her softly on the mouth. "Welcome to New Orleans," he whispered softly. "Are you glad you came with me now?"

Aimee refused to concede quite yet, feeling somewhat stubborn as she watched the smug look on his face. "I shall have to become more acquainted with the city and our work before I can make a complete judgment," she replied primly.

"To hell with our work!" He laughed, pulling the cover off her body and pressing her nakedness to his. "Give me your sweet self in bed every night like you were last night and I won't ever write another report to that sly Talleyrand." He reached down with his lips and teeth to nip and bite at her neck and jawline, causing her to protest mildly as she tried to wriggle out of his grasp.

"Lucian, you are being outrageous!" she protested, but couldn't help the laughter that bubbled up inside of her as he continued to tease her gently.

For a few moments they tussled on the bed, each one trying to gain the advantage over the other. Breathless, Aimee tried to slip out from underneath him, only to find that she was locked into place by the strength of his legs and arms. Laughing uncertainly, she pushed against his chest, seeking to dislodge him, but that, too, failed, leaving her panting a little and staring up into those vivid blue eyes that were smiling down at her victoriously.

"So—now that I have you where I want you," he began, bending his head to kiss her ear and follow the line of her jaw, "what shall I do with you, I wonder?"

"Lucian, we must get up!" Aimee urged, wriggling beneath him. "Our hosts are probably already at breakfast and they will be wondering where we are!"

"Nonsense. If I know Dominic, he is doing exactly what I am doing—making love to his new wife! Besides, does it matter if they are wondering what we are doing, my dear?" he queried her. "They would never be discourteous enough to *ask* what kept us from breakfast—do you think?"

Aimee flushed deeply. "Oh, you are terrible!" she cried, moving her hips to try to squirm from beneath him.

"Darling, if you continue to do that, I'm afraid this session of lust will be quite short," he reprimanded her, kissing her on the mouth and moving his hands to that silken spot between her thighs.

"Lucian!"

"Hmm?" His lips moved down to her breasts and began torturing them most delicately, until Aimee surrendered to the demand clamoring inside of her to be released. Her hands went up and around his neck to caress the tender nape and swirl through the thick sable of his hair. With a sigh of surrender, she opened herself unconditionally to his passion, forgetting for the moment about her hosts, their secret mission for France—and everything else . . .

More than an hour later, feeling languorous and satiated, Aimee lay in bed listening to her husband giving a servant orders for hot water to be brought up for a copper tub so that both he and

Aimee could wash themselves before dressing. She watched him move from the door, splendid in his nakedness as he stripped himself of the breeches he had hastily donned. From beneath the modest veil of her lashes she could look at the entire length of him—from the handsome, well-chiseled features of his face down his body to the muscular calves and the well-shaped feet. He was standing lightly on those same feet, watching her in bed, wondering, and rightly so, if she was feigning sleep.

Making a quick decision, he came forward lightly. Then, with a quick motion, he drew off the protective cover of the bed-clothes, displaying her own nudity and causing her to sit up, making a quick stab at the covers before she faced him angrily.

"I didn't think you were asleep," he explained with a mocking note.

"What if I wasn't?" she challenged him. "Does that mean that you can pull the covers off of me any time you desire? What if a servant came in?"

"They would knock first," he reminded her, amused at her guilty sputtering. "What's the matter, little wife? Didn't you want me to think you were looking at me? Is that something a modest and proper wife wouldn't do?"

She sputtered again, trying to find a retaliatory comment for him, but failing dismally.

He laughed and launched himself on the bed next to her. "Aimee, I don't want a 'modest and proper wife'! I want a woman I can trust, someone I can have fun with and who never tries to deceive me with these petty games that women seem to love playing on their spouses."

"Petty games!" she snorted. "I would say that men are equally good at playing those, too!"

"And how would you know?" he teased her. "You are such an innocent, my dear!"

She was speechless, irritated more than a little by the smugness of his attitude. Thankfully, before she could burst out with some angry little remark that she would have later regretted, there was a knock at the door, signaling the return of the servant with the required water. Quickly, Aimee grabbed the covers over herself and Lucian clutched at a piece of them, enough to cover the most strategic area of his nudity, before bidding the servant to enter. Respectfully, the man set the huge basin of steaming water inside the door, explaining that cool water was collected in the large jar outside the French door of their room on the balcony.

Lucian thanked him and, after he'd left, he padded over to the balcony in order to bring in the jar of water.

"Lucian, you—you're undressed!" Aimee objected, seeing that he was about to open the door that led out into the interior patio.

"Yes?"

"Well, what if—what if someone sees you?" she wondered, experiencing a twinge of something—jealousy?—at the thought of another female seeing what she had every right to!

"Then they will know how very lucky you are!" He laughed, winking at her. She flounced back on the bed at his arrogance, telling herself she didn't care if the whole city saw him!

A few minutes later, having mixed the water in the large copper tub, Lucian glanced over at Aimee, who was still fussing in bed, and bowed to her, indicating the copper tub. "After you, my dear?" he offered gallantly.

Aimee would have liked to retort with something stinging, but realized that the idea of a warm bath sounded quite heavenly, so she prudently closed her mouth and stepped over to the tub, still dragging half the bedcovers with her.

"Aimee, are you going to wash those, too?" Lucian wondered, pointing at the covers. "I'm afraid there's not enough room for you and me and those also."

"You and me?" she repeated, blinking. "Why, you can't possibly think I'm going to bathe with you in the tub at the same time!"

"That's exactly what I think. Now, be a good girl, drop the covers and step into the tub before I lose all patience with you," he said good-humoredly. "Not to stretch a point, but by now the St. Cyrs are probably wondering why we haven't shown ourselves this morning—and if we don't get dressed and downstairs soon, Dominic will be up here to see if there is anything wrong."

"But I can't bathe with—with a man!" Aimee cried, not ready to give up that part of her privacy.

"Not just any man, but your *husband,*" Lucian reminded her, pulling the covers from her fingers to expose her nakedness. "Lord," he groaned, "you do tempt me, even though by all rights I should be unable to perform after all that you've already put me through!" He reached over and grazed a rosy nipple with his hand.

"All right, I'll bathe with you, but you must promise not to—do that!" Aimee said.

He grinned with a positively lecherous air. "I promise."

She glanced at him distrustfully, then stepped into the tub, moving to one end to make room for him. The water rose up over the sides and splashed on the floor so that Aimee was glad for the tile that surrounded it on all sides, protecting the rug from getting wet. With Lucian facing her at the opposite end, she leaned back against the lip of the tub and felt the warm water swirl around her shoulders and breasts. Her knees were showing above the water, as she had folded her legs to make room for Lucian, but he seemed to have other ideas as he stretched his out on either side of her and wriggled his toes against her hips. Lazily, Aimee reached for soap and lathered her arms and breasts, though Lucian protested that he would be more than happy to perform that service for her. She turned her nose up at him and continued soaping herself.

"The least I could do is soap your back," he told her when she'd finished most of the other parts of her body.

She conceded that it would be impossible for her to do it herself and reluctantly relinquished the soap cake to him. Smiling, Lucian watched her squirm around and present her back to him. Slowly, he soaped around her shoulder blades and down her spine to the small of her back, cunningly pulling her closer against him so that their legs were stretched out to the other end of the tub.

Aimee, aware of his tactics, felt a somewhat familiar probing at the cleft of her buttocks through the water and nearly jumped up. Lucian laughed at her response and leaned over to kiss her neck.

"Darling, I'm sorry, I can't help it, you know! Just try to ignore it—and maybe it will go away."

"I doubt it," she replied with an exaggerated stoicism that brought more laughter from her husband.

He reached around her to caress her full, uptilted breasts, his hands sliding over her smooth, wet skin and causing tiny goose bumps to stand up all over her body. Restlessly, Aimee moved in the water, but he held her fast, one hand sliding down her stomach to disappear in the water.

"Lucian, didn't you say something about being in a hurry?" she questioned, although her breath was coming faster as he manipulated a most sensitive part of her anatomy.

He nuzzled the back of her neck, licking her shoulder enticingly. "Did I say that?" he murmured.

Unable to help herself, Aimee leaned back against his chest, bringing her knees up in the water and letting them rest against the sides of the tub. She closed her eyes in a heat wave of sensual ecstasy, concentrating on his fingers and letting him have his way until a great bubble seemed to burst inside of her and she felt a series of sharp tingles reverberate throughout her body. Releasing a long sigh, she wasn't sure if she should say anything to Lucian or not, but he seemed to know how much pleasure he had given her, for he leaned down to bring her face around to his so that he could kiss her.

"You are a devil," she whispered beneath her breath when he took his mouth away.

"And you are my most willing victim!" He laughed. "And now, my dear, you must soap me!"

She took the soap from him and proceeded to apply it vigorously to his chest and neck, glancing at him coyly, before sliding her hands beneath the water to wash the lower half of him. Her fingers came up against something hard and resistant and she grasped it almost instinctively, watching her husband's eyes widen at the pleasure he received from her touch. Leaning back against the tub, it was now his turn to be totally captivated by her will, and, encouraged by his response, she took the tumescent organ in both hands and soaped it first with the soap cake and then with her hands, so that Lucian groaned with pleasure and leaned forward abruptly to push her backward against the other side, kneeling in front of her and pushing himself into her. With a gasp, Aimee felt his hardness filling her up, the swift, sure strokes, and then the release. She lay back against the tub, feeling spent, wondering what other sexual pleasures she would be introduced to in the near future.

He looked into her languorous eyes and smiled encouragingly. "You are a most willing and apt pupil," he informed her. "But I suppose I have ruined the purpose of the bath, my sweet."

Aimee sighed, feeling him disengage himself from her, before standing up to grab a towel from a nearby chair. He toweled himself dry, then offered her one, wrapping it cozily around her while he helped to dry her.

"I am wondering," she remarked impishly, as they started to dress, "if we are ever going to get out of this room!"

He laughed and pulled her over to kiss her soundly, hugging her close before releasing her in order that they both could finish dressing. "I admit to acting like a man who's been famished for too long, Aimee. You must forgive me and put it up to the effects of the long sea voyage." He winked at her. "Besides, I'm afraid that once we get serious about our mission here, we won't have time for such love play."

"Surely *you* will find time," Aimee said, returning his wink after settling a fresh silk gown over her head. She turned her back to her husband so that he could do up the fastenings.

"I should hate to disappoint you, my sweet," he said, fastening her gown and bestowing another kiss upon her hair. "Shall I call a maid to help you with your chignon?" he inquired.

She shook her head. "I can do it very well, I suppose, after nearly eleven weeks of doing it on board ship. Just give me another minute and I'll be ready to accompany you downstairs."

When she was ready, he escorted her out to the interior hallway of the house, where they soon found the dining room, led on by all sorts of delicious smells that wafted throughout the house. Inside, Dominic and Violette were already seated. At Dominic's inquiring look, Lucian shook his head with a laugh and cocked an eyebrow toward his wife, making Aimee blush and causing Dominic to have a hard time in restraining his laughter.

After the usual polite conversation, Violette suggested that she and Aimee tour the city that day. There were several places in which they could lunch, and that way the men would be free to do whatever business they had to do, without feeling the need to return home until the dinner hour. Aimee thought it a marvelous suggestion and agreed enthusiastically to the city tour, anxious to see this transplanted French metropolis.

"Actually, it's a mixture of French, Spanish, American, English, German, and even a little Dutch," Violette told her as they stood in the hallway later, donning bonnets and shawls and pulling on their gloves.

After the two men had taken their leave, Aimee and Violette settled themselves in the open carriage, stretching up their sunshades against the bright sun that had appeared from behind morning clouds.

"We must make a stop at my dressmaker," Violette told Aimee, eyeing her gown approvingly. "When she finds out that I have a guest who has just come from Paris, she will not rest until she makes copies of your gowns. She really is a very good dressmaker and sends to Paris for sketches of gowns, but, alas, the mails are sometimes very slow and she can be five years behind the fashions."

It was on the tip of Aimee's tongue to question the need, in this backwater place, to be fashionable, until she realized how cruel that would sound to Violette, whose entire world was this city of New Orleans. "I would be happy to talk to your dress-maker," she said warmly, feeling guilty that she had even thought what she had. Violette was so friendly and sweet, so intent on making Aimee feel welcome that it would be a terrible thing for her to sound unappreciative.

They drove through the streets, Aimee enchanted by the fa-çades of the red-brick and white-stucco houses, all with their numerous balconies facing the street. In some cases, the balcony was only a small, railed platform under one window; in other cases it extended the entire front of the second story of a build-ing, the wrought iron twisted into delicate scrolls and lacy pat-terns.

"It is very beautiful," Aimee remarked, noticing one splendid-looking house whose upper-story balcony extended the length of the front and even curved around the corners to continue down the sides.

"The wrought iron is imported from Spain," Violette told her. "We want to teach the slaves who work in the city's smithies to copy it, as it would prove less expensive, and we would have a ready supply for the many homes that are being built."

They passed the corner of Toulouse and Levee streets, where Violette pointed out the newly built governor's residence. "That is where our current governor, Manuel Gayoso de Lemos, re-sides," she informed Aimee. "He is a competent man, I suppose, but I wish you had visited when the Baron de Carondelet gov-erned this territory. Ah, he was such a gentleman, Aimee. All of the people loved him and were sorry to see him go, for he truly worked for the welfare of the citizens."

"But isn't it hard for you as a Frenchwoman to be governed by the Spanish?" Aimee asked with interest.

Violette shrugged. "As long as they govern fairly, I suppose it makes little difference what nationality the governors are. Actu-ally, when we were under French rule, my mother told me things were much worse, for the King at that time couldn't afford to send us provisions and materials. We were ignored for many years and left to fend for ourselves. When Spain took over our territory, they brought order and peace to our land. Our economy has thrived over the years."

"Then the citizens of New Orleans are happy under Spanish rule?"

Violette smiled. "Prosperous. But there is no doubt that, deep down in the hearts of all the French descendants, there is the wish to become one of France's territories once more." She shrugged.

"If it happens, I can only hope that the French will govern as wisely as the Spanish have."

Aimee nodded thoughtfully, wondering suddenly at Talleyrand's motives behind wanting this territory back in French hands. Would he help it to grow and develop, or would he use it for some other purpose—perhaps to dump unwanted French goods or to use in some kind of military maneuver? Perhaps it would be better to leave these people alone.

Silently, she leaned back in her seat and watched the array of houses and shops pass before her eyes. Her interest was piqued at their arrival upon the great square of the city, called the Place d'Armes. It was thrilling to watch soldiers go through their orderly drills to the beat of drums and the blast of trumpets, no matter whose uniforms they wore. In evident appreciation of the ladies' interest, several of the officers doffed their plumed hats and bowed toward the carriage so that Aimee shaded her face with her umbrella in embarrassment. Violette laughed at her discomposure and assured her that the officers always reacted that way when a lady's carriage came upon the square.

They stopped to step inside the Saint Louis Cathedral for a moment, Violette remarking that she had not made her confession yet this week. It struck Aimee, who had also been brought up as a Roman Catholic, that she had not been to confession for many years. She knelt in a pew and looked at the sculpture of Christ on the crucifix, knowing that He somehow understood and forgave her. By the time Violette had finished, Aimee, too, was done, feeling an inner contentment at having made her peace with God. The killing of Faron, the stealing—all had been put to rest. Now she must look to the future—her future with Lucian. She realized suddenly that this marriage with him had come to mean much more than the fulfillment of a bargain between them. Despite the fact that the ceremony had been brief and unemotional, she would not have changed it for a wedding mass with all the pomp and ceremony, the beautiful gown and the hundreds of guests. Although she was not sure exactly what love was, she realized that she felt happy and safe with Lucian—that there was not another man with whom she would want to spend the rest of her life. It only mattered that he must feel the same way, she decided. While it was true that he enjoyed her physically, he must learn to trust her, to share everything with her and to care for her with a deepening commitment that would only grow with the years.

"What are you thinking of with such a serious look on your

face?" Violette wondered as they came out of the church back into the bright sunlight.

Aimee laughed self-consciously. "I was thinking of my husband," she replied honestly.

Violette nodded. "You love him very much," she commented matter-of-factly.

Aimee stared at the other woman for a moment. "Yes," she said finally, "I do love him, Violette."

"And he loves you," the Creole continued. "There is no doubt that he does. Dominic commented on it after we retired. Something in his eyes when he looks at you, the way he touches you —it is unmistakable, my friend."

Aimee's smile widened at the possibility as they returned to the carriage and continued their ride, heading for the shop of Violette's dressmaker.

Several hours later, after the trip to the dressmaker's, several visits to relatives and acquaintances of Violette's, and a hearty lunch at an elegant tearoom, the two young women arrived back at the St. Cyr abode, feeling the need for the siesta that was such an ingrained Spanish custom. After leaving her hostess, Aimee took off her gown and, clad only in her cotton chemise and stockings, she stretched out on the bed, trying not to blush at certain memories she shared on that piece of furniture with her husband.

Yes, she realized now that she loved Lucian. And Violette assured her that Lucian loved her. Aimee felt happy at the news, anxious to see her husband again and show him how much she trusted him to make her life complete. At the thought of his tall, handsome form striding through the door, her pulse leaped and she hugged the covers to her breast, thanking God for the intensity of the joy she felt. She envisioned the two of them, returning to France after this was all over, settling down on a parcel of land from Beautreillis, or perhaps an estate that had been left to him by his father. It would all be so very simple, she thought. Of course, they must finish what they had to do for Talleyrand, so that they would be free to lead their own lives without further interference from the wily politician. She conceded that it might be difficult at first to halt the wanderlust that was evident in her husband's psyche, but surely once they were settled down, starting a family, there would be the same change in Lucian that her brother, Etienne, had undergone. Etienne had been a wild one, having such a need for adventure, she recalled. But when the adventure began to pale and he realized that he was lonely without the security of home and hearth, he had grasped at the opportunity that Talleyrand had bestowed, returning to the castle and taking a wife with whom he was already starting a family. His passion for glory had subsided and he was content to be a good husband and provider. Lucian, too, would prove to be just as content, she thought.

While she was indulging herself in such pleasant schemes, Aimee was surprised to see the embodiment of her thoughts appear in the bedroom doorway. With a sign of welcome, she rose from the bed to run on bare feet to her husband. Her face was alight with joy and she reached up to put her arms around him.

But to her consternation, he did nothing more than bestow a token peck on her cheek. Looking at him closely, she could see the weariness in his eyes.

"What is it?" she wondered.

Wordlessly, he walked to a chair and sank down in it. "I've just come from a meeting with Governor Gayoso," he explained. "Not a very pleasant meeting, although he did his best to appear charming and affable. I'm afraid I might have irritated him somewhat with my bald accusation that he was growing rich off the illegal collection of duties on ships in New Orleans, and no wonder he would not welcome a takeover by the French government." He looked bleakly at Aimee. "I'm afraid I lost my temper."

"Well, and what is so terrible about that?"

"A spy, a man with a mission, cannot lose his temper, Aimee," he explained carefully. "That is sheer stupidity and the quickest way to find yourself out in the cold. I'm afraid I saw some correspondence between the governor and a General James Wilkinson, who happens to be an officer in the United States Army, which indicated strongly that this Wilkinson is a double agent for Spain. A rather jarring note."

"But why?" Aimee asked quickly. "What does it matter to you if a man is selling American secrets to Spain?"

Lucian leaned back in his chair, then gazed steadily at his wife, as though wondering if it would be easier to attempt an explanation or just to leave things go. With a shrug, he obviously came to the decision to leave things stand, for he made no attempt to explain the significance of his findings.

"Don't bother yourself about it," he commanded somewhat snappishly. "Just let's drop the subject. I've got a damnable headache already from the course of the day and too much imbibing of some Spanish brandy that Gayoso dispenses rather freely to his guests."

"But tell me, Lucian. I want to understand. I—"

"Aimee, please, can't you respect my wishes?" he demanded.

She felt as though he had slapped her. "I . . . only thought we had agreed to trust each other," she said slowly, looking down at the rug.

He laughed rather disdainfully, the effect of having too much to drink and of the disappointment he had experienced. "I've learned to trust no one, my dear."

"Lucian, how can you expect me to help you if you don't tell me—"

He stood up and faced her angrily. "Aimee, I don't expect you to help me," he informed her curtly. "Do you really think that I needed you for this mission? Good God, woman! Haven't you realized that I brought you along for one thing? It's much easier having a warm body there for the taking than exerting the energy and taking the trouble to go out and assuage the body's needs elsewhere. You were the bone that Talleyrand threw me just so that I would take this assignment!"

Lucian watched as his wife's face grew red and then paled suddenly while her mouth tightened. He realized that he was angry, that he had said things that he shouldn't have said, but he was not prepared for the coldness in her voice as she confronted him.

"I see," she said, her words very deliberate. "I am glad that you have informed me of my exact function in all this, Lucian. I must admit to more than a little confusion, especially when you were so . . . tender . . . last night and this morning. But I suppose you're just a little more considerate than most lovers. You must forgive my ignorance, but I promise I will learn fast."

"Aimee," he began, sighing deeply, realizing that he had hurt her with his barbs, "I'm sorry, I—didn't really mean all that. Of course you mean more than just some paid doxy. You—"

"Yes, I know, I am your wife, isn't that right?" Her brows drew downward and her green eyes hardened. "Well, you needn't worry about that dragging you down, Lucian, for remember how easily a divorce can be obtained once we return to France. Perhaps then you can involve yourself in the life of some other homeless girl who is just as gullible as I was! Believe me, once we set foot on French soil again, I will be just as anxious as you to sever our relationship!"

Lucian realized too late that he had made a terrible error.

"Aimee, I don't *want* to end our relationship," he told her evenly. "I—there are so many things that you can't be aware of! Things that have nothing to do with you, but everything to do with me and my work. I'm sorry if you can't understand, but these are things upon which a nation depends, and I—"

"I don't care, Lucian," she said coolly, retrieving her gown and sliding it over her head.

He took a step toward her, one hand raised in a gesture of truce. "Aimee, let's not quarrel. You know I care for you—and I know you care for me. After your response last night, you can't lie to me about it."

She eyed him from emerald eyes that were cold enough to freeze. "No, I can't lie about my response," she admitted, "but, then, you aren't the only one who can use people for their own purposes, Lucian."

He reared back as though she had physically attacked him. "You expect me to believe that you used me—for some kind of stud service," he asked sarcastically.

She shrugged and sat down at her dressing table, eyeing him in the mirror. "I don't care what you believe," she said calmly.

For a long moment he looked at her, undecided as to how to break down her icy barrier. Then with a terrible oath, he strode out of the room, slamming the door behind him—and leaving his wife to lay her head on the dressing table and cry her heart out.

28

The days that followed were miserable ones for Aimee. After the initial anger had subsided, she felt a deep hurt at what Lucian had said to her—especially after having just discovered her true feelings for him. How could Violette have said he loved her when all he wanted from her was the physical relief he could get from any whore on the street? And yet, he had tried to explain and she hadn't let him. She knew that he had been disappointed about something, and he'd said he'd been drinking too much. Yet, how could he have been so cruel? He had told her he didn't trust her—and the feeling still rankled even after nearly a week.

And now she was expected to be his bright and sparkling wife, pretending to be wonderfully happy as they attended the fête given by the Spanish officers' wives this evening. It had been hard enough pretending in front of Violette, whose dark eyes seemed to see through the charade. She had been polite enough to say nothing, but there was always a question there, and Aimee had found herself becoming more and more adverse to facing that question.

She glanced listlessly at herself in the mirror, noting the high color in her cheeks and the dread reflected in her eyes. She wondered if Lucian was dreading tonight as much as she was. Certainly, it had been painful when he had expressed his wish of sleeping on a divan at night instead of in their bed. She hadn't realized how much she would miss his tall, strong body draped protectively around hers in sleep. As a result, she had slept very little and now felt rather drained and wrung out, hardly in any condition to appear lighthearted this evening. And yet, she knew she couldn't back out of it, plead some excuse. Lucian had informed her curtly of how important it was to him for her to make an appearance. Aimee wished she could have told him that it was too bad and that he could take someone else to the fête, but she had almost been glad of a reason to be with him, even in such a charade as this.

When she heard his knock on the door, she stood up quickly, knowing her color had automatically deepened, but she couldn't help the vibrant pulse of her heart as she looked at the figure of her husband in his splendidly cut breeches and cutaway coat that was molded to his wide shoulders, making him so handsome it took her breath away.

As far as Lucian was concerned, Aimee was the loveliest woman he had ever seen, in the low-cut, high-waisted watered-silk gown of a golden-peach shade that made her skin seem like velvet. There was such an urge in him to run to her and take her in his arms, to tell her everything she wanted to know so that she would understand; yet, he hesitated, unused to having to woo a woman to his side. Why couldn't she be like other women? he'd grumbled to Dominic last night. Why did she have to be so damned independent? Why couldn't she understand that he hadn't really meant what he had so stupidly let burst forth in anger? It was damned hard for him to tell her he was sorry—and even then she had dismissed him coldly, as though she could have truly cared less if he'd gone out and shot himself. Well, he would let her stew a little while longer. Surely she would make an offer of peace—and he would grab at it, but not too quickly, he told himself.

"You look beautiful tonight," he told her formally. "It shall be my honor to escort you to the fête as my wife, Aimee."

She smiled just as formally. "Thank you, Lucian. Is it chilly outside? I wasn't sure which wrap to bring."

Their formality with each other maddened him, but he nodded swiftly. "Yes, there is a chill in the air—perhaps you'd best bring a heavy shawl."

She went and retrieved it from the armoire and presented herself to him. "I'm ready, then."

Hiding his frustration, Lucian extended his arm and she took it hesitantly, as though, he thought angrily, she thought he might try to snatch her into his arms. The thought occurred to him briefly, but he rejected it quickly, afraid that she might reject him so completely he would never be able to try a reconciliation at a later date.

They walked in silence downstairs and outside to where Violette and Dominic were awaiting them in the carriage. Everyone exchanged salutations and then settled into a rather glum ride to the governor's quarters on Toulouse Street.

Aimee was glad the ride was not long. She was relieved when Lucian helped her out and was escorting her inside the long, one-story residence that was quite large and built in the Spanish style with many grilled windows. Once inside, she hoped to make herself invisible, perhaps even get lost in one of the ante-chambers until the party was over. She really didn't think she could keep up this masquerade all evening.

Inside the lights were blinding, the rooms overly warm, and the people so ingratiating that Aimee felt her teeth on edge. One after another, the Spanish officers clicked their heels and bowed in front of her, their white teeth gleaming beneath their black moustaches and the black eyes eyeing her with such arrogance she wanted to slap them. Their wives were not much better, ex-claiming over her gown, demanding all the latest news from Paris, pulling her into their midst with a determination that left Aimee feeling as though she were being pulled by invisible strings, like some puppet. She looked for Violette and saw her conversing in another group, her dark eyes animated as she waved her fan back and forth to keep the heat from settling on her. Dominic and Lucian were involved in conversation with sev-eral of the officers as well as a thin, dark Spaniard of middle age with hawklike features. Aimee wondered if that was General Gayoso, the governor of the Louisiana Territory.

Trying to make as little commotion as possible, she edged her way over toward the men, hoping to pick a time when she could complain of a headache to Lucian so that he might take her home early or have someone else do it. In doing so, she realized she could hear their conversation and found herself listening with a great degree of interest as Lucian related to the Spaniards the details of the French revolution and the type of government that ruled under the Directory. He spoke lightly of Talleyrand and of the Foreign Minister's hopes for continued prosperity in the Louisiana Territory.

"Yes, I can imagine Talleyrand might hold a great deal of interest in our province since for nearly four years he has been pushing for negotiations between our country and his for a deal to return Louisiana to France," the middle-aged man was saying with a sinister smile.

"That is true enough, General Gayoso," Lucian returned aff-ably. "But your people have proved quite stubborn about giving up so rich and promising a land."

Gayoso shrugged. "It seems only natural that we should ex-tend out from the borders of Mexico. After all, this new United States would like nothing better than to march her settlers into our territory and claim it for themselves."

"Perhaps that would not be such a bad thing," Lucian sug-gested softly. "In that way, you would have people settling the land, clearing it, and making it productive—all for the glory of Spain."

"Ah, señor, but would it be for the glory of Spain? I think not. More for the future glory of the United States. Certainly, there have been many rumors in the past few years of wars and alliances to separate the Louisiana Territory from the rest of Spanish influence. Why, only two years ago when their President Adams took office, there was a group of Americans led by a senator from Tennessee who wanted to try to form an alliance of Creek and Cherokee Indians and English to take the two Floridas and Louisiana away from Spain."

"And what did you do about that?" Lucian wanted to know, his blue eyes vivid as he tried to conceal his great interest.

"I'll tell you what he did about it!" The new man who had just spoken had only just arrived on the scene, Aimee noted. He was a corpulent man with thinning hair, a large nose, and a wide mouth, dressed in a blue officer's uniform with gold braid. He seemed at home in this Spanish setting, although it was obvious that he was not a Spaniard himself. Upon seeing him, Gayoso's mouth turned down sourly and his dark eyes gazed at him with obvious distrust.

"So, General Wilkinson, you have honored our little fête with your unexpected presence," he said, making quick introductions between the general and Lucian, whose blue eyes narrowed at the intruder.

Aimee remembered this man's name being mentioned when she and Lucian had fought. Hadn't he said something about Wilkinson's being a spy, too? She smiled wryly—the two of them ought to get along beautifully together.

But, to the contrary, Lucian and Wilkinson were eyeing each other rather doubtfully, circling each other almost warily, as though each was aware of the other's occupation and wasn't about to say anything that might incriminate them.

Lucian finally said, "And you were saying, General Wilkinson, something about what happened when the senator from Tennessee tried to mount an alliance against Spain to take away Spanish territories?"

General Wilkinson nodded carefully. "Ah, yes, I was saying that there were those who brought their complaints to my attention and tried to . . . persuade me to make myself the Washington of the West, to form an army and take Kentucky out of the Union in order to establish a separate republic as a kind of buffer between the United States and Spanish territory."

"And, of course, you wisely declined," Lucian prompted with a scathing smile.

Wilkinson's smile was oily. "Of course, I am a loyal patriot to my country, Mr. Napier. But you must remember that this sort of thing is not unusual here. The interests of our New England merchants and tradesmen are not the same as those of the southern planters or of the many Americans living in the western territories and states beyond the Appalachians. It is quite difficult for the whole to come together and quite easy for each part to try to break away from the others."

"I'm sure it is," Lucian agreed.

"Yes. And the map of the United States is not at all reassuring. The Atlantic sea coast is practically indefensible against British sea power; the northern border is open to British attack from Canada. And, of course, our good friends the Spanish hold Florida and the Louisiana Territory west of the Mississippi River. All of this combines to make the Americans pretty nervous."

"But there is no need to be nervous because of us," Gayoso added smoothly. "We are peace-loving people who only desire to govern what is ours. The trouble comes when those westerners try to bully our officials along the river, or bring trouble to our fair city when they float their goods down on flatboats. Many times they have become drunk and disorderly, initiating fights between our people and theirs, causing fires and raping our women. They are a disgrace!"

"The Americans in the western lands are full of schemes," Wilkinson agreed, warming to his tale. "They plan variously to ally themselves with Spain, to become Spanish subjects, or to establish a separate nation of their own—or even to launch an attack down the Mississippi River to capture New Orleans."

"Or even, upon capturing New Orleans, to turn west to attempt the conquest of Mexico?" Lucian suggested softly, watching the American general's corpulent face pale considerably.

Gayoso, too, saw the change and glared at his "friend" suspiciously. "If the westerners are thinking that, they are doomed to an unpleasant shock, I'm afraid, for we will certainly give up none of our land to them," he stated firmly.

Lucian smiled. "But, I am sure, General, that General Wilkinson is quite aware of that fact. He has most likely reported it already to his government." He looked to the general for confirmation.

General Wilkinson sputtered for a moment, then nodded. Lucian turned away from him for a moment and his eyes fell on

Aimee, standing on the fringe of a small group of ladies whose conversation had obviously been disinteresting to her. He could see the knowledge in her eyes as they touched on the form of the fat American general. Swiftly, without thinking, he walked over to draw her forward in order to introduce her to the two men.

Aimee curtsied to the two generals, wishing that Lucian had left her out of this, but determined to show him that she could play the game as well as he, if required to.

Sweetly, she turned to General Gayoso, complimenting him on the liveliness of the party and the splendid beauty of his mansion. Then, equally as honey-voiced, she turned her attention to the round General Wilkinson, whose small eyes were roving quite freely—and irritatingly—over her figure beneath her close-cut gown.

"General Wilkinson, have you come alone to the party?" she questioned with a little pout.

His smile was positively lecherous. "I'm afraid so, madame. My . . . uh . . . wife is in rather poor health. She's not used to the climate here, having come from Philadelphia, a city to the north, you see."

"The daughter of one of the influential families of Philadelphia," Gayoso interjected, obviously having some intimate knowledge of the American's background.

For a moment, Wilkinson looked almost embarrassed, but quickly recovered himself and smiled with considerable charm at Aimee. For all his slippery swinishness, she could see that he might have some ability to manipulate people, hence the reason for his promotion to general. Certainly this man could not have distinguished himself in battle; he seemed more the type that might slink away while the blood of brave men drained onto the battlefield. She found herself disliking him instantly and turned back to General Gayoso.

"General, I must confess to being pleasantly surprised by your city. I had thoughts of a virtual swampland, a backwoods town without leadership or direction, but find instead a lovely town with friendly people, governed quite ably by a most charming administrator."

Gayoso preened visibly at her compliments. "Thank you, señora. Such a lovely lady cannot but brighten our festivities. You must let me introduce you to several of the influential citizens of our city." He bent his elbow and she placed her hand lightly on his sleeve, not even looking at her husband as she sailed away on the Spanish governor's arm.

Wilkinson followed her leavetaking keenly, eyeing the tall man beside him with a mixture of jealousy and suspicion. "So, Mr. Napier, you are lucky enough to have in your possession a true treasure."

"Thank you, General Wilkinson. Yes, I admit to having quite a bit of luck actually," he agreed, his eyes narrowing as they met the gaze of the general.

The latter smiled flatly. "Luck's a funny thing, you know. It can come and go so that first you think you're on top of the world, and the next thing you know—something goes terribly wrong and you can do nothing about it. I wouldn't rely on luck too much, Mr. Napier. I think we both could agree that luck has very little to do with the whole scheme of things."

"You're right, of course. Although some men seem luckier than most, General, their luck is bound to run out sometime. And then it's time for the vultures to move in."

General Wilkinson looked at the other man curiously. "I was just thinking, Mr. Napier, haven't I heard somewhere that you own land in Virginia?" he queried.

Lucian smiled and, bowing, he walked silently away from the general, leaving him more than a little confounded and wondering if he had said too much.

Later that evening as the dancing was beginning, Aimee sought out her husband, hoping to persuade him to take her home early; unfortunately, she could not find him anywhere. Where he had gone she wasn't certain, but she quickly realized that there would be no chance for her to escape once the dancing began, for, already, several young officers had requested a dance from her.

During the course of the evening, she danced with General Gayoso twice, doing her very best to remain charming and sparkling, determined that Lucian could find no fault with her on that score. Unfortunately, General Wilkinson demanded equal time and, for some reason, Aimee could hardly find it in her heart to be courteous to him. Something about him made her feel soiled as he took her about the waist.

"Well, Mrs. Napier, I must say I envy your husband for finding such a jewel as you. Where did you meet him?"

"In Paris," she replied quickly.

"I see. Had you known him for a long time before you were married?"

"Long enough, General," she replied rather pointedly.

"I suppose you must have had an exciting time of it during the revolution," he went on, switching the subject adroitly.

"It was hardly exciting, General, when each day one didn't know whether or not he would be arrested. False charges were flying about the entire country. I lost my father to the guillotine because of just such charges."

"I'm sorry to hear it, madame." His hand on her waist squeezed her unnecessarily, causing Aimee to miss a step in her surprise. Quickly, he was all fatherly concern. "What's the matter, my dear? Do you feel faint? Shall I walk you to the window for some fresh air?"

She shook her head no, but he insisted, pulling her over to a window and standing next to her in the alcove, so close that his breath fanned the curls in front of her ear.

"There, now, is that better?" he inquired solicitously.

She nodded. "Much better, and now you must excuse me, General, I—"

"Excuse me, madame, but I would like for you to stay here for a moment longer. You see, I'm certain that you must love your husband and that you want the best for him. I just want you to give him a little message for me—don't meddle in affairs that don't concern him. Do you understand me?"

"General Wilkinson, I'm afraid I don't—"

"There's no need to appear coy, madame. I'm sure we both understand each other perfectly. Your husband is putting his nose into affairs that don't concern him—and that can be very dangerous. Tell him to leave things to me. He is only muddying the waters, and that could be quite disastrous for his . . . er . . . employer. If he's trying to pin anything on me, he can forget it, because I cover my tracks too well for that. It will only end up badly for him, and there's no reason for anyone to cause grief to such a lovely young lady as yourself. *I* certainly would not want to be the one to put a tear in those beautiful eyes."

"General Wilkinson, if you wish to make these remarks known to my husband, why don't you tell him yourself?" Aimee suggested, although a small tide of fear washed over her as she realized that Lucian could make many enemies in his trade.

"Because, my dear, I truly feel that he will listen to *you* more than he would put credence in the words coming directly from me." He made a little bow to her and left abruptly, disappearing beyond the crowd of dancers on the floor so that Aimee was left staring after him, wondering what his message could possibly mean to Lucian.

She was not much enlightened by her husband when she saw

him again. Spotting him in the crowd, she hurried over to him, a little breathless as she asked him to dance with her. Lucian seemed pleased and took her onto the floor, his hand tight about her waist, drawing her close against him.

"Where have you been?" she asked him quickly.

"Talking with guests," he returned noncommittally, staring down into her green eyes and marveling at the perfection of her features.

"So have I," she returned, oblivious to the softness in his eyes as he looked at her. "In fact, that fat American general seemed quite intent on talking to me. I could barely escape him!"

Instantly, one of Lucian's dark brows drew downward in consternation. "What do you mean?" he demanded with a touch of arrogance at the thought that that swine should make his wife feel uncomfortable.

"I mean he wanted to make sure I gave you a message." She repeated it to him and watched as Lucian's vivid blue eyes narrowed and darkened. "Well?" she questioned him. "What does it all mean, Lucian? Are you really in danger from him? To tell you the truth, I'm not sure who seems more menacing—Gayoso, with his slick, sinister charm, or Wilkinson, with his overt warnings. I'm confused—and afraid for you."

"Don't be," he assured her while his mind was working quickly. Obviously, Wilkinson knew more about his reasons for being in New Orleans than he had thought. Perhaps now those reasons were no longer valid if Wilkinson had spoken the truth to Aimee. Of course, how far could one trust a man like Wilkinson? Perhaps the best thing to do would be to lie low—in effect, to do as Wilkinson had suggested. A watch-and-wait attitude might prove most beneficial at this point, although time was against such an attitude.

"Lucian?" Aimee's voice brought him back to the present. "You stepped on my foot," she accused him.

He smiled charmingly. "I'm sorry. Didn't you know what a terrible dancer I was when you married me?" he asked teasingly.

She grimaced comically and he laughed. His eyes roved over her face and he pulled her closer. "Aimee, can we call a truce?" he suggested.

Immediately, she stiffened, not wishing to be reminded of the things he had said to her. "What—what do you mean?" she asked, wanting to gain time in which to think more clearly.

"You know what I mean," he reprimanded her. "I don't like fighting with you. I don't like sleeping on the divan when I'd much rather be sleeping beside you. To be honest, I hate this tension and strain between us. I can't think, food seems unpalatable, and I just don't give a damn about what happens in this work I'm doing."

After a long moment of silence, she nodded, looking down at the floor where their feet automatically moved in time to the music. "I don't like fighting with you either," she admitted with a sigh. "I've felt awful this last week."

He let out a low sigh of relief. "I'm glad to hear you say it, my dear, for I've felt exactly the same. Let's be friends now."

"Now? And what about the future?" she asked in a small voice.

His eyes clouded for a moment. "I can't be certain about the future, Aimee," he said honestly. "Not because of my feelings for you, but because of this rather uncertain life I lead."

"We lead," she corrected him with a little smile.

He nodded. "Yes, I suppose we are in this together, but you have to understand, Aimee, that there are certain things I simply cannot tell you now. Delicate negotiations, secret deals—they're things I really don't want you involved in. I know you are an intelligent and resourceful woman, but—"

"You still don't trust me?" she inquired sadly.

He wouldn't answer, but his eyes pleaded with her to understand.

Aimee felt a rising tide of resentment, but pushed it down determinedly. All right, then, she thought, she would simply have to earn his trust—as he would have to earn hers. She would be his friend, she would be his wife, but the rest would have to wait until this immediate situation was taken care of.

"All right, we'll call a truce for the duration of this mission," she said carefully. "But once we return to France, Lucian, we must talk about our . . . commitment to our marriage."

He seemed pleased at her words and kissed her lightly on the cheek. "Darling, I'm so happy to hear you say that. There's no sense in punishing ourselves just because of some silly misunderstanding."

"Yes," she agreed, and realized that the music had stopped. Slowly, she disengaged herself from his arms, feeling a twinge of regret that their conversation had somewhat spoiled her enjoyment of dancing with him. Immediately, a young officer was standing in front of her expectantly, and Lucian, instead of rescuing her, bowed correctly and walked away to speak once more with Governor Gayoso.

The rest of the evening passed in a whirl for Aimee. She would have liked to leave early, but Lucian was too busy trying to pick the brains of all the Spaniards present, and Dominic and Violette were having much too good a time to think of leaving early. It was much later that Aimee saw General Wilkinson moving toward her, and, though she tried to outmaneuver him, he cornered her and asked her for the next dance. More than a little afraid to refuse this mysterious and seemingly dangerous man, she accepted unwillingly, feeling annoyed as he pressed his stomach paunch against her during the waltz.

"Did you give your husband the message I told you?" he inquired pleasantly, letting his small eyes peep into her neckline from his vantage point close against her.

She nodded stiffly.

"Good. I knew I could rely on your natural wish to protect your husband from any unpleasantness." They danced silently for a moment and then he continued: "Do *you* know why your husband is here in New Orleans, my dear?"

"I would deem it no business of yours, General Wilkinson," she said stiffly, "if I did."

He smiled. "Very loyal of you, Mrs. Napier, but let us say that you do know his reasons for being in New Orleans at this particular time. Don't you think it would be to his advantage to leave here and return to the capital?"

"Why would we wish to return to Paris now?" she inquired carefully.

He looked at her in surprise. "I'm not speaking of Paris," he replied, "but of Philadelphia, the present capital of the United States. However, my reports have confirmed that Washington City is to be the new capital and that the administration should be moving in sometime next year."

"Why should we go to this Philadelphia?" Aimee wondered. "My husband has no business there, I can assure you. Perhaps, General, you have gotten some faulty information yourself."

He smiled thinly. "I don't think so, Mrs. Napier, although I have been put in a position to receive incorrect information several times. No, I do think that Philadelphia would be the place he'd like to go. After all, it's the Americans who want this territory very badly. The French wouldn't know what to do with it if it was presented to them with a blue ribbon."

"You are speaking of my countrymen, General," Aimee reminded him coolly. "I can assure you, we would know precisely what to do with it."

"Hmm. And what is that, if you don't mind my asking, madame?"

Aimee opened her mouth to tell him of the grandiose schemes of Talleyrand himself, but suddenly she saw the shifty expression about Wilkinson's eyes. She hesitated, wondering if the general was trying to glean some secret information from her. Certainly, she didn't feel she was privy to very much of that sort, but the general could, perhaps, put whatever she told him to some unorthodox use, while at the same time discredit Lucian and gum up his work here in New Orleans. Resolutely, she closed her mouth and stared at him challengingly.

"General, if you have asked me to dance merely to interrogate me, I shall have to complain to General Gayoso. I certainly don't care for this kind of treatment."

Immediately, Wilkinson was all oily smiles and obsequiousness. "Of course, madame, I understand. I was only expressing a real interest in the politics of France these days. Reports are so muddled at times that one cannot make head or tail of things in your country."

When the music ended the dance, Aimee was more than a little relieved. She didn't like General Wilkinson at all. She hurried to where Violette was conversing with several young women and was glad when Violette pulled her into the circle. For the next hour, she talked of fashions and Frenchmen, trying hard not to smile when the Spanish señoras wondered if it was true that all Frenchmen were very amorous and more than generous as lovers. Aimee explained that her experience was not vast enough to make a realistic comment on these things, but that her husband had proven himself more than adequate.

Violette laughed at the tactful answer, squeezing Aimee's arm and telling her what a diplomat she was. "I saw you and Lucian dancing earlier," she whispered when they had a spare moment. "You seemed much happier than I've seen you in days."

Aimee smiled. "We had . . . a little misunderstanding," she explained briefly. "I think we've patched things up."

"Good! It is such a shame when two such extraordinary people cannot come to terms with each other, especially when it is obvious that they are very good for each other."

"I thank you for your concern, Violette," Aimee said softly, sincerely. "You have proven yourself a very good friend, and I am grateful. I have realized since I've come to your city that in the past I have had very few women friends. I don't know why, really, unless it was just that my life was in such a shambles from the beginning of the revolution. At any rate, I want to thank you for being my friend."

"You are more than welcome, Aimee," Violette said warmly. "We shall have a wonderful time while you are with us, right?"

Aimee nodded, hoping her words would prove to be true.

29

Spring burst into full bloom in New Orleans, accompanied by the usual drenching rains and the riot of color from wisteria, crepe myrtle, and all the other flowers that Aimee delighted in gathering into bunches to display in the St. Cyr home. The days had gone by smoothly. She and Lucian shared any information they received, although she realized she did more sharing than he did. Of course, most of her information she deemed fairly trivial: a slight comment by a French Creole's wife that she wished France would hurry and take over the governing of the territory; a hint that several of the higher-class families had written letters to the government of France, expressing their most sincere hopes that the Directory would continue negotiations with Spain on their behalf. Not all the people, of course, were in favor of a French takeover. The Spaniards were content with their government, and the few Americans Aimee had met seemed intent on persuading the United States to take a more active role in trying to buy the land from Spain.

There had been several incidents with American rivermen, many having to be locked up in the calaboose after all-night drunkenness and destruction of wharf property. Truly, Aimee thought, they seemed a loose-moraled and sodden lot, a poor representation of their country. When General Gayoso threatened to close the river to their transportation because of their rowdiness, he received several threatening letters in return, as well as voiced opinion by many upstanding citizens of New Orleans that their economy would be ruined if the goods from the Americans were not allowed into the port. Gayoso had been forced to back down from his threat, although he imposed stricter fines and punishment on the rivermen who were caught disobeying the laws.

If the days had gone smoothly, Aimee thought, the nights had gone even better. Lucian had been very attentive and tender and their lovemaking had taken on an intensity that left her breathless and blushing. She had found that she enjoyed the tenderness, the mutual affectionate holding and touching . . . and what came after. She sometimes wondered if she was turning into a loose woman, but a few discreet conversations with Violette assured her that she was only behaving in a healthy fashion.

The two women had grown closer in friendship and Aimee felt toward her like a sister. They enjoyed each other's companionship and very seldom quarreled. If they did quarrel, they were always certain to patch up the argument within a few hours. Aimee was quite content living in New Orleans, and little by little her longing for France and what little homesickness she had first experienced were leaving her. Then, too, it was comforting to receive letters from Etienne, usually once a month, informing her of progress on the castle, the state of his wife's pregnancy, and the crop production on the de Chartres lands. Aimee was happy for him and very grateful that he had settled down and convinced himself that the glory of the de Chartres name and estate were more important than the glory of France.

Toward the end of April, Violette told Aimee that they would be going out to spend several days at the plantation home of her parents, Andre and Catherine Aubremont, in order to celebrate her father's birthday and to escape some of the humidity that clung to New Orleans after all the rains they had been receiving. Already the mosquitoes were out and Aimee had been glad of the netting that surrounded Lucian's and her bed.

Aimee was excited at the prospect of meeting Violette's parents and also of seeing more of the country surrounding New Orleans. She knew that farther south, toward the Gulf coast, there was very little but swamplands and bayous, but closer to the city and north of it there was excellent soil that nurtured the crops that were planted and promised to make all the planters very rich men. Violette had told her that after several seasons of planting indigo and being all but wiped out from the insect that had destroyed it, her father had planted sugarcane for the last three years and had already begun making huge profits. They had been able to add on to the original plantation house so that it was looking quite respectable now. Aimee could hear the obvious pride in Violette's voice, but when she teased her about keeping Dominic in New Orleans, Violette simply laughed and told her that Dominic was no farmer at heart. He preferred to live off his family's money and dabble in land speculation, perhaps even run for public office in the near future.

As the day arrived for the trip to Aubremont House, Aimee packed her bags carefully, packing also for Lucian, pressing his things next to hers with a slight shiver of joy, feeling the fact of their intimacy expressed so physically by such a slight thing as their clothing in the same bag. He would be meeting them at the plantation later that afternoon, as he and Dominic were going to be busy making the rounds of the taverns and public houses, gleaning whatever information they thought might be useful.

Once in the carriage with Violette, Aimee leaned eagerly out the window, watching as they drove out of the Vieux Carré and started toward the less settled part of the city. The houses were less grand and beautiful here, but still charming, she thought, feeling generous. The April day was cloudless for a change and the bright sunshine beat down on the green grass and the riotous tangle of flowers that seemed to grow everywhere. Once they had left the city proper and were well on their way along a country mud road, she could see the huge cedar trees that grew close to the river, the gray Spanish moss hanging quaintly from their branches. Cypress trees and willows also grew along the riverbanks, and Violette pointed out the wildflower bushes of azaleas and honeysuckle that lent their sweet scent to the fresh air.

Less than an hour later, they were turning into a tree-lined drive, layered with crushed oyster shells that shone whitely in the sun beneath the dappled shade of the tree branches. The drive seemed long to Aimee, who was eager to see the house itself — and when it did come into view, she held her breath at the sheer size of it. Three-storied with long wings on both sides, it looked as though it could hold ten families instead of one, she thought. Six tall pillars made of white Italian marble stood grandly in front with a wide veranda, extending the length of the house on the second story and hammered in the delicate cast iron that she had seen before in the New Orleans homes.

"Good heavens, it does take the breath away!" she exclaimed to Violette, who nodded.

"My father has too much of the grandiose scheme when it comes to architecture. I told him that one day this building would prove to be a white elephant, but he insists he is saving it for the day when Dominic and I decide to live in the country. Of course, he wants it filled with grandchildren. I told him that my sister, Charlotte, could do the honors very well, for she and her husband, Jean, already have three. But Charlotte prefers Natchez to New Orleans, and she and Jean will probably not move south."

"Will Charlotte be here for your father's birthday?"

"Of course, as will my three brothers, all of whom are a disgrace to the family since they have refused to marry so far. Naturally, Jacques is only fourteen and cannot be expected to be pursuing young ladies yet, but the other two are already in their twenties and have not been able to find the lady of their choice yet." Violette smiled at Aimee and gave her a warning look. "You'd best stay away from them, lest they try to sweep you off your feet and take you away from Lucian."

"Oh, Lucian wouldn't mind!" Aimee teased airily.

"Ha! He would be so jealous, Dominic would have to hold him back from challenging poor Michael and Richard to a duel!"

"Michael and Richard?"

Violette giggled. "Yes. You must remember that my mother is an American by birth, and she insisted on naming two of her children with American names. My father has never forgiven her, and claims that their very names are the reason they have not yet married. Of course he's not serious, but it still goads my mother at times when he brings up the subject."

"Your parents sound delightful!" Aimee returned.

She soon found that Andre and Catherine were every bit as wonderful as she had hoped. They immediately made her feel welcome, while the rest of the family was very kind and courteous. The two older brothers did have a propensity to eye her as though sizing her up for an auction, but Aimee found she could forgive them when she realized how intensely their father was pushing them to marry. Andre complained loudly of the fact that his sons were still bachelors and said that Charlotte was the only one of his children who had pleased him with three grandchildren. Charlotte, a taller version of Violette, preened and leaned against the arm of her husband, who looked distinctly self-conscious.

After being in the house for only a few hours, Aimee soon realized from what an energetic family Violette came. She was asked to go riding, go swimming, or go fishing. Would she like to ride over the plantation fields? Would she like to see the slave quarters? Did she like to boat on the river? She felt as though she were in the eye of a hurricane and was relieved to hear the arrival of Dominic and her husband. Hurrying to his side, she felt she had been rescued and leaned against Lucian as he put an arm around her shoulder and hugged her close.

After more introductions were made, everyone settled down to an enormous dinner, so that afterward Aimee wanted nothing more than to be shown to her room and collapse on the bed. After Catherine took them upstairs to the second floor, Lucian closed the door firmly and turned to his wife, a questioning smile on his lips.

"Oh, not now," Aimee pleaded, pressing a hand to her stomach. "I'm afraid you'd get very little cooperation from me right now, Lucian, for I feel as though I've swallowed a bushel basket!"

"Nonsense! A little exercise is the best thing for such overindulgence," he teased her, coming over to take her face between his hands and kiss her with growing passion.

Aimee laughed and shook her head. "Dearest, you shall have to find another exercise, then, for I need to rest first."

For a moment, he looked extremely disappointed, but then shrugged and informed her he would, in that case, return downstairs to discuss plans with Dominic to return to New Orleans for a few hours the next day. At her look of disappointment, he assured Aimee that he would not be gone all day and would return in plenty of time for the birthday party. With a sigh, she watched him take his leave, then shrugged and removed her gown, lying down on the bed.

A few minutes later, Violette knocked on her door and entered, clad in a dressing gown. She saw Aimee's discomfort and laughed, accusing her of eating too much, then cocking her head suddenly and looking at her more closely.

"Mon Dieu!" she exclaimed suddenly. "You—you are not *enceinte,* are you, my friend?"

Aimee started at the idea and immediately pressed a trembling hand to her abdomen, as though checking for some telltale swell beneath her chemise. It came to her suddenly that she had missed her menses last month. She hadn't really thought of it, attributing it to the change in the climate and the food, but now, as she thought more and more about the possibility, she realized she might actually have conceived Lucian's child.

"Well?" Violette wondered out loud.

A hesitant smile shaped Aimee's mouth as she stared at her friend. "I—I cannot be sure, Violette, but I think—yes—I might be with child."

"Ha!" Violette clapped her hands. "You would make my father proud!" she teased her. "But have you said anything to Lucian?"

"No, I only just discovered it myself—and I still cannot be
sure. Aren't you supposed to be sick when you're having a baby?
I feel quite well, except for the discomfort from too much dinner."

Violette shrugged. "I know very little about such things, but
perhaps Charlotte could explain further. I'm sure not every
woman reacts the same to a pregnancy—perhaps you will be
lucky enough not to get sick."

"Oh, Violette, I can't believe it!" Aimee said, struggling off
the bed and running to the full-length mirror to look at her figure.
"Lucian's baby! It's—it's really so unexpected—I mean, how
will he react to the news that he might be a father!" Before Violette could frame an answer, Aimee found herself giving herself
one. He wouldn't be pleased, she felt sure. How could he be? A
child would only complicate their marriage and his work. She
would be less inclined to travel. What if they were called back to
France in the next few months? She shuddered to think of ocean
travel while she was pregnant. Oh, no, Lucian would not be
pleased at all, she was suddenly sure. Almost protectively, her
hands went to her stomach, pressing inward, demanding to know
now if a new life grew there.

Violette was aware of the changing emotions on Aimee's face
and could read the uncertainty there. "Are you worried about
Lucian's reactions?" she guessed accurately.

Aimee nodded, unable to lie to the other woman about her
reservations.

"Then you should tell him quickly so he can become used to
the idea over the next months," she returned matter-of-factly. "I
have seen most men go wild with joy and pride once their wives
tell them they are going to be fathers. It will probably be the
same with Lucian."

Aimee was not so sure, but she declined to tell Violette
that. After all, she and Violette had never really discussed the
secret reasons for Lucian's arrival in New Orleans, and she
wasn't sure how much Dominic confided in her about those
things. She felt a sudden sense of panic within her at the
thought that Lucian might be angry about the baby. And yet,
he had certainly never tried to protect her from becoming pregnant. Perhaps he thought that if she did get pregnant, it would
leave him free to get on with his work without interference
from her. Yes, that could very well be it, she decided unsteadily. If she was pregnant, he could more easily push her out of

his life—she would become the quiet and docile wife, her world bounded by the needs of the child.

Wait, she told herself suddenly, realizing she was on a downhill slide of emotional panic that threatened to drive her crazy. Conjectures were fruitless, really—she must confront Lucian with the possibility of her pregnancy. Only then could she discover the truth of his feelings.

"You will tell Lucian tonight?" Violette asked.

"Yes," Aimee responded. "You must promise to say nothing to anyone—not even to Dominic—until I have talked with Lucian." Her green eyes stared at the other woman as though testing her loyalty.

"I will say nothing until you tell me it is all right," Violette promised. She came over suddenly and hugged Aimee around the shoulders. "And don't look as though you are about to be put in front of a firing squad, my friend. Everything will work out, I'm sure. It is very foolish for you to imagine all sorts of things before talking with Lucian. As for me, if my opinion counts for anything in all of this, I am delighted! Of course, I fully intend for you to make me the godmother!" She hugged her again and was surprised to see the tears in Aimee's eyes.

"Oh, Violette, you are a true friend!" she cried, putting her face on her shoulder and giving full rein to her tears. "Whatever would I have done without you?"

Violette patted her back comfortingly with one hand. "I expect you would have made a complete mess of things," she retorted with a twinkle in her black eyes.

After Violette had gone to dress for the evening, Aimee sat alone in front of one of the long French windows, trying to keep calm despite the fact that she knew very soon her husband would come back up to see if she had finished with her nap and was ready to return downstairs for the evening. It would be a social night of conversation and cards—a passion of these Creoles, she knew, from playing many hands with Violette and Dominic.

She was only just beginning to calm the rapid beat of her heart when Lucian opened the door to their bedroom, presenting himself to her with an engaging grin. "Good evening, sweetheart. It promises to be quite a riotous evening, for already Charlotte's husband and brothers have threatened to take our measure in the card games planned for tonight. They even proposed gambling for small stakes, but I'm afraid my luck at cards is so terrible that I quickly talked them out of that. Dominic backed me up, for he probably thought it would be quite ungallant of them to take his guest for all his money in one night!" He stopped suddenly, aware that Aimee was not joining in his jest. "What's the matter?" he asked bluntly, coming closer to put his hands on her shoulders as she sat in the chair watching him.

Aimee pushed her tongue out to lick her lips, sliding it along the upper one while she cast about in her mind for the best way to broach the subject. Lucian watched her rather curiously.

"Are you not feeling well?" he wondered solicitously.

"I—I think I—might be—p-pregnant!" she stammered on a small explosion of sound, afraid to meet his vivid blue eyes as they bore into hers.

For a long moment, there was silence above her and her heart sank. Then she felt Lucian, pulling her up by the arms, enfolding her against him, pushing her head into his shoulder. Suddenly, all her fears seemed to come to a head, and for the second time that evening she burst into tears.

Lucian allowed her a few moments to get it all out of her system, while his hand rubbed along her spine soothingly. Finally, when she had quieted somewhat, he pushed her away just enough to tilt her chin up so he could look into her eyes.

"Are you unhappy about that possibility?" he asked her softly.

She shook her head. "I—I don't know."

"Did you think I would be angry?" he guessed.

She nodded. "Are you?" she questioned abruptly.

"No."

Her eyes held a glimmer of hope. "I thought that perhaps you would think it a terrible inconvenience, considering the reason we are here in New Orleans. It—it might complicate matters quite a bit, especially if I have to travel before the baby is born."

"It doesn't matter," he said firmly. He took her hand and led her to the bed, sitting down next to her with one hand loosely clasped about her waist. "Darling, don't you think I know what can happen when two people have indulged themselves as amorously as you and I have in these past weeks? If I hadn't wanted you to get pregnant, there are means I could have used to prevent it. Of course, I admit that we are still on rather tentative ground as far as the lasting relationship of our marriage, but perhaps this will serve to cement it. I care for you very much, Aimee. No, that's not right. I might as well admit that I love you, for I do."

Aimee's heart leaped at the news and her eyes were shining and wide, staring up into her husband's with hope—and something else.

He smiled down at her. "Have I surprised you, my love? What kind of man do you think I am? My God! I think I've loved you for a very long time, but being a man and somewhat stupid about certain things, I've not wanted to admit it to myself, afraid that you might not return that feeling."

"Oh, Lucian, I do love you!" she whispered, reaching up to put her arms around his neck in order to kiss him.

He kissed her thoroughly, then pushed her gently back onto the bed, his hands intent on the fastenings of her chemise. "Why else would I have displayed such an inordinate amount of interest in a common little pickpocket, a street urchin who carried about some demented idea of revenge that would have scared off a saner man?" He laughed, exposing her breasts and kissing each of them gently. "I couldn't bear the thought of you in prison, nor the idea that you could very well get your pretty little neck stretched on the gallows for shooting that bastard Faron. I was willing to promise Talleyrand the moon if it meant getting you out of there!"

"Oh, Lucian, I—I don't know what to say!" she told him, her hands smoothing his hair and lacing her fingers through the curls at the back of his neck.

"I think you do!" he teased her, sucking softly at the stiffening nipples that tempted him unbearably.

"I love you," she said, feeling as though a great weight had fallen from her shoulders. No more subterfuge or silly games, she told herself, and the idea brought such relief and joy that she passionately pressed her body to his, causing a quick response in him.

"So there'll be no more worries, no more doubts about this baby?" Lucian questioned her, even as he stood up for a brief moment to remove his breeches before rejoining her on the bed.

"*If* I am going to have a baby," she reminded him with a smile, parting her legs and feeling his welcome entrance.

"Darling, if you're not—I promise I can take care of that immediately," he promised with a little laugh, applying himself diligently to the problem.

* * *

Some hours later, Aimee and Lucian made their appearance downstairs, Aimee looking radiant and a bit flushed, and Lucian's face bearing the telltale traces of pride that told Violette he knew about Aimee's suspicion of pregnancy. They confirmed that when Lucian proposed a toast to his first child, bringing about happy applause from the Aubremont family, with Dominic coming over to pat him heartily on the back and promising rather smugly that he supposed he had been laggard in his own duty. He eyed Violette leeringly and returned to her to lay a proud hand at her waist. Andre noticed the movement and felt inordinately pleased at the whole business, telling himself that he could probably expect more grandchildren in the near future.

The rest of the evening passed pleasantly with cards and conversation. Charlotte was more than willing to pass on all her knowledge about pregnancy symptoms and the birth experience, and Violette's mother passed on little tidbits that she had gleaned from having five children of her own. Aimee felt quite content and surrounded by warmth and friendship. She looked over at her husband and caught him watching her with a great deal of pride. With a smile, she acknowledged him and her green eyes sparkled when he gazed back at her with blatant lechery. It was hard to imagine, she realized, ever leaving this kind of warmth and friendliness. The thought of Paris, of those cold and unloving streets where she had seen death and lawlessness, made her shiver imperceptibly. Did she really want to return to that place of bad memories? Did she want to bring a child back there?

Aimee thought about such plaguing questions, wondering what Lucian might say if she suggested they remain here. After all, what difference did it make? Talleyrand was a long way away. She knew that Lucian sent him orderly reports every two or three weeks, and once he had completed his service, surely there would be nothing to bring him back to Paris. But could Lucian give up the life to which he had become accustomed? It was a big question—one which she would have to ask him at a later date. She knew he enjoyed New Orleans, that he was close to Dominic. Yet, perhaps he had done this same thing many times before —become close to people, only to return to Paris sooner or later to receive more orders for more adventures. What would he truly think if she asked him to stay here in New Orleans, to make this their home? It was true that the city's future was uncertain. Who knew if France would eventually be able to wrest it from Spanish hands? Could she live under a Spanish government? There were many unanswerable questions floating about in her mind, but the thought of finding all the answers filled her with a sudden fatigue. Perhaps it would be best to just let things happen naturally —many times that was the best way. She must begin thinking of the baby growing inside her. She was sure now that she was with child. Certainly someone as vibrant and potent as her husband could not fail to impregnate her after the many nights of sensual pleasure they had experienced together. She hugged the thought inside of her that she would love to have a little sable-haired son with his father's blue eyes—but perhaps a golden-haired daughter with emerald-green eyes that matched hers would be just as delightful!

30

Summer followed a short spring and the temperatures began to soar, bringing with them an uncomfortable stickiness that seemed nearly unbearable to Aimee as the effect of her pregnancy became more noticeable. The mosquitoes were especially vicious and it seemed she always had three or four red, swelling bumps on her arms that would itch her mercilessly on those nights when she felt drenched in perspiration, too hot to stay close up against Lucian. She hated not being able to cuddle with him at night, but they both agreed it was impossible even when the occasional breeze blew warmly through the open windows. Aimee became more irritable and her mood swings were a mystery to Lucian, who, many times, could only watch helplessly as she burst into angry tears or moped about the room in a depressed state.

Aimee was certain he was growing to hate her, for he seemed to stay away from her more and more, especially in the evenings when he and Dominic would prowl the public houses. Sometimes, Lucian would tell her casually that they had seen General Wilkinson moving about the city, and Aimee would feel an instant moment of fear, knowing that Wilkinson had warned Lucian about nosing into his affairs. She tried to make her husband promise to be very careful, but he would shrug his shoulders and assure her cockily that in exercising too much caution he might miss out on a valuable piece of information.

On occasion, Aimee would ask to see a report that he wrote to Talleyrand, but Lucian usually found some excuse not to show it to her, making her think that she had become totally useless in her capacity to help him with his work. Violette tried to cheer her up, but the heat and Aimee's stubborn resistance eventually wore down her enthusiasm and the two of them would very often sit idly, reading or sewing, wondering when their husbands would return, and feeling horribly bored at their own inactivity.

It didn't help matters much in the two women's view when Violette found out that she, too, was pregnant in early July. "Two cranky females," Dominic had joked, but the dangerous looks he had received from those women had made him realize instantly that he had said the wrong thing. Unlike Aimee's early stage of pregnancy, which had been relatively sickness-free, Violette had to endure violent spells of vomiting that left her weak for hours afterward. The physician assured her that the sickness would pass eventually, but it was hard to convince Violette of that as she lay, helpless to move, with a cool washcloth pressed over her eyes. At such times she would express her opinions as to why on earth she ever thought she wanted to have children.

Finally, though, as high summer gave way to September, Violette found some relief from her illness and Aimee began to feel quite well, almost like her old self again. Nearing her sixth month of pregnancy, she was astounded at the swelling round-ness in her belly, ordering the dressmaker to let out the seams of all her summer gowns in order to be as comfortable as possible.

She and Violette begged the men to take them out on the town in the evening, anything to feel once more in the mainstream of the city. Dominic and Lucian relented one evening and surprised them with tickets to the theater. Violette informed an excited Aimee as they dressed that evening that French comedians flee-ing from the French revolution had come from Santo Domingo and opened the first theater in New Orleans some years before. It had first been nothing more than a hired hall, but such was the enthusiasm of the Creoles attending the theater that never again was the city without a full season of performances. The theater had only recently been relocated to Saint-Peter Street, between Bourbon and Orleans, not too far distant from the St. Cyr home. Regular performances in classic drama, opera, ballet, and panto-mime were given at the Saint-Pierre Theater, which was always packed and assured of a sell-out crowd, hence the need for ticket purchasing well in advance.

Despite the usual warmth and humidity of the September eve-ning, both Aimee and Violette dressed as elegantly as they could stand, surprising their husbands with the evident desirability of two such pregnant wives. The two men exchanged winks and promised themselves to enjoy this night to the fullest, both during and after the theater performance.

"I think you are growing more beautiful," Lucian whispered to Aimee as they sat in the carriage opposite the St. Cyrs. "It seems that having babies must agree with you."

"Except for the change in temperament," she whispered back with a woeful air.

Lucian smiled. "I can't blame you for that, my dear. Everyone in the city has been edgy with this damned sticky weather. The sooner autumn arrives, the better it will be. The mosquitoes have already caused enough suffering for one season, and I've heard rumors of spotty outbreaks of fever caused from the miasma coming off the bayous and swamps." He put a protective arm around her shoulders.

"There is nothing wrong with me that three more months of patience won't cure," Aimee replied pertly, delighting her husband with her return of spirit.

He sighed, pressing his lips against her hair. "I am so glad to hear you sound like the old Aimee," he told her. "I've missed her."

"So have I!" Aimee laughed.

They arrived at the theater, where the crowds were milling about before the performance, buying cooled ginger beer and other drinks from vendors seated along the banquette. To one side, and looking very out of place, stood a rough-looking crowd of red-shirted men, smoking cigars and cursing coarsely in language that caused a bright flush to come to the cheeks of any women who happened to pass by.

"American rivermen," Violette said with a note of distaste. Her mouth twisted in irritation. "Dominic, they won't be allowed inside, will they?"

"Of course not," he assured her quickly. "I'm surprised they've come this far from the river, actually. Usually, they find their pleasures along the riverfront houses that keep them well supplied with women and drink." He cast an anxious look at Lucian. "Do you think they're looking for trouble, my friend?"

Lucian shrugged. "The night patrol will be by in a while and set them straight. I'm sure we needn't concern ourselves about it."

He and Dominic led their wives inside the building, which seemed to hit Aimee with the force of a blast furnace. All these people crammed together in one space made her feel faintly nauseated, and she turned to Violette, who was obviously having the same difficulty.

"Have we time to take the air before the performance begins?" she asked Lucian, who had begun shouldering his way through the crowd in order to get to their seats.

He frowned back at her. "We'd best find our seats now, Aimee. I have a feeling it's first-come, first-served tonight. This comedy must be very good to elicit such a response."

"Perhaps the people are just rabid for an evening out after trying to stay inside to escape the heat for the past few weeks," Violette suggested, leaning heavily against Dominic, her expression somewhat pained as she fought back rising nausea. Carefully, Dominic picked his way through the crowd to the seats inside.

Once they were seated, Aimee admitted to feeling a little better, although poor Violette continued to look pale and strained. The first act was barely appreciated by the two young women, as each was more concerned with her own feelings of sickness. By the second act they felt better and were able to laugh and guffaw with the rest of the audience.

As the curtain fell on the second act, one of the performers came out to center stage, looking somewhat uncertain and anxious. Clearing his throat, he faced the audience and spoke loudly. "Ladies and gentlemen, I have just been informed that our honorable governor, General Gayoso, has died this evening."

The news seemed to hit the audience like a bolt of lightning. Everyone stood rooted to their seats, unable to believe the governor had died, just like that. Only yesterday he had been seen drilling the soldiers in the Place d'Armes. Lucian and Dominic exchanged looks.

"What do you think?" Dominic asked his friend, his eyes hooded.

Lucian shrugged. "I think there might have been a particular reason for Wilkinson to have been in the city these past few days, but God knows we'll never be able to prove anything. The man's too cunning to leave any traces. Then, too, we could be mistaken, and he might have had nothing to do with it. There are enough French, Spanish, and American spies in this city for any one of them to have done the deed, hoping that by his death they could throw the territory into anarchy and allow their own governments to move in."

Aimee, following her husband's conversation with difficulty, realized he was talking as though Gayoso's death could have been murder. She shivered at the possibility, realizing how very much in danger her husband was in in his profession. Many of the people were already getting up to leave, because the performer had announced that the rest of the show would be canceled out of deference to the general's death. With relief, Aimee stood up, glad that they would soon be out of this hothouse. Next to her, a little sigh from Violette told her that the other woman was feeling the same way.

As they walked out to the colonnaded entrance, Aimee could see that the rivermen were still lounging drunkenly outside, making disparaging remarks to several of the gentlemen who were hard-pressed not to challenge them. One hotheaded young Creole actually returned the ribald comments, causing the rivermen to take offense and quickly surround him. Instantly, Dominic and Lucian leaped to his aid, leaving Aimee and Violette to watch wide-eyed as a full-fledged scuffle began, with others joining in the foray.

Pressed well back from the action, Aimee watched as Lucian engaged in a fierce fistfight with a bullet-headed man who looked to be twice the size of her husband both in height and girth. Fearfully, she watched Lucian take a hamlike fist to the stomach, nearly gagging herself when he doubled over in pain. But quickly, with unbelievable speed, he straightened up, bringing his own fist with him to crack weightily into the other man's lantern jaw. The giant staggered, then roared out in his anger and his pain, crouching down as though to pounce on Lucian. Aimee watched anxiously, wondering if her husband was about to be crushed into the floorboards.

The fight raged on for nearly an hour, with the rivermen finally seeming to be getting the worst of it, especially as reinforcements came for the citizens in the form of the patrol. Aimee watched as several rough-looking men were taken away in carts to the newly built jail near the Cabildo. Others, including several of the victorious citizens, were taken to the Charity Hospital of Saint Charles, nursing broken bones, bruised ribs, and bloody noses. Fortunately, neither Lucian nor Dominic was hurt seriously.

"With Gayoso's unexpected death, there'll be chaos until a new governor can be assigned from Spain," Lucian reflected as they made their way to the waiting carriage.

Dominic nodded. "The legislative assembly will have to act quickly to set up some sort of interim government. Tomorrow morning I will attend the meeting and suggest sending for someone from Cuba who can take over the authority until Spain decides who to send us. At least that will be much quicker than waiting for several months for word from the Spanish throne."

"I agree. Do you think I can accompany you?"

Dominic shrugged. "I don't see why not. We'll leave first thing in the morning in order to have some time to talk privately with key legislators."

"But, darling, you promised that tomorrow you would accompany me to the park," Aimee interrupted quickly, sensing that she was about to lose her husband once more to his duty.

"I'm sorry, Aimee, but you must understand how important this is. With Gayoso's death, who knows what plots are hatching in the city and north in the western territories? It would be just like Wilkinson to try to lead an army of Americans in here and ruin everything. He may be crafty and manipulative, but his timing could be all wrong."

"And that would jeopardize France's attempts to buy the land?" Aimee queried.

Lucian nodded. She sighed in defeat and imagined another hot, dull day on the morrow. But then she brightened. She and Violette could take a drive along the river. It would be cooler than staying at home all day, and they might even go as far as Violette's parents' home. The idea of a visit with the gregarious Aubremonts appealed greatly to her, and she resolved to make the suggestion to Violette later that evening while the men discussed their strategy for the assembly tomorrow.

The next morning started out in a very ordinary way. After Lucian had left, Aimee bathed and dressed, then ate a light breakfast with Violette as they discussed their plans for the day. Both young women were in high spirits at the thought of a country drive, and even the weather seemed to be cooperating, for the heat had diminished a little and the humidity seemed even to have lessened.

"I wish the men could have accompanied us," Aimee said as they settled into the carriage, "but at least we'll not be confined indoors today. I should think the outing is owed us after that terrible fiasco at the theater last night."

Violette agreed immeasurably, spreading her umbrella out behind her to protect her pale skin from becoming sunburned. Aimee did likewise and the drive proceeded pleasantly through the Vieux Carré. They passed the Ursuline convent and waved at the little charges of the good sisters who were dressed in dark blue uniforms. Aimee wondered if her daughter—if she had one —would attend a convent school. She recalled her own bad memories of the convent in Orléans, then quickly put it out of her mind.

Their driver, an old and trusted servant who had been in the Aubremont household for many years, started the horses on the river road. The black man's grizzled head glistened with sweat beads in the sun and Aimee wondered how he could stand being folded into the tight costume and high collar of his station. The idea made her feel warm again and she fanned her face with a handkerchief, idly watching the passing scenery, admiring the bending cypresses that arched out over the mighty gray-green river. Beside her, Violette had begun to doze a little. All seemed serene and peaceful.

Then, suddenly, as they rounded a bend in the river road, Aimee's eyes flew open wide as she perceived a gang of rivermen struggling with a flatboat that had become entangled in swamp weeds. Their curses and oaths floated back to her and she leaned forward to suggest to the driver that they not pass too closely to these potentially dangerous men, but it was too late, for the Americans had already seen the approaching carriage and were waving it down, indicating they required assistance.

Hesitantly, the Negro servant slowed down the carriage a safe distance away and proceeded to walk over to the rivermen. Aimee could see them talking and she wondered what they were asking the servant to do, for he continued to shake his grizzled head while pointing back at the two ladies in his care. Obviously, she thought, they wanted his help in extricating the flatboat from the weeds and tree branches, and he was refusing because Aimee and Violette were in his company.

A disparaging remark was uttered by one of the men, and another leaned over to seize the servant by the lapels of his coat, shaking him until his head rolled back and forth. Disgustedly, they let him drop, unconscious, to the ground and proceeded toward the carriage, intent on using it and the horses to help pull the flatboat out of the water, or at least to retrieve the cargo on board.

Frightened, Aimee shook Violette awake and leaned over the high seat to grab at the reins. With a jerk, she started the horses, climbing awkwardly into the seat in order to better control them. Seeing her maneuver, the rivermen began running toward her, yelling at her to stop and aid them. But Aimee was too frightened to help these rough men. She had seen what they could do, how their tempers flared, at the theater last night—and she wanted no part of them.

Swinging the carriage around at a dangerous angle, she whipped the horses to a gallop, hearing Violette's squeal of protest as she was slammed up against the side of the backseat. Nearly unseated herself, Aimee hung onto the reins for dear life, for the horses, sensing an untrained hand on the reins, were beginning to bolt. Wildly now, the carriage was careening along the river road, leaving the shouting rivermen far behind.

Gritting her teeth, Aimee leaned down low, keeping her eyes straight ahead as she tried to pull on the reins in order to get the horses under control once more. The leather slipped continually from her hands, so that she was unable to get a good grip on it.

"Stop, Aimee! You will have us both killed!" Violette was screaming, bouncing around in the backseat and trying to keep her seated position and protect her stomach at the same time.

"I can't stop them!" Aimee cried back over her shoulder. She leaned forward to try to get a better grip and the horses strained in front, bringing her to a half-crouched position in the driver's seat. Abruptly, she jerked the reins and the horses reared up with dilated nostrils.

For a moment, she felt as though her arms were pulled out of their sockets—and then she was losing her footing, flying through the air and landing with a sickening thud on the ground, rolling over and over while she heard Violette screaming somewhere behind her.

Aimee lay quietly on the ground, her head filled with a buzzing noise and her body suddenly wracked by some terrible pain that gripped her in the small of her back and threatened to break it in two. She heard another woman screaming—and realized it was herself.

Clutching her belly, she brought her knees up so that she was curled into a tight ball, trying to deflect the pain somehow. Oh, God, she felt as though she were going to die from the pain! Please, someone help her not to lose her baby! *Violette, help me!* she screamed in her mind.

With her eyes gradually losing their ability to focus, Aimee could nevertheless see a tall, broad-shouldered figure looming up over her suddenly. She screamed out loud as he bent down to pick her up, the pain shooting with horrible intensity through her spine. Her eyes focused cloudily on a red-shirted chest—and she realized that one of the rivermen must have followed them and was here now. Holy Mother! What would he do to them! Trying to fight the pain and her slow roll into unconsciousness, Aimee beat at him weakly, begging him to let her go, but to no avail.

"Quiet, now, you crazy woman!" the man was saying with a sharp twang in his voice. "Christ, you done killed your baby already—don't kill yourself, too!"

They were the last words that drifted to Aimee as she swooned quietly into a dead faint.

31

A week later, Aimee had just been released from the hospital and been allowed to return home, her head lying disconsolately against her husband's shoulder. Her mind was a jumble of emotions, all of them very painful—there was the sense of devastating loss that her baby had died, too small to live outside his mother's body; there was also a peculiar hesitancy in her relationship with Lucian. He had not blamed her, nor had he questioned her on the sensibility of taking a long drive with only an old servant to protect two pregnant young women. Still, there was a twinge of something in those keen blue eyes when he looked at her—and she wondered if he no longer loved her. It had been the baby's presence that had brought out his admission of love for her. Would that declaration be rescinded because the baby was gone? There were so many questions in her mind, so much confusion about her own changing feelings toward Lucian. It had certainly not been his fault that she had lost the baby, yet her mind accused him illogically of caring more about his work than about her and their child. Surely, if he had kept his promise and accompanied her on the drive, none of this would have happened. She *knew* she was being illogical, but was helpless to stop the dangerous train of thought. Then, too, there was anger deep inside her—anger at the wasted life, at her own stupidity, and at the Americans who had inadvertently caused it all.

Even though it had been one of the rivermen who had seen her and Violette to the hospital, she lumped all of them together. The rivermen were Americans—and therefore she hated Americans because of the part they had played in her terrible loss. Nothing Lucian could say to her could make her change her mind. She regarded all Americans as uncouth and dangerous, hardly fit to have their own country. Surely it would have been better had the British massacred every last one of them instead of surrendering to them in ignominy. Her vengeful thoughts upset Lucian greatly. After all, he was one-half American. The thought of ever meeting her mother-in-law was totally repulsive to Aimee in her current

371

state of mind. Lucian's mother was one of *them*—one of the
despised Americans.

Violette, who had been fortunate enough to have remained
unharmed in the carriage when it was stopped, saw the distress
and the emotional strain in the sad green eyes of her friend, but
she, too, was powerless to change it. She felt almost guilty for
having survived without losing her own child, and when Aimee's
eyes had focused pointedly on her rounding abdomen, Violette
had very nearly gone off into tears.

But now that the first terrible week was over and Aimee was
returning to the St. Cyr home, everyone hoped that things would
begin to resume some sort of normality. Aimee fervently hoped
so and was determined not to place guilt or blame on Lucian or
Violette, or anyone else. Only her abiding dislike of all things
American remained with her and she refused to talk about it to
Lucian.

When he suggested, with extreme gentleness, that there would
be other babies to love and nurture, Aimee had turned away from
him sharply, closing her ears to the possibilities. She did not want
to think of babies now. How could Lucian be so insensitive to her
grief? Did he not care enough about the child? Did he not care
enough about her? Such questions spiraled her into despair—a
dangerous road from which she realized she must move away.

Once back inside the spacious and lovely home of the St.
Cyrs, Aimee's natural recuperative powers helped her back to
health at an amazing speed. Even so, as she grew stronger every
day, her eyes followed Violette's thickening body and she could
not let go of the dark grief that threatened to become the center of
her being.

One afternoon toward the last of October, when the heat had
diminished and the southern autumn was in full bloom, Violette
found Aimee in the interior patio, daydreaming as she gazed
broodingly into the splashing waters of the fountain. Carefully,
Violette came up to her, sensing the grief inside the other
woman.

"Aimee?"

She started violently, unaware before then of Violette's presence. As always, her eyes automatically swerved down to the
bulging abdomen and Violette saw the unconscious tightening
around her mouth.

"May I sit with you?" Violette asked softly.

Aimee nodded listlessly, dabbling her hand in the water.

"Aimee, we must talk," Violette began, taking a deep breath

and plunging on. "I know that you still carry much grief for your unborn child, my friend. I sympathize with you—we all do. You don't know how much your sadness affects all of us."

"Why should you be sad?" Aimee asked her bitterly. "You still have a child."

"Yes, by the grace of God, I do," Violette agreed gently. "And you, too, will have another child someday, I am sure of it. I truly believe, my dear, that things happen for a reason. Please don't misunderstand me. I would never have hoped for the loss of your baby—and yet, perhaps it has something to do with a destiny that is still unfulfilled. You and Lucian, so newly married, still with so many things unclear in your marriage. Yes, I have seen the looks you give each other and I sense there is uncertainty between you."

"That is none of your business, Violette," Aimee said stiffly.

Violette shrugged, determined not to take offense. "It is the business of a concerned friend to help another friend," she replied gently. "And I do consider you my friend, Aimee. Nothing you do will change that."

Aimee stole a glance at the other woman, beginning to feel rather churlish. "I'm sorry, Violette. I know I have proven to be rather trying these past days, but you cannot understand the pain I am going through. Lucian and I—" She stopped and shrugged. "Well, it's just as you say, we are uncertain about our feelings now. And there is so much else mixed up in it—the fact that I am away from what little family I have, my ambiguous feelings toward my homeland, the fact that Lucian is half-American. I cannot seem to rid myself of the notion that the Americans are not to be trusted."

"But Lucian is your husband, Aimee, not some nameless riverman!" Violette said quickly. "He cares so much for you, but you are blotting him out and he cannot find a way to breach the defenses you have erected!"

"He doesn't want to!" Aimee sighed. "I am simply a useless appendage now!"

"Nonsense! You only see yourself that way. But what did you do before you became pregnant? Certainly you did not feel an extension of your husband! You seemed a proud, independent woman when I first met you. You are still that same woman!"

Aimee laughed sadly. "I don't know, Violette, whether I am the same woman or not!"

"Pooh! You are wallowing in your own self-pity now and it is most unbecoming, I can assure you!" Violette reprimanded her with a sharpening tone.

Aimee was silent, knowing in her heart that Violette was offering her the best of advice. If only she could take it! What she had said was true enough. Before she was pregnant, she had done very well just being Lucian's wife—and before that she had managed to survive as an unmarried woman. Why should everything change just because of a terrible accident? She *was* still the same woman!

Looking over at Violette, with tears beginning to seep from the corners of her eyes, Aimee smiled and nodded. "Oh, Violette! Whatever would I do without you? How is it I have survived twenty years without a friend such as you?"

"I have no idea!" Violette said, smiling, too, through the tears.

Gradually, from that day forward, Aimee began picking up the pieces of her life, renewing her interest in her marriage and in New Orleans and in the work that was so important to Lucian. She insisted he tell her of his findings and lent her own brand of advice, whether he asked for it or not. There was still a great deal of uncertainty in her personal feelings for her husband, but she was determined to stop wallowing in self-pity and make something useful of her life. She had come to New Orleans to help her husband, and she could certainly do so. She was careful to keep her ears open when dining at the homes of prominent families in New Orleans and managed to find a special talent for drawing out confidences from many of the Spanish ladies, who expressed a quiet dread about the unpredictability of their future in New Orleans.

An interim governor was sent over from Cuba at the beginning of the year 1800, the Marquis de Casa Calvo, whose authoritarianism could sometimes be galling to the people, but whose reserved and diplomatic charm could at other times entice his citizens into believing that he was one of the best governors since the beginning of Spanish rule.

It was in January of 1800 that important papers reached Lucian in New Orleans with news that could only be called sensational. The Directory, having been deemed incompetent because of its many political and military blunders, had been voted out of office in the elections of 1799, but the Directory had had the vote annulled once again as it had the year previously. There had been a division of power within the five-man Directory, with Paul

Barras squaring off against his now-archrival Sieyès, who had become master of the Directory and both Councils through the liberal use of money and other bribes. Napoleon Bonaparte had learned of this chaos in August of 1799 and had sailed secretly from Egypt to France, arriving in Paris in October of that year.

Talleyrand wrote that Sieyès was already conspiring to overthrow the Directory and assume total control, but needed a military general with an army to help him gain his objective. Bonaparte had cunningly feigned neutrality and offered his services. The Council of Ancients had convoked the Legislature to meet on November 10 at Saint-Cloud and had ordered Bonaparte to take command of the troops of Paris. Delirium had broken out in Paris when the beloved general was given so much power. The cries of the people called out for Bonaparte to lead them, and Barras, Sieyès, and the rest of the Directory had been forced to resign so that the executive body ceased to function.

In the midst of this chaos, Bonaparte had gone to the two Councils to address them, but both had reacted strongly against him and were determined that he not become their new leader. However, the army, under Bonaparte's control, and led by his good friend General Murat, went storming into the hall of the Council of Five Hundred, and those good men fled immediately. The Council of Ancients now proved themselves more docile and adjourned both chambers, appointing a provisional government of three consuls until a new constitution could be completed. This had been at the suggestion of Napoleon Bonaparte himself, Talleyrand wrote—and Aimee could fairly picture the sardonic smile with which Talleyrand would favor those frightened little men of the legislature. He had already concluded that out of the three consuls—Sieyès, Ducos, and Bonaparte—it was Bonaparte who would prove himself the most capable leader and would soon arrogate himself to the supreme position. By the new Constitution of 1799, Napoleon Bonaparte was named First Consul, with two innocuous assistants as second and third consuls after Ducos withdrew from politics and Sieyès settled himself into making political statements on his own private soapbox.

"Talleyrand writes most astutely that the Constitution of 1799 was mostly the work of Bonaparte himself," Lucian said as he perused the last letter in the packet. He looked up at Aimee, who was staring off into space, her mind trying to understand what this new political aspect would do to the government of France. "The three consuls have pledged fidelity to the Republic, to liberty, equality, and the representative system of government, but

Talleyrand suggests strongly that Bonaparte has other ideas in mind. This new Constitution was designed primarily to assure the placement of power in his hands."

"So the people have guillotined a King and replaced him finally with a general," Aimee murmured thoughtfully. "Unless, of course, this Napoleon Bonaparte proves himself unequal for the task of governing a nation. He must understand that it is quite different from governing an army."

"I had occasion to meet the little general," Lucian said. "He seems to be a man in full charge of his own destiny." He held up the last letter he had been reading. "According to the new Constitution, Bonaparte as First Consul will have most of the power in his hands—the appointment of ministers, ambassadors, officers of the army and navy, judges and other civil officials. He holds the right to make war and peace. This could mean that Talleyrand might have found the right person to press his suggestions as to the future of the Louisiana Territory. Now he only has to persuade one person of the validity of his plans." He appeared to be thoughtfully turning over the possibilities in his mind. "Of course, that presumes that Talleyrand can retain Bonaparte's favor."

"Knowing the wily Talleyrand, he should be able to without very much trouble," Aimee stated flatly. "Did he say anything of his chances?"

"Not in so many words. I gather he had to think about the consequences of revealing too much in case this packet had been confiscated by the authorities before getting out of France."

"So, what is our position here in New Orleans?" Aimee asked practically.

Lucian shrugged. "We will continue to sift out the feelings of the populace toward French control and send reports back to Talleyrand. I have no doubts that he will use them as evidence for Bonaparte's agreement to take back the territory from France. Meanwhile, I am sure that the United States cannot but be viewing these new developments in France with some trepidation. Obviously, they will be renewing their efforts with Spain in order to come to some kind of agreement."

"Do you think they will come to an agreement?" Aimee wondered, feeling distaste at having the beautiful city of New Orleans come under American control. "Surely Spain would not sell this territory to a fledgling country with very little to barter with!"

Lucian shrugged. "I don't know what the Spanish are thinking, Aimee. I would bet my very last franc, though, that our old friend General Wilkinson knows. I am certain that he is under the pay of Spain to provide details of American army strength and border tactics, but there is no way to prove that."

"What do you care if he is under the Spanish influence and working against the United States?" Aimee asked. "If it keeps the Americans from floating their people down the river to New Orleans, I am all for it!"

Lucian glanced sharply at her. "Darling, all Americans are not like the rivermen you've seen. In fact, they are a very small portion of the populace, and are not representative at all. In my dealings with the citizens of the United States, I have come to think of them as closely matched in their ideals with the original intentions of the French. They, too, want liberty, equality, and fraternity. They seem to be doing better at it than your countrymen," he added softly.

Aimee was not about to admit to any such thing, and Lucian smiled, standing up from his desk and walking over to where she sat in a chair in the library. "Come, come, my wife, what has happened to that open mind of yours? You cannot simply hate an entire people because of one tragic incident. It would be grossly unfair!"

"I don't view it so," she retorted, turning her nose up determinedly.

He put both hands on either arm of her chair, effectively closing her in. "You are proving to be stubborn and intractable, my love."

She winced at the use of the endearment, but he pretended not to notice, intent on the play of light from the window across her face, lightening her green eyes and bringing out a gold sheen in her hair. She had allowed it to grow again since they'd been in New Orleans and now it was long and thick, curling of its own accord despite her insistence on brushing it back into a high-crowned chignon.

"You really are much too beautiful for me to think about Talleyrand and his machinations," he murmured, leaning over to kiss her mouth.

Instinctively, Aimee tilted her head up to receive his kiss, but when his hands moved from the chair to her shoulders, she recoiled. Instantly, Lucian drew back, reacting as though she had slapped him by her body's rejection of his amorous advances. Aimee bit her lip, feeling humiliated and angry at her own reactions, but helpless to stop them for some reason. With tightened lips, Lucian straightened and walked to a cabinet where he poured himself a quick brandy.

"Would you like one?" he offered when he was sure the anger would not show in his voice.

Aimee hated this pretense. It was always like this. Although they worked together well and could converse intensely about many subjects, sex was not one of them anymore. Since she had lost the baby, there was a strange reluctance in her to enjoy the physical part of her marriage. She knew Lucian suffered greatly from it and told herself he probably had to find relief in the whorehouses along Rampart Street. But in spite of her raging jealousy at imagining him with other women, doing the things to them that he had done with her, she could not bring herself to respond to his sensuous nature. It was as though that part of her had died with the baby. It was intolerable for both of them, but they were stolidly determined to deny its existence.

"No, I don't want a brandy," she told him levelly, wishing she could close her eyes and get drunk to her eyeballs, just so that she might come to him as a whole woman again.

Lucian shrugged and took another one himself. "So, what were we discussing?" he mused, half to himself. "Ah, yes, Talleyrand and his probable suggestion to General Bonaparte that this whole Louisiana Territory could somehow be used for the glory of France. Bonaparte, being a military man, might find the suggestion most appealing."

"That would be good for New Orleans," Aimee said carefully.

"Perhaps, although they seem to be flourishing under Spanish rule."

Aimee shrugged, knowing the argument would get them nowhere—and that neither of them was really interested in continuing it now.

Her heart ached for the closeness they had shared so briefly together, but that now seemed a thing of the past. She waited for Lucian to say something, but found him staring at her rather bleakly.

"Do we have plans for this evening?" he finally inquired rather formally.

She shook her head.

"Then I shall be going out." The statement was direct, yet somehow evasive.

Aimee swallowed and turned her head to hide the tears. It was her own fault, she told herself. How could she expect Lucian to remain true to her when she had changed so drastically from the woman he had married?

In March of that year, Violette's baby was born, intensifying the feeling of upheaval within Aimee. The baby was a beautiful girl, dark-eyed and dark-haired, with so much hair on her head that Violette joked she would have to cut her daughter's hair by the time she was six weeks old. Dominic was very proud and he and Lucian had gone out to drink to the baby's health. Aimee had held the precious bundle with great awe, gazing at the tiny hands and feet and being unable to help herself from thinking about her own child. How beautiful he, too, would have been, she told herself.

Violette knew the emotions that were passing through her friend's mind and tried to help her, although it was not an easy task. The past hurt and anger came once more to the forefront of Aimee's mind and she turned away from Lucian even more decidedly. Violette watched Lucian go out in a black anger one evening and wondered if this time he would return.

Once her anger had been spent, Aimee, too, wondered if Lucian would return that evening. Her pride hated to admit that he could not stand to be with her for any length of time. Her anger was unreasonable and nothing he said could keep her from spilling the acidic comments that bubbled within her. She accused him of not loving her, of using her for his own nefarious purposes, of not caring enough about their marriage or their dead baby. Lucian had given up in angry frustration, knowing he had to leave or throttle her.

Aimee went to bed feeling miserable, unable to sleep, wondering where Lucian was. She didn't want to imagine him in the arms of another woman, but the image continually popped into her mind. By the time he returned home in the middle of the night, Aimee was so relieved that he had come home at all that she didn't even mind the telltale reek of perfume mixed with the fumes of alcohol on his breath. He staggered into their room, going over to his usual place on the divan.

Aimee watched him in the half light through her lashes and felt her heart lurch with pity, a feeling she knew he would reject immediately. But then her pulse became more rapid as she saw him stop before settling on the divan and turn back toward the bed. Stiffening unconsciously, she barely breathed as she watched him stagger toward her, pulling off his clothes indiscriminately as he went.

"Aimee?" he whispered into her face, the smell of alcohol making her cough uncontrollably. "You're awake, then."

She opened her eyes, all pretense forgotten. "How could I not be awake after all the noise you've made," she returned tensely.

With easy strength, he reached down and rolled her over onto the other side of the bed. "I'm sleeping in here tonight," he informed her, slurring the words before flopping down next to her. Possessively, he reached for her body beneath the covers, angered that she wore a nightgown. Snatching at it in irritation, he succeeded in ripping the delicate material and leaving her naked. "That's much better," he told her, hiccoughing and leaning toward her to gather her rather unsteadily into his arms.

"Lucian, please. I—I don't like it when you're like this," she said, seeking to free herself from his hold.

"I don't give a damn what you like," he informed her. "You are my wife! Dammit, woman! I want to feel myself inside you!"

She winced at the directness of his words. "No doubt you've been feeling your way all around the riverfront of New Orleans," she said accusingly.

He laughed as though she had said something funny. "I'd like to go hump some mindless whore on the wharf," he told her, "but fortunately—or unfortunately—I could never make myself do it. No, my loving little wife, I could only think of those huge, green eyes of yours and the sadness I see in them every day. And I'm afraid I just lost all desire—whoosh! Right out the window, you see!"

Her mind latched onto this important declaration and she clung to it as he lowered his head to kiss her. For a moment she resisted, but he pushed her forward, against his chest, with one hand behind her head, pushing her face to his. "Dammit! Kiss me!" he ordered.

Helpless to refuse, Aimee opened her mouth and obliged him. It was a shock to feel his tongue on hers, to find it exploring the soft interiors of her mouth and running sensually on the inner side of her teeth. She could taste the brandy and the whiskey, but surprisingly it somehow didn't bother her as she felt a once-familiar spark of desire begin deep in the secret recesses of her body.

"Christ, how I want you!" he groaned when he stopped kissing her, moving his hand from the back of her head to caress her jaw with a sudden tenderness. "You've made me wait too long for this, wench!" he told her.

She smiled up at him bravely, wanting him suddenly to take

his revenge on her. She had been a fool! "I have waited too long, too," she whispered.

She heard his surprised intake of breath and then he was kissing her again, slow and powerful kisses that sucked the breath from her lungs and made her strain her neck toward him. She was powerless to resist his expertise, feeling her limbs going soft and tingling, unable to move as they lay unresisting on the bed. He was not gentle with her, and she did not want him to be. His mouth and tongue evoked shivers in her flesh, his hands caressed her, stroked her. Her nipples grew taut from his lips and her whole body caught fire from his touch. Without too many preliminaries, his knee parted her thighs and she arched upward instinctively as he entered her, driving so hard that she gasped in pain.

Only then did he quiet, as though, in finally achieving his goal, he could afford to be languorous in the enjoyment of it. Aimee lay beneath him, feeling a deep throbbing between her legs, bringing her knees up to wind tightly around his hips and waist. Her heels dug softly into his back and her hands tightened their hold around his neck.

"God, Aimee, I've ached for this moment!" he said, kissing her face and neck and suckling her breasts like a starving man.

Aimee felt thrills of pleasure running through her as he moved within her and her arms clung fiercely to him, her heels digging harder, urging him to love her with fury. Her whole body felt awash with an intense desire that built and built inside her. She felt his hands cupping her breasts, bringing them to his mouth, then one hand sliding between their bodies, seeking the tiny bud of sensuality between her thighs, manipulating it even as he continued to stroke within her so that she thought she would go mindless with the wondrous pleasure of it. The pleasure washed over her in waves and she heard herself calling his name in a voice that deepened with her passion.

Rising up, with his hands on either side of her, he hovered above her in order to lengthen his strokes and give her even more pleasure. Aimee dug her fingers into her breasts, seeking her release with breathless abandon as she thrust her hips forward and back, feeling him growing even more turgid within her. He was prolonging the act until she could barely stand it and a ragged cry burst forth from her lips—sweet music to his ears.

Her hair was damp on the pillow, her entire body slick with a thin sheen of perspiration that had nothing to do with the weather. His, too, was moist, and their flesh made wet, slapping sounds against each other as they moved together toward the culmination of their passion. For Aimee, there was no one else, and she knew that Lucian would be the only man to draw this response from her flesh. He knew how to draw every drop of reserve from her nature and reduce her to some half-mad, passionate woman, as abandoned as any whore and just as shameless in her need. He brought her to the peak of frenzy and she cried out in demand for fulfillment.

Obligingly, he quickened his movements, lowering himself once more so that he could hug her against him, his mouth glued to hers as they reached the peak of ecstasy together. With tongues fencing furiously, they felt the explosive climax, so intense it left both of them shaking, their bodies continuing to throb from the aftereffects for several moments afterward.

Finally, Lucian rolled to the side, his breathing rapid, his chest rising and falling from his efforts. Almost timidly, Aimee moved sideways to lay her head on his chest and place one hand next to her cheek. Lucian reached his own hand down to stroke back her wet hair. Neither one of them spoke.

In the morning, Aimee awoke first, gazing down into her husband's face as he slept, memorizing every feature with a loving tenderness that caused a happy thrill to course through her. She watched him awaken, trying not to laugh at the bloodshot eyeballs that attested to his heavy drinking of the night before. When Lucian awoke he looked at her with a comic grimace, lifting one hand tentatively to his head, as though checking to see that it was still attached to his body.

"Was I very drunk?" he asked her.

She nodded with a mocking look in her green eyes that reproached him.

"But—it wasn't a dream, was it? We did—"

"We did," she affirmed with a grin, kissing him on the tip of his nose.

He let out a sigh of relief. "Oh, God! I thought I'd been dreaming!"

"I'm glad you weren't dreaming," she told him, kissing him again.

He eyed her with a wry mockery. "We've wasted too much time, Aimee," he told her, laying aside any pretense. "I want you as a wife—not just a co-worker or a conversation partner. I want —what we had last night. I want all of you!"

She purred like a contented kitten, rubbing her cheek against his chest. "I'm sorry for these past months, Lucian. I suppose I didn't deal very well with—with what happened to me. I somehow held it against you—even though I knew none of it was your fault. I had to blame someone, I suppose, and I could not face the blame myself. I understand that I've lost a baby, and I will always keep that memory in my heart—but, more importantly, I realize now that I don't want to lose a husband, too. You have become very important to me, my love."

He sighed contentedly. "You don't know how good that sounds, Aimee. I had begun to give up hope—I suppose that's why I was continually drowning my sorrows in brandy."

"Let's begin again," she told him, leaning up on her elbow to look into his eyes. "Let's shut the world out and concentrate on us."

32

Unfortunately, shutting out the world seemed quite impossible as events unfolded during the next months. As Violette's daughter grew stronger and even more adorable, events were taking shape in the world outside that would have repercussions on all of them. Napoleon Bonaparte was proving himself an able and ambitious leader, and once things had settled down at home, he concentrated on destroying his enemies. In June of 1800, he achieved a decisive victory against the Austrians at Marengo. His armies were winning all over the European continent and he felt the surge of power like heady wine, making him more interested in Talleyrand's subtle suggestions of extending French influence outside the sphere of Europe. Through Talleyrand's correspondence, Lucian found out that Bonaparte had agreed to end the sea war between France and the United States and also to hasten negotiations between France and Spain for the acquisition of the Louisiana Territory. Bonaparte formally offered peace to the United States, repealing decrees of harrying American ships and telling the American government that he would be receptive to any delegation they would send to France. Lucian could imagine Talleyrand's sense of a victory at hand. Bonaparte was buttering both sides of his bread, accepting delegations from the United States and reopening conversations with Spain with respect to New Orleans and the Louisiana Territory. After putting his stamp of approval on both these projects, he promptly ordered a wholesale increase of the French Navy and then returned to war.

In the fall, Lucian learned that a three-man American delegation to Paris had concluded a peace with Napoleon. Talleyrand also hinted a treaty had been signed between France and Spain that would decide the fate of the North American territory. Lucian wrote back anxiously for further enlightenment, but Talleyrand refused to release the secret terms of the treaty and, instead, ordered Lucian to the new United States capital of Washington City. There he would make contact with the French ambassador and the newly elected President, Thomas Jefferson.

Aimee received this news with trepidation. She had no inclination to go to Washington City. She pleaded with Lucian to disobey Talleyrand's request and stay in New Orleans; she was happy here with Violette and Dominic and their little Lenore. Despite Aimee's obvious reluctance, Lucian insisted that they must leave as soon as possible.

"But why?" Aimee wanted to know. "Why can't we remain here and build a home for ourselves, Lucian? I don't care if we aren't able to return to France in the future!"

"Darling, you know you're being ridiculous!" Lucian returned practically. "I can't imagine you giving up the future right to see your brother—your only living relative—and his family."

"But I don't *want* to go to Washington City!" Aimee reiterated firmly. "I don't want to have to be elegant and sociable for these rough, crude Americans! New Orleans has become my home in these last two years. We are to get a new governor soon who promises to be even more open-minded and indulgent than our current one. We—"

"Sweetheart, Juan de Salcedo is an officer in the Spanish Army—he will not be indulgent, believe me. In fact, he may even stir up old troubles between the citizens and the Spanish soldiers here. I have heard he is iron-willed and believes in the direct, dictatorial powers of the Spanish hierarchy. The only thing New Orleans can hope for is quick transferral into French or American hands!"

"But, what if the French do take over control?" Aimee argued. "Certainly that would be the very thing we've been waiting for!"

"But then Talleyrand would have complete jurisdiction over our welfare," he told her practically. "He would have us arrested, put in jail—anything he wished, actually, for we would be French citizens liable for our actions to the French government. He could very easily have us labeled traitors for refusing to follow his commands as Foreign Minister!"

"Oh!" Aimee cried, putting her hands over her ears, as though refusing to hear any more of his justifiable arguments. What a coil they had gotten themselves into! One thing was certain: she would have to give in with as much grace she could muster and follow her husband to Washington City. The thought still filled her with a mixture of revulsion and panic, but she could see that—for now, at least—there was nothing else to be done.

"All right." She sighed heavily. "I will go with you, Lucian, but you must promise me that we will return to New Orleans someday soon! I couldn't bear the thought of leaving Violette and her sweet little Lenore forever!"

He came and put his arms around her to hug her close. "All right, my sweet, I promise we will return as soon as it is possible."

"I—I suppose you will be wanting to visit your tobacco farm in Virginia while we are there," she said grudgingly, shuddering at the thought of having to meet his mother and grandmother. She could imagine the pair of them, crude women with a washerwoman's language and worse manners. Two women running a large estate—it was completely unheard of in France!

"Yes, we will visit the tobacco farm," he told her quickly. "I would like for you to meet my mother and grandmother. I know they will love you immediately."

She tried to smile and ended up looking forlorn. Lucian laughed at the look on her face and assured her it would be nothing like standing up before a firing squad, whereupon his irate wife pushed him away quickly and glared at him.

Two weeks later, in mid-January of 1801, almost exactly two years since they had come to New Orleans, Aimee and Lucian bid an emotional good-bye to the St. Cyrs, Aimee and Violette crying on each other's shoulders, while the baby added to the poignancy by wailing loudly in her mother's arms. Lucian gripped Dominic's hand firmly, each knowing without words that they would miss the other's friendship deeply.

"You will be careful," Dominic said softly, looking into his friend's blue eyes. "Washington City is a veritable nest of spies, all trying to do their jobs and discredit one another. It is full of the vipers' intrigue and you must tread very carefully, my friend."

"I do have a foot in since I have already met President-elect Jefferson," Lucian reminded him with a careless smile.

"Still, you must take care," Dominic advised him sternly. "You have Aimee to think of, too, remember."

"I will remember," Lucian said with more gravity and clasped his friend's hand in a hard shake.

A few minutes later, they were aboard their ship, which would take them back out to the Gulf of Mexico, then around the tip of Florida, and up the eastern Atlantic coastline to the fledgling city of Washington on the shores of the Potomac River. Aimee waved her handkerchief until her hand and arm were sore with the effort. Slowly, the ship slipped from her mooring place and cast out into the river, moving farther and farther away, until the wharf was very small and Violette and Dominic were no more than dark specks on the riverbank.

Turning to her husband, Aimee cried softly on his shoulder, afraid she would never see her friends again. Although Lucian had promised her to return, who knew what plans Talleyrand would have for him once he finished whatever work he had to do in Washington? Her heart sank at the notion that, as long as Talleyrand pulled the strings, they would never be free to do as they wished.

"What is it, darling?" Lucian murmured in her hair. "I know how sad you feel at leaving New Orleans, but you must believe me when I say you will see it again someday."

She nodded, pressing her handkerchief to her nose and sniffing. "Yes, of course, Lucian. I just hope that time can be soon."

He smiled and patted her soothingly. "I shall have to see what Talleyrand has in mind for me. He said in his last letter that there would be instructions awaiting me upon our arrival in Washington."

"Will we stay at the house with your mother?" Aimee asked anxiously.

"No, since that might prove a little inconvenient. My plantation is about forty miles southwest of the new capital. I've already sent letters, arranging for us to rent a home in Alexandria, a city about six miles south of Washington."

"We won't be staying with friends, then?" For some reason, the idea appealed to Aimee. Although she loved Violette dearly, the idea of being in a home of their own pleased her greatly. She realized it would be the first time she and her husband would have had a home to themselves. "And I can decorate in whatever way I wish?" she asked him excitedly.

He smiled to see the animation return to her lovely face. "Of course. I'm sure I can spare something from my accounts in Virginia to liven up the house. I don't know if there'll be much furniture already in it or not. Ordinarily, I would say there would be, but since this house has been unoccupied for some time, I don't know. Who knows, my dear, you may be able to start from scratch and decorate to your heart's desire." He kissed her on the tip of her nose. "That would please you, my sweet?"

She nodded. "Very much. I would make everything very French in flavor—just to irritate these American bumpkins!"

He laughed out loud. "They aren't all *bumpkins*, little wife.

Remember that many of them are descended from old, aristocratic families originally from England."

Her face resembled that of someone who had just bitten into a sour apple. "Ugh! In that case, they should prove even more uncouth!" she amended.

"You are a terrible snob!" he accused her, even as his arms went around her to press her lightly against him.

The ocean voyage was tedious, though not as long as the one from France to New Orleans. Still, the days seemed to go by faster than Aimee would have wished, as each one brought them closer to their destination. She could not shake the anxious feeling she felt every time she thought of meeting Lucian's mother. Would the woman like her? Would they get along well? She wanted to appear the most mannerly and genteel young woman that Lucian's mother would ever meet, but she was still insecure about meeting this mysterious woman, who was, after all, an American. Lucian had never even told her of their marriage, which gave her no comfort, since that meant her very existence would be a shock to his mother. Perhaps she already had someone else in mind—someone *American*—whom she thought would make the perfect wife for her son.

When she confessed her insecurities to her husband, Lucian simply laughed and told her she was being foolish—that his mother would love her instantly, just as he had.

The end of the voyage came too soon, as Aimee awoke one morning and came out on deck to see the wide Chesapeake Bay laid out before them. The ship pointed into it and she looked anxiously along the coastline, noting the river flats close by, climbing to gentle hills in the distance—the blue hills of Virginia, Lucian told her with a note of pride to his voice. Virgin forest and swampy creeks spread out all around the sides of the bay, so that this looked very much like a land that had barely been discovered, much less one that could hold the capital of a new nation.

The bay flowed from the Potomac River, Lucian explained, which they would see presently as they continued their voyage upriver. The captain had told them they would anchor just outside the mouth of the river that evening, so that they could arrive in the port of Alexandria early the next afternoon.

Aimee went to sleep, feeling restless and on edge, refusing Lucian's gentle overtures at lovemaking so that both of them finally went to sleep feeling rather surly. The next morning,

Aimee watched from the ship's railing as they entered the broad and serene Potomac River, which would lead them northwest to the city of Alexandria, just within the limits of the ten-mile-square District of Columbia, named after the explorer Christopher Columbus, Lucian had explained to her.

By lunchtime they had arrived, and Aimee looked out anxiously to the river wharf, noting the warehouses lining its riverbank and the merchant ships that stood at its docks. Beyond the warehouses, she could see a prosperous little Colonial town with shuttered houses that had gabled roofs, tiny dormers, and cobblestone streets in front. This city, as well as the city of Georgetown, farther upriver, was a tobacco-shipping port, Lucian explained, pointing out the rows of hogsheads that were used to store the tobacco when it was shipped out. They stood neatly in open crates, ready to be boarded up and brought on board several waiting schooners. All in all, Aimee was surprised to realize how bustling and industrious this city actually was. It reminded her a lot of New Orleans in its activity, if not in its architecture.

By the time they had come ashore and had hired a carriage to take them to Prince Street, she was beginning to feel rather welcome here. The people along the wharf seemed friendly enough, and they were not, by any means, all rivermen with hard faces and calloused hands. There were many merchants, dressed in fashionable clothing and with perfectly polite manners. Although many of them still adopted the old style of wearing their hair powdered or in wigs, Aimee was favorably impressed and relayed this information to her husband, who smiled to himself and watched as his wife gazed out the window of their carriage. Along the stretch of the river, there were many shops and warehouses, above which dormered windows attested to the fact that the upper stories were used as homes for the merchants' families. They passed several shops and taverns, as well as an apothecary shop, which, Lucian pointed out, had been established for some ten years and had gained a fine reputation of dispensing the correct medicine in the exact amounts required. One of the finest taverns in the little city, Gadsby's Tavern, would serve as a good place to have a meal this evening, Lucian suggested, since they would not have the luxury of having their meals cooked by a servant, until Aimee was able to hire a cook and maids.

The idea of being so in charge of her own destiny appealed greatly to Aimee, who, at twenty-one years of age, had still not had the opportunity to run a household of her own, something many young women her age had been doing since the age of sixteen. Marriages, Lucian told her, were encouraged at an early age, and, he reminded her, had she not been married to him, Aimee herself would have been considered an old maid, despite the fact that she was in blooming health and still three months away from her twenty-second birthday.

Finally, they arrived in the two-hundred block of Prince Street, a place of residence for many of the gentry of Virginia. Most of the houses were identical on the outside, pressed close to the brick sidewalk and all bearing their red-brick, three-story façades with a certain amount of regal grandeur. Aimee liked the effect of the dormers on the upper story and the white trim, incorporating classical motifs into the design. Also, the half circle fan light over the door met with her approval, for it helped to give the whole façade a graceful air of stateliness.

Inside, she was heartened to see lovely wood moldings around the ceilings and halfway up the walls, which were all painted in a soft gray. She told Lucian she would like to cover some of the walls with rich fabrics, perhaps silk or damask, to give them texture. Lucian smiled softly to see her growing interest in their house and complimented himself on having the real estate agent pick out the perfect home. There was not much furniture in the house. Most of what remained was done in heavy mahogany, which Aimee declared she would change to add gilt and enamel pieces, which had been so popular in France when she left. Fortunately, there was a bed left in one of the upstairs bedrooms, with a mattress that would serve until something better could be found. Linens had been stacked neatly in a heavy press on one wall of the bedroom, and to Aimee's relief it looked as though they would have no difficulty with their sleeping arrangements.

Lucian assured her there would have been no difficulty even without a bed in the house, since he would have been content to sleep on the floor as long as she was beside him. Aimee laughed at him, then ran to kiss him on tiptoes, wriggling out of his arms as he tried to keep her from running off into the next room.

"I'm very glad you like it," he told her, following her into the room. "You had me worried on the voyage from New Orleans. I was sure you would take one look at the house and promptly declare your refusal to stay here!"

She glanced back at him, her green eyes sparkling. "I have since rethought my position, my dearest husband," she informed him confidently. "And now that I can see I shall be very busy in the next few months while you take care of whatever it is you must, I will be very happy, indeed."

"I suppose decorating is dear to every woman's heart," he murmured, watching her with loving eyes as she flitted about the room. "You are exactly like my mother, Aimee."

The mention of his mother effectively served to douse some of Aimee's high spirits, but then she refused to lose her feeling of euphoria and brushed lingering worries aside, telling herself she would deal with them when the time came.

"When can I begin to buy new furniture?" she asked Lucian, glancing back at him over her shoulder as they descended the staircase.

"As soon as you like," he returned complacently. "I think you should also see to the employment of a few servants to help you in your endeavors. Tomorrow or the next day, we'll ride to Chesterfield Hall, where you will meet my mother and grandmother. They can help instruct you on where to find the best servants for the tasks at hand."

"But I am perfectly capable of doing that myself," Aimee returned quickly.

"I know, my dear, but I still want you to meet them. Please accept any help they may offer, for it will be offered in the spirit of love and kindness, you can be sure."

Aimee continued to grumble for a few moments, then sighed and shook her head, realizing she must begin to be gracious about his mother's probable influence on their lives while they were in Virginia. If Lucian's mother proved too domineering, Aimee resolved she would just turn a deaf ear to her proposals and do as she liked. After all, Lucian could not blame her for being concerned about this meeting. He hadn't even bothered to tell her when they had married that he had family still living—hadn't even told her he was half American. His little deception might prove rather uncomfortable for him now, but that was his own doing, she assured herself.

After dressing for dinner, they went to the tavern Lucian had mentioned earlier and settled down to a truly fine dinner of fowl and rich meat pies. Aimee drank a little too much wine in her nervousness, and by the time they returned home she was feeling somewhat adventurous and ran up the stairs, laughing loudly while Lucian pursued her. He caught up with her in the bedroom, exactly where she had hoped he would, and proceeded to undress her slowly and sensuously, taking the time to nibble every inch of her flesh in the process.

Swooning from the wine and the newness of everything and from her husband's ardent caresses, Aimee leaned back in his arms and let him carry her to the bed, depositing her on it and then stepping back to divest himself of his own garments. As always, Aimee marveled at the lean, corded muscles that stretched tautly in his arms and legs and banded across his back and chest.

"A superb physical specimen," she pronounced, watching him smile with a masculine smugness that delighted her.

Immediately, he leaped on the bed next to her, and for some time neither of them got to sleep.

33

"There's the house now," Lucian said with a note of growing pride in his voice as he pointed out the three-story pillared house of red brick.

Aimee leaned farther out the carriage window, intent on seeing this home that belonged to her husband's family. It was, she admitted, very beautifully laid out, with a large middle section of three stories and two side sections, each one story high, housing the kitchen on one side and the guest quarters on the other, he told her. The main portion of the house was bedecked with square columns that lent it considerable grandeur, as well as a balcony on the third story, just beneath the roof line, where a slanted roof rose steeply upward, topped by a charming colonnaded captain's walk. Lucian told her of the times he had climbed up to the captain's walk and taken his grandfather's telescope to look far past the gentle hills of Virginia to the sparkling sea beyond.

"Oh, Lucian, it's easy to tell that you were very happy here," she told him, her green eyes soft and dewy. "Were you happier here than in France, when your father took your mother to Paris?"

He shrugged. "They are so different, there is no comparison," he replied rather evasively. "Look, there is my mother on the porch, waving to us! She's so anxious to meet you, I know."

He had told her earlier that he had sent a message to his mother on the evening they had arrived in Virginia to tell her that he was bringing his new bride to see her. Aimee unconsciously leaned back inside the carriage, as though loath to expose herself to the eyes of her mother-in-law. She tried to shake the feeling that she was on the auction block here. After all, she was already married to Lucian—nothing was going to change that fact, no matter whether his mother approved of her or not. Anxiously, after smoothing the deep green velvet of her skirts, she pulled the warm, fox-lined cape around her shoulders. Unlike the warm climate of New Orleans, Virginia had a definite winter feeling about it on this late February day, and Lucian had been obliged to purchase hurriedly several outerwear garments for both of them upon their arrival.

Today, in fact, there had been a light dusting of snow on the ground, making the house and surrounding grounds seem even prettier and more enchanting, Aimee thought. It had surprised her to realize how much land her husband owned, and she realized that, without knowing it, she had married a wealthy man. The thought brought her little comfort today, though, for she was to meet this man's equally wealthy mother. Having come from a family that, although noble, had been very poor, Aimee felt her back stiffening, as though readying herself for a challenge. Carefully she composed herself, although she felt the involuntary tightening of her stomach muscles as the carriage stopped in the curved drive and Lucian jumped out ahead of her to open the door and greet his mother.

Before he could help his wife out, Martha Napier was rushing down from the porch steps, hugging her shawl about her narrow shoulders and launching herself at her son with a glad cry of welcome. Lucian held out his arms to her and hugged his mother close. Martha, her hair already showing speckles of white among the exact sable color of her son's, cried unashamedly upon holding her son in her arms.

"Oh, Lucian, I'm so happy to see you again!" she cried, obviously having missed her son greatly during his sojourn in Paris. "Hurry, you must bring your wife inside and warm yourselves in the parlor. I've had Sam stoke the fire up high, and there's hickory aplenty out back to lay on. Your grandmother is waiting impatiently inside. I told her the weather was far too cold for her to stick her nose out, but she is about to burst with eagerness to meet your bride—as we all are, my son!"

With some curiosity, but also with a warm smile on her face, Martha Napier peered inside the carriage, trying to make out the features of her new daughter-in-law. "My dear, forgive me for hanging on to my son! Come out and I'll show you inside the house. We are most anxious to meet you and welcome you into our home, my dear."

Feeling the tight constriction in her chest become somewhat eased by the warmth in that voice, Aimee stepped outside with her husband's aid and faced the woman she hadn't even known existed when she married her son. She saw a woman of about fifty, tall like her son, and with a straight-backed grace that was evident in the sweep of her hand and the tilt of her elegant head. Her blue eyes were warm and crinkling, the lines of age fanning out from the corners in a comforting way that reminded Aimee sharply of her own mother.

"I am so happy finally to meet you, Aimee," Martha was saying heartily, taking her mittened hand to pull Aimee closer. "Come inside at once, my dear, before your poor feet become frozen out here!"

"Thank you," Aimee replied a bit awkwardly, not knowing what to call her.

As though guessing her predicament, Martha tucked her mittened hand into the crook of Aimee's arm and patted it familiarly. "Please call me Martha, my dear. I realize this must all be very new for you yet, and a bit awkward still. Lucian's grandmother's name is Frances, and I'm sure she would be pleased to have you call her so."

"You are very kind, Martha," Aimee replied as they navigated the icy steps and hurried across the porch inside the doorway. Once inside, as they stood in a wide hallway, covered with braided rugs and pieces of satinwood furniture, Aimee took off her outerwear, noting the pert, little coffee-colored servant who took her wrap from her. Everything seemed spotless and she marveled at the quiet elegance of the interior of the house. They entered a parlor, the walls of which were covered in light blue silk that matched the swagged drapes at the long windows. Seated on a dark, damask Chippendale sofa was an elderly lady with powdered white hair done high on her head, similar to the style of Madame Pompadour when she had been mistress to Louis XV. A coquettish little curl streamed over her left shoulder, lying against the whiteness of paper-thin skin above the deep décolleté of her low-waisted, full-skirted dress.

"May I present Lucian's grandmother, my mother, Frances," Martha said smoothly, leading Aimee over to the older woman.

"I am so pleased to meet you," Aimee said, taking the hand extended out to her and curtsying easily.

"Well, it is about time that scamp married!" Frances Sheridan said in a high voice. "Martha and I were beginning to wonder if he would ever settle down and quit his rambling ways. He was in that accursed France more often than he was here!"

Martha colored at the insult done their guest, but Aimee shook her head, indicating there was no need for embarrassment.

Lucian hurried over to present himself to his grandmother, assuring her that he would be staying put—for a little while, at least—and that he wanted to remind her that his new bride was a Frenchwoman.

"A Frenchwoman! How odd that you should marry a woman from France!" his grandmother insisted rather garrulously. "I had always thought that you intended to marry a fellow Virginian!"

"Grandmother, don't be nasty," Lucian said with genuine fondness. "Aimee is a dozen times more charming than anyone I have ever met in Virginia, excluding yourself, of course. She is from Orléans, a city outside Paris."

"How did you manage to escape that horrible revolution?" Frances wanted to know, leaning forward eagerly.

"I—"

"Her family was killed during the revolution," Lucian offered quickly. "Her father was from the nobility. He was guillotined during the Great Terror, Grandmother."

"I'm so sorry," Martha said sympathetically. "And you lost your mother, also?"

"Yes." Aimee nodded, feeling a rush of tears gather in her eyes. "My mother and all of my brothers but one were killed by a madman, a butcher who took advantage of the general chaos of the country to put his ideas of revenge into practice. He was a *monster!*"

"How did you escape?" Frances demanded to know.

"I was not at the castle when this monster came to exact his revenge. I had been sent to a convent to receive my education. My oldest brother, Etienne, survived also because he was away from home. Together, we journeyed to Paris in order to find the man who had caused us so much suffering."

"And did you find him?" Frances commanded implacably, her faded blue eyes sharpening on Aimee's face.

"I did."

"And?"

"I killed him," Aimee said simply, staring back into the old woman's eyes as though daring her to reprimand her for the deed.

For a moment, everyone in the room was quiet. Aimee was aware of her heart beating wildly, wondering if she had said too much, if she had presented herself as a cold, vengeful young woman who was a murderess on top of being an "accursed" Frenchwoman. And then a smile cracked the thin lips of the old dowager and she rubbed her paper-thin hands together with something like glee.

"Good for you, girl, you've got spirit! The bastard deserved nothing less!"

If she was shocked at such language from her, Aimee didn't show it, for she smiled, too, feeling somehow accepted into this family and relieved and happy at the same time. She glanced over at Lucian, who winked at her as though to say she had said exactly the right thing. Martha smiled and nodded her head as though to say she, too, approved. Aimee felt quite at home.

"Sit down beside me, my dear," Frances said imperiously, patting the space on the divan with a welcoming hand. "I want you to tell me about your life in France—and how did you meet my grandson?"

Aimee seated herself and launched into a discussion of her meeting with Lucian, of her existence in Paris when she had lived with her aunt and made do as best she could. Frances murmured little words of encouragement when Aimee faltered over some of the worst of the times and expressed her sentiments loudly when Aimee told her of the horrors of the Reign of Terror. By the time she had drunk her third cup of hot tea, she felt quite cozy and even felt close to this gregarious old woman, who retained quite a bit of the regal serenity and the commanding stature of her younger days. Only her rheumatism, she said, held her back from doing all the things she used to love to do, like ride the horses and walk around the tobacco fields, watching the field hands at work and supervising the storage of the precious tobacco leaves.

"Martha has no sense for such things," Frances complained, eyeing her daughter accusingly. "And since Lucian is always about somewhere else, we're forced to rely on a hired foreman, more's the pity. Perhaps you can use your considerable influence to get him to settle down and attend to his duties here," Frances suggested.

Aimee smiled and shook her head. "I'm afraid my influence is actually very little," she confessed. "You see, I didn't even want to come here at all. I enjoyed New Orleans during our time there; we had made many friends and I'd grown comfortable with the way of life there. I tried to persuade Lucian to remain in New Orleans, but he refused. You see how little I can influence him."

"You must become a little wiser—and that comes with age, my dear," Frances assured her, patting her hand stoutly. "But you say you liked New Orleans? My dear, that is a *Spanish* territory. How could you possibly have wanted to stay there! Everyone knows they are the most dictatorial people in the world! I wouldn't live under their rule for the world!"

"Actually, their influence was felt very little," Aimee hastened to reply. "We were seldom aware of them, except for the drilling of the soldiers in the square."

"Ah, but such a decadent nation," Frances went on, refusing

to listen to any other opinion. "I hope to God that new President, Jefferson, can do something about them being on our back door-step! If he can't settle the thing peaceably, I'm all for going in and taking what should rightfully be ours. God knows, this continent stretches from east to west, ocean to ocean—someday it shall all belong to the United States, as well it should be!"

Martha exchanged a glance with her daughter-in-law. "My mother is very proud of her country," she explained quickly.

"As we all should be!" Frances put in emphatically. "This country will be greater than any of those decadent European nations that are constantly fighting among one another, weakening themselves in the process. Now with this new general . . . what is his name?" She looked to Lucian for help.

"Napoleon Bonaparte, Grandmother," Lucian supplied.

"Yes, this Bonaparte! Pah! He won't last long, mark my words—none of them do. Now, if he were here, an American, then he might have a chance, for we are still open to change, new ideas, a growing process. France—ha! It is too late for him there!"

"We shall see, Grandmother," Lucian suggested tactfully. "It matters very little to the United States who sits on the throne, of course, just so long as whoever it is treats us with respect. Somehow, I don't think this Bonaparte will do that. He is quite devious about getting what he wants—of course, that means getting what is good for himself and not always what is good for France."

"Then the people will throw him out eventually. They'll turn on him, just as they turned on their King," Frances said emphatically.

"He is not as stupid or complacent as Louis the Sixteenth was," Lucian returned smoothly. "Neither does he have a wife whom he allows to lead him about by the nose."

"Harrumph! Lucian, I'll not have you telling me that my opinion is wrong in this matter!" Frances responded a bit acidly. She looked over to her daughter. "Martha, when is dinner to be? I must admit to being tired now. Will you ring for one of the girls to help me up the stairs to my room? I'll take a short nap before we eat." She glanced over at Aimee. "You understand, don't you, my dear? If I don't rest, I'm afraid I may end up nodding over the soup course at dinner. One of the evils of getting old, I'm afraid." She patted her hand once more, then stood up with the help of a handsome ivory cane. When one of the black servants arrived, she left the room slowly.

"My mother has . . . strong opinions about nearly everything," Martha remarked somewhat apologetically.

"I think she is wonderful," Aimee replied truthfully. "She says what she thinks—and that is rather refreshing."

"I'm glad you like her. She will be very pleased," Martha responded with warmth.

"I only hope I can gain her favor—as well as yours, Martha," Aimee said with a little shyness, not wanting to be too bold.

"I can assure you, anyone Lucian had the good sense to marry already has my favor, as well as my mother's." Martha laughed, glancing at her son with a ready smile. "I despaired of ever having him married. I was afraid this plantation would have to be sold someday because there would be no heirs to run it."

"No, Mother, I've told you before," Lucian interjected seriously, "I can't promise you that I shall ever stay to run this plantation. I love it here, yes, but there are other things I feel compelled to do. Also, I've already promised Aimee that after our visit here is ended, we will return to New Orleans."

Martha's brows went up interrogatively. She looked at Aimee, who suddenly felt as though she had done a terrible thing by making Lucian promise to return to New Orleans with her. But, then, after a moment of silence, Martha shrugged.

"So? Then one of your sons will come back and love it as I do," she murmured softly.

Once ensconced in their assigned bedroom, Aimee dropped into a chair and propped her feet up on a hassock, staring at her husband as though seeing him for the first time. He noticed her look and stood in front of her, legs akimbo and his fists on his hips.

"What are you staring at, wife?" he asked her jovially.

"At you," she said pointedly. "It is very hard for me to reconcile the mocking policeman, the dangerous spy, with the man I know as the son of Martha Napier, and the grandson of Frances Sheridan. How did you ever become an agent of France, Lucian? With your background, it seems so unlikely."

He shrugged. "My father was an officer in the French Army. At a very young age, I was introduced to soldiering and the military ways of life. Despite some childhood vacations here in Chesterfield Hall, for the most part I followed my father everywhere. When he was killed, I lost my taste for soldiering, but I still enjoyed the intrigues of war, the behind-the-scenes deals that can truly make or break an army, no matter who wins the battle. I became adept at my work."

"And sold your services to the highest bidder?" she queried, with raised brows.

Another shrug. "My loyalty has always been to my country."

"But this United States is also your country," she pointed out quickly. "How can you turn your back on her?"

His keen blue eyes sharpened as they returned her stare. "So, what would you have me do, wife? Spy for both countries?"

She shook her head quickly and the sharpness went out of his glance. "No, of course not. I know that you love France and that you want to help her attain the greatness that your grandmother seems to think will always be elusive. And yet, there is a great love in you for this country, for this Virginia estate. The pull on you is strong, Lucian."

"Yes, I admit it. Perhaps that is why I stay away from this place more than my mother would like. It would be very easy to settle down with a pipe between my teeth and a cool drink in my hand while my slaves would raise the tobacco and big profits would make me even wealthier. But that kind of life has no adventure, no real meaning for me."

"You mean you cannot live without some danger?" she asked him steadily. And he nodded. "But you have a wife now," she went on. "And someday you will have a family. I won't have our son following you around in your spying missions, like you followed your father around in his military escapades."

He looked uncomfortable for a moment. "We will have to cross that bridge when we come to it," he said finally.

"But, Lucian, you can't just push it out of your mind," she returned. "I love you, but I can't go on living a life in which we're constantly on the move. At some point, after a child, or perhaps even before, I'll want to make a real home for us!"

"Darling, you've got to trust me on this," he said, kneeling suddenly in front of her and laying his hands on her knees. "I know it is hard for you now, but believe me, soon there will come a time when we won't be moving around, when we—"

"When? When will that be?"

He stood up again and paced for a moment. "Soon," he said definitely.

It was on the tip of her tongue to press him for a more specific time, but she realized suddenly that she was only putting him under greater strain. He needed all his wits about him for the delicate mission that he must undertake for Talleyrand. He would be assisting the French ambassador, in a somewhat clandestine manner, to learn which way the wind blew in Washington City concerning the alliance with the English. Jefferson had hinted before that if the French did not prove satisfactory allies, the Americans would have little choice other than to marry themselves to the British. Needless to say, this had not gone over well in the French government. Lucian was to feel his way around the city, find out what the British were up to, and report on it to Talleyrand. If the Americans decided to ally themselves with the British, he was to report it immediately so that the French could take quick action to retaliate. War on the high seas could be renewed and many ships and men would be taken before Jefferson even knew what was happening. The trump card might even be the purchase of the Louisiana Territory from Spain. If France had truly negotiated such a deal, they could use that land as leverage against the United States. Either way, Talleyrand must keep the Americans guessing as long as possible as to the French intentions. Bonaparte needed time to expand his navy and consolidate his victories on the Continent. Only when he had defeated his enemies there could he turn his attention to the English—and to any allies they might have made in the interim.

Thinking of all this and seeing the closed, tense look on her husband's face, Aimee sighed and shoved her own doubts aside. As long as they were together, she supposed she would have to be content for the time being. Perhaps, as Violette had told her after she'd lost the baby, God had seen the outcome of that drive along the river road as the wind of destiny, of fate. If she had come to term and delivered a son to her husband, how much more pressure would that have put upon him? And, too, she felt certain that Martha and Frances would have been much more vocal about their staying here at Chesterfield Hall. The longed-for heir—they would not let him out of their sight very easily.

"Lucian, I'm sorry," she said, catching him off guard. "I know you have so much on your mind that my badgering you does more harm than good."

He drew her into his arms with a grateful smile. "Do you realize what a treasure I have found in you?" he stated, nuzzling the side of her neck.

She arched her back, unconsciously striving for contact with him, pushing her breasts into his chest, grinding her hips against his in a blatant invitation that even a lesser man could not have let go by unchallenged. Quickly, watching each other with burning eyes and without shame, they undressed slowly, seductively, drawing out the moment as long as they could stand it. Then, with a low groan, Lucian picked her up in his arms and carried her to the braided rug before the fireplace. When Aimee questioned him silently with raised brows, he smiled ruefully.

"This used to be my bedroom, sweetheart. I know from experience—the bed creaks!"

She wrinkled her nose and laughed, but the laughter died away quickly as he lowered himself beside her and proceeded to make exquisite love to her. Tenderly, he let his lips wander as they would, from her soft, shining hair to her forehead, down her nose and slanting against her lips, which opened beneath his. His hands caressed the perfect globes of her breasts, brushing the nipples with his open palms, before coming back to massage the entire breast in light movements that soon caused a tingling sensation in both of them. Meanwhile, he continued to kiss her, weaving his tongue in and out of her mouth, curling around her own so that she lay back, her eyes closed, enjoying the pleasurable sensations he was producing inside her body.

When his mouth left hers and started downward, she pushed him away for a moment, gazing up into his eyes with a sleeping passion. "Show me what to do for you," she whispered huskily, seeing the pleasurable surprise in his eyes.

Eagerly, she pushed him down on the rug and let her mouth cover his while she brushed at his chest with her hands and used the same movement on his nipples as he had used on hers. With the palm of her hands, she brushed against them until they stiffened, emboldening her to bring her mouth to them, licking and biting at them quite lasciviously until she heard her husband moan deep in his throat.

Feeling flushed with her triumph, she let her hands roam lower, down over his hard, flat stomach, feeling the muscles beneath the skin as they rippled involuntarily in eager anticipation. More hesitantly, she felt the crispness of his pubic hairs, tangling her fingers in them, before bumping against the hard shaft of his manhood. Curiously, she raised herself up, looking down at this wondrous gift that could pleasure her so. Cautiously, she grasped it, hearing the loud whoosh of his breath as she did so. He gasped out the movement he wanted from her and she obeyed, watching with heightened breathing as the flesh darkened and stiffened beneath her touch.

"Darling, finish it!" he groaned aloud, his eyes closed. "Ride on top of me, my beautiful wife!"

Hesitantly, Aimee swung her leg across him, straightening up and then lowering herself carefully, feeling the hot shaft of his manhood nudging between her thighs most suggestively. With a quick movement of his hips, he positioned it beneath her. Then, with his hands on her hips, he pushed her downward. She gasped, her breath tearing away from her throat, as that pulsing member was pushed deep inside her. For a moment she stiffened. Then, at his urging, she relaxed and sat astride him, rocking gently back and forth, to his delight. Feeling more sure of herself as she saw the pleasure registered on Lucian's features, Aimee leaned forward on her knees and wriggled her bottom deliciously against him so that he rolled his eyes upward and warned her to be careful lest he lose himself too quickly. She smiled with triumph, bringing her hips up and down with slow, strong strokes that seemed to madden him further.

Finally, Lucian could stand it no longer, and he quickly put his hands around her waist and lifted her up and down, pressing his own loins against her faster and faster until he exploded inside her. Aimee watched the pleasure cross his face, intent on the emotions she could see in this new position. Slowly, she relaxed against him, lowering her upper body so that she could press her breasts against his chest.

Cupping her face in his hands, Lucian opened his eyes and leaned forward to capture her lips once more. "My God, woman, you'll be the death of me!" he swore softly, nibbling her lips and gazing at her with pleasure-filled eyes.

"Oh, no!" Aimee said quickly, moving on top of him once more. "You can't possibly die on me, my darling. I'm enjoying this much too much!"

34

The few days they visited at the tobacco farm were idyllic for Aimee and Lucian. There was feisty and uplifting conversation with Lucian's grandmother, who seemed to enjoy mightily getting a rise out of her grandson's new wife, although she never pushed it to such an extreme that it would get in the way of their newfound friendship. Martha was the very antithesis of what Aimee had expected and dreaded. She had welcomed her new daughter-in-law with love and warmth, making Aimee feel so welcome that she felt she had known the woman her whole life. Many was the time that she found herself comparing the woman favorably to her own, dead mother—and this made her feel even closer to her.

Despite the wintry chill, Lucian insisted on taking Aimee around the perimeters of his land. They had bundled up in warm clothing to ride horses around the wintry whiteness of his many acres. They had ridden past the slave quarters, square, two-room buildings, each with its own plot of ground to grow vegetables in the spring and summer months. Some of the women were house slaves, but many of the others were field hands and spent these winter months doing light chores in their own homes and seeing to the needs of their husbands and children. Most of the men were employed in cleaning out and refurbishing the tobacco warehouses and storage areas, anticipating an early spring so that they might begin planting soon.

The overseer was a pleasant, bluff man in his late forties who seemed to enjoy his work greatly. It was easy to see that Lucian trusted him implicitly and that the overseer respected his absent master very much, despite the difference in their ages. Jovially, he had insisted the two of them come into his home, a one-story, white-brick building that housed five rooms and was quite well appointed, Aimee thought as she greeted the wife and three children of the man.

As they rode back to the Hall, Aimee watched the mist-white breath of her horse blowing out into the cool air and commented to Lucian about how well run the place seemed, certainly more efficient than many of the lands in France on which the peasants had worked for years.

"We are newer and have learned from the mistakes of the European countries," he said gravely. "Although I cannot justify the attitudes of some of the owners of these plantations in the way they treat their slaves and hired help, I refuse to treat my people with anything less than human respect."

"And it shows in their love for you," Aimee said proudly, feeling her heart swell at the thought that this wonderful man was her husband.

They returned to the house and a lovely lunch that Martha had prepared herself. Sitting at the dining table, listening to the wealth of conversation on so many subjects drifting around her, Aimee felt at peace. Although the memories of New Orleans still tugged at her heart, she realized this place was also very close to her heart and that she would certainly insist on visiting Chesterfield Hall many times throughout the years—especially, she thought with sudden longing, when she once more conceived a child. Martha had hinted more than once how much she longed for grandchildren, and Aimee had thought determinedly that she was more than willing to supply them. The thought made her smile, then blush, as she caught her husband's eye across the table. Lucian returned her smile, his blue eyes wicked as they divined the reason for her blush.

Later that afternoon, they packed their bags and, with teary good-byes, bade farewell to Frances and Martha to return to their rented house on Prince Street in Alexandria. Martha had given her names of two reputable furniture houses in the area, and also several recommendations on acquiring servants for the house.

Within a week after returning home, Aimee had hired a cook and two serving maids who would see to all the housework. She had purchased some furniture, including tables and chairs, and heavier pieces done in the Chippendale style that combined the graceful lines of Queen Anne furniture with the more elaborate rococo. There was a new linen press with Chinese-carved motifs and a library bookcase done in a Gothic style that seemed to draw the eye as it stood majestically against one wall of the newly redecorated study, which she had papered in soft tones of brown for her husband. She bought mahogany-and-gilt, mirrored sconces for the walls, French porcelain vases made in Sèvres, and a Hepplewhite-style mahogany linen press that she would use for extra storage.

Their bedroom she saved for last, ordering a soft, spring-green fabric with a rich texture for the walls, and several large Turkish carpets for the wooden flooring. The bed would stay, but she purchased a new mattress, for the old one had too many lumps in it, she had discovered. She surveyed the room with satisfaction, amazed at how quickly she had been able to find everything and hire workers to do the room exactly as she wanted it. Lucian, too, was favorably impressed and declared he had never realized the extent of his wife's talents until now.

At the very beginning of March, Lucian told her that they would be attending the new President's inauguration on the fourth. Only two days away, Aimee was slightly miffed that Lucian had waited until the last possible moment. Fretting out loud, she declared she had nothing fit to wear, upon which Lucian burst into laughter.

"I didn't think you cared how you looked to these 'crude, rough Americans'!" he told her, not able to resist the temptation. "I do believe that's how you described them earlier."

"Oh, you would throw that back in my face!" she accused him, half seriously.

"Well, you did say—"

"I said a lot of things that were stupid and immature!" Aimee returned quickly. "I have the grace, I believe, to admit that, and I would thank my husband to let the matter drop! Now, tell me, what shall I wear to the inauguration?"

Finally, it was decided that she would wear a high-waisted, round-necked dress of sky-blue velvet with a matching hat and reticule, as well as a small capelet edged in ermine to keep her warm should the weather prove unseasonably cold.

On the appointed day, Aimee settled herself in the carriage and prepared to meet this newly elected President of the United States with a great deal of caution. Despite her changing feelings toward the Americans, she still could not trust them completely, especially since she knew that their relations with her mother country were a bit strained, to say the least. She wondered how Lucian and she would be perceived, coming as they did from one of those "old, decadent" European nations, but Lucian assured her that President Jefferson was quite the diplomat and had always loved France, having lived there for several years before the outbreak of the revolution.

Still, Aimee felt many reservations surface as they were ferried across the river, and she found herself in the new District of Columbia. To her surprise, this capital of a new nation looked more like a frontier trading settlement than the seat of government. The streets were unpaved and there were very few light poles anywhere along them. There were no grand avenues, only fields and trees and the river. She could see men in powdered wigs and knee breeches with their ladies wading through the street mud on their way to the inauguration at the unimposing Capitol building, which stood on top of a small knoll called Jenkins Hill. Nobody seemed to care that it was an untidy town, provincial and possibly poorly managed. It was truly a town of trade more than a town of government, and Aimee told her husband so.

Lucian smiled grimly. "Yes, it really is not very impressive when you think of Versailles or Paris or London, is it, my dear? Yet, their intentions are good, and I feel certain someday it will take its place among the great capitals of the world."

"How can you be so sure that this country will survive that long?" Aimee asked with an edge in her voice.

He shrugged. "When you meet Thomas Jefferson and the others of his Cabinet, you may change your opinion," he promised.

Aimee felt dubious about that, but kept her opinions to herself. She was willing to be fair, although she wondered why anyone would want to live in this conglomeration of swamps and river flats, much less build a capital here. When Lucian explained that this site had been chosen by George Washington himself, the first President of the United States, because of his ties to Virginia and the fact that he had had to compromise between a site in the industrial north and the agrarian south, Aimee still could not think of a more unpromising location. Surely, it should at least resemble a capital and not a farming community, she remarked archly, whereupon Lucian laughed and assured her that was exactly what the southern states enjoyed about the new capital. They preferred a loosely knit central government and favored their own states' rights.

"A capital that resembles nothing more than a trading town is preferable to them, rather than the grandeur of a Versailles," he explained easily.

"But it doesn't impress foreign dignitaries," she offered promptly.

"That's true," Lucian agreed. "In fact, I've heard that any foreign minister who is sent to America considers it the worst possible assignment, for it means they will have to live in Washington City, where there is, as yet, no culture, no art galleries, no museums, and little chance for stage or opera shows."

"So what do we do while we're here?" Aimee asked on a sigh, realizing how dreadful this assignment could very well turn out to be.

"The city is full of intrigue," Lucian returned with a sparkle in his blue eyes. "A hornet's nest of spies and agents that makes it all very exciting and worthwhile, in my opinion!"

They went on, managing to keep from getting stuck in the mud of the road, until they arrived in front of the newly finished portion of the Capitol building, the north wing of which would be obliged to hold both Houses of the Legislature, as well as the six Supreme Court justices and the fledgling Library of Congress, until other buildings could be started. The only three official government buildings, Lucian told her, that had been begun to be constructed were the Capitol building, the Treasury building, and the President's mansion, as it was known. He pointed out the clearing that ran from the Capitol building to the President's house and told her that was to be Pennsylvania Avenue, although right now she could see trees felled to either side of it and only an unpaved stretch of road stopping at what looked like a half-finished house and continuing on the other side as a muddy little path leading through the woods.

Carefully, she alighted from the carriage and followed her husband up the steps inside the sandstone building that was most unimposing. Inside, there was a press of people—too much noise, too much heat despite the chill outside. She was glad for the small fan she had tucked into her sleeve and brought it out now to wave in front of her face, wrinkling her nose at the myriad of smells she perceived in the tight room. Somewhere in front of her, she knew the newly elected President was taking his oath of office, but in the crowd, she could distinguish very little. She stood next to Lucian, hoping that her toes would not get stepped on in their thin satin slippers and that she wouldn't be trampled on when it came time to exit.

The ceremony lasted too long for comfort, and Aimee was more than relieved when it was over. After the ceremony, Thomas Jefferson, only the third man to be elected President in this new nation, left the Capitol to return to his house. The officials, workmen, and the public simply followed him down the muddy stretch of Pennsylvania Avenue to the house, where a general reception was to be held.

Upon arrival at the President's "mansion," Aimee caught her breath in surprise. *This* was considered a fit place for the highest office-holder in the land to live? she wondered. Why, it wasn't even finished, and all around it were pits dug into the swampy terrain filled with tools and bricks and discarded materials. It resembled a house sitting in the middle of a squalid junk pile, while flowing in front of it, to the south, was a canal. When Aimee questioned her husband in alarm, Lucian, looking distinctly uncomfortable, admitted the place was barely suitable as an abode, but that plans were being made to drain the canal and put an avenue in its place.

The inside, Aimee thought, was not much better, for it was little more than a cold, bare shell full of workmen and rubble, with no permanent stairs to lead up to the six upper-story rooms, and only two rooms finished downstairs with very little light or heat. Looking out one of the windows, Aimee could see carpenters' shacks and pits for mortar and plaster surrounding the house. There were no lawns, paths, or stables. She felt her opinion of this new nation begin to plummet sharply. Why, this was a disgrace! It was ludicrous! Across from the north entrance of the house, Lucian admitted there was a racetrack where the local gentry raced their thoroughbreds, and between the house and the racetrack was a swampy area that was known simply as the President's Square, a veritable slap in the face, Aimee thought.

"Lucian, this is a disgrace—especially with all the foreign dignitaries here," Aimee whispered as they made their way around the two rooms and up a temporary flight of stairs, after which they came into an oval room furnished as a drawing room with crimson fabrics, decorated, someone said, by the previous President's wife, Abigail Adams.

"Jefferson has a great many plans for it," Lucian replied defensively. "He is a pretty good architect and has drawn up a whole set of drawings that will add colonnades to either side. And once the canal is drained and the swampy square filled in, I'm sure he will have trees and shrubbery planted that will make this look more fitting for a President to live in."

"How can you be so sure?" Aimee wondered with a frown. "Isn't it true that Jefferson is a widower? There'll be no lady's touches to soften the usual formality of a man's taste. This could very well be a horrid place once he's done with it!"

"The President does have two married daughters who live away from Washington, but they will certainly be visiting quite often. Also, even though the Vice-President, Aaron Burr, is also a widower, the new Secretary of State, James Madison, has a vivacious little wife who will be the designated hostess during Jefferson's term. She is said to have a wonderful sense of decor, and no doubt will be called upon to exercise it."

Aimee truly doubted that anything could be done with this house, but she decided to complain no more, realizing that her doubts had probably been mirrored on her face, and she didn't want to cause undue attention. Already, she had noted a tall, rather handsome man, perhaps forty years old, who had been staring at her for several minutes. He was being quite rude, actually, and she turned away from where he was standing at a window, hoping to discourage such blatant scrutiny. Probably some impossible American who had no manners to speak of, she thought snobbishly.

They moved into an oval yellow room that someone jokingly said would be known as the Ladies' Drawing Room, since this was the room designated by the President's daughters as their place of entertainment when they visited their father. Aimee caught a glimpse of one of the daughters, a tall, fair-haired young woman who seemed to enjoy her position as official hostess for the inaugural celebration.

But then her attention was diverted as her husband took her arm firmly and pushed her forward through the crowd in order to introduce her to the President himself. Aimee was favorably impressed upon getting her first good look at Thomas Jefferson. She took in the tall, large-boned, slim man, who, although he was nearly sixty, still stood erect and sinewy. He had angular features, a ruddy complexion, and sandy hair that was thinning slightly on top. His carriage seemed relaxed and he was, she thought, rather pleasant-looking on the whole, although his hazel-flecked gray eyes displayed an impressive wealth of learning and intelligence as they watched this young woman being brought forward.

"Mr. President, may I present my wife, Aimee de Chartres Napier, of France," Lucian said proudly as Aimee curtsied grandly, despite the fact that she felt perspiration dotting her forehead and wondered if her chignon was wilting under the press of humanity.

"Welcome to our country, Mrs. Napier," Jefferson said in a deep, pleasant voice. "I have long admired the French people and have hoped for many years that they might find a true and lasting republic as we here, in the United States, have. Alas, it seems more than ever that they have not the consistency to operate under the rule of the people, but need more direct control from a single man to decide their fate."

Aimee had to catch her breath in order to keep from staring openmouthed at this man who had immediately launched into a political discussion with a woman he had only just met. Recovering her aplomb, she responded carefully, "Our government is still in transition, Mr. President. Unfortunately, we have had many years of rule under one man, and it is very hard to unburden ourselves of that."

Jefferson smiled, pleased with her wit and intelligence. "That is quite true, Mrs. Napier. It is hard to unburden oneself of the yoke once it has been cast on. Even for our young nation, having only so recently delivered ourselves from the tyrants across the ocean, it was difficult to tear ourselves away from a steady economy, a sense of belonging to one nation. Only through strong and courageous men can this be accomplished." He turned to Lucian. "And you, Mr. Napier, shall you prove to be one of those courageous men? I know you have extensive acreage not very far from here. Your dear mother has had me over twice for excellent luncheons at which I thoroughly enjoyed the witty conversation of your grandmother. Tell me, do they have plans to visit the capital?"

Lucian smiled. "The weather is not conducive to my grandmother's state of health, Mr. President, but I can assure you they will be up when the weather turns warm in the spring." He bowed and led his wife away, promising to make a more personal visit sometime after the excitement of the change in administration had died down.

"What do you think, sweetheart?" he asked Aimee when they were out of earshot of the President.

"He is a most learned man, Lucian," she replied carefully. "I am glad that he favors the French; yet, his favoritism is not uncritical."

"I know he is fond of most things French. In fact, he has stated that he would like to decorate his house in the French style. But I do believe he was mightily confounded when the French revolution did not bring about the same governmental tendencies that the American revolution did."

Aimee nodded to a small, dark-haired, balding man who was standing a few feet away from the President, wondering who he was.

"That is the new Vice-President, Aaron Burr," Lucian commented. "He is a rather hot-tempered man who needs some restraint if he is going to carry out the duties of his office. He hails from New York, a state totally different in temperament from our lazy, easygoing Virginia. Here you have the classic differences between the north and the south. Hopefully, the two together will be able to appease both sections of the country and help bring the nation forward."

"You don't seem too pleased with the Vice-Presidential choice," Aimee said thoughtfully.

"I would rather have seen James Madison in that position since he is a longtime cohort of Tom Jefferson. But he will make an able Secretary of State, as he has had extensive background in foreign affairs."

He nodded discreetly to a small, slender man with a fair complexion and light hair who was standing a little by himself, conversing with a vivacious, dark-haired lady who seemed bent on making the man smile. Aimee noticed immediately the strong features and deepset eyes, but what impressed her most were the dignified bearing and the elegant clothes of the man, who seemed quite vain and more than a little arrogant.

"Who is he?" she wanted to know.

"Alexander Hamilton, our former Secretary of the Treasury, and the leader of the Federalist Party, which advocates a strong central government and close ties to Great Britain. He looks a bit uncomfortable surrounded by all these republicans, don't you think?" He laughed.

"He favors Great Britain, a country from which this nation only just freed itself?" Aimee asked, not understanding. "That would seem a most foolish loyalty."

Lucian shrugged. "He does not see it so. He has professed to despise the French notion of liberty and equality for everyone; that is why he doesn't see eye to eye with Jefferson, who wrote the Declaration of Independence for the United States. His interests are those of the north, since he, like Burr, is from New York. In fact, I have heard he is retiring from active politics to go into private law practice and write essays on the wisdom of a strong, central government."

"I don't think I want you to introduce me to him," Aimee said, with a shudder. "He would not appreciate the addition of two Frenchmen to his nation, I'm sure."

"Oh, I've had some uproarious conversations with the man on my previous visits here," Lucian assured her. "Believe me, he can roar like a lion, but there is not an evil bone in the man's body. He loathes violence. In fact, it was a tragedy when, only recently, his oldest son was killed in a duel. Hamilton would like to outlaw the practice altogether and have anyone convicted of participating in a duel sent to prison."

"How sad that is about his son," Aimee said sympathetically, revising her opinion of the man a little.

"And there," Lucian went on, pointing out the powerful people in Washington, "is the illustrious John Marshall, who you may recall from the infamous XYZ Affair that caused such a furor here in the United States and rather badly discredited our own dear Talleyrand for his part in offering the Americans access to the government heads in exchange for bribes to him. It was quite uncharacteristic of Talleyrand, quite stupid, actually. Now that same John Marshall, who was one of the dignitaries sent to France and then removed in anger, is the Chief Justice of the Supreme Court. The explanation of the laws of the Constitution and their practical application are in his hands. Would you like to meet him, my dear?"

She shook her head. "I don't think we would be favorably received, Lucian. He may still be antagonistic toward all things French." She glanced up at him curiously. "How can you be so calm and cool in the midst of all these men who would like nothing better than to see you drawn and quartered if they knew of your mission for Talleyrand?"

"Hush, my dear, there'll be no loose talk among so many who, as you say, would be quite interested in such information."

"Like him, over there?" Aimee nodded to the tall man who had been watching her earlier from the window. "He has been following us with his eyes all evening, until I get the uncomfortable feeling that we are the ones who are being spied upon!"

Lucian looked casually in the man's direction, then stiffened upon recognizing the interested party. "That is Garth Cabot, my dear, a rather nasty man whose allegiance is tied directly to the English. He is, to put it simply, an English spy, placed here in Washington City for the express purpose of giving aid to those like Hamilton and Burr who favor the English. He would like nothing better than to bring about the destruction of the political careers of Jefferson and Madison. A dangerous man, little one, and one I would prefer you not get involved with."

"But he is quite handsome," Aimee remarked teasingly. "And it is almost a relief that he is not one of these Americans with their intense party loyalties and infighting. Goodness, it's really a wonder that anyone can get elected to the office of President here!"

"Darling, Cabot has his own brand of loyalty—to himself!

Just be careful if you find an occasion where you are obliged to speak with him."

"Is he married?" Aimee wondered curiously, looking about for a woman who might seem to belong to him.

"Yes. His wife, Lianne, is an invalid, though. She only occasionally is able to get up from her bed and attend any social functions, although she enjoys entertaining in her own home and is really quite a bright hostess among the mud and swamp of Washington. They live in a home in Georgetown, a river port quite similar to Alexandria that is just to the northwest of the capital."

Lucian stopped suddenly as he saw Garth Cabot begin to move toward him from the window. Aimee felt her husband tensing as though preparing himself for an underhanded blow that might come from any angle. She couldn't help the tension that she herself felt, wondering if this man would pose a real threat to the safety of herself or her husband.

Upon closer inspection of the man, Aimee realized he was not as handsome as she had first surmised. There was a look of cunning in his hazel eyes that made her shiver, and when he smiled his mouth resembled nothing more than a wary wolf baring his fangs, a condition heightened by the sharpness of his nose and chin.

"So, Napier, I see you have come back to the United States. The last time I saw you—let's see, in Philadelphia, wasn't it?"

"Yes," Lucian confirmed with formal courtesy, shaking the man's proffered hand briefly.

"And this time, it seems, you have arrived with someone quite unexpected—and quite lovely," he went on, bowing over Aimee's hand. His fingers touched hers and she felt as though she had been scalded. "Madame, you have lightened these dreary hours for me considerably and I look forward to seeing more of your delightful company."

"This is my wife, Aimee," Lucian responded aggressively.

"Ah, then you must make the acquaintance of my own dear wife," Cabot added swiftly. "I insist, madame, that you must present yourself at my home in Georgetown at your earliest convenience." He touched her hand once more with his lips. Then, with a mocking smile to Lucian, he made his way through the crowd and disappeared.

"I don't like him," Aimee said, wiping her hand on the skirt of her dress.

"Unfortunately, most everyone else in Washington City thinks him quite charming," Lucian said. "He has seduced a number of wives among the government workers, all for the good of his country, no doubt," he added with a twist of his lips.

"You are not blameless yourself in that area," Aimee reproached him gently.

"Ah, but I was not married when I conducted myself with ease through the political boudoirs," Lucian reminded her with gentle mockery.

Aimee took out her fan and moved it back and forth in front of her face. She suddenly felt tired and wanted to return to the house on Prince Street, to feel her husband close against her, with his arms wrapped protectively around her.

"Darling?" she asked suddenly. "Can we leave now? I have seen enough of the people here and would rather be alone with my handsome husband."

"But they are just putting out the food," he told her in surprise. "Afterward, there'll be plenty of time for conversation and time for you to introduce yourself to many of the prominent ladies of the city. It could help—"

"Please, Lucian," she responded. "I would like to leave!"

He shrugged. "All right, my dear, if you are so insistent, although I believe we are passing up a golden opportunity."

How anyone would be able to remember a new face in all this press, Aimee could not imagine. To her it would be useless time spent to remain and try to converse with these women.

Gratefully, she settled back in the carriage seat, snuggling close to her husband, trying not to grit her teeth at every muddy bounce and jolt of the carriage. The idea of existence in this new and rough city filled her with a quiet dread and she could well imagine how any foreign diplomat would feel in the same situation. She remembered, upon meeting the French ambassador a few days before, the look of resigned displeasure on the face of his wife, which, she thought, must be mirrored in her own eyes. For the first time in many weeks, she thought longingly of New Orleans, picturing the sunny weather, the friendly faces, and the sense of cultured elegance that she was missing so sorely.

35

· · · · · · ·

The days in their cozy home in Alexandria took on a routine
sameness that at first soothed Aimee's spirit and then caused her
restless nature to come to the fore. Spring had finally come to
Virginia in mid-April and she felt the need to break her routine
and become once more immersed in the affairs of her husband.
Upon receiving an invitation to a small tea at the home of Mrs.
Lianne Cabot, she promptly accepted without thinking, or wondering, what reaction Lucian might have.

When he returned that evening from his duties with the French
ambassador, she informed him of her decision and he frowned,
gazing curiously at her. "Why did you accept, Aimee, when you
know how dangerous the man is? Believe me, he is not a friend
of the French, and I cannot see any reason for him to be friendly
toward you—unless he is trying to seduce you and learn my
secrets."

Aimee flushed at his directness. "I'm tired of sitting here,
purchasing furniture or doing shopping. There is no excitement in
my life," she said with a challenge. "You've managed to shut me
out of yours and . . . even our time together in the evening is . . .
well, not what it was," she ended a bit awkwardly.

Lucian's keen blue eyes narrowed and his mouth turned down
in a mocking frown. "What, have I been neglecting you too
much, my dear?" he asked her in the voice of a father talking to a
spoiled child. "Really, I had thought my first duty was to that
country you are constantly harping about, and to the preservation
of our place here in Washington society. I'm afraid the wife of a
spy cannot always claim adventure, my dear, no matter what your
earlier notions were. Most of the time it is a rather tedious business."

"Yes, I'm beginning to find that out!" she snapped back irri-
tably, hating the way he was talking down to her.

"And so what do you propose to do about it? Land yourself in
the spider's web? You may find yourself in more trouble and with
more adventure on your hands than you might like, my dear."

"I am going anyway," Aimee returned stubbornly. "It is only

for ladies, and I don't see the harm in making her acquaintance. After all, you said she was one of the most brilliant hostesses in Washington. Surely, I will have occasion to meet many of the wives of the government officials. Who knows—I may be able to glean some information that will make our assignment here end all that much quicker. And that would be most satisfactory to me!" She turned on her heel and flounced out of the room, leaving a husband who wondered whether he should follow her and make passionate love to her or bend her over his knee and spank her soundly.

A few days later, Aimee, having dressed with especial care on this afternoon of her societal debut, was deposited in front of an imposing residence on Twenty-eighth Street in Georgetown. Carefully smoothing down any wrinkles in the skirt of her gown, Aimee walked up to the front door and knocked firmly with one gloved hand, awaiting the arrival of a servant, who opened the door quickly and bade her come in. Her wrap was taken and she was guided into a long, high-ceilinged salon where the central figure was easily the gilt-haired woman who sat rather laconically in a wheelchair, her bright eyes listening avidly to the conversations of several women all at the same time.

Upon seeing a new arrival, she wheeled her chair slowly toward Aimee, smiling invitingly and holding out her hand for Aimee to take. Carefully, the woman rose from the chair in order to greet her guest properly.

"I am Lianne Cabot," she said in a low-toned voice. She was not quite what Aimee had expected: a small-boned, pretty-faced woman with expressive blue eyes and a bow-shaped mouth that seemed to be perpetually puckered in a soft pout of distaste. Her cheeks were full, her hands dimpled, and her dress of the very finest material.

"Good afternoon, Mrs. Cabot. I am Aimee Napier."

"Yes, of course. My husband told me how beautiful you were, and I can see that for once he was correct. You see, my husband thinks most women are beautiful, at least those that are not required to use a wheelchair to get around," she added acidly. But then her face brightened. "Welcome to my home, my dear. Please come in and I will make introductions for you. I entertain quite often and many of the ladies present have been coming to my salon for a long time. Of course, it has been hard getting used to this muddy city—I prefer to remain indoors for obvious reasons. Still, I do get around as well as possible." She settled herself back in the chair and moved into the center of the room, calling for everyone's attention.

Aimee felt uncomfortable as the ladies present stared at her as though assessing her worth and what she might be able to bring to their little gathering. The names passed by her quickly: Mrs. Laird, wife to John Laird, who was the owner of one of Georgetown's first great tobacco warehouses; Mrs. Washington Bowie, wife of the prosperous ship owner and godson of George Washington; and the wife of Gilbert Stuart, the portrait painter. All blended together as their rouged cheeks and darkened eyes appeared in front of her with blatant curiosity.

"Is it true that you have lived in Paris?" someone asked her quickly.

Aimee nodded. "Yes, I lived there for several years after the revolution," Aimee replied.

"Oooh! You must tell us about the revolution. I mean, was it as terrible as they say, with blood staining the street cobblestones red and little children being taken to the guillotine after refusing to name their fathers in a conspiracy?"

"No, of course not, those tales are stretched out of proportion," Aimee replied hastily. She prepared herself for a host of questions, most based on mistaken notions and misinformation that the ladies had received from unreliable sources. It seemed that she must have talked for the better part of two hours before Lianne Cabot, with a graceful wave of her white hand, indicated that food was served and everyone could retire to the dining room for tea and biscuits.

Aimee was reminded that this woman was English by birth. The servants were all white with clipped, British accents and a stiff bearing that matched their collars and contrasted greatly with her own staff of warm, easygoing blacks. The tea service was beautiful and very expensive. Everything was elaborately decorated to give the overall impression of wealth and ease. The women ate sparingly, complaining about the tendency to gain weight with the tedium they were exposed to in this rough capital city. By and large, they all seemed to resent their husbands' dragging them away from the cultured flavor of Philadelphia to this frontier town that could not even boast proper street lighting.

Aimee sat quietly, her plate in her lap, trying not to eavesdrop, but unable to stop herself. It made her feel a little ashamed that she had expressed these same feelings to Lucian not so many days before. The complaints sounded so shallow and obnoxious on the lips of others that she shuddered to think how she must have sounded to her husband.

She was beginning to think that Lucian had been right and she shouldn't have come when Lianne brought herself over to where Aimee was sitting, rather isolated, and favored her with a warm smile. "You look as though you are not enjoying yourself, my dear," she noted.

Aimee shook her head, determined to lie as gracefully as possible. "Oh, no, I am having a good time, Mrs. Cabot. I just feel a little out of place, since I am not an American like so many of these good ladies."

"I am not an American either," Lianne informed her. "I was born in London, but that does not mean that we cannot be friends. I know that our countries are at war, and that our husbands probably do not like one another at all, but we should be courageous enough to overcome that bias. We have much in common, I'm sure. Won't you call me Lianne? It would make me feel much closer to you."

Aimee nodded uncertainly, not quite sure what this woman was up to. There was something untrustworthy about her, although Aimee could not quite put her finger on it. Maybe it was the simple fact that their husbands did hate each other and that their countries were fighting an all-out war. Those facts could not be easily erased, despite Lianne's reasons for wanting them to be.

"You know, it is really so foolish of France and England to be making war on each other. If they would unite together, they could probably rule the entire world. This pitiful little nation, without a decent capital, would have no recourse against the might and determination of our two countries." Lianne sighed. "But, of course, that would take a miracle, and I do not envision that happening, much to the relief of countries like this United States."

"Our countries could never get along," Aimee interjected, "mostly because the people are so different."

"And the rulers," Lianne added pointedly. "This new young general—what is his name?—Bonaparte! Yes, what do you think of him, my dear? Have you ever met him? I have heard all manner of things about him, from the fact that he is a military genius to the equally stunning opinion that he can make love to two or three women every night. He has the stamina of a stallion and can service any number of women without tiring. Rather a titillating advantage, don't you agree?" She laughed, her eyes appearing rather languorous as she imagined such a lover.

"I would not want to be his wife in that case," Aimee returned with wit.

Lianne stared at her a moment, then laughed again. "You are very sharp, my dear. I applaud Lucian Napier for finding a gem like yourself. Of course, he has always had the luck with women. Naturally, he has built something of a reputation among the ladies around here, having sampled many of them for himself, you see. He—"

"Lianne, I don't see the point of this conversation," Aimee said rather sharply, standing up from her chair to move away from her.

"Well, my dear, I simply thought you knew what an adventurer your husband was among the ladies. Notice, I do say *was* —which is more than I can vouch for my own husband!" There was that bitter edge to her voice once more and Aimee couldn't help feeling a little pity for her. It must not be easy being married to a man like Garth Cabot, confined to an invalid's existence while her husband made merry with the ladies of the town— some of them probably in this very room.

"My dear, must you go already?" Lianne wanted to know, taking Aimee's hand as though to keep her here forceably.

"I really can't stay too long," Aimee replied vaguely. "Look, many of the others are already calling for their wraps."

"Most of them have children waiting for them at home," Lianne replied. "Whom do you have waiting for you, my dear Aimee?"

The mark hit its target and Aimee sagged visibly back into the chair.

"Wait here while I see my guests out the door, and then you and I will have a nice little conversation," Lianne promised.

Aimee watched the animation on her face as she bade good-bye to the ladies. She seemed genuinely to like each one of them, but Aimee felt it was all a charade, a charade that hid the real bitterness she felt about her physical condition and the character of the husband she was bound to. Curiously, she watched her manipulations and the bright, soothing conversation she scattered about her like so many petals. When the ladies had all gone, Aimee stiffened, seeing the woman returning to her, noting the pouting smile on the red mouth.

"Ah, they have finally all gone." She sighed, bringing her chair up in front of Aimee's. "Now we can truly talk, my dear. I can see that you are not happy here, and I'm wondering what it is that makes you stay. Surely, you are free to return to France at any time, are you not? Or is there some trouble in your family that keeps you in exile?"

"No, I could return to France if I wished it," Aimee returned slowly. "But, I'm afraid, my husband is not free to leave right now."

"I see. His duties with the French ambassador?"

Aimee nodded. "We have only just arrived from New Orleans and—"

"New Orleans! Now, there is a city I should like to visit," Lianne said, her blue eyes gleaming.

Prompted by her words, Aimee obligingly told her of the loveliness of the city that mixed the French and Spanish so well— and that would put this city of Washington to shame.

"Yes, I've heard there is some ambiguity about the eventual government in that city," Lianne went on, watching the change of emotions cross Aimee's expressive face. "The Spanish have a tenuous hold at best—and your own France would like nothing better than to lay hands on all that country. It would make quite a good feather in Bonaparte's cap, wouldn't it?"

"Yes, I suppose it would, but I have no idea if that will ever come about," Aimee said truthfully. "The Spaniards delegate authority with maximum efficiency and a minimum amount of aggravation to the citizens. I believe it is true that the citizens would like to be under French control once more, and yet, if that happy event is not forthcoming, they will still be content under the Spaniards."

"What about the British? Are there many in the city from my nation?" Lianne wondered curiously. "Surely we are hardy explorers along with the French and Spanish. Our empire stretches wide throughout North America, and I've no doubt we would like to seize a hold on part of this vast Louisiana Territory."

"I'm sure you are right about that, although—with your husband's connections—you would probably have more information than I on the subject," Aimee returned, beginning to realize that the woman was after information, information she would obligingly turn over to her husband. With a kind of irritation at herself, she tried to think back on all she had said and wondered if she had revealed too much.

Lianne realized that her guest was beginning to understand the intricacies of "small talk" in Washington and quickly backed away from her aggressive stance. Instead, she sought to placate the younger woman. "I'm sorry if I've seemed overly curious," she remarked smoothly, "but I do get very little chance to go anywhere, except where my husband is stationed. We usually follow the government—"

"What exactly does your husband do?" Aimee interrupted with a deceptively pleasant smile on her face.

Lianne paled, then recovered herself. "He works with the British delegation at the embassy, of course. He is one of the secretaries there."

"I see. I'm sure it is quite an interesting job."

"Yes, although I must admit that *I* do not find it all that interesting. Believe me, I would be much happier back in my native country, where I still have family. But a woman's duty is to follow her husband, no matter what, isn't it?" she ended, nodding her head toward her weakened legs.

Aimee nodded absently, then asked, "What exactly is the nature of your ailment, Lianne?"

The latter smiled gently. "My physician puts it all up to a delicate health, my dear, but I am inclined to think it is the changes in the weather here that have afflicted me so. I was never confined so often to a wheelchair in London."

"But that city has its share of dampness and cold," Aimee pointed out.

Lianne shook her head. "Still, there's no accounting for a change in climate and the difference in having those you love surrounding you."

"I could go anywhere, as long as my husband is with me," Aimee said softly.

"Ah, then you are an exception, my dear. A woman truly in love with her husband—a novel idea, here in the city of intrigues where morals are tossed about with such ease one would think they were on a tennis court!"

Aimee laughed and the other woman smiled, this time with genuine warmth. "You *are* different from so many of the wives I've met," Lianne continued, cocking her head to one side. "I suppose most of us who've been here the longest have . . . uh . . . lost our souls, or at least a piece of them. Yours seems still to be intact, Aimee."

"I would hope so." Aimee sighed uncertainly.

Lianne did not press her this time, and for a few minutes the two women sat in companionable silence, sipping from their tea cups. Then a man's footsteps were heard in the hallway outside and Lianne was looking up, her face a mixture of pain and love as she beheld her husband standing in the doorway. Garth Cabot's hazel eyes wandered over the domestic setting and a grin shaped his mouth.

"How nice to see you again, Mrs. Napier!" he said heartily, coming over quickly to take her hand. "Lianne, I wasn't aware that you had made Mrs. Napier's acquaintance," he said, planting a perfunctory peck on his wife's cheek.

"I sent her an invitation to my tea today and she kindly consented to come," Lianne explained, watching each movement her husband made as though making a mental picture in her mind.

"Ah, and did you enjoy yourself, Mrs. Napier?"

Aimee nodded. "Yes, it was interesting meeting many of the other wives of the city. I'm afraid I'm not very good at making friends in a strange city. It takes me a long time to feel comfortable. Your wife was very kind in helping to make me feel welcome here."

Lianne sent her a look of gratitude and Aimee suddenly felt very sorry for this woman, who was obviously caught in a battle between her jealousy of her husband's affairs and her love for him. Meanwhile, Garth was watching her with particular attention, causing a slight blush to heat up Aimee's cheeks. She realized she did not like his eyes on her, even with the protection of his wife's presence. She had the distinct feeling that, were Lianne not here, he might try to take advantage of her.

"Well, I suppose I should be going," she said quickly, standing up to place her tea cup back on the sideboard. "Lianne, thank you for the lively afternoon. I would very much like for you to visit me whenever you have the time." She took the other woman's hand in hers and smiled. "I mean that. I think we have a common bond that goes beyond being strangers in a strange land. I hope to see more of you."

"As I hope to see more of you!" Garth put in smoothly, coming over to take her hand once more. "If you will allow me, I would be more than happy to see you to your carriage," he added.

Aimee would have refused, but he was holding on to her hand so tightly and seemed so disinclined to accept a refusal that she nodded in order to avoid any potential scene. Upon receiving her wraps, she walked outside to the front bricked sidewalk, Garth Cabot's hand firmly over hers as it lay on his arm. At her carriage, she turned to thank him and was aware of a smoldering desire in his eyes that shocked her with its intensity. She stepped back involuntarily, an uncertain smile trembling on her lips.

"My dear Mrs. Napier, you must know that you have won me

over completely," Garth Cabot was saying in a low, seductive voice. "I shall be looking forward to the next time we meet."

"Thank you, Mr. Cabot. I—please tell your wife that I hope to see her again soon."

He smiled as though dismissing the woman awaiting him inside the house. "My wife is of delicate health as you know, Mrs. Napier. Any company she receives is a great delight to her. Have I your promise that you will come again? If so, I shall endeavor to make sure that I am here at your arrival."

"I—will come again," Aimee said swiftly, wanting to get away from this man and his pressured intentions.

He seemed satisfied. With a final kiss to her hand, he released her to the safety of her carriage. Aimee heard the door close with relief and did not look back to see him standing on the curb of the street, watching the carriage with a look of treacherous design on his face.

36

—•—•—•—

"Darling, must we go to this party tonight?" Aimee asked, as the maid brushed her hair so that it shone brilliantly with a golden glimmer that would have rivaled newly minted gold. "It seems I have been to so many dull and tedious affairs in the past three months—"

"Now, now, Aimee," Lucian said with a smile, enjoying watching the heavy silk of her hair brushed into lustrous gold. "Remember, we must do our duty. The French ambassador has been quite ill for the past week and will be unable to attend. You and I will be filling in for him, and we must be there. It would not look good for France were the whole British delegation to show up while no one of any import was there on the French side."

"Oh, I suppose you are right." She sighed, dreading the thought that Garth Cabot would be there. The last few parties they had been to, he had made it a point to dance with her as often as possible so that she could imagine the whispers that must be floating about Washington about them. Lucian had brushed them aside disdainfully, but Aimee was aware that her husband was not impervious to their insinuations. In this capital city, the people thrived on rumors and gossip—the juicier the better. Everyone knew politicians were terribly unfaithful specimens, and it was almost a game trying to guess who was sleeping with whom. Aimee found it childish and sometimes quite irritating, but there was nothing she could do about it.

She stood up after the maid had finished working her hair into a complicated coiffure that made her resemble a Grecian goddess. Even her dress was in the same theme, for this was a masquerade ball and everyone was required to wear a costume. She glanced at Lucian in his Roman soldier's outfit and her heart beat crazily at the thought that this handsome, interesting man was her husband. She smiled widely and ran over on impulse to throw her arms around him and kiss him soundly on the mouth.

Lucian returned the kiss, nearly crushing her against the hard leather of his breastplate. "You are beautiful tonight, Aimee. I

425

will certainly be the envy of every man at the masquerade."

"And I will be the envy of all the women," she replied, wrinkling her nose at him. Then she sighed. "Actually, I would rather just be happy with you and not have to worry about those awful twinges of jealousy I feel whenever another woman looks at you possessively," she confessed.

He smiled. "I never knew you were truly jealous, Aimee. I thought you were much too smart for that when you know how much I love you." He kissed her again.

Aimee bit her lip and turned away from her husband, reflecting on her feelings in connection with his work and his propensity to draw women toward him at all the social functions in Washington. It was easy to see that he must have made himself quite irresistible to women in the days before his marriage. She wasn't sure why he had ever given that up to settle down with just one woman, but he always assured her that he had realized she was the one woman he loved and respected enough to do just that. Other women might be dazzling and witty, and he certainly enjoyed being around them—but when it was time to go to bed, Aimee would always be his partner.

Still, it was hard to see her husband thrown into situations where he was obliged to be close to other women in order to ferret out their husbands' secrets. It seemed somehow dishonoring to their marriage, yet he always explained patiently that it was just part of his work as an agent and could not be avoided. Aimee knew he was telling her the truth, but it still galled her to see him dancing unnecessarily close to another woman, or watching as some young flirt leaned over to allow him the luxury of looking inside the cleavage of her gown.

Perhaps that was why she was especially sensitive to Garth Cabot's attentions to her. She knew how she felt when other women plied her husband—and she was equally aware of how Lucian must feel to see her with another man, especially with Cabot, who was his avowed enemy.

"Will the President be there tonight?" she asked as they got into the carriage. She had not spoken to Jefferson since that first time she had seen him during the snowy atmosphere of his inauguration. She recalled how the tall, raw-boned man who had just marked his fifty-eighth birthday seemed to fit in naturally with the expanse of water, woods, and open fields half circled by low hills that was Washington City.

"I believe he has hinted that he might come," Lucian replied, putting an arm about his wife as they were driven the few short miles to the home of William H. Dorsey, whose manor house, Dumbarton Oaks, in Georgetown, was one of the most impressive homes in the area. This party was to celebrate his appointment as the first judge of the Orphan Court. He had been appointed by Jefferson to protect the homeless children of the district.

Upon arriving, they were greeted convivially by their host and hostess and then entered the impressive interior of the house, where many of the guests were already engaged in lively conversation and partaking of the excellent food and wine. It was hard to pick out who was whom, but Aimee spied a delicate and pale Helen of Troy seated in a wheelchair and excused herself from her husband to say hello to Lianne Cabot.

"Aimee, that is you under that gold mask, is it not?" Lianne laughed.

Aimee giggled and nodded. "Is my disguise so transparent, then?" she wondered.

"Indeed, yes, for how can one hope to cover up such extraordinary beauty!" came the unwelcome voice of Garth Cabot behind her.

Aimee stiffened and turned to see Garth dressed elegantly as one of the King's French Musketeers. "You see, my dear, how I honor your country with my choice of costume," he remarked cunningly, leaning over her hand.

Behind her, Aimee could hear the sharp intake of Lianne's breath. "Garth, you're embarrassing Aimee. Now, go on and do whatever it is you're supposed to be doing while she and I have a good talk."

He smiled and withdrew, promising to see Aimee again when the dancing started.

"I wish it were possible for me to dance with my own husband." Lianne sighed heavily, watching Cabot's tall figure in the crowd. "Perhaps, in that case, he wouldn't be pestering you so much, Aimee!"

Aimee blushed at the other's keen powers of observation. "I don't mind," she lied, "although it would appear unseemly if we are dancing together too much, don't you agree?"

"My dear, it is so obvious to me that you love your husband, I could never take any rumors to heart, so have no worry on that score," Lianne assured her with warmth in her voice.

Aimee breathed a sigh of relief. "I—was afraid that I might offend you—"

"Nonsense! My husband cannot resist a pretty face and, yours being one of the prettiest, I'm not at all surprised at his interest in you. And, of course, since you are the wife of one of his political rivals, I'm sure he enjoys irritating your husband at the same time. A pity, your husband couldn't dance with me and irritate Garth as well!" Lianne laughed thoughtfully at the idea, though Aimee could hear the hint of sadness in her voice.

They talked pleasantly for the better part of an hour when Lucian came to interrupt them, begging Lianne's pardon while he took his wife to be presented before the President, who had arrived late, not even bothering to be in costume, dressed in a careless manner. It was easy for Aimee to understand why the cultured people from Georgetown on the high ground looked across with a mixture of disdain and envy at the simple honesty and ideals of this farmer President.

Aristocratic by birth and taste, Jefferson nevertheless championed the common man. In a very materialistic age, he had brought to government in the few short months of his Presidency an idealism and breadth of vision that were wisely tempered by political shrewdness. As he had said to everyone at his inaugural address, he prized freedom more than order and placed human welfare above the rights of property.

His hazel eyes were keenly perceptive as they touched on those people who were milling about him. Aimee thought he seemed to be able to see into the hearts of the men around him and she wondered, with a little shiver of dread, if he could divine Lucian's unsavory occupation. Perhaps he knew—he must know of the number of spies who besieged any capital. If he did, he never showed it by look or action as he bent formally over Aimee's hand, complimenting her on her choice of costume.

"My dear Mrs. Napier, how appropriate for you to have chosen a costume depicting those founders of civilization, the philosopher's country. You look very charming tonight," he told her with unusual gallantry.

"Thank you, Mr. President—but where is your costume?" she replied with a touch of coquetry that seemed to delight Jefferson.

"I have come as Everyman tonight," he replied with a smile.

Aimee curtsied. "Then I salute you, Everyman, for without you none of us would be here tonight!"

"Well spoken, madame," Jefferson returned. "You sound like a patriotic American citizen! If it were not for your charming French accent, I would suspect that Lucian has been lying about your nationality."

"We are patriots, too, in France, Mr. President," Aimee reminded him softly.

"Ah, yes—France," he intoned in a deep voice as his brows drew downward, almost without his own volition. "France," he repeated, drawing Lucian aside. Aimee moved with them automatically.

"Rumors have been circulating that France has finally pressed Spain to hand over the territory of Louisiana," Jefferson said in a grave voice. "I have heard that Spain has signed away the entire territory for the Grand Duchy of Tuscany—a bad bargain for the Spanish, I would say, but I have also heard that this upstart Napoleon Bonaparte has some marvelously persuasive powers. What do you think, Lucian? Should I believe these rumors?"

Lucian cocked a disbelieving eyebrow, then glanced anxiously to where his wife was standing. "Mr. President, I have heard these same rumors, but as yet, we at the French Embassy have received no official word of any bargain struck between the French and the Spanish. I am sure should any word come, the French ambassador will call upon you immediately."

"Now, that's a damned lie if ever I heard one," Jefferson returned bluntly. "If it is true, I'll not hear it from the ambassador. No, I shall have to hear it from less direct channels. It would hardly be in Bonaparte's interest to make such negotiations public knowledge—not while he is still fighting a war with Great Britain. They have quite a bit of strength in their territory in North America. Canada alone is an extensive province. If they thought that the French had taken control of the Louisiana Territory, it could provoke war on this continent—a war that Bonaparte could not handle with all his navies tied up with the British. And if that day ever comes, God help the United States." Jefferson's troubled face turned toward the window, as though he were seeing beyond the events of the moment and into the future. "No, my friend, America's best hope for survival lies in taking advantage of Europe's trouble."

Lucian cleared his throat and eyed Aimee once more. "Mr. President, I think this discussion would best be aired at another time and in another place. If you will excuse me, my wife is waiting for me to ask her for the first dance." He bowed and took his leave, taking Aimee to the next room, a large, wooden-floored salon that had been cleared of furniture except for the large dais at one end of the room where an orchestra had just begun playing. Effortlessly, Lucian took Aimee in his arms to begin the popular waltz.

"The President was telling you a lot that will certainly fill a report to Talleyrand," Aimee pointed out as they danced. "Was he wise in divulging so much information to a Frenchman? Perhaps he tells Mr. Cabot the same thing."

Lucian shrugged. "Jefferson has always been blunt, but he is also very shrewd. I think that may have been a warning, couched in very oblique terms."

"A warning! To whom?" Aimee scoffed. "Do you really think that Talleyrand has finally achieved his dream and acquired the Louisiana Territory, Lucian? If that is the case, then we can return to New Orleans and once more be on French soil! Oh, I know that Violette would be so joyful if it is true!"

"But we don't know for sure," Lucian added hastily. "Talleyrand won't give me anything but the barest bones of information. I do know that a treaty was signed between France and Spain, but I don't know exactly what it entailed. It could have been for rights to the port of New Orleans. The French could use it as a base of operations for their navy vessels should they seek to bring the war with Britain over here."

"Do you think Bonaparte would do that?"

"I don't know. He seemed a man of great vision. His plans for France could be more far-reaching than any of us could assume."

Aimee sighed and Lucian asked her what was wrong. "It's just that I feel suddenly sorry for Mr. Jefferson," she said softly. "He is a man of such high idealism—imagine coming to a masquerade as Everyman! I think it would break his heart to have to come to blows with another republic."

"But France is no longer a republic," Lucian reminded her gravely. "In fact, with all the power in Bonaparte's hands as First Consul, it comes very close to being a dictatorship!"

"And so what was the revolution for?" Aimee wondered with a shrug of her shoulders.

"It was the exasperation of a thousand years rolled into a violent explosion of feeling," Lucian returned. "Yes, I know the explanation is much too simple to encompass all the details of what happened in the last twelve years, but, in essence, that *is* what it has come to mean to many people. They revolted against the injustice of a system. It worked—at least it got rid of that particular system. But now they are facing a new kind of kingship. And this Bonaparte has already been called a military genius, and a man of the people. He may do what all the Bourbon Kings could not—unify France under one man. No more all the little provinces and principalities. He has even talked of simplifying the legal code of the country. It seems an overwhelming task, and one which will take a long time to accomplish. That is why I see this Bonaparte as keeping his place as head of the country for a long time."

"But the people do love him," Aimee said thoughtfully.

Lucian nodded. "It remains to be seen what his plans are for the Louisiana Territory. Until I can pin down Talleyrand on something definite, I am as much in the dark as Jefferson is. I do know that he was bent on commissioning his secretary, Meriwether Lewis, to explore the territory and see if there was some kind of natural passage to the Orient. But he cannot go in now, for he has no idea who the territory belongs to. These rumors have been rife in Europe, by all reports, and certainly the British think they are true. I've heard our friend Cabot has been nosing about the French Embassy trying to verify them."

"I wouldn't trust him for a moment," Aimee said quickly.

Lucian looked down at his wife. "He seems to have taken an interest in you, my dear. I must caution you to be very careful what you say when you are in the presence of Garth Cabot. Naturally, you will repeat none of what Jefferson said earlier to me."

Aimee glared up at him, stung to think he would think her so loose-tongued. "Of course I will say nothing. Do you think I encourage the man's attentions?"

"I am sure you do not," Lucian returned, kissing her slightly on the nose. He looked beyond her to where Garth Cabot was watching them from beside his wife. "But you may be able to find out something useful either from him or his wife. I know from experience that Cabot ordinarily keeps his silence on political matters, but if you—"

"Lucian! I told you before, I will not prostitute myself to gain information for you or Talleyrand!" Aimee interrupted angrily.

He realized he had made a mistake and sought to soothe her ruffled feathers. "Darling, I'm sorry, I didn't mean that at all. I just meant that, in the course of normal conversation, if you hear anything which might be of interest—"

"I understand," she said coolly.

The rest of the dance was finished in rather distant silence. Lucian knew that Aimee was angry with him, and Aimee was not ready to forgive him his lapse of trust in her, or his inference that information must be obtained at any price. It rankled to think that many women relied on their beauty to seduce a man's tongue in this city—and that her husband would even *think* of including her in such an unsavory group.

When the dance was over, Lucian escorted her to the side of the dance floor, then immediately went to ask the wife of John Marshall to dance. Aimee watched as the Chief Justice himself came to ask her for the next dance, a Virginia reel that seemed totally out of character for this coldly intelligent man whose iron control, Lucian said, concealed the talents of a master political strategist. Fortunately, he was pleasant enough as a dance partner and Aimee found herself smiling at him at the end of the dance.

Unfortunately, the smile lost some of its brilliance when she perceived Garth Cabot bowing in front of her to ask for the next dance, another waltz that put her in closer contact with him than she would have wished. She spared a glance for Lianne, who was chatting determinedly with several ladies, then concentrated on the dance, hoping that it would be over with soon.

"Mrs. Napier, you are extremely light on your feet," Cabot said, smiling down at her. "I suppose it is true what they say about Frenchwomen—that one of the two things they do best is dance."

Aimee refused to rise to the bait of that unfinished phrase, afraid to find out what he might claim was the other thing Frenchwomen did best. She simply smiled her thank-you and tried not to feel uncomfortable as his hand tightened about her waist. Out of the corner of her eye, she could see her husband dancing with the vivacious Dolley Madison, the wife of the Secretary of State and the official hostess of the President's mansion.

"I said, do you miss France very much?" Garth Cabot asked for the second time. He smiled. "You are not listening to me, Mrs. Napier. I do believe you are watching your husband with Mrs. Madison with a rather jealous look in your eye."

"I certainly am not!" Aimee returned in irritation. "Mr. Cabot, I'm afraid you don't understand how much love there is between my husband and me. How could I possibly feel jealous when I know that he is simply doing his duty as a gracious dance partner —just as you are doing?"

He laughed. "Mrs. Napier—let me call you Aimee," he went on without asking permission. "Aimee, I think we both know that I find you most attractive. Frenchwomen have always intrigued me, and I must say that you are one of the most intriguing I have yet come across. Really, I cannot imagine how Lucian managed to latch on to you. His reputation has been less than savory in regard to his choice of women in the past. In fact—"

"Mr. Cabot, this discussion is pointless, sir, and if you don't wish me to leave you dancing alone on this floor, I would suggest you drop it immediately!" Aimee interrupted with an angry flush.

His hazel eyes sparkled with undisguised delight. "God, you are marvelous!" he whispered, drawing her closer against him so that her breasts were pressed lightly against the front of his waistcoat. Slowly, he was leading her toward the long French windows on one side of the room, intent on getting her out onto the decorative balcony that overlooked an immense rose garden, Dumbarton Oaks's greatest pride. Before Aimee was aware of what he was about because of her own anger, he had whisked her outside, where a moonlit June night lit up the park. Immediately, she pushed him away and stood staring at him for a moment, her green eyes sparkling with anger like twin emeralds.

"Mr. Cabot, if you will kindly escort me inside!"

"Stay with me a moment longer, Aimee, I beg you," he said softly. "I must tell you how lovely I find you, how much you have attracted me from the first moment I saw you at the inauguration! Please don't spurn me—I want only to worship you!" He came closer and grabbed her about the waist, jerking her forward to be crushed against his chest.

"Aimee, I have needs . . . that my wife is unable to fulfill! Please let me—"

"Mr. Cabot, let me go!" Aimee cried, beginning to feel a little frightened, although the sound of music was coming comfortingly through the open windows. "If you don't release me, I shall scream and I—"

"Don't be foolish. Don't you think your husband has indulged in a few tête-à-têtes while he has been in the capital? It is practically required behavior in this place, I can assure you!"

"I don't believe you for a minute!" Aimee hissed, bringing her hands up to push at his chest. "And you—you should be ashamed of yourself for flirting with your wife's friend! I find it despicable behavior, Mr. Cabot!"

"Damn my wife!" he said, an angry note entering his voice. Squeezing her against him, he bent his head down to capture her mouth, searing it with his, pulling her lips back to thrust his tongue between them outrageously.

"Cabot, you will release my wife immediately!" Lucian's voice reached them and guiltily they sprang apart. He looked to Aimee's flushed face and bruised mouth and felt hot rage spread through his veins. With two steps he was beside the Englishman, his hands pressed into fists.

"Lucian, no!" Aimee cried when she realized that the two of them would start a fistfight right there on the balcony. Already humiliated enough, as she realized several other guests had arrived on the scene, she tried to grab her husband's arm to bring him away.

Lucian snarled at her angrily, "Let me deal with this, Aimee! If you hadn't been so damned foolish as to get yourself in this situation—"

She dropped her hand, stung at his fury. "I did not get myself in this situation!" she cried. "Do you think I wanted him to bring me out here!" She stopped in renewed embarrassment as she saw the dozens of interested faces staring at her. "Please take me home!"

"Not until this is settled! Cabot, I believe I am forced to salvage my honor and that of my wife! If you will set the time, I am at your service tomorrow for pistols!"

"Lucian! Garth! What is going on here?" The President himself had arrived on the scene, and Aimee wished fervently she could drop through the floor and disappear. "I'll not have any of this foolish dueling!" he proclaimed seriously. "Both of you can discuss your differences in a civilized manner. My God! Your two countries may be at war, but I'll not have you bringing that war to this arena!"

"This cad has tried to force his attentions on my wife!" Lucian returned hotly. "I'll not stand by and see her honor besmirched by this jackal!"

"I was doing nothing wrong!" Cabot defended himself airily. "You can ask the lady herself if she was in any danger with me!"

Jefferson turned to Aimee, who wanted nothing more than to wake up from this nightmare. "I—I wasn't in any danger," she whispered, hating herself for lying, but desperate to save her husband from being wounded in a duel—or worse.

For a moment, she looked over at Lucian's white face, his lips tensed in a cruel travesty of a smile. She swallowed hard, knowing how he must hate her for the lie. He probably would not understand her wish to protect him from any harm.

"Then perhaps we should all leave you and Mr. Cabot out here," he said softly, his blue eyes dangerously narrowed. "Then you can resume your . . . uh . . . discussion."

"Lucian, your wife is only protecting you!" Jefferson said quickly, aware of the sacrifice Aimee had made. "Don't be a damned fool about it and get your dander up! Mr. Cabot, I believe your actions were both unnecessary and completely ungentlemanly in this affair," he went on harshly, staring at the Englishman. "If you will excuse yourself from this house, I will speak to the English ambassador about your behavior tonight. Another episode like this one and I shall request your removal back to England, sir!"

Jefferson's public reprimand probably hurt worse than any pistol wound that Cabot might have received in a duel of honor. Smarting from the humiliation, Cabot bowed jerkily and quickly pushed his way through the crowd to find his wife and take her home. Aimee was relieved to see him go, although she knew that he was probably an even deadlier enemy to her husband than he had been before. She hoped he would be sent back to England, and the sooner the better. Her only loss would be the friendship of Lianne, whom she genuinely liked.

She felt Lucian's hand on her arm, squeezing it tightly as he pulled her through the crowd and out to the vestibule, where a servant was already waiting with their wraps. When the carriage was called, each retired into icy silence, waiting for the other to apologize. By the time they returned home, Aimee feared they would go to bed without speaking at all. No matter that it galled her to be the first one to speak, she decided she could not go to bed without some try at reconciliation.

As they entered their bedroom, she turned abruptly to her husband. "Lucian, I'm sorry for what you *think* happened back there. I can assure you that Garth Cabot is a wolf hiding behind the elegant trappings of a gentleman, but that is no reason for you to challenge him to some foolish duel to assuage your pride!"

"And why is it that I found you and him kissing on the balcony when I arrived?" Lucian questioned angrily, pacing the floor as he began to take off parts of his costume. "It is hard to believe that you were not enjoying it since you didn't seem to be protesting very hard!"

Aimee stiffened with shock. "Then you saw only what you wanted to see!" she assured him with just as much anger. "I did not want Garth Cabot to kiss me. Neither did I wish to dance with him! As I recall, *you* were the one who wanted me to put myself in contact with him in order to discover his little secrets!"

He had the grace to look a bit ashamed as he recalled his own words to that effect. He was silent for a moment, struggling out of the breastplate. Despite his difficulties, Aimee was determined not to run to his aid. She simply watched him impatiently as he finally worked himself free, throwing the armor to the floor in a reaction of anger.

"All right!" he said. "I suppose I did intimate that, were you to find yourself in a situation such as the one tonight, you should make the most of it to gain Cabot's trust, but I—I didn't realize how much it would hurt to see you in his arms!" He faced her and his blue eyes held the pain of his remembrance of seeing his beloved wife pressed so intimately against another man.

Aimee understood. "It would hurt me just as much to see you holding another woman close against you," she admitted with a small smile, trying to brush aside the rankling anger. She refused to hold on to such a destructive emotion, when she only wanted her husband to understand why it had happened. "I feel nothing at all toward Garth Cabot. I only tolerate him because I truly enjoy my conversations with his wife. Despite the fact that our countries are at war, Lianne is an intelligent, understanding woman whom I like very much. It is a shame that she is married to a man like Garth, who causes her such pain."

With a sigh of exhaustion, Lucian settled himself into a chair and leaned his head back, closing his eyes. "I'm sorry for jumping to conclusions," Lucian finally told her. "I've been on edge lately. This thing with the Louisiana Territory is maddening. I don't trust Talleyrand to give me the truth of the matter—and I can't be sure why he is withholding such information from me."

"Talleyrand is such a wily fox, he probably has his reasons." Aimee shrugged, walking quietly to stand next to her husband. She knelt beside his chair and laid her head trustingly on his knee, feeling the need to be close to him until all the previous anger was gone. A tiny thrill shot through her when she felt his hand on the top of her head, idly stroking the shining gold of her hair.

After a few minutes, that same hand grew bolder, throwing out the pins that held up the heavy tresses so that they hung down in a golden cascade and he could pick them up and feel the silky stuff in his fingers. Aimee turned to face him, her chin digging into his knee as she eyed him with the beginnings of an amorous sparkle in her eye.

"You are quite a saboteur," he told her with an amused grin. "I was determined not to forgive you easily; in fact, I had every intention of sleeping downstairs tonight. But it seems my usual defenses are nothing compared to your will. I'm afraid I simply cannot hold out against you."

"Might that be because you are in love with me, dear husband?" Aimee chided him gently.

He shrugged playfully and said teasingly, "Love is for children, wife. You and I have what is known as an understanding between us—it is not the same thing at all!" His blue eyes twin-

kled with amusement as they watched her stand up in front of him
and begin to untwine the Grecian garments from around her body.

"I see," she said, playing the game with him. "Then—this
understanding between us—it must be a very strong commitment, mustn't it?"

"Indeed, it is!" he assured her, feeling his own response to her
unveiling of her charms. "In fact, I would say that it precludes
the idea that there shall be other 'understandings' between anyone else but ourselves! You do understand me!"

Aimee laughed and pushed the last of her garments aside,
stepping out to stand gloriously naked in front of him. "Lucian
Napier, you are a terrible tease, and I'm not sure whether you are
truly deserving of all the love I lavish on you!" She danced out of
his reach, sticking out her tongue and twisting sensuously like
some pagan dancer in front of him. "I cannot do more than dance
for you until I hear an avowal of love!"

Lucian watched her in delight. Just like some naked pagan
goddess, she danced and spun about, alternately teasing and
taunting him until he felt feverish with his need for her. Licking lips suddenly gone dry, he smiled at her, his blue eyes
caressing the length of her nakedness. "You tempt me beyond
reason, wood nymph! I cannot be responsible for my actions, I
assure you!"

She laughed again and moved her hips sexually so that he
abruptly stood up from the chair and divested himself of the rest
of his clothing. His nakedness revealed that he was aroused and
Aimee pointedly gazed at that part of him that was saluting her
stiffly.

"Come here, dammit!" He laughed, reaching out to grab her.

Aimee danced nimbly away and he took a more belligerent
stance, watching her keenly and waiting for his chance to pounce
on her. She continued to dance and weave back and forth, her
eyes growing cloudy with her own desire as she was caught up in
the sensual movements of her body. Suggestively, she glanced
toward the bed, then back at her husband.

"Do you love me, then?" she asked in a throaty whisper.

"I would be a fool to say no!" he told her, moving carefully
toward her so that she would be hemmed in against the bed.

"You didn't answer my question!" She laughed.

With a spring, he knocked her back onto the bed, his body
covering hers as he rained kisses on her face and neck, pushing
his hips against hers as they both tumbled backward to the mattress. He caught her lovely face in his hands and pressed his

mouth to hers, seeking unconsciously to erase the memory of Garth Cabot's mouth. Aimee returned his kiss eagerly, feeling joy burst through her.

"I love you—you know damned well I love you, Aimee!" Lucian said, rising up on his elbows to lock glances with her.

"Then we are lost, for I love you, too!" Aimee said teasingly, tracing his upper lip with a roving finger. "If I had my way, we would tell Talleyrand to go to Hades and begin to live our own lives, Lucian! I wouldn't care where it was, as long as we were together and were happy. You know how much I like your mother and grandmother. I could even be happy at Chesterfield Hall, except for the fact that I would miss New Orleans and Dominic and Violette. But I—"

"Hush!" he interrupted, clasping her breasts and burying his face in her shoulder. "You talk too much!" he murmured.

37

In October, Lucian received an unexpected message from Talleyrand, ordering him back to Paris for a few months. Although Aimee begged to go back with him, Lucian was adamant that she remain in Washington City. He was unsure as to the reason for this command and wanted Aimee to be well out of danger. At the mention of danger, Aimee blanched and clung to her husband, not understanding why he felt uncomfortable with these orders from Talleyrand.

The few days before he set sail were spent making dizzying, desperate love that brought her to the heights of passion, only to be plummeted downward again when the euphoria wore off and she remembered that her husband would be leaving her soon. Pressing him as much as she dared, she tried to find out the reasons for his sense of unease, but he refused to divulge anything, telling her only that with the new power on the throne, he could not be sure of anything.

"Lucian, please let me go with you!" she pleaded with him on the morning of his arrival at the docks to take ship back to France. "I would a thousand times rather be with you than alone here in this foreign country."

"Darling, you are not alone. My mother and grandmother insist that you stay with them for most of the time. You will be safe and well protected. I'm sorry that you cannot go, but even Talleyrand expressed his desire that you remain here." Lucian disengaged himself gently from her clinging hands. "Aimee, you are a very strong woman, and I have no fears that you will be able to take care of yourself in my absence. I promise to be gone no longer than necessary, my love. It will be as much pain for me as it is for you, I can assure you."

"No," she said stubbornly. "You love this kind of adventure and uncertainty, while I abhor it! No doubt you will enjoy your little vacation in Paris while I remain here, stuck in this provincial little town with men like Garth Cabot just waiting to—"

"Aimee, don't have our parting be in anger," he said gently, turning her face up to his and bestowing a kiss on her mouth that

439

took her breath away. "God knows I love you more than my own life!"

She tried to staunch the ready tears that threatened to spill over at any moment. "But how long will you be gone?" she persisted.

"As long as Talleyrand commands," he answered evasively. "I promise to send a note to your brother and visit him if at all possible. I have your letters for him and his wife in my baggage. Now, promise me that you will be careful while I am gone."

"I only wish I could travel back to New Orleans and stay with Violette and Dominic," she said grudgingly.

"That would be very foolish," Lucian told her gravely. "I have no idea what Talleyrand wishes to talk with me about, but it probably has something to do with that same city and the territory surrounding it. Now, until I know for sure whether or not it belongs to France, I do not want you leaving the neutral ground of the United States. Jefferson knows I am going, as does the French ambassador—both of them will help you if you find you need their assistance."

"Small recompense for months without my husband," she added sourly.

He smiled. "Think of me and my loneliness," he told her lovingly. "I shall miss you very much."

She smiled back bravely, although tears once more threatened. "Oh, Lucian, I do love you! Please take care of yourself and write me whenever possible. Despite the naval war between France and Britain, mails have been getting through, so I won't hear of that as an excuse when you return!"

He kissed her deeply. "I love you!" Then he was up the gang-plank, leaving Aimee to watch him, the tears flowing freely and dropping onto her cheeks as she waved her handkerchief to him until her arm ached. He waved from the ship and she could see his figure at the railing long after the ship left the docks and began to make its way down the majestic Potomac toward the Chesapeake Bay and the open sea.

Dejectedly, she walked back to the carriage and commanded the driver back home, trying not to think of the many long months that stretched out ahead of her. The voyage home and back alone would take nearly four months, and who knew how long Talleyrand had in mind to keep him in Paris? She only wished she knew more about this spy work. Was it very dangerous? Could Talleyrand be accusing Lucian of not doing his job—of sending faulty reports? The possibilities frightened her and she refused to think of them. Surely, he was not going to be taken away from his duties here, for in that case Talleyrand would have had Aimee accompany Lucian on the journey back to France. No, she would just have to wait for the better part of two months until Lucian arrived in France and was able to get some correspondence to her. The idea caused her to lean back heavily in the seat cushions, closing her eyes and trying to imagine life here in Washington City without her husband.

Well, she told herself, he had expressed his trust in her ability to take care of herself, and she would certainly show him that she could do just that. No use in crying over spilled milk, when the ship had gone and there was nothing that was going to bring Lucian back sooner than Talleyrand wished it. She supposed she could send Lianne a note, but she hated to imagine the look on Garth Cabot's face when he knew she was alone. She didn't trust the cunning Englishman at all and only wished it had been him being called back to England instead of her own husband being ordered back to France.

Arriving back at the town house on Prince Street, she set about answering correspondence from the wives of the politicians she had met over the last months. She smiled at the invitation to tea from the vivacious Dolley Madison. She had come to enjoy the plump little woman's company, despite the fact that she was a terrible flirt and loved to chance her wiles upon every handsome man in town. She had flirted with Lucian on a number of occasions, but he had been so charming about turning her aside that Dolley had liked him all the better for it, and her liking had automatically extended to his French wife.

Well, she thought, Lucian had not forbidden her to attend social functions, and she supposed that she ought to take the ladies up on some of the invitations rather than sit here running out of things to do. Who knew what information she might glean for Lucian from the chitchat of the women at these gatherings? Although most of them were quite empty-headed and concerned only with superfluous things, there were a number of women who were fairly active in their husbands' work and enjoyed enumerating the good points of their husbands' activities. Such proud observations were often the clues to the inner workings of the government, and Aimee was always attentive when she was invited to one of these social functions. At times she felt a little guilty receiving the confidences of these trusting women—but then she would tell herself she was simply helping her husband and that she was doing it for the glory of France.

France, though, seemed very far away to her now. Farther and farther away as her husband sailed toward it. She hoped the voyage was a good one for him and realized that she didn't envy him that trip. She had never especially liked travel by ship, yet she would have voyaged twice as far if she could have been with Lucian.

Aimee thought longingly of Violette and Dominic and of little Lenore, who must be a healthy active toddler by now. She felt a compulsion to have her own child, and deep disappointment that she had not gotten pregnant again yet. Was there something wrong with her? She tried not to be drawn into such dangerous introspective questioning, but without Lucian, she admitted it would be easy to fall into the trap of self-absorption. Determinedly, she answered her correspondence and accepted several invitations just to keep herself busy. She planned, too, to visit her mother-in-law and crusty old Frances in a few days; perhaps she would extend the visit to a week or more. She truly enjoyed the company of both women and felt somewhat blessed that she had had the good fortune to find herself the daughter-in-law of a woman like Martha.

During the next few days, Aimee kept herself determinedly busy. She attended as many social functions as she could fit into her schedule. At several of them she went out of her way to shine toward the other guests and found several of them nodding her way rather speculatively, wondering if she would become the next brilliant hostess to enter the social scene of the political capital. Aimee would smile and shake her head, telling them she had no wish even to try to eclipse the lively Dolley Madison or the witty Lianne Cabot, or any of the others who were at the top of the social list. No, Aimee told herself with firm resolve, that kind of life was not for her. This social whirl was only a way of passing the time until her husband returned—and, hopefully, until they could return to New Orleans, which still held such a special place in her heart.

It was odd, she thought, how the scene of the most tragic event in her life— the loss of her baby—could hold such splendid memories for her. But it didn't matter; she only knew she had felt at home among the Creoles and their lacy, iron balconies and the slow cadence of life among the plantations. Here in Washington City, everything was rushed and vibrant, filled with an intense anticipation that kept everyone on his toes. It would be exhausting even for the heartiest of people, and Aimee could feel the fatigue growing.

She arranged to close her town house for the entire month of November in order to spend it with Martha and Frances, who welcomed her with open arms. Aimee stood quietly inside the wide hallway of Chesterfield Hall and breathed in the smells and sounds of the plantation house, trying to think of Lucian as a young boy here.

Evenings were filled with card games and storytelling, Aimee eager to hear whatever the other two women could tell her about her husband. When they, in their turn, pressed her on the nature of Lucian's work or the reason for his abrupt departure for France, she adroitly maneuvered them away from the subject or made some offhand remark to the effect that she herself knew very little about the political scene and would have to wait, as they would, for Lucian's letters to begin arriving.

One evening, when the temperature had dropped, causing freezing rain to ice the roads, making them quite impassable, Aimee sat cozily with Martha in front of a roaring fire, drinking hot tea and speaking of frivolous things. Frances had gone to bed early, for the cold weather affected her joints and she felt more comfortable lying down.

"When do you expect Lucian to return to America?" Martha asked suddenly, eyeing her daughter-in-law speculatively.

Aimee shrugged. "I really don't know. His work for the ambassador is really too much for me to follow most of the time. I gather that he was called back by the Foreign Minister —perhaps because of a change in French policy toward the United States."

"Do you think there will be war between us?" Martha asked solemnly.

Aimee paled at the thought. "I . . . don't know," she answered truthfully. "I sincerely hope not, Martha."

"Would you find it hard to take sides, Aimee?" she wondered.

"France . . . is my homeland, the country where I was born," she hedged carefully. "I have learned to respect the United States for a great many things, not the least of which is their ability to learn the lesson of their revolution. France learned very little, for I've heard the peasants' lot has hardly been helped from all the violence and bloodshed. It was a useless revolution for them. Perhaps the bourgeoisie gained some ground, but already Bonaparte has established a new order of 'aristocracy.' They are comprised mostly of his numerous family members and military companions, but still it is not that different from the nobility of old."

"Do you think the peasants will become so dissatisfied that they will rise up again and bring this new head of state down?" Martha queried, interested in the intelligent ideas Aimee was expressing.

"Perhaps," Aimee replied thoughtfully. "Lucian has told me, though, that this Corsican general is very adept at manipulating popular opinion in his favor. With the victory against the Austrians last year and the peace treaty signed with them just last February, I'm sure the people believe he can do anything—even win the war against the English."

"What do you think?"

"I think the English are quite different from the Austrians. For one thing, the English have the greatest navy in the world and could harass French shipping forever if they wished. You remember what happened to the French when Admiral Nelson destroyed all of our navy in Egypt. It was a crippling blow. Now, Lucian says that Bonaparte is trying desperately to rebuild the navy, but that it will take a long time; meanwhile, the English have definite control of the seas."

Martha nodded. "It is very frightening to think of that control when one lives close to the ocean," she said softly. "I remember the horrors of the American revolution, and I would not want to live through another like it. Oh, it might not have had the blood and gore that sensationalized the French revolution, but any war, believe me, is terrible."

Aimee nodded grimly. "The innocent lives that are needlessly lost," she commented, tears coming to her eyes as she thought of her father's death. "I shall never forget the injustice of my father's execution."

"Your father must have been quite a man to have borne such an intelligent, astute daughter," Martha commented warmly. "I'm sorry not to have met him."

"You would have liked my mother, too," Aimee said softly. "She was a gentle woman who hated violence and wanted only to bring up her family in peace. Her murder was a violation of all that is good in the world." She choked up suddenly and felt the hot tears spilling over onto her cheeks. "I miss her," she said simply, "even after all these years—and even after taking my revenge against her murderer. I wish she could have met Lucian."

For a moment both women were silent, each with her own

thoughts as the fire crackled in the grate and the sound of the freezing rain pelted against the windowpanes. Finally, Martha said gently, "My dear, I certainly do not propose to take the place of your dear mother, but please feel toward me as you would toward her if you wish. I can assure you that I feel you are more than my son's wife—you are like a daughter to me. I enjoy your company immensely, and only wish you had come to meet me sooner."

Spontaneously, with a little sob, Aimee reached over and hugged the older woman. "You are so kind to me," she said, wiping the tears from her cheeks with an unsteady hand. "And to think I was so afraid of meeting you!"

Martha smiled and hugged her close. "The very same emotion I felt myself!" She laughed, not without a touch of irony.

Two days later, the weather seemed to do a complete turn-around and the temperature climbed into a springlike range. Frances enjoyed the sunshine as she sat, covered with a shawl, on the veranda of Chesterfield Hall, with Aimee close by her. Martha was busy inside the house, so the two sat in companionable silence for a time, until Aimee's keen eyes noted a horseman coming up the road toward the house. She stood up, shading her eyes with her hand, trying to make out the features of the tall man on the horse.

"Why, I do believe that it's the President, Mr. Jefferson!" she said with some surprise, looking down at Frances.

"Tom Jefferson!" Frances repeated. "Goodness, he hasn't visited in a month of Sundays. Honey, be a good girl and call Martha out. Perhaps he'll be staying for luncheon!"

While Aimee hurried to do as she was asked, Thomas Jefferson reined in his horse and tied it to the hitching post, just as his small retinue came up the drive behind him. He walked up to where Frances was rocking and bowed deeply, a smile creasing his care-worn face.

Frances smiled, too, and wagged a finger at him. "Still trying to impress the ladies, Thomas?" she asked him. "You always said you could ride better than anyone else and would try to prove your prowess to all of us!"

He laughed. "I just got tired of the sedate, presidential pace my companions were setting and decided to give the horse his head. It felt good, believe me, Frances."

"If it weren't for this damned arthritis, I'd be on a horse next to you!" Frances assured him heartily.

Martha came out with a welcoming smile, followed by Aimee, who was still showing her surprise that the President would actually come to visit them. It would be unheard of in France. She couldn't even imagine King Louis ever setting out to visit any of the commoners. Of course, here in America there was supposed to be no division between the highest office holder of the land and the lowest servant. She found her esteem for the fledgling nation improving by leaps and bounds.

"Mr. President, how nice for you to visit," Martha was saying.

Jefferson took both hands in his and looked at her thoroughly with a smile. "Martha, there's no sense in being so formal with me just because your daughter-in-law is watching. You know you can call me Thomas—and have been doing so for years since my own dear Martha consented to be my bride." For a moment, the pain of his beloved wife's early death shone in the hazel eyes, but quickly passed as he bowed to Aimee. "Good morning, Mrs. Napier. A lovely morning for riding, don't you think?"

She curtsied and smiled. "I'm not much of a rider myself, Mr. President," she confided.

"The wife of a bona fide Virginian not much of a rider—why, it's preposterous! Mrs. Napier, you must remind me of that fact the next time your husband is in town, for I will make sure he does not neglect your riding lessons any longer." His tone was teasing and Aimee found herself enjoying the company of this bluff, serious man who before had seemed somehow formidable to her.

He sat down easily in a chair, pulling it close to Frances, and the two other women found seats and did likewise. Meanwhile, the rest of the President's party had arrived and were quickly dispatched to the kitchen to be given something to eat, though some would have preferred to stay close to the President. Jefferson, however, waved them on, declaring he would like to have some private conversation with three of the loveliest ladies in Virginia.

"Now, my dear Mrs. Napier, I must ask you if you've heard yet from your absent husband?" Jefferson asked pleasantly.

Aimee shook her head. "It is too soon yet," she answered with a sigh.

"I'm anxious to find out why he was recalled so quickly to France," Jefferson admitted anxiously. "The French ambassador will tell me nothing, and I must admit to feeling a degree of frustration in all of this."

"If you like, when I hear from him, I will send word to you," Aimee offered, feeling on shaky ground because of the nature of her husband's "business." She wondered, not for the first time, what would happen if Jefferson knew that his good friend Lucian Napier was really a spy for France, listing America's secrets in reports to Talleyrand to help him find out the weaknesses of this country. She felt ashamed of her husband's work and could not quite meet the honest, warm eyes of the President.

There was an awkward silence. Then Martha asked quickly, "What have you been doing to your house, Thomas? We have heard reports that you are actually trying to clean up some of the mess surrounding it."

Jefferson sighed. "Ah, give me my beloved Monticello to that half-finished shell any day, my dear. It's true I'm trying my best to make the thing livable, but it is slow work at best. The worst of the junk has been carted out of the grounds and I've had a post-and-rail fence erected around the property, but with the winter weather coming soon, work will be slowed. Poor Mrs. Madison complains bitterly at having to entertain in rooms without adequate heat, and my two daughters are even worse. They do try hard to accommodate themselves to the place, but I can understand why they don't visit more often than they do. God, I miss the company of women sometimes, I don't mind telling you."

"You've done very nicely without them!" Frances intoned rather belligerently. "You've introduced a . . . dramatic informality to the Presidency that that northeasterner Adams didn't know anything about—he and his snooty wife, Abigail. Pah! You'd make twenty of the two of them together, Thomas!"

"Thank you, Frances, for your faith in me," Jefferson replied with a twinkle in his eyes. "I must say, though, that I've heard this democratic informality, as you call it, acclaimed by my followers as true to the genius of the republic—but just as many of my enemies regard it as cheap in the debased fashion of . . . uh . . . French radicals, if you'll pardon the comparison, Mrs. Napier."

Aimee nodded, flushing a bit, but really taking very little offense. She knew very well that such sentiments were not those of Jefferson himself, for he had professed on more than one occasion to love things French and had even proceeded to order furniture in the Louis XVI style, importing much of it from French furniture makers at great personal cost.

"So you have been trying to beautify our new capital," Martha said to break any awkwardness, returning to her earlier subject. "I know that earlier this fall you planted poplars along Pennsylvania Avenue."

"A quick-growing tree," Jefferson said with a nod. "I've ordered the planting of the slower-growing oaks and elms that will take decades to shade the street that poor L'Enfant envisioned as broad and stately. But in time it will come to pass and his vision will be realized, mark my words, ladies." He looked at Aimee. "I take a great personal interest in this new capital, my dear. Trees, houses, wharves, stonework on the new Capitol—nothing escapes my notice, despite my necessary musing over deeper matters. I keep hoping that my example will force others to follow it, for we need citizen participation in the affairs of an ever-expanding and complex republic."

"It is hard for people to think about anything but their own lives," Aimee answered. "They enjoy complaining about the muddy streets and the impossible swamps that still exist in the capital, but as long as they are safe and comfortable in their own homes, they do very little about it."

"Good observation, my dear, but, alas, that is the essence of human nature. Of course, if I put them all to visit in the President's house for a week, perhaps they will see how uncomfortable it is and take pity on me!" He laughed. "Ah, but the basic problem is in attracting private capital to the new city so that it won't be dependent solely on federal expenditures. I've tried to do it by encouraging new banks and by giving priority on the principal streets as locations for private business. I've even ordered more river-wharf construction for the private sector."

"I'm sure it will do some good," Martha said comfortingly, and Jefferson looked to her gratefully.

Martha turned to Aimee. "Did you know that our President is a great collector, my dear?"

Aimee shook her head, at which Jefferson launched into a description of some of the many books he had collected over the years for his private library. It seemed to Aimee that he collected everything: scientific instruments, books on science, art, agriculture, seeds, furniture, maps, and surveying instruments. Archly, she observed that he was as bad as a pack rat, which provoked a hearty round of laughter from the President.

"I suppose I just want to make sure that *somebody* collects these things that represent the beginnings of our nation," he said thoughtfully. "In future generations, they will take on a greater importance as representatives of a time when this nation was but an infant. Someday, I hope it will grow into a strong adult, able to hold its own with the mighty nations of Europe."

"I have the utmost faith in it," Frances declared stoutly, rapping her cane against the floor of the veranda. "It just pains me to think that I will be long dead when that comes about!"

"As shall all of us, I'm afraid, my dear Frances," Jefferson returned with a sad smile.

Martha stood up, breaking the President out of his poignant reverie. "You must stay for luncheon, Thomas. The cook is preparing some of your favorites and will be very insulted should you refuse. Besides, all of your men have already been offered food and drink, and we cannot be remiss in having the President leave us a starving man!"

"Ah, dear lady, I could never starve in your witty presence. It feeds my intellect to engage in such stimulating conversations with you and your family. God, I do miss your son quite sorely, for his wit is nearly as sharp as his mother's!" And with this gallantry, he followed the ladies into the dining room, assisting Frances to a chair, then seating himself at the head of the table upon Martha's insistence.

Throughout the meal, he continued to talk and Aimee marveled at his ability to eat and converse at practically the same time. He was such an informal man, so at ease among the three ladies present, that she felt quite comfortable with him, almost as though he were an old friend, as indeed he seemed to be of Lucian's family.

"Yes," he was saying, as the third course was brought out from the kitchen, "I want the President's house to take on a French flavor. I want, moreover, the quality of the food and drink to take precedence over any elaborate protocol that the foreign dignitaries would like to see foisted on me. Equally novel to them, I think, would be to see the quality of conversation one could get at my house match the quality of the food and drink."

"Your house would become a quite curious blend of home and palace," Aimee said thoughtfully.

"That's it, exactly!" Jefferson cried. "Mrs. Napier, you've hit it exactly. A blend of dignity and informality that makes it easy for senators and representatives to come together for a meal and good conversation, where private citizens might mingle with the official guests to the mutual advantage of all!"

"It seems a remarkable deviation from the usual trappings of government," Martha stated. "Do you think it will work?"

"Of course it will work!" Frances interrupted crossly. "Thomas is the President, after all, and he certainly can do as he likes—and damn the rest of them!"

38

•-•-•-•-

December was crisp and chilly that year, not at all unpleasant, so that Aimee was able to get around town quite easily. She continued her social visits and was included in most of the livelier parties around Christmastime, which was celebrated in the capital with quite a deal of fanfare. French, English, German, and Spanish customs seemed to intermingle and entwine during the holiday festivities, and Aimee thought she had never eaten so many different kinds of food in her life. She missed Lucian terribly during all these occasions and at times found herself giving in to depression as she cried at night in bed, but these episodes were few and far between, as she continued to tell herself that soon she would see him again. In fact, she had received two letters from him already, encouraging messages of love that had heartened her considerably. He said very little about why he had been recalled by Talleyrand, only that there had been some scandal involving the Minister of Police, Fouché, and that Talleyrand had wanted him in Paris during the investigation. He mentioned that he had met and talked with Napoleon Bonaparte and had found the man quite capable as the leader of the French people, although his ambition was truly boundless, and Lucian wondered if he would be content to remain merely First Consul. He wrote jokingly that, had Bonaparte been able to prove he had even one drop of royal blood in his veins, he would have declared himself King immediately!

After Christmas, Aimee received a visit from Lianne Cabot, something of a surprise, since Aimee had studiously avoided her and her husband at most of the functions, not wanting to involve herself with Garth Cabot while Lucian was away.

"Merry Christmas, my dear!" Lianne smiled, being helped to the door by two servants, one behind her carrying the wheelchair.

"Merry Christmas, Lianne!" Aimee exclaimed, showing her surprise as she ushered everyone inside, where Lianne was quickly installed in her chair, and the servants were sent to the kitchen to remain while the two ladies talked.

"You haven't visited me in so long that I took it upon myself to come to see you," Lianne began, her bright eyes troubled as they saw the guilty look cross Aimee's face. "What is it, Aimee? Is it because of my husband?"

Aimee stood up and clasped her hands together, avoiding Lianne's inquisitive eyes for the moment. "You know what happened at the masquerade that one evening, Lianne," she pointed out reasonably. "Lucian was very angry, and the two of them would have dueled had it not been for Jefferson's intervention. I don't want to find myself in a compromising position like that again."

"I assure you, I've talked to Garth about it and he has promised me to behave like a gentleman toward you," Lianne put in sweetly. And then at the look of doubt Aimee bestowed upon her, Lianne said, "Please believe me, Aimee. Garth can be a terrible womanizer, but when confronted with a jealous husband, he backs down pretty quickly. I know he and Lucian dislike each other, but that is no reason for us to avoid each other's company. I like you, Aimee, and, to tell you the truth, I find you quite refreshing in this town, where most of the women are mere ornaments, there to help their husbands get ahead in politics. I feel proud, too, that we can be friends despite the war that continues to rage between our two countries. I think it makes us somehow better than the norm. Do you know what I mean?"

Feeling vastly uncomfortable, Aimee nodded. "Yes, I understand, Lianne, but you must understand that I cannot quite believe your husband is going to behave in any different vein from what is his habit."

Lianne pouted, looking quite perturbed that Aimee refused to believe her. "But you mustn't turn your back on *me!*" she protested quickly. "Surely we can still be friends despite our husbands!"

Aimee sighed. "I suppose we can, Lianne, but it will be difficult. I simply do not trust Garth. For one thing, even though we may be able to rise above the rages of our countries, I know he and Lucian cannot. Lucian has a deep love for France, as I'm sure your husband has for England. There is no room for friendship there."

"I wonder about your husband's supposed love for France," Lianne said with a cunning look in her bright eyes. She ran a finger through her hair to push aside an errant gilded lock. "It seems to me he holds a great deal of love for America.

Haven't you noticed how well the President treats him, and, setting aside the fact that he already has property in Virginia, wouldn't you think he would rather be situated in Paris than in Washington?"

"Lianne, as you know, a diplomat seldom gets to choose the place where he is stationed by his government. Lucian has accepted his appointment with good grace. It is by happy circumstance that he also has family here, but I can assure you, were he to be recalled permanently to Paris, he would go in an instant!"

Lianne shrugged, backing away from the subject. "All right, Aimee. See how easily I can be persuaded! Yes, Lucian's heart is all for France—and I suppose yours is, too. But let's put all that aside for now and just be friends while we're here in Washington. It is so difficult to find women capable of discussing intelligent subjects wittily—"

"And incapable of feeling amorous intentions toward your husband?" Aimee guessed with a wry smile.

Lianne reddened. "Ah, you have caught me there, my friend. Yes, I suppose it's true, you are one of the minority when it comes to those women my husband can find as easy marks for his flirtatious manner." She looked away and for a moment was quiet, a look of resigned pain in her eyes. "I, too, was very easily caught in his spell. When I found out that this handsome, sophisticated man wanted to marry me, a girl who had never been out of her country house, I nearly died of excitement. Although my father had money, I never dreamed in my unsophisticated naïveté that Garth might consider that a reason to court me. He had come to know my brother through various common business interests. One day, my brother brought home this handsome stranger from London. I was sixteen, and most of the boys who lived close to me were nothing more than acquaintances. I was always in delicate health even then, and many of them stayed away because I couldn't ride a horse or dance as long as most of the young girls in the county. And yet, despite the fact that I felt inadequate, Garth made me feel as though I was the most beautiful, the most intelligent, and fascinating young woman he had ever met."

"It sounds like true love," Aimee remarked gently, feeling sorry for this woman who had been so cruelly conned by an avaricious man.

"It was true love—on my part," Lianne agreed. "Garth—I don't know if he ever really loved me or not, but he enjoyed making me think he did. As I said, I had very little experience with men. When Garth kissed me for the first time, he was so gentle, so wonderful, that I thought my heart would burst. My health even improved dramatically so that, very soon, I was riding with him through the hills of Kent, dancing at all the cotillions. The other young men grew interested, but I spurned all of them with haughty disdain. They had not loved me before—only Garth had loved me then, and I was so . . . so painfully grateful to him." She sighed.

"And he took advantage of your gratitude?" Aimee guessed.

Lianne nodded, not quite meeting the other's eyes. "I suppose I wanted him to take advantage of it," she said softly. "Soon kisses weren't enough and I knew how much he wanted to become my lover. It had never before occurred to me that any man would ever want to love me physically."

"But you are lovely," Aimee interjected sincerely, noting the bright gilt of her hair, and the small-boned frame that would cause any man to want to protect her.

She shrugged. "I never thought of myself as lovely. My father had been disappointed in me from the time I evidenced ill health. His only wish was that he could marry me off without delay. He was not a bad father, really, he just disliked intensely anything having to do with sickness or disease. When my mother contracted a cancer a few years ago, I think he went through more discomfort than she did. When she died, it was almost as though my father started living again."

"How terrible!" Aimee exclaimed, feeling her heart go out to this woman. She remembered with tenderness her own father and felt very lucky to have had such a warm, understanding man for a parent.

"I suppose he can't help himself. Some people just react that way to sickness," Lianne stated matter-of-factly. "I truly think Garth might be one of those like my father, for ever since my health deteriorated again, he has been very . . . distant. You see, when he asked me to marry him, I was in what you might call 'full bloom,' and he saw how quickly I had recovered from my poor health while under his influence. I suppose I disappointed him when I didn't continue that recovery after we were married. I never knew until a year later that my father had settled quite a large sum on my dowry and that Garth had made sure he would control every penny of it. When I did find out, my health started deteriorating again. Added to that were three miscarriages in the first three years of our marriage, and all my energy just seemed to seep away."

"Three miscarriages! You poor thing!" Aimee commiserated, remembering how ill she had felt after her one.

"Garth grew angry with me because he realized I would probably never have children. He made me think that was the only reason to have sex—to create children. Since I could not do that, he withdrew from me and began to seek his pleasures elsewhere. I couldn't believe he could be so vindictive, and I withdrew even more into my own pain. Eventually, I needed a wheelchair more often than not. The physicians told me my muscles would atrophy in time if I didn't exercise them. I didn't care, so I didn't heed their warnings. Now it is too late, I suppose. But it was too late a long time ago for Garth and me. I only wish sometimes that I would die and be done with it, but unfortunately my illness is not that kind of disease. It seems I am just repeating the pattern of my parents—Garth is more uncomfortable with my poor health than I am."

"Lianne, he is being terribly cruel to you," Aimee said quickly. "You can't let him continue this way. You are lovely and worth much more than he is! You must make yourself get better. Surely there are exercises, practices—"

"It is too late for that, Aimee," Lianne said without bitterness. "I am content—no, not content, but resigned to the fact that I will never get much better than I am today. Garth has accepted that, too. He has not been a true husband to me for many years, yet I can still be useful to him in my own way. I entertain, put on the mask of the perfect hostess, smiling at all those insincere women who can't wait to sink their claws into my husband behind my back. Sometimes I find myself wanting to scream out my anger at their false friendliness, but then I realize that would be a most foolish mistake. For if I cannot hold on to my reputation as a most brilliant hostess, I would become very much alone. There would be no reason for anyone to come to see me—and I couldn't stand the loneliness. I couldn't stand it, Aimee," she said bleakly. "And so, you see, back goes the mask and I smile at the women who have committed adultery with Garth, knowing how much they enjoy being included in my parties."

"Then you shouldn't invite them!" Aimee said angrily. "Why should you surround yourself with insincere women who haven't an ounce of honesty in them?"

"Because," Lianne said, "I have found that most of the

women are like that. If I didn't include them, there would be very few women at my parties." She looked hopefully at Aimee. "That is why I cannot lose you as a friend, Aimee. When I realized that Garth had designs on you, I wanted to kill him for taking another friend away from me. But when you didn't give in to his little games, I thought perhaps there was a chance for true friendship between us." She smiled. "You are so lucky to have a husband like Lucian. I can see the love you feel in both your eyes, and if I can be a part of it, in even the tiniest way, I will feel well recompensed for the time I spend with those other heartless creatures."

"Oh, Lianne, you make me feel rather foolish," Aimee said, feeling a hint of tears as she realized how much it had probably cost this woman to reveal her history and her inner feelings. "Of course I am your friend. I will not let Garth stand in the way of that. Knowing what you have told me, I feel better able to deal with any . . . advances he might make toward me in the future. Thank you for telling me."

"You—you won't stay away anymore?" Lianne asked.

Aimee shook her head.

Lianne released a sigh of relief. "I am so glad to hear you say that, my good friend. Please remember that should you ever need anything, you can count on me to help you in any way I can."

After that visit, Aimee spent a good deal of time with Lianne. They shopped together and visited, Aimee insisting that Lianne get out as much as possible. Slowly, and without Lianne realizing it, Aimee was urging her out of the life of ill health into which she had allowed herself to sink. Aimee never believed in giving up, no matter how bad the odds were, and she communicated this feeling to Lianne, who laughingly told her she was better for her than any medicine a physician could prescribe.

The two friends shared confidences, Aimee telling Lianne how much she would like to return to New Orleans one day. She shared letters from Violette and news of little Lenore's first steps and that babble of words with which she was experimenting. The days went by faster than Aimee could ever have imagined, and although she continued to miss Lucian, she realized there were more constructive ways of using her time than mooning over an absent husband. The nights were most difficult still, and sometimes she would lie awake restlessly, tossing and turning, wishing he were there to make love to her. Her passionate nature had barely been tapped by her husband, and she was determined that when he finally returned she would show him how very much she loved him.

January of 1802 came and went and still America was ignorant of the truth of the treaty between Spain and France. Jefferson could not find out if the Louisiana Territory had changed hands, and this proved most frustrating for him. He suspected that Bonaparte was deliberately withholding the truth to keep the British from trying to continue the war in New America, a war that Bonaparte could not afford right now with all his forces concentrated in Europe as he began to carve it into portions as he saw fit. Jefferson felt positive that Bonaparte cared nothing for the United States, whose friendship or enmity was unimportant to him, but he was willing to use America to claw at the British. Perhaps this reasoning might be helpful to Jefferson in the months to come. The United States was still politically fragile, virtually without an army and navy and without a true friend in the world. Her best military defense lay in the fact that her territory was chiefly a wilderness, a fact not lost on Jefferson as he sat in his half-finished mansion and debated inwardly his ideas on the schemes of Bonaparte.

Desperate for news, he dispatched Robert Livingston as ambassador to France with a scheme to ask France to sell West Florida to the United States. Presumably, if France was receptive to the idea, it would indicate that the rumors were true and that the Louisiana Territory was now under French control. If France disclaimed possession of the Floridas, then Livingston was to ask France to assist the United States in purchasing West Florida from Spain. At the same time, Charles Pinckney was sent as ambassador to Spain and was told to ask the Spanish if the United States could buy West Florida. Here again, the reason was to see who really held the land. But the strategy got Jefferson nowhere, for France said it didn't own West Florida and Spain refused even to discuss it.

Aimee was surprised when, one day at the end of February, she was summoned to the President's mansion by a harried-looking Thomas Jefferson. Bidding her to sit down in one of the new chairs that had just arrived from France, he seated himself opposite her, his raw-boned hands lying on his knees for only an instant before they began moving actively across his chest, showing his anxiety.

"Mrs. Napier, forgive me for this hasty summons," he began diplomatically enough. "I'm afraid I have had no news from your absent husband and was wondering what you have heard from him."

Aimee was somewhat taken aback by this direct approach and thought for a moment on how best to proceed without revealing any secrets that Lucian might not wish to be made known. "I have heard very little," she remarked truthfully. "It seems, according to his last letter, that France and England are moving closer to some kind of truce. Lucian feels that Bonaparte is trying to gain time to improve his naval forces." That, she felt, was probably already known to Jefferson through his own agents in France and England.

"Yes, yes," he commented quickly. "But has he heard anything of the territory of Louisiana?"

The bluntness of the question once more gave Aimee pause. "I don't know, Mr. President. I suppose there is very little he can put into a letter for fear the authorities might go over it before it gets to the mail channels. I am sure that when he returns he will make some kind of report to the French ambassador here. You will be informed of anything . . . pertinent."

"Mrs. Napier, you make a damned cunning diplomat yourself," Jefferson acknowledged rather impatiently. He stood up, clasping his hands behind his back. "I don't mind telling you, madame, for I'm sure you've already heard rumors that my political career is in jeopardy. So is the precarious unity, if not the very existence, of this infant nation. While we sit here, ignorant of the truth, God knows what those despots across the ocean are planning to do. I'm sure all of them could not care less whether we survive. In fact, several are probably planning our eventual demise."

"Mr. President, certainly you have the means to defend yourself!" Aimee protested, not wanting to be drawn into a feeling of pity for this country.

He shrugged. "We shall not discuss this now, madame. Defense will do one very little good if one does not know from which flank the blow will come. To the north, we have Canada, firmly under British control and much larger than our small nation. To the west and south we have Spain—at least that is what I hope. Spain has become decadent and weak in the past century and will prove easy enough to bargain with should it ever come to that, but if that territory is owned by France and the ambitious Bonaparte, I shudder to think what plans he carries for us. Already, Spain has grown rather pompous because she feels she has France's friendship. The new Spanish governor, Juan de Salcedo, has issued a decree forbidding the granting of land in Louisiana to citizens of the United States. That slap in the face was followed by the high-handed suspension of the right of deposit at New Orleans, which has been negotiated in the treaty of 1795. It is bringing quite a stir from the westerners in Kentucky and Tennessee, I can assure you."

Aimee nodded, admitting, "My friends in New Orleans wrote to me of that, Mr. President. But Violette also said that the Spanish government intervened and reopened the port to them, and that the action had been based on an individual decision made by Salcedo himself."

Jefferson stared at her. "By God, common citizens know more about these things than the President himself. I only just received word that Salcedo had backed down from his stance after the westerners threatened to float down the Mississippi and take possession of New Orleans by force. Believe me, Mrs. Napier, it was quite touchy for a while there with the Kentuckians threatening to secede from the Union if they did not gain our protection for their scheme. No protection, no allegiance, was their claim. You see how very fragile this nation is with all the various interests among the different groups. I worry constantly about such political schemes that have allies among my political enemies, and even some of those in the Republican Party."

Aimee knew he was referring to the Vice-President, Aaron Burr, whose hotheaded ideas were a thorn in his side and who, rumor had it, would like nothing better than to establish his own state under a separate flag. But, of course, nothing could be done against him while none of these things could be proven. It was up to Jefferson to keep a close eye on his second-in-command.

"Rumors are constantly floating about in this city of intrigue," Jefferson went on thoughtfully. "I have heard that Bonaparte, by secret treaty, has reacquired for France the port of New Orleans and certain territories in the Mississippi River basin that France had earlier ceded to Spain. This was done at the insistence of Foreign Minister Talleyrand. *If* this is true, then any scheme to attack New Orleans or the Mississippi River territories would be an attack upon a France much more dangerous than the decadent Spanish empire."

"You plan to attack New Orleans, Mr. President?" Aimee asked in surprise and with some alarm.

He looked at her quickly, as though realizing to whom he

had been speaking. "No, the United States has no plans to take such action unless we are threatened first," he said reassuringly. "But there are many groups in the western states that would welcome the notion of putting New Orleans under the American flag."

"But, they must listen to you as their President!" Aimee stated confidently.

Jefferson laughed rather sarcastically. "My dear Mrs. Napier, since when do hotheaded rabble-rousers listen to anyone? You must know from your experiences during the French revolution that people embroiled in passionate issues seldom have the sense or patience to listen to reason. I just don't want anything to happen while I am in the dark as to whom we are actually dealing with west of the Mississippi!"

"If Lucian knows, I am sure you will know, too, very soon, Mr. President," Aimee said soothingly.

"I certainly hope so, Mrs. Napier. If Bonaparte does own New Orleans and he decides to send ships to attack the British here, the English would attack up and down the Mississippi River, and that would be one hell of a mess, if you'll pardon me for saying so!"

Aimee had learned, from the many parties she'd attended and from her discussions with Lucian, something about the political life in America. In her need to offer some kind of substantial advice to an obviously desperate man, she said to Jefferson, "You do have the option of becoming allies with the British, Mr. President. That would protect your boundaries—and the British seem to be the real threat, since they are already along your borders in strong numbers."

He shrugged. "Marry ourselves to our old enemy," Jefferson remarked with a weary sigh. "Yes, it might protect us for a time, but it could prove political suicide for me, since my fellow southerners are all pro-French and anti-British. Also, it could prove potentially ruinous to the United States should the British decide to 'improve' on such an alliance to the point of recovering their lost colonies! Quite a few northeastern merchants would be more than willing to have their states reattached to England—and, no doubt, many of them are plotting to that end, my dear. They regard me as an insane, atheistic Jacobin and are very distrustful of all southerners and their ways."

"Then ally yourself with the French," Aimee pointed out reasonably.

He shook his head. "An equally dangerous option, Mrs. Napier, since those same pro-Britishers in New England wouldn't stand for it. And it would probably provoke a British attack on the United States."

"Then you must remain neutral," Aimee suggested firmly. "At least by nonalliance with either country you prove to both that you wish to remain out of their differences."

"How simple it sounds," Jefferson commented wearily. "But mighty countries seldom accept the neutrality of a potentially harmful country. I worry constantly about the outcome of this war between England and France. An ultimate victory by Bonaparte would be a mixed blessing; if France has reacquired former French territories in the Mississippi River basin from Spain, then France obviously means to reestablish herself in North America. French bayonets along the Mississippi River would be just as unfriendly—and as unwelcome—as British ones, madame. That is why my best hope is to discover whether it is true that Bonaparte now holds title to New Orleans and its surrounding lands," he continued, reaffirming his position. "If it is true, then I should try to make a deal with Bonaparte to secure some kind of right or claim to free passage down the Mississippi River and free trading rights at New Orleans. This would at least defuse the explosive plans of the would-be filibusters. If the United States could acquire a foothold of its own on the Gulf coast, even if it were served by some river other than the Mississippi, I would be content."

"What if you could buy the city of New Orleans from its owner, whoever that may be?" Aimee speculated, although she abhorred the thought of the city going into American hands if there was a chance that the French had reacquired it.

"It might protect the city from a British fleet, should the English decide to seize it the moment another European war erupts. By all accounts, a truce should be likely between France and England very soon. This would not necessarily put an end to British ambitions in North America, but it might at least cause them to postpone whatever designs they might have until they have first settled accounts with the French."

"And give you a little breathing room," Aimee noted with a smile.

The President nodded, returning her smile, although his brow was still lined with his worries. "I am, madame, an ardent revolutionary, not a pacifist as some might label me. My fervent hope is that this nation will grow strong while the European nations bleed themselves white. Then I can drive the lot of them out of the Western Hemisphere and create a single, great republic of intelligent and well-educated farmers in both North and South America."

"A very grandiose scheme, Mr. President," Aimee said softly, surprised at hearing such lofty ambition emanate from this man.

"A modern utopia"—he smiled—"but probably as elusive as some mythical kingdom in a storybook. The people are too diverse even in these original colonies ever to be totally united."

"Many people thought the same of the diverse provinces of France," Aimee pointed out, "and yet Bonaparte has promised to unite them all under one single cause—the future glory of France."

"The future glory of France," Jefferson mused. "And I seek the future glory of America. Tell me, Mrs. Napier, what do you think of this—passion for glory that men constantly seek? Do you think it is worth all the time and trouble, the glorious statements and the numbing battles, the dead and the wounded?"

Aimee shook her head. "My father used to say that nations are forged with the blood of men, Mr. President. The saying holds true throughout the centuries of civilization, and I expect it will continue to hold true as long as there are new places to explore and conquer."

"But one day the earth will be used up—and there will be nothing new to explore," Jefferson said, half to himself. "And then, I wonder where the glory will come from." He looked over to Aimee and smiled. "Ah, but such a rhetorical question deserves no answer. We must stick to the tangibles, eh, Mrs. Napier?"

"I can only hope, Mr. President, that my husband will return soon and that he will be able to enlighten you on these matters," she said respectfully. She was awed by the trust this man had placed in her and flattered that he had chosen to discuss such lofty matters with one who was not even a citizen of his country. But, then, Jefferson was known for his unorthodox methods of reaching decisions. Perhaps that was what made him so fascinating, Aimee thought.

As she left the President's mansion and traversed the muddy canal in her carriage, she wondered what Talleyrand might give to know all the things she had been told in confidence by Jefferson. For a split-second, she imagined using the information as a bargaining tool in exchange for permanent placement in New Orleans, but almost immediately rejected such an idea. Crafty Talleyrand, with all his intrigues and plots, would hear nothing from her lips about this, she decided firmly. Jefferson had placed his confidence and trust in her—and she would not break that trust.

39

It was mid-April and Aimee was resigned to the fact that she would be celebrating her twenty-third birthday alone, without her husband. Although she felt his absence keenly, she consoled herself with the thought that she would enjoy the celebration to which Martha had invited her. Riding out to Chesterfield Hall, she heard the songbirds in the trees and watched the burgeoning fields with delight and pride that all of this belonged to her husband. It was, Martha had told her, almost as large as the ten thousand acres of Monticello that belonged to Thomas Jefferson.

All around, spring was in the air, and Aimee felt a restlessness within her own body as she realized she had been without a husband for six months. Briefly, she wondered if he had remained faithful to her during his stay in Paris, then chided herself even for thinking such negative thoughts. She would have to trust him—she *did* trust him. She only wished he would hurry and return to her.

As always, Martha was waiting for her on the veranda, her arms open in a gesture of love and welcome. Frances was her usual crotchety self, although her arthritis had improved with the warmer temperatures. She immediately launched into a discussion of the perils of being old versus the perils of being young. Aimee laughingly told her there were too many to enumerate and kissed the woman lovingly on the cheek, receiving the usual perfunctory hug for her trouble.

It was well into evening and dinner was over, the cake already eaten, when the ladies retired to the small drawing room to sit and converse quietly as was their wont on these occasions. There was an air of comfortable companionship that was very appealing to Aimee—and at this moment, New Orleans seemed very far away. She had received a letter from Violette two days before telling her of the excitement in New Orleans as rumors continued to run rampant that France would soon be taking control of the city. Lenore had turned two in March—a fact that amazed Aimee, who remembered her as an infant. Another surprise had been the announcement that Violette was pregnant once again, to the delight of her parents and Dominic, who had, she reported, decided he wanted a large family to fill the plantation house he hoped one day to build. The baby was due in October and Violette expressed her hope that it would be born on French soil.

"Such a lazy day it has been," Martha commented, busy with needlework as she glanced out the window. "Did you enjoy your birthday, my dear?" she asked Aimee.

The latter nodded vigorously. "I couldn't have asked for anything better—unless it was to have my husband back home again."

"The scamp's been gone far too long!" Frances agreed in skeptical tones. "He should never leave such a beautiful young wife alone this long. It's quite foolish of him, really."

"I agree."

All three ladies turned to the doorway and Aimee let out a cry of shock as she perceived Lucian standing in the hall, gazing in at the three of them with an amused grin. Jumping up from her chair, she ran into her husband's arms, laughing and crying, unable to believe he was really home after so long a time. Lucian kissed her mouth, her ears, her wet cheeks, expressing his happiness at being reunited with her again.

"God, how I've missed you, my love!" he said, pressing her cheeks between his hands to look into her eyes. "You've grown even lovelier since I saw you last."

"What do you expect!" Frances returned grumpily, although she, too, was happy to see her grandson home again. "Did you think she'd be pining away to bare bones while you were gone!"

"No, Grandmother, I was sure you would keep her from doing such a thing!" Lucian laughed, grabbing Aimee's hand to take her with him as he went to kiss Frances and then his mother.

As he greeted Martha, Aimee could only stand next to him staring at him to make sure he was really there. She let her eyes travel lovingly over the sable-dark hair that curled roguishly at his white collar, proclaiming the need for a visit to the barber. They traveled to the sun-browned face, even more deeply tanned from his exposure on board ship, and to the vivid blue eyes that were crinkled now with laughter as his mother related their celebration of Aimee's birthday. His mouth was turned up in a smile—that mouth that could be so tender

when he kissed her, she thought with a little shiver. She longed
to feel his kisses right now, to have him throw her on the floor
and make love to her, but it would be impossible to have him
alone to herself for at least the time it would take him to talk
to his relatives. She chafed impatiently at the wait and felt his
hand pressing her waist, as though to tell her he understood
and was just as impatient as she was.

"You've done a good job of surprising us all!" Martha
laughed, calling for something to eat for her son, who professed
that he was, indeed, famished.

"I wanted to be home in time for my wife's birthday," Lucian replied with a tender smile in Aimee's direction. "When I
went to Prince Street, I had the horrible idea that she might be
at some social function and I would make a fool of myself by
breaking in on it and carrying her away with me. When the
servants told me she was out here, I took the time to bathe the
travel stains off and change my clothing so I could present
myself in halfway decent fashion." He leaned down and kissed
the top of Aimee's head. "God, it was so good to see all three
of you together in such harmony. It gave me such a feeling of
content, I find it hard to describe. Suffice it to say that I love
you all dearly!"

"And I love you very much, Lucian!" Aimee whispered into
his ear, taking the moment to nibble teasingly at it.

He hugged her closer and she could feel the thrill that ran
through her at his nearness. It was all she could do to watch him
eat quietly, chafing in her seat while she imagined them together
upstairs in their bedroom. She wished that they were in their own
home in Alexandria, but told herself it wouldn't matter if they
were in the Capitol building itself! She would be the most loving
and ardent wife her husband could ever imagine.

Finally, the questions subsided, and Martha, sensing their
need to be alone, announced she was ready to retire, taking a
protesting Frances with her. Tenderly, Lucian put an arm about
his wife's waist and walked upstairs with her to their room.
Once inside, he closed the door and pulled her possessively
into his arms, his mouth crushing hers as his tongue pushed
itself inside to fence delicately with hers. They kissed a long
time, a slow, leisurely kiss that seemed to draw the very breath
out of Aimee.

She could feel his hands tangling in her hair as he loosened
it from its pins, could feel the insistent pressure of his touch on
the back of her neck. A half-recalled sense of tingling, of

excitement suppressed for too long, rose within her. She looked warily into the blue eyes that melted into hers.

"I am at your mercy," she whispered, trembling a little as she saw the fire in his eyes at her words.

"As I am at yours," he told her, bringing her chin up with one hand so that her mouth tilted once more into his. He was kissing her again, with slow, hot lips that leisurely molded her mouth to his as his hand dropped from her chin to her waist, then around to her back to press her closer.

Aimee felt his arms tremble as he held her as though he were deliberately holding himself back, fighting the urge to take her quickly. That knowledge, coupled with the expertise he was showing with his kisses, flooded her even more with hot passion. He bent her backward in his arms so that she was arched against him, her breasts straining against the delicate fabric of her gown.

Suddenly, he picked her up in his arms and placed her gently on the bed, staring down at her while he undressed, throwing his clothing haphazardly into the four corners of the room. When he was naked, he lay down beside her, supporting himself on one elbow as he leaned over to kiss her again. His lips parted hers again, sending a thrill up her backbone. Her mind seemed to be swaying, darkening, blotting out the reality of the room and the house—filled with only the knowledge of his presence, his warm, splendid nakedness against the soft fabric of her gown. It seemed somehow indecent, almost lecherous that she should still be dressed while he was totally exposed to her. It gave her a quiet sense of power and, with a boldness that made him gasp, she ran her hands down the length of him, catching hold of that part of him that had stiffened in his passion.

Gently, she moved her hand on him so that he lay back for a moment, his eyes closed, his breath coming faster. Then, at once, he pushed her hand away, springing up with a low growl. Like a suddenly awakened tiger, he pounced on her, pulling at the fastenings of her gown so that he could peel it away from her shoulders to expose the uptilted globes of her breasts.

"Dammit, woman! You'd torture me with your caresses—and now I'll torture you with mine!" he whispered, his hands fondling her breasts while his mouth came down to enclose a turgid nipple. Slowly, lovingly, his tongue came out to lave the darkening point, drawing lazy circles around it until his lips closed over it and sucked gently, driving her crazy with passion.

He moved to the other, his hands continuing to caress her, moving down slowly to her hips and belly, feeling the satiny smoothness of it with a sigh. His teeth, sharp and ungentle, bit at the nipple he held in his mouth, causing Aimee to arch toward him in unrestrained desire. Apologetically, he licked at it and Aimee felt a subtle tingling shoot down to her toes.

With a sigh, she felt his hands on the juncture of her thighs, brushing the springy hair that grew there before going lower to the moist heat between. Gently, his fingers worked magic on her flesh so that Aimee threw her head from side to side on the bed. With a smile, he continued to pull her gown down to her ankles, and then, with a careless toss, it landed somewhere on the floor along with the rest of her garments.

Now they were both naked, and Aimee, anticipating what was bound to happen, arched her body up to him, opening her knees to welcome him. But he was not yet ready to satisfy her raging passion. With a low laugh, he kissed both her breasts, then moved slowly down to her belly, bestowing little nips on the smooth flesh before dipping lower to that part of her that she was sure must be fairly steaming with her passion.

Masterfully, his dark head dipped down and she felt his mouth working wonders so that she wanted to scream and groan aloud with the marvelous feeling of it all. Her hands were clasping his head, pressing it against her, and she thought she would die from the shivering, tingling sensations running through her. Finally, everything seemed to tighten into one large ball of pleasure and she felt it explode inside of her, making her legs tremble with reaction. Lying back, feeling the perspiration breaking out on the smooth flesh of her body, she was dimly aware that he was kissing her once more along her inner thighs, torturing her exquisitely, bringing her back with breathless passion so that in a very short time she experienced yet another explosion that left her exhausted.

"No more!" she cried, wanting him against her, wanting his mouth on hers and his body pressed against her.

Obligingly, he moved up, joining his body to hers. She felt the hard length of him slide easily into the well-prepared opening, fusing them together as his mouth came down hard on hers. With a deep sigh, she clung to him, wanting him as deep inside of her as was possible. Her hands were tight around his neck, her legs arching upward to clasp him around the hips.

"Oh, Lucian!" She sighed when she could draw a breath to speak. "I have missed you so!"

"Not half as much as I have missed you, my beloved!" he replied, kissing her again and beginning to move deeply and surely within her.

There was no more time for talk as he brought her once more to the threshold of almost painful pleasure that seemed to course through her body with a breathless urgency that left her gasping. When he could stand it no longer, his movements became faster and she could feel the tingling hardness of him filling her up, followed by the climactic moment when she knew he had spent himself. With a groan he kissed her, his body trembling with the force of his release. Aimee clasped him close, kissing him back with passionate frenzy, feeling her own response catch fire inside of her.

After several seconds, he lowered himself gently against her, putting most of his weight on his elbows as he gazed down at her with eyes still narrowed with his passion.

"Aimee, I love you!" he whispered, kissing her again.

"I love you, Lucian!" she replied, returning his kiss ardently.

"My grandmother is perfectly right—I *have* been foolish to stay away so long. How could any man in his right mind leave such a passionate little vixen behind?" he teased, placing a kiss on the tip of her nose.

"I agree completely." Aimee sighed.

He moved off her, his body still pressing against hers from the side. "God, it's good to be home with my wife," he said softly. "Every day I was in Paris, I thought of you, Aimee. I found myself wishing I might find you by some miracle at that little boardinghouse in the Montmartre. I walked the streets of Paris, thinking I would see that charming face of yours watching me from some street corner. Alas, it was all a foolish fantasy."

"Nevertheless, I am flattered by it," she said delightedly.

"And did you miss me as well?" he demanded, gazing down at her with brows drawn down in mock anger.

"Too much," she admitted with a smile. "Especially at night, I'm afraid."

"Ah, what a greedy little wench you are!" He laughed, hugging her against him. "But I'm sure there were some amusements during the day?"

She shrugged. "The usual gatherings and teas that seem to be the way of life here in the capital. In fact, I have to admit to thinking that I would make a very good politician's wife, should you ever decide to run for office somewhere. You would have been quite proud of me if you could have seen me mingling with all the other politicians' wives!"

"God forbid I should ever seek public office!" Lucian exclaimed with a suddenly weary air. "It is enough that I do what I already do!"

Aimee turned on her side to face him, leaning on her elbow. "Your mission? Talleyrand?"

"Ah, God, it is a long and involved story, my dearest. It seems that my old friend Fouché had been involved with some royalists who were planning on overthrowing Bonaparte. Even though the Minister of Police prides himself on his ability to conceal his motives, he made a mistake this time and Bonaparte caught him. For a few months he was actually out of favor, but then Bonaparte realized he needed him too much and finally reinstated him. It was all a political farce, really. Everyone else in the plan was sent to prison, but our wily Fouché escaped such a fate. Clever man—too clever, I think, for one day he will end up going too far and he'll be tripped up."

"Was that the reason why Talleyrand had you come all the way from America?" Aimee wondered in astonishment.

Lucian looked uneasy. "No, not exactly. He had had word that there was an informant within the organization who was leaking information to the British. For a time, I suppose they suspected me, but the culprit was soon caught and I was released from any suspicion." He leaned back and closed his eyes for a moment. "Much has happened while I've been in Paris," he said, almost to himself.

"Did you find out if the treaty with Spain is fact?"

"Talleyrand did not ever come out and state baldly that France and Spain had come to an agreement on the Louisiana Territory," he said warily, "but he did intimate the fact. But the most important news is that the Peace of Amiens was signed just last month between France and England. The war is over—at least for now."

"But that is wonderful!" Aimee exclaimed.

"I suppose it is," Lucian agreed lightly, "and yet, it will present many problems for Jefferson and the United States. With both countries freed from the responsibilities of war in Europe, they will have the leisure to turn their attention to the Americas."

"Jefferson has already expressed his fear that this might happen," Aimee remarked thoughtfully. She missed the surprised look her husband bestowed on her. "The poor man is desperate to know the fate of New Orleans."

"I wish to God I knew the truth," Lucian replied, "but, apparently, Bonaparte wants the thing kept secret until he feels the time is right to reveal the terms. Meanwhile, the American ministers have been dangling on at the French Court, trying to sniff out the truth of his secret pact with Spain, fairly jittery with anxiety and humorlessly prattling away about shipping losses and their natural rights to navigate the wilderness rivers. Talleyrand, as usual, has been amusing himself by inventing complicated and graceful evasions of their queries and by telling them the most charming lies imaginable, all of which they swallow with amazing grace!"

"What do you think will happen?" Aimee asked.

"Sooner or later, Jefferson will have to make a decision on what he *thinks* has happened between France and Spain—and then he will act according to his own conscience and the wishes of his constituents. It will be a damned difficult decision no matter which side he chooses to believe. He knows that Bonaparte has brought unity and internal peace to France. Now with the new peace with Great Britain, he has also brought external peace to his country. If there is to be a new France in his vision of greatness—a vision planted there by Talleyrand, I'm quite sure —then it will have to be built in stages."

"What do you mean?"

"First, the position of the Caribbean islands must be secured. After the revolution in Santo Domingo, Bonaparte is aware of the strategic importance of recapturing that island for France as a refueling station. Second, he will probably try to convert the Gulf of Mexico into a French pond for the exclusive use of his naval warships. The third and most logical step after that would be to attack Canada from the south and return it to France."

"I feel certain the British would have quite a lot to say about that, especially if they entered into this new peace with good intentions."

"Bonaparte is using the time gained by this peace to further his own ambition. Even Talleyrand admitted it," Lucian commented with a sigh. "The English aren't stupid; I'm sure they've already suspected Bonaparte of such tactics, but they could probably use the time themselves to think up new strategies and reinforce their army and navy. You can be sure that Garth Cabot has been busy trying to find out Jefferson's position in regard to both

France and Great Britain. If the English think that America is leaning toward France, they would not hesitate to begin a war with them."

"But popular opinion has been going against France recently," Aimee pointed out.

"It is a fact, though, that Jefferson and Madison still cling to the rather romantic notion that there should always be friendship between the great republics of the United States and France. Poor Robert Livingston, the American ambassador to France. I saw him while I was in Paris and the poor man is nearly chewing his nails up to the elbows trying to find out what he can about New Orleans. He finally asked Talleyrand point-blank if there was such a pact that had given France the right to the port city, and Talleyrand blandly denied it. But unless France means to go to war with Spain, then no French force can occupy New Orleans unless there actually is a treaty."

"It seems a fine coil—no one being truthful, Jefferson left to deduce what he can—"

"And the First Consul and his able Foreign Minister on top of it all like cocks on a dung heap!" Lucian remarked, showing his irritation.

"Darling, if New Orleans is in French hands, then perhaps we will be able to return there soon," Aimee returned soothingly, bringing her hands up to brush at his chest, feeling the pleasant ripple of muscles that moved under her hand.

Lucian was silent for a moment. Then he said, with a voice grown husky once more with desire, "Let's not talk about it anymore! It's a sad comment when a man's return home to his lovely wife can be marred by all this political talk! Perhaps I am in the wrong business, my love, for I certainly will not have a strain on our marriage from all of this."

"I would hardly call it a strain!" Aimee giggled, feeling her husband's hands begin to explore the curves and hollows of her body. "Perhaps it even lends a certain . . . uh . . . excitement to it!"

Lucian laughed. "I don't agree at all. I think it would all be much better were I to tell Talleyrand to go to hell and become a gentleman farmer, growing tobacco on my Virginia estate. Could you picture yourself as the wife of such a man, waiting in her chair on the porch, needlework in hand, while a dozen children play in the yard?" he wondered, nuzzling her neck with his lips.

"A dozen?" she squeaked, jumping as he nipped the hollow of her throat.

"At least," he murmured, moving up to her lips. "And I would suggest we begin to work on that immediately, Mrs. Napier," he ended huskily, molding her body to his and beginning the delightful love play that Aimee knew would send the familiar tingling sensations coursing through her body, to be climaxed by the joining of their bodies. She settled back on the mattress and hugged her husband close, losing herself in the wonder of their lovemaking.

40

●─●─●─●

Apprehension grew by leaps and bounds in the muddy new capital city of the United States, as news of the Peace of Amiens was received and rumormongers insisted that now there would be nothing to stop either country from making war on America. American public opinion had already begun to turn against France, but that feeling was intensified now that suspicions had arisen that France intended to make the Gulf of Mexico a "French pond" and the whole of the Louisiana Territory into a "new France" that would effectively threaten the power of the United States.

Lucian, aware of the rumors and very concerned about their effect on the political climate, wrote back to France, warning Talleyrand that he must make some conciliatory gestures to the Americans or they would be forced into that "marriage" with Great Britain that Jefferson abhorred in order to protect their own borders. The states of Kentucky and Tennessee were veritable hotbeds of sedition and activism that caused new lines of worry to mark the President's brow.

The summer months passed with isolated incidents in several of the states; in many cases the flareups had to be put down with the use of force. Even so, hotheaded leaders, funded secretly by various dissatisfied factions, rose up to fill the settlers' heads with dreams of floating down the Mississippi River and taking New Orleans as their natural right. Jefferson had his hands full with the increasingly intricate juggling act that included balancing the friendship of France against England, even though he still did not know for sure if France had acquired New Orleans from Spain.

As Lucian had predicted, France, without the worry of England barking at her heels, was looking toward America, intent on regaining the revolutionary island of Santo Domingo, which had revolted against France a few years before. Bonaparte sent a fleet of fifty thousand veterans of war under the command of his brother-in-law, General Leclerc. He effectively wiped out the black republic, and even before the final battle was won there, fast packet boats bearing news of this expedition arrived in the United States. Added to that was the ominous news that the British fleet was poised just off of the island of Jamaica, prepared for action if necessary.

For Jefferson, war with France was still unthinkable, but equally so was Bonaparte on the Mississippi River. He continued to hope that England and France would go to war again, with his second option being an alliance with Great Britain if French warships arrived in New Orleans. He wrote to Livingston, his ambassador to France, saying that the day when France took possession of New Orleans would fix his intentions forever. He maintained it would seal the union of America and England and would enable the two countries to work together to maintain exclusive possession of the oceans. He reiterated that this was not a state he sought or desired by any means; it would be adopted only if France forced it upon the United States. He gave this letter to Victor Du Pont, who had acted as the President's private messenger before, with orders that Du Pont was to disclose the contents to Livingston, Talleyrand, and Bonaparte exclusively. Du Pont suggested that the United States try to buy New Orleans and the Floridas; it would be cheaper than taking France to war—a war they would probably lose anyway.

Lucian heard of the letter and shook his head in frustration, telling Aimee that all this talk was unavailing if Bonaparte and Talleyrand meant to build an empire, which he was strongly beginning to suspect.

At the same time, there came news from Santo Domingo that the French Army had fallen victim to yellow fever and couldn't press on to New Orleans, if that was, indeed, its intended goal. In Washington, Jefferson breathed a little easier since now he was given some time, despite the reports from France indicating that Bonaparte had already ordered another fleet and army to sail directly to New Orleans.

The capital was in a state of constant flux, opinion swaying back and forth, verging many times on hysteria, fueled by rumors from English spies and French spies alike. Garth Cabot was one of the instigators of a rumor that spread concerning the ultimate wisdom of settling their differences with Great Britain in order to counterattack France effectively should her warships arrive on the horizon. He urged everyone to write to the President demanding that he give up his delicate balancing act and side, once and for all, with England.

Added to these fears, the Spanish intendant in New Orleans had once more canceled American trading privileges in New Orleans and on the river. He said, simply, that they no longer existed. The fear in Washington was that the French had put the Spanish up to this. Despite the governor's action, though, American rafts and keelboats continued to ply the river, their crews saying they could float on it as they damned well pleased, provided they paid the port duties and fees like any other foreigners. The governor of the territory was forced to back down under this unexpected stance. The westerners claimed an easy victory, reinforcing the fact that they felt the navigation of the river was rightfully theirs. They certainly did not admire the Spanish—their religion, or anything else about them. Still, the western shrieks of outrage carried to Washington, demanding that the fees be discontinued, because to many of these settlers, veterans of the American revolution, "taxes" was a fighting word and one not likely to be taken lightly. They wrote to Jefferson saying that being asked to pay port duties was tantamount to being denied the Mississippi River. They began to form their own state militias and sent angry statements to Congress, saying they would take New Orleans themselves, and to hell if it meant war with France!

Jefferson's dilemma continued: if he concurred with the westerners, it would mean an alliance with the English in a war against France, which would show the policy of his political rivals, the Federalists, as correct, and the policy of his own party, the Republicans, as wrong. He refused to make a choice, hoping his popularity among the westerners would continue long enough to give him time until war would inevitably break out again between France and England.

But time was rapidly slipping away as reports came in from France that Bonaparte was spending over two million francs to equip a new fleet to set sail for the Americas. In London, the government was considering sending its own fleet there first, unless the Americans decided to take New Orleans themselves.

Lucian was gone much of the day during the weeks that followed and Aimee worried constantly for him, afraid that with public opinion so high against France, the people might physically turn against anything or anybody from that country. Lucian warned her to stay indoors as much as possible, for already there had been incidents of stones being thrown through their windows and ugly signs being painted on their doorstep. Aimee was not so much afraid for herself as for her husband, who must constantly make the trip across the river to the capital in order to confer with the French ambassador.

She received a call from Lianne one day in late November and was so grateful for a guest that she declared she would keep the other woman there all day just so she wouldn't find herself talking to the walls! Lianne offered her sympathy for the change of events and settled down in her chair with an unexpected warning to Aimee.

"Garth has grown quite relentless in pursuing ways to discredit the French dignitaries—and your husband, especially," she admonished her in all seriousness. "I am fearful of some scheme he has cooked up, which he refuses to discuss with me. I am worried, terribly worried, that Lucian may wind up falsely accused of something if he is not careful. Garth has been spending money like water. I wish I knew what he was up to!"

Aimee's eyes had widened with her fear and she licked her suddenly dry lips anxiously. "What do you mean, Lianne? Do you think he plans some physical attack?"

Lianne laughed rather bitterly and shook her head. "No, Garth is much more subtle than that, my dear. He would just as soon destroy a man's reputation and hound him out of town than attack him physically. I believe he is really something of a coward where physical confrontation is required."

"But what can I do to protect Lucian?" Aimee worried, rubbing her hands together. "He refuses to remain at home, insisting that he has his work to do in Washington. I practically begged him to stay home today, but he treats me like a child!"

"Men are like that in a crisis," Lianne observed with a sniff of disdain. "They think their women will fall apart like corn-husk dolls, but what they don't realize is that our spines are just as stiff as theirs!"

Aimee nodded. "So Garth is bent on destroying Lucian. But, why?"

Lianne looked into Aimee's green eyes, her own holding a wealth of honesty. "My dear, he hates Lucian—and he hates you because you would not allow yourself to fall victim to his wiles. He has a wealth of pride, more than enough for two men! The fact that you are French only adds to his determination. My husband . . . uh . . . works closely with the government of Great Britain to work for their interests."

Aimee knew that Garth was a spy for England, but she and Lianne had never come out and admitted it in so many words.

That Lianne knew that Lucian was a spy, Aimee was not sure of, but she suspected that if Garth was aware of it, so was his wife. Tactfully, they both avoided the subject.

"But you have no idea what Garth is planning?" Aimee asked anxiously.

Lianne shook her head. "No, I'm sorry. I wish I did, but I thought I should at least warn you that something was afoot. He will use any underhanded tactics he can, and has been dispensing money too liberally not to cause some suspicion in my mind."

"But, even if I tell Lucian, he will probably shrug it off and tell me not to worry!" Aimee cried, feeling sudden anger at her husband's insistence that nothing was going to happen. She had too many memories of vindictiveness in people, leading to tragedy for those she loved—and she was determined that she was not going to lose her husband to such a thing.

"If he won't listen to you, tell him he is making a terrible mistake," Lianne returned. "He should think of your welfare above his own, surely!"

"I don't know, I don't know," Aimee remarked, shaking her head. "He is so involved in his work in the capital that I wonder if he thinks of me at all sometimes. It has been such a strain on both of us, with all this negative opinion against France and all these false warnings and rumors that continue to circulate that Bonaparte is going to send his fleet to conquer the United States!"

"I understand, my friend, and I insist that, should something dire happen to Lucian, you must come to me immediately. I know you would be hesitant because of Garth, but he is so seldom at home these days I don't think it would make any difference. Then, too, sometimes the safest place is the least suspected, don't you agree?"

Aimee did not know what to think. "I could go to Chesterfield Hall and stay with Martha and Frances."

"You may not have the time to go there. If something happens to Lucian, your mother-in-law may find herself under suspicion also. I beg you to promise me to come to me should anything happen, Aimee! There is nothing Garth would do to you in my own house, I promise you!"

Aimee was still skeptical, but promised she would come. Lianne breathed a sigh of relief and leaned over to clasp Aimee's hands. "My dearest friend, I could never forgive myself should something happen to you because of my husband. You have shown yourself so kind and loyal to me, even with the hostilities between our two countries, that I can do nothing but everything within my power to help you."

Two days later, the warning became reality. Aimee was sitting quietly in the small salon, trying to concentrate on a letter she was writing to Violette, when a loud knocking on the door interrupted her train of thought. Flying to answer it, certain it had something to do with her husband, she opened it to perceive a contingent of men in uniform, their faces very stern. The officer in command proceeded to read a lengthy document, the gist of which said that her husband was suspected of a plot to dispatch pro-French forces to Kentucky in order to overthrow the governor of the state and lead the Kentuckians on a march to the Mississippi River valley to take over the territory for France.

"But—this is preposterous!" Aimee sputtered. "President Jefferson couldn't possibly believe such lies!"

"Mrs. Napier, I haven't come to debate the truth of the document, only to inform you of it and to tell you that we are seeking your husband for questioning. Do you have knowledge of his whereabouts?"

It was on the tip of her tongue to snarl out that he was on his way to Kentucky with his invisible troop of pro-French forces, but she gulped back the sarcastic words with difficulty. "He is in the capital, of course, attending to legitimate work for the ambassador from France."

"Thank you, madame. We won't trouble you further, but we do suggest you remain in the city. Do not attempt to leave its perimeters or we may be forced to place you under house arrest!"

Aimee watched them go, feeling her heart like lead in her breast. Lucian would be arrested! She was very frightened. After all, her husband, even though she knew he had no plans to take over the Mississippi valley for France, was a spy under the pay of Talleyrand. If President Jefferson found out about his clandestine activities, God knew what he would do to him. She wasn't sure of the laws and punishments meted out in this country, but she could imagine what would happen under the same circumstances in France. The diplomatic immunity extended to the ambassador and his direct staff would be sidestepped in such a case. Lucian could wind up in prison for a very long stay—or even worse! She dared not even think of that, her hand clutching at her throat as though she was finding difficulty in breathing.

Her mind flew to the instigator of this insidious plot—Garth Cabot! Her green eyes froze into chips of emerald ice as she wondered how much it had cost him to think up such an elaborate net of lies. And the worst of it was that she could not even denounce him as an English spy, for fear of the repercussions it would bring on her own husband.

Quickly, not even bothering to change clothes, she ordered a horse saddled and galloped pell-mell to the house of Garth Cabot in Georgetown, chafing at the delay of the ferry. Once at the house, she jumped down from her horse and ran to the front door, shaking the brass knocker off its hinges in her haste to talk with Lianne.

To her surprise it was not Lianne, but her husband, who answered the door. For a moment, she was nonplussed. Before she could recover, Garth was smiling a cunning smile and ushering her into the house, closing the door firmly behind her.

"Why, Mrs. Napier—my dear Aimee, how nice of you to visit when I am at home for a change! Lianne is upstairs napping, but you and I can converse quite pleasantly while you wait—"

"I have no wish to speak with you!" Aimee interrupted tightly. "You know perfectly well what has happened to my husband! And all because of *your* little machinations!"

He appeared dumbfounded and Aimee congratulated him on his acting abilities. "What are you saying, my dear? What has happened to Lucian?"

"He has been arrested."

"Arrested!" Garth was hard-put to hide his smile of satisfaction. "Do you know why?"

"I know that *you* must have had something to do with it," Aimee answered quickly, shoving aside the hand he had put on her arm to lead her to a chair. "You hate my husband for reasons that are as disgusting as you are! You hate him because you were unable to seduce his wife and you realized that he is much more of a man than you could ever be!" She stood there watching his eyes darken with suppressed anger.

"I think you overestimate your charms, my dear," he said when he had recovered his aplomb. "I would not hate a man simply because his wife proves herself naïve and ungrateful for another man's attentions." He laughed cynically. "If that were the case, I would be more likely to direct my hatred at the wife, not the husband. But, I'm afraid, you seem to be under some delusions, my dear, for I had nothing whatsoever to do with your husband's arrest."

"You are a liar!"

His mouth tightened and his eyes narrowed as his hand shot out to tighten painfully around her wrist. Holding back the tears of pain, she faced him, unwilling to back down from her stance. "I resent your insults, Mrs. Napier," he said bitingly. "I must say I would suspect the sanity of your condition right now. You come here with your hair in disarray, still attired in a morning gown, and spit out insults in my own house! I will not stand for it, I can assure you!"

"You are loathsome!" Aimee snarled, beside herself with rage as he continued to pretend no knowledge of the reason for her husband's arrest. "You are not even man enough to admit to me what you have done!"

His face paled and his grip on her wrist tightened ominously. "Madame, you truly go beyond hospitality's dictates," he said in a low voice. Pulling her into the salon, he closed the doors quickly, keeping hold of her wrist. "I will not have your mad screechings disrupting my wife's rest!"

"You care nothing for your wife!" Aimee accused him. "Lianne has already confided in me the details of your marriage!"

Losing his calm, Garth reached his free hand out and slapped her viciously across the face. "I'll not have a common little French tart discussing the details of my private life behind my back!" he roared, nearly beside himself with rage. "You have wormed your way into my wife's good graces—for what purpose I have yet to find out. But I can easily put a stop to that, let me assure you! I can forbid you ever to come to this house again. Or, if that fails, I can very easily forge some letter implicating you in the same plot as your husband."

"Like you forged the letter implicating my husband?" she challenged, her eyes revealing their suspicions.

He stared at her, realizing he had said too much. Then, with a supremely confident smile, he released her wrist and watched her as she rubbed it, wincing from the pain. "You are most intelligent, Aimee. I am—almost impressed by you. In fact, I would say that you are too intelligent to continue allying yourself to your husband and his losing cause. Yes, I know what his purpose is in Washington City. He is a spy for France, reporting to Foreign Minister Talleyrand himself. It was quite easy to find out this information—your husband is not quite as professional about his work as he might like his wife to believe."

Aimee was silent, hoping he would continue talking. It would keep him away from her, and she hoped Lianne would be awakened by all the commotion and come downstairs to her aid. She sensed that there was something innately dangerous about this man who stood before her, chuckling over his cleverness. Although she told herself she was too angry to be afraid, it still worried her to be alone with him. She edged farther toward the door, watching him with her keen eyes, alert to any sudden move he might make.

"What?" he asked her suddenly. "No protestations of her husband's innocence! No remarks about the nefarious dealings of my own work here in the capital. Surely, you are wise enough to know that I, too, work secretly for my government. Fortunately, there are at least two dozen other spies in this city. Actually, the process is quite normal—and I daresay all capitals expect some amount of intrigue. It is only when we overstep our bounds—as your husband did—and get mixed up with the politics of a nation that we are severely punished for it."

"My husband certainly did no such thing," Aimee interjected staunchly. *"You* were the one who was behind this fabrication of lies."

"If I were, you can bet I made very sure your husband would not be able to escape the net. I have made the acquaintance here of a man who is very, very good at forging signatures," he said with a hint of smugness. "For a high price, he will do anything you require, even forge Jefferson's handwriting! It could be quite amusing, don't you think, sending a forged letter to the French stating that the United States is ready to make war on them! How delightful to watch that uncouth Jefferson scramble around like a beheaded chicken, trying to find out why the French naval fleet is bearing down on the Atlantic coast. Of course, it would be child's play for Bonaparte to force the Americans' surrender—and then equally easy for British troops from Canada to storm southward and kick out the French forces, already weary and depleted from their battles with the Americans. And then this upstart United States would be right back where they belong, within the welcoming arms of their mother country." He smiled broadly. "A tantalizing prospect, my dear, wouldn't you say?"

"I would say your grandiose schemes are bound to backfire in your face!" Aimee declared. "I am quite sure my husband will be able to get out of this tangle you have placed him in, and then I suggest you watch out for your own scurvy hide!" she added, sounding braver than she felt.

"Ah, my poor Aimee. You carry such delusions about your husband's strength and judgment. I think it is high time you realize he is nothing compared to a *real* man!" And he came toward her, like a cat stalking a mouse, his eyes never leaving her face as it paled visibly at his tactics.

Backing up slowly, Aimee felt her back placed against the drawing room doors. Desperately, she reached behind her with her good hand, seeking the door latch that would free her from this dangerous man. But before she could find it, he pounced on her, knocking her to the floor so that they rolled around for a moment, each of them trying to gain the upper hand. Unaccustomed to such physical tactics from a man, Aimee's strength was rapidly depleted and she found herself crushed beneath his weight, staring up at him with fright and rage mixed in her green eyes as she tensed to see what he would do next.

With a low, triumphant laugh, he bent his head to plant unwelcome kisses on her face and neck, even more horrible to Aimee as she recalled her husband doing the very same thing the night before as they made love together. With one arm stretched across her neck, threatening to choke her should she move, Garth Cabot reached down with his other hand to push down the neckline of her morning gown and grasp her breast roughly.

Fighting the urge to faint, if only to save her senses from the torture she knew she could expect from this man, Aimee tried to bite him, but each time she moved her head, he would increase the pressure of his arm against her throat until she could scarcely breathe. He lowered his mouth to suck at her breast while his hand moved lower among the folds of her skirt, seeking the womanly softness of her.

In growing panic, Aimee did the only thing she could—she screamed at the top of her lungs. Dismayed at her tactic, Garth was shaken up enough to release his arm from her throat, enabling her to scream again before he sent her a blow to the side of her face, making her head wobble on her neck and the room seem to dip and swirl around her for a moment. Enraged, he would have done more physical harm to her, except that he heard his wife's voice from upstairs, demanding to know what was happening.

"I have no love for my wife, but she can still be useful to me!" he growled, gritting his teeth in his frustration. "It seems, my dear, you have escaped me again, but I assure you, there will be another time." He released her and stood up, pulling her up with him. "I suggest you fix your gown before my wife arrives downstairs," he added smoothly.

"I shall tell her everything!" Aimee warned, fumbling with the front of her gown, her head still not steady after the blow he had delivered.

"No, you won't," he assured her maliciously. "If you say anything to my wife about this incident, I can promise you your husband will not have to prove his innocence to the President, for he will be killed before he can even gain a release from jail. Do not think my threats are idle, Aimee, for it is a very easy thing to place a few sacks of gold in the hands of the proper people—and arrangements can very easily be made."

Aimee stared at him in alarm. The man was mad with his obsessive hatred of her husband. She realized it would be wise to pretend to believe his threats, at least for the time being. Accusations against him in front of Lianne would do very little good, anyway, for there was nothing she could truly accomplish. She would have to bide her time—and wait for the chance to catch this man in a compromising situation. Meanwhile, she must think of the safety of Lucian. With this thought in mind, she straightened her gown and tidied her hair, just before the bump of the wheelchair on the hall floor told her that Lianne was downstairs.

With one last warning look from beneath his upraised brow, Garth stepped to the doors in order to open them, having already straightened his own clothing. With a suave smile, he leaned over to kiss Lianne, not noticing the look of distaste on the face of his wife.

"My dear, look who has arrived to see you," Garth said pleasantly.

"I heard a woman's scream," Lianne stated flatly, looking from one to the other of the two occupants of the room.

"I . . . fell, slid on the rug," Aimee lied quickly, hating the triumphant sparkle in Garth's eyes. "I'm afraid I managed to land quite a good bruise on my cheek," she added, in order to explain the reddening swell on the side of her face.

"Goodness, you need that attended to immediately to keep it from swelling worse!" Lianne cried, immediately concerned for her friend. "Come to the kitchen with me, my dear, and I'll have the cook doctor it up for you. She's marvelous with her home remedies and will have you feeling much better directly. Garth, perhaps you should offer our guest a brandy?"

"An excellent suggestion," Garth concurred, walking to the

side-board to pour the liquid into a glass. He came back to Aimee and held it out to her, the smug superiority in his smile infuriating her all over again, but she was careful not to release her anger this time and, smiling almost invitingly, she tossed the contents down, forcing herself not to choke.

"You did that very well," he commented in an undertone.

"And now, Aimee, come with me to the kitchen. Garth, were you on your way out?" Lianne queried pointedly, looking at her husband speculatively.

He bowed, the perfect diplomat. "As a matter of fact, I was, my dear. If you and your charming guest will excuse me, I have some necessary matters to see to in Washington." He glanced meaningfully at Aimee, then hurried out of the room, leaving the two women alone.

Lianne stared at her friend for a moment. Then, gently, she asked, "And now, can you tell me what really happened, Aimee?"

"I already told you, Lianne. I fell when I slipped on the rug and landed rather awkwardly against one of the side tables. My face hit one of the legs and I—"

"Did my husband do this to you? Is it because of what he caused to happen to Lucian? There's no sense in lying, Aimee. Garth is gone and none of what you tell me shall leave my lips, you can count on that. I already know that he forged a letter to implicate your husband in a treasonous plan to break away some part of the United States from the government. I have become quite adept myself at spying on my husband's correspondence. It passes the lonely hours and gives me rather a good feeling, knowing that someday I might be able to use any evidence I can glean against him."

"Oh, Lianne!" Aimee sat down in a chair, feeling suddenly weary. "I wish there were some way I could disentangle myself from all of this without involving you, but, unfortunately, there isn't. Yes, you are correct. Garth attacked me in here, thinking you were still asleep upstairs. If I hadn't been able to scream, I feel certain he would have carried out his intended rape of me."

"My poor Aimee—how horrible! I'm sorry that I was not awake to greet you the moment you arrived. I had no idea Garth would act this quickly against your husband!" She wheeled herself forward to lay a sympathetic hand on her friend's. "My husband is a brute, Aimee. Please accept my heartfelt apologies for the despicable way in which he treated you!"

"Thank you, my friend, but there is no need for you to apologize." Aimee leaned her head back against the chair, feeling her swollen cheek smarting painfully.

"There's no need for you to go back to the kitchen. I'll have the cook bring her medicines out here. Poor dear, I—I hate Garth for what he's done to you!" She wheeled herself out of the room, leaving Aimee alone for a few moments before returning with the cook and a soothing compress for her face.

When some of the swelling had subsided and the pain had been subdued, Aimee turned to Lianne with tears in her eyes. "Lianne, I can't bear the thought of Lucian being gone from me again, so soon after he returned from France. Everything is so topsy-turvy in this world! I am truly beginning to hate this place for all the trouble it has caused Lucian and me. I want to return to New Orleans!"

"Hush, my dear. I understand that you're distraught, but I'm sure your husband will be able to extricate himself from this plot of Garth's. President Jefferson is very fond of Lucian, and I'm sure that will play some part in all of this. He won't allow him to languish for very long without a chance to defend himself."

"I don't know," Aimee murmured. "The Americans have gone against the French; they are afraid that Bonaparte will send troops to conquer them. They will not want to disbelieve the lies Garth will be spreading freely about the capital. It may be more difficult than you think for Lucian to prove his innocence. With public opinion against him, he may not be able to count on Jefferson's friendship." She leaned her head in her hands, feeling fatigue settling around her. "I am tired to death of all of this constant strain and the worry about our property being damaged or our persons being attacked in the street. This place has been driven half mad with the fear of war, Lianne. I feel as though I am being hounded—and yet I am forced to stay until my husband consents to leave."

"My dear, I wish there were something I could do," Lianne answered worriedly. "Unfortunately, if I should offer you shelter with me, I could not be sure what Garth would do."

Aimee shuddered delicately. "I could never remain under the same roof as Garth Cabot, Lianne," she said firmly. "No, I am better off in my own home. If worse comes to worst, I can go for aid to the French ambassador. Perhaps he can put me up in his quarters until Lucian is released from jail."

"You could go to Jefferson yourself and plead your husband's case," Lianne suggested, trying to form a plan for Lucian's defense. "You surely know most of your husband's activities; you could vouch for his innocence."

Aimee shook her head. "I can't vouch for him in all truth, Lianne, for Jefferson is well aware that my husband comes to the capital alone every day. There is a lot of time in between his leaving me in the morning and returning at night—he could well believe Lucian did have a hand in the plot Garth has woven into the letter."

Lianne sighed. "Then, I'm afraid, you will just have to wait and keep faith in Lucian's ability to find a way out of this snare, Aimee. And know that you can rely on me throughout your difficulties. I will not turn on you because I might worry about my reputation, believe me! If you need anything, please let me know, and if it is within my power, I will certainly help you!"

"Thank you," Aimee said simply, gratefully. "It is some comfort to know that I have a friend like you through this thing."

41

·—·—·—·—·

As the days went by, Aimee was to become even more grateful for Lianne's continued support. Everyone else in the capital shunned her as though she had the plague. There was such anxiety and distrust toward the French that most people were of the opinion that Lucian Napier was guilty of the charges and that his wife, most likely, had been in on the plot with him. They were surprised that she had not been arrested also. But if Jefferson was naïve enough to allow the woman free rein in the streets of the capital, they were certainly not stupid enough to allow her into their homes!

Aimee had gone twice to the President's house to speak personally with Jefferson, but each time the servants had turned her away with some lame excuse so that she finally accepted the fact that he was not going to speak with her. She had asked to see her husband in jail, but that request, too, was denied her. She could do nothing but cool her heels and wait for the outcome of the investigation. John Marshall himself, a very able lawyer, had looked into the matter, indicating how grave it was in this time of uncertainty.

Lianne was supportive, but Aimee could not bring herself to go to the other's house because of the possibility that she might run into Garth there. Once, she had seen him in the streets of Alexandria and had quickly ordered her driver to turn around and return home. Garth had seen her, and though he could have followed her on his big, blood-bay gelding, he had not done so, probably because the crowds would have wondered why the Englishman was going after the wife of the French anarchist.

Still, he enjoyed playing a cat-and-mouse game with her, presenting himself twice at her door with a solicitous look on his cunning face. Once he had come when the servant was away at the market and Aimee had answered the door. Upon seeing him, she had tried to slam the door in his face, but he had shouldered his way inside, pushing her easily out of the way.

"So, I see your husband is still safely ensconced in jail, my dear. More's the pity for a healthy young woman like yourself. Tell me, Aimee, are you finding it lonesome without a man to take care of your needs?"

"Get out of my house, Garth Cabot!" she said angrily. "I shall call one of my servants to get the watch and have you thrown out for harassing me!"

"How sympathetic do you think they would be to the wife of the French traitor?" he wondered silkily, moving toward her. "Do you think they would care if she were raped or not?"

"You wouldn't dare risk your own reputation!" Aimee snarled at him, backing away when he continued to move closer.

Idly, he pointed a finger and let it slide along the smooth expanse of her exposed bosom, which was rising and falling quickly with her agitation above the deep cut of her high-waisted gown. Angrily, Aimee slapped his hand away, distressed that he could continue to be so bold.

"You might be worth a man's reputation," he commented idly, his hand dropping to her waist.

"I can't imagine Garth Cabot being so foolish!" Aimee rushed on, hoping to dissuade him from doing anything that would ignite his sexual desires. "I'm sure there are plenty of other women who would be glad to make themselves available to you!"

He laughed. "That's true enough, my dear. There has always been an availability in Washington City, but, alas, the quality is sometimes lacking. You, on the other hand, continue to be *unavailable*, which makes the quality seem even better, if you catch my meaning. Why don't you surrender to me, my dear? I can assure you that I could very easily use my considerable contacts in the capital to release your husband from jail. Why do you continue to fight me? Surrender to me once and I will let your husband go free."

For a moment, Aimee actually wavered, so desperate was she to secure Lucian's freedom. But the idea of facing him after being unfaithful was so distasteful, so alien to her values, that she dismissed the idea quickly. Looking up into Garth's eyes, she felt her heart quicken with her anger. "You will never have me!" she cried. "Not even if my husband should go to his death as a traitor—I would *never* surrender to you, Garth!"

"Then you are a fool, madame," he said solemnly. And, turning on his heel, he was out the door and gone, much to her intense relief. She collapsed into a chair and rubbed her eyes, telling herself that her nerves were wearing thin from this game that Garth Cabot went on playing with her. She could not continue to fence with him, for sooner or later he would be able to reach past her defenses, and then she would be lost.

"Oh, Lucian!" she sobbed to herself. "I want you so much —I need you so much! Please come home to me soon."

A few days later, she received a note from the President, requesting her presence in the drawing room of the President's mansion at two o'clock in the afternoon. Surprised, but elated at the chance to talk personally with Jefferson, Aimee dressed very carefully for her interview. She must not appear too regal, she thought, and yet she did not wish to make him think she had come to grovel. She chose a tasteful pale blue gown of watered silk, the long sleeves of which were banded in narrow bits of velvet ribbon at the wrist, the forearm, and the elbow, with a matching row of three bands along the hem. The décolleté was scooped, modestly cut, so that only her upper chest was exposed, and for extra measure she tucked a fine fichu of white cambric inside the bodice. She had her maid dress her hair in a conservative chignon, bringing her bangs forward and leaving only a trace of tendrils around her ears, pulling the rest into a neat twist at the back of her head. When she felt she was ready, she selected a long fur-lined cape to protect her against the December chill and took a deep breath to still her wildly beating heart.

As her carriage drew nearer to the President's mansion, she nervously clasped and unclasped her hands, hoping that she would not show her intense anger and fear on her face before the President. She kept telling herself that Jefferson was an impartial, fair man who would listen to reason.

Once inside the President's house, though, her resolve began to weaken as soon as the President's personal secretary showed her into the small drawing room, furnished entirely in French period furniture, even down to the ormolu clock from Limoges. Mr. Lewis's face was grim, as though he did not quite approve of all these French things any more than he approved of the young Frenchwoman who stood among them. He left her alone for a few minutes, during which time Aimee took a moment to check her appearance one last time in the ornately carved French mirror.

"A woman's eternal fussing over her appearance is one of her most endearing qualities," a voice intoned with a hint of amusement.

Aimee turned to face Thomas Jefferson and swallowed air

involuntarily in her nervousness. His slight smile was encouraging, although she was aware of the ability of politicians to don any mask they chose.

"Please sit down, Mrs. Napier," the President said, indicating a straight-backed chair close to the fireplace. He waited for her to sit, then seated himself across from her, leaning forward slightly, as though to see into her eyes better as the flames were reflecting in them. "Were you surprised to receive my note?" he asked casually.

She nodded. "Yes, I was under the impression that you had no wish to see me, Mr. President, because I have already called twice at this residence since my husband's arrest."

He nodded. "I am aware of that, Mrs. Napier, but I must tell you that, politically, it would have been a grave mistake for me to see you at that time. It would have hurt your husband's cause more than it would have helped. The attitude of the people toward your country was very suspicious, and for me to have been seen, welcoming the wife of the French traitor into my home, would have been a political mistake."

"My husband languishes in jail and you worry about your damned politics!" Aimee burst out before she could stop herself.

Jefferson frowned. "Madame, you will keep your temper with me and watch your words carefully. These charges against your husband are very serious, indeed, especially with the political climate here. Having only recently returned from France, he is under even more suspicion by the people."

"What about your suspicions, Mr. President?" Aimee inquired, gaining hold of her temper and able to keep her voice down.

"I have all the faith in the world in Lucian Napier," he said. "For reasons which I cannot now explain, I have put quite a bit of trust in your husband. I know him to be intrinsically a good man, and I have my doubts about the authenticity of this document that was presented to me as his letter to whatever pro-French forces he was supposed to be whipping up against us."

"Then you believe the letter was forged?" Aimee questioned eagerly.

Jefferson put his hand up. "As I said, Mrs. Napier, I am in no position to release your husband without proof of his innocence. Whoever would have forged such a letter has a wide range of contacts that could be used to further weaken the unity of this country. I have my own suspicions as to who these people are, but since I lack proof against them, my hands are tied. My own

Vice-President plots against me, and I can do nothing there, either. It is quite frustrating, my dear madame, when you think that I am supposed to have so much power, and yet it seems in reality I have very little."

"But that is what your country wanted when you broke away from England," Aimee pointed out. "You did not want another kingdom."

He smiled. "You are right, of course. The idea of a Kingdom of the United States does not sit well on the tongue, don't you agree? It smacks of the pomposity of the Old World, and that is what we are trying to get away from."

"But what has this got to do with my husband's innocence?" Aimee asked impatiently. She had not come to debate the good versus the bad about various systems of government—she wanted her husband back safely as soon as possible.

"Ah, I know how impatient you are to have Lucian back with you, Mrs. Napier, but I'm afraid you must wait a little longer. The tide of opinion is turning a little, and very soon it will be safe for me to release him."

"Does that mean you truly believe him innocent, Mr. President?" she wondered. "But if that is the case, how can you hold an innocent man in jail. Isn't that against the very laws you helped to set up in this new country?"

The President looked a bit nonplussed at her knowledge. "Mrs. Napier, you make me wish that all women had your good sense. I'm afraid you are correct that every man should be treated as innocent in this country until proof can be brought as to his guilt, but in this case, because of the mood of the people, I think it safer to keep Lucian where he is. Developments have come about that will hasten his release, I can assure you."

"What are these developments?" she asked, relieved that at least the nature of Lucian's work as a French spy had obviously not come to light.

Jefferson hesitated a moment, then said, "I have received a note from the Spanish government in Madrid, asserting that the governor of the Louisiana Territory has acted without their knowledge or consent. I am going to show this communication to Congress in the morning, hoping that tempers there and in the western territories will be somewhat assuaged. Of course, in reality, Spain is not the real threat, but at least it is something concrete to alleviate anxiety, especially for those Kentuckians who were ready to storm the city of New Orleans at any moment. Now that their free trade is once again assured, I can turn my attention to the problem of Napoleon Bonaparte."

He stood up, clasping his hands behind him and taking a few turns about the room, as though thinking carefully on his words. "I have decided to accept that the secret treaty between France and Spain is a reality, that the Louisiana Territory, including the port of New Orleans, has been turned over to France. Tomorrow I am going to inform Congress of my decision. It is the French who are to be feared, for I do not know for sure what their intentions are in regard to this vast new territory they have acquired. I am not even certain of the boundaries of that territory. But all of this forces me to do something that I cannot do without a great deal of distaste—seek an odious British alliance."

"But, Mr. President, you have said before that such an alliance could be very dangerous, not only for your political future, but the future of your country!" Aimee exclaimed, surprised that the President had finally weakened enough to accept such terms of defeat, for defeat it was in a way for America to have to go back to the very same country against which it had fought so bitterly only two decades ago to bring about its own liberty.

"I am aware of that," Jefferson said, sighing heavily, "but there is nothing else that can be done to protect ourselves from what people see as a direct threat to our very security—our very existence as a nation. I have instructed the American Embassy in London to discuss the possibility of a military alliance between the United States and Great Britain, in the event of war with France."

Aimee was silent, aware of how much this had cost Jefferson. He had ordained his own political downfall as well as that of his party, in all probability. She wondered, suddenly, how much of the information that Lucian had been able to glean through his workings in the capital and had sent on to Talleyrand had brought Jefferson to this impasse. She hated to think that some secret knowledge of the weakness of America had been passed on to Talleyrand, who would certainly know how to use it to his own advantage. Still, France was the country of her birth, the country that held the graves of her parents and brothers—that held one living brother still. She thought longingly of the Castle du Beautreillis, recalling the wonderful things Lucian had told her about the improvements Etienne had already been able to make on it. She supposed she should be grateful to Talleyrand for that, at least, although the gratitude tasted bitter on her tongue.

"You are strangely silent, Mrs. Napier," Jefferson said suddenly, studying her from beneath hooded lids. "You are thinking of your homeland?" he guessed.

She nodded. "I was thinking how very proud I should be that France is improving her strengths, her greatness—her glory. And yet, I have also come to care for this adopted country. After all, it is the country of Lucian's birth," she ended thoughtfully.

"I had hoped one day that this country would know the power and glory that Bonaparte now seeks for France," Jefferson admitted. "The birth of a nation is so fraught with turbulence and discord; it seemed fitting that after the terrible struggle we went through to become free, we should remain so, unencumbered by any political entanglements from Europe. Unfortunately, our isolationist policy is not destined to work."

"I'm sorry," Aimee said simply, feeling there was nothing else she could say.

Jefferson nodded. "So am I, my dear." He was silent for a moment, then recovered himself. "So, I do hope you understand that Lucian must remain in jail until this matter can be cleared satisfactorily. I doubt that the forged letter will stand up in any court of law, but channels must be gone through, madame. I should think, though, that you should have your husband back with you by the beginning of next year."

"Thank you, Mr. President," she said sincerely.

She left the President's house, thoughtfully mulling over what Jefferson had just revealed to her. She realized how well Garth Cabot had timed his plan and hated him all the more for it. She hoped she could place her complete trust in Jefferson's goodwill and judgment and that in another month, at most, she would have her husband back again.

The days were long until the first of January, 1803. She wanted to visit with Martha, but was unable to leave the city without risking her own arrest. Confined mostly to her own house, she paced the floor restlessly, hoping the day would come soon when she would be able to welcome Lucian back into her arms. Despite her confinement, she was able to dispatch mail and receive it from her friends in New Orleans. It gave her some comfort to read of the ordinary events in their lives. In October, Violette had been delivered of a healthy son, whom she had named Andre, after his proud grandfather. He was perfect, Violette wrote, her joy overflowing into the ink on the paper. She wondered if Aimee had been able to conceive yet—and Aimee had to smile bitterly, thinking how very little time there seemed to be for concentrating on making a baby. One needed a husband who was home every night, and she did not have that luxury now.

Restless by the second week in January, Aimee rode over to Georgetown to visit Lianne. She hoped that Garth was not at home, but as long as Lianne was awake, she had no fear of him now. She was surprised to see Dolley Madison having tea with her friend, but smiled invitingly at her, glad to see an old and familiar face after going so long without the company of others. Dolley, although a bit strained at first, eventually capitulated completely, telling Aimee how distressed she had been at the news of Lucian's arrest and how she was very sure that soon he would be freed.

"I cannot imagine that charming husband of yours being anything but an honest and law-abiding man," Dolley confided as she sipped her tea.

"I thank you for your confidence," Aimee replied, wondering sardonically where Dolley had been all these weeks, while she had been alone and without friends, save for Lianne Cabot.

As though she could read her mind, Dolley said dramatically, "I have been so busy with my duties as the official Washington hostess that there has scarcely been time to make any social calls. Poor dear James is quite piled over with work because of all this excitement in the government. Did you know, my dear, that President Jefferson has received a letter from Victor Du Pont, in Paris, who says he's been led to believe that France might possibly sell New Orleans and both Floridas to the United States for ...oh...I think the figure was six million dollars!" She tittered behind her fan. "Of course, it still hasn't been confirmed that France even *owns* the territories, but, goodness, one doesn't know what to believe with all the rumors and gossip flying about!"

"What does the President think?" Aimee inquired with interest.

Dolley shrugged. "My dear, I probably oughtn't to say anything about it, but I do love to talk, you know. I think he wants to send Mr. Monroe over to France to join Ambassador Livingston to see about making the purchase! If France won't sell New Orleans, his orders are to bargain for at least some part of it—a little site on the riverbank where the United States could maintain a dock and a warehouse. The President is so excited about this unforeseen event!"

"It could be the key to keeping him from having to make an alliance with England!" Aimee said thoughtfully.

Lianne laughed. "Garth will be so disappointed to find out about these events!" Upon noting the stares the two other ladies gave her, Lianne added quickly, "Don't worry, I won't breathe a word of it to him. Let him find out on his own. He prides himself on his detective work—I'll see how long it takes him to hear the news!"

"You are quite an unusual woman," Dolley said, then laughed her usual carefree laugh, which was so infectious. "Most wives I know would hardly be able to wait to tell their husbands!"

"I am not so bound to Garth as some wives are to their husbands," Lianne said pointedly.

"Speaking of husbands, *when* is yours supposed to be able to return home?" Dolley asked Aimee interestedly. "I know the President has ordered his cell fixed so that it is practically a hotel room!"

Aimee was surprised to hear it. "I didn't know," she admitted. "I haven't had any correspondence from my husband since his arrest six weeks ago."

"Ah, well, I'm sure he'll be home soon—as I must be immediately, or dear James will be very angry with me. I was only to stay an hour, and here I've let another forty-five minutes go by. My dear, it was so wonderful to see you again!" she said to Aimee. "Please don't remain a stranger. Perhaps if an agreement is reached with France, there will be no need to worry about falling from favor again. I certainly hope that is the case!"

After Dolley had gone, Aimee shook her head, telling herself that the woman was undefeatable. Lianne agreed good-naturedly, though she privately thought the wife of the Secretary of State was somewhat empty-headed and frivolous. Still, she made a most amusing conversationalist, so one could learn to put up with the rest of her personality.

"Garth will be home soon." Lianne sighed, glancing at the clock on the mantel. "I know how much you wish to avoid any confrontation with him, my dear, so I think it best you were on your way back home."

Aimee nodded and stood up quickly. Suddenly, her head

began to spin and she was forced to sit down again, looking rather bewildered as she tried to stop the nauseating spin before her eyes. Lianne watched her fearfully, wondering if she had caught some fever. It was entirely possible with all the swampland about, but the yellow fever usually attacked in the summer.

"What's the matter, my friend? You have gone quite pale," she said.

"I—I just had a moment's dizziness," Aimee replied, putting a hand to her forehead. "There, it has passed already." She stood up again, then suddenly let out a cry.

"What is it!" Lianne demanded, reaching out to steady her friend.

Aimee began to laugh. "Oh, my goodness, Lianne, how very stupid of me! There's nothing wrong with me—I'm simply going to have a baby!"

"A baby! Are you sure?"

Aimee nodded happily. "Yes, I remember thinking that I was long overdue for my monthly blood flow, but I attributed it to the stress I've been undergoing. I didn't even think it could be a baby, I suppose because Lucian's been gone so much."

"But it only takes once." Lianne smiled, arching her eyebrows teasingly.

Aimee laughed again. "Oh, he will be so happy when I tell him!" she remarked gaily. "I remember these same symptoms with my first pregnancy. Oh, Lianne, this one must come to term; it simply must!"

"It will," Lianne promised. "You will take good care of yourself and do everything you are told to do by the physician. I will give you the name of my own doctor if you wish."

"Thank you, Lianne. Oh, I am so happy—I only wish Lucian were here to listen to my news! I don't think I can wait much longer to tell him!"

Garth arrived unexpectedly in the hallway and stood at the entrance to the salon, his eyes narrowing at the evidence of joy written on the faces of the two women inside. He himself had had a terrible day, and he asked sourly, "What gives you the right to be so happy?" He put a hand to his throbbing temples. "Bah! The day has been worse than terrible!"

"You must have heard the news from France," Lianne remarked with secret glee.

He glared at her. "I see you know about it already."

"Dolley Madison was over for tea; she can't keep anything to herself."

"What are you doing here?" he asked Aimee. "Your husband has been the cause of this damnable headache of mine!"

"Oh, Garth, don't be ridiculous!" Lianne said protectively. "Lucian is in jail! How could he be the cause of anything?"

"He was released an hour ago," Garth responded soberly, "for lack of sufficient evidence. His release comes on the heels of these new developments with France. But I have the feeling that Jefferson is chasing rainbows on this deal with Bonaparte. I can't imagine the ambitions of the man will allow him to give up a third of an entire continent!"

"I don't care what you think!" Aimee replied gaily, too happy to have her spirits dampened by Garth's sourness. Her husband had been released from jail and she was carrying his child—the world was perfect for her! After Aimee gave Lianne a hug, she avoided Garth and hurried outside, telling the driver to go as fast as humanly possible.

Anxiously, she fidgeted in the carriage the entire way home. Once they'd arrived in front of the house, she fairly bounced out of the carriage and ran to the front door, opening it to find her husband getting ready to go out in search of her.

"Why is it that whenever I return home from a long absence, I never find you here?" he grumbled mockingly. But then he was taken aback by the small whirlwind that launched herself at him. Laughingly, he tried to steady himself, holding her close against him as she kissed his face and eyes and cheeks and ears in a sudden frenzy. "Wait! Wait!" He laughed. "Good God, I'll stay away weeks at a time if this is the kind of welcome I receive whenever I return!"

"You'll not be separated from me again!" Aimee vowed soberly. She stood a little away from him and her green eyes were brilliant with love. "I'll not let anything ever again stand in the way of our being together! If you go to prison, I'll simply move in with you! If you're sent back to France, I'll follow you there, even if you forbid it!"

"Such devotion is priceless!" He smiled, bringing her close again and hugging her tightly. "I am truly the luckiest of husbands!"

"And the luckiest of fathers!" she crowed, delighted to see the joy seeping into his blue eyes as he stared at her, speechless. "Yes"—she nodded—"it is quite true, Mr. Napier, you are going to be a father!"

"When—when did this happen?" he stammered, his eyes automatically descending to her stomach. "I—did you know before I was arrested?"

She shook her head. "I found out only today. Oh, Lucian, I am so happy! I know that this time we'll have our baby and it will be born healthy and beautiful!"

He laughed and nodded and swung her around in his arms. "Oh, darling, you have made this a joyous day to remember. Here I thought I would be the one on center stage, but you have once again upstaged your husband!"

"Forgive me," she said, "but I was not about to wait to tell you!"

"Aimee, I couldn't have asked for a better homecoming," he said, bending down to kiss her passionately. He felt the response in her body and thought hungrily of the bed upstairs that awaited them. "It seems," he remarked in a shaky voice, "that we are destined for passionate reunions, my love."

She nodded. "But, Lucian, before we go to bed, you must tell me what happened," she said seriously. "I was so concerned. I had called twice at the President's mansion and he wouldn't receive me. Then, totally unexpectedly, I received an invitation from him to call on him to discuss your imprisonment! I didn't know what to think! He said he believed you were innocent, but he couldn't release you because of the political climate—and I wanted to tear away every bar of that jail until I found you. I could imagine you being treated most unfairly by your American guards!" She paused for breath before going on. "And then I met Dolley Madison at Lianne Cabot's today and she said you were practically living in a hotel room—and then Garth Cabot came in and said you were the cause of his headache—"

"Stop! You're going to faint from lack of breath!" Lucian laughed, pulling her into the sitting room and pushed her into a chair while he drew up a hassock and sat at her feet, holding both her hands in his.

"Darling, I will try to explain everything to you," he said seriously, looking into those great, green eyes and wanting to jump right into them. "I'm sure, by now, you know the reason I was arrested was because of a trumped-up charge involving me in an attempt at rebellion against the United States. The charge was totally ridiculous, as Jefferson well knew. But you are right—because of the high feeling against all things French, and because of my attachment to the French Embassy, I was held over in jail until things could be straightened out satisfactorily."

"But that was grossly unfair, holding you in jail because of public opinion!" Aimee raged.

Lucian held a finger to her lips. "Ssh! My love, let me continue. I'm anxious to have you all to myself upstairs, and the sooner I can say what I have to say, the more quickly we can be together!"

Aimee flushed and kissed the finger he held to her lips, making him grin lecherously. "Ah, if you aren't careful, I will turn you into a limp rag doll before the night is over!"

She smiled bravely. "You'd best be careful yourself, dear husband, or you may end up in the same condition!"

He laughed, reaching up to kiss her, then resumed his explanation in a more serious vein. "In the meantime, while I was jailed, so much was happening on the political front. Jefferson has convinced himself that the French have reacquired New Orleans and has further convinced himself that the only hope for the United States lies in a military alliance with Great Britain. Since then, though, word has come of a possible bargaining point. Bonaparte may decide to sell the land France now owns to the United States for the money he needs to continue the war for the conquest of Europe. That relieves some of the strain on the political climate here in Washington—enough to finally release me from jail."

"I still think it is outrageous that Jefferson would hold you so long!"

"Darling, I was treated very well. I suppose they were wary of the fact that I might slip information to you to send to France."

Aimee sniffed disdainfully. "Here I was so worried about you, and you were practically enjoying a vacation!"

"Not quite," he assured her, his blue eyes devouring her. "And now, if there are no more questions?"

She looked surprised. "You mean, that is all? But what happens now? Do you think that Jefferson is right in presupposing that France does own New Orleans?"

"I am sure of it. We both know that was Talleyrand's dream."

"And Talleyrand will not be keen on selling his dream to the Americans," Aimee added quickly.

Lucian nodded his agreement. "Maybe not, but Bonaparte will probably override him. Can't you see the irony of it? All these years, all the negotiations with Spain over a tract of land that Bonaparte probably realizes would be impossible for him to defend as he turns his sights on conquering Europe! He probably thinks if the Americans want New Orleans, he'll offer it *plus* the

Floridas and get both of them off his hands for the money he needs to outfit his army and navy. Instead of selling the Americans the rights to float the Mississippi River, he'll just sell them the whole damned river, and make a pretty profit in the bargain!"

"Talleyrand will fight the idea," Aimee predicted.

"He will fight it, but the power belongs to Bonaparte. The man is making a meteoric rise to power. There is nothing and no one going to stop him, short of an assassination attempt, and the people love him too much for that to happen."

"So Jefferson will finally get what he has always wanted— secure boundaries for this fledgling nation," Aimee said thoughtfully. "Such a coup for him will probably win him another term as President."

"You are probably right, my love," Lucian stated, standing up and pulling her to stand beside him. He put an arm about her waist. "And now, if there are no more questions, I suggest you and I retire for the evening. Tell the servants not to disturb us— and that we will be sleeping in in the morning, madame!"

42

It was an idyllic time for the two lovers as they passionately renewed their love for each other. Aimee felt truly blessed and, as she felt her body beginning to change in preparation for the nurturing of a new life, she was quite content to remain in the background as her husband renewed his work in the capital. If there was a subtle change in him, she was slow to notice it, for she was so at peace with the world at large. She and Lucian visited Martha and Frances, who were both overjoyed at the news of having a new baby in the family. The tobacco was just being planted and Martha insisted that Lucian take Aimee for a ride around the fields, showing to her all that would someday be her child's inheritance.

Aimee looked at the rolling, muddy hills with the rows of neatly planted crops and her heart felt saddened, for she knew that, although she loved Martha and Frances dearly, her heart was not here in these green Virginia hills, despite their breath-taking beauty. Of late, she had been thinking of France, of the Castle du Beautreillis, and she felt an inordinate longing to return to the land of her birth, to bear her own firstborn there.

When she first broached the subject of returning to France to Lucian, he simply stared at her as though she had gone mad. But when she insisted on talking about it, he shook his head and invented some excuse to avoid the subject. France, he told her seriously, was not the same country she remembered. Bonaparte—or Napoleon, as he liked to be called now—had instituted sweeping changes throughout the provinces and cities. Tax reform, the penal code, a new and blooming aristocracy had all replaced those orders she remembered.

"I know, Lucian," she argued gently. "I know there are bound to be changes, but I long to see them for myself. I want to see Etienne again and his growing family. I want to see the castle where I played as a little girl and where my mother and brothers are buried."

"Darling, don't you think it is just the craving of a mother-to-be, this longing for the places filled with nostalgia? Surely, you can't mean that you're unhappy here, can you?"

She shook her head. "No, I cannot say that I'm unhappy, but I—I thought our stay here was only a temporary one and that, someday, we would be going home."

They were in a soft meadow, between two groves of oaks on the boundary of his tobacco plantation. The soft, early spring breeze brought the sounds of the slaves as they sang to themselves while they worked the muddy ground, coaxing it to bear new life for another season. Lucian gazed at his lovely wife, barely showing her early pregnancy, and thought how heartbreakingly beautiful she seemed to him at that moment. That he loved her was something he had known for a very long time, but he was constantly amazed at how that love had grown and changed over the time he had known her. Without her, he realized, his world would be considerably poorer and he would be a most unhappy man. And now, as he gazed at her and saw the love shining in those marvelous green eyes of hers, he hesitated in what he was about to say, wondering if he would lose her because of it.

Aimee watched him, sensitive to the changes of emotion that were reflected in those blue eyes she loved so dearly. "What is it, Lucian? Are you so unhappy at the idea of return- ing to France, even though you know how much it means to me? Surely, you cannot reject your own country—for it is your country, too!" Her eyes were beseeching. "I am tired of the constant vigilance required in your work, my dearest, and tired of feeling uprooted and homeless in this new land. I want my baby to be born surrounded by a sense of permanence, of a real home!"

"Aimee," Lucian began gently, "I love you so very much that you know I would do anything to ensure your happiness. But—it is impossible for me to return to France and make my home there for the rest of my life. America is my home; I have always loved it, and my love has grown during the time we have been here. I had hoped that you would come to feel the same way—I thought you *were* feeling the same way as I. I don't want to leave here, Aimee," he ended.

She looked at him in astonishment. Astounded by this unex- pected turn of events, she could not think of anything to say for a moment. And then, finally, she asked, "Why? Why do you feel this way, Lucian? Don't you want to return to France, your *true* homeland? I thought you had an endless passion for glory—look to the glory of France! She will become one of the mightiest nations on earth—perhaps the mightiest! How can you claim to love America more?"

"Darling, no. This place is my true homeland, and I want my child born an American. My feelings have always been ambiguous toward the land of my father's birth. I believe now that America offers real freedom and that there is a much better chance for a bright future here for our child! Napoleon's rule grows increasingly tyrannical in France, and the republican ideals of the revolution have quickly given way to one man's greed and ambition. I don't want that legacy for our child. I want him never to know the shackles of ignorance and want. Here he can be free to live whatever life he wishes!"

"Lucian, don't do this to me—to us!" Aimee cried stubbornly. "How can you refuse this request?"

"Darling, please try to look at things rationally. I know you are thinking of the child, but if that is so, then you should be able to see the rightness of bringing him up in a free and democratic country. I want the best for him—and for you! I cannot believe that returning to a France grown quickly as decadent as it was under the Bourbons is the best place for our family to live!"

"You—you are being obstinate!" Aimee accused him. "You knew—you promised me that you would not be here permanently." She looked at him hopefully. "You cannot leave the employ of Talleyrand; you said so yourself! What if he orders you back to France?"

"I won't go."

She was incredulous, her happiness shattered as she believed her husband a traitor to his responsibility and to his country. She stood there, struggling with her conflicting emotions, fighting her love for him and weighing it against her own feelings of displacement and homesickness. Why was he refusing her this? Why could he not take her back to France, at least for the birth of their child? "Lucian, I can't believe you are saying these things to me," she said sharply. "You—you were jailed here, for heaven's sake! How can you have good feelings toward such a place?"

"Darling, you were imprisoned in Paris, and yet your memory has faded and you embrace the city as though it were the place of the gods! I don't understand your wishing to return there when you, yourself, hated the place! Would you want your child brought up in the streets of Paris, watching the homeless orphans begging on street corners and stealing from merchants' windows?"

"He would not be a homeless orphan!" Aimee declared quickly.

"Darling, believe me when I say I want the best for us. Stay here, please!"

"I cannot stay in Washington—not in this political swamp of hypocrites and intrigue and falsehoods! If not France, then why not New Orleans, at least! I love Violette dearly, and I know you and Dominic were good friends! Lucian, take me there for the birth of our baby—and we can talk of the rest later."

Lucian turned away from her, squaring his shoulders and taking a deep breath. "Aimee, I cannot leave the capital now," he told her sharply. "It is impossible at this time with everything that is happening. I have responsibilities."

"I thought you had renounced your responsibilities!" Aimee countered in considerable bewilderment. "And, besides, what about your responsibility to me and to the child?"

"You are angry now," he told her firmly. "I don't want to discuss this further now, when you are merely working yourself into a lather over it. We have plenty of time to discuss this again, later."

"But—"

"Aimee, I told you my feelings on the subject. I don't want this to escalate into a full-blown argument between us," he commanded her.

Aimee would have continued, but she realized he was right, that they were both in bad moods, and any continuance of the argument could lead to a bitter fight and hurt feelings on both sides. She did not want to hurt him—she loved him! But she became all the more stubborn about seeing France again, because he had refused her so churlishly. If he had backed down even the tiniest bit, even to letting her go to New Orleans for a visit with Violette, she might have swallowed her pride and accepted his decision, but now she was firmly resolved in her decision to go to France—with or without him!

In the days that followed, she was careful not to bring up the subject again, and Lucian, thinking she had accepted his decision, put aside any concerns to concentrate on the business at hand. Life went on as usual, which necessarily meant many interruptions with all the excitement brewing because of the deal being worked out with France. Monroe had sailed for France in

March, at the same time Jefferson had received word that the French fleet was iced in at some Dutch port and wouldn't be able to sail for several weeks. He hoped that before that happened, his emissaries would be able to work out the beginnings of a deal with Napoleon.

Unknown to him, Napoleon had already met with his Foreign Minister, Talleyrand, and the Minister of Public Treasury, François Barbé-Marbois, in early April. Napoleon had told both men that war would break out with the British once more, possibly as early as May. For this, France would need all its navy in European waters to bring an army to British shores. So, Napoleon declared, he had decided to sell the Louisiana Territory to the United States, since he could not defend it and would lose it to the British anyway, in all probability. Talleyrand, seeing his dream slipping from his fingers, argued angrily for peace, not war. He pleaded with Napoleon that he couldn't allow an American empire to belong simply to the Americans, but Napoleon said he must defeat the British first. Then, he said, he could turn his attention back to America. Talleyrand argued that it would be too late—that he was passing up a golden opportunity, but Napoleon was adamant. "They ask me for one town in Louisiana," he told his ministers, "but I will cede them the whole colony without any reservations. In return, you will ask for fifty million francs!"

Meanwhile, Monroe had arrived in Paris with orders that permitted him to bid as high as ten million dollars for New Orleans and East and West Florida and a guarantee of free navigation of the Mississippi River. Jefferson had further told him that he could offer France free trading rights for their French ships in the port of New Orleans and that, if necessary, the United States would forever guarantee French possession of Louisiana west of the Mississippi River.

When Marbois told Monroe that Napoleon was willing to sell the entire territory for fifty million francs, he was shocked. Although the offer was very tempting, where could they get that kind of money? Marbois wanted an answer immediately, so that Monroe was unable even to send a message back to Jefferson for his answer.

And then, mysteriously, a man from the British government showed up to inform Monroe that he was empowered to offer ten million dollars at six percent interest per year for the purpose of helping the Americans buy the territory. Obviously, the British spies had done their work well and knew of the deal. They certainly did not want Napoleon in Northern America as a threat to Canada, and the government simply decided to loan whatever monies were necessary to ensure that America was able to take over the territory.

On April 30, a bargain was struck. The United States agreed to pay sixty million francs for Louisiana and twenty million francs to American shipowners to satisfy their claims against France. After the negotiations were over, Monroe and Livingston wondered if the Constitution allowed the government to buy foreign lands, but it was too late for regrets; they had just more than doubled the size of their young nation, a heady feeling indeed!

Meanwhile, in Washington, Jefferson anxiously awaited word from his emissaries on the progress of the negotiations. There was a feeling of euphoria in the air, and in May, as Napoleon had predicted, when England and France once more declared war, the joy of the Americans knew no bounds.

In direct opposition to this celebration, Aimee sat glumly in her house, five months pregnant with her child and chafing at the bit, for Lucian had insisted she remain carefully indoors, not wanting a repeat of what had happened to her in New Orleans. Although she argued with him that she would be very careful, he demanded she stay inside and not jeopardize her health or the life of the child. Aimee felt confined and resentful. Lucian seemed happier than she had seen him for a long time, while she felt miserable. It wasn't fair that she was made to sit at home with nothing to do while he cheerfully went off every morning to do God-knew-what! He had stopped reporting to the French ambassador, he told her, and that left her wondering what he did. He was vague, at best, and she wondered if he had truly turned traitor and was actually working as an agent for the Americans now. She kept her suspicions to herself, but her heart sank to think that she didn't know her husband at all. She had always thought him loyal to a cause, strong and impervious to outside pressures, but now she understood that he was as human as anyone else. And although he would never sink to the lowly depths of someone like Garth Cabot, this sudden realization that she could not be sure of him frightened her very much.

The longing for France continued inside of her and she let it grow by leaps and bounds, obstinately refusing to listen to her heart, which told her she would truly be happy only with her husband—no matter where that was! Restless for company, she disobeyed Lucian's orders and went to see Lianne.

The latter was more than pleased to see her friend, her eyes sparkling at the increasing evidence of her pregnancy. "Aimee, you are looking wonderful! I was about to come and see you myself!" she exclaimed. "I was wondering if you had decided to become a hermit and stay in your house until the birth of your child!"

"Not by my own choice"—Aimee sighed—"although Lucian would heartily approve!"

Lianne gazed at her sympathetically. "Men are such dolts when their wives are having their first child. They would like to encase them in glass and keep them safe from a huge assortment of imagined evils—when really fresh air and exercise are some of the best things you can get. I remember my physician in England telling me that when I was carrying my first child. I didn't believe him at first, but when I tried his advice, I realized I felt much better for it. Unfortunately, I suppose I just wasn't meant to have children—and I lost the baby."

"You would have made a wonderful mother, Lianne," Aimee commented with warmth in her voice.

"But Garth would have made a terrible father," she returned with a half smile filled with self-mockery. "It is lucky for the children that they did not come into this world, saddled with an adulterous, unethical father and a weak, easily defeated mother. What sad children they would have been, don't you think?"

"No! I don't think that at all! I think you would have been strong for them and you would never have let Garth influence them in any way. Knowing your husband, he would have been more than content to have left them alone and in your care anyway!"

"You are probably right!" Lianne laughed, although there was a bitter note in the laughter. "Still, I suppose God or fate or whatever it is that guides our destinies must have known what he was doing." She gazed dreamily in front of her. "Still, it would have been lovely to have a child—a human being of my own to mold and nurture and bring to adulthood!" She shook her head suddenly, wiping a tear from her eye, then smiling brightly at Aimee. "I don't want to appear maudlin. I suppose it's just in the air. Garth is furious at the recent turn of events. With the war commencing again between England and France and America looking to buy the lands west of the Mississippi, all his plans have gone awry. I do suspect him of plotting to bring in British ranks from Canada, but it will be impossible now that England must once more concentrate on Europe."

"I'm glad of it. Despite my love for you, Lianne, I have no love for your country, I must admit. I suppose it is just the age-old rivalry our countries have borne for hundreds of years. I doubt that it will ever truly be vanquished."

"I agree." Lianne laughed. "But without such enmity, what would they do? If there were peace in the world, the politicians would become bored and the soldiers could not make any money on which to live. Wars create booming economies in these countries, my friend."

"They also create death and hardship," Aimee added softly.

Lianne shrugged. "Tell me," she began, changing the subject, "how is Lucian doing these days? Garth seems to think he has something up his sleeve, but can't quite figure out what. He tells me that Lucian has been acting strangely, snooping into British affairs and meeting with Jefferson clandestinely in the President's mansion. Has he turned traitor to France?"

"I don't know," Aimee said truthfully. "I have begged him to return with me to Paris, but he refuses. Ever since his stay in jail, he has been acting strangely in regard to his work, but he won't discuss it with me. He keeps telling me that he doesn't want me to be upset—it isn't good for the baby. He doesn't realize I am more upset when he keeps me in the dark like this! I hate his sneaking around, keeping his doings secret from me. It makes me believe he doesn't trust me—and that is a real thorn in my side!"

"Do you trust him?" Lianne asked her.

Aimee hesitated. "I—I am finding it increasingly hard," she finally admitted. "If he would only talk to me—"

"Don't let him go, Aimee," Lianne urged her. "Make him talk to you, tell him how important you feel about it. Surely, if he loves you, he will tell you everything you want to know."

"I don't know, Lianne. He has been so secretive of late—"

"It isn't another woman, is it? Since you're pregnant—?"

Aimee blushed and shook her head. "No, I think I'm more than enough for him." She laughed a little self-consciously.

"I'm relieved to hear it," Lianne said vigorously. "If I thought he was turning into someone like Garth, I think I would shoot him myself!"

Aimee stood up from her chair and paced the room restlessly, walking to the window and back to where Lianne watched her curiously. "Lianne," she suddenly burst out, "I am thinking of returning to France—on my own. Since Lucian won't go with me, I could return alone. I have my brother, Etienne, living there, and I am sure he would take me in."

"You would be miserable without Lucian," Lianne pointed out.

"But I am miserable *now!*" she told her. "I'm confused and upset at his lack of faith in me. I want a permanence in my life. I won't live here for the rest of my life—I just don't feel as though I belong."

"Then what about New Orleans?" Lianne suggested reasonably. "You've always had a desire to return."

"Lucian won't make a decision on that now. He claims he has too many responsibilities here in Washington. I hate him when he says that—giving me that look that tells me he doesn't trust me enough to tell me any more!" She slumped into a chair, biting her lip and frowning thoughtfully. "I feel if I don't do something to make him sit up and take notice of my feelings, he will soon forget me, placing me carefully on some high shelf where I'll be 'safe' and he won't have to be bothered with me, while I grow fat and ugly with this baby!"

"Hush, Aimee! You want this child very much, you know that! As for the other, I cannot advise you. I have never had the strength to leave my own husband despite his constant betrayal of my loyalty. How can I tell another woman to leave hers?" Lianne ran a hand through the bright gilt of her hair and sighed. "It has to be your own decision, my friend, but do be wise in this. I wouldn't want anything to happen to you!"

"Don't worry." Aimee smiled reassuringly. "I can take care of myself. For many years I was virtually alone in Paris. I have learned that there are ways of protecting oneself in such circumstances."

Lianne looked doubtful. "But now that you are with child—"

They both looked up suddenly as a sound came from the hallway. In surprise and some alarm, Aimee saw Garth Cabot enter into the drawing room, a crafty smile curving his mouth. Suddenly, she wondered how much he had heard before he had made his presence known. Anger, mixed with suspicion, coursed through her veins and she frowned at the man, causing his grin to widen even farther.

"Good afternoon, ladies. What a pleasant surprise to find you here!"

"Hello, Garth, you are home early," Lianne remarked, eyeing

her husband thoughtfully. "Have you heard any more of the war between France and England?"

He shrugged. "I hardly think that to be a fitting topic of discussion for two such lovely ladies," he observed gallantly. He seated himself in an armchair and watched the two women with pleasure. "You are looking well, Aimee," he noted, his eyes going to the rounded curve of her stomach, faintly visible beneath the light silk of her gown.

Automatically, Aimee pressed a hand protectively to her abdomen, her suspicions aroused. "You are being unusually pleasant today," she observed, remembering many times when he had allowed the gentleman's mask to slip and reveal the wolf beneath.

"I am behaving in exactly the same way that any man would who comes home to find two charming females there," Garth responded. "My day at the home of the British ambassador has been a good one; I was invited to luncheon with President Jefferson along with the rest of the ambassador's party, and the day is very beautiful outside. I would be a cur to be put in a foul mood after such a gratifying afternoon."

Aimee nodded, still unbelieving. Lianne smiled haltingly. "Have you heard more on the proposed purchase of the western lands?" she wondered.

Garth favored her with a smile. "Nothing yet, my dear, but I believe that Monroe is to return in the next few weeks, and then, I'm sure, the news will be posted all over Washington. If the purchase has been made, it will be a real coup for Jefferson and will ensure his reelection to office next year. If not, then he is no worse off than before, and perhaps Monroe has been able to work out a deal with the French."

"Did you happen upon my husband today?" Aimee asked, rounding her eyes innocently, although she was testing him deliberately to see if the mask would fall under such baiting.

For a moment, a look of hatred crossed Garth's face, but he covered it quickly and nodded. "Yes, I did see Lucian, as a matter of fact. He was with the President when the ambassador's party arrived for lunch. He seemed to be in some deep discussion. I wonder, my dear, has your husband been given new employment by President Jefferson? He seems to spend a great deal of time there. Personally, I have my doubts about his continued loyalty to France."

Aimee whitened, but she could offer no dissension to his opinion, for she herself shared it. Still, Garth's aspersions of disloyalty about her husband irritated her, and she looked at him with narrowed eyes.

He noted her look and smiled mockingly. "Your husband displays a curious blend of agility and cunning when it comes to being in the right place at the right time," Garth said conversationally. "I applaud him for that, for it is a quality necessary to anyone in political life. Yet, I do begin to wonder what exactly he is doing. Can it be that he is revealing French secrets to Jefferson—for some exorbitant sum of money that will enable him to expand upon his tobacco plantation?"

"Lucian would never do that!" Aimee burst out quickly. "There may be *some* men you know who would sell their countries for gold, Garth, but my husband is not one of them!"

"Aimee, don't upset yourself," Lianne interjected, casting a glance of annoyance at her husband. "Garth, you have no proof of such accusations. I suggest you keep yourself from uttering them in my presence, and the presence of my friend."

Garth glanced at her with a look of dismissal. "My dear wife, you know very little of what goes on in the capital. Here, in this comfortable Georgetown home, you are pampered and protected, free to conduct your little parties and listen to the vapid discussions from those brainless wives who believe their husbands are essential to the workings of the government. The truth is often less charming, I can assure you." He glanced again at Aimee. "But, if my conversation is tiresome to you ladies, I will excuse myself." He stood up and bowed. "Good afternoon, Aimee. I suppose we shall be seeing much more of you, once the child is born. I'm sure that your husband plans to make his home here—what with his new connection to Jefferson."

Then he was gone, having done what he had deliberately set out to do—sow the seeds of discontent and suspicion in the minds of the two ladies remaining.

43

As summer flowered on the Potomac, Aimee grew more and more uncertain of her feelings. She felt a strong pull back to the land of her birth—yet, her love for her husband was very strong, urging her to remain with him, to keep faith in him until he could offer an explanation of what he was doing. But his continued long absences, his short, clipped answers to her questions, were not conducive to expanding her trust in him. Finally, not knowing what else to do, she began to make plans for her own secret return to France. Carefully, she composed a note to her brother, Etienne, apprising him of her later arrival by ship, possibly as early as August. Mentally, she counted, realizing that would give her just enough time before the baby's birth in September. She would have to make the decision now, or she would not be able to travel until after the birth of her child. And once that event occurred, she was certain that Lucian would never allow her to go—certain that she herself would not be able to make the decision to go.

It was the end of a gloriously sunny day and Aimee had amused herself by taking a long walk around the town of Alexandria, stopping at her leisure in several shops, breathing in the fragrant summer air and feeling joy in the fact that her child had become quite active during this, the beginning of her sixth month. She remembered the look of pride in Lucian's eyes when he had watched her get dressed that morning, and her steadfastness had wavered slightly as she thought of her husband. And yet, if he truly loved her, he would follow her, she thought stubbornly. She could not continue without his trust.

When Lucian returned from Washington City that evening, he seemed in excellent spirits, hugging her tightly and twirling her around in the hallway until she let out a squeak of protest for him to put her down. He obliged her and kissed her soundly.

"You are the most wonderful wife a man could hope for," he proclaimed, kissing her again for good measure. "Darling, things are happening quickly now, and very soon we will know what the outcome of all our machinations and maneuverings are. Monroe should arrive in less than a fortnight!"

"How wonderful for you!" Aimee replied with a shade of sarcasm coloring her words. "I suppose then you will write Talleyrand and share the information with him?"

He looked at her, tilting his head as though to view her from a better angle. "Aimee, you don't sound very happy about things," he observed. "Is it the baby? Are you uncomfortable, my dear?"

With a snort of disgust, she eyed him, hands on hips. "There is nothing wrong with me!" she began. "The baby is fine—that is all you care about anyway, isn't it? That and your grand secret plans—or whatever you've been up to lately!"

He realized this was only the beginning of a temper tantrum, which he hurried to nip in the bud. "Aimee, I love you," he said patiently. "The baby is only an addendum to our love—you know that! We both want this baby very much, and it's only natural that I'm concerned for your health!"

"I'm as healthy as a horse!" she said quickly.

He smiled. "I'm very happy to hear it, but I wouldn't want you to take any risks."

"You don't want me to do anything!" Aimee exclaimed angrily. "You don't want me to go to the capital with you. You don't want me to visit friends, or meet anyone or go anywhere! I'm to stay docilely behind, the pregnant wife, unfit to go outside or to accompany you on your political jaunts. Why, Lucian? What is it that you're up to? Have you so forgotten your principles and values that you can turn traitor on your own country? I don't understand what has happened!"

Lucian rubbed his eyes wearily and ran a hand through the sable of his hair. "Aimee, I promise I will be able to discuss everything with you in due time. Negotiations are so tentative, so delicate right now, that it would be too risky to tell you everything. I would be betraying someone's trust, and I—"

"And *my* trust means nothing, I suppose!" she threw at him.

"Darling, it means everything to me," he countered sincerely. "And I promise—"

"I am sick of your promises!" she cried, giving her anger full release. It felt wonderful to blow up and she let herself go, letting loose the tide of doubts and anger she had been storing inside of her for so long. "Ever since I met you, I have never really been in on your confidences, have I? Everything you do must be kept secret from your own wife! Most men share their work with their wives, at least to the point of telling them what it is they actually do! I can't say that about you—everything is secret, delicate negotiations! I am sick of it! I'm your wife, Lucian! I'm carrying your child! You owe me explanations, but you refuse to give them to me!"

Lucian, despite himself, was showing signs of his own anger, equally as strong, after weeks and months of hard work and strain. "I don't owe you any explanations!" he returned sharply. "What I'm doing is something you wouldn't understand, Aimee. It involves the fates of many men and whole countries. Are you so shallow that you can think only of yourself and your own curiosity?"

She stepped back abruptly, astounded by the vigor of his counterattack. "You accuse me of thinking only of myself?" she repeated. "How can you, when you know I am thinking of *us*—of our marriage and our future! I can't live with a man who has no trust in me! How can you expect me to trust you when the feeling isn't mutual!"

"Aimee, most women don't even think about trust. They just accept their life as the wife of a man who must do a job. It doesn't matter what that job is. Why is it that I have been unfortunate enough to be saddled with a woman who must stick her nose into affairs that don't concern her?"

"I see—so now you accuse me of being a meddling wife who doesn't know her place, is that it? Well, I don't care what other wives do or feel, I only care about my own feelings and how I feel toward you, my husband! And right now—I don't feel good, Lucian. You are shutting me out!"

"Dammit! You'll just have to be patient!" he returned.

"I am running out of patience, Lucian. You expect too much of me!"

"Aimee, I'm not going to discuss this anymore with you. We're both upset and tired and I don't want to feel this way. You and I—"

"Lucian, will you take me back to France to have my baby?" she asked suddenly, directly, her green eyes watching him with an unnatural urgency.

He looked at her as though she had gone crazy. "No, of course not. I've already told you, Aimee, our future no longer lies with France—that is all behind us now. We can build a much better future here, in America. I can't believe that you truly wish to return there. Aimee, you don't understand the changes—even your brother, Etienne, has been caught off guard by the sweeping reforms that Napoleon is determined to bring about."

"Why do you keep giving me these stupid excuses?" Aimee asked him. "The real reason is because you've turned traitor to your own country, haven't you? Haven't you?"

There was silence, during which time they both stared at each other. Finally, Aimee turned away, reading in his silence his damning assent to her words. With shoulders drooping in her disappointment, she began to walk upstairs, her feet clumping heavily on the wood, as heavy as her heart felt in her breast.

"Aimee?" He stood at the bottom of the stairs, watching her, fighting the urge to run after her and fold her into his arms.

"I don't want to talk to you now," she replied bitterly and closed the bedroom door against him, hoping he would have the decency not to pursue her. Once in her room, she lay on the bed, sobbing as though her heart was broken. He had driven an invisible wedge between them—a wedge of deceit that she could not overcome. All of her love cried out to him to tell her that she was mistaken, that this was not really true, but she knew it was. Her values, her morals instilled in her by her father so long ago, could not be played with so easily. She hated dishonesty, hated the practice of deception, whether played on a grand scale or on a personal one. It was hard to see the tall, solid statue of her husband crumbling before her eyes, his feet made of mere clay instead of the golden substance she had once thought.

"Oh, Lucian!" she sobbed. She clasped her stomach as the baby kicked vigorously. "Poor baby," she whispered soothingly. "Poor little baby."

Later that evening, Aimee heard her husband's footsteps slowly coming up the stairs. She held her breath and closed her eyes, pretending to be asleep as he slowly opened the door to their bedroom.

"Aimee?" He walked to the bed to see if she was awake and she felt his hand reach out tentatively to touch her shoulder. "Aimee, I know you're not asleep," he said softly.

When she refused to answer him, he sighed, then turned away to undress. When he was naked, he slipped into bed beside her, bringing her close against him, despite her initial resistance. She felt his warm breath on her neck as he pulled her hair to the side and kissed the tender nape. A low sigh escaped her when his lips traveled provocatively to her shoulder and from there back down her shoulder blade to her spine. Tenderly, his hands came around to unfasten the front of her gown and slip it down her arms to her waist. Silently, he finished undressing her, moving her this way and that to accommodate him.

When she was naked, he stretched her out next to him, kissing her face softly, warmly—kissing her lips lightly, then her jaw-line, her cheekbones, and the front of her ears. His hands gently caressed her breasts, bigger now since her pregnancy, softly brushing the hardening nipples with the palms of his hands. Lightly, he leaned down to take each point in turn into his mouth, nuzzling them easily.

Despite her earlier anger, Aimee felt herself responding to his tenderness. Slowly, her eyes opened and she stared into the blue depths of her husband's gaze. Without words, they looked at each other. Then he brought his mouth to hers, kissing her softly again, but slowly increasing the pressure until the kiss sprang into passionate life and her arms came up to fold around his neck.

They kissed a long, leisurely time and then he moved down her neck to her chest and the slopes of her breasts, licking the sensitive flesh while his hands moved lower to the swell of her belly. Gently, he caressed the tightening skin, drawing back in surprise when he felt the pressure against his hand from within.

"It's kicking," she whispered with a little laugh.

"Should I stop?" he wondered, and when she shook her head with a languorous sigh, he smiled and gently rubbed her belly again.

He kissed her once more, then gently turned her on her side, letting his mouth trail moist imprints around her shoulder and down her spine to the middle of her waist. He moved with her, positioning himself spoon-fashion behind her, bringing his hand down to caress her intimately between her thighs from behind.

Aimee sighed again, shivering with the first sexual tingles that began to flow over her body. Languidly, she moved her legs to better accommodate his manipulative fingers, feeling a surge of warmth deep within her, made all the more sensational by his continued kissing of her back and the upper swell of her buttocks. Gently, he brought himself closer and she felt the hard length of him pushing insistently against her lower body. Moving to ac-commodate him, she gasped at the sensation of feeling when he entered her, arching reflexively and throwing her head back against the pillow. When he moved, she cried passionately and felt his mouth at her neck while his hand came around to clasp one swelling breast.

Together they moved slowly, drawing out the pleasure until Aimee thought she could stand no more. Her hips moved faster as she pressed herself urgently against him, seeking the release that she knew would come soon. Obligingly, Lucian quickened his thrusts, clasping her close against him, burying his lips in her hair as he released his seed deep within her.

Aimee cried out softly at the crest of her passion, feeling delicious waves passing in widening circles from her belly outward. She felt the baby kick in protest and smiled to herself as Lucian's hand came down protectively to touch her stomach. When his thrusts had subsided, he lay against her, still inside of her, as though needing the added closeness for a longer time.

"Aimee—"

"Ssh! Don't talk," she whispered urgently.

He settled against her silently and Aimee closed her eyes, feeling his warmth and protectiveness against her. How could she leave this man? She knew he loved her very much. The thought of his nefarious tactics, his deceit in turning away from his own government to help the government of this new United States, still concerned her, but she realized suddenly that she could deal with that. He was right—she could wait until the right time when he would be able to explain everything to her. There would be an explanation as soon as possible, he had promised her. Well, she would believe in him a little longer. She would wait and, if he wasn't honest with her after the baby was born, she would think what to do then. But, oh, God, she did love this man! She loved him so much and she so wanted him to trust her. Whatever was the reason for what he was doing, she would try to understand, she told herself. She snuggled closer against his welcome maleness and smiled to herself, thinking how foolish she had almost been. Certainly, she would have been a fool walking onto some ship bound for France, leaving behind a man like Lucian.

For the first time in many weeks, her sleep was unclouded by dreams of leaving her husband. She awoke refreshed, thankful to feel him close against her in almost the same position in which sleep had caught them. Gently, she let her hand slide down the length of his arm, feeling the powerful muscles beneath the skin that rippled pleasantly at her touch.

"You're awake," he whispered, nibbling her ear.

"Yes."

"Did you sleep well?"

"I slept wonderfully. Lucian?" She extricated herself from his grasp and turned to her other side to meet his blue eyes. "Lucian, I love you," she said simply.

He smiled, his eyes showing his relief. "I love you, Aimee."

He cocked one dark eyebrow knowingly at her. "And now, what would you say to another exquisite session of making love like last night?"

"In the morning? But you have to go—"

"I want to be with my wife for a little while this morning. The rest of the world can go to hell!" He laughed, hugging her against him and kissing her soundly.

44

It was quite late when Lucian finally bade her farewell for the day. Aimee stood on the front step, waving gaily to him, nearly hugging herself with her secret joy. Somehow, she felt as though a great weight had been lifted from her, a weight she had been carrying around for some time now. She loved Lucian; nothing else mattered! It was all so simple, really. She busied herself with some sewing she needed to do for the baby's nursery. While she was busy with that, she realized that she had sent the letter to her brother advising him of her coming. Feeling a sudden alarm that poor Etienne would be waiting for her, wondering where she was and possibly worried that something had happened to her during the ocean voyage when she didn't show up at the docks at Brest, she quickly sat down to write another letter to him, telling him of her change in plans. She explained briefly that her trip would have to be postponed, saying only that it was due to the baby's imminent birth. She did not feel like sharing her doubts with her brother. Although she loved Etienne, she knew he had problems of his own and would not welcome the news of her own worries.

Since it was such a beautiful day outside, she decided to have her driver take her down to the docks so she would deliver the letter to the ship's office, thereby ensuring that it would be dispatched on the first available ship to France. Cheerfully, she dressed in a light, mauve gown that gave her plenty of room for her burgeoning belly, tying the wide ribbon of a matching hat beneath her chin. She felt in such a good mood, she even stuck a posy in her hatband, telling herself she felt quite frivolous after the discovery last night that she loved her husband more than anything else in the world.

"You are a lucky man, Lucian Napier," she said to her reflection in the mirror. "With such an understanding wife, you should go far in this world!" She blew a kiss to her double in the mirror, then ordered the carriage brought out and was happily ensconced in the open seat, her sunshade outspread behind her, on her way to the docks.

The river wharf was unusually busy today. Plenty of ships had been coming in with goods and the workers were all busily carrying crates back and forth and tagging boxes and baggage for distribution to various warehouses. Aimee walked among all the activity, fascinated by the bounty laid out before her. There were containers of furniture from France, articles from the islands in the Caribbean, sugarcane from New Orleans, and various foodstuffs from New York and Boston. Everything was a veritable beehive of activity and she watched with fascination as men moved cargo about, shouting and barking orders to one another, cursing ripely when a box was lowered to the dock and shattered because of careless handling.

"Why, Aimee, whatever are you doing down here?"

Aimee turned around, nearly bumping into Garth Cabot, who was in the act of removing his hat with a courteous action. He smiled down at her, his eyes going from her person to the ships bobbing on the Potomac. Aimee stepped back, nervously feeling the need to keep her distance.

"Good morning, Garth. What are you doing down here?" she asked pointedly.

"I'm overseeing some materials being unloaded from that ship," he answered easily, nodding toward a British vessel in the harbor. "The ambassador wants them in his office right away. He's expecting letters from London on the war and his instructions on how to present our concerns to President Jefferson."

"I see," Aimee replied without much interest. If she knew Garth Cabot, he was probably trying to smuggle secret papers on board that ship without any of the dock officials being any wiser. She began to walk away from him, nodding her good-bye, intent on hurrying to the ship's office in order to get her letter mailed out on the first available ship.

Unfortunately, now that she had chanced upon Garth Cabot, it was going to be very hard to rid herself of him. He offered his arm in gallant fashion and she took it hesitantly, eager for him to go, but not wishing to appear afraid of him. He escorted her to the offices and waited outside as she took care of her business. When she returned back outside, he bowed again and asked what he could do for her.

"Nothing, thank you," she said with a slight smile. "I'm just on my way home again."

He looked down at her curiously. "You know, when I saw you here on the docks, I was sure that you had come to book passage back to France, Aimee."

"Why would you think that?" she asked him sharply. "Were

you eavesdropping when I told Lianne of my tentative plans?"

"Yes," he admitted. "It was unintentional, I can assure you. You were conversing when I came home that day and I just happened to catch the end of the discussion. So—are you still planning to leave?"

She shook her head. "No."

"But, why not? From the sounds of the conversation, you were quite adamant in your decision. I got the feeling you were very angry with Lucian about something and quite willing to release yourself from him and return alone."

"My plans have changed, Garth. I've since realized that my place is here—or wherever my husband is."

He nodded. "Your husband is a most persuasive man, I suspect."

She colored and turned away from him abruptly, intent on finding her carriage and returning home. But it was not to be that easy, for once again he caught up with her and she could feel his unwelcome hand beneath her arm.

"Aimee, don't run away from me," he chided her softly. "Let me see you safely home. I would really feel much better if you would allow me to."

She shook her head. "It isn't necessary, Garth, I have my own carriage here."

"No, I insist," he said stubbornly. "Besides, I could drop you off at my house on the way to the capital. Lianne has been pining for you, complaining that you haven't been by in so long. I can't bear any more of her complaints, and she'd be delighted with me for having brought you over."

"Well..." Aimee hesitated. She liked the idea of visiting Lianne, but still didn't trust Garth at all. "I'll go see her later this afternoon," she said swiftly, putting a frown on Garth's face. "You can tell her that."

"But I insist—"

"No, thank you," she said firmly, snapping her sunshade up right beneath his nose and turning abruptly to return to her carriage.

She told herself she was well rid of him, but to her surprise he appeared at her shoulder once again. She was about to make some scathing remark to him, truly losing patience, when he pulled her beneath the shade of one of the overhanging roofs of a warehouse, cluttered with crates and boxes that had been put there in preparation for storage.

"Aimee, I'm afraid I must insist that you accompany me," he

said roughly, catching her arm and pulling her toward him.

"Garth, let go of me!" she cried. "You're hurting my arm—"

"Dammit! I'll do more than that if you don't listen to me. I want you to come with me peaceably, or—"

"Garth, let me go, or I'm going to scream and every dockhand around will come running. You will wind up looking very foolish," Aimee told him, feeling more indignant than fearful at having to employ these unusual tactics. "What in the world do you think you are doing?"

With a low whistle from Garth, two very rough-looking men came out from behind the warehouse, each one looking as if he was ready to take on a dozen rowdies in a fight. With a nod to her, Garth stepped back and the two men advanced to grab her arms and keep her from getting free. Quickly, Garth stepped away, looking quite nonchalant as he slipped back out to the open wharf once more as though nothing had happened. Aimee gazed up at the two who still held her arms, getting ready to scream as they leered threateningly at her. What in God's name was Garth doing? Was he going to have her killed by these two river thugs? Her fear of this type of man was increased as she remembered the rowdies in New Orleans when she had lost her baby. A hysterical fear constricted her throat, making her unable to scream for a moment—for one precious moment that gave them time to quiet her permanently. With a vicious grin on his face, one of them brought his fist back and then forward, landing it neatly close to her temple.

Aimee felt her knees buckle and then her body sag against the one who was still holding her. Still half conscious, she felt one of them lift her up in his arms. Like a wounded bird, she stirred against him, trying to swim back to life, but it was of no use as a dense blackness seemed to close in around her. She heard someone saying, "Give the woman air! She's fainted!"

And someone else called "Hey, there, this woman's with child—you'd best get her to a physician immediately!"

She wanted to scream out that they were kidnapping her— why, she didn't know, but her mouth refused to work and she finally let herself sink into the black oblivion.

Aimee stirred a little, fighting her way back to consciousness. She tried to lift her head, but the effort seemed too much for her and she let it fall back on something soft. Her arms automatically came up to hug around her belly and she opened her eyes, feeling the dull throb at her temple like some vast band tightening around her forehead like a vise. Carefully, she willed the room to stop swaying and dipping, then gazed around at her surroundings, trying to focus her eyes on the objects in the room—for it was a room; she could discern that much. There was a high window on one wall letting in what looked like late-afternoon sunlight. Where was she—and what time was it?

Groggily, she forced herself to sit up on the pile of blankets upon which she had been laid. She seemed to be in what might have been part of an old barn at one time. She looked about at the high stone walls, wishing she were tall enough to see out the one narrow window, but it was up too high. There was an assortment of old cupboards against the walls and several hooks embedded into the stone so that she surmised this had once been the tackroom. The floor had been swept clean in most places, although dirt had been allowed to collect in the corners of the room where spider webs caught the rays of the dying sun. There was very little furniture in the room, only the old cupboards, a small table, and two chairs. The blankets upon which she'd been lying had been thrown haphazardly into the semblance of a bed. She could see no other signs of life and looked toward the low door that was the only way in or out of the room, wondering if her unknown jailer would appear shortly.

Steadying herself, she got to her knees, then slowly stood up, reaching back to lean against one wall until her head stopped spinning. With careful steps, she walked to the door, trying to open it, although she was sure it was locked and barred from the outside. The door would not budge under the pressure of her hand and she sighed with frustration. She felt no fear yet.

Surely, Garth Cabot was waiting outside for her to wake up, and when he made his appearance she was going to tell him exactly what she thought of this stupid little trick. Why he had gone to all this trouble to kidnap her, she was not sure, but when she made him realize that her husband would find her very soon, she felt positive she would be able to persuade him to release her. Garth was, after all, a very shallow and spineless man who would cave in easily under pressure. This was probably his idea of some kind of twisted joke, but she would soon set him straight on what she thought of it!

She paced the room in growing frustration, watching the last rays of the sun hit the wall before dying out altogether. All around her on the outside, she could hear night noises: the screech of a barn owl, the barking of dogs somewhere in the distance, the soft, summer cadence of the crickets in the grass. Despite the summer warmth outside, she felt chilly within the stone walls and rubbed her bare arms in her short-sleeved dress, wishing she had brought a shawl with her. Hesitantly, she reached down for one of the blankets, relieved to find it passably clean, and wrapped it around her.

When no one arrived after at least an hour of darkness, Aimee went to the door once more and pounded on it with her fists. "Hello!" she called. "Is anyone there?" No answer.

She ground her teeth in anger and went to the cupboards to look for something with which to pry open the door. There was nothing; they were all empty. She glanced around the darkened room, lit only by the moonlit window, trying to find something with which to open the door, but could see no useful tool in sight, and it was too dark to go rummaging behind the cupboards or in the corners. She had a fear of spiders and was loath to go too close to their webs.

Once again, she went to the door, pounding as hard as she could on it, until her fists felt bruised and burning from contact with the splintery wooden door. Had they simply left her alone here? she wondered, beginning to feel the first signs of fear. What was Garth's plan? Why had he done this? Surely it *was* Garth's doing, wasn't it? She hadn't dreamed that episode on the wharf this morning—or was it this morning? Had a whole day already passed? She was becoming disoriented in the darkness and her body began to shiver uncontrollably as she tried to grab hold of her fear.

She turned to the door, pounding on it until her flesh was scraped and bloody, yelling at the top of her lungs for someone to come to her. Nothing. Not even a sound of footsteps outside or a horse—nothing! Fear clutching at her stomach, Aimee backed away from the door and sat down heavily on the pile of blankets, drawing the one around her even tighter. She felt the baby moving within her and hugged her stomach protectively, feeling slow tears begin to squeeze from her eyelids. Why was he doing this to her? she wondered. Was he mad?

She rocked gently back and forth, holding her belly and trying not to give in to the urge to scream her head off. Trying to remain calm, she stretched back out on the blankets, telling herself that Lucian was probably already aware of her absence and on his way to Garth's house. He would know that Garth would have something to do with this! He would suspect him immediately and then Aimee would be found! She hugged this hopeful thought inside her, trying to ignore the gnawing hunger pains that mingled with the angry kicking of the baby inside her stomach.

Indeed, Lucian had returned home already and found his wife had been gone most of the day. Upon questioning the servants, he learned that she had been driven to the wharf that morning. When he asked the driver what had happened, he shrugged, claiming he had driven Mrs. Napier to the docks that morning, waited until late afternoon for her to return from her business, and then finally had come home, thinking she had gotten a ride with a friend or some other acquaintance.

"You mean you did not search for her once an hour had passed?" Lucian asked incredulously. "Didn't you think something might have happened to her?"

The wiry little man shook his head, dumbfounded. "No, sir. She told me to wait. She said that she had business at the ship's office—"

"The ship's office?"

"Yes, sir. Something about the first ship back to France, I remember her saying, sir, but I'm not sure—"

"The first ship back to France! Did she—did she have any baggage with her?" Lucian demanded, paling as an idea came to mind. Good God! She hadn't carried out her threat to return alone to France—not after last night! Feeling the beginnings of panic, Lucian hurried outside to have a horse saddled in order to get down to the wharf to question the dock official. It seemed forever as he careened through the streets, urging his horse to a dangerous gallop as people walking along the street jumped aside, the men raising their fists and shouting protests after him.

Once at the wharf, Lucian went straight to the office, relieved to see that someone was still there. Pounding on the door, he burst into the office, surprising the bespectacled man behind the desk.

"Yes, sir, what—"

"I need to know if a woman was here today!" Lucian shouted, leaning on the desk and facing the man with blazing eyes. "She is a tall woman, with blond hair and green eyes—you'd never forget the eyes if you saw her. She would be very obviously with child—"

"Oh, yes, sir, I do remember doing some business with such a woman. As you say, the eyes are hard to forget. A very lovely young woman—"

"Dammit, man! What was the business she transacted? Was she buying passage on board one of the ships?" Lucian demanded, his heart in his throat. He knew there would be no way of bringing her back now, for the ships had all set sail on the tide and were a good three or four hours out of Alexandria already on their way to the open sea.

"Let me see, now," the clerk said slowly, eyeing the man before him warily. He riffled through a sheaf of papers, glancing down to check passenger lists. "What was the name, sir?" he asked timidly.

"Mrs. Lucian Napier. She would have obtained passage on a French ship bound for the port of Brest! Hurry, man, I must find out quickly!"

Obligingly, the man continued his inspection, finally shaking his head. "She's not on any of the official passenger lists, sir, unless, of course, she used a different name."

"A different name!" Lucian hadn't thought of that. He groaned aloud. Although he doubted she would do such a thing —for there would be no reason to disguise herself—he still could not be sure that she might not have done so in order to keep her final destination secret from him. For what reason, he had no idea. The only place she would go would be to her brother's estate in Orléans. He wiped a hand across his forehead and glared at the innocent clerk in front of him. "Thank you, sir!" He stormed out of the office, much to the relief of the official, who immediately put up a "Closed" sign on the door to prevent any other lunatics from coming inside before he was able to slip away for the evening.

Meanwhile, Lucian wandered around the docks a little longer, looking for some clue, he knew not what. Suspiciously, he eyed the rowdies who always inhabited such areas, many of them from the shantytown across the river known as "Swampoodle." Surely, he thought, none of these men would have remembered seeing a young woman on the docks this morning. Still, it was worth a try, he thought, willing to do anything to get information on his wife's whereabouts.

"Ho, there!" he called out to a group of rivermen who eyed him suspiciously, flexing their fists as though readying for a fight. "Listen, if any of you have been here since this morning, can you tell me if you saw a woman this morning, a tall, fair-

haired woman who was with child? She would have come in a
fine carriage on her way to the ship's office. Did any of you see
such a woman?" he asked hopefully.

The men laughed and guffawed. "Now, damn me, but I've
seen a hell of a lot of fancy women today!" One man laughed
deeply. "All fine and pampered-looking, going about their business with nary a glance at us, let me tell you!"

"But this woman is my wife," Lucian said desperately. "The
servants said she was dressed in a mauve gown and matching hat.
She is pregnant—"

"Aw, now, I remember some pregnant wench being helped
away because she'd fainted," said one of the men—a boy, really,
not as old or as hardened yet as his fellows. He cocked his head
at Lucian, holding out his hand for money.

Quickly, Lucian dug into his pockets and threw several gold
pieces into the boy's hands. The boy's mouth fell open and he
quickly stuffed the coins into his pocket. "Here, now, I'll tell you
anything you want to know!" he crowed, eyeing his comrades
with a smug attitude.

"You're sure my description fits the woman you saw?" Lucian
demanded.

"Aye, it does. She was a tall woman, about five or six months
along with her baby. I remember seeing her blond hair fall out
from underneath her hat when some man picked her up after
she'd fainted. She looked very sick, I can tell you that much, and
there were two men who must've chanced upon her. They helped
her away."

"These two men—were they gentlemen?" Lucian asked hopefully.

The boy laughed. "Hardly that, sir. More like me, I'd say,
rough men who I'd be surprised would take any interest in a lady
of the ton."

"Where did they take her?"

He shrugged. "I don't know. I remember them bringing her
out from behind a warehouse, and then I got interested in something else." He shook his head. "None of my business, you
know, what happened to a perfect stranger!"

"I understand," Lucian said, gritting his teeth and feeling additional frustration at learning so much, only to be kept from
discovering the last vital link. "Then you don't know if she was
taken on board a ship or back to where the carriages were
parked?"

The boy shook his head. "Like I said, no reason to watch anymore once the excitement died down."

"All right, thank you," Lucian said, passing a hand over his face. It seemed there would be nothing more to be gained by loitering here, so he quickly went back to his horse, returning to Prince Street at a much slower pace than he had left it. Where could she be? Could she have come down in order to take a ship back to France? Could she really have left him despite the closeness they had shared last night and this morning? He refused to believe it. He loved her too much to think she could have betrayed him in this way. Surely, she would have at least left some sort of note, an explanation for him to read.

His thoughts grew bleaker as he wondered about her alone on board ship, sailing for France, a country in which he no longer had any interest. In fact, it was very unlikely he would ever return there, not now. He thought of the reasons behind his hesitancy to tell her the truth about his work. Then he shook his head quickly, feeling she should have waited for the explanation he was bound to give her once this Louisiana Territory purchase was finished. Everything had been so unexpected, so quickly unraveled, that there had been no time to tell her everything in detail. He had been sure that she loved him enough to trust him. And yet, he realized with a twinge of shame that he hadn't trusted her enough to tell her what was happening. From the beginning, he had lied to her—and now it seemed she was paying him back in his coin, leaving him without telling him anything.

By the time he returned to his house, his shoulders were sagging with his feelings of rejection and betrayal. A spark of anger flared briefly at the woman who had twisted his feelings so, had caused him to become separated from the polished, cool-headed spy who had never let feelings get in the way of his duties. She had brought him to this, only to leave him! How could she have gone!

And then came the sudden thought that perhaps she hadn't gone. Perhaps she was still here—somewhere, letting him think she had gone, but in reality hiding away until the baby was born. But, no! He immediately rejected such a loathsome idea as unworthy of her. If she was angry with him, she would never stoop to such a cruel trick to make him suffer. He was sure of that much, at least. But, then, where was she? What if she had gone down to secure passage on board one of the ships, then fainted and been taken somewhere—but where? The hospital, perhaps? He hadn't thought of that in his haste to check out the docks.

Quickly, he spurred his horse once again, taking the opposite direction of Prince Street and hurrying to the hospital, which had been set up not too long before, mostly for charity cases. Bursting into the vestibule, he nearly sent the on-duty clerk into hysterics, before calming her down enough to explain himself. When she checked her records and found no indication of any such woman having been brought in that day, his shoulders slumped and he turned away quickly, realizing this was just one more dead end.

But if she had fainted, where would two rough rivermen have taken her? The answer made his blood run cold, and he refused even to think of it. No, he would not let himself imagine his lovely wife abused by the likes of those two and then left to find her own way home—or, worse, to be brought up in the river the next day. He shivered uncontrollably at the idea and put such thoughts from his mind determinedly.

When he returned to his home, he slumped down into a chair, refusing dinner, unable to think of eating with so much on his mind. He came up with various notions, then dismissed them quickly. He might have suspected Garth Cabot of putting some disgusting plan of his to work, except for the fact that Aimee had been telling him for so long that she wanted to return to France. Would Garth have helped her leave America? Lucian shook his head quickly at the notion. Despite the satisfaction Garth might get from seeing the two of them separated, he would never be generous enough to help anyone in such a way. He was the type of man who was too concerned with his own well-being to help anyone else. Still—and Lucian leaned forward, clasping his hands and frowning deeply—Garth Cabot could have easily had something to do with Aimee's disappearance. He turned the possibilities over in his mind, but everything kept coming back to the fact that Aimee had *wanted* to return to France, and so that would explain her being driven down to the docks. If that had, indeed, been Aimee who had fainted, it would have been easy to transport her on board a ship on which she had already booked passage. He could hardly believe that Aimee would have fainted—unless something was wrong with the baby! Such fears only led to worse feelings of total inadequacy as he realized there was nothing he could do but wait.

"Damn! If she was leaving for France, she would have left me a note!" he cried out loud. "I know she wouldn't have just sneaked away on a ship without telling me she was going!"

Again he thought of last night and their tender lovemaking.

No! She wouldn't have left him after that—there must be some other explanation! The only other person who might know something of what had happened would be Lianne Cabot, he decided reasonably. He glanced at the clock; it was nearly ten. Should he wait until morning, or go right away? If he went now, he would probably come up against Garth Cabot, since Lianne had probably gone to bed already. The idea of facing Cabot was an interesting one, and Lucian could feel his fists flexing automatically, as though savoring the thought of planting them in Cabot's smirking face.

But, no, he could wait until morning, when Lianne would be alone. He felt reasonably sure that the woman would know something, and she might be more easily persuaded to speak openly without her husband around. It would do him very little good to go over there tonight. With that decision made, he went upstairs to stretch out on the bed, knowing already that he would not be able to sleep.

45

•—•—•—•

Lucian blinked his eyes at the dawn, rolling off the bed to walk unsteadily to the washstand in order to throw water on his face to help him come awake. He took the towel and wiped his face, then felt along his chin, aware of the overnight growth of beard that should be eradicated before he paid his call on Lianne. He felt an itching need to speak with her quickly; time was of the utmost importance. Although he wasn't sure she would be able to shed light on Aimee's disappearance, he did know that she would be aware of her feelings and would probably be able to tell him what plans she had made.

After making himself presentable, Lucian called for his horse and immediately headed across the river to Georgetown. It was still early enough that the ferry was not yet too busy, and he was able to get to the Cabots' house in good time. Impatiently, he sounded the brass knocker, relieved to see the majordomo answer the door, inquiring as to what his business was.

"I must see Mrs. Cabot immediately!" Lucian barked, shouldering his way into the hall before the surprised servant could stop him.

"Really, sir, it is terribly early and Mrs. Cabot is still abed!"

"I will wait, then. It is a matter of utmost importance, and I'm sure when you inform Mrs. Cabot that Mr. Lucian Napier is waiting for her, she will not be upset at being awakened."

The servant bowed and Lucian sat down in the drawing room, his eyes going absently over the decor. So, this was the home of that rat Cabot, he thought dispassionately, trying to imagine Aimee seated here conversing with Lianne. He was left waiting only half an hour when he heard Lianne making her way slowly downstairs with the help of her maid. He hurried into the hall to help her into her wheelchair, then wheeled her into the drawing room.

"Mr. Napier, I admit to being somewhat surprised to see you here," Lianne began, bidding him to be seated. "I'm afraid if it is my husband you have business with, he isn't here. He left very early this morning."

"Do you know where he was going?" Lucian asked quickly, suspiciously.

Lianne looked taken aback. "No, of course not," she replied after a moment.

"I have come here to talk to you," Lucian informed her. "My wife has . . . disappeared. She was gone when I returned home last night and hasn't returned."

Lianne nodded. "She has been telling me that she was thinking of returning to France—"

"Exactly. Just how much did she tell you? Do you know if she did, in fact, book passage for France yesterday? You must tell me, Mrs. Cabot, for I am very worried about her. Now that she is with child, it might be very dangerous for her to try to return to France."

Lianne's brows went up as she gazed thoughtfully at the handsome man seated across from her. "You love her very much, don't you? Forgive me for prying, but you see, I also care a great deal about your wife. She has been a true friend to me—and I would not have her hurt for the world. I am aware of her unhappiness in your marriage."

"Why? Why should she be unhappy? I love her more than my own life!" Lucian protested quickly.

Lianne shrugged. "Who knows what is in the heart of a person? But I do know that she was very upset because you would not trust her enough to tell her what you were doing with your visits to the capital. She believes you are a traitor to your country and have 'gone over to the other side,' so to speak. I don't think she would have ever even thought of leaving for France if this hadn't happened."

Lucian frowned. "There are many good resons for me to keep certain things from her," he protested. "She should be able to accept that!"

"Obviously, she cannot," Lianne remarked steadily. "At any rate, she did speak to me about returning to France, although I could see that her heart wasn't truly in it. She was trying to think up excuses *not* to go!"

"Then you don't think she would have gone?" Lucian asked hopefully.

"I don't know. I do know that she loves you very much and that she is confused with this new baby on the way. She told me she couldn't bring a child into the world, not being able to trust its father. I think she was unhappy simply because you weren't treating her as a wife anymore, but simply as the mother of your heir apparent. I'm sorry if that sounds too simplistic, but it's probably true for most women, although most don't go to the same lengths as your wife!"

"But you don't truly think she would have left me of her own accord," Lucian stated urgently. "I did find out that she was at the wharf yesterday and that she had been to the ship's office—for what reason, I don't know. The clerk looked up the passenger lists of all the outbound ships heading for France, and her name was not on any of them. Still, he told me she ·might have used another name—"

"Aimee could not be so underhanded," Lianne returned promptly. "She is a very honest person. I don't think she would have tried to delude you like that. I also don't think she would have slunk away like some criminal without first telling you her plans, or at least leaving you a note."

"I agree completely," Lucian said with relief. "Then, she didn't go to France. I am fairly certain of that now."

"So, do you think she might have gone to Chesterfield Hall to visit your mother?" Lianne asked. "I know she is very fond of her."

"No. It's very curious because the carriage driver told me he waited until late afternoon, but she never returned from her business at the docks. Then a boy down by the river told me there'd been a pregnant woman earlier that day who had fainted and been taken away by two rivermen."

"Two rivermen! Good heavens!" Lianne exclaimed, lines of concern etching her face. "Have you spoken to the patrol? Perhaps they might have some knowledge of something suspicious going on."

Lucian shook his head. "I didn't think of them. I assumed she had either left on board some ship, or perhaps had come here to you for some reason."

"I haven't seen her, I'm sorry to say," Lianne responded sadly. "But, surely, someone must have seen where those two men took her."

"It doesn't seem that way. I've heard nothing since my arrival home last night. If she was taken somewhere, I think she was taken without her own approval," he said. His blue eyes gazed directly into Lianne's. "Do you think . . . would your husband have anything to do with this?"

Lianne whitened. "I can't imagine Garth doing something so terrible, Mr. Napier," she remarked, somewhat taken aback by the question.

"But he . . . he was *interested* enough in my wife to harass her while I was in jail. Aimee told me there were several times where he . . . was guilty of conduct unbecoming to a gentleman. I'm sorry to have to say it, Mrs. Cabot, but I can't discount the fact that your husband was attracted to my wife. I don't think he was used to facing rejection and carried around a great deal of resentment because she had not responded to his advances." Finally, it was out, and he wasn't about to back down on what he'd said. He was sorry if he'd hurt the woman, but she must already know of her husband's philandering ways.

Lianne avoided his eyes for a moment, gazing at the opposite wall as though digesting all that he had just told her. "Mr. Napier, you are quite right. My husband is very fond of women. I'm afraid that I . . . can no longer see to his . . . needs." She blushed painfully, but brought her eyes back to stare into Lucian's. "He did find Aimee attractive, even more so because she did not return the feeling. I knew this—and I knew it might eventually destroy our friendship, but I tried to make Garth understand that she was happily married to you and that he shouldn't try to destroy something so beautiful."

"Did he understand?"

Lianne shook her head in distress. "No, I'm sure he didn't. In fact, my husband cannot stand any kind of rejection, Mr. Napier, no matter from a woman, or from something to do with his occupation. He . . ."—she cleared her throat—". . . he hated you because you seemed very successful at what you were doing here in Washington City. He has always prided himself on a job well done." She leaned forward in her chair, her eyes staring straight into his. "Let us be candid, Mr. Napier, you and my husband both do the same thing, although it is for two very different countries. As an agent for France, you must know of all the double-dealing and intrigue that accompany the job. It is very exciting for Garth. But beyond the excitement is the knowledge that his superiors are highly pleased with his work.

"When this whole idea of the United States purchasing the Louisiana Territory came to light, Garth was furious. He had been working for the exact opposite to happen. England was sure that France had reacquired the territory long before President Jefferson was. Garth received orders to keep the United States from entertaining thoughts of buying the territory from France. He worked very hard—but not hard enough, I fear. In fact, when another British agent was empowered to offer a loan of quite a bit of money to the United States in order to complete the purchase,

Garth was badly humiliated. His work had been for nothing and, in fact, he had received a severe reprimand for his inability to keep the President from sending peaceful emissaries to discuss the purchase. The British had been poised on the borders of Canada, ready to take over the entire Mississippi River if need be. War with Spain would have been inevitable, but it would be minor compared to a double-edged war with France—one battleground in Europe, and another here in North America. It was intolerable for the powers in England to have France here in North America, but when they heard of Jefferson's plans to purchase the territory, they decided it would be better to help the Americans to acquire it."

"The easier to relieve them of it in the future after they've taken care of Napoleon," Lucian remarked sardonically.

"Mr. Napier, you know very well that all of this must stay between us. If Garth ever found out that I had told you, he would leave me. And despite his faults, I have come to realize that I cannot lose him." Lianne's eyes were brimming with tears. "I know that our marriage is a sham to you, but Garth, in his own way, needs me. I am the positive strength that he can always count on."

"Don't worry yourself needlessly, Mrs. Cabot. We had learned of the British plans to try for a takeover of the upper Mississippi valley. Jefferson has his own spies at work, for we both know there is no trust between England and America. But what has this to do with Aimee's disappearance? I know that Cabot hates me, but why would he do something to Aimee?"

"I don't know that he has," Lianne remarked swiftly, "but I do know that he blamed you for things going wrong. After his humiliation at the collapse of his plans to head off Jefferson, he heard that you had seemed to be able to heap yourself with glory—in fact, that you enjoyed a close relationship with the President, the exact kind of relationship that his superiors had been ordering him to cultivate. He needed to be on the inside in order to continue gathering information, and he couldn't do that with you in the way. Jefferson had obviously chosen France over England, and the English ambassador was very much perturbed by that news. Another humiliation for Garth."

"And he knew after the episode with the forged treasonous letter that he couldn't touch me," Lucian said, beginning to understand. "So, he might try to get me to resign through Aimee—is that right?"

Once again, Lianne shrugged. "I cannot know that for sure,

Mr. Napier. I know he was working toward that end. He wanted you out of the way in order for him to worm his way into Jefferson's confidence. He held to the idea that you were poisoning Jefferson against him. He couldn't tolerate that, of course, and vowed to unseat you in whatever way possible." She looked away from him again. "He overheard Aimee telling me of her plans to go to France. He told me later that he would enjoy seeing that happen, for it would be the quickest way to ensure your own removal from the scene."

"Do you think he would have forced her on board a ship?" Lucian wondered, standing up with his intense agitation. "Do you think he might have paid those rivermen to put her on board —against her will? Perhaps she fought them and they had to take measures to keep her quiet." His face paled and his mouth tightened at the notion that anyone would touch Aimee violently. "If your husband has anything to do with this, he'll have to answer to me!" he cried unsteadily. "The bastard has gone too far this time!"

"Mr. Napier, I beg you to keep your temper!" Lianne protested. "I know how you must feel, but one thing I'm sure of— Garth would never hurt your wife physically, especially now that she is with child. If she is on her way to France, you can be sure she is fine—bewildered, but physically unharmed."

"I wish I could be as sure of that as you are," Lucian growled menacingly. "But how can we know for sure if Cabot did put her on a ship bound for France? Could he have had any other plans? Might he have taken her somewhere else, for instance?"

Lianne shook her head. "I don't think so. Why would he wish to keep her here? It would be in his better interests to get her out of the country, in order for you to follow her, giving him time to gain Jefferson's confidence while you were gone."

"Unless he simply wants me to *think* that she has left the country," Lucian responded, calming himself with an effort. "He wouldn't necessarily have to place her on a ship, but if he made me think she was gone, I would make haste to get on the next boat out. It would accomplish the same thing."

"But where would he take her?" Lianne wondered. "And why would he keep her here?" She met Lucian's glance and her cheeks flushed deeply. "But Garth wouldn't—I mean, Aimee is six months pregnant. Surely, he wouldn't think—"

"I don't know what he might do. You say his reputation is on the line. His superiors are already after him to bring about results. He's had a great many disappointments in his profession lately, all brought about by me, according to him." He tightened his hands into fists and closed his eyes, trying not to picture Garth and Aimee together. "By God, if he touches one hair of her head, I'll kill the bastard!" he said through gritted teeth. He swung on Lianne, his blue eyes flashing his accusations. *"You* knew he was capable of this, Mrs. Cabot, and yet you didn't warn my wife about him. You must help me find her now. The more I think of it, the more I'm sure that he has her locked away somewhere. Think of the friendship she bore you, for God's sake! Think of that innocent life she carries inside her!"

Lianne burst into tears, putting her hands to her face. "I swear I didn't think he would ever do such a thing. He was constantly throwing his wrath at you, claiming that you were the only one who was standing in his way—"

"That's ridiculous!" Lucian interrupted savagely. "This place is crawling with agents, all trying their damnedest to get close to the President."

"But none of them has been able to get as close as you have," Lianne pointed out, reaching for a handkerchief to dab at her eyes.

Lucian sighed. "Mrs. Cabot, I'm sorry if I've upset you. But, please, you must talk to your husband when he returns this evening. Tell him that you have heard of Aimee's disappearance and suspect him of being behind it. Tell him I have decided not to leave for France and that, if he is holding her somewhere, it will do him very little good."

"All right." Lianne nodded. "I will try to find out something for you, but Garth has been so secretive lately, I'm not sure that he will be willing to confide in me." She looked up at Lucian, her eyes still moist. "I will do everything I can to help you find your wife, Mr. Napier. Please believe me."

"I believe you, Mrs. Cabot," Lucian said in a gentler tone, although he was still raging inside as his hatred of Garth Cabot crystallized. "Please let me know the minute you find out *anything*. I want my wife home with me!"

Aimee had awakened about the same time as Lucian that morning, feeling heavy-lidded and disoriented, focusing with bleary eyes on the walls that surrounded her. Everything came back quickly to her and she winced as she moved her hands, staring down at the still-raw scrapes on her knuckles. Painfully, she stood up, stretching and working the kinks out of her back. Her hands went to her stomach, where hunger pains were causing her a great deal of discomfort. At least the baby had quieted and she didn't have to deal with his kicking on top of everything else. She patted her rounded belly thoughtfully, allowing herself a smile as she whispered to the baby how good he was being this morning.

Then she walked about her prison room, trying to figure out some way to get out of here and find out exactly where she was. There were no sounds outside that would indicate she was in a place where people lived. Obviously, whoever had brought her here had decided they did not need to keep watch, as there was no way she was going to get out. They had simply left her alone. She sat down wearily in one of the chairs, trying to think of reasons for this strange set of events. Why would Garth Cabot have brought her to this place?

She sat thinking for a long time, trying not to think about the hunger pangs that were becoming more and more demanding. She'd eaten nothing since her breakfast yesterday morning, and already she was beginning to feel a bit faint for lack of food. Her ears picked up the sounds of a horse's hooves in the distance; it seemed as if they were coming nearer. With hope in her heart, she stood up, wishing she could see out the window. For a moment, she thought of placing one of the chairs on the table and trying to stand on it to see out, but quickly rejected the idea, imagining what would happen if she lost her footing. If she hadn't been pregnant, it might have been a good idea, but there was no reason to risk her life or the baby's when the rider, in all probability, would make himself known shortly.

Quickly, she composed herself, brushing the dust out of her dress and folding the blanket she'd been using over a chair. Tentatively, she felt at her temple, noting that the swelling had gone down, but there was still a painful soreness when she touched it. She brushed her golden mane with her fingers, trying to find enough pins left in her hair to twist it into a reasonable chignon. Whoever it was, she didn't want to seem at a disadvantage by appearing to him to look like a hoyden!

The horse whinnied outside as the rider dismounted. Aimee heard booted feet outside and then a door creaked open in an adjacent room. Footsteps walked heavily across the boarded floor and then stopped in front of her door. Aimee tensed, facing the door, waiting to see whose face would confront her.

The sound of a bar being slid across the door, followed by a key turning in the lock, was the explanation as to why it would be impossible for her to push the door down to escape. The door opened, swinging heavily on newly oiled hinges—and revealed the face of Garth Cabot, watching her with a look of insolent satisfaction in his cold eyes that made her shiver involuntarily.

"You are awake, I see," he remarked, stepping inside and closing the door behind him. In his hands he was carrying a knapsack, and Aimee's eyes went to it hopefully. He smiled and held up the sack before tossing it carelessly on the table. "Yes, there's food inside, little mother. I'm sure your belly's been growling all night."

Without even bothering to respond to him, Aimee seated herself at the table and opened the sack, relieved that he had brought her some repast. Without even looking at him, she bit into the chicken leg, pulling out the container that held cool spring water and washing the food down with thirsty gulps. She could feel Garth's eyes on her, watching as she ate, but she didn't care. She was hungry and she must gain strength if she was going to outwit this man and win her freedom.

"Did you sleep well?" he asked absently, walking about the room before seating himself next to her in the only other chair.

She favored him with a frown. "What do you think, Garth? I am not accustomed to sleeping on a pile of blankets!"

"I'm sorry I wasn't able to get you a real bed, my dear, but these preparations were made in a hurry and I couldn't think of everything." He watched her devour a plum and carefully handed her a napkin with which to wipe the juices from her fingers.

"Why have you done this?" Aimee demanded suddenly, beginning to feel full and able to attack him with more strength. "Why have you brought me here?"

"I think it must be fairly obvious," Garth remarked easily.

"Then I must be exceedingly thick-skulled, because I do not see anything as being obvious, except that you have gone beyond the bounds of 'professional competition' with my husband. That *is* what this is all about, isn't it?"

He smiled. "Would you like me to say that I don't give a damn about your husband—that it's you I want?" He laughed at the cool look she gave him. "My dear, you truly are priceless. I must say your composure under stress is remarkable. You are the only woman of my acquaintance who could look her kidnapper in the eye like that and make him feel like some underling."

"I'm sorry, Garth, but I can't help wondering at all these dramatics," she said levelly, trying not to let her real fear show. She was afraid, although he was not yet aware of it. She was afraid for her baby more than for herself and she realized she would do anything to protect it. "You didn't kidnap me, bring me here to this godforsaken place, then show up a day later to tell me how remarkable a woman you think I am!"

He laughed, enjoying her spirit. "By God, you are wonderful! I never realized the spirit in Frenchwomen; perhaps I've been missing out by keeping my seductions to these coarser American wives, whose wit is all homespun from the good earth! I shall have to remember that in the future." He leaned toward her leeringly. "Or perhaps you are just the exception, my dear. Ah, little spitfire, what a fascinating mistress you would have made me."

"Garth, you're talking nonsense," Aimee returned sardonically. "Tell me why you've really brought me here."

He shrugged. "It's quite simple, really. I want your husband gone—back to France on the first available ship out. With Lucian assuming you have already left for France yesterday morning, it will not be long before your loving husband follows you to bring you back. In the meantime, I will be able to find out Jefferson's plans for the Mississippi River valley—his strengths, his plan of defense; in short, everything we need to know in order to launch an attack on it from Canada."

"But England is at war with France. They can't possibly be thinking of attacking the United States!" Aimee protested.

"Not yet, my dear, but in a few years' time such information will prove invaluable to them. Do you really think that England, the greatest country in the world, is going to stand back and allow this upstart little nation to strengthen its tiny muscles! How ridiculous! We fully intend to get our property back, I can assure you, once we've beaten Napoleon soundly. The man is just as much an upstart as America, and we intend to have them both in our pockets in a few years!"

"Garth, I have a feeling this little scheme is all yours. I can't imagine the British ambassador giving his stamp of approval to something so implausible."

"It's not implausible! You are right that the ambassador is allowing me to act on my own in this, but I know it will work. I've already found out that Jefferson plans to send an expedition into the Louisiana Territory sometime in July, led by his secretary. It will officially be called the Lewis and Clark Expedition, and its purpose will be to explore the entire territory and set its boundaries on maps. I've convinced London that it would be a very good idea to send along one or two special English agents on this expedition in order to make our own survey and plan strategic locations to set up attack points. As I said before, this information cannot be used immediately, but in a few years, when France is beaten, London will be ready for my plans."

"And then you will be a hero?" Aimee guessed.

He nodded. "Perhaps not a hero, but I will have redeemed myself from the drubbing I took from your husband earlier this year. I'm afraid I was rather caught off guard about this entire Louisiana Purchase, whereas your husband seemed to be on top of everything. He must either employ superior tactics of gaining his information, or he is working as a double agent." He rubbed his chin thoughtfully. "I must say, the idea appeals to me, but, unfortunately, in my position as adjutant to the ambassador, I cannot move about so freely."

"So all of this is just a charade?" Aimee demanded angrily. "You went to the trouble of hiring two river thugs, kidnapping me, and keeping me out here just for some kind of revenge on my husband?"

"It's not only a matter of revenge," he informed her coolly. "It also makes good business sense, my dear. In this way, I'll get rid of Lucian for a good four or five months—the time it will take him to catch a ship back to France, find out that you never left America, and then return here to find you. In five months a lot can be done for putting my plan into motion. Once the expedition is off, there will be no way Lucian can stop it or even inform the leaders that there will be spies planted in their midst."

"But what makes you so sure he will think I have left for France?" Aimee wondered.

"My dear, you played completely into my hands in that respect. You went down to the ship's office to post your letter. When your husband hears that you went to the office, he will think you have gone to get passage back to France on board the first French ship sailing. As that ship left yesterday on the tide, he will assume you were on it. After all, you *were* thinking of returning to France, weren't you? Your husband must be aware of your unhappiness. He will rightly assume that you've left without telling him. And, being the loving husband that he is, he will immediately take the next ship out."

"And what if he doesn't?"

"My dear, he *will!* What else can he do? I have found in my business that every man has a weakness, no matter how strong he seems, how impenetrable—there is always some weakness that can be found and used to one's advantage. *You,* my dear, are Lucian Napier's weakness. He will do anything to keep you—even to running after you on a wild-goose chase across the Atlantic Ocean! It really is very funny when you think about it. Your husband, arriving in Paris, searching frantically for his lovely wife, making inquiries and finding out she never arrived. He will look the fool! Talleyrand won't appreciate his leaving his post, either. I daresay his humiliation will equal—if not exceed—my own of a few months ago. Yes, I can honestly say it will do my heart good to hear of that!"

"Garth, you forget one thing—your wife, Lianne," Aimee said softly.

"What do you mean?"

"Lianne knows you too well. Even if you haven't told her of your grandiose scheme, she will wonder about it. If no proof can be found that I have left on the French ship, she will begin to believe that you had something to do with my disappearance. She is well aware of your hatred for Lucian!"

He shrugged. "Bah! Lianne is my wife and loyal to me. Do you think she would say anything to your husband about her suspicions? I don't think so!"

"Then you no longer know your wife, Garth. Your infidelities have been crushing to her; you practically flaunt them in her face, making her feel her own inadequacies quite painfully. If you speak of revenge against my husband, you had better start thinking of the revenge your wife could take on you!"

Garth stood up fretfully, frowning as he considered her words. "No, I think you are bluffing, my dear. Lianne's loyalty to me far outweighs any friendship with you. Who would she have if I left her? Who else would put up with her delicacy, her lack of sexual interest, her constant complaints? She knows that she would be alone if she ever turned on me—that by itself will keep her from doing so."

Aimee keenly felt her own doubts about Lianne's ability to stand up to her husband, but she told herself that she must believe in her; otherwise, Garth would win the game and Lucian would be on his way to France and eventual ruin. She thought about the fact that their baby would be born without its father being there, and she sagged visibly.

"So, you are going to keep me here until when?" she asked, striving for calm.

He gazed at her speculatively. "At least until your husband takes ship for France. After he leaves, then we'll see. It depends on you, my dear. I must have time to implement the plan. The Lewis and Clark Expedition will probably not leave until mid-July, according to the documents I saw."

"Garth, you must at least give me time to prepare for my baby's birth!" Aimee protested, feeling the walls beginning to close in around her. "I'll be seven months along by the time the expedition leaves!"

"Well, then that should be incentive enough for you to be a model prisoner," he returned mockingly. "Believe me, my dear, I didn't wish to do this at all, but your husband forced my hand! It would be better for me if you weren't pregnant now, but time was of the utmost importance, and since everything played so neatly into my hands, I saw no reason not to take advantage of the opportunity presented." He leaned toward her again, his mouth lecherously composed into a smile. "Ah, how much more fun we could have together if you didn't have that big belly, my dear. I would show you how wrong you were to refuse my advances the first time."

"Then I am doubly glad of my pregnancy!" Aimee blurted out angrily. "Is this the only way you know to get women to allow themselves to be seduced by you, Garth?" she taunted him. "Must you hound them constantly, as you did me?"

"My dear, you flatter yourself." He yawned. "I haven't hounded you at all. Oh, I admit to teasing you now and then, but there are plenty of women in the capital who are easily available —bored politicians' wives who have nothing better to do than make love to someone new and spout off the details of their husbands' jobs. Actually, this spy business is quite rewarding in its way. I'm sure even your loving husband has reaped the benefits, my dear," he ended with a parting shot that hit home.

Aimee crimsoned and stood up from her chair, turning her back to her tormentor. Finally, she turned to face him. "All right, Garth." She sighed, feeling tired and sick at heart at her imaginings about her husband's reasons for keeping his recent activities secret from her. "If you are intent on keeping me here until this expedition leaves, you can at least bring me some changes of clothing."

He seemed surprised at her sudden capitulation. "That's it, then!" he wondered. "No more spitting and fighting? You've come to accept my plan?" He cocked an eyebrow at her curiously. "I would have expected more spunk from you, Aimee. Somehow, you disappoint me."

"I'm sorry to be a disappointment, Garth, but my energy has to be saved for my baby. I want a change of clothing and decent food—at the very least! You can't expect me to stay here without those essentials."

"And in return for these considerations?" he asked pointedly.

She sighed. "I'll not press charges against you once you release me, if that's what you mean." She eyed him sharply. "I could, you know. I could bring all of this up to Jefferson himself and you would be returned to England in disgrace!"

"The day you do that, your husband is a dead man, my dear. And don't think he would be safe just because I've gone back to England. It is a simple matter to pay any one of my more dangerous acquaintances to do the job for me. Think about that, my dear, should you wish to tell anyone of your adventures." He stood up and came closer to her, his face showing his concern. "After all, I am only asking you to be reasonable about this. Once your husband is on that ship and the expedition has left, I will take you back to your home as though nothing had happened. No one will be the wiser. You can tell people in town that you were at your mother-in-law's for a month of rest."

"And what will I tell Lucian when he returns from France?" Aimee queried.

"That, my dear, is your problem!"

46

Lianne Cabot composed herself in a straight-backed chair, determined that she would not fall back on the visual drama of her wheelchair when she confronted her husband with her suspicions. Lucian's words earlier that day had planted several seeds of doubt in her mind and she was determined to find out if her husband was, indeed, behind the disappearance of Aimee Napier. She heard his voice in the hallway as he came in from the stable and waited patiently for him to greet her, as was his usual custom.

"Good evening, my dear," he said casually, coming in to plant a chaste peck on her pale cheek. "I trust you had a good day?"

"How was your day?" she asked, ignoring his question.

He shrugged. "Full of the usual political nonsense. You wouldn't be interested, my darling." He walked to the sideboard to pour himself a brandy. He noticed the absence of her wheelchair. "You must be feeling very well today," he commented, downing the brandy in one swift gulp.

"Yes, I am feeling stronger today," she returned, her bright eyes searching his face for any sign of deception. "I—I heard that Aimee Napier has been missing for two days, with no sign whatsoever as to where she might have gone."

"Hmm. Aimee Napier, you say?" Garth repeated with a slight frown. "How do you know she's missing, my dear? Was she to have visited you?"

"No, but her husband paid me a call to ask me if I knew her whereabouts," Lianne remarked quietly. She noticed a slight stiffening in her husband's face—or was that just her imagination? "Of course, I told him I had no idea where she might be," she went on smoothly.

He seemed to relax. "Good. I wouldn't want him pestering you anymore. I'm surprised he had the gall to come to my house, considering our differences."

"I don't think he considers those differences very important when it comes to the safety of his wife," Lianne went on. She glanced at her husband. "Would you mind pouring me a brandy, Garth? I think I might need one this evening."

He did as she asked, handing the glass to her with a wary air. For a moment they looked at each other—husband and wife, hardly more than polite strangers for many years now. Garth saw the look of strain about her eyes and mouth, but the determination in her bright, direct gaze nearly unsettled him.

"You seem on edge, my dear," he commented. "I'm sure Napier's visit must have had something to do with that. I'll have him arrested the next time he trespasses on our property. I'll not have him upsetting you like this!"

She sighed. "Garth, if I'm upset, it is because I realized just today that for a very long time I haven't been aware of my own husband. We've lived together as husband and wife to all outward appearances, but we both know the truth is that it has all been a calculated charade. You, as the English spy, must be sure to have the look of a comfortable businessman, an assistant to the English ambassador—and so having a wife and a nice home in the most affluent part of the new capital is very important to you. It doesn't matter that you haven't been a real husband to me in a very long time."

"My dear, your illness—"

"I am not disclaiming any of the blame," she interrupted before he could go on. "I realize that a man with your appetites would find it very hard to be married to a woman who can no longer satisfy those appetites. I am aware of your . . . many indiscretions, Garth, and I have accepted them. I suppose in a twisted kind of way I've thought of them as some sort of punishment for my own inability to be a good wife and mother."

"Lianne, you—you're talking nonsense!" Garth protested, totally caught off guard at the honesty his wife was displaying.

"I am not talking nonsense, I'm simply speaking the truth," Lianne said softly. "I know it is something you are uncomfortable with, my dear husband, especially in your occupation. But, I'm afraid, that it is something I must have from you tonight."

He poured himself another brandy and swished it around in his glass, watching her over the rim. "Lianne," he began quickly, "I don't know what has brought about this sudden surge of honesty, but—"

"Please, let me finish," she said, holding up her hand. "Lucian Napier came to me today because he wanted to know if I knew anything of his wife's disappearance. He wondered if, possibly, *you* could have something to do with it."

Garth's surprise was genuine as he realized that Lucian was much more clever than he had surmised. Would the man not take the bait? he wondered nervously. He knew he needed time to proceed with his plan. He missed the fleeting expression on his wife's face—an expression of despair, of sadness.

"Garth, do you know where Aimee is?" she asked him directly.

For a minute, under the sudden strength of that gaze, he fluctuated—but years of training, of hard discipline, made his backbone stiffen and he was able to stare back at her unblinking. "No, my dear."

She continued to look at him, her eyes bright with unshed tears. "Garth, if you are lying to me—"

"Why do you think I would lie about something like that?" he countered, letting anger tinge his words with self-righteousness. "Why in God's name would I know anything about Aimee's disappearance? I have no claim on her! If her husband cannot keep an eye on her, that is his affair!"

"But you—you have shown an interest in her before," Lianne said delicately. "Aimee is a very lovely young woman."

"There are many lovely young women in Washington City, my dear," Garth reminded her offhandedly. "That is no reason to suspect me of any wrongdoing. Is Napier so damned jealous that he runs to my wife to lay out all his gross suspicions at her feet? It's damned irritating—and damned ungentlemanly of him to boot. The man has no tact at all."

"He's in love with his wife," Lianne commented with a sigh. "He's afraid for her and doesn't know what to do."

"Has he checked with the patrol, the police? Perhaps they know something," Garth suggested, feeling safe enough that his two rivermen accomplices were, by now, well on their way to Kentucky to join the other rabble-rousers with plenty of gold in their pockets.

"I'm sure he has," she answered, biting her lip worriedly.

"But, then, why would she have left him? Where could she have gone?" Garth asked, setting the trap as neatly as he could. "Is there somewhere she might go if she felt she could not remain here in Washington City any longer?"

"She has a brother in France," Lianne remarked.

"Aha! Perhaps, then, she has returned there," Garth summed up, downing his brandy with a neat twist of his wrist.

"But why would she go back to France when she loves Lucian and he is here?" Lianne wondered with concern. "She is over six months gone with child, Garth. She would not leave her husband of her own accord!"

He shrugged. "Who knows the workings of a woman's heart? Surely, she has reasons—reasons that perhaps she could not even tell you, my dear. Has Napier checked with the clerk down at the ship's office? He could certainly look at the passenger lists—"

"He has already done so." Lianne sighed.

"And?"

"Her name was not on any of the lists, but the clerk told him that she might have used an assumed name for purposes of disguise. I truly can't imagine Aimee doing something like that."

"But you don't know what was driving her! Perhaps she and Napier had an argument. Perhaps she decided she could no longer live with him."

"She *was* thinking of returning to France," Lianne admitted, trying to think, trying to wade through this morass of information.

"So there you have it! By all accounts she probably went down to the shipyard that morning and took passage to France on one of the French ships anchored there." He walked over to Lianne and patted her soothingly on the shoulder. "Don't worry, my dear, I'm sure she's quite safe. All her husband has to do is take the next ship out for France and he should be able to arrive just before the baby is due. Explanations can be made, forgiveness accepted, and they will be no worse off than before."

"But what if she hasn't returned to France?" Lianne wondered. "What if something truly terrible has happened to her?"

"Like what?" he asked.

"Well, what if she went to the docks and was . . . kidnapped, taken away by some rivermen?" Lianne asked in a frightened tone of voice. "When Lucian went down to the docks to investigate, he did find out that a young woman had fainted that morning and had been carried away by some rivermen!"

Garth steadied himself, reminding himself that the two men were long gone by now. They would be the only ones besides himself able to supply clues to Aimee's disappearance. He breathed a little easier, but the collar of his shirt still seemed constricting. He passed a finger around his neck to loosen it.

"Lianne, there are probably dozens of women who frequent the docks during the day—not all of them of the best reputation! It could have been anyone!"

She shrugged. "I don't know. Lucian . . . thought perhaps you had arranged to have her kidnapped!"

"For what purpose?" he asked her with a little laugh.

"You do hate him," she answered levelly. "Garth, don't tell

me that you don't. You've complained about him to me too many times. You've gone out of your way to discredit him with the administration; you've even gone to underhanded means to have him arrested—"

"You mean that forged letter?" he asked, with a little shake of his head. "Ah, my dear, that should tell you I've learned my lesson. Yes, I'll admit to doing my best to discredit the man. I wouldn't be a very good agent for my country if I didn't try my damnedest to get rid of a possible threat. But that has nothing to do with the man's wife! I've run up against opponents before, and you know I've always managed to come out on top. I will again this time, believe me!"

"But at what cost!" Lianne cried. "You're obsessed with the ruination of this one man, Garth! I don't know why. Of course, I realize that things have not been going the way you wish. Jefferson continues to lean toward the French, and despite your appeals to his Vice-President, Burr is not the man Jefferson is. I remember your scheme to coerce several of the most influential businessmen in the northeast to band together and pledge their allegiance to Great Britain—break off from the United States and declare their own country!"

"And it would have worked, too, had Jefferson not arrested the leaders!" Garth protested, his eyes reflecting his anger. "Without them, the rest of them were like cows, following whoever held the authority!"

"You have had many disappointments piling up in the past several months, Garth. I think, perhaps, it has affected your judgment of the situation. You are doing the very best job you can for your country! You should be proud of that!"

"Dammit, Lianne! I received my commission from King George's own hand!" Garth said proudly. "I've done the best work I could possibly do for our country! Someday, it will enable them to gain a foothold in this country again, and then they will bring war upon this United States and show them the power of a *real* nation! This piddling swamp of fields and trees is nothing compared to the grandeur of London. Do you think they can hope to compete with such greatness?"

Lianne stared at her husband. He was married to his government, she realized suddenly. He was in love with his country, and England would always take first place in his heart, no matter where he obtained physical gratification for his male needs. No woman could hope to compete with an entire nation! She realized that he would do anything to add to the power of England, and she was suddenly sure that whatever scheme he was turning over in his mind now, he had used Aimee as some sort of weapon in order to keep Lucian from getting wind of it.

Composing her face, she asked him deliberately, "And what do you think Lucian Napier should do about his problem?"

Garth settled himself, realizing that he had been spouting off rather ridiculously a moment before. Looking a trifle chagrined, he smiled insincerely at his wife. "How should I know? Do you really think Napier would accept any suggestion I happened to make? He would suspect anything I said, I'm sure!"

"Then, tell me, and I will tell him it was my suggestion," she went on unperturbed. "After all, the poor man will probably come back here tomorrow demanding to be told what I've found out."

"Damn him, then!" Garth burst out in irritation. "The man has no right to come here, bringing his domestic problems with him."

"Garth, Aimee is my friend. I told him I would help if I could."

"Then tell him to go back to France! That that is where she has gone, in all likelihood!" he responded tightly. "If the fool hasn't realized that himself, then he doesn't deserve to be an agent for his country!"

The next morning, Lianne relayed the suggestion to Lucian when he arrived just after breakfast. Without telling him everything, she relayed much of the conversation between Garth and herself.

"So, what do I do?" Lucian wondered bleakly. "Do I leave on the first available ship back to France? I cannot believe she would have left me. Yet, if you think your husband was telling the truth and I have no other clues—"

Lianne shook her head. "I would definitely advise you *not* to leave for France, Mr. Napier, for I am quite certain that Aimee is still here in the United States. I don't know where, and I'm not precisely sure why, but I do think Garth knows something of her disappearance. He would never—*never*—have made any suggestion to you as to what to do unless it suited his purposes. If he wants you to leave for France, it is because he wants you gone for some reason."

"But why would he take Aimee away?"

"For insurance purposes—and to make you think she is truly gone," Lianne explained. "Ah, yes, I've learned something from watching my husband for ten years, Mr. Napier. He is quite cunning and very ruthless. He loves his country very much, and the recent humiliations he has suffered are worse than if he had been embarrassed in front of a lover!" She shrugged. "He feels you were instrumental in those humiliations, and so he has decided to repay you in kind."

"But, how? I cannot think why he wants me out of the country! What scheme has he hidden beneath his hat?"

Lianne shook her head. "I know he would never tell me that. You'll have to find that out for yourself, Mr. Napier." She smiled mockingly. "After all, that *is* your profession, is it not?"

Lucian nodded. He realized that he must find out what plan Garth Cabot was about to implement. If he could intercept that plan before it reached its culmination, he might have Cabot over a barrel and would be able to force him to divulge what he had done with Aimee. He was trying hard to control his anger and keep his hatred of Cabot from surfacing, for he realized the worst thing he could do would be to call the man out now. If he intimated he knew anything of his plans, it would ensure that he would never find Aimee!

"So, you think he wants me out of the country, safely on my way to France to join Aimee? Hmm. Perhaps I could set up a fake departure, make him think that I have left. That might ease him into playing his cards more out in the open."

Lianne agreed. "But you must not let him know that you have only pretended to sail from here, Mr. Napier, for that will endanger Aimee needlessly. As long as he feels confident that his plan will work, I feel sure he will not harm her."

"Then I must find a hiding place of my own."

Lianne thought for a moment. "There's an old estate just on the border between Maryland and Virginia that belongs to an English friend of Garth's. It's about a two-hour ride from here; no one lives there anymore. His friend had a new house built a few miles away from the old one, which has pretty much fallen into disrepair. There used to be an old stone barn there, if I remember right. I was only out there once—"

Lucian shook his head quickly. "A two-hour ride is too far away, Mrs. Cabot. I need to be closer in order to follow Garth's moves in Washington more carefully."

"Then, perhaps, you can count on your friends in Washington to find a place for you," Lianne suggested practically.

"Yes, but I'll have to wait until a French ship arrives in port. I'll make arrangements to buy passage on board her, and when she leaves, I'll conveniently not be on her. I'll buy the captain's silence with gold, should your husband decide to question him just to make sure."

"Do you have any idea when the next French ship is due in?"

"I hope very soon, Mrs. Cabot," he answered her wearily.

47

Aimee paced her prison restlessly. She was tired of being held captive in this place! The next time Garth came to see her, she would demand that he release her immediately. She had been here for two weeks already and no longer saw any humor in the situation. She tried to think of Lucian, wondering if he had gone to France yet to find her. Would he have stepped into the trap Garth had set? She didn't see why not. There would be no other clues to lead him to her, and he would, after an investigation that yielded nothing, decide that was where she must have gone. The only thing holding him up would be an arrival in Alexandria of a French ship. With the war raging between France and England, it would take some time for one to stop in America. She shuddered to think that it could take several weeks! The longer Lucian remained in Washington, the longer it would take before Garth released her.

At least, she thought with a sigh, she was well fed. Sometimes she felt like a cow being fattened up for the final slaughter. Garth brought enough food to feed several people and, indeed, sometimes he partook of a repast with her. She was becoming grateful for his infrequent visits and looked forward to the days when her food supply began to dwindle, for she knew that would bring him back with more and she would have someone to talk with for a few hours. Despite the fact that he had once been intent on seducing her, the fact of her pregnancy had seemed to change his disposition toward her. He had never touched her in any way that she might construe as lascivious. His conversation, she found out, could even be quite witty and lively. He talked of the "pseudo court" at Washington City, a kind of smaller scale of the grand scheme of Versailles or Whitehall, with Dolley Madison doing her best in posing as the queen and Jefferson making a woefully inept king regent. His mockery of the greats of this country frequently made Aimee smile involuntarily. She realized that he truly did look down on this new nation and had every expectancy of seeing it rejoined to Great Britain at some future date. That he felt this new Louisiana Territory was the key to war with the United States was obvious as he warmed to his plan, telling her of the careful groundwork he had laid out for its fruition.

She realized that this was a novelty for the English spy, too. She was, quite literally, a captive audience, and he used her to his own advantage. As an agent for his country, he had always had to maintain silence about his clandestine doings, but now, with her safely imprisoned and unable to reveal his plans, he enjoyed talking about them, showing his pride in his own cleverness. Aimee came to realize the immense pride of the man, and she began more easily to understand how he had felt when Lucian seemed to be usurping some of his glory. There was always a fierce competition between agents for as much information as they could get, and Lucian had proved very competent at obtaining exactly what was needed for his country. Garth was unused to such expertise, for in his own experience he had been able to outshine most all the other agents. This was something new for him.

The days turned into weeks and Aimee thought she would go mad from the enforced inactivity. Although this place was not as small as a prison cell, she still felt a kind of claustrophobia within its walls and longed for Garth to let her take the fresh summer air outside during his infrequent visits. But as time passed and no French ship had arrived in Alexandria, Garth became more taciturn and moody, fearing exposure of his plan before Lucian would leave.

Finally, the day came when she heard the bar being passed along the door and the key turning in the lock. She stood up from where she had been sitting listlessly, a relieved smile crossing her face as she realized it was Garth.

He came through the door, a pleased look about him, and she hoped that, finally, he was going to release her. "Good morning, Aimee!" he greeted her excitedly. "I am very pleased to tell you, my dear, that your husband has left for France today. A French ship came into port two days ago, divested itself of cargo from France, and took on passengers and American cargo. Your husband was on the passenger list. I even took the precaution of speaking directly to the captain this morning before the ship sailed, and he assured me that a Mr. Lucian Napier had come aboard that morning with his traveling bags."

Aimee felt a mixture of emotions run through her: relief that this meant her ordeal in this prison was over, and a twinge of sadness that her husband would soon be an ocean away from her, thousands of miles away when their child was born. She looked down at her belly, which had, incredibly, grown larger in these past weeks. She was nearly seven months pregnant, but she thought she could not possibly go another two months before delivering. She was already very uncomfortable and the heat inside the barn had been torture for her in the past few days.

"So," she commented quietly, "Lucian has done what you expected, Garth. You have won."

He smiled broadly. "Yes, my dear, your husband has played quite nicely into my hands. You, I must say, have proven yourself a model prisoner, my dear," he added quickly.

"And now you must keep your promise to release me," she reminded him.

He scratched his chin, watching her closely. "Not so fast," he said suddenly. Aimee jerked her head up to stare at him, a cold fear churning in her stomach. Had she misjudged this man during these past weeks? Was he really a cold and corrupt liar who would go back on his word?

"But you promised you would release me after Lucian left for France," Aimee said hesitantly.

"I know, my dear, but, you see, I have just realized how much you know of my plan. I think it might be very stupid of me to release you now. Your friendship with Jefferson has been noted before. It would be a very easy thing for you to send word to him that two English agents have been planted in the Lewis and Clark Expedition. It would ruin my lofty plans, my dear."

"Garth, you cannot do this to me!" she cried, feeling bitter disappointment like a lump in her breast. "You promised that you would let me go! I have told you that I will not press charges of kidnapping against you. I will not tell Jefferson of your plan—I swear it! What do I care about his expedition? My loyalties will always remain with my own country, France!"

He rubbed his chin and shook his head, continuing to stare at her speculatively. "I just don't know, my dear. Trust comes hard to a man in my profession. I only just realized how well acquainted you actually are with my plan." He shrugged his shoulders. "I am afraid I must delay your release until the expedition gets off safely with my men in its ranks."

"No! You can't do this to me! Damn you!" she cried, running toward him to claw at his hateful face.

He caught her wrists and thrust her away from him. She nearly lost her footing at the violence of his action, but righted herself quickly and glared at him. "How can you do such a thing,

Garth? Have pity on me in this heat, for heaven's sake!" she pleaded.

He shook his head. "You'll have to remain here a little longer, my dear. It won't be much more, I would think. With your husband gone, it will be an easy thing to have my men join the expedition before Jefferson knows anything about it. Once that is accomplished and they have left on their journey, I will release you—you have my word on it!"

"Pah! Your word means nothing!" she shouted, beside herself with indignation. The thought of remaining imprisoned in these four walls for another two or three weeks nearly drove her crazy. She glared at her jailer with hatred in her green eyes, wishing there was some way she could overpower him and get away. But, once again, she realized there was no way she could escape in that manner, for it would be too dangerous for the growing child inside her—and she could not take a risk with Lucian's child. She must keep it safe for him.

"I've brought you a gown and more food," Garth was saying casually, opening a knapsack to display a servant's dress of bright calico with a snowy-white apron and a new pair of shoes. "It's a summer weight and should be comfortable enough within these stone walls. Actually, they should keep out most of the heat, my dear. Just don't move about too much and you should be fine."

"Garth," Aimee said wearily, "you mustn't keep me in here much longer. I—I'm nearing the end of my seventh month."

He nodded. "Don't worry, nothing will happen to you or your child, I can assure you. The expedition is set to leave July 15, if all goes according to plan. There will be plenty of time for me to return you to your home before the birth of the child."

He set out the food he had brought—mostly fruits and vegetables, as they held up better in the summer weather. There was a little dried, smoked pork and beef and a cotton cloth wrapped around a fresh loaf of bread. Aimee gazed dully at the food. She hardly felt like eating in this heat. She longed for a plentiful supply of water, but Garth had brought only two containers of it—barely enough to last her the amount of time he was usually gone. She grabbed one container thirstily and drank quickly, wishing there was some way she could have a bath. But the idea was incongruous in this setting. Her spirits sank further.

Garth watched her, a gnawing worry inside him despite his resistance to her charms. It was odd, this concern for her, he told himself. She was only a woman—an enemy, really, a member of the French nation, wife to a dangerous spy for France. He should have no worries for her. This was war and he had taken her prisoner—where was the wrong in that? Yet, seeing her visibly wilting in front of him, his heart was touched and he knew a moment's regret at the impasse that had brought him to take this desperate measure. Could he trust her enough to take her back to Alexandria? Would she tell Jefferson of her knowledge of the foreign agents planted in the expedition? Would Jefferson believe her? He shook his head, telling himself he could not afford to take that chance. Pushing aside his concerns for her, he turned away abruptly to take his leave. A man in his position could not afford to go soft on account of a woman—that was the easiest road to ruin.

"Good-bye, my dear," he said gruffly. "I will see you again very soon. Take heart, you've not much longer in these rough quarters."

She said nothing, staring back at him with hatred and a loss of hope. As the door clicked behind him, she could only listen to the key in the lock, the bar sent home across the wood. Then she sat down listlessly and stared at the bounty he had brought.

"Oh, Lucian!" she cried aloud, burying her head in her hands. "I miss you so much, my love. Where are you now?" She thought of him on board the French ship on his way to France to search for her. What would he think when he arrived in Orléans to question her brother and found she had never come—that, in fact, she had sent a letter to Etienne, telling him she had decided to stay in Alexandria with her husband. Would he think her dead? Murdered? She wept bitterly at the time she was losing—the time *they* were losing to be together. She so wanted to be with him, to have his child with the comfort of his presence beside her. She continued to sob for a long time after Garth Cabot had left, wondering if she would ever see her husband again.

Lucian stood within the shadow of a town house, watching the front door of Garth Cabot's home. In the early morning sunlight, he could see the figure of his enemy standing on the porch step, squinting up at the sun and wearing a pleased smile, like a man who had found himself in the most agreeable of circumstances. He was pulling on his riding gloves in preparation for riding to the capital, Lucian was sure. He himself had a horse waiting behind the protection of some enveloping shrubbery. When Garth mounted his horse and swung him around in the direction of Washington City, Lucian hurried to mount his own horse and follow him.

The going was agonizingly slow for Lucian in his desperate impatience. Garth was taking his time, tipping his hat to a bevy of lovely ladies on their way to breakfast at one of the new, fashionable restaurants that had begun to spring up about the city. He stopped to chat with two gentlemen acquaintances, then crossed the swampy creek that separated Georgetown from the capital proper. Lucian was careful to keep well out of sight, his eyes sharp as the man swerved down a street that would take him in the opposite direction of the English ambassador's head-quarters. Lucian urged his mount to a trot so as not to lose his quarry as they passed through a more heavily populated area. Finally, Garth stopped in front of a building whose storefront façade proclaimed it was a printer's shop. He tied his horse up and proceeded through the front door.

Carefully, Lucian tied his own horse and walked toward the building, eyeing the side door in the rough clapboard and won-dering if he should try that way or enter boldly through the front. If Garth was still within and he saw Lucian, he would know immediately that Lucian was on to him and it might put Aimee in more danger.

It was an agonizing decision, but he realized he must find out what Garth was doing inside that building. The thought came to Lucian that Aimee could even be inside there, held a prisoner. Hope sprang into his heart as he pictured himself barging into her room and releasing her. And yet, he couldn't be sure; he must be careful until he found out more.

Cautiously, he crept to the side door, leaning toward it and listening for any sounds within. He could hear nothing and put his hand on the doorknob, feeling sweat breaking out on his brow as he turned it. Slowly, very slowly, he opened the door, praying it would let out no telltale squeak. After opening it an inch, he peered inside, perceiving a narrow hallway off which were sev-eral doors as well as a low archway that led into the main part of the printer's shop.

Lucian opened the door wider and stepped inside, walking first to the archway and peering around inside to see a long, low counter on the other side of which was a printer's press and three men going about their work. He did not see Garth Cabot and surmised that he must have gone from the shop into one of the doors leading off the hall.

Retracing his steps, he stopped at the first door and listened, hearing nothing. Cautiously, he opened the door to look inside. Stacked up high were boxes and crates, carrying printer's supplies and paper. A sound from the room next door alerted him suddenly and he swiftly entered the storeroom, leaving the door open a fraction of an inch so that by pressing his eyeball to the opening he could see something of what was going on.

"So, you will be ready to leave on the fifteenth?" Garth was saying to a man who had followed him out the door. "I have all your papers filed correctly. Lewis has already agreed to include you in the expedition; he needs a trained botanist who will be able to describe the flora and fauna of the territory at length. Of course, your other reports—the ones we've already discussed—will be kept secret and turned over to me when you return to Washington. Is that understood?"

"Yes." The man spoke in a clipped accent that was distinctly British. "When will I receive the money, Mr. Cabot?"

"There will be half awaiting you in your room at the hotel tomorrow morning. The other half is the collateral that will ensure me of your cooperation. You will receive it when I have the reports in hand."

"I see. But how do I know I can trust you, Mr. Cabot, if you don't mind my asking?" the man continued cautiously.

Cabot laughed. "We must trust each other, my man. You do the necessary work for me and my government, and you will be amply rewarded. If you decide to scuttle your mission and go over to the Americans, you can be sure you'll receive nothing else." Cabot's voice was menacing. "Of course, I do have ways of disposing of unworthy agents. I'm sure you understand."

The man nodded.

"Good. Then it is settled. You can gather your things and I'll meet you at the Grover's Hotel in Georgetown tomorrow morning."

Lucian watched as the two men took their leave of each other. So, he thought, Cabot had decided to plant an English agent in the Lewis and Clark Expedition. He was surprised he hadn't thought that he might try something like that. Of course, with Aimee's disappearance, he had been able to think of little else but her plight—exactly what Cabot had been counting on.

Lucian relaxed against the wall of the storeroom, giving Cabot time to get beyond the store before he himself left. His mind worked quickly; it would be a simple matter for him to forewarn Jefferson and have the man removed, but not too quickly. They would wait until the expedition reached the stopover point of St. Louis; in that way Cabot would never know his plans had gone awry until it was too late to do anything about it. Lucian smiled to himself, pleased at the unexpected gift he had received by following Cabot this morning. Then his smile faded as he realized he had not found out what he had come for. He still did not know where his wife was, or even if Cabot was really holding her somewhere. The man was quite clever and would probably not tip his hand until well after the French ship was out to sea, too far to turn around should Lucian have a change of heart.

Grinding his teeth in frustration, he cautiously slipped out into the hall and back out into the alleyway from the side door. He noted that Cabot's horse was gone and hurried to his own, hoping to catch up with him again in case he should leave any clues as to Aimee's whereabouts. To his chagrin, he was unable to find out which direction he had taken and risked exposure himself by remaining so highly visible during the day. Regretfully, he took his horse in the direction of the rooms that he had taken until the time when he could find his wife. There would be time this evening, under cover of night, to inform Jefferson of the agent planted in the expedition. Jefferson could deal with the matter from there.

Meanwhile, he was still no wiser as to where Aimee was, and the fact infuriated him to no end. Mentally, he counted the months of her pregnancy and realized she had less than two months left before the baby was due. The skin on the back of his neck prickled with anxiety as he realized that she could be in a great deal more danger as the time of the baby's birth grew closer. He remembered when she lost the baby in New Orleans, and the fear twisted inside him at the thought of her losing this child, too. If she did—or if anything happened to her—Cabot would pay with his life, he swore it!

Unfortunately, as much as he wanted to tear into Cabot now, he would find no satisfaction yet, not until Aimee was safe. He would have to confer with Jefferson tonight and hope for some clues from the questions he had asked before. He tried not to think of his wife under the power of that bastard Cabot . . . tried not to think of her in pain or discomfort, scared or lonely in whatever place she was being kept prisoner. He found himself hoping that she *had* left on one of the ships to France; at least he would feel better about her safety.

The days continued to pass slowly for Aimee, still incarcerated in the old barn. She was growing huge, she thought, passing a hand over her stomach. The temperature was oppressive, but Garth had been right—the stone walls did help to keep most of the heat out; with only one window, there was not enough sunlight getting in to heat up the interior very much. She paced constantly, needing the exercise to keep her bones from getting stiff and her mind from going crazy. She was not the sort who had ever found herself held to the indoors. She remembered with longing the long vistas of meadow and field at the Castle du Beautreillis, the thousands of acres surrounding Lucian's tobacco plantation; even the mucky swampland was preferable to being buried inside this tomb, she thought with frustration.

If Garth did not release her on his next visit, she would break down and plead with him to take her outside, at least for a short walk. Her confinement was too taxing on her emotionally, and she knew she could not last much longer inside these walls. Now she knew what Lucian must have felt during his imprisonment, a wrongful punishment inflicted upon him when Garth had forged the letter implicating him in the plot against the United States. She gritted her teeth. Always it was Garth responsible for their woes! She hated the man! If only there was some way to best him, to foil his grandiose schemes, but she knew there was nothing she could do, and such thoughts only made her all the more frustrated.

When he finally visited her again, she eyed him coldly, waiting to see what he would say. Garth was aware of her emotions and came immediately to the point.

"The expedition has left," he said with very little expression. "The men should be across the Alleghenies in a few days, and from there they can proceed to St. Louis for the beginning of the actual exploration. Once in St. Louis, my agent has instructions to send me a letter, letting me know that everything is well. When I receive that letter, you will be free to return to your home."

"And when do you expect the letter?" Aimee asked, an urgency in her voice.

He shrugged. "No later than the first of August. You must be patient only a little while longer, my dear."

"What you ask of me is grossly inhumane!" she cried, her frustration bursting forth. "How can you expect me to sit quietly while you tell me I shall have to remain in this hole for another two weeks?"

He shrugged again. "I'm sorry, Aimee, but there is nothing else for me to do until I'm sure my plans have not been foiled."

"You bastard!" she cried between her teeth. "You bloody bastard! I swear that if anything comes of this—if anything happens to my baby because of your scheme—I'll kill you myself!"

He scoffed at the idea. "Calm yourself, my dear. Such language sounds ill on your sweet lips."

"Don't think I can't kill you, Garth!" she warned him with a sneer. "I've killed a man before." She saw the surprised look on his face. "Oh! You didn't know about that, I see. I'm surprised. I would have thought your investigations into the past of your victims were more thorough! Yes, Garth, I've killed a man! Shall I tell you what it felt like to squeeze the trigger that ended his putrid life forever?"

Garth's hazel eyes had grown larger upon hearing such unexpected information emanate from this woman standing in front of him, her belly bulging beneath the servant's gown he had brought her. It seemed ludicrous that she could ever have even contemplated killing a man, he thought. Was she lying to him? He shrugged. It hardly mattered. "Nothing will happen to you or your baby," he told her quickly. "There's no need for such threats, my dear. Remember, without me you would quickly starve to death or succumb to the heat without water! I wouldn't be making such warnings if I were you!"

Aimee realized the truth of his words and backed down a little from her belligerent stance. "All right, we shan't talk of threats or of murder now, Garth." She gazed at him with blazing green eyes. "But you must let me out of this place for a little time outside! Do you wish to drive me mad? I cannot endure another two weeks of this unless you allow me outside for a little while now."

He hesitated. It seemed highly unlikely that she would try to escape. Of course, he really couldn't trust her—yet, he could understand her need to be outside. He gazed around him at the uninviting room and his heart knew a moment's pity for her. She was nothing more than a pawn in the battle between himself and Lucian Napier. He supposed he could let her outside for a while. He nodded.

"All right, you can go outside, but if you try to run away—"

She laughed almost hysterically at the idea. "You won't have to worry about that, I can assure you, Garth! As you know, you have me at a distinct disadvantage, and I will not endanger myself or my baby by attempting anything foolish!"

He seemed satisfied. "Come along, then. I can't be away from the city for too long."

He took her arm to help her over the threshold and into the

next room, which was in a condition even worse than her own cell, many of the boards having rotted away, allowing spaces in between. When they entered the outside, Aimee closed her eyes for a moment and felt the sun on her face. With a smile, she welcomed it, holding out her arms to feel it on her body. Garth urged her forward and she delighted in the simple feeling of the grass beneath her shoes, the caress of the summer breeze against her cheeks, the sounds of the insects all around her that signaled life.

Garth noted her enjoyment and realized how very little it had cost him to bring it about. It gave him an odd kind of pleasure to see the smile on her face, to notice the way the breeze lifted her hair from her cheeks. He felt almost sorry that he had had to do this to her. But immediately he stifled the unwelcome feeling, telling himself that it had been necessary. After all, she wasn't as innocent as she seemed if she had truly killed a man. Although Garth was relentless in his profession and used many means to gain information, he had never resorted to murder by his own hand. The whole idea of taking a man's life made him squeamish. He enjoyed the risks he took and the praise that was heaped upon him by his superiors for a job well done, but if he had been asked to become an assassin for his country, he knew he could not have done it. He might pay another man to do the job, but he was incapable of carrying it out himself.

Aimee was unaware of the direction of her captor's thoughts. She was engrossed by the soft grass; the warm sun, and the delicate wildflowers that were growing in a cluster a few yards from the broken-down barn. Squatting down with some difficulty, she picked several blossoms, bringing them to her nose to smell their delicious fragrance. She sat down heavily in the grass, leaning back on her hands and closing her eyes, lifting her face like a sunflower to the morning sky. Ah, she could have remained there forever, she thought with pleasure. The thought of having to go back into the barn filled her with dread and, for a fleeting moment, she opened her eyes to gaze at Garth standing nearby, wondering if it would be possible to escape from him.

Quickly, though, she forced the thought away. It would be risking too much harm, she knew. She found herself on the edge of cursing the luck that had brought her a baby at this time. If she hadn't been pregnant, she could have easily skipped away from her captor, mounted his horse, and rode like the wind for Washington City. But, as it was, she had no alternative but to sit there and enjoy herself for as long as Garth would allow. Immediately, she realized she would not have traded this baby for anything else in the world. She said a quick prayer to God, asking Him to forgive her for even thinking that she would rather not have been pregnant. She would take no chances on losing this child, she told herself shakily. Her eyes went upward to the clear blue of the sky and she asked God's forgiveness for her irrational thoughts.

Ah, but where was Lucian? she wondered sadly. Where was the father of this baby who kicked and moved so strongly within her? She leaned farther back and put one hand on her stomach to feel the life within. His baby, she thought with a soft smile—oh, God, pray keep them both safe.

48

•─•─•─•

Lucian stood next to Jefferson and frowned at the piece of paper he had just been handed. It seemed that his old friend General James Wilkinson, whom he'd met in New Orleans, had written to the Spanish intendant in New Orleans warning him of the Lewis and Clark Expedition and suggesting that the Spaniards had every right to arrest the Americans if they wandered into Spanish territory. This certainly put a hitch in things while the expedition waited for further word from Jefferson on whether to proceed into the territory.

"Damn!" Lucian swore softly, throwing the letter down in irritation. "Wilkinson must be a secret agent for the Spanish! How else could one explain the sympathies he expresses?"

Jefferson shrugged. "The man is too wary to have put his signature to the paper," he pointed out, showing Lucian that the letter was, indeed, unsigned.

"But it's so obvious he's behind it," Lucian protested. "Why don't you have the bastard arrested?"

Jefferson shook his head. "I can't go about arresting every alleged agent in the United States, Lucian! Besides, what does it matter? There are more than two hundred thousand Americans in the Mississippi River valley, compared to only sixty-four thousand French and Spanish Creoles. The Spaniards would not have enough men to get through, even if they wanted to."

"But the Spanish ambassador hinted at dire consequences," Lucian pointed out.

"His warning to Madison might have sounded dire, but in reality there's very little he can do. His government threatens to suspend the treaty they made with France to cede them the territory of Louisiana since France had said they would not cede the territory to any other power when Spain sold it to them. France will just tell them it is too late to void the treaty, since they no longer hold the land. The territory is ours now, and I fully intend to explore it! I'm sending word to the expedition to tell them to proceed." He signed the order and set it aside, glancing up at his friend with concern.

"Have you heard anything more of your wife?"

Lucian shook his head grimly. "Either Cabot is too damned clever for me, or the truth is that she really did leave for France."

Jefferson shook his head sympathetically. "I know how hard this has been for you, my friend. Are you sure you want to continue with your work now? I mean, I would understand if you—"

"No, I keep thinking that the expedition is somehow the key to Aimee's release," Lucian said determinedly. "Cabot is waiting for something, some sign from his man that things are going as planned. Because of this damned unexpected delay, he's probably cooling his heels waiting for word and not about to release my wife until that time."

"You've tried following him?"

Lucian nodded. "To no avail. He's extremely careful and clever and continues to lose me. I have figured out that she's not being held here in the city or anywhere across the river. All I can hope for is that he'll release her soon."

"I'll get the order out to the expedition as soon as possible," Jefferson promised quickly. "If that will help to release your wife all the sooner, Wilkinson and his threats can go to hell!"

Lucian smiled bitterly. "I just hope she's able to hold on through all of this." He glanced at the calendar on Jefferson's desk and felt a shiver of dread run down his spine as he realized that this was already the second week of August. As far as Aimee had been able to calculate, the baby should come around the first part of September. He hoped she had not miscalculated . . .

Lianne watched curiously as her husband got dressed. "I thought the ambassador had released you from your duties because of your illness this week," she remarked, referring to a stomach disorder that had plagued Garth because of some tainted fish he had eaten a few days before. "Why don't you stay home? You're still not completely over it."

He glanced at her and continued to hurry into his clothes. "I've got something I must attend to today, my dear."

"An appointment?"

"Yes, you could say that. I'm two days late and my . . . er . . . contact will be quite worried at my absence." He finished knotting the cravat and put his coat on, despite the midsummer heat that settled heavily in the room. Absently, he kissed his wife and then went downstairs to make arrangements with the British ambassador's secretary, who had been filling in during his absence.

Lianne frowned to herself, remembering how ill her husband had been. He was still not feeling well, for she had heard him tossing and turning during the night, and this morning his face had been shiny with sweat and pale as death; yet, he insisted on keeping this appointment. She wondered.

Making a quick decision, she called for a servant to take her downstairs the back way and had a carriage quietly readied for a drive. Should Garth become suspicious, she would simply inform him that she was going out for some air and would probably be stopping at Dolley Madison's house for morning tea. That story would appeal to him, as he would instruct her to gather whatever information she could from the talkative wife of the Secretary of State.

"Where shall we be going this morning?" the driver asked politely, once his mistress was settled comfortably in the seat behind him.

"We're going to be taking a rather long drive, Tolliver," she replied, opening her sunshade and leaning back against the soft cushions. The suspicion had been growing inside of her for some time. She had heard from Lucian that all his efforts to find Aimee had been in vain and that he was fast losing patience, increasingly worried about the approaching due date for the baby to arrive. He had told her he didn't think Aimee was anywhere within miles of Washington or Georgetown, and he was unable to follow Garth, who was too elusive for Lucian to keep up with him.

She remembered suggesting to Lucian that he hide out in the old abandoned barn, but now she thought it might have made a suitable hiding place for Garth to have taken Aimee. Surely, if she were not in the city, there was no other place where he could be sure that no one would chance upon her. It was an isolated spot some two hours from the capital along the Maryland border. Quickly, she scribbled a note, making an instant decision. It might be a wild-goose chase, but if it wasn't she realized that she would need Lucian's help.

"Take me to Mr. Lucian Napier's house, Tolliver, on Prince Street in Alexandria. I've got to leave this note with him before we proceed." It would be going out of the way, but if he was home, it would be well worth the extra time spent.

The driver whipped the horses up and Lianne prayed that her husband would not step outside before she had gone. It would save any explanations that might relay her nervousness to him. Possibly, he had even decided he was too ill to ride that day—she hoped that was the case. Still, she could be wrong about this and wind up taking the drive for nothing. But what else had she to do? she thought ironically. And, God knew, if she could help in any way possible to find her friend, she would do it.

"Please hurry," she commanded the driver crisply, craning her neck as they rounded the corner to see if her husband had left the house yet. No, his horse was still there. She continued to urge the driver to greater speed, chafing at the wait they had at the ferry.

Once they were across the river, Tolliver obliged Lianne by putting the horses through their paces, arriving speedily at the house on Prince Street. Lianne gave the driver the letter and watched, with a sinking heart, when the servant who answered the door shook her head, indicating that Lucian Napier was not home. In any event, the instructions on the note were as precise as she could remember. If Lucian kept to the border, he would most certainly come upon the farm and would be able to ask directions at the main house. She gave her driver instructions and he headed back to the ferry, and from there proceeded in a north-westerly direction, following the lazy course of the Potomac River.

Lianne continued to urge Tolliver to greater speed, feeling that she must hurry. The beautiful majesty of the river, the rolling hills of Maryland, and the bright sunshine overhead were all lost on her as she strained forward in her seat, hoping desperately that Aimee would be there when she arrived. It was a long shot, but it would make sense if Garth had taken her there. The place was isolated, not far from the river, and it would be easy for him to lose anyone who might be trailing him because of the twisting road and the hills and trees that would make it extremely difficult for the one following who did not know where he was going.

She felt perspiration trickle down her rib cage beneath the dress and drip from beneath the brim of her hat. Nervously, she licked her dry lips, her eyes fixed on the sparkling river alongside which they raced almost recklessly. The driver had given the horses full rein and the animals were responding, galloping strongly despite the oppressive August heat.

Finally, nearly two hours later, they came upon a stretch of plowed fields. Lianne instructed the driver to pass this by and turn away from the river toward the low foothills to the north. She strained forward, her eyes searching for the tall, round turret of the old barn.

"There it is!" she cried, nearly jumping up in her excitement. Indeed, the crumbling stone walls and adjacent wooden boards still stood exactly as she remembered, nestled in a valley. There was no one around, no sign of life at all. The heat settled lazily on everything, oppressive and still, and Lianne felt a sudden, dreadful feeling inside.

"Hurry!" she said to the driver. "Go inside and see if anyone is in there!"

"Yes, madam." The driver stopped the horses and jumped down from his seat, wondering what in the world his mistress was doing in this isolated space. Uneasily, he walked into the outer room, looking around and finding no one. Wait! What was that noise? He drew back from the barred door, hearing soft noises within. A prickling along the base of his spine made him wonder if this place might be haunted.

"Do you see anyone?" Lianne's voice came to him in the still air.

"I hear . . . something, madam," he called back, "from inside the stone walls."

"For God's sake, man, open the door!" she called back swiftly.

With some hesitation, the driver cautiously drew back the bar, then realized he could not open the door without the key. Setting his shoulder against the iron and wood, he shoved as hard as he could, but to no avail. Quickly, he went back to the carriage and explained his dilemma to his mistress.

"You need a key?" she asked with keen disappointment. She hadn't thought of that. "Can't you force the door?" she queried urgently.

He shook his head. "Not by myself, madam. It's extremely heavy."

"Well, then, help me down and carry me inside. I want to see if what I am looking for is here."

Obediently, Tolliver did as she asked, depositing her on an old piece of crate that had been overturned in the anteroom. Lianne pressed her ear to the door. Indeed, yes, there were noises coming from the other side! Excitedly, she banged on the door, trying to catch the attention of whoever was inside.

"Aimee! Aimee, are you in there?" she cried out as loudly as she could.

There was no answer, only the continued sounds of groaning, as though someone were hurt or in pain. Lianne felt fear catch at her heart. "Aimee, answer me! Is that you? Are you all right?" She stared at the door with loathing, beating her hands against it until they felt raw and swollen. "Aimee, answer me!" she repeated. "For pity's sake, my friend, are you in there? Are you hurt?"

Still no answer. Lianne thought she would go crazy with the waiting. She turned to the driver once again. "Tolliver, you must find a way to get in there. I'm sure someone is inside in pain! Please, think of something!"

Obligingly, the servant hurried to grab a piece of wood, then attempted to force the door with it, but to no avail. Other methods proved the solidity of the door, and Lianne's heart sank. How could this happen? Here she was, so close, yet she could not reach her friend! It must be Aimee; she was almost sure of it now. And judging from the sounds inside, she was unconscious—perhaps sick! She shuddered to think of the consequences to Garth should Aimee die inside there. Lucian Napier would tear him apart, and she would not stop him.

"Aimee, please answer me!" she pleaded, feeling tears of frustration well up in her eyes. "Please, please, answer me!"

"What are you doing here, Lianne?"

She turned around swiftly to behold the angry face of her husband staring at her. For a moment, both of them could only look at each other, she with the realization that she had been right in her suspicion, and he with the equally shattering realization that she knew of his deception.

"Open this door, Garth!" she demanded in a low voice, loathing him for what he had done. "Open it immediately!"

He glanced warily at her. "Why?"

"You know why!" she screamed. "Aimee is in there! I can hear her—and it sounds as though she is in pain! What have you done to her?"

"I've done nothing to her," he sneered. "I meant to ride out to check on her a few days ago, but that damned sickness got hold of me, preventing me from doing so." He indicated the knapsack of food and water at his side, seeing no need to pretend innocence anymore. "I've come to give her provisions."

"You'll let her return with me immediately!" Lianne cried shrilly. "I'll not allow you to keep her here one more minute, Garth. You've gone too far with this!"

"Dammit! I hadn't planned to keep her so long!" he returned defensively. "But I can't release her until I've received word from one of my agents in St. Louis! I've not come this far with my plan to see it all ruined!"

"Open the door!" Lianne commanded. "I don't give a damn

about your plan! You've nearly ruined an innocent girl's life because of your stupid pride! Open it!"

For a moment, he hesitated, glancing at the servant, who, he was sure, would never openly attack his master. Then they both heard the loud groan that penetrated from the room within. His already pale face seemed to turn pasty and sweat broke out on his forehead. What if Lianne was right? What if Aimee was sick? Hastily, Garth reached a decision. If she wasn't sick, there was no need to panic. He would force Lianne to promise not to reveal Aimee's whereabouts until after the message came from St. Louis. She was his wife, after all, and owed him loyalty.

"All right, I'll open it!" he grumbled, pulling out the key.

He opened the door and peered inside. Lianne struggled to her feet, and with the driver's help, she went inside the room, her breath stopping in her throat as she gazed down at her friend.

Aimee was writhing on the makeshift bed, clutching her stomach and emitting continuous groans from her mouth, punctuated by rapid, shallow breaths. All around was the stench of her slops. She had been sick, Lianne could see, and on top of that, it seemed that she was in labor. She turned back to Garth, who was looking sick himself.

"Give me some water, for mercy's sake! This girl needs our help!" She searched for something to wet with the water so she could wipe off Aimee's face. In frustration, she tore off a piece of her dress and used it to wipe Aimee's face gently, kneeling painfully beside her, but unaware of her own discomfort as she recognized the greater pain of her friend. "Oh, God, please help me in this," Lianne prayed, knowing she must find the strength to do everything she could to save her friend and the innocent life that was trying to make its appearance in the world.

"Aimee?" she asked gently, bringing the water to her lips and watching as she drank greedily. "Aimee, it is I, Lianne. My poor child, do you know me?"

Aimee's eyes opened, cloudy and distant, struggling to focus on the shadowy face above her. It seemed she had been in pain forever. She could no longer remember when the cramps had begun to tear at her bowels, causing her to retch violently. A gush of water had flowed from between her legs, making her aware of the fact that her baby was coming early. She had been so frightened; there had been no one to help her. But now . . . who was this who bent over her and talked so soothingly? The voice was familiar, but she felt the pain too much to try to figure out who it was.

"Help me!" Aimee begged the face above her. "My baby—"

"Oh, God, Aimee, I'll do everything I can for your baby," Lianne responded. She felt her tears dropping on the material of her skirt as she leaned forward to try to make Aimee as comfortable as possible. She glanced at Tolliver and Garth, who were staring at the scene in amazement and fear. "Tolliver, don't stand there gawking! Help me make her more comfortable!" When Garth would have come forward to assist, Lianne fixed him with a stare of hatred. "Don't you touch her!" she declared savagely. "You've done enough already!"

Quickly, Lianne unfastened Aimee's dress to give her more room to breathe. The air in here was stale, the heat heavy, but it was better than taking her outside in the open. Gently, she raised the girl's skirts, trying to see if the baby's head had appeared yet. She felt a sense of fear; she had never assisted at the birth of a baby—she had never even had her own baby! What did she know of these things? All she could remember was the pain of her miscarriages and the sense of loss that had accompanied the pronouncement that her babies were dead. Well, by God, she wasn't about to let that happen to this baby!

Gritting her teeth, Lianne pushed up her sleeves, taking off her bonnet so she could wrap a torn piece of her gown around her head to keep the perspiration from dripping onto Aimee's body. When the driver would have stood up to leave, Lianne put a restraining hand on his arm.

She looked at the man trustingly. "Tolliver, you've got to help me with this," she said gently, but with a steel edge in her voice that made the servant nod. "Have you ever seen a baby born before?"

He nodded. "My wife's had four, madam," he said. "I watched the first two being born."

"Good. Then you'll have to help me along. This baby's going to be born any minute, so we haven't time to go fetch a doctor. She's going to need all the knowledge you have, Tolliver."

"There's nothing to having a baby," Tolliver answered quickly. He stared down at the girl, who continued to writhe, bringing her knees up to her belly in her attempt to push the child out.

"Give her more water," Lianne directed, "while I do what I can to make her comfortable."

They both hovered protectively over the young woman while Garth sat dejectedly in a chair, his head in his hands. Never had anything like this happened to him before. What had gone wrong? Damn that Napier—if it hadn't been for him!

Suddenly, he lifted his head, his ears picking up the sounds of a horse's hooves in the distance. Who could that be? He half stood up, but before he could straighten all the way he saw Lucian Napier striding quickly through the door.

Lucian was halted abruptly as he gazed at the scene before him. Garth Cabot was half crouched over a chair, eyeing him balefully, his mouth automatically twisted in a leering sneer. Next to the opposite wall, on a mound of blankets, he could see someone rolling about, making a great deal of noise, while two people bent over her, barely looking up to glance at him. In surprise, he saw that one of them was Lianne Cabot. Then . . . was that Aimee? Fear and anger choked him as he strode forward to gaze down at his beloved wife. What he saw maddened him further. His wife, his lovely, sensible little wife!

"What is happening?" he asked jerkily.

"She is having her baby," Lianne returned swiftly. "She was nearly delirious when we arrived. I don't know how long her labor has been, but she looks to be quite close to delivery. My driver, Tolliver, helped his wife birth two of their children. He's going to help me with this."

"A servant is going to help my wife give birth?" Lucian queried incredulously. He seemed stunned for a moment. "Why?" he asked. But he already knew. He turned around slowly to eye the perpetrator of his wife's suffering. "You!" he raged, his face reddening, his fists clenching in front of him. "You did this to her, you bastard—I'll kill you!"

Before Garth could recover enough to run outside, Lucian was on him, knocking him to the floor. A terrible rage seized him and he drove his fists into the other man's face, satisfied to see blood spurt from his nose and mouth. An animal rage, an indescribable need to maim this man who had caused his wife to suffer like this, possessed Lucian and a red mist seemed to settle before his eyes. Again and again he pounded at the man in front of him, unaware of any blows he was receiving in kind. He would kill the bastard—he would kill him!

He felt someone behind him, trying to drag him off, but he shook him away as though he were no more than a fly, intent on his driving need to beat the man beneath him into a bloody pulp. If Aimee died because of this man's desire for revenge, he would not be responsible for his actions!

"Lucian! Lucian! Stop that!" Lianne's voice finally reached him through the rage that had made him blind and deaf to her first appeals. "He isn't worth your anger, but your wife needs your help!" she pleaded with him. "Lucian, she needs you now!"

Hesitantly, he stopped his fists in midair, turning to see Aimee struggle to give birth to her child—*their* child. Cabot was forgotten as Lucian scrambled off him, leaving him lying nearly unconscious while he hurried to his wife. Gently, he knelt beside her head, smoothing back the golden hair that had darkened with perspiration.

"Aimee—God, how I love you!" he said, choking on sudden tears. "Don't leave me now, my darling! I beg you—be strong for my sake!" He leaned forward, weeping unashamedly as he prayed to God for the life of his wife and child.

Aimee opened her eyes, the long lashes flittering above her cheeks. She looked up and felt the splash of tears on her forehead, making her blink rapidly before she could focus on the face above hers. Was she hallucinating? Or was she dead? Had she lost the baby? Was that really Lucian's beloved face above her?

"Lucian," she said softly, coming slowly to her senses. Then she winced and closed her eyes once more as the pain knifed through her back and closed in around her abdomen.

Lucian looked down at her with hope. "Aimee? Yes, it's Lucian, my dearest. I'm here with you."

Her hand crept upward to grasp his and he took it gently, not minding the pain when she squeezed hard as another contraction hit her. Lucian looked over to Lianne, who was unfolding a white apron from the knapsack that she had next to her. Carefully, she placed it between Aimee's legs on top of the blankets in preparation for the baby's arrival. She glanced up and met his eyes, eyes that had darkened with pain upon seeing the ordeal his wife was experiencing. He was looking at her like a drowning man—looking to her for life, and Lianne hoped she would prove capable for the task.

Lianne smiled a little timidly at Lucian. "I can see the baby's head," she said. "Tolliver says it won't be long now."

Lucian gazed over to the man next to him. "Thank you," he said simply. The servant reddened and nodded.

A heartfelt groan of pain escaped Aimee's clenched teeth and she panted hard, bearing down as she brought her knees up again. Lianne positioned herself between Aimee's legs and brought the apron up to receive the baby.

"The head—the head is out!" she cried excitedly. Then: "Now the shoulders! Good, Aimee! Push a little more, my friend!"

"Come on, darling!" Lucian urged gently. "It's almost over," he said as he attempted to soothe her, bringing his face close to hers to plant a kiss on her cheek.

Aimee pushed down again and let out a yelp of surprise as she felt the baby slide from within her. "Ah!" She sighed aloud, squeezing her husband's hand once more. She looked up at him with a half smile, unable to believe he was actually here with her.

"You didn't go to France?" she asked softly.

He shook his head. "I knew you wouldn't leave me like that," he told her in a husky voice. "I wish to God I could have found you sooner, my love, and saved you this pain."

"I would have had the pain anyway," she said with a sigh. Then she looked down to where Lianne was busy rubbing the baby, cleaning out its mouth and shaking it gently to make it breathe. Aimee smiled in delight upon hearing her baby's first cry. "What is it?" she asked.

"You have a son, my friend," Lianne informed her with a wide grin. She was crying at the same time. "A healthy son who doesn't seem at all upset at his arrival in a deserted barn."

"Thank God!" Lucian said with a heartfelt sigh. "My darling, I thank you for our son," he said simply, kissing Aimee gently on the mouth. He felt the response of her lips against his.

"And now, if you would like to hold your child, I will see to your wife," Lianne directed briskly, feeling quite proud of herself for the job she had accomplished. She winked at Tolliver, whose stiff British sense of propriety made him redden under such a circumstance, but he winked back all the same, allowing himself a generous smile of congratulations for the assistance he had lent.

Lucian stood up, cradling his son close against his chest and staring down into the lazy blue eyes that were half closed. A wealth of love for this innocent little creature stirred inside his breast, and he wondered at how much he could feel for his son— and for the mother of his son. He smiled to himself, thanking God for such a miracle. Now all that remained was to get them both home and comfortably ensconced in a real bed. The thought made him glance to where Garth Cabot was stirring feebly on the floor, his face an unrecognizable mass of cuts and bruises. He pushed the rage back down deliberately, wanting nothing to mar his good feelings about the birth of his firstborn. He glanced back at Lianne.

"Is she well enough to travel? I want to get them both out of here as soon as possible. I want to bring them home!"

"Yes, I think if we are careful to secure her to the seat, we can carry her back in the carriage. I can hold the baby on my lap. You know, Aimee has been through quite an extraordinary ordeal—"

"Yes, but she's as strong as a horse," Lucian replied, receiving a smile from his wife, "as she is very fond of reminding me from time to time."

49

Aimee sat comfortably in a well-upholstered chair on the veranda of Chesterfield Hall, her son fast asleep against her breast. Next to her, Martha and Frances gazed now and then at the newest member of their family with a mixture of awe and delight. Each had exclaimed that little Philippe looked very much like his father with his dark hair and blue eyes. Aimee had been pleased at the resemblance, for he was then sure to be one of the most handsome men around when he grew up.

"Oh, my dear, when I think of all you went through!" Martha sighed reflectively. "It nearly breaks my heart to think of the unnecessary pain and suffering that . . . that brute put you through!"

"He should have been hanged!" Frances spoke up angrily.

"Hush! Let's not talk of it," Aimee said quietly. "It's all over now, and Philippe and I are safe. I shall never forget that Lianne probably saved my life and the life of my son."

"Pah! She's the wife of that British bastard!" Frances snapped.

"Mother, she *did* save Aimee's life," Martha admonished gently. "I cannot judge her by the same standards as I do her husband." She glanced sympathetically at her daughter-in-law. "You were sorry to see her go, weren't you, my dear?"

Aimee nodded, remembering that day nearly two weeks ago when she had bid good-bye to her friend. Philippe had just turned one month old and Aimee was feeling very well, despite the ordeal she had been through. A physician had made a thorough examination of her and remarked that she was truly lucky to have had such a strong constitution. Because of her quick recovery, which Lucian insisted was all but miraculous, Aimee had been able to travel down to the docks at Georgetown to see Lianne off to England.

Making an effort, Lianne had stood up from her wheelchair and walked to greet Aimee as she got down from her carriage. The two women had gazed warmly at each other for a moment, before each had moved forward to clasp the other in a fond embrace. Aimee had stared into her friend's eyes, a wealth of love and understanding reflected in her own.

"I am sorry to see you go," Aimee had said with sincerity, realizing she would miss Lianne terribly.

The other had shrugged. "I don't have much choice, do I? President Jefferson has virtually sent Garth packing. He's loath to go, for he's to be brought before his superiors once we arrive in London. A fitting punishment for a proud man like him, Aimee, believe me. He'll always bear the scars inflicted by your husband's fists, but what awaits him in England will hurt much worse, I know."

"Must you go with him?" Aimee had asked gently, searching out the truth in her friend's eyes.

Lianne nodded. "Yes, my friend, I must. Hopefully, he will at least have come to respect me a little for the stand I made against him in your behalf. I don't know what will happen between us in the future, but at least I have recovered some of my own pride and self-respect, which were sadly lacking before. I thank you, from the bottom of my heart, for bringing them back to me," she had finished, her eyes bright with unshed tears.

Aimee felt tears very close to the surface and she smiled thoughtfully at the Englishwoman. "I don't know what will happen between England and the United States, Lianne. Garth seems to insist that war is inevitable; perhaps it is, but I know that no matter what else happens, you and I will always be friends."

Lianne nodded. "Always," she murmured, hugging her one last time.

And then they had parted, with Tolliver helping her up the gangplank to the ship where Garth Cabot waited sourly, refusing even to look in Aimee's direction. His career had been ruined by his own greed and stupidity, she realized. She remembered how, when they had returned to Washington, he had parted from their company with a slight sneer, even though it had pained his cut lip.

"So, now you have your wife back and a new son, Napier!" he said bitterly. "And you will see to it, no doubt, that Jefferson has me sent back to England in disgrace. But do not look too triumphant yet, for the hour in which you expose me to Jefferson will be the hour in which I expose you as an agent of France! I doubt that the President will be so friendly to you then!"

With utmost calm, and a flickering smile of mockery, Lucian gazed back at the man who had hated him enough to put his wife's life in danger. "You may tell Jefferson with my compli-

ments, Cabot, for, you see, I am, in actuality, an agent of the
United States." At Cabot's indrawn breath, Lucian's smile widened. "I'm afraid it's true. My loyalties have always been with
this new republic, my poor, blind unfortunate! I have served its
government from the very beginnings in any way I could. I have
used my ties in France as an instrument to gain worthwhile information for Jefferson ever since he was Washington's Secretary of
State."

"But—but—you reported to Talleyrand himself!" Cabot had
sputtered in disbelief.

Lucian's blue eyes mocked Garth in pity. "So I did! But the
information I sent to France was harmless to the United States'
interests; it was information that could have been gleaned by
anyone on the ambassador's staff. It was the information I *received* from an unsuspecting Talleyrand that proved most beneficial to the American government. So you see how unwise it was
for you to have instigated Jefferson to turn against me, Cabot, for
it was a game that you could *never* win."

The knowledge had shattered Cabot and he had left a truly
broken man. Utterly defeated, he would go back to England to
await his final fate.

As Aimee sat in her reverie, she thought about all that had
been revealed to her by her husband in these past days. At first
she had been incredulous, as disbelieving as Garth Cabot that her
husband could actually be an agent for the United States. The
surprise had turned to hurt that he had not seen fit to trust in her
enough to reveal his true dealings long before now. Lucian was
aware of her hurt, had explained that the plans involving the
Louisiana Territory and New Orleans had been so delicate that he
could trust no one, yet Aimee had still been unable to put her
feelings aside.

It was late that evening when Lucian had arrived back at
Chesterfield Hall from Washington City, filled with good news
about the expedition's progress and the outlook for increased
trade in New Orleans and the rest of the towns along the great
Mississippi River. His triumph had been dampened somewhat by
the quiet look he had received from his wife, whose uncertainty
was written all over her lovely face.

After dinner, when they were alone in their room, having put
Philippe to bed for the night, Lucian faced his wife, his blue eyes
gazing warmly into hers. "Darling, I'm sorry for not having
trusted you before with all of this. I suppose part of it was that it

was all so complicated, really. You had been led to believe I was an agent for Talleyrand, and you already hated the thought of my being a spy at all, if you recall. I suppose I didn't want you to hate the idea any more than you already did. When you expressed your reservations about coming to the United States, I didn't think it was the best of times to reveal my own loyalties."

"But, if you had told me before you left for France—or at least before you were put in jail, which I realize now was also a lie!" she returned.

He looked slightly chagrined. "Yes, I admit that I was actually on a mission for Jefferson in the northeast while I was supposedly in jail. I'm sorry, my love, but it was the only way I knew how to protect you! I thought the less you knew, the less danger you would find yourself in. I thought ignorance would be your best defense. Alas! Cabot proved me dangerously wrong!"

She relented a little at the pain in his eyes. "But you couldn't know how much he hated you!" she responded quickly.

He nodded, his mouth tightening with the memory of it. "No, but I should never have allowed you to be so vulnerable to him. I was aware of his underhanded manipulations, especially after that forged letter he made up to get me in trouble with Jefferson, but I did nothing to protect you from them. I suppose, in my male vanity, I thought I could continue to provide you with protection just because of my connection with the President. I'm sorry I was wrong, my dearest. It nearly cost me my wife!"

He came to her, putting his arms around her tenderly, feeling a token resistance, before she sighed and clasped her hands behind his neck. They stood like that for a long time, each one holding the other, aware of their deepening love. Finally, Aimee looked up at him, her eyes brilliantly green.

"I'm afraid I can do nothing else but love you for the rest of my life, Lucian Napier," she told him with a smile. "After everything I have been through with you, I think we make a very good match. What do you think?"

He bent down to capture her lips with his. "I agree most heartily, wife," he answered her. "And now, how do you feel about making love with your lusty husband, who has missed that part of our relationship quite sorely for the past seven weeks?"

She frowned mockingly at him. "I was wondering when you would get around to asking me that!" She giggled, pulling his head down and kissing him lasciviously.

They began slowly to undress each other, taking as much time as they could to prolong the anticipation that was building up inside both of them. When they were naked, Lucian picked her up in his arms and deposited her on the bed, lying next to her so that he could look into her magnificent eyes, while his fingers began to play passion's music on her taut body.

"And to think," he joked softly, "that I was saving my trump card in case you proved recalcitrant!"

"And what was that trump card?" she murmured, beginning to feel desire spread throughout her body as his hands caressed her with expert care.

"I have just completed a deal whereby we now own a few thousand acres of good river bottom land just upriver from New Orleans. From the looks of the plans, it abuts several acres that have only recently been bought in the name of Dominic St. Cyr; it's where he plans to build a beautiful house for his wife and two children."

"What!" Aimee opened her eyes wide, staring incredulously at her husband. "B-but what about President Jefferson . . . your responsibility to the American government!" she sputtered unbelievingly.

"I'll have to inform him of my immediate retirement!" He chuckled, then kissed her lips while his hands brushed her breasts, feeling them tightening with desire. "I'm sure he'll find some post for me in the new Louisiana Territory," he added, becoming more and more amorous as his wife's body responded deliciously beneath him. "Something suitable for a gentleman farmer."

"Or a gentleman spy?" she wondered with a little laugh before giving herself up to the tender demands of her husband.